SOCIAL
PROBLEMS
Private Troubles and

Public Issues

SOCIAL PROBLEMS

Private Troubles and Public Issues

EDITED BY

ARNOLD BIRENBAUM
WHEATON COLLEGE

EDWARD SAGARIN
CITY COLLEGE OF NEW YORK

Charles Scribner's Sons · New York

For *C. Wright Mills*

to whom we are indebted for much inspiration, as well as for an essay from which we have borrowed the title for this book

CONTENTS 🏵 🏵

INTRODUCTION ❧ ❧

THE MEANING OF ANALYZING
SOCIAL PROBLEMS 🌿

What kind of country is the United States? Where have we been and where are we going? What is the quality of life in the space age? Are we the "last best hope of mankind" or have we "lost the lucky star" under which our poets believed we once lived? How do we know where we are at?

America in the last third of the twentieth century is a nation of opposites and contradictions. We have placed men on the moon through the brilliant application of scientific knowledge and planning, yet there is hunger in the land. Our cities contain monumental office buildings and huge cultural centers, while traffic and industry unspectacularly suffocate the city dweller and poison the animal and plant life of the waterways. American diplomats conclude treaties to limit the testing of nuclear weapons, while nearly a million troops (and as many as half a million at one time) test new weapons in military operations off our shores. And so it goes. . . .

The American experiment which began several hundred years ago also contained antagonistic elements. We sought to build a national identity outside of the traditional feudal and class distinctions of Europe, but at the expense of the native American Indian and the enslaved African. The great adventure of this country has not ended; what lies largely behind us is the smugness and certainty of past decades, those complacent and styleless years following World War II, when partial affluence was regarded as cause to create an American celebration, a celebration of what may never have been there. America, some proclaimed, had solved or was on the way to solving most of its social problems without violence, by institutionalizing an equitable way of settling class grievances through the two-party system. Many of those who hailed these successes were once social critics of the left who, overreacting to their acceptance by established elites and to Stalinism, ended by renouncing their former critique of capitalism. Still other erstwhile critics withdrew from political discussion into cultural criticism, there

3

to find solace and acceptance in the university, the foundation, and the little magazine.

Intellectuals, who in the 1930s saw Franklin D. Roosevelt as a conservative reformer, now asserted that technology had created such abundance under corporate capitalism that there was no need for critiques of American political economy from the left, but need only for answers as to how to put this technology to work. American thinkers found themselves in "an age of happy problems," and critical analysis based on faith in an alternative model of social reality was regarded as unnecessary and dangerous, an oversimplification of events and problems. Daniel Bell and others, in announcing "the end of ideology" of the 1930s, grandiosely proclaimed the end of all critical ideology. In so doing, they created an ideology of anti-ideology, simplifying it into slogans without solutions for current problems, into commitment without analysis.

Curiously and ironically, it was Daniel Bell who, in a brilliant examination of the recent history of the sociology of industry, demonstrated the necessary connection between analysis and commitment, going far beyond slogans to practical suggestions for making factory work more meaningful. In "Work and Its Discontents," Bell indicated the analytical distortions in the work of both the scientific management and the human relations schools of industrial sociology precisely because he held to an alternative vision of social reality. Not only was Bell committed to certain values which lead to the selection of the problem for study, but he ably went beyond the established views about work because he did not accept management's interests as dominant and, therefore, its way of understanding the relationship between men and their work. But let us now return to the relationship between the events of the 1950s and concern for the study of social problems.

The key to the end of critical thought in the Eisenhower years was the staggering abundance produced under capitalism. The apparent success of the economic system in raising the standard of living for many Americans, if not for all, called into question Marxian analysis of the capacity of mature capitalism to thrive except at the expense of the working class. The increasing impoverishment of the people who toiled in factories and shops, once considered necessary to maintain profits for large corporations which found it more and more difficult to acquire competitive advantage by making improvements in techniques of production or transportation, was abandoned in favor of an analysis of a land moving toward permanent affluence.

Three developments were omitted from this analysis which made the prediction inaccurate with respect to the United States. First, the involvement of the federal government in the economy as regulator, consumer, and subsidizer of production, starting during the Great Depression in the 1930s and continuing through World War II and the cold war, made it possible to manipulate the economy and maintain high employment at fairly satis-factory wages. Secondly, the expansion of credit and installment buying to almost everyone in America kept consumer purchases up and stimulated production. Finally, American economic interests were able to dominate foreign markets, control natural resources in other lands, and establish business and factories abroad, thus producing high rates of profit and insuring continued high dividends for investors and good wages for Ameri-can employees at home.

These economic and political developments seemed to render obsolete much of the analysis of conventional left thinking, particularly with regard to political and ideological militancy of the working class and its role in social change. Did it eliminate *all* criticism and analysis? One might argue that in order to examine the growth of corporate capitalism in the 1950s and 1960s, new ideas are needed. Indeed today and in the future, the focus should include the effects of quantitative abundance and organizational control on our living patterns and ways of thinking; for it is possible that although we are on the verge of freedom from material necessity, we remain oppressed in more subtle ways. We do not suffer from an embarrassment of riches but from a dearth of options as to how to put the riches we make to work and what to do with our economic and personal freedom. Despite the perpetuation of many problems of underdevelopment and inadequate distribution of resources, America, in the words of C. Wright Mills (some-times considered the most important social critic and problem-oriented sociologist of the period following World War II), has become an *over-developed nation,* one in which

. . . the standard of living dominates the style of life; its inhabitants are possessed, as it were, by its industrial and commercial apparatus: collectively, by the mainte-nance of conspicuous production; individually, by the frenzied pursuit and mainte-nance of commodities. Around these fetishes, life, labor and leisure are increasingly organized. Focused upon these, the struggle for status supplements the struggle for survival; a panic for status replaces the proddings of poverty.[1]

Despite his prophetic awareness of the entrapments of power and afflu-ence, Mills did not devote much direct attention in his work to the rage, hopelessness, and despair experienced by those who have been systemati-cally excluded from the acquisition of basic commodities and the produc-tion of useless ones. While the general standard of living has improved for all Americans during the past twenty-five years, black people and other minorities have not advanced at the same rate as whites; nor have they come to share the same opportunities for advancement that those of the dominant group have. Moreover, there are many poor whites who feel excluded from these processes of development, which have been unevenly distributed to the various segments of contemporary American society.

This sense of increasing deprivation experienced by those who are marginal to an affluent society is only one aspect of the relationship between overdevelopment and exclusion. Of equal significance are the ways in which an affluent society depends upon personal motivation and concern for increasing one's standard of living in order to maintain a demand of a high magnitude and constancy for mass-produced commodities. An important consequence of this social and economic configuration is cultural and psychological: economic standardization restricts the proliferation of a variety of life styles, lest they encourage underconsumption of standardized products. In turn, those from minority groups—the blacks, the Mexican-Americans, the Indians, the Puerto Ricans, or even the poor whites of the Cumberlands—may well reject white middle class values of consumption; when they seek to preserve their culture, they threaten the motivational foundations which underpin or buttress these economic arrangements.

Those minority group members who are made into effective production workers and pursuers of a more affluent way of life are often forced to give up ways of living which validate their identities as individuals not entrapped in the commercial and industrial apparatus. Many such people gain economic and social integration in society at a tremendous cost to their dignity. Assuming that our ways are better, we always ask members of oppressed minorities to give up their identity and old ways, and we discount the possibility that they have something to contribute to our lives.

The preceding discussion seeks only to examine some of the rich social, cultural, and psychological implications of Mills' concept of the *overdeveloped nation* and is not meant as a rejection of the concept; rather, we intend to expand its analytical power in examining the motivational and cultural contradictions in an affluent society. Furthermore, as will become evident momentarily, there is no suggestion made here that cultural hegemony is a necessary component of an industrial society but merely an outcome of particular processes of economic and technological growth. As students of society, we must be able to say whether new social and cultural forms are possible: that is, what *can* be as well as what currently exists. Otherwise our work tends to close horizons rather than to open them; it tends to reinforce existing social arrangements and implies to others that what is must always be an unalterable reality.

Mills' criticism of the United States was based on the positing of an alternative—a properly *developing society* which deliberately supported the cultivation of alternative styles of life as its central concern. He envisioned such a society as using abundance and technology in the service of self-realization and individual uniqueness:

... decisions about standards of living would be made in terms of debated choices among such styles; the industrial equipment of such a society would be maintained as an instrument to increase the range of choices among styles of life.[2]

Mills complemented his critique of American intellectual life by examining American social structure; specifically, he strove to reveal the emergence of new centers of power through the growth of bureaucracy in industry, government, and the military. Moreover, he showed that the communications apparatus of the country was dominated by these power centers, which used them to justify these far-reaching changes in American life. Cultural activities no longer created alternative life styles but instead were used in the service of maintaining the illusion of individuality. Along these lines Mills attacked the general complacency of men of ideas who failed to respond to underlying changes in social structure except by celebrating them, retreating into apathetic resignation that nothing could be done, thereby insuring the continued domination of the forces of centralization. The intellectuals were now in the service of those who controlled the means of communication, and the ideas they generated served the interests of the decision-making elites who sought their counsel and bought their schemes to make things run more efficiently. At a time when Mills saw the development of crucial problems in American society, intellectuals were helping to legitimate established social relationships rather than challenging them.

The sociology of intellectual conformity which Mills documented in the late 1950s came out of a personal sense of malaise in an apparently untroubled era. As a professional sociologist, he also criticized his own discipline, condemning equally the scholasticism of those who claimed to be theorists and who avoided the major issues and developments of the time, and the formalistic empiricists who overconformed to the techniques of the physical sciences, producing studies whose results they were highly confident of, but which had low informative value; indeed what they said may have been true, but it had little significance.

Such developments in sociology may have been disappointing but were not surprising to Mills following his own analysis of the relationship between changes in social structure and intellectual life. Sociology was becoming a highly differentiated and specialized discipline in the 1950s. Aside from the distinction between theory and research, a number of substantive specializations emerged, such as political sociology, formal organizations, small groups, and demography. These developments fit in well with the modernization of the universities, beginning in the 1920s, which served industry and government by providing centers for the performance of complex research efforts in the physical sciences and training large numbers of personnel to man the slots in these institutional spheres. Graduate education in sociology reflected these needs, stressing the acquisition of techniques of data-gathering rather than substantive knowledge and its meaning. The knowledge value of sociological research was judged by tests of statistical significance and the precision of sampling techniques, rather than the implications of the findings.

These developments in sociology were spurred on by the quest of sociologists to become academically respectable and powerful. They, therefore, emulated the physical sciences in the development of quantifiable knowledge rather than the humanities in hopes of altering their condition. There developed an overconformity to the norms of the physical sciences without raising questions as to whether their techniques were useful in obtaining valid information about social arrangements. Since sociology was often and still is confused in the public mind with social work and social reform, many members of the discipline eschewed the study of social problems as a way of correcting this distorted image.

Most recently, Alvin Gouldner, in the *Coming Crisis in Western Sociology* (1970), examined in great detail the relationship between American social structure and the organization and content of sociology. As one who regards himself as the inheritor of Mills' role of internal critic of the discipline, Gouldner has attempted to restore the sociologist-as-intellectual, with all his moral values and concern for the development of the self, to the center of the sociological enterprise. We agree with Gouldner insofar as he regards the sociologist as one who lives *for* his work rather than living off it. It is only in this way that sociologists can avoid becoming apologists, justifiers, and sanctifiers of existing social arrangements and alternatively, that sociology can eschew responsibility for the management of those groups of people who either voluntarily or involuntarily deviate from assuming and performing in an uncomplaining way the demarcated roles of consumers and uncreative producers in an advanced industrial society.

The question must be raised, both for Gouldner and for ourselves, as to what has led us to recognize the failure of the conventional approaches of contemporary orientations in sociology. For many of us, these approaches were far removed from our motivations to become sociologists and from our major emotional and intellectual concerns, maintaining in us a state of unease and malaise in a smooth society. Finally, it must be noted, that our alienation from these trends made us responsive to the emerging social reality of the 1960s—the rebellions of black people, the search of youth for authentic life styles, the increasing consciousness of women, and the autonomy implicit in efforts of voluntary and involuntary deviants to define themselves in relation to the larger society—a new, dynamic and conflict-ridden society in which the theoretical constructs of conventional sociology have less and less understanding or meaning.

In contrast to these complex changes taking place in the development of sociology that Gouldner attacks most eloquently, the founders of the major intellectual traditions in the field—Karl Marx, Emile Durkheim, and Max Weber—had made no effort to separate theory from research in their substantive writings. They did not base their interest in the problems they undertook to investigate on a desire to accumulate knowledge for its own sake, but rather their interest was a reflection upon and reaction to the immediacy of their experiences and to the quality of life in their times. In each case they sought to understand society historically, dealing with the changing relations between concrete agents and agencies. Most importantly, the classical sociologists of the nineteenth and early twentieth centuries were critical spirits who made no sharp distinctions between concern with sociological problems and social problems. For these men society could be known by the problems which it chose to ignore or confront. Yet, their ultimate concern was with what has been called "big" sociological problems: e.g., the origins of capitalism, the transition from traditional to modern society, the nature of social integration in a modern society. They could, by virtue of this orientation, not only include the study of social problems in their analysis, but could illuminate their writings by what was of vital concern to them and to others as members of society. Their writings were full of vitality because they expressed shock and outrage.

Until recently, and even to this day for many respected members of the profession, sociology has rarely challenged the accepted view of social reality, probably because sociologists, like others in the modern world, lost the "capacity to be astonished" by the events taking place around us. Most contemporary sociologists write for a professional or preprofessional audience; their writings removed from contemporary life, from controversy and conflicts. Social problems are regarded as "strains," explained away or encompassed within the same conceptual framework which accounts for order and stability. In particular, the writing of theory has acquired the properties of a theology dealing with social problems; uncertainty and disappointment are explained away in an unexcitable and unexciting way.

While we do not wish to belabor the internal controversies of the discipline in this anthology, we do find that Talcott Parsons, for example, the major theoretical spokesman for functional analysis, which is the most popular orientation among contemporary sociologists, regards all existing arrangements as adaptive for the continuation of social systems. Such may be the case, but excluded from his understanding of the operation of social systems are the human costs of adaptation as functional alternatives to rebellion or major efforts at social transformation. Parsons rarely deals with the central question, raised by numerous critics: "for *whom* are these arrangements adaptive?" Avoidance of that question in the center of one's analysis reveals a failure on the part of such eminent figures to get involved in fundamental research and theorizing about the social sources of the human aspects of society: suffering, powerlessness, social isolation, meaninglessness, self-estrangement. No connection is made between these conditions of human existence and the extent to which they are directly or indirectly related to existing social arrangements. The language of functional theory is most unreceptive to these concerns; it is euphemistic and remote from human feeling and aspirations and sheds no light on social problems because it avoids raising questions about the place of sociology and the members of the discipline in relation to social problems.

To the extent that this occurs, the sociological enterprise becomes less of an intellectual adventure as it becomes a legitimate part of the academic establishment. Its historical origins go unremembered, that is, the concern with the consequences of the Industrial and French revolutions and, in particular, the removal of ascriptive restrictions upon human activities. Its capacity to create knowledge, which gives the knower a way of coming to grips with the world and a means to alter his condition, has been deeply threatened by concern with technique, precision, and grand speculation. In this pathway, sociology has become innocuous, producing no dangerous or subversive ideas, rarely calling into question any current practices or conceits.

One way out of this dilemma is to recognize the failure of sociology to remain autonomous and deal with the consequences of this for the field and those we hope to reach outside of it. In order to overcome the estrangement between the current practices of sociology and its responsibilities in a developing society, the conditions must be created for an authentic dialogue between opposing and contradictory visions of social reality. Accordingly, the field of social problems provides an excellent site to do this, since it brings into sharp focus these opposing styles of living. However, these problems cannot be fully understood unless it is clear that sociology is willing and able to confront this task. In creating the conditions for genuine discussion, the discipline of sociology may best insure itself an independent future.

Three elements are necessary to create these conditions: (1) the establishment of the moral independence and responsibility of sociology to investigate social problems through formulating the values of the discipline; (2) the development from these premises of a paradigm or analytical tool for the study of social problems; and (3) the creation or movement toward a definition of social problems based on these premises which would allow the student to draw out the implications of a social problem for establishing personal and collective priorities. In this search, we hope to arrive at a method which would allow people maximum control over their own lives. Insofar as sociology has its roots in the social life from which it was born, thought and action are bound together. Recognition of this unity is a basic premise for the establishment of a developing society.

The meaning of sociology is related to problems derived from a complex and changing world. The study of the maintenance, modification, and dissolution of social order, and, conversely, the problem of how human freedom can be achieved, derive from the experiences of the last two centuries. Yet, these problems are also universal to the extent that human beings are not indefinitely plastic, nor are they uninfluenced by other men. Too often in the past sociology has avoided these problems in order to free itself from the moralistic label of telling others what should be. In so doing, it has failed to tell society about what is possible, or what can be. To study only what exists has its dangers for freedom, since it provides no opportunity for men to make an imaginative leap beyond what exists to what is possible.

Maintaining a healthy skepticism about these conditions does not necessarily mean that one can then be free to study what one wants. Whenever sociology serves a client or even when no client is involved, investigations often avoid the central problems for the peripheral ones. Values influence one's work at every level: from problem selection, to choice of method appropriate to solve the problem, to drawing out the implications of the findings. Each stage in the process of investigation involves choices. The sociologist must always be aware and make others aware of which values are involved and what is at stake. This is the moral side of sociology and herein lies its responsibility: if we do not determine the threats to freedom and order as well as the "functions" of the institutions and groups we study, then we are merely obliging technicians who have no claim that others should listen to us except that we provide useful, satisfying, and reliable information. For sociology to make a serious claim upon the world, it must be free to be concerned with the profound problem of the relationship between freedom and order. How can this be done?

Sociology must become concerned with social issues and priorities as well as those events or phenomena ordinarily regarded as social problems. What can be done is to provide the intellectual framework for both understanding and action. It cannot wait until others define a social problem before recognizing its existence but must engage in the defining process itself, clarifying and establishing relationships among the problem, the social structure, and the ideology (or nonideology) of the problem.

This critical spirit in sociology is invaluable in contributing to the growth of human freedom and social development. Criticism should also present a reasoned vision of alternative social forms and consciousness. Debunking of society and official explanations of how order is maintained and how much freedom exists is a purposeful social activity only when it avoids cynicism and nihilism about the possibilities for change. This can be done to the extent that the discipline presents alternative models of social reality which are responsive to previously unmet human needs.

The study of social problems is one way of validating this claim to autonomy and responsibility. It means getting at the inner problems and the core relationships which are hidden by the usual efforts to avoid or confront a particular social problem. It means locating the social costs for the solution of a problem, as well as the new freedom or new constraints derived from it. Finally, it must be determined how a problem reaffirms or challenges the taken-for-grantedness of different groups' views of social reality.

In order to make this kind of analysis possible, a general model to the approach of social problems is needed, free of many of the assumptions which have plagued those who have sought to study this field. These assumptions have often led either to an emphasis on descriptive presentations of the problems, or to a concentration on the defining process. In both approaches, there may be a failure to capture the relationship between social problems, social structure, and the beliefs about the problems. Yet it is possible, we believe, and in fact necessary to provide an approach or model of analysis which eschews these commonly assumed notions.

Social problems are defined and interpreted by the agents of social control in society even while they are barely socially visible, although the problems may exist when the social control agencies have not recognized them or have chosen to ignore them. However, the study of social problems cannot be separated from the solutions or explanations proffered by those actors (usually referred to as "people in power") who are designated by society to deal with them. Often heads of government agencies, elected officeholders, religious leaders, and directors of voluntary organizations will participate in the process of recognition and definition of a problem. This effort involves protecting their interests, perpetuating their own power, and hence perpetuating and protecting the very beliefs and interests that they should be calling into question. The head of a government agency already overburdened with tasks may seek to prevent the general public from becoming concerned with the problem, or will attempt to get the problem defined in such a way so that he can free himself of responsibility. Alternatively, an underutilized agency or one which is running out of tasks may seek to get the problem defined in such a way that the problem will become its responsibility. The head of such an agency may offer an alarming and horrifying number of examples showing the rapidity of the spread of some social evil, real or imagined, accurate or exaggerated. Thus, the presence or absence of a particular problem from public discussion is a condition to be analyzed.

It requires investigation of the cultural designs for society and the structural arrangements which make for the failure or success in turning "private troubles" into "public issues."

Such an independent perspective on social problems requires that the following aspects of social reality *not* be taken for granted: (1) that a uniformity of belief exists about all social problems so that they are regarded as universally abhorred by all the members of society and to the same degree; (2) that there is a one-to-one correspondence between attitudinal and behavorial performance by societally designated agents and agencies for the elimination of a particular social problem; (3) that all members of society, despite their differential location in the social structure and the different roles that they must perform, have equal access, opportunity, and responsibility to solve these problems; or, finally, (4) that all social problems are solvable or resolvable without major structural transformations of social relations and consciousness via equivalents to or actual social revolutions.

To avoid these assumptions, the analyst of social problems may attempt to locate an Archimedean point outside of society, an impossibility for man studying man. Instead we wish to go beyond this fruitless quest to perhaps an equally unrealizable but more useful one for our purposes. Without assuming the inevitability of a newer world, one in which human freedom and community might prevail, we will seek to use these irreducible dimensions of man as a way of making assertions about contemporary social problems, their interrelationships, and their priorities. Without such a vision, utopian if you will, we cannot begin to develop a mode of analysis which escapes from the conventional view that social problems can be studied independently of social structure and of beliefs about the problems.

There is no assumption in this view of a newer world that it can be accomplished by sociologists, social planners, or social workers; it can only be brought to fruition by men doing for themselves, producing a planning society rather than a planned society. What the analysis of social problems can do is make clear the relationships, contradictions, and well-nigh irreconcilable antagonisms that exist in contemporary America. This paradigm—in the form of a series of interrelated questions—seeks to provide a lever to change one's world: for if one is to make history, he must do it for himself, knowing full well that within him and all other men there exists a human spirit to be realized.

A paradigm is nothing more than a heuristic device, a guide to the explorer. It is a model of how one can make sense from or impose a structure on social reality. The purpose of this device is to raise questions which must be asked if problems are to be adequately defined and analyzed. These questions are not rhetorical devices to alert the reader to the ramifications of a particular subject but are both a way of understanding material pertaining to particular problems and a mode of analysis for further independent study of such matters and issues as are omitted from this collection or which may arise at a later point in time. Some of these questions are of a general order, concerning the nature of advanced industrial society and the kinds of possibilities and constraints found there. Others are of a more specific character, involving the interplay between social problems, social structure, and belief systems. Finally, a third set of questions must be posed, about the relations between the type of society we live in, contemporary actors and agencies, and the possibilities for freedom and community.

A Paradigm for the Study of Social Problems

What are the characteristics of an advanced industrial society? What are its achievements and what are the penalties of living in it? Has technology led to greater or lesser control over the environment? Has the centralization of the state, the protective and allocative agency of society, created greater or lesser personal security and a minimal level of distributive justice? Has the transition from traditional to modern society created new problems, or was it done at the expense of groups in society which have never been recompensed for their losses? Has the transition left some men or all men without a communal orientation, a sense of social integration and, therefore, with psychic closure? Are meaningful relationships available between members of different sectors of society? Is there a mutuality of obligations and common outlook? What is the meaning of America's superpower status for our relations with other nations? How does this relationship to the larger world affect the quality of life at home? Which of our values are threatened and which of them are achieved by our international relationships?

Who benefits from the continued existence of a social problem? Which institutions, organizations, and agencies control their interpretations and practical interventions? What are the justifications for the continuation of a social problem, and what justifications exist for its solution? What models of social reality are used to create these justifications and solutions? Who controls their application? Which sectors of the population are penalized by a problem's existence?

Can human freedom be realized at the expense of a sector of society? How much repression is necessary to maintain social order? Are there alternative means to establishing social integration other than by conformity to a generalized set of norms? Can one control one's own life without having control over the sources of power in modern society? Are these sources of power divisible among many sectors of society? Does an egalitarian conception of society necessarily demand that everyone be like everyone else? Are social diversity and social justice possible in the same society? Do modern-day social problems and their solutions create more or less freedom for self-realization? In what ways can solutions for social problems create the conditions for self-realization?

Our first set of questions provides us with a way into the public issues and private troubles of American society and attempts to avoid, as C. Wright Mills noted, the recasting of public issues into private troubles, a process which only leads to the consideration of our problems as unalterable through collective activity. First, we will deal with the most general social problems of this nation in order of magnitude and in so doing hope to generate intellectual awareness and concern about our current situation. There is no attempt here to imply that solving our environmental problems, for example, should be done at the expense of the race problem or by ignoring the monumental power of the United States in the world at large. Rather, we begin with the recondite problems of all industrial societies—past, present, or future: the destruction of the environment as a means of improving the standard of living. In turn, we examine the economic conse-quences of affluence and the failure to regulate it with regard to poverty, unemployment, and displacement of workers by the introduction of sophis-ticated techniques of production. A third aspect of this kind of society—its relationship to the nonindustrial or newly industrializing world—is con-sidered in the light of the consequences of our power and policies control-ling and shaping billions of people who have different life styles and cultures from ours.

Next we turn to more specifically American issues in the examination of the mysteries and mystifications of race and racism, within the context of our advanced industrial society and in relation to the roots of the American experience of wanting to be somebody. Similarly, problems of violence and disorder, crime and justice, and the family and sexuality are placed in the framework of a society that rarely deals with its past or future.

Throughout the essays run the themes implicit in the third set of ques-tions: the problems of self, particularly and peculiarly modern in origin; concerns that cannot be contained or labeled in neat topic headings, but must be continuously examined in every selection presented in this anthol-ogy. For if we cannot examine the self in all of our work, if we cannot find room for self-expression in our society, if we cannot develop into the persons that we want to be through the solution of our social problems as well as in other ways, then why work, why analyze them, why consider alternative ways of living? It is through this set of questions that the ultimate meaning of social problems is uncovered and the dialectic between self and society, with the human self as creator as well as product of society, is recognized and engaged in by all.

Accordingly, perhaps the single most important contribution that sociology has made to the study of man has been to demonstrate the importance of group life and the meaning of membership for the development of the self and for self-determination. Insofar as one can make a real impression upon the world and realize unspoken dreams, it is through relations with others. One of the fundamental conditions for this possibility is that members of society regard each other as being irreplaceable: that is, making a moral claim or obligation upon each other which is binding for all. Recognition of each member's competency to make that claim, and reflexively, to recognize when to respond to another's claims, is the foundation of social life. This condition for freedom and order is realized when men have arrived at a shared definition of their obligations to each other which also recognizes their diversity and the ultimate voluntary nature of such relationships. This constitutes a consciousness of unity, a general will, in Rousseau's language, but not a unified consciousness in which all think and act alike. A social problem exists when the collective society is rent by, at the very least, a public recognition that there is a sector of society, represented by its practices, which threatens or prevents others or themselves from establishing or maintaining their claims to membership.

This situation endangers both social integration and self-realization to the extent that we begin to regard others, or are regarded by them as not being fully competent members of society. To the extent that the origins and scope of particular problems can be determined, we can locate responsibility, thereby making moral claims ourselves and recognizing precisely which values are at stake. In this sense the act of analyzing a social problem is the first step toward establishing the conditions for human freedom: for we are recognizing the claims of membership upon us both through our vocation and independent of our specific roles and functions. Moreover, we go to such responsibilities freely and lovingly; indeed, our own self-realization depends upon others being free: we gladly join in this effort of emancipation.

NOTES

1. C. Wright Mills, "Culture and Politics," in *Power, Politics and People: The Collected Essays of C. Wright Mills,* ed. Irving Louis Horowitz (New York: Oxford University Press, 1967), p. 240.
2. Ibid.

I

PROBLEMS OF THE
ECOSYSTEM ❧ ❧

ECOLOGY: THE NATURAL HISTORY OF A SOCIAL PROBLEM 🙥

Ecology is an old word, but a new discovery, nonetheless, in sociology. It was a key word in the language of the Chicago school, the center of sociological studies and learning in America for two decades. Here, scholars studied the relationship of man to his environment, the effect of the environment upon human behavior, and the reverse, how human behavior effects changes in the environment. Urban sociology was born in the Chicago arena, where Louis Wirth, drawing upon Simmel, outlined how man adapts to life in the cities and how city man is different from rural man. One recalls with nostalgia that era of sociology and the place of ecology in it, for it is removed as if by centuries from the world we inhabit today (a world that is becoming increasingly uninhabitable), and yet, from the Chicago sociologists-ecologists there did emerge the first glimmer of understanding of the social-environmental problems that now surround us: the dual and yet interrelated matters of an overcrowded and highly polluted planet. However, the Chicago ecological school, focusing as it did on the microcosmic, on the relationship of a small portion of the population to a small amount of space, could not have seen the dimensions of the ecology problem as they appear to man today.

As a social issue, which it indubitably is, pollution and overpopulation involve some peculiar matters. For one thing, there appear, at least at first glance, to be no good guys and no bad guys on the question of pollution. Does not everyone, literally everyone, want clean air, living and breathing space, chirping birds in the springtime, and cities without deafening noise? Where is the social conflict that is at the bottom of crime and deviance, the decline of morality, poverty amid affluence that thrives in a land that emanates an ideology of equality? Nevertheless, everyone wants a world

19

without crime and without poverty, just as all people want clean air and uncontaminated food. In both types of problems, one is confronted with the question of whether life and business are to be continued as usual, with only the slightest patchwork reforms, or whether the desire for solution to these enormous problems will carry us to their root causes.

Aside from the question of the population explosion, which seems to have interested and disturbed man (although pondering over it, he did little about it) for many centuries, it would have been surprising to discover anything on the deterioration of the environment in a social problems book only a few years ago. There were essentially two reasons for this omission. First, only a few persons were concerned with environmental deterioration. Of these, hardly anyone saw it as a problem that would so soon engulf us, and most people had a blind confidence that science, particularly physical science, would provide all the answers. Secondly, those who did view it as a serious problem saw it as primarily biological in nature, something that was neither caused by man, nor that could be controlled, changed, and corrected by him. Looking back at both of these naïve views, it seems to make absurd the oft-repeated statement that a problem becomes a social problem when it is recognized as such by a considerable number of influential people. Perhaps by that time, like a creeping malignancy in the human body, it is too late.

Not that no one was interested in the environment in years gone by; some were, and they were not considered crackpots. If occasionally they sounded an alarm that our raw materials were being depleted, the depletion never seemed so great that it would affect those now living. As for their grandchildren or unborn great-great-grandchildren, so far away unborn that it was hard to imagine them as being or as beings (much less feel concern over the world that they would inherit), it was believed that somehow new technological advances would replenish these materials. If forests were being depleted, new ones would be planted to take their places. New deserts might be created, new arid land that once was arable, but irrigation and other advances would make the once barren deserts green. The extinction of a given species, the whale or the buffalo or some lovely bird that once flew across the meadows, was unfortunate, but who except the professional conservationists could really be concerned? Without the whale, there would be other sources of valuable oils and of meat, and for the biologists who warned that man was upsetting the balance of nature, it was hardly conceivable that the vast sea would not be able to create its own evolutionary modifications. One could join these conservationists in campaigns against the wearing of leopard coats, knowing that the spotted feline faced extinction, but the people who did support such campaigns (and few wore leopard coats anyway) considered the leopard a zoological curiosity, a thing of beauty to gaze upon from the safe vantage point outside the bars of the cage. Who then thought that this was one small, even infinitesimal, part of the grand problem of saving the world so that it could remain habitable for men and life of any form?

A few persons did, but they generally fell into two categories: the alarmists and the demographers (many of whom, by the way, were alarmists of a different type). Some people are always predicting the apocalypse and the Armageddon, and they often develop religious ideas to account for the coming deluge. As James Baldwin reminded us, God said to Noah, "This time the flood, the fire next time." Some heard the voice of the Lord, and made dire predictions. Generally, however, these people had little scientific backing; and if they envisaged an earth on which there would not be enough oxygen for all the people to breathe, or enough space to move about (except up and down, perhaps), they did so with the authority of those who were later to see flying saucers. If their warnings were not heeded, it was because they could not be taken seriously, and this may have been a tragedy for mankind, because they were hitting close to the target of truth.

As for the demographers, their concern with overpopulation was attracting attention, although in America the vast westward expansion, the continued need for labor, the relative affluence for a considerable portion of the population, and the knowledge that there was enough food to go around and enough space in which to live (even if some people did not have enough of either, that was a socioeconomic or distributional problem, not a demographic one) left the specter of a severely overpopulated planet far enough away so that it did not become a daily concern. Overpopulation was a matter for India, China, and other lands. The doubling of the American population in sixty years (the last doubling had taken over a century, and the next one, at this rate, would be in about thirty-five or forty years) had not yet made this a crowded land unable to support its people, except for the poor residents of inner cities. Although demographers warned, even they did not foresee the ecological crisis as a combination of population growth too fast for the world to adapt to, too great for the world to support, and affecting and being affected by other events. What the demographers failed to emphasize was the unbalanced distribution both of resources and of population. If America had no overpopulation problem, it was not only because of its seemingly unlimited space, but also because of its lion's share of the world's resources. Vast stretches of still undeveloped land only concealed the grim realities of the social-psychological conditions that would develop in a rapidly urbanizing nation.

Perhaps ecology came into its own with the bombing of Hiroshima and Nagasaki, not only because men now believed that science had the power to blow the planet to smithereens and leave nothing for posterity, but also because radiation suddenly became a household word, and a frightening one at that. As atomic scientists debated about the possible short- and long-term effects of radiation, a larger and larger audience of frightened, interested people all over the world became increasingly concerned. Cows grazing on grass far from the atomic blasts were producing milk that had radioactive substances in it, which some authorities claimed were present in dangerous quantities. Charges were made that leukemia and other diseases could be traced to increases in radiation. Although not confirmed, there were reports that the incidence of higher infant mortality followed wind currents after test blasts occurred. People speculated on radiation causing genetic defects, and others on its causing sterility. Pat Frank wrote a novel entitled *Mr. Adam* about a world in which all males except one (he happened to be in a lead mine at the time) were made sterile as a result of atomic radiation.

Only a few years ago in 1962, and yet centuries ago, an obscure biologist with the style of a novelist and the hard facts of a scientist wrote a book that became a best seller in America and was widely distributed abroad. Entitled *Silent Spring,* Rachel Carson's work won eight awards (mainly from conservationist groups). Author Carson sounded an alarm such as no other writer had before, although there had been murmurings of fear about the matters she discussed. Her book was directed mainly against the use of chemical insecticides, particularly their promiscuous and indiscriminate use, with special attention given to the use of DDT.

Rachel Carson's book opens with an epigraph in the form of a dedication to and quotation from Albert Schweitzer: "Man has lost the capacity to foresee and to forestall. He will end by destroying the earth." Her work was widely read, widely praised, widely attacked, and from the viewpoint of those in positions of power, who might have done something about the situation that she described, widely ignored. The title of her book was lovely but ill-chosen, for it left people with the impression that she was talking about the same thing that conservationists had discussed for generations: a world without birds in the backyard, on the lawn, and in the park, a world devoid of chirping sounds and mating calls. All of this would have been tragic enough for those sensitive to the beauties of nature; however, for Carson this was certainly a secondary consideration. She traced the chemical poisons from the insects to the birds, from the plants to the rivers to the fish, how the poisons were stored and not excreted, and finally accumulated until they reached levels of toxicity threatening not only man's lovely sights and sounds, but his food supply as well. She was concerned with the balance of nature, not because it was wrong or sinful to upset it, but because in so doing man was committing unlimited harm to himself by protecting one crop for one year: a problem to which she was not insensitive, for she suggested that such crop protection could take place in other ways.

When first published, *Silent Spring* met furious denunciation by many sectors of the popular media as well as by the hired scientists of the insecticide, agricultural, aerosol, and other industries; yet, today this same book reads like a mild understatement of what is already taking place. A decade ago Rachel Carson was charged with implying that our whole way of life (capitalism, democracy, and particularly the laissez-faire economy) was destroying us. Now, she is honored for her foresight, but ironically those who honor her now deny that she ever attacked the American way of life: now she is heard as another but more eloquent voice of the conservationist, one interested in birds, not in the remaking of a system that has killed them. However, we will miss the most important lesson of her work if we do not investigate why, for seven or eight years after her book was published, no one in a position of power would attempt to institute the changes she suggested. One can be sure, such an investigation will not take place.

Just a few years later the 1970s opened as the decade of ecology. Everyone has discovered pollution; it was the most popular word in the new language of politics. Candidates opposed pollution the way they opposed sin and wickedness, and with just as little idea of what they could do about it. They favored clean air the way they favored motherhood (which, by the way, is no longer that much in favor). An ecology handbook today reads like the prophetic words of doom. Deafening noises may worsen if the sonic boom becomes a reality, with young urban dwellers already as hard-of-hearing as were elderly persons some years ago. The sounds that surround us: zooming planes, screeching brakes, the sirens of fire and police engines as well as ambulances racing against death, transistor radios blasting away on the streets and in the parks, so that the moment of silence between the honking of horns is eerie, all epitomized when one pushes the button of an elevator, the door closes, and Muzak comes forward to bombard you.

The air: filled with smoke and gasoline fumes, with evil smells, putrid as if everything were coming from the sewers, which perhaps it is. The food: filled with toxins. Even the ocean, the vast and almost limitless ocean, becomes polluted. And the outlook is for population growth and a worsening environment. Except that all this may be a self-defeating prophecy: by telling us that it will get worse, we may all be aroused to make it better. Perhaps we have not turned the wrong corner of the maze and found that there is no way out; perhaps we have reached a point of return. It is here that sociology comes in: the task of the scientist is to analyze in order to predict and to control.

Already there is a danger that the ecology issue can be put to great misuse. If only the rebellious youths, hippies and Yippies, long-haired and short, can be united in the fight for clean air and quiet cities, against poisonous foods and toxic fumes, then their energies and anger can be deflected in directions unthreatening to the institutionalized power structures of the nation. The generation gap can be closed, the president and the radical youth can smile together before television cameras; reconciliation can be the order of the day: a great national unity to save the environment. And until this unity is forged, and these energies are so channeled, war continues (with its defoliation, radiation, and other environmental destruction), racism continues, poverty goes on, undernourishment gets worse.

It is a grand plan: ecology as a made-to-order program not to save pure air but to permit the putrid air of racism and war to go unhindered. It would be a tragic irony if this were the major consequence of the new interest in ecology, to which Professor Ritchie Lowry has given the name "religecology": bridging the important social chasms by an ecology crusade. Yet, it is unlikely that this will occur, for the deeper interests of youth and of many others are challenging the old order of things and are not fickle; they may diminish in intensity but they do not die. Incited by an incident, an event, or a charismatic individual, they flare up again. The old causes will remain alive until the issues are settled.

Still there is another reason that any hope that sociology will become the theme of reconciliation must be abandoned. Those dedicated to the solution of the demographic and the environmental problems have found that they do not have allies, they have opponents, if not enemies, in a society in which the retention of international power positions and the aggrandizement of corporate profits are priorities that must take precedence before one can think of fresh air, of milk free from radiation molecules, or of great lakes that have not become immense sewers. The corporation has no other business than to make profits, writes one of America's leading and most prestigious economists, and he speaks not for himself but for an entire economy. The cleaning of the air must be done in opposition to General Motors and Ford, even though it might seem that they are cooperating, giving a research grant and offering a helping hand to laboratory technicians working on the problem. These companies, like other giant corporations, can become sensitive to a problem only when an aroused public compels them to be, challenges their very right to continue to pollute, takes them to court, pickets, writes, denounces, and shouts vigorously and vociferously at stockholders' meetings. And thus it was with DDT, and so it will be with all other environmental polluters. It will be dangerous if everyone starts wearing the same button in a great display of national unity, all proclaiming that we should save the environment or all hailing an Earth Day or a Clean Atmosphere Week. If this does occur and we are lulled into the belief that wearing buttons does any good, and if we do not see in many of those distributing and wearing such buttons the very opponents whose activities must be so vigorously combatted, we will then, in fact, be doing ourselves harm and defeating our all-important cause.

We start this section with an article by Garrett Hardin, professor at the University of California at Santa Barbara. His article might well be directed toward any area of modern human activities, not exclusively the control of population and the securing of human existence on an insecure planet. For Hardin argues, and most persuasively, that lack of planning and cooperation are today incompatible with survival. Whatever may have been the merits in times gone by of laissez-faire economy and the industrial growth that was spurred by the Protestant ethic of competitiveness, today these characteristics have become disastrous. Each man, corporation, or even each nation, left to its own, without outside control and obligation or responsibility to others, will in advancing its interests injure his neighbor and himself perhaps even to the point of extinction.

From the biologist Paul R. Ehrlich's best seller *The Population Bomb*, we select his most factual material: the constantly accelerating rate of growth, where it is taking us, and how fast we are getting there. Lord Ritchie-Calder continues the same theme, but makes the vital link from demography to pollution: what can happen to a world in which a city might have a billion (not a million, but a billion) people, or more, what this does to an underfed world, to industrialization and its resultant smog, to the air we breathe and the garbage we try to dispose of. The author presents no answers, except cooperation, planning, and control, but this raises the question of who controls and for whose benefit.

Robert L. Heilbroner, economist and social critic, examines the threats of environmental pollution, radiation, the exploitation of the fast-diminishing natural materials neither inexhaustible nor magically replaceable, as the public naïvely tends to believe, by "synthetics" (which of course must be synthesized from natural products). Heilbroner places the entire problem in a socioeconomic perspective. He counterposes the economic predictions of John Stuart Mill to those of Karl Marx: will capitalism reach a stationary apex or must it expand unceasingly; and to this he adds a third possibility —the decline and destruction of Western civilization. Why Western, one might ask.

We end this section with an essay by Gene Marine that originally appeared in *Ramparts*. Here, the author places the ecological crisis as a conflict between the needs of the common people and the capitalist exploitative corporate powers. Reading his documented article, one must be skeptical of the ability of American power groups to come to grips with the ecological crisis, and one must look with considerable suspicion upon their new-found concerns.

As a social problem, ecology (like other social problems but even more so) requires a cooperative effort, not of profitmakers or profiteers and their

victims, but of scientists of many backgrounds and disciplines. Ecology
requires a degree of international cooperation that the world has not seen
(although UNESCO and WHO are beginnings) and a downgrading of
profits in favor of public welfare. A solution of environmental problems
involves, in short, that oft-used phrase: the reordering of priorities, which
means the reallocation of resources and the review and ultimate revision of
many basic values that are cherished by many Americans, not only profit
and private property, but individualism as well.

In this book we discuss the social problems that arise out of the American
dream, born here of those born here or coming to these shores from abroad,
that everyone can be somebody. Without solving the ecology problem, not
only will he not be a somebody, he will be a nobody.

THE TRAGEDY OF
THE COMMONS ❧ *Garrett Hardin*

At the end of a thoughtful article on the future of nuclear war, Wiesner and
York[1] concluded that: "Both sides in the arms race are . . . confronted by
the dilemma of steadily increasing military power and steadily decreasing
national security. *It is our considered professional judgment that this
dilemma has no technical solution.* If the great powers continue to look for
solutions in the area of science and technology only, the result will be to
worsen the situation."

I would like to focus your attention not on the subject of the article
(national security in a nuclear world) but on the kind of conclusion they
reached, namely that there is no technical solution to the problem. An
implicit and almost universal assumption of discussions published in profes-

SOURCE: Garrett Hardin, "The Tragedy of the Commons" *Science,* (December 13, 1968),
1243–1248. Copyright 1968 by the American Association for the Advancement of Science.
Reprinted by permission of the author and publisher.

sional and semipopular scientific journals is that the problem under discussion has a technical solution. A technical solution may be defined as one that requires a change only in the techniques of the natural sciences, demanding little or nothing in the way of change in human values or ideas of morality.

In our day (though not in earlier times) technical solutions are always welcome. Because of previous failures in prophecy, it takes courage to assert that a desired technical solution is not possible. Wiesner and York exhibited this courage; publishing in a science journal, they insisted that the solution to the problem was not to be found in the natural sciences. They cautiously qualified their statement with the phrase, "It is our considered professional judgment. . . ." Whether they were right or not is not the concern of the present article. Rather, the concern here is with the important concept of a class of human problems which can be called "no technical solution problems," and, more specifically, with the identification and discussion of one of these.

It is easy to show that the class is not a null class. Recall the game of tick-tack-toe. Consider the problem, "How can I win the game of tick-tack-toe?" It is well known that I cannot, if I assume (in keeping with the conventions of game theory) that my opponent understands the game perfectly. Put another way, there is no "technical solution" to the problem. I can win only by giving a radical meaning to the word "win." I can hit my opponent over the head; or I can drug him; or I can falsify the records. Every way in which I "win" involves, in some sense, an abandonment of the game, as we intuitively understand it. (I can also, of course, openly abandon the game—refuse to play it. This is what most adults do.)

The class of "No technical solution problems" has members. My thesis is that the "population problem," as conventionally conceived, is a member of this class. How it is conventionally conceived needs some comment. It is fair to say that most people who anguish over the population problem are trying to find a way to avoid the evils of overpopulation without relinquishing any of the privileges they now enjoy. They think that farming the seas or developing new strains of wheat will solve the problem—technologically. I try to show here that the solution they seek cannot be found. The population problem cannot be solved in a technical way, any more than can the problem of winning the game of tick-tack-toe.

What Shall We Maximize?

Population, as Malthus said, naturally tends to grow "geometrically," or, as we would now say, exponentially. In a finite world this means that the per capita share of the world's goods must steadily decrease. Is ours a finite world?

A fair defense can be put forward for the view that the world is infinite; or that we do not know that it is not. But, in terms of the practical problems that we must face in the next few generations with the foreseeable technology, it is clear that we will greatly increase human misery if we do not, during the immediate future, assume that the world available to the terrestrial human population is finite. "Space" is no escape.[2]

A finite world can support only a finite population; therefore, population growth must eventually equal zero. (The case of perpetual wide fluctuations above and below zero is a trivial variant that need not be discussed.) When this condition is met, what will be the situation of mankind? Specifically, can Bentham's goal of "the greatest good for the greatest number" be realized?

No—for two reasons, each sufficient by itself. The first is a theoretical one. It is not mathematically possible to maximize for two (or more) variables at the same time. This was clearly stated by von Neumann and Morgenstern,[3] but the principle is implicit in the theory of partial differential equations, dating back at least to D'Alembert (1717–1783).

The second reason springs directly from biological facts. To live, any organism must have a source of energy (for example, food). This energy is utilized for two purposes: mere maintenance and work. For man, maintenance of life requires about 1600 kilo-calories a day ("maintenance calories"). Anything that he does over and above merely staying alive will be defined as work, and is supported by "work calories" which he takes in. Work calories are used not only for what we call work in common speech; they are also required for all forms of enjoyment, from swimming and automobile racing to playing music and writing poetry. If our goal is to maximize population it is obvious what we must do: We must make the work calories per person approach as close to zero as possible. No gourmet meals, no vacations, no sports, no music, no literature, no art. . . . I think that everyone will grant, without argument or proof, that maximizing population does not maximize goods. Bentham's goal is impossible.

In reaching this conclusion I have made the usual assumption that it is the acquisition of energy that is the problem. The appearance of atomic energy has led some to question this assumption. However, given an infinite source of energy, population growth still produces an inescapable problem. The problem of the acquisition of energy is replaced by the problem of its dissipation, as J. H. Fremlin has so wittily shown.[4] The arithmetic signs in the analysis are, as it were, reversed; but Bentham's goal is still unobtainable.

The optimum population is, then, less than the maximum. The difficulty of defining the optimum is enormous; so far as I know, no one has seriously tackled this problem. Reaching an acceptable and stable solution will surely require more than one generation of hard analytical work—and much persuasion.

We want the maximum good per person; but what is good? To one person it is wilderness, to another it is ski lodges for thousands. To one it is estuaries to nourish ducks for hunters to shoot; to another it is factory land. Comparing one good with another is, we usually say, impossible because goods are incommensurable. Incommensurables cannot be compared.

Theoretically this may be true; but in real life incommensurables *are* commensurable. Only a criterion of judgment and a system of weighting are needed. In nature the criterion is survival. Is it better for a species to be small and hideable, or large and powerful? Natural selection commensurates the incommensurables. The compromise achieved depends on a natural weighting of the values of the variables.

Man must imitate this process. There is no doubt that in fact he already does, but unconsciously. It is when the hidden decisions are made explicit that the arguments begin. The problem for the years ahead is to work out an acceptable theory of weighting. Synergistic effects, nonlinear variation, and difficulties in discounting the future make the intellectual problem difficult, but not (in principle) insoluble.

Has any cultural group solved this practical problem at the present time, even on an intuitive level? One simple fact proves that none has: there is no prosperous population in the world today that has, and has had for some time, a growth rate of zero. Any people that has intuitively identified its optimum point will soon reach it, after which its growth rate becomes and remains zero.

Of course, a positive growth rate might be taken as evidence that a population is below its optimum. However, by any reasonable standards, the most rapidly growing populations on earth today are (in general) the most miserable. This association (which need not be invariable) casts doubt on the optimistic assumption that the positive growth rate of a population is evidence that it has yet to reach its optimum.

We can make little progress in working toward optimum population size until we explicitly exorcize the spirit of Adam Smith in the field of practical demography. In economic affairs, *The Wealth of Nations* (1776) popularized the "invisible hand," the idea that an individual who "intends only his own gain," is, as it were, "led by an invisible hand to promote . . . the public interest."[5] Adam Smith did not assert that this was invariably true, and perhaps neither did any of his followers. But he contributed to a dominant tendency of thought that has ever since interfered with positive action based on rational analysis, namely, the tendency to assume that decisions reached individually will, in fact, be the best decisions for an entire society. If this assumption is correct it justifies the continuance of our present policy of laissez-faire in reproduction. If it is correct we can assume that men will control their individual fecundity so as to produce the optimum population. If the assumption is not correct, we need to reexamine our individual freedoms to see which ones are defensible.

Tragedy of Freedom in a Commons

The rebuttal to the invisible hand in population control is to be found in a scenario first sketched in a little-known pamphlet[6] in 1833 by a mathematical amateur named William Forster Lloyd (1794–1852). We may well call it "the tragedy of the commons," using the word "tragedy" as the philosopher Whitehead used it[7]: "The essence of dramatic tragedy is not unhappiness. It resides in the solemnity of the remorseless working of things." He then goes on to say, "This inevitableness of destiny can only be illustrated in terms of human life by incidents which in fact involve unhappiness. For it is only by them that the futility of escape can be made evident in the drama."

The tragedy of the commons develops in this way. Picture a pasture open to all. It is to be expected that each herdsman will try to keep as many cattle as possible on the commons. Such an arrangement may work reasonably satisfactorily for centuries because tribal wars, poaching, and disease keep the numbers of both man and beast well below the carrying capacity of the land. Finally, however, comes the day of reckoning, that is, the day when the long-desired goal of social stability becomes a reality. At this point, the inherent logic of the commons remorselessly generates tragedy.

As a rational being, each herdsman seeks to maximize his gain. Explicitly or implicitly, more or less consciously, he asks, "What is the utility *to me* of adding one more animal to my herd?" This utility has one negative and one positive component.

1. The positive component is a function of the increment of one animal. Since the herdsman receives all the proceeds from the sale of the additional animal, the positive utility is nearly $+1$.

2. The negative component is a function of the additional overgrazing created by one more animal. Since, however, the effects of overgrazing are shared by all the herdsmen, the negative utility for any particular decision-making herdsman is only a fraction of -1.

Adding together the component partial utilities, the rational herdsman concludes that the only sensible course for him to pursue is to add another animal to his herd. And another; and another. . . . But this is the conclusion reached by each and every rational herdsman sharing a commons. Therein is the tragedy. Each man is locked into a system that compels him to increase his herd without limit—in a world that is limited. Ruin is the destination toward which all men rush, each pursuing his own best interest in a society that believes in the freedom of the commons. Freedom in a commons brings ruin to all.

Some would say that this is a platitude. Would that it were! In a sense, it was learned thousands of years ago, but natural selection favors the forces of psychological denial.[8] The individual benefits as an individual from his ability to deny the truth even though society as a whole, of which he is a part, suffers. Education can counteract the natural tendency to do the wrong thing, but the inexorable succession of generations requires that the basis for this knowledge be constantly refreshed.

A simple incident that occurred a few years ago in Leominster, Massachusetts, shows how perishable the knowledge is. During the Christmas shopping season the parking meters downtown were covered with plastic bags that bore tags reading: "Do not open until after Christmas. Free parking courtesy of the mayor and city council." In other words, facing the prospect of an increased demand for already scarce space, the city fathers reinstituted the system of the commons. (Cynically, we suspect that they gained more votes than they lost by this retrogressive act.)

In an approximate way, the logic of the commons has been understood for a long time, perhaps since the discovery of agriculture or the invention of private property in real estate. But it is understood mostly only in special cases which are not sufficiently generalized. Even at this late date, cattlemen leasing national land on the western ranges demonstrate no more than an ambivalent understanding, in constantly pressuring federal authorities to increase the head count to the point where over-grazing produces erosion and weed-dominance. Likewise, the oceans of the world continue to suffer from the survival of the philosophy of the commons. Maritime nations still respond automatically to the shibboleth of the "freedom of the seas." Professing to believe in the "inexhaustible resources of the oceans," they bring species after species of fish and whales closer to extinction.[9]

The national parks present another instance of the working out of the tragedy of the commons. At present, they are open to all, without limit. The parks themselves are limited in extent—there is only one Yosemite Valley —whereas population seems to grow without limit. The values that visitors seek in the parks are steadily eroded. Plainly, we must soon cease to treat the parks as commons or they will be of no value to anyone.

What shall we do? We have several options. We might sell them off as private property. We might keep them as public property, but allocate the right to enter them. The allocation might be on the basis of wealth, by the use of an auction system. It might be on the basis of merit, as defined by some agreed-upon standards. It might be by lottery. Or it might be on a first-come, first-served basis, administered to long queues. These, I think, are all the reasonable possibilities. They are all objectionable. But we must choose—or acquiesce in the destruction of the commons that we call our national parks.

Pollution

In a reverse way, the tragedy of the commons reappears in problems of pollution. Here it is not a question of taking something out of the commons, but of putting something in—sewage, or chemical, radioactive, and heat wastes into water; noxious and dangerous fumes into the air; and distracting and unpleasant advertising signs into the line of sight. The calculations of utility are much the same as before. The rational man finds that his share of the cost of the wastes he discharges into the commons is less than the cost of purifying his wastes before releasing them. Since this is true for everyone, we are locked into a system of "fouling our own nest," so long as we behave only as independent, rational, free-enterprisers.

The tragedy of the commons as a food basket is averted by private property, or something formally like it. But the air and waters surrounding us cannot readily be fenced, and so the tragedy of the commons as a cesspool must be prevented by different means, by coercive laws or taxing devices that make it cheaper for the polluter to treat his pollutants than to discharge them untreated. We have not progressed as far with the solution of this problem as we have with the first. Indeed, our particular concept of private property, which deters us from exhausting the positive resources of the earth, favors pollution. The owner of a factory on the bank of a stream— whose property extends to the middle of the stream—often has difficulty seeing why it is not his natural right to muddy the waters flowing past his door. The law, always behind the times, requires elaborate stitching and fitting to adapt it to this newly perceived aspect of the commons.

The pollution problem is a consequence of population. It did not much matter how a lonely American frontiersman disposed of his waste. "Flowing water purifies itself every ten miles," my grandfather used to say, and the myth was near enough to the truth when he was a boy, for there were not too many people. But as population became denser, the natural chemical and biological recycling processes became overloaded, calling for a redefinition of property rights.

How to Legislate Temperance?

Analysis of the pollution problem as a function of population density uncovers a not generally recognized principle of morality, namely: *the morality of an act is a function of the state of the system at the time it is performed.*[10] Using the commons as a cesspool does not harm the general public under frontier conditions, because there is no public; the same behavior in a metropolis is unbearable. A hundred and fifty years ago a plainsman could kill an American bison, cut out only the tongue for his dinner, and discard the rest of the animal. He was not in any important sense being wasteful. Today, with only a few thousand bison left, we would be appalled at such behavior.

In passing, it is worth noting that the morality of an act cannot be determined from a photograph. One does not know whether a man killing an elephant or setting fire to the grassland is harming others until one knows the total system in which his act appears. "One picture is worth a thousand words," said an ancient Chinese; but it may take 10,000 words to validate it. It is as tempting to ecologists as it is to reformers in general to try to persuade others by way of the photographic shortcut. But the essence of an argument cannot be photographed: it must be presented rationally—in words.

That morality is system-sensitive escaped the attention of most codifiers of ethics in the past. "Thou shalt not . . ." is the form of traditional ethical directives which make no allowance for particular circumstances. The laws of our society follow the pattern of ancient ethics, and therefore are poorly suited to governing a complex, crowded, changeable world. Our epicyclic solution is to augment statutory law with administrative law. Since it is practically impossible to spell out all the conditions under which it is safe to burn trash in the back yard or to run an automobile without smog-control, by law we delegate the details to bureaus. The result is administrative law, which is rightly feared for an ancient reason—*Quis custodiet ipsos custodes?*—"Who shall watch the watchers themselves?" John Adams said that we must have "a government of laws and not men." Bureau administrators, trying to evaluate the morality of acts in the total system, are singularly liable to corruption, producing a government by men, not laws.

Prohibition is easy to legislate (though not necessarily to enforce); but how do we legislate temperance? Experience indicates that it can be accomplished best through the mediation of administrative law. We limit possibilities unnecessarily if we suppose that the sentiment of *Quis custodiet* denies us the use of administrative law. We should rather retain the phrase as a perpetual reminder of fearful dangers we cannot avoid. The great challenge facing us now is to invent the corrective feedbacks that are needed to keep custodians honest. We must find ways to legitimate the needed authority of both the custodians and the corrective feedbacks.

Freedom to Breed is Intolerable

The tragedy of the commons is involved in population problems in another way. In a world governed solely by the principle of "dog eat dog"—if indeed there ever was such a world—how many children a family had would not be a matter of public concern. Parents who bred too exuberantly would leave fewer descendants, not more, because they would be unable to care adequately for their children. David Lack and others have found that such a negative feedback demonstrably controls the fecundity of birds.[11] But men are not birds, and have not acted like them for millenniums, at least.

If each human family were dependent only on its own resources; *if* the children of improvident parents starved to death; *if,* thus, overbreeding brought its own "punishment" to the germ line—*then* there would be no public interest in controlling the breeding of families. But our society is deeply committed to the welfare state,[12] and hence is confronted with another aspect of the tragedy of the commons.

In a welfare state, how shall we deal with the family, the religion, the race, or the class (or indeed any distinguishable and cohesive group) that adopts overbreeding as a policy to secure its own aggrandizement?[13] To couple the concept of freedom to breed with the belief that everyone born has an equal right to the commons is to lock the world into a tragic course of action.

Unfortunately this is just the course of action that is being pursued by the United Nations. In late 1967, some thirty nations agreed to the following:[14]

The Universal Declaration of Human Rights describes the family as the natural and fundamental unit of society. It follows that any choice and decision with regard to the size of the family must irrevocably rest with the family itself, and cannot be made by anyone else.

It is painful to have to deny categorically the validity of this right; denying it, one feels as uncomfortable as a resident of Salem, Massachusetts, who denies the reality of witches in the seventeenth century. At the present time, in liberal quarters, something like a taboo acts to inhibit criticism of the United Nations. There is a feeling that the United Nations is "our last and best hope," that we shouldn't find fault with it; we shouldn't play into the hands of the archconservatives. However, let us not forget what Robert

Louis Stevenson said: "The truth that is suppressed by friends is the readiest weapon of the enemy." If we love the truth we must openly deny the validity of the Universal Declaration of Human Rights, even though it is promoted by the United Nations. We should also join with Kingsley Davis[15] in attempting to get Planned Parenthood-World Population to see the error of its ways in embracing the same tragic ideal.

Conscience is Self-Eliminating

It is a mistake to think that we can control the breeding of mankind in the long run by an appeal to conscience. Charles Galton Darwin made this point when he spoke on the centennial of the publication of his grandfather's great book. The argument is straight-forward and Darwinian.

People vary. Confronted with appeals to limit breeding, some people will undoubtedly respond to the plea more than others. Those who have more children will produce a larger fraction of the next generation than those with more susceptible consciences. The difference will be accentuated, generation by generation.

In C. G. Darwin's words: "It may well be that it would take hundreds of generations for the progenitive instinct to develop in this way, but if it should do so, nature would have taken her revenge, and the variety *Homo contracipiens* would become extinct and would be replaced by the variety *Homo progenitivus.*"[16]

The argument assumes that conscience or the desire for children (no matter which) is hereditary—but hereditary only in the most general formal sense. The result will be the same whether the attitude is transmitted through germ cells, or exosomatically, to use A. J. Lotka's term. (If one denies the latter possibility as well as the former, then what's the point of education?) The argument has here been stated in the context of the population problem, but it applies equally well to any instance in which society appeals to an individual exploiting a commons to restrain himself for the general good—by means of his conscience. To make such an appeal is to set up a selective system that works toward the elimination of conscience from the race.

Pathogenic Effects of Conscience

The long-term disadvantage of an appeal to conscience should be enough to condemn it; but has serious short-term disadvantages as well. If we ask a man who is exploiting a commons to desist "in the name of conscience,"

what are we saying to him? What does he hear?—not only at the moment
but also in the wee small hours of the night when, half asleep, he remembers
not merely the words we used but also the nonverbal communication cues
we gave him unawares? Sooner or later, consciously or subconsciously, he
senses that he has received two communications, and that they are contradictory: (i) (intended communication) "If you don't do as we ask, we will
openly condemn you for not acting like a responsible citizen"; (ii) (the
unintended communication) "If you *do* behave as we ask, we will secretly
condemn you for a simpleton who can be shamed into standing aside while
the rest of us exploit the commons."

Every man then is caught in what Bateson has called a "double bind."
Bateson and his coworkers have made a plausible case for viewing the
double bind as an important causative factor in the genesis of schizophre-
nia.[17] The double bind may not always be so damaging, but it always
endangers the mental health of anyone to whom it is applied. "A bad
conscience," said Nietzsche, "is a kind of illness."

To conjure up a conscience in others is tempting to anyone who wishes
to extend his control beyond the legal limits. Leaders at the highest level
succumb to this temptation. Has any president during the past generation
failed to call on labor unions to moderate voluntarily their demands for
higher wages, or to steel companies to honor voluntary guidelines on prices?
I can recall none. The rhetoric used on such occasions is designed to
produce feelings of guilt in noncooperators.

For centuries it was assumed without proof that guilt was a valuable,
perhaps even an indispensable, ingredient of the civilized life. Now, in this
post-Freudian world, we doubt it.

Paul Goodman speaks from the modern point of view when he says: "No
good has ever come from feeling guilty, neither intelligence, policy, nor
compassion. The guilty do not pay attention to the object but only to
themselves, and not even to their own interests, which might make sense,
but to their anxieties."[18]

One does not have to be a professional psychiatrist to see the consequences of anxiety. We in the Western world are just emerging from a
dreadful two-centuries-long Dark Ages of Eros that was sustained partly by
prohibition laws, but perhaps more effectively by the anxiety-generating
mechanisms of education. Alex Comfort has told the story well in *The
Anxiety Makers;*[19] it is not a pretty one.

Since proof is difficult, we may even concede that the results of anxiety
may sometimes, from certain points of view, be desirable. The larger question we should ask is whether, as a matter of policy, we should ever encourage the use of a technique the tendency (if not the intention) of which is
psychologically pathogenic. We hear much talk these days of responsible

parenthood; the coupled words are incorporated into the titles of some
organizations devoted to birth control. Some people have proposed massive
propaganda campaigns to instill responsibility into the nation's (or the
world's) breeders. But what is the meaning of the word responsibility in this
context? Is it not merely a synonym for the word conscience? When we use
the word responsibility in the absence of substantial sanctions are we not
trying to browbeat a free man in a commons into acting against his own
interest? Responsibility is a verbal counterfeit for a substantial *quid pro quo*.
It is an attempt to get something for nothing.

If the word responsibility is to be used at all, I suggest that it be in the
sense Charles Frankel uses it.[20] "Responsibility," says this philosopher, "is
the product of definite social arrangements." Notice that Frankel calls for
social arrangements—not propaganda.

Mutual Coercion
Mutually Agreed Upon

The social arrangements that produce responsibility are arrangements that
create coercion, of some sort. Consider bank-robbing. The man who takes
money from a bank acts as if the bank were a commons. How do we prevent
such action? Certainly not by trying to control his behavior solely by a
verbal appeal to his sense of responsibility. Rather than rely on propaganda
we follow Frankel's lead and insist that a bank is not a commons; we seek
the definite social arrangements that will keep it from becoming a commons.
That we thereby infringe on the freedom of would-be robbers we neither
deny nor regret.

The morality of bank-robbing is particularly easy to understand because
we accept complete prohibition of this activity. We are willing to say "Thou
shalt not rob banks," without providing for exceptions. But temperance also
can be created by coercion. Taxing is a good coercive device. To keep
downtown shoppers temperate in their use of parking space we introduce
parking meters for short periods, and traffic fines for longer ones. We need
not actually forbid a citizen to park as long as he wants to; we need merely
make it increasingly expensive for him to do so. Not prohibition, but
carefully biased options are what we offer him. A Madison Avenue man
might call this persuasion; I prefer the greater candor of the word coercion.

Coercion is a dirty word to most liberals now, but it need not forever be
so. As with the four-letter words, its dirtiness can be cleansed away by
exposure to the light, by saying it over and over without apology or embarrassment. To many, the word coercion implies arbitrary decisions of distant

and irresponsible bureaucrats; but this is not a necessary part of its meaning. The only kind of coercion I recommend is mutual coercion, mutually agreed upon by the majority of the people affected.

To say that we mutually agree to coercion is not to say that we are required to enjoy it, or even to pretend we enjoy it. Who enjoys taxes? We all grumble about them. But we accept compulsory taxes because we recognize that voluntary taxes would favor the conscienceless. We institute and (grumblingly) support taxes and other coercive devices to escape the horror of the commons.

An alternative to the commons need not be perfectly just to be preferable. With real estate and other material goods, the alternative we have chosen is the institution of private property coupled with legal inheritance. Is this system perfectly just? As a genetically trained biologist I deny that it is. It seems to me that, if there are to be differences in individual inheritance, legal possession should be perfectly correlated with biological inheritance—that those who are biologically more fit to be the custodians of property and power should legally inherit more. But genetic recombination continually makes a mockery of the doctrine of "like father, like son" implicit in our laws of legal inheritance. An idiot can inherit millions, and a trust fund can keep his estate intact. We must admit that our legal system of private property plus inheritance is unjust—but we put up with it because we are not convinced, at the moment, that anyone has invented a better system. The alternative of the commons is too horrifying to contemplate. Injustice is preferable to total ruin.

It is one of the peculiarities of the warfare between reform and the status quo that it is thoughtlessly governed by a double standard. Whenever a reform measure is proposed it is often defeated when its opponents triumphantly discover a flaw in it. As Kingsley Davis has pointed out,[21] worshippers of the status quo sometimes imply that no reform is possible without unanimous agreement, an implication contrary to historical fact. As nearly as I can make out, automatic rejection of proposed reforms is based on one of two unconscious assumptions: (i) that the status quo is perfect; or (ii) that the choice we face is between reform and no action; if the proposed reform is imperfect, we presumably should take no action at all, while we wait for a perfect proposal.

But we can never do nothing. That which we have done for thousands of years is also action. It also produces evils. Once we are aware that the status quo is action, we can then compare its discoverable advantages and disadvantages with the predicted advantages and disadvantages of the proposed reform, discounting as best we can for our lack of experience. On the basis of such a comparison, we can make a rational decision which will not involve the unworkable assumption that only perfect systems are tolerable.

Recognition of Necessity

Perhaps the simplest summary of this analysis of man's population problems is this: the commons, if justifiable at all, is justifiable only under conditions of low-population density. As the human population has increased, the commons has had to be abandoned in one aspect after another.

First we abandoned the commons in food gathering, enclosing farm land and restricting pastures and hunting and fishing areas. These restrictions are still not complete throughout the world.

Somewhat later we saw that the commons as a place for waste disposal would also have to be abandoned. Restrictions on the disposal of domestic sewage are widely accepted in the Western world; we are still struggling to close the commons to pollution by automobiles, factories, insecticide sprayers, fertilizing operations, and atomic energy installations.

In a still more embryonic state is our recognition of the evils of the commons in matters of pleasure. There is almost no restriction on the propagation of sound waves in the public medium. The shopping public is assaulted with mindless music, without its consent. Our government is paying out billions of dollars to create supersonic transport which will disturb 50,000 people for every one person who is whisked from coast to coast three hours faster. Advertisers muddy the airwaves of radio and television and pollute the view of travelers. We are a long way from outlawing the commons in matters of pleasure. Is this because our Puritan inheritance makes us view pleasure as something of a sin, and pain (that is, the pollution of advertising) as the sign of virtue?

Every new enclosure of the commons involves the infringement of somebody's personal liberty. Infringements made in the distant past are accepted because no contemporary complains of a loss. It is the newly proposed infringements that we vigorously oppose; cries of "rights" and "freedom" fill the air. But what does "freedom" mean? When men mutually agreed to pass laws against robbing, mankind became more free, not less so. Individuals locked into the logic of the commons are free only to bring on universal ruin; once they see the necessity of mutual coercion, they become free to pursue other goals. I believe it was Hegel who said, "Freedom is the recognition of necessity."

The most important aspect of necessity that we must now recognize is the necessity of abandoning the commons in breeding. No technical solution can rescue us from the misery of overpopulation. Freedom to breed will bring ruin to all. At the moment, to avoid hard decisions many of us are tempted to propagandize for conscience and responsible parenthood. The temptation must be resisted, because an appeal to independently acting consciences selects for the disappearance of all conscience in the long run, and an increase in anxiety in the short.

The only way we can preserve and nurture other and more precious freedoms is by relinquishing the freedom to breed, and that very soon. "Freedom is the recognition of necessity"—and it is the role of education to reveal to all the necessity of abandoning the freedom to breed. Only so, can we put an end to this aspect of the tragedy of the commons.

NOTES

1. J. B. Wiesner and H. F.York, *Sci. Amer.* **211** (No. 4), **27** (1964).

2. G. Hardin, *J. Hered.* **50,** 68 (1959); S. von Hoerner, *Science,* **137,** 18 (1962).

3. J. von Neumann and O. Morgenstern, *Theory of Games and Economic Behavior* (Princeton Univ. Press, Princeton, N.J., 1947), p. 11.

4. J. H. Fremlin, *New Sci.,* No. 415 (1964), p. 285.

5. A. Smith, *The Wealth of Nations* (Modern Library, New York, 1937), p. 423.

6. W. F. Lloyd, *Two Lectures on the Checks to Population* (Oxford Univ. Press, Oxford, England, 1833), reprinted (in part) in *Population, Evolution, and Birth Control,* G. Hardin, ed. (Freeman, San Francisco, 1964), p. 37.

7. A. N. Whitehead, *Science and the Modern World* (Mentor, New York, 1948), p. 17.

8. G. Hardin, Ed. *Population, Evolution, and Birth Control* (Freeman, San Francisco, 1964), p. 56.

9. S. McVay, *Sci. Amer.* **216** (No. 8), 13 (1966).

10. J. Fletcher, *Situation Ethics* (Westminster, Philadelphia, 1966).

11. D. Lack, *The Natural Regulation of Animal Numbers* (Clarendon Press, Oxford, 1954).

12. H. Girvetz, *From Wealth to Welfare* (Stanford Univ. Press, Stanford, Calif., 1950).

13. G. Hardin, *Perspec. Biol. Med.* **6,** 366 (1963).

14. U Thant, *Int. Planned Parenthood News,* No. 168 (February, 1968), p. 3.

15. K. Davis, *Science* **158,** 730 (1967).

16. S. Tax, ed., *Evolution after Darwin* (Univ. of Chicago Press, Chicago, 1960), vol. 2, p. 469.

17. G. Bateson, D. D. Jackson, J. Haley, J. Weakland, *Behav. Sci.* **1,** 251 (1956).

18. P. Goodman, *New York Rev. Books* **10** (8), 22 (23 May 1968).

19. A. Comfort, *The Anxiety Makers* (Nelson, London, 1967).

20. C. Frankel, *The Case for Modern Man* (Harper, New York, 1955), p. 203.

21. J. D. Roslansky, *Genetics and the Future of Man* (Appleton-Century-Crofts, New York, 1966), p. 177.

TOO MANY PEOPLE
❧ *Paul R. Ehrlich*

Americans are beginning to realize that the undeveloped countries of the world face an inevitable population-food crisis. Each year food production in undeveloped countries falls a bit further behind burgeoning population growth, and people go to bed a little bit hungrier. While there are temporary or local reversals of this trend, it now seems inevitable that it will continue to its logical conclusion: mass starvation. The rich are going to get richer, but the more numerous poor are going to get poorer. Of these poor, a minimum of three and one-half million will starve to death this year, mostly children. But this is a mere handful compared to the numbers that will be starving in a decade or so. And it is now too late to take action to save many of those people.

In a book about population there is a temptation to stun the reader with an avalanche of statistics. I'll spare you most, but not all, of that. After all, no matter how you slice it, population is a numbers game. Perhaps the best way to impress you with numbers is to tell you about the "doubling time" —the time necessary for the population to double in size.

It has been estimated that the human population of 6000 B.C. was about five million people, taking perhaps one million years to get there from two and a half million. The population did not reach 500 million until almost 8,000 years later—about 1650 A.D. This means it doubled roughly once every thousand years or so. It reached a billion people around 1850, doubling in some 200 years. It took only 80 years or so for the next doubling, as the population reached two billion around 1930. We have not completed

SOURCE: Paul R. Ehrlich, *The Population Bomb* (New York: Ballantine Books, 1968), pp. 17–35. Copyright © 1968 by Paul R. Ehrlich. Reprinted by permission of the publisher.

the next doubling to four billion yet, but we now have well over three billion people. The doubling time at present seems to be about 37 years.[1] Quite a reduction in doubling times: 1,000,000 years, 1,000 years, 200 years, 80 years, 37 years. Perhaps the meaning of a doubling time of around 37 years is best brought home by a theoretical exercise. Let's examine what might happen on the absurd assumption that the population continued to double every 37 years into the indefinite future.

If growth continued at that rate for about 900 years, there would be some 60,000,000,000,000,000 people on the face of the earth. Sixty million billion people. This is about 100 persons for each square yard of the Earth's surface, land and sea. A British physicist, J. H. Fremlin,[2] guessed that such a multitude might be housed in a continuous 2,000–story building covering our entire planet. The upper 1,000 stories would contain only the apparatus for running this gigantic warren. Ducts, pipes, wires, elevator shafts, etc., would occupy about half of the space in the bottom 1,000 stories. This would leave three or four yards of floor space for each person. I will leave to your imagination the physical details of existence in this ant heap, except to point out that all would not be black. Probably each person would be limited in his travel. Perhaps he could take elevators through all 1,000 residential stories but could travel only within a circle of a few hundred yards' radius on any floor. This would permit, however, each person to choose his friends from among some ten million people! And, as Fremlin points out, entertainment on the worldwide TV should be excellent, for at any time, "one could expect some ten million Shakespeares and rather more Beatles to be alive."

Could growth of the human population of the Earth continue beyond that point? Not according to Fremlin. We would have reached a "heat limit." People themselves, as well as their activities, convert other forms of energy into heat which must be dissipated. In order to permit this excess heat to radiate directly from the top of the "world building" directly into space, the atmosphere would have been pumped into flasks under the sea well before the limiting population size was reached. The precise limit would depend on the technology of the day. At a population size of one billion billion people, the temperature of the "world roof" would be kept around the melting point of iron to radiate away the human heat generated.

But, you say, surely Science (with a capital "S") will find a way for us to occupy the other planets of our solar system and eventually of other stars before we get all that crowded. Skip for a moment the virtual certainty that those planets are uninhabitable. Forget also the insurmountable logistic problems of moving billions of people off the Earth. Fremlin has made some interesting calculations on how much time we could buy by occupying the planets of the solar system. For instance, at any given time it would take only about 50 years to populate Venus, Mercury, Mars, the moon, and the moons of Jupiter and Saturn to the same population density as Earth.[3]

What if the fantastic problems of reaching and colonizing the other planets of the solar system, such as Jupiter and Uranus, can be solved? It would take only about 200 years to fill them "Earth-full." So we could perhaps gain 250 years of time for population growth in the solar system after we had reached an absolute limit on Earth. What then? We can't ship our surplus to the stars. Professor Garrett Hardin[4] of the University of California at Santa Barbara has dealt effectively with this fantasy. Using extremely optimistic assumptions, he has calculated that Americans, by cutting their standard of living down to 18% of its present level, could in *one year* set aside enough capital to finance the exportation to the stars of *one day's* increase in the population of the world.

Interstellar transport for surplus people presents an amusing prospect. Since the ships would take generations to reach most stars, the only people who could be transported would be those willing to exercise strict birth control. Population explosions on space ships would be disastrous. Thus we would have to export our responsible people, leaving the irresponsible at home on Earth to breed.

Enough of fantasy. Hopefully, you are convinced that the population will have to stop growing sooner or later and that the extremely remote possibility of expanding into outer space offers no escape from the laws of population growth. If you still want to hope for the stars, just remember that, at the current growth rate, in a few thousand years everything in the visible universe would be converted into people, and the ball of people would be expanding with the speed of light![5] Unfortunately, even 900 years is much too far in the future for those of us concerned with the population explosion. As you shall see, the next *nine* years will probably tell the story.

Of course, population growth is not occurring uniformly over the face of the Earth. Indeed, countries are divided rather neatly into two groups: those with rapid growth rates, and those with relatively slow growth rates. The first group, making up about two-thirds of the world population, coincides closely with what are known as the "undeveloped countries" (UDCs). The UDCs are not industrialized, tend to have inefficient agriculture, very small gross national products, high illiteracy rates and related problems. That's what UDCs are technically, but a short definition of undeveloped is "starving." Most Latin American, African, and Asian countries fall into this category. The second group consists, in essence, of the "developed countries" (DCs). DCs are modern, industrial nations, such as the United States, Canada, most European countries, Israel, Russia, Japan, and Australia. Most people in these countries are adequately nourished.

Doubling times in the UDCs range around 20 to 35 years. Examples of these times (from the 1968 figures just released by the Population Reference Bureau) are Kenya, 24 years; Nigeria, 28; Turkey, 24; Indonesia, 31; Philippines, 20; Brazil, 22; Costa Rica, 20; and El Salvador, 19. Think of what it means for the population of a country to double in 25 years. In order just to keep living standards at the present inadequate level, the food available for the people must be doubled. Every structure and road must be duplicated. The amount of power must be doubled. The capacity of the transport system must be doubled. The number of trained doctors, nurses, teachers, and administrators must be doubled. This would be a fantastically difficult job in the United States—a rich country with a fine agricultural system, immense industries, and rich natural resources. Think of what it means to a country with none of these.

Remember also that in virtually all UDCs, people have gotten the word about the better life it is possible to have. They have seen colored pictures in magazines of the miracles of Western technology. They have seen automobiles and airplanes. They have seen American and European movies. Many have seen refrigerators, tractors, and even TV sets. Almost all have heard transistor radios. They *know* that a better life is possible. They have what we like to call "rising expectations." If twice as many people are to be happy, the miracle of doubling what they now have will not be enough. It will only maintain today's standard of living. There will have to be a tripling or better. Needless to say, they are not going to be happy.

Doubling times for the populations of the DCs tend to be in the 50- to 200-year range. Examples of 1968 doubling times are the United States, 63 years; Austria, 175; Denmark, 88; Norway, 88; United Kingdom, 140; Poland, 88; Russia, 63; Italy, 117; Spain, 88; and Japan, 63. These are industrialized countries that have undergone the so-called demographic transition—a transition from high to low growth rate. As industrialization progressed, children became less important to parents as extra hands to work on the farm and as support in old age. At the same time they became a financial drag—expensive to raise and educate. Presumably these are the reasons for a slowing of population growth after industrialization. They boil down to a simple fact—people just want to have fewer children.

This is not to say, however, that population is not a problem for the DCs. First of all, most of them are overpopulated. They are overpopulated by the simple criterion that they are not able to produce enough food to feed their populations. It is true that they have the money to buy food, but when food is no longer available for sale they will find the money rather indigestible. Then, too, they share with the UDCs a serious problem of population distribution. Their urban centers are getting more and more crowded relative to the countryside. This problem is not as severe as it is in the UDCs (if current trends should continue, which they cannot, Calcutta could have

66 million inhabitants in the year 2000). As you are well aware, however, urban concentrations are creating serious problems even in America. In the United States, one of the more rapidly growing DCs, we hear constantly of the headaches caused by growing population: not just garbage in our environment, but overcrowded highways, burgeoning slums, deteriorating school systems, rising crime rates, riots, and other related problems.

From the point of view of a demographer, the whole problem is quite simple. A population will continue to grow as long as the birth rate exceeds the death rate—if immigration and emigration are not occurring. It is, of course, the balance between birth rate and death rate that is critical. The birth rate is the number of births per thousand people per year in the population. The death rate is the number of deaths per thousand people per year.[6] Subtracting the death rate from the birth rate, and ignoring migration, gives the rate of increase. If the birth rate is 30 per thousand per year, and the death rate is 10 per thousand per year, then the rate of increase is 20 per thousand per year $(30 - 10 = 20)$. Expressed as a percent (rate per hundred people), the rate of 20 per thousand becomes 2%. If the rate of increase is 2%, then the doubling time will be 35 years. Note that if you simply added 20 people per thousand per year to the population, it would take 50 years to add a second thousand people $(20 \times 50 = 1,000)$. But the doubling time is actually much less because populations grow at compound interest rates. Just as interest dollars themselves earn interest, so people added to populations produce more people. It's growing at compound interest that makes populations double so much more rapidly than seems possible. Look at the relationship between the annual percent increase (interest rate) and the doubling time of the population (time for your money to double):

ANNUAL PERCENT INCREASE	DOUBLING TIME
1.0	70
2.0	35
3.0	24
4.0	17

Those are all the calculations—I promise. If you are interested in more details on how demographic figuring is done, you may enjoy reading Thompson and Lewis's excellent book, *Population Problems.*[7]

There are some professional optimists around who like to greet every sign of dropping birth rates with wild pronouncements about the end of the population explosion. They are a little like a person who, after a low temperature of five below zero on December 21, interprets a low of only three below zero on December 22 as a cheery sign of approaching spring. First of all, birth rates, along with all demographic statistics, show short-term fluctuations caused by many factors. For instance, the birth rate depends rather heavily on the number of women at reproductive age. In the United States the current low birth rates soon will be replaced by higher rates as more post World War II "baby boom" children move into their reproductive years. In Japan, 1966, the Year of the Fire Horse, was a year of very low birth rates. There is widespread belief that girls born in the Year of the Fire Horse make poor wives, and Japanese couples try to avoid giving birth in that year because they are afraid of having daughters.

But, I repeat, it is the relationship between birth rate and death rate that is most critical. Indonesia, Laos, and Haiti all had birth rates around 46 per thousand in 1966. Costa Rica's birth rate was 41 per thousand. Good for Costa Rica? Unfortunately, not very. Costa Rica's death rate was less than nine per thousand, while the other countries all had death rates above 20 per thousand. The population of Costa Rica in 1966 was doubling every 17 years, while the doubling times of Indonesia, Laos, and Haiti were all above 30 years. Ah, but, you say, it was good for Costa Rica—fewer people per thousand were dying each year. Fine for a few years perhaps, but what then? Some 50% of the people in Costa Rica are under 15 years old. As they get older, they will need more and more food in a world with less and less. In 1983 they will have twice as many mouths to feed as they had in 1966, if the 1966 trend continues. Where will the food come from? Today the death rate in Costa Rica is low in part because they have a large number of physicians in proportion to their population. How do you suppose those physicians will keep the death rate down when there's not enough food to keep people alive?

One of the most ominous facts of the current situation is that roughly 40% of the population of the undeveloped world is made up of people *under 15 years old*. As that mass of young people moves into its reproductive years during the next decade, we're going to see the greatest baby boom of all time. Those youngsters are the reason for all the ominous predictions for the year 2000. They are the gunpowder for the population explosion.

How did we get into this bind? It all happened a long time ago, and the story involves the process of natural selection, the development of culture, and man's swollen head. The essence of success in evolution is reproduction. Indeed, natural selection is simply defined as differential reproduction of genetic types. That is, if people with blue eyes have more children on the average than those with brown eyes, natural selection is occurring. More genes for blue eyes will be passed on to the next generation than will genes for brown eyes. Should this continue, the population will have progressively larger and larger proportions of blue-eyed people. This differential reproduction of genetic types is the driving force of evolution; it has been driving evolution for billions of years. Whatever types produced more offspring became the common types. Virtually all populations contain very many different genetic types (for reasons that need not concern us), and some are always outreproducing others. As I said, reproduction is the key to winning the evolutionary game. Any structure, physiological process, or pattern of behavior that leads to greater reproductive success will tend to be perpetuated. The entire process by which man developed involves thousands of millenia of our ancestors being more successful breeders than their relatives. Facet number one of our bind—the urge to reproduce has been fixed in us by billions of years of evolution.

Of course through all those years of evolution, our ancestors were fighting a continual battle to keep the birth rate ahead of the death rate. That they were successful is attested to by our very existence, for, if the death rate had overtaken the birth rate for any substantial period of time, the evolutionary line leading to man would have gone extinct. Among our apelike ancestors, a few million years ago, it was still very difficult for a mother to rear her children successfully. Most of the offspring died before they reached reproductive age. The death rate was near the birth rate. Then another factor entered the picture—cultural evolution was added to biological evolution.

Culture can be loosely defined as the body of nongenetic information which people pass from generation to generation. It is the accumulated knowledge that, in the old days, was passed on entirely by word of mouth, painting, and demonstration. Several thousand years ago the written word was added to the means of cultural transmission. Today culture is passed on in these ways, and also through television, computer tapes, motion pictures, records, blueprints, and other media. Culture is all the information man possesses except for that which is stored in the chemical language of his genes.

The large size of the human brain evolved in response to the development of cultural information. A big brain is an advantage when dealing with such information. Big-brained individuals were able to deal more successfully with the culture of their group. They were thus more successful reproductively than their smaller-brained relatives. They passed on their genes for big brains to their numerous offspring. They also added to the accumulating store of cultural information, increasing slightly the premium placed on brain size in the next generation. A self-reinforcing selective trend developed—a trend toward increased brain size.[8]

But there was, quite literally, a rub. Babies had bigger and bigger heads. There were limits to how large a woman's pelvis could conveniently become. To make a long story short, the strategy of evolution was not to make a woman bell-shaped and relatively immobile, but to accept the problem of having babies who were helpless for a long period while their brains grew after birth.[9] How could the mother defend and care for her infant during its unusually long period of helplessness? She couldn't, unless Papa hung around. The girls are still working on that problem, but an essential step was to get rid of the short, well-defined breeding season characteristic of most mammals. The year-round sexuality of the human female, the long period of infant dependence on the female, the evolution of the family group, all are at the roots of our present problem. They are essential ingredients in the vast social phenomenon that we call sex. Sex is not simply an act leading to the production of offspring. It is a varied and complex cultural phenomenon penetrating into all aspects of our lives—one involving our self-esteem, our choice of friends, cars, and leaders. It is tightly interwoven with our mythologies and history. Sex in man is necessary for the production of young, but it also evolved to ensure their successful rearing. Facet number two of our bind—our urge to reproduce is hopelessly entwined with most of our other urges.

Of course, in the early days the whole system did not prevent a very high mortality among the young, as well as among the older members of the group. Hunting and food-gathering is a risky business. Cavemen had to throw very impressive cave bears out of their caves before the men could move in. Witch doctors and shamans had a less than perfect record at treating wounds and curing disease. Life was short, if not sweet. Man's total population size doubtless increased slowly but steadily as human populations expanded out of the African cradle of our species.

Then about 8,000 years ago a major change occurred—the agricultural revolution. People began to give up hunting food and settled down to grow it. Suddenly some of the risk was removed from life. The chances of dying of starvation diminished greatly in some human groups. Other threats associated with the nomadic life were also reduced, perhaps balanced by new threats of disease and large-scale warfare associated with the development of cities. But the overall result was a more secure existence than before, and the human population grew more rapidly. Around 1800, when the standard of living in what are today the DCs was dramatically increasing due to industrialization, population growth really began to accelerate. The development of medical science was the straw that broke the camel's back. While lowering death rates in the DCs was due in part to other factors, there is no question that "instant death control," exported by the DCs, has been responsible for the drastic lowering of death rates in the UDCs. Medical science, with its efficient public health programs, has been able to depress the death rate with astonishing rapidity and at the same time drastically increase the birth rate; healthier people have more babies.

The power of exported death control can best be seen by an examination of the classic case of Ceylon's assault on malaria after World War II. Between 1933 and 1942 the death rate due directly to malaria was *reported* as almost two per thousand. This rate, however, represented only a portion of the malaria deaths, as many were reported as being due to "pyrexia."[10] Indeed, in 1934–1935 a malaria epidemic may have been directly responsible for fully half of the deaths on the island. In addition, malaria, which infected a large portion of the population, made people susceptible to many other diseases. It thus contributed to the death rate indirectly as well as directly.

The introduction of DDT in 1946 brought rapid control over the mosquitoes which carry malaria. As a result, the death rate on the island was halved in less than a decade. The death rate in Ceylon in 1945 was 22. It dropped 34% between 1946 and 1947 and moved down to ten in 1954. Since the sharp postwar drop it has continued to decline and now stands at eight. Although part of the drop is doubtless due to the killing of other insects which carry disease and to other public health measures, most of it can be accounted for by the control of malaria.

Victory over malaria, yellow fever, smallpox, cholera, and other infectious diseases has been responsible for similar plunges in death rate throughout most of the UDCs. In the decade 1940–1950 the death rate declined 46% in Puerto Rico, 43% in Formosa, and 23% in Jamaica. In a sample of 18 undeveloped areas the average decline in death rate between 1945 and 1950 was 24%.

It is, of course, socially very acceptable to reduce the death rate. Billions of years of evolution have given us all a powerful will to live. Intervening in the birth rate goes against our evolutionary values. During all those centuries of our evolutionary past, the individuals who had the most children passed on their genetic endowment in greater quantities than those who reproduced less. Their genes dominate our heredity today. All our biological urges are for more reproduction, and they are all too often reinforced by our culture. In brief, death control goes with the grain, birth control against it.

In summary, the world's population will continue to grow as long as the birth rate exceeds the death rate; it's as simple as that. When it stops growing or starts to shrink, it will mean that either the birth rate has gone down or the death rate has gone up or a combination of the two. Basically, then, there are only two kinds of solutions to the population problem. One is a "birth rate solution," in which we find ways to lower the birth rate. The other is a "death rate solution," in which ways to raise the death rate—war, famine, pestilence—*find us.* The problem could have been avoided by *population control,* in which mankind consciously adjusted the birth rate so that a "death rate solution" did not have to occur.

NOTES

1. Since this was written, 1968 figures have appeared, showing that the doubling time is now 35 years.

2. J. H. Fremlin, "How Many People Can the World Support?" *New Scientist,* October 29, 1964.

3. To understand this, simply consider what would happen if we held the population constant at three billion people by exporting all the surplus people. If this were done for 37 years (the time it now takes for one doubling) we would have exported three billion people—enough to populate a twin planet of the Earth to the same density. In two doubling times (74 years) we would reach a total human population for the solar system of 12 billion people, enough tc populate the Earth and three similar planets to the density found on Earth today. Since the areas of the planets and moons mentioned above are not three times that of the Earth, they can be populated to equal density in much less than two doubling times.

4. "Interstellar Migration and the Population Problem." *Heredity* 50: 68–70, 1959.

5. I. J. Cook, *New Scientist,* September 8, 1966

6. The birth rate is more precisely the total number of births in a country during a year, divided by the total population at the midpoint of the year, multiplied by 1,000. Suppose that there were 80 births in Lower Slobbovia during 1967, and that the population of Lower Slobbovia was 2,000 on July 1, 1967. Then the birth rate would be:

$$\text{Birth rate} = \frac{80 \text{ (total births in L. Slobbovia in 1967)}}{2,000 \text{ (total population, July 1, 1967)}} \times 1,000$$
$$= .04 \times 1,000 = 40$$

Similarly if there were 40 deaths in Lower Slobbovia during 1967, the death rate would be:

$$\text{Death rate} = \frac{40 \text{ (total deaths in L. Slobbovia in 1967)}}{2,000 \text{ (total population, July 1, 1967)}} \times 1,000$$
$$= .02 \times 1,000 = 20$$

Then the Lower Slobbovian birth rate would be 40 per thousand, and the death rate would be 20 per thousand. For every 1,000 Lower Slobbovians alive on July 1, 1967, 40 babies were born and 20 people died. Subtracting the death rate from the birth rate gives us the rate of natural increase of Lower Slobbovia for the year 1967. That is, 40 − 20 = 20; during 1967 the population grew at a rate of 20 people per thousand per year. Dividing that rate by ten expresses the increase as a percent (the increase per hundred per year). The increase in 1967 in Lower Slobbovia was two percent. Remember that this rate of increase ignores any movement of people into and out of Lower Slobbovia.

7. McGraw-Hill Book Company, Inc., New York. 1965.

8. Human brain size increased from an apelike capacity of about 500 cubic centimeters (cc) in *Australopithecus* to about 1,500 cc in modern *Homo sapiens.* Among modern men small variations in brain size do not seem to be related to significant differences in the ability to use cultural information, and there is no particular reason to believe that our brain size will continue to increase. Further evolution may occur more readily in a direction of increased efficiency rather than increased size.

9. This is, of course, an oversimplified explanation. For more detail see Ehrlich and Holm, *The Process of Evolution,* McGraw-Hill Book Company, Inc., New York. 1963.

10. These data and those that follow on the decline of death rates are from Kingsley Davis's, "The Amazing Decline of Mortality in Underdeveloped Areas," *The American Economic Review* 46 (May 1956), 305–318.

POLLUTING THE ENVIRONMENT
✌ *Lord Ritchie-Calder*

To hell with posterity! After all, what have the unborn ever done for us? Nothing. Did they, with sweat and misery, make the Industrial Revolution possible? Did they go down into the carboniferous forests of millions of years ago to bring up coal to make wealth and see nine-tenths of the carbon belched out as chimney soot? Did they drive the plows that broke the plains to release the dust that the buffalo had trampled and fertilized for centuries? Did they have to broil in steel plants to make the machines and see the pickling acids poured into the sweet waters of rivers and lakes? Did they have to labor to cut down the tall timbers to make homesteads and provide newsprint for the Sunday comics and the celluloid for Hollywood spectaculars, leaving the hills naked to the eroding rains and winds? Did they have the ingenuity to drill down into the Paleozoic seas to bring up the oil to feed

SOURCE: Lord Ritchie-Calder, "Polluting the Environment," *The Center Magazine,* 2, no. 3 (May 1969), 7–12. Reprinted by permission from *The Center Magazine,* a publication of the Center for the Study of Democratic Institutions in Santa Barbara, California.

the internal-combustion engines so that their exhausts could create smog? Did they have the guts to man rigs out at sea so that boreholes could probe for oil in the offshore fissures of the San Andreas Fault? Did they endure the agony and the odium of the atom bomb and spray the biosphere with radioactive fallout? All that the people yet unborn have done is to wait and let us make the mistakes. To hell with posterity! That, too, can be arranged. As Shelley wrote: "Hell is a city much like London, a populous and smoky city."

At a conference held at Princeton, New Jersey, at the end of 1968, Professor Kingsley Davis, one of the greatest authorities on urban development, took the role of hell's realtor. The prospectus he offered from his latest survey of world cities was hair-raising. He showed that thirty-eight per cent of the world's population is already living in what are defined as "urban places." Over one-fifth of the world's population is living in cities of a hundred thousand or more. Over 375,000,000 people are living in cities of a million and over. On present trends it will take only fifteen years for half the world's population to be living in cities, and in fifty-five years everyone will be urbanized.

Davis foresaw that within the lifetime of a child born today, on present rates of population increase, there will be fifteen billion people to be fed and housed—over four times as many as now. The whole human species will be living in cities of a million and over and the biggest city will have 1,300,000,000 inhabitants. Yes, 1.3 billion. That is 186 times as many as there are in Greater London today.

In his forebodings of Dystopia (with a "y" as in dyspepsia, but it could just as properly be "Dis," after the ruler of the Underworld), Doxiades has warned about the disorderly growth of cities, oozing into each other like confluent ulcers. He has given us Ecumenopolis—World City. The East Side of Ecumenopolis would have as its Main Street the Eurasian Highway, stretching from Glasgow to Bangkok, with the Channel tunnel as an underpass and a built-up area all the way. West Side, divided not by railroad tracks but by the Atlantic, is already emerging (or, rather, merging) in the United States. There is talk, and evidence, of "Boswash," the urban development of a built-up area from Boston to Washington. On the Pacific Coast, with Los Angeles already sprawling into the desert, the realtor's garden cities, briskly reënforced by industrial estates, are slurring into one another and presently will stretch all the way from San Diego to San Francisco. The Main Street of Sansan will be Route 101. This is insansanity. We do not need a crystal ball to foresee what Davis and Doxiades are predicting—we can see it through smog-colored spectacles; we can smell it seventy years away because it is in our nostrils today; a blind man can see what is coming.

Are these trends inevitable? They are unless we do something about them.

I have given up predicting and have taken to prognosis. There is a very important difference. Prediction is based on the projection of trends. Experts plan for the trends and thus confirm them. They regard warnings as instructions. For example, while I was lecturing in that horror city of Calcutta, where three-quarters of the population live in shacks without running water or sewage disposal, and, in the monsoon season, wade through their own floating excrement, I warned that within twenty-five years there would be in India at least five cities, each with populations of over sixty million, ten times bigger than Calcutta. I was warning against the drift into the great conurbations now going on, which has been encouraged by ill-conceived policies of industrialization. I was warning against imitating the German Ruhr, the British Black Country, and America's Pittsburgh. I was arguing for "population dams," for decentralized development based on the villages, which make up the traditional cultural and social pattern of India. These "dams" would prevent the flash floods of population into overpopulated areas. I was *warning,* but they accepted the prediction and ignored the warning. Soon thereafter I learned that an American university had been given a contract to make a feasibility study for a city of sixty million people north of Bombay. When enthusiasts get busy on a feasibility study, they invariably find that it is feasible. When they get to their drawing boards they have a whale of a time. They design skyscrapers above ground and subterranean tenements below ground. They work out minimal requirements of air and hence how much breathing space a family can survive in. They design "living-units," hutches for battery-fed people who are stacked together like kindergarten blocks. They provide water and regulate the sewage on the now well-established cost-efficiency principles of factory-farming. And then they finish up convinced that this is the most economical way of housing people. I thought I had scotched the idea by making representations through influential Indian friends. I asked them, among other things, how many mental hospitals they were planning to take care of the millions who would surely go mad under such conditions. But I have heard rumors that the planners are so slide-rule happy they are planning a city for six hundred million.

Prognosis is something else again. An intelligent doctor, having diagnosed the symptoms and examined the patient's condition, does not say (except in soap operas): "You have six months to live." He says: "Frankly, your condition is serious. Unless you do so-and-so, and unless I do so-and-so, it is bound to deteriorate." The operative phrase is "do so-and-so." One does not have to plan *for* trends; if they are socially undesirable our duty is to plan *away* from them, and treat the symptoms before they become malignant.

A multiplying population multiplies the problems. The prospect of a world of fifteen billion people is intimidating. Three-quarters of the world's present population is inadequately fed—hundreds of millions are not getting the food necessary for well-being. So it is not just a question of quadrupling the present food supply; it means six to eight times that to take care of present deficiencies. It is not a matter of numbers, either; it is the *rate* of increase that mops up any improvements. Nor is it just a question of housing but of clothing and material satisfactions—automobiles, televisions, and the rest. That means greater inroads on natural resources, the steady destruction of amenities, and the conflict of interest between those who want oil and those who want oil-free beaches, or between those who want to get from here to there on wider and wider roads and those whose homes are going to collapse in mud slides because of the making of those roads. Lewis Mumford has suggested that civilization really began with the making of containers—cans, non-returnable bottles, cartons, plastic bags, none of which can be redigested by nature. Every sneeze accounts for a personal tissue. Multiply that by fifteen billion.

Environmental pollution is partly rapacity and partly a conflict of interest between the individual, multimillions of individuals, and the commonweal; but largely, in our generation, it is the exaggerated effects of specialization with no sense of ecology, i.e. the balance of nature. Claude Bernard, the French physiologist, admonished his colleagues over a century ago: "True science teaches us to doubt and in ignorance to refrain." Ecologists feel their way with a detector through a minefield of doubts. Specialists, cocksure of their own facts, push ahead, regardless of others.

Behind the sky-high fences of military secrecy, the physicists produced the atomic bomb—just a bigger explosion—without taking into account the biological effects of radiation. Prime Minister Attlee, who consented to the dropping of the bomb on Hiroshima, later said that no one, not Churchill, nor members of the British Cabinet, nor he himself, knew of the possible genetic effects of the blast. "If the scientists knew, they never told us." Twenty years before, Hermann Muller had shown the genetic effects of radiation and had been awarded the Nobel Prize, but he was a biologist and security treated this weapon as a physicist's bomb. In the peacetime bomb-testing, when everyone was alerted to the biological risks, we were told that the fallout of radioactive materials could be localized in the testing grounds. The radioactive dust on The Lucky Dragon, which was fishing well beyond the proscribed area, disproved that. Nevertheless, when it was decided to explode the H-bomb the assurance about localization was blandly repeated. The H-bomb would punch a hole into the stratosphere and the radioactive gases would dissipate. One of those gases is radioactive krypton, which decays into radioactive strontium, a particulate. Somebody must have known that but nobody worried unduly because it would happen above the troposphere, which might be described as the roof of the weather system. What was definitely overlooked was the fact that the troposphere is not continuous. There is the equatorial troposphere and the polar troposphere and they overlap. The radioactive strontium came back through the transom and was spread all over the world by the climatic jet streams to be deposited as rain. The result is that there is radio-strontium (which did not exist in nature) in the bones of every young person who was growing up during the bomb-testing—every young person, everywhere in the world. It may be medically insignificant but it is the brandmark of the Atomic Age generation and a reminder of the mistakes of their elders.

When the mad professor of fiction blows up his laboratory and then himself, that's O.K., but when scientists and decision-makers act out of ignorance and pretend it is knowledge, they are using the biosphere, the living space, as an experimental laboratory. The whole world is put in hazard. And they do it even when they are told not to. During the International Geophysical Year, the Van Allen Belt was discovered. The Van Allen Belt is a region of magnetic phenomena. Immediately the bright boys decided to carry out an experiment and explode a hydrogen bomb in the Belt to see if they could produce an artificial aurora. The colorful draperies, the luminous skirts of the aurora, are caused by drawing cosmic particles magnetically through the rare gases of the upper atmosphere. It is called ionization and is like passing electrons through the vacuum tubes of our familiar neon lighting. It was called the Rainbow Bomb. Every responsible scientist in cosmology, radio-astronomy, and physics of the atmosphere protested against this tampering with a system we did not understand. They exploded their bomb. They got their pyrotechnics. We still do not know the price we may have to pay for this artificial magnetic disturbance.

We could blame the freakish weather on the Rainbow Bomb but, in our ignorance, we could not sustain the indictment. Anyway, there are so many other things happening that could be responsible. We can look with misgiving on the tracks in the sky—the white tails of the jet aircraft and the exhausts of space rockets. These are introducing into the climatic system new factors, the effects of which are immensurable. The triggering of rain clouds depends upon the water vapor having a toehold, a nucleus, on which to form. That is how artificial precipitation, so-called rainmaking, is produced. So the jets, crisscrossing the weather system, playing tic-tac-toe, can produce a man-made change of climate.

On the longer term, we can see even more drastic effects from the many activities of *Homo insapiens,* Unthinking Man. In 1963, at the United Nations Science and Technology Conference, we took stock of the several effects of industrialization on the total environment.

The atmosphere is not only the air which humans, animals, and plants breathe; it is the envelope which protects living things from harmful radiation from the sun and outer space. It is also the medium of climate, the winds and the rain. These are inseparable from the hydrosphere, including the oceans, which cover seven-tenths of the earth's surface with their currents and evaporation; and from the biosphere, with the vegetation and its transpiration and photosynthesis; and from the lithosphere, with its minerals, extracted for man's increasing needs. Millions of years ago the sun encouraged the growth of the primeval forests, which became our coal, and the life-growth in the Paleozoic seas, which became our oil. Those fossil-fuels, locked in the vaults through eons of time, are brought out by modern man and put back into the atmosphere from the chimney stacks and exhaust pipes of modern engineering.

This is an overplus on the natural carbon. About six billion tons of primeval carbon are mixed with the atmosphere every year. During the past century, in the process of industrialization, with its burning of fossil-fuels, more than four hundred billion tons of carbon have been artificially introduced into the atmosphere. The concentration in the air we breathe has been increased by approximately ten per cent; if all the known reserves of coal and oil were burned the concentration would be ten times greater.

This is something more than a public-health problem, more than a question of what goes into the lungs of the individual, more than a question of smog. The carbon cycle in nature is a self-adjusting mechanism. One school of scientific thought stresses that carbon monoxide can reduce solar radiation. Another school points out that an increase in carbon dioxide raises the temperature at the earth's surface. They are both right. Carbon dioxide, of course, is indispensable for plants and hence for the food cycle of creatures, including humans. It is the source of life. But a balance is maintained by excess carbon being absorbed by the seas. The excess is now taxing this absorption, and the effect on the heat balance of the earth can be significant because of what is known as "the greenhouse effect." A greenhouse lets in the sun's rays and retains the heat. Similarly, carbon dioxide, as a transparent diffusion, does likewise; it admits the radiant heat and keeps the convection heat close to the surface. It has been estimated that at the present rate of increase (those six billion tons a year) the mean annual temperature all over the world might increase by 5.8° F. in the next forty to fifty years.

Experts may argue about the time factor or about the effects, but certain things are observable not only in the industrialized Northern Hemisphere but also in the Southern Hemisphere. The ice of the north polar seas is thinning and shrinking. The seas, with their blanket of carbon dioxide, are changing their temperatures with the result that marine life is increasing and transpiring more carbon dioxide. With this combination, fish are migrating, even changing their latitudes. On land, glaciers are melting and the snow line is retreating. In Scandinavia, land which was perennially under snow and ice is thawing. Arrowheads of a thousand years ago, when the black earth was last exposed and when Eric the Red's Greenland was probably still green, have been found there. In the North American sub-Arctic a similar process is observable. Black earth has been exposed and retains the summer heat longer so that each year the effect moves farther north. The melting of the sea ice will not affect the sea level because the volume of floating ice is the same as the water it displaces, but the melting of the land's ice caps and glaciers, in which water is locked up, will introduce additional water to the oceans and raise the sea level. Rivers originating in glaciers and permanent snowfields (in the Himalayas, for instance) will increase their flow, and if the ice dams break the effects could be catastrophic. In this process, the patterns of rainfall will change, with increased precipitation in areas now arid and aridity in places now fertile. I am advising all my friends not to take ninety-nine-year leases on properties at present sea level.

The pollution of sweet-water lakes and rivers has increased so during the past twenty-five years that a Freedom from Thirst campaign is becoming as necessary as a Freedom from Hunger campaign. Again it is a conflict of motives and a conspiracy of ignorance. We can look at the obvious—the unprocessed urban sewage and the influx of industrial effluents. No one could possibly have believed that the Great Lakes in their immensity could ever be overwhelmed, or that Niagara Falls could lose its pristine clearness and fume like brown smoke, or that Lake Erie could become a cesspool. It did its best to oxidize the wastes from the steel plants by giving up its free oxygen until at last it surrendered and the anaerobic microörganisms took over. Of course, one can say that the mortuary smells of Lake Erie are not due to the pickling acids but to the dead fish.

The conflict of interests amounts to a dilemma. To insure that people shall be fed we apply our ingenuity in the form of artificial fertilizers, herbicides, pesticides, and insecticides. The runoff from the lands gets into the streams and rivers and distant oceans. DDT from the rivers of the United States has been found in the fauna of the Antarctic, where no DDT has ever been allowed. The dilemma becomes agonizing in places like India, with its hungry millions. It is now believed that the new strains of Mexican grain and I.R.C. (International Rice Center in the Philippines) rice, with their high yields, will provide enough food for them, belly-filling if not nutritionally balanced. These strains, however, need plenty of water, constant irrigation, plenty of fertilizers to sustain the yields, and tons of pesticides because standardized pedigree plants are highly vulnerable to disease. This means that the production will be concentrated in the river systems, like the Gangeatic Plains, and the chemicals will drain into the rivers.

The glib answer to this sort of thing is "atomic energy." If there is enough energy and it is cheap enough, you can afford to turn rivers into sewers and lakes into cesspools. You can desalinate the seas. But, for the foreseeable future, that energy will come from atomic fission, from the breaking down of the nucleus. The alternative, promised but undelivered, is thermonuclear energy—putting the H-bomb into dungarees by controlling the fusion of hydrogen. Fusion does not produce waste products, fission does. And the more peaceful atomic reactors there are, the more radioactive waste there will be to dispose of. The really dangerous material has to be buried. The biggest disposal area in the world is at Hanford, Washington. It encloses a stretch of the Columbia River and a tract of country covering 650 square miles. There, a twentieth-century Giza, it has cost much more to bury live atoms than it cost to entomb all the mummies of all the Pyramid Kings of Egypt.

At Hanford, the live atoms are kept in tanks constructed of carbon steel, resting in a steel saucer to catch any leakage. These are enclosed in a reënforced concrete structure and the whole construction is buried in the ground with only the vents showing. In the steel sepulchers, each with a million-gallon capacity, the atoms are very much alive. Their radioactivity keeps the acids in the witches' brew boiling. In the bottom of the tanks the temperature is well above the boiling point of water. There has to be a cooling system, therefore, and it must be continuously maintained. In addition, the vapors generated in the tanks have to be condensed and scrubbed, otherwise a radioactive miasma would escape from the vents. Some of the elements in those high-level wastes will remain radioactive for at least 250,000 years. It is most unlikely that the tanks will endure as long as the Egyptian pyramids.

Radioactive wastes from atomic processing stations have to be transported to such burial grounds. By the year 2000, if the present practices continue, the number of six-ton tankers in transit at any given time would be well over three thousand and the amount of radioactive products in them would be 980,000,000 curies—that is a mighty number of curies to be roaming around in a populated country.

There are other ways of disposing of radioactive waste and there are safeguards against the hazards, but those safeguards have to be enforced and constant vigilance maintained. There are already those who say that the safety precautions in the atomic industry are excessive.

Polluting the environment has been sufficiently dramatized by events in recent years to show the price we have to pay for our recklessness. It is not just the destruction of natural beauty or the sacrifice of recreational amenities, which are crimes in themselves, but interference with the whole ecology —with the balance of nature on which persistence of life on this planet depends. We are so fascinated by the gimmicks and gadgetry of science and technology and are in such a hurry to exploit them that we do not count the consequences.

We have plenty of scientific knowledge but knowledge is not wisdom: wisdom is knowledge tempered by judgment. At the moment, the scientists, technologists, and industrialists are the judge and jury in their own assize. Statesmen, politicians, and administrators are ill-equipped to make judgments about the true values of discoveries or developments. On the contrary, they tend to encourage the crash programs to get quick answers— like the Manhattan Project, which turned the laboratory discovery of uranium fission into a cataclysmic bomb in six years; the Computer / Automation Revolution; the Space Program; and now the Bio-engineering Revolution, with its possibilities not only of spare-organ plumbing but of changing the nature of living things by gene manipulation. They blunder into a minefield of undetected ignorance, masquerading as science.

The present younger generation has an unhappy awareness of such matters. They were born into the Atomic Age, programmed into the Computer Age, rocketed into the Space Age, and are poised on the threshold of the Bio-engineering Age. They take all these marvels for granted, but they are also aware that the advances have reduced the world to a neighborhood and that we are all involved one with another in the risks as well as the opportunities. They see the mistakes writ large. They see their elders mucking about with *their* world and *their* future. That accounts for their profound unease, whatever forms their complaints may take. They are the spokesmen for posterity and are justified in their protest. But they do not have the explicit answers, either.

Somehow science and technology must conform to some kind of social responsibility. Together, they form the social and economic dynamic of our times. They are the pacesetters for politics and it is in the political frame of reference that answers must be found. There can never be any question of restraining or repressing natural curiosity, which is true science, but there is ample justification for evaluating and judging developmental science. The common good requires nothing less.

ECOLOGICAL ARMAGEDDON

❧ Robert L. Heilbroner

Ecology has become the Thing. There are ecological politics, ecological jokes, ecological bookstores, advertisements, seminars, teach-ins, buttons. The automobile, symbol of ecological abuse, has been tried, sentenced to death, and formally executed in at least two universities (replete with burial of one victim). Publishing companies are fattening on books on the sonic boom, poisons in the things we eat, perils loose in the garden, the dangers of breathing. The *Saturday Review* has appended a regular monthly Ecological Supplement. In short, the ecological issue has assumed the dimensions of a vast popular fad, for which one can predict with reasonable assurance the trajectory of all such fads—a period of intense general involvement, followed by growing boredom and gradual extinction, save for a die-hard remnant of the faithful.

This would be a tragedy, for I have slowly become convinced during the last twelve months that the ecological issue is not only of primary and lasting importance, but that it may indeed constitute the most dangerous and difficult challenge that humanity has ever faced. Since these are very large statements, let me attempt to substantiate them by drawing freely on the best single descriptive and analytic treatment of the subject that I have yet seen, *Population, Resources, Environment* by Paul and Anne Ehrlich of Stanford University. Rather than resort to the bothersome procedure of endlessly citing their arguments in quotation marks, I shall take the liberty of reproducing their case in a rather free paraphrase, as if it were my own, until we reach the end of the basic argument, after which I shall make clear

SOURCE: Robert Heilbroner, "Ecological Armageddon," *The New York Review of Books* (April 23, 1970). Reprinted with permission from *The New York Review of Books*. Copyright © 1970 Robert Heilbroner.

some conclusions that I believe lie implicit in their work.

Ultimately, the ecological crisis represents our belated awakening to the fact that we live on what Kenneth Boulding has called, in the perfect phrase, our Spaceship Earth. As in all spaceships, sustained life requires that a meticulous balance be maintained between the capability of the vehicle to support life and the demands made by the inhabitants and the craft. Until recently, those demands have been well within the capability of the ship, in its ability both to supply the physical and chemical requirements for continued existence and to absorb the waste products of the voyagers. This is not to say that the earth has been generous—short rations have been the lot of mankind for most of its history—nor is it to deny the recurrent advent of local ecological crises—witness the destruction of whole areas like the erstwhile granaries of North Africa. But famines have passed and there have always been the new areas to move to. The idea that the earth as a whole was overtaxed is one that is new to our time.

For it is only in our time that we are reaching the limit of earthly carrying capacity, not on a local but on a global basis. Indeed, as will soon become clear, we are well past that capacity, provided that the level of resource intake and waste output represented by the average American or European is taken as a standard to be achieved by all humanity. To put it bluntly, if we take as the price of a first-class ticket the resource requirements of those passengers who travel in the Northern Hemisphere of the Spaceship, we have now reached a point at which the steerage is condemned to live forever —or at least within the horizon of the technology presently visible—at a second-class level; or a point at which a considerable change in living habits must be imposed on first class if the ship is ever to be converted to a one-class cruise.

This strain on the carrying capacity of the vessel results from the contemporary confluence of three distinct developments, each of which places tremendous or even unmanageable strains on the life-carrying capability of the planet and all of which together simply overload it. The first of these is the enormous strain imposed by the sheer burgeoning of population. The statistics of population growth are by now very well known: the earth's passenger list is growing at a rate that will give us some four billion humans by 1975, and that threatens to give us eight billion by 2010. I say "threatens," since it is likely that the inability of the earth to carry so large a group will result in an actual population somewhat smaller than this, especially in the steerage, where the growth is most rapid and the available resources least plentiful.

We shall return to the population problem later. But meanwhile a second strain is placed on the earth by the simple cumulative effect of *existing* technology (combustion engines, the main industrial processes, present-day agricultural techniques, etc.). The strain is localized mainly in the first-class portions of the vessel where each new arrival on board is rapidly given a standard complement of capital equipment and where the rate of physical and chemical resource transformation per capita steadily mounts. The strain consists of the limited ability of the soil, the water, and the atmosphere of these favored regions to absorb the outpourings of these fast-growing industrial processes.

The most dramatic instance of this limited absorptive power is the rise in the carbon dioxide content of the air due to the steady growth of (largely industrial) combustion. By the year 2000, it seems beyond dispute that the CO_2 content of the air will have doubled, raising the heat-trapping properties of the atmosphere. This so-called "greenhouse" effect has been predicted to raise mean global temperatures sufficiently to bring catastrophic potential consequences. One possibility is a sequence of climatic changes resulting from a melting of the Artic ice floes that would result in the advent of a new Ice Age; another is the slumping of the Antarctic ice cap into the sea with a consequent tidal wave that could wipe out a substantial portion of mankind and raise the sea level by 60 to 100 feet.

These are all "iffy" scenarios whose present significance may be limited to alerting us to the immensity of the ecological problem; happily they are of sufficient uncertainty not to cause us immediate worry (it is lucky they are, because it is extremely unlikely that all the massed technological and human energy on earth could arrest such changes once they began). Much closer to home is the burden placed on the earth's carrying capacity by the sheer requirements of a spreading industrial activity for the fuel and mineral resources needed to maintain the going rate of output per person in the first-class cabins. To raise the existing (not the anticipated) population of the earth to American standards would require the annual extraction of 75 times as much iron, 100 times as much copper, 200 times as much lead, and 250 times as much tin as we now take from the earth.

Only the known reserves of iron allow us to entertain such fantastic rates of mineral exploitation (and the capital investment needed to bring about such mining operations is in itself staggering to contemplate). All the other requirements exceed by far all known or reasonably anticipated ore reserves. And, to repeat, we have taken into account only today's level of population: to equip the prospective passengers of the year 2010 with this amount of basic raw material would require a doubling of all the above figures.

I will revert later to the consequences of this prospect. First, however, let us pay attention to the third source of overload, this one traceable to the special environment-destroying potential of newly developed technologies.

Of these the most important—and if it should ever come to full-scale war, of course the most lethal—is the threat posed by nuclear radiation. I shall not elaborate on this well-known (although not well-believed) danger, pausing to point out only that a nuclear holocaust would in all likelihood exert its principal effect in the Northern Hemisphere. The survivors in the South would be severely hampered in their efforts at reconstruction not only because most of the easily available resources of the world have already been used up, but because most of the technological know-how would have perished along with the populations up North.

But the threats of new technology are by no means limited to the specter of nuclear devastation. There is, immediately at hand, the known devastation of the new chemical pesticides that have now entered more or less irreversibly into the living tissue of the world's population. Most mothers' milk in the United States today—I now quote the Ehrlichs verbatim— "contains so much DDT that it would be declared illegal in interstate commerce if it were sold as cow's milk"; and the DDT intake of infants around the world is twice the daily allowable maximum set by the World Health Organization. We are already, in other words, being exposed to heavy dosages of chemicals whose effects we know to be dangerous, with what ultimate results we shall have to wait nervously to discover. (There is something to think about in the archaeological evidence that one factor in the decline of Rome was the systematic poisoning of upper-class Romans from the lead with which they lined their wine containers.)

But the threat is not limited to pesticides. Barry Commoner predicts an agricultural crisis in the United States within fifty years from the action of our fertilizers, which will either ultimately destroy soil fertility or lead to pollution of the national water supply. At another corner of the new technology, the SST threatens not only to shake us with its boom, but to affect the amount of cloud cover (and climate) by its contrails. And I have not even mentioned the standard pollution problems of smoke, industrial effluents into lakes and rivers, or solid wastes. Suffice it to report that a 1968 UNESCO Conference concluded that man has only about twenty years to go before the planet starts to become uninhabitable because of air pollution alone. Of course "starts to" is imprecise; I am reminded of a cartoon of an industrialist looking at his billowing smokestacks, in front of which a forlorn figure is holding up a placard that says: "We have only 35 years to go." The caption reads, "Boy, that shook me up for a minute. I thought it said 3 to 5 years."

I have left until last the grimmest and gravest threat of all, speaking now on behalf of the steerage. This is the looming inability of the great green earth to bring forth sufficient food to maintain life, even at the miserable threshold of subsistence at which it is now endured by perhaps a third of the world's population. The problem here is the very strong likelihood that population growth will inexorably outpace whatever improvements in fertility and productivity we will be able to apply to the earth's mantle (including the watery fringes of the ocean where sea "farming" is at least technically imaginable).

Here the race is basically between two forces: on the one hand, those that give promise that the rate of population increase can be curbed (if not totally halted); and on the other, those that give promise of increasing the amount of sustenance we can wring from the soil.

Both these forces are subtly blended of technological and social factors. Take population growth. The great hope of every ecologist is that an effective birth control technique—cheap, requiring little or no medical supervision, devoid of taboos or religious hindrances—will rapidly and effectively lower the present fertility rates which are doubling world population every thirty-five years (every twenty-eight years in Africa; every twenty-four in Latin America). No such device is currently available, although the Pill, the IUD, vasectomies, abortions, condoms, coitus interruptus, and other known techniques could, of course, do the job, if the requisite equipment, persuasion (or coercion), instruction, etc. could be brought to the 80 to 90 percent of the world's people who know next to nothing about birth control.

It seems a fair conclusion that no such world-wide campaign is apt to be successful for at least a decade and maybe a generation, although there is always the hope that a "spontaneous" change in attitudes, similar to that in Hungary or Japan, will bring about a rapid halt to population growth. But even in this unlikely event, the sheer "momentum" of population growth still poses terrible problems. Malcom Potts, Secretary General of International Planned Parenthood, has presented a shocking statistical calculation in this regard: he has pointed out that population growth in India is today adding one million mouths per month to the Indian subcontinent. If, by some miracle, fertility rates were to decline tomorrow by 50 percent in India, at the end of twenty years, owing to the already existing huge numbers of children who would be moving up into child-bearing ages, population growth in India would still be taking place at the rate of one million mouths per month.

The other element in the race is our ability to match population growth with food supplies, at least for a generation or so, while birth control techniques and campaigns are being perfected. Here the problem is also partly technological, partly social. The technological part involves the so-called "Green Revolution"—the development of seeds that are capable, at their best, of improving yields per acre by a factor of 300 percent, sometimes even more. The problem, however, is that these new seeds generally require irrigation and fertilizer to bring their benefits. If India alone were to apply fertilizer at the per capita level of the Netherlands, she would consume half the world's total output of fertilizer. This would require a hundredfold expansion of India's present level of fertilizer use.

Irrigation, the other necessary input for most improved seeds, poses equally formidable requirements. E. A. Mason of the Oak Ridge National Laboratories has prepared preliminary estimates of the costs of nuclear-powered "agro-industrial complexes" in which desalted water and fertilizer would be produced for use on adjacent farms. It would require twenty-three such plants per year, each taking care of some three million people, just to keep pace with present world population growth. Since it would take at least five years to get these plants into operation, we should begin work today on at least 125 such units. If we assume that no hitches were encountered and that the technology on paper could be easily translated into a technology *in situ,* the cost would amount to $315 billion.

There are as well other technical problems of an ecological nature associated with the Green Revolution—mainly the risk of introducing locally untried strains of plants that may be subject to epidemic disease. But putting those difficulties to the side, we must recognize as well the social obstacles that a successful Green Revolution must overcome. The new seeds can only be afforded by the upper level of peasantry—not merely because of their cost (and the cost of the required fertilizer), but because only a rich peasant can take the risk of having the crop turn out badly without himself suffering starvation. Hence the Green Revolution is likely to increase the strains of social stratification within the underdeveloped areas. Then, too, even a successful local crop does not always shed its benefits evenly across a nation, but results all too often in local gluts that cannot be transported to starving areas because of transportation bottlenecks.

None of these discouraging remarks is intended in the slightest to disparage the Green Revolution, which represents the inspired work of dedicated men. But the difficulties must be kept in mind as a corrective to the lulling belief that "science" can easily offset the population boom with larger supplies of food. There is no doubt that supplies of food *can* be substantially increased—rats alone devour some 10–12 percent of India's crop, and insects can ravage up to half of the stored crops of some underdeveloped areas, so that even very "simple" methods of improved storage hold out important prospects of improving basic life-support, quite aside from the longer term hopes of agronomy.

Yet at best these improvements will only stave off the day of reckoning. Ultimately the problem posed by Malthus must be faced—that population tends to increase geometrically, by doubling; and that agriculture does not; so that eventually population *must* face the limit of a food barrier. It is worth repeating the words of Malthus himself in this regard:

Famine seems to be the last, the most dreadful resource of nature. The power of population is so much superior to the power in the earth to produce subsistence for man, that premature death must in some shape or other visit the human race. The vices of mankind are active and able ministers of depopulation. . . . [S]hould they fail in this war of extermination, sickly seasons, epidemics, pestilence, and plague, advance in terrific array, and sweep off their thousands and ten thousands. Should success still be incomplete, gigantic inevitable famine stalks in the rear, and with one mighty blow, levels the population with the food of the world.

This Malthusian prophecy has been so often "refuted," as economists have pointed to the astonishing rates of growth of food output in the advanced nations, that there is a danger of dismissing the warnings of the Ehrlichs as merely another premature alarm. To do so would be a fearful mistake. For unlike Malthus, who assumed that technology would remain constant, the Ehrlichs have made ample allowance for the growth of technological capability, and their approach to the impending catastrophe is not shrill. They merely point out that a mild version of the Malthusian solution is already upon us, for at least half a billion people are chronically hungry or outright starving, and another 1½ billion under or malnourished. Thus we do not have to wait for "gigantic inevitable famine"; it has already come.

What is more important is that the Ehrlichs see the matter in a fundamentally different perspective from Malthus, not as a problem involving supply and demand, but as one involving a total ecological equilibrium. The crisis, as the Ehrlichs see it, is thus both deeper and more complex than merely a shortage of food, although the latter is one of its more horrendous evidences. What threatens the Spaceship Earth is a profound imbalance between the totality of systems by which human life is maintained, and the totality of demands, industrial as well as agricultural, technological as well as demographic, to which that capacity to support life is subjected.

I have no doubt that one can fault bits and pieces of the Ehrlichs' analysis, and there is a note of determined pessimism in their work that leads me to suspect (or at least hope) that there is somewhat more time for adaptation than they suggest. Yet I do not see how their basic conclusion can be denied. Beginning within our lifetimes and rising rapidly to crisis proportions in our children's, a challenge faces humankind comparable to none in its history, with the possible exception of the forced migrations of the Ice Age. It is with the responses to this crisis that I wish to end this essay, for telling and courageous as the Ehrlichs' analysis is, I do not believe that even they have fully faced up to the implications that their own findings present.

The first of these I have already stated: it is the clear conclusion that the underdeveloped countries can *never* hope to achieve parity with the developed countries. Given our present and prospective technology, there are simply not enough resources to permit a "Western" rate of industrial exploitation to be expanded to a population of four billion—much less eight billion—persons. It may well be that most of the population in the under-developed world has no ambition to reach Western standards—indeed, does not even know that such a thing as "development" is on the agenda. But the elites of these nations, for all their rhetorical rejection of Western (and especially American) styles of life, do tend to picture a Western standard as the ultimate end of their activities. As it becomes clear that such an objective is impossible, a profound reorientation of views must take place within the underdeveloped nations.

What such a reorientation will be it is impossible to say. For the near future, the outlook for the most population-oppressed areas will be a continuous battle against food shortages, coupled with the possible permanent impairment of the intelligence of much of the surviving population due to protein deficiencies in childhood. This pressure of population may lead to aggressive searches for *Lebensraum;* or as I have frequently written, may culminate in revolutions of desperation.

In the long run, of course, there is the possibility of considerable growth (although nothing resembling the attainment of a Western standard of consumption). But no quick substantial improvement in their condition seems feasible within the next generation at least. The visions of Sir Charles Snow or the Soviet academician Sakharov for a gigantic transfer of wealth from the rich nations to the poor (20 percent of GNP is proposed) are simply fantasies. Since much of GNP is spatially nontransferable or inappropriate, such a huge levy against GNP would imply shipments of up to 50 percent of much movable output. How this enormous flood of goods would be transported, allocated, absorbed, or maintained—not to mention relinquished by the donor countries—is nowhere analyzed by the proponents of such vast aid.

The implications of the ecological crisis for the advanced nations are not any less severe, although they are of a different kind. For it is clear that free industrial growth is just as disastrous for the Western nations as free population growth for those of the East and South. The worship in the West of a growing Gross National Product must be recognized as not only a deceptive but a very dangerous avatar; Kenneth Boulding has begun a campaign, in which I shall join him, to label this statistical monster Gross National Cost.

The necessity to bring our economic activities into a sustainable relationship with the resource capabilities and waste absorption properties of the world will pose two problems for the West. On the simpler level, a whole series of technological problems must be met. Fume-free transportation must be developed on land and air. The cult of disposability must be replaced by that of reusability. Population stability must be attained through tax and other inducements, both to conserve resources and to preserve reasonable population densities. Many of these problems will tax our ingenuity, technical and socio-political, but the main problem they pose is not whether, but *how soon* they can be solved.

But there is another, deeper question that the developed nations face—at least those that have capitalist economies. This problem can be stated as a crucial test as to who was right—John Stuart Mill or Karl Marx. Mill maintained, in his famous *Principles,* that the terminus of capitalist evolution would be a stationary state, in which the return to capital had fallen to insignificance, and a redistributive tax system would be able to capture any flows of income to the holders of scarce resources such as land. In effect, he prophesied the transformation of capitalism, in an environment of abundance, into a balanced economy, in which the capitalist both as the generator of change and as the main claimant on the surplus generated by change, would in effect undergo a painless euthanasia.

The Marxian view is of course quite the opposite. The very essence of capitalism, according to Marx, is expansion—which is to say, the capitalist, as a historical "type" finds his *raison d'être* in the insatiable search for additional money-wealth gained through the constant growth of the economic system. The idea of a "stationary" capitalism is, in Marxian eyes, a contradiction in terms, on a logical par with a democratic aristocracy or an industrial feudalism.

Is the Millian or the Marxian view correct? I do not think that we can yet say. Some economic growth is certainly compatible with a stabilized rate of resource use and disposal, for growth could take the form of the expenditure of additional labor on the improvement (aesthetic or technical) of the national environment. Indeed, insofar as education or cultural activity are forms of national output that require little use of resources and result in little waste product, national output could be indefinitely expanded through these and similar activities. But there is no doubt that the main avenue of traditional capitalist accumulation would have to be considerably constrained; that net investment in mining and manufacturing would effectively cease; that the rate and kind of technological change would need to be supervised and probably greatly reduced; and that as a consequence, the flow of profits would almost certainly fall.

Is this imaginable within a capitalist setting—that is, in a nation in which the business ideology permeates the views of nearly all groups and classes and establishes the bounds of what is possible and natural, and what is not? Ordinarily I do not see how such a question could be answered in any way but negatively, for it is tantamount to asking a dominant class to acquiesce in the elimination of the very activities that sustain it. But this is an extraordinary challenge that may evoke an extraordinary response. Like the challenge posed by war, the ecological crisis affects all classes, and therefore may be sufficient to induce sociological changes that would be unthinkable in ordinary circumstances.

The capitalist and managerial classes may see—perhaps even more clearly than the consuming masses—the nature and nearness of the ecological crisis, and may recognize that their only salvation (as human beings, let alone privileged human beings) is an occupational migration into governmental or other posts of power, or they may come to accept a smaller share of the national surplus supply simply because they recognize that there is no alternative. When the enemy is nature, in other words, rather than another social class, it is at least imaginable that adjustments could be made that would be impossible in ordinary circumstances.[1]

There is, however, another possibility to which I must also call attention. It is the possibility that the ecological crisis will simply result in the decline or even destruction of Western civilization, and of the hegemony of the scientific-technological view that has achieved so much and cost us so dearly. Great challenges do not always bring great responses, especially when those responses must be sustained over long periods of time and require dramatic changes in life styles and attitudes. Even educated men today are able to deny the reality of the crisis they face: there is wild talk of farming the seas, or transporting men to the planets, of unspecified "miracles" of technology that will avert disaster. Glib as they are, however, at least these suggestions have a certain responsibility when compared to another and much more worrisome response: *Je m'en fiche.*

Can we really persuade the citizens of the Western world, who are just now entering the heady atmosphere of a high consumption way of life, that conservation, stability, frugality, and a deep concern for the distant future must now take priority over the personal indulgence for which they have been culturally prepared and which they are about to experience for the first time? Not the least danger of the ecological crisis, as I see it, is that tens and hundreds of millions will shrug their shoulders at the prospects ahead ("What has posterity ever done for us?"), and that the increasingly visible approach of ecological Armageddon will bring not repentance but Saturnalia.

Yet I cannot end this essay on such a note. For it seems to me that the ecological enthusiasts may be right when they speak of the deteriorating environment as providing the *possibility* for a new political rallying ground. If a new New Deal, capable of engaging both the efforts and the beliefs of this nation, is the last great hope to which we cling in the face of what seems otherwise to be an inevitable gradual worsening and coarsening of our style of life, it is possible that a determined effort to arrest the ecological decay might prove to be its underlying theme. Such an issue, immediate in the experience of all, carries an appeal that might allow vast improvements to be worked in the American environment, both urban and industrial. I cannot estimate the likelihood of such a political awakening, dependent as these matters are on the dice of personality and the outcome of events at home and abroad. But however slim the possibility of bringing such a change, it does at least make the ecological crisis, unquestionably the gravest long-run threat of our times, potentially the source of its greatest short-term promise.

NOTES

1. Let me add a warning that it is not only capitalists who must make an unprecedented ideological adjustment. Socialists must also come to terms with the abandonment of the goal of industrial superabundance on which their vision of a transformed society rests. The stationary equilibrium imposed by the constraints of ecology requires at the very least a reformulation of the kind of economic society toward which socialism sets its course.

AMERICA THE RAPED

Gene Marine

I: Who Needs a Swamp?

Fifty years ago, more or less, Americans rose up in anger against the rape of their country.

The fight of a few dozen men, led by giants—Roosevelt, Pinchot, Muir,

SOURCE: Gene Marine, "America the Raped," *Ramparts Magazine* (April 1967), 34–45. Copyright 1967 *Ramparts Magazine, Inc.* Reprinted by permission of the editors.

Powell—was against the uncaring lumbermen who despoiled hill and valley and left eroding soil and sick rivers in their wake; against the unthinking farmers and stockmen who replaced precious and fertile grasslands with thorn scrubs and dust bowls; against the stupid hunters who wiped out a hundred species and endangered a hundred more.

Left when the battle had ended were the national and state parks and forests, a mushy purr-word—"conservation"—and a vague conviction that except for a few renegade lumber companies and mining firms, the rapine had ended. In fact, it has hardly begun.

The old rapists—the lumbermen and miners and utilities companies—are still with us, though today they substitute seduction for rape wherever possible. The Georgia-Pacific Company still strips virgin Douglas fir from California's northern coast, but today it also contributes a few thousand dollars to a study of the habits and habitats of the American eagle.

Fortunately for the rest of us, a dozen groups have arisen to keep the old rapists in check. But while they try, the new rapists are loose upon the land; theirs, still, are the vicious, violent techniques of the *laissez-faire* turn of the century. They are not, for the most part, employed by lumber companies or mining companies—but by you and me. They work for the Port Authority of New York and New Jersey, or for the state highway commissions; the U.S. Forest Service or the National Park Service; the Army's Corps of Engineers, the Bureau of Reclamation or the Bureau of Public Roads.

They are called Engineers.

They build bridges and dams and highways and causeways and flood control projects. They *manage* things. They commit rape with bulldozers.

They are hard to fight off, because they must be fought with words, and the weapons are inadequate. In New Jersey, there is a fantastic land of wonders, still substantially as it was when the glaciers retreated thousands of years ago. It is called the Great Swamp. The Engineers want to put a jetport on it—an absurd and irreversible crime. But—who needs a "swamp"?

The salt marshes of the Georgia coast have become an outstanding laboratory for the study of the interactions of life; there, the University of Georgia has learned much of how shrimp and other seafood depend on the unusual estuarine conditions for their life. Yet Dr. Eugene Odum, the leading researcher in the field, reports that "we are often asked, 'Of what value is the salt marsh?' or 'What can be done with all that wasted land?' "

The Engineers know: build a dam, build a levee, build a wall, dredge, fill, *change*. The marsh grass will die, the phytoplankton will die, the algae will die—and thus the shrimp and the bass will die, but the Engineers don't care. What good is a salt marsh? Who needs a swamp?

The "conservationists" can lose an isolated battle over a grove of trees or a factory on a river. We will survive, and so will trees and rivers. But the Engineers are not only straining to dam the Grand Canyon and the last wild stretch of the Missouri, to wall off the rich estuaries of Long Island and fill in the Great Swamp. They are in every section of every state, ripping, tearing, building, changing.

Theirs is a rapine from which America can never, never recover.

II: The Bug of Bermuda

In 1944, a retired American industrialist, who owned a handsome home in Paget Parish, Bermuda, decided that the place would look nicer with a few decorative shrubs around the house.

He looked around, but he didn't see anything he liked. The landscape was dominated then—as it had been 332 years earlier when the first British colonists arrived—by groves of Bermuda cedars, many of them as high as 50 feet tall. Their reddish-brown, knotty wood was a Bermuda staple, not only as firewood and lumber but as a raw material for souvenirs, as coffin material, and—in cross-section, so tough were its fibers—as flagstones. Most important to the island, rows of these tall, aromatic evergreens gave Bermuda its tropical flavor, served as windbreaks for crops, and were anchors for the soil to keep it from being washed into the ever-precious rain water supply on which the island colony depends.

There were two million Bermuda cedars.

They're too big for decorative shrubs, however, and the prosperous American decided to import a few shrubs from a mainland nursery. They were carefully inspected at both ends, but inspectors overlooked at least one pregnant *Carulaspis visci*—a scale insect which reproduces (without need for mates) throughout most of the year. Distributed by wind, it attaches itself to a plant, drills into a twig, grows a protective "scale," and repeats the process.

One year after the American imported his shrubs, the Bermuda legislature appropriated £14,000 to exterminate the insects before the insects exterminated the Bermuda cedar. The powerful insecticides that might have reached the *Carulaspis visci* under their protective scales couldn't be used, lest they get into the water (on the mainland at about the same time, we were happily pouring DDT all over everything). Imported ladybird beetles, which control the scale insect in Ontario, weren't successful—there are beetle-eating lizards in Bermuda which don't exist in Ontario.

Four years later—five years after the prosperous American decided to decorate his grounds—the Bermuda legislature gave up. The appropriations now are for removing dead cedars to where you can't see them from the road. There are no windbreaks left to protect the banana plants, whose leaves are shredded and dried by wind; Bermuda now imports bananas.

Ecology is the study of how things fit together, or, if you prefer, the study of the interactions between life forms and their environment. We know very damned little about it, but Engineers know—or act as if they know—absolutely nothing.

Most of us have had to learn a little ecology in the past few years, in order to deal with the political problems of radioactive fallout and air and water pollution. Some of us learned about the concentration of strontium-90. Others of us learned that a harmless scattering of DDT (0.02 parts per million) in the water of Clear Lake, California, was concentrated by plankton (to 5 parts per million), concentrated again by fish (to several hundred parts per million), and ultimately killed the grebes that ate the fish. In the tissues of the birds, DDT concentration was 1600 parts per million.

The government builds dams and highways, levees and reactors, and every one rips into an ecological system far more complex than anyone yet understands. "No one," says Dr. Odum, who is one of the world's leading ecologists, "has yet identified and catalogued all the species of plants, animals and microbes to be found in any large area, as for example, a square mile of forest." But science in government is dominated by the Engineers, and the government is doing almost no work in ecology, giving almost no grants, encouraging almost no one. Instead, as could be expected of Engineers, they spend millions studying things that somebody wants to manage.

When most people think of ecology—if they've ever heard of it at all—they tend to think of food chains: minnows eat mosquitos, bream eat minnows, bass eat bream. Odum calls it the grass-rabbit-fox chain.

But there is far more to ecology than food chains and gross changes in the environment. The ignorant use of DDT and its widespread effects (it has been found in the fat of Antarctic penguins) is something most people know about; but Dr. LaMont Cole of Cornell, among others, has pointed out what we *might* have done.

Proteins—the "building blocks" of everything alive, including you and me—are nitrogen compounds. But nitrogen is a scarce element—90 per cent of all the nitrogen there is can be found in the air, and plants can't use it directly. They depend on certain bacteria, and on blue-green algae, to convert the nitrogen to ammonia, which they can use. On top of that, there are a couple of other kinds of bacteria which change the ammonia into nitrate, which is the way most plants actually do use it. You and I get our nitrogen mostly from the plants. Even then, it would all disappear except for still other bacteria, which recover the nitrogen from dead plants and animals and turn it back into ammonia. Finally, all the nitrogen in the world would have turned into ammonia a long time ago, except for still other types of bacteria which can regenerate molecular nitrogen from nitrate.

DDT kills bacteria, and nobody has ever known exactly *what* bacteria. If DDT had proven to be toxic to any of the types of bacteria mentioned above, man—in his unthinking attempt to kill a few plant pests—would have wiped himself off the face of the earth.

This is not the kind of thinking that concerns the Engineers. They not only do not care whether they push a freeway through a wildlife refuge, nor whether they flood the Grand Canyon with a dam, they don't care whether they wipe out our only chance to understand the ecology of vast regions of the earth, and thus, perhaps, keep from killing ourselves. It is the Engineers who pollute our air and our water—and they may yet do worse than that. They may drown most of us.

What with industrialization and its attendant burning of carboniferous fuels, we have managed since 1900 to raise the amount of carbon dioxide in the atmosphere by at least ten, and possibly 15, per cent. Normally, of course, there is always carbon dioxide released; we breathe it out; but the overall ecosystem can handle that and break it down, even allowing for the population growth. Burning all that coal and wood and fuel oil is releasing it faster than the atmosphere can handle it. Dr. Thomas Malone dispassionately told a Congressional committee last year that the effect of this additional carbon dioxide:

has been to increase the temperature in the lower atmosphere—that is, the troposphere—by about 0.2 degrees C and to decrease the temperature in the upper atmosphere—that is, the stratosphere—by about 2 degrees C.

. . . The implication of this situation is related to the volume of water contained in the masses of ice in the polar regions. If the earth is warmed, the ice melts and the sea level would be raised so high that, were it to happen, we would probably have to swim home from this building this morning.

The buildup of CO_2, to put it simply, lets the sun's heat in, but it doesn't let the heat back out again when the earth radiates it. It's called, cutely enough, the "greenhouse effect." Sunday supplement stuff, of course—except that Dr. Malone added that the danger "is something we must resolve in a matter of decades. The situation could become serious by the end of the century." That's 33 years from now.

Possibly the best and most dramatic example of the failure of the Engineers to understand what they're doing is demonstrated by our attempt to create a completely artificial, if temporary, ecosystem: the space capsule.

The Russian manned satellite contains air—plain, simple old air, like the stuff you and I used to breathe before we moved to the city. When we Americans set out to build a capsule, however, we found out that it leaked —and in order to keep it from leaking, we would have had to make the capsule much heavier.

Leave it to us, said the Engineers. We'll make the ecosystem just that much more artificial, but we'll solve the problem. Pure oxygen can be used, at only one-fifth the pressure of air; you won't have to plug the leaks so tight, you can use rockets with less thrust; it'll all work out fine. And indeed it did—until the first astronauts for the first time confronted the fact that you can have a spark, or even light a match, in air—but not in oxygen. The Engineers improved on nature and killed three men.

Usually, of course, the dangers of ecological destruction are less dramatic. For instance, we've been extremely successful in developing and growing hybrid corn. As a result, we've almost lost hundreds of corn varieties that fell by the wayside—thereby making it impossible to experiment with new hybrids, discover possible new disease-resistant strains, or make any other use of the genetic information stored in these varieties.

This is one of the most difficult concepts of conservation to communicate —and the one least understood by conservation groups. From wanting to save the redwoods because they're pretty, some organizations have progressed to wanting to save a particular group of redwoods because of its ecological value.

But few people have yet reached the idea of the conservation of genetic information—the idea that we ought to keep every species of animal or plant alive, and in its own ecosystem, because we have no way of knowing what characteristics of what animal, plant or microbe may someday prove to be in some way valuable. The variety of corn that is not grown today, because it isn't economical in competition with today's hybrids, may be the variety which will prove, tomorrow, to be resistant to an as yet unforeseen disease. A byproduct of the whooping crane may be tomorrow's wonder drug. The ecology of the Long Island estuary may provide the clue that enables us to project a more viable ecosystem for a space station.

Everything fits together. Everything. And nobody seems to care, least of all the rampaging, rapist Engineers.

III: Alligators and Aerojet

I have a frightening map of central and southern Florida. Published by the U.S. Army Corps of Engineers, it shows in glorious red and green the existing and proposed network of canals, levees, dams, pumping stations and control centers with which the Corps is transforming all of the bottom of the state. To anyone who has even heard the word "ecology," the map is a horror. It is a bland and terrifying symbol of the triumph of the Engineers and the rape of America.

The key to the existence of southern Florida—not its Miami Beach economic existence, but its ecological existence—is the flow of water. From the central part of the state, water flows into Lake Okeechobee. From there it does not so much flow as seep southward and southwestward, across vast acres of sawgrass dotted with higher areas (or "hammocks") that bear shrubs and trees. On these hammocks for centuries lived the Seminoles, feeding off the 150-odd species of fish, the dozens of species of birds, living in harmony with deer and alligator, moccasin and panther. Finally, the water flows into Florida Bay, mixing with the salt water of the ocean to form one of the richest estuarine areas in the world.

"This tremendous productivity," explains Roger Allin, superintendent of Everglades National Park, "is in part dependent upon gradual salinity gradients from fresh to sea water across a broad estuarine belt. The major aquatic species to a degree are abundant because they have free access to whatever proportions of the salt gradient they need at different times in their life cycle."

The productivity of a fluctuating water system is, or should be, well known to anyone who has ever seen a rice paddy—the richest and most productive artificial agricultural ecosystem man has ever created. But the Engineers have decided to divert all the overflow from Lake Okeechobee into "drainage control canals" directly to the Atlantic Ocean and the Gulf of Mexico, leaving the park to get most of its water from local rain. You don't have to be an expert to know that's going to louse up the whole Everglades bit. Actually, the Corps of Engineers is charged by Congress with the responsibility for providing water to the park—but that works out better on paper than in fact. In fact, the water it "controls" from Okeechobee south is stored under the administration of something called the Central and Southern Florida Flood Control District, which was set up in 1949, two years after the national park was established.

"The way it has worked out," says Miami newspaperman John Pennekamp, "is that five unpaid men, who meet once a month, exercise enormous power on a project about which they cannot have the knowledge that comes with day by day application." One of the five men manages his own investments at Kissimmee, one is a real estate operator at Melbourne, one is an agriculturist at South Bay (part of the Corps operation involves completely draining the area just south of the lake to open it up for agricultural development, and to hell with the water flow), one is an insurance man in Coral Gables, and the fifth sells Chevrolets at Fort Pierce.

The results of all this water management are dramatic.

In May 1961 (the park counts its alligators in May), along the Shark Valley loop road and in that area, park officials counted 375 adult alligators and 75 young. Every year since, the numbers have declined, until in May 1966, in the same area, they counted only 24 adults—and no young. There are similar effects on a number of other animals and birds.

The park, then, is slowly dying, thanks to the Engineers. Outside the office window of Superintendent Allin, just inside the park boundary near Homestead, woody brush dominates a landscape that should be mostly sawgrass and a few hammocks. It is what happens when year after year is dry, and it will take years to restore the area to its "natural" form. In nature, of course, wildfire is the ecological restorer (serving also the function of decomposing much of the organic material for reuse), but Park Service policy is against even controlled burning.

Inconspicuous on the garish Corps of Engineers map is a short red line, running a few miles northwest from Barnes Sound and crossing U.S. Highway 1, labeled "C-lll." It is a canal that already exists; when I was there it had a "plug" in it, but by the time you read this the plug will have been pulled, unless some completely unexpected intervention has taken place.

C-111 has two avowed purposes. One of them is that ubiquitous excuse for anything the Engineers want to do: flood control. The canal will take the fresh water that flows "overland" in a southwesterly direction into the park, and divert it into Barnes Sound—thus changing, when and if it works, the salinity of the sound and probably of whole sections of Florida Bay. When there isn't fresh water to divert, the salt water of the sound will come up the canal and—through overflow and seepage—change salinity in the other direction.

The second purpose of C-111 is to provide a channel for barge transportation to a plant operated by the Aerojet-General Company. C-111 is openly called "the Aerojet canal," and true or not, it is widely believed that Aerojet's tremendous political influence as a prime defense contractor bolsters the Engineers' determination to ignore the protests of the Park Service and virtually everyone else about the opening of the canal.

The water which will not flow into the park carries the nutrients which are needed by the park's vegetation and wildlife, and nobody yet knows who needs which nutrients. But even more important, according to Allin, are "the diluting effects of these waters which will be diverted to Barnes Sound. Without question, salinities in Florida Bay will be increased and circulation retarded. The eastern portion of this area could well become nothing more than a brine basin within a few years." Scientists at the Marine Institute in Miami have already determined that changes in the salinity level in the Everglades estuary are lethal to the young and the eggs of nearly all marine species.

Within the alluded area, says Allin, are 60 per cent of the park's roseate spoonbills, 25 per cent of the great white herons, 15 per cent of the American eagles and 95 per cent of the dwindling number of crocodiles (not alligators)—among other species. All of these birds and animals are already in the "rare and endangered" classification.

Of course the Park Service has complained. The Engineers, however, have answered. We'll pull the plug, the Corps has said, "to see what damages would occur and thereby justify the Service's claim that a plug is necessary"!

The Corps of Engineers has legal authority over "the execution, operation, maintenance and control of river and harbor and flood control improvements authorized by law, and the administration of laws for the protection and preservation of navigation and navigable waters in the United States." Its permit regulations make clear what the Corps' orientation is: ". . . the decision as to whether a permit will be issued must rest primarily upon the effect of the proposed work on navigation . . ."

The law does require the Engineers of the Army to "coordinate application for permits" with the fish and wildlife people of the federal government and the affected state, but it doesn't require the Engineers to pay any attention to their recommendations, except to transmit them to the applicant. In the New York-Long Island area alone, the federal Bureau of Sport Fisheries and Wildlife, from 1962 to 1965, recommended denial of 24 dredge-and-fill permits; 16 of the permits were issued anyway. During the same period the Bureau recommended that 35 other projects be approved only with restrictions intended to protect fish and wildlife; 21 of these projects were authorized by the Engineers without restrictions.

Not only in southern Florida and on Long Island, of course, do the Engineers run wild. The Corps' Gathright Dam, on the Jackson River in Virginia, will flood the state-owned Gathright Wildlife Management Area. The last natural estuary area in the Puget Sound complex, near Tacoma, is threatened by a project to dredge out the bay and construct a railroad yard.

Nor are all the Engineers in the Army. On the Little Tennessee River in Tennessee is some of the last free-flowing, unspoiled river country of the Southeast, famous for trout fishing and for scenic values; the Engineers of TVA are about to destroy it with Tellico Dam. The Duke Power Company will threaten the entire Savannah River and destroy four of its wild tributaries—the Toxaway, the Whitewater, the Horsepasture and the Thompson— with a development in South Carolina. In Alaska, the proposal to build Rampart Dam—which would involve sweeping changes in the entire ecology of central Alaska—still stirs nationwide controversy.

If it isn't a dam, it's a highway. In New Jersey—the fourth smallest state in the union—studies now project 40 additional superhighway lanes across the state in the next few years. A proposed federal parkway will destroy Vermont's famous Long Trail on the ridgetops of the Green Mountains. Another is aimed through the wilderness of the Spruce Knob-Seneca Rocks National Recreation Area in West Virginia. Still other projects will pave

Franconia Notch in New Hampshire and Cumberland Gap, between Virginia and Kentucky, for interstate highways.

They are everywhere, the Engineers. And so pervasive in our nation is the Engineers' mentality that a law passed last year to establish "a coordinated, long-range national program in marine science" is called the Marine Resources and Engineering Development Act. California Democrat George Brown, Jr., during a Congressional hearing on the shortage of ecologists, put it into a single sentence: "Might I suggest that we could solve the problem . . . if we retitled these ecologists as biological systems engineers and let the Department of Defense finance them?"

IV: You Go Through Sedro Woolley

Some atlases show it as Highway 17A, but it's marked as Route 20. Rod Pegues of the Sierra Club in Seattle told me that it was the best road to take if I wanted to see unspoiled land in the Great Cascades. "If you go through Sedro Woolley," he said, "you're on the right highway."

The road escapes the shoreline civilization quickly, and winds lazily up the lovely and unspoiled Skagit River, a deep and enchanting mint green with the beginnings of spring runoff—now loafing its way through a wide valley, now hurtling whitely through a narrow gorge. On both sides of the river and road, creeks as varied as their names, and falls ranging from tiny trickles to crashing cataracts, contribute their share of the precious water to the river. The Engineers and their angry steel-and-concrete rapine seem far away.

But atop the Skagit, within Mount Baker National Forest, are the three dams of the Seattle Power and Light Company, "City Light" to Washingtonians. Each is ugly, and the river grows stunted and ugly as you approach the first of them. They have spawned an ugly town, Newhalem, with the depressing standardized look of company towns everywhere.

This area is north of the proposed Great Cascades National Park and the wilderness area proposed as a part of it, but the land is the same, and when I got out of the car, I could only do what thousands have done before me: stare at the awesome mountains and wonder what kind of idiots we are.

I was forced to admit that the dams weren't really hurting anything. The Skagit is as beautiful today a little way below Gorge Dam as it ever was, the fish still swim, the microorganisms still thrive. And would I give up the electricity that drives the typewriter on which I write, that lights the paper I write on?

A few feet from where I stood on the bridge, the Forest Service is building a picnic area, carefully cleared in tiny patches beneath the firs. There are lavatories, and I wondered idly whether, over a period of time, their nutrients will change the land and perhaps the lake, itself artificial. The road at whose temporary end I had stopped will eventually cut its way all across the range; it was the subject of a conservationist fight, now lost, and of course it will change, as any road changes, the meaning of the land it touches. But can I believe that it will seriously damage the Great Cascades?

"They call us preservationists," Stewart Brandborg told me in Washington, D.C. "It's supposed to be kind of a dirty word. They say we're trying to 'lock up' the land. But all we think is that some of it ought to be left completely alone."

Brandborg is executive director of The Wilderness Society, which is just what it sounds like. The high point of the Society's existence was passage in 1964 of the Wilderness Act, which froze 54 areas within national forests as "wilderness areas," to remain essentially untouched by man, and provided for the possible designation of a number of other areas now within national parks or other federally owned and administered lands. Some people—lumbermen, for instance—don't like the act at all.

There isn't anything wrong with that. We can't save all our forest and ask for wood as well. Far better that the lumbermen should do their "harvesting" under the careful control of the foresters of the Department of Agriculture—who will see (as state forestry agencies usually do not) that the logging is selective, that new seeding is done, that roads are not built up the middle of streams and that they are reseeded, too, after their immediate use—than that the slopes should be logged bare and left to erode, the roads left in the streams to destroy the life there.

In his office in the Everglades National Park, Superintendent Roger Allin expressed to me his pride that "a little old lady in a wheelchair can come here and really see the Everglades." She can, too. And she should be able to, as she should be able to see the Great Swamp or the Great Smokies or the Great Cascades.

But the inheritors of Pinchot, who sought to combine conservation with access and use, still fight with the disciples of Muir, who urged the preservation of wilderness. The Sierra Club and the Wilderness Society, their opponents charge, are made up of "backpack snobs"—people with the time and the money (and the youth and the energy) to go on mule trips or afoot into the deep wilderness, and who consequently want it saved for themselves, although the great majority of American vacationers expect, and have a right to expect, more of the amenities—including the right to see the Cascades as I did, with my car in sight and its warmth to retreat to.

The critics are partly right. There was a hearing, for example, on the Park Service's proposal to include 50,000 acres of Lassen Volcanic National Park under the Wilderness Act. The Wilderness Society, urging a larger wilderness area, said in part that "the Horseshoe Lake road should be closed in order to provide a quality wilderness camping opportunity that would afford some relief from the standard, congested campgrounds." The Society argued no special wilderness value for the additional area, much less any ecological importance; only the snobbish-sounding appeal for a "quality" area away from the "standard" places where the peasants go.

There is no need for such conflict, no more than there is any need to fight every work of man—such as City Light's dams or the cross-Cascades road. A trip up Route 20 proves (or would if the power lines were underground) that we can have dams and the Skagit too; and where the ecological pattern is repeated again and again, we can spare one riverhead to the demands of convenience. It proves that we can have a road for spoiled city dwellers or people in a hurry—like me—and still have plenty of space in the Great Cascades for the backpackers.

In fact, what it demonstrates best is that we *must* have both, and in plenty. The demands on Yosemite and the Great Smokies are already too great. We can kill a national park or a national forest by choking it to death with campsites; before that happens, we must somehow assure that some of the cars, some of the little old ladies, go elsewhere this year.

On my way back from the top of the Skagit, I stopped at a tiny restaurant which is the only building in Newhalem not owned by Seattle Power and Light, and talked with the couple who operate it. Last year, I learned, the power company took 24,000 people through a tour it operates for visitors; easily twice that many, perhaps more, must have visited the area, and visited it deliberately, because the road does not yet go anywhere else.

"Is that too many people?" I asked, because the woman behind the counter obviously loved the stark and snow-clad mountains and the green and gentle river.

"No," she replied, after a moment. "But one of these years it will be."

Interlude: Goodby, Ruby Tuesday

Goodby, Ruby Tuesday,
Who can hang a name on you
When you change with every new day?—
Still I'm gonna miss you.
　　　　　　　　　—The Rolling Stones

Save the cable cars.
Save the Grand Canyon.
Save the Hudson, the roseate spoonbill, the Metropolitan Opera House, the Missouri, the coyote, the epiphytic algae.

What shall we save, and why?

Would anyone die for the roseate spoonbill?

Probably. And probably only because they are pretty. But we need a better reason to save things. There are pretty highways—as any advertisement for American automobiles or Greyhound Bus makes clear. There are pretty bridges, and pretty dams, and pretty artificial lakes (and were they endangered, I should want to save some of them). Some of the best fishing is in artifically stocked streams, and some of the best camping is in artificially managed forests.

I have before me, as I write, a stack of literature begging me, or anyone else who will listen, to save a quarter million acres of wilderness on the upper Selway River in Idaho. A vast area of land has been put into wilderness, but a corridor has been left, which is now, according to one leaflet, "threatened by logging and roads!" Nowhere in this literature is there any argument as to *why* I should save it, except simply to keep it from being logged.

But *something* has to be logged, and without roads, I, for one, will probably never see *any* of the upper Selway. I am willing to urge that the upper Selway ought to be saved, if someone points out that logging this particular corridor will endanger the watershed ecology, or make a meaningful difference to the rest of the already selected wilderness area. But none of the literature makes these points, and I have to reply that we can't save everything.

Without a sense of the ecosystem, we will not only fail to rally support for particular projects, we will fail to save some of the things that ought to be saved. The beauty of redwood stands, or of the Grand Canyon, is obvious; but there is no overwhelming conservationist support for the proposed Great Basin National Park, which would preserve an ecosystem unique in the world.

In fact, this point is almost sure to be lost even amidst the raging fight over the redwoods. There will be a Redwoods National Park, but chances are that it will be in the wrong place. The National Park Service is proposing a park in the Mill Creek area on the Smith River; the Sierra Club and others want a park on Redwood Creek, further south. The Mill Creek proposal would include about 15,000 acres and would cost about $56 million. The Sierra Club's Redwood Creek proposal would include 90,000 acres and cost $140 million. Secretary of the Interior Udall says the Redwood Creek proposal would "break the back of the conservation fund."

But conservationists rarely argue the real importance of the Redwood Creek proposal. It is the last chance to save a complete, or nearly complete, redwood ecosystem. The proposed park area embraces nearly all of the watershed of Redwood Creek, while the Mill Creek proposal takes in only a tenth of the Smith River watershed, and that tenth is at the bottom.

On Bull Creek, further south in California, there stood, until a decade or so ago, Rockefeller Forest, a state-owned stand of virgin redwoods, maintained in preservation. Between 1947 and 1954, the unprotected area above Rockefeller Forest was logged by private lumber companies; a fire followed, and in the winter of 1954–55, northern California was hit by severe storms.

The naked slopes of upper Bull Creek couldn't hold the water they had once been able to retain, and in the classic pattern of erosion, the river rose even higher, and in its turn undercut its banks to create more erosion, the circle ever widening until finally, in the Rockefeller Forest, the ground was cut from under the mighty—and "protected"—redwoods, and hundreds of them fell to the gnawing water. Logging has ceased now on upper Bull Creek—but every winter more redwoods fall.

Bull Creek is the reason why the Redwoods National Park should be on Redwood Creek and should embrace the entire 90,000 acre proposal of the Sierra Club—regardless of cost—not because the trees are taller or because there is a pretty beach. A few trees at the bottom of a river are not an ecosystem in the redwood country, and if you kill the ecosystem you're only kidding yourself about saving the trees.

We could, if we wanted to, rebuild the Metropolitan Opera House. But we can't put the redwoods back in Rockefeller Forest. That, it would seem, is the key to answering the question, "What should we save?"

We should have, we must have, national parks with campsites and lakes for boating. But we should *save* species and ecosystems.

V: Everybody Should Break an Ankle

In a lawsuit in San Francisco a few years ago, an attorney was trying to recover damages for a workman who had broken his ankle on the job, and on the stand, a doctor testifying for the insurance company was vigorously insisting that no permanent damage had been done. The ankle, the doctor insisted, was as good as new. "In fact," the doctor argued, "the cartilage that has grown up at the point of fracture is actually stronger than the original bone."

The attorney turned to the jury, raised an eloquent eyebrow, and turned back to fix the doctor with a withering stare. "Tell me, doctor," he asked, "do you recommend this type of fracture to all your patients?"

All across the United States, the Engineers recommend fractures as improvements on the national ankles. In almost every case, the fracture is in the public pocketbook, either immediately or in the long run.

On a foggy January afternoon, I drove slowly up Route 9D in New York, a winding, occasionally dangerous road that follows the east bank of the Hudson. To my immediate left, railroad yards, dumps and frequent junk-piles occupied the foreground; in the middle distance the brown and dirty but still impressive river went past in the other direction, occasionally as much as five miles wide; beyond, in the distance, the false fronts of the Palisades, looming and impressive even though I knew that their backs have been quarried away, looked somberly down.

Where a tunnel pokes through Breakneck Ridge, I stopped, left the car in the parking lot of the deserted Breakneck Lodge, and climbed down the bank to walk across the New York Central tracks and stand on the shore. Across the Hudson—narrow and hurrying at this point—was Storm King Mountain.

The ridge behind me was, and is 295 higher than Storm King's 1,340 feet; but Breakneck Ridge is simply there. Storm King rises directly and abruptly from the rushing river, and in its presence, even from the other side of the river, I felt that sense of helpless puniness that men are apt to feel in the presence of nature.

The Engineers of the Consolidated Edison Company feel no such puni-ness. Storm King, they decided, was the ideal place for a pump storage plant.

A pump storage plant is a simple thing, though not in itself an economical one. Its function is to suck up water, and to pump it to a high reservoir. Then, at peak periods when the company needs to deliver a lot of power, the reservoir releases the water to fall back into the river, and the plant uses the falling water to generate electricity.

When conservationists protested the plans to build the plant, Con Ed promptly responded, not only that "we need the power" and that taxes and payroll would benefit the village of Cornwall (which rose magnificently to the bait), but that the care which Con Ed would give the site would actually improve its scenic values. The company also said it would build Cornwall a riverfront park—which the town welcomed, partly because a park built without state or federal funds could be restricted to local citizens, thus keeping out "undesirable" visitors from New York City. Guess what that means.

But we have heard all that before. A seacoast away, the Pacific Gas and Electric Company proposed to deface California's beautiful Bodega Head with a reactor and to call the result "PG&E's Atomic Park." Public pres-sure forced PG&E to surrender (temporarily) its reactor plans, and on the Hudson, Con Ed finally, and grumpily, agreed that it could bury its 800-foot-long plant, pump its water up and let it fall through a hidden tunnel, and put the necessary power lines underground instead of allowing them to march through Yorktown on steel towers.

Now the trick is to talk fast, loud and long about how it's all going to be underground—and to hope that nobody will notice the 240-acre reservoir out in the open behind Storm King, in the middle of a treasured forest that is used as a study area by Harvard's botany department and which includes trails maintained by the New York-New Jersey Trail Conference.

Con Ed would like it, too, if everybody would shut up about fish. Somebody committed the *faux pas,* in hearings before the Federal Power Commission, of pointing out that striped bass—beloved of fishermen from Long Island to South Carolina—go up the Hudson to spawn, and that something like 85 per cent of them spawn in the Storm King area. That gigantic "straw" through which Con Ed plans to suck up river water can suck up fish and larvae and eggs just as easily.

The FPC granted Con Ed the permit to build its Storm King toy, but some citizens who wouldn't quit took it all to court, and won from the United States Court of Appeals a historic decision:

> The Commission's renewed proceedings must include as a basic concern the preservation of natural beauty and of national historic shrines, keeping in mind that, in our affluent society, the cost of a project is only one of several factors to be considered.

The broken-ankles-are-better philosphy often comes out as the philosophy of "maximum use" (or, sometimes, "multiple use"). Industrial polluters of water, as parodied by the Conservation Foundation's Russell Train, put it this way:

> A stream has a natural capacity to assimilate waste. This assimilative capacity (which depends upon the availability of free oxygen in the stream) is a natural resource. Conservation means wise multiple use of natural resources. Therefore, it is 'true conservation' to use the assimilative capacity.

Having quoted it, Train proceeds to tear it apart, but it hardly seems necessary; its sophism is self-evident. It is similar to the argument that underground transmission lines should never be used because they raise the cost of power, or that pollution abatement devices can't be installed because they raise the price of manufactured goods. "Following this approach," Train said in a different speech, "child labor would never have been abolished."

Over a hundred years ago, Henry David Thoreau gazed with sick horror on the work of Engineers on the Concord River, and wrote: "Poor shad, where is thy redress . . . who hears the fishes when they cry?" Today, approximately a hundred miles away, the Yankee atomic plant on the lower

Connecticut River threatens to destroy the highly productive shad run in the river. Cooling towers will be installed only if the plant decides the fish are being hurt—which may be far too late.

VI: The Effluent Society

Once upon a time there was a lake.

It was a thing of magnificent beauty, left a breathtaking blue by departing glaciers. It was 30 miles wide in some places, nearly 60 in others, and more than 240 miles long. Ten thousand square miles of lake, over 200 feet deep, it lived on a still larger sister to the north, and fed a somewhat smaller sister to the east.

In 1669, a white man—Louis Joliet or Jolliet—saw the lake, and soon forts and settlements sprang up.

Today, Lake Erie is virtually dead. Detroit, Cleveland, Buffalo, Akron, Toledo and a dozen other cities pour millions of *tons* of sewage into the lake every *day*. Some of it is fairly carefully treated; much of it (especially Detroit's) is not.

The Detroit River, which feeds Lake Erie, carries every *day,* in addition to Detroit's largely untreated sewage, 19,000 gallons of oil; 100,000 pounds of iron; 200,000 pounds of various acids; and two million pounds of chemical salts. The fertilizer used on the farms of Ohio and Pennsylvania and New York drains into streams which pour into the Erie. Paper mills in the Monroe area of Michigan pour volumes of pollutant waste into the lake. Steelmakers pour in mill scale and oil and grease and pickling solution and rinse water. The Engineers of the Army dredge the harbors and channels of the area and dump the sludge into the middle of Lake Erie.

Normally, a lake receives from various sources a certain amount of nutrient material, which is consumed by plankton or algae or bottom vegetation or bacteria. The fish eat the plankton and the algae, the bacteria mess around with the nitrogen, a couple of hundred other processes simultaneously take place, and it all works out.

So you dump a bunch of sewage or fertilizer or other biologically rich material into the water, and the algae, for instance, grow faster than the fish can eat them. Algae are life forms just like you and me, but (like you and me) in large numbers they stink. They also use up whatever free oxygen might be in the water, which makes it tough for the other life forms. Beaches become covered with algae in the form of slime, and so does the surface of the lake. The lake, in ecological terms, "dies."

Lake Erie has had it.

At first glance, the solution seems easy: Stop. It may not save the lake, but at least it can be kept from getting any worse. Simply make it illegal to put anything into the lake that can remotely be construed as a pollutant.

But there's another problem. If you don't put it into the lake, what are you going to do with it?

There are a number of sophisticated techniques for dealing with a lot of water pollution. There's sand-bed filtering. There's a method called electrodialysis (one sizable California town, some of whose citizens don't know what they're drinking, gets all of its water from the electrodialysis of "waste water," mostly irrigation runoff and sewage). There's another called reverse osmosis.

The problem is that every method leaves you with *something*. After you've separated the water out, what do you do with what you separated it out of? Bury it? An urban unit of one million people produces, believe it or not, 500,000 tons of sewage a day (that's everything in the sewer, not just the most obvious component, and much of it is industrial waste). Even after you take the water out, you'll need a pretty big cemetery. Burn it? We have enough air pollution problems as it is.

Sewage aside, that same urban unit of a million people produces, every day, another 2000 tons of solid waste that has to be disposed of. On top of that, it throws into the air, every day, 1000 tons of particles, sulfur dioxide, nitrogen oxides, hydrocarbons and carbon dioxide. In 1963, American mines, every day, discarded 90,400,000 tons of waste rock and tailings. In 1965, every day, 16,000 automobiles were scrapped (joining from 25 to 40 million already on junkpiles).

Every year, America manufactures 48 billion cans, 26 billion bottles and jars, 65 billion metal and plastic caps, virtually all of which become, almost instantly, solid waste (and aluminum cans and Saran wrap don't degenerate easily like easy-rusting steel cans and paper). Of the eight billion pounds of plastics we produce, only ten per cent is reclaimed. Of the one and three quarters million *tons* of rubber products, only 15 per cent is reclaimed.

The pollution of the air is the form of pollution that most people know most about, but ecologists have some concern here, too. Nobody knows, for instance, what happens if you take one pollutant out of the witches' brew that city dwellers breathe; the chemical interactions are so complex that to take away the hydrocarbons and nitrous oxides that come out of auto exhausts may lead to difficulties with the remaining pollutants that no one can now predict.

While we search, perhaps not as frantically as we should, but at least with increasing concern, for someplace to put our solid, liquid and gaseous wastes, the Engineers gaily produce new ones. In the rush to find new sources of clean water, the technique that has most captured the popular imagination is the desalinization of sea water.

But when you've finished the desalinizing, what you have left is a bunch of hot brine. You can't dump it back into the ocean on the spot; you'll raise the temperature considerably and thus endanger all the offshore life. Besides, you'll just raise the salt concentration near your intake and have to take it all out again in your next batch.

The Engineers assure us that we can get rid of sulfur dioxide in the air and stop the ecological damage done by big dams on watersheds if we will only turn to nuclear power; but nuclear plants create radioactive wastes and "thermal pollution." Thermal pollution—the alteration of the ecosystem by changing the water temperature—is what's killing the shad near the Yankee atomic plant on the Connecticut River.

Even sewage, spewed out in large enough amounts, raises water temperature. "Sharks have appeared in waters off southern California," Congressman George P. Miller points out, "where they never previously appeared, and the studies made indicated that the slight rise in temperature through the disposal of sewage changed the ecology and caused the water to become suitable for the sharks. These are the things," the Congressman added in the understatement of his career, "that we don't know very much about."

Ultimately, it is reclamation and reuse that hold the only hope for escape from slow death by pollution. The reclamation and reuse of water is already possible, and can be done by some methods without the creation of too much solid waste. A method is being developed to make it far more economical to reclaim steel from junk automobiles. Sulfur can be reclaimed, albeit expensively, from the sulfur dioxide of stack gases. Electric automobiles, still a difficult conception for most of us, can be a reality whenever we're ready; it's a simple matter of cost.

Cost, and learning to know what we're doing—both when we fight pollution and when we pollute. In a Senate hearing early in 1966, Senator Gaylord Nelson of Wisconsin talked with Assistant Interior Secretary Stanley Cain (himself a noted ecologist):

SEN. NELSON: I notice that they have now filled in 200 square miles of San Francisco Bay. It was about 520 square miles and it is now down to 300-and-some square miles of water. . . .

SEC. CAIN: To my knowledge there is no general ecological study being made of the bay and the damage of this filling. I can say, however, that the Bureau of Commercial Fisheries has been engaged for a few years now on a study of Tampa Bay, where perhaps between 15 and 20 per cent of the bay has been filled behind bulkheads and, in producing the material for the fill, there has been about an equal percentage of the bay that has been dredged. These studies reveal that after 10 years of dredging, the bottom is, in effect, a biological desert. . . .

SEN. NELSON: So after it is all filled, the ecologists will be able to tell us what happened to it?

SUGGESTED READINGS

George Borgstrom, *The Hungry Planet* (New York: Macmillan, 1965).

Rachel Carson, *Silent Spring* (Boston: Houghton Mifflin, 1962).

Paul R. Ehrlich, *The Population Bomb* (New York: Ballantine Books, 1968).

Paul R. Ehrlich and Richard L. Harriman, *How to Be a Survivor* (New York: Ballantine Books, 1971).

Richard A. Falk, *This Endangered Planet* (New York: Random House, 1971).

Frank Graham, *Since Silent Spring* (Boston: Houghton Mifflin, 1970).

Samuel Z. Klausner, *On Man in His Environment* (San Francisco: Jossey-Bass, 1971).

Gene Marine, *America the Raped* (New York: Simon and Schuster, 1969).

Joseph L. Sax, *Defending the Environment* (New York: Alfred A. Knopf, 1971).

Osborn Segerberg, Jr., *Where Have All the Flowers Fishes Birds Trees Water & Air Gone?* (New York: McKay, 1971).

II

PROBLEMS OF ECONOMIC
POLICY ❧ ❧

POVERTY, UNEMPLOYMENT, AND AUTOMATION

A society may be judged by the way it responds to the members it defines as "most superfluous," that is, by the way in which it does or does not provide the minimal requirements necessary to sustain a human life and make that life worth living. Human dignity is a vague abstraction to those who possess it; however, it is an elusive but concrete thing to those who are denied it. In a society that evaluates people by the money that they spend and the work that they do, not having a stable income or a stable occupation is tantamount to being a nonmember, going unrecognized and unrespected in everyday dealings with others who are better off or who work steadily. To be poor in America, especially if you are black or a member of some other oppressed minority and/or rural in origin, is to be invisible; you just don't count, you cannot make your weight felt. Witness the manner in which the aged are politely but prematurely buried in "golden year" settlements, or the disregard for the Poor People's March in 1968, ending in the mud and despair of Washington, D.C.

Yet, those who launched and led the march of the poor, that futile effort to make themselves visible, were able to accomplish several things that altered their relationship to the larger society around them. First, they did organize to provide the basic services for themselves that were otherwise acquired through dependent relations with others or never received at all. Second, they reduced the apathy that often accompanies poverty and unemployment, finding within themselves the will to become independent and to be recognized as rightful members of this society. Finally, they directed their efforts toward Washington, the seat of national power and policy making, and in so doing made it clear to themselves and the rest of the nation that poverty and unemployment are not merely the result of the absence of jobs in the labor market, or due to the whims of the economy, but are the direct responsibility of the government.

As early as the first Truman administration, Congress established this responsibility as belonging to the federal government. The Full Employment Act was the recognition that not only would the federal government coordinate trade, but it would make sure that jobs were available to all those who sought work. While this bill was intended to provide employment for the recently demobilized veterans of World War II, during a period of expected depression, it also established the direct accountability of the government for all aspects of economic policy, not just those which business wished to delegate to it.

This assumption—that the federal government must be responsible for all aspects of economic policy—is a necessary one for a number of reasons, resulting from the continued and necessary intervention of the federal government, both directly and indirectly, in the maintenance of the economic stability of the country. Through its regulative and supervisory agencies, most notably the Federal Reserve Bank, the government has a determining role in setting the amount of capital available for financing the expansion of industry and home building, making money for investment plentiful or scarce. Consequently, it can increase or decrease the number of jobs available in the private sector of the economy. The federal income tax structure does regulate the redistribution of wealth in the country, both in regard to private and corporate wealth, which makes it possible to guarantee a minimum wage and, within the limits of economic productivity, a minimum annual income for every citizen. Finally, the federal government is the country's largest purchaser and employer of labor, providing a stable demand of great magnitude and constancy such as is needed in an advanced industrial society. By maintaining what economists call "aggregate demand," the federal government also generates many services and consumer industries to supply the people working for it and its contractors, thereby, creating more jobs indirectly via its direct intervention in the economy. The fluctuations in the economy of such diverse states as California, Washington, and Utah are understandable to a great degree in terms of the defense industries and military installations located in those areas.

A related problem of national policy has to do with the introduction of those labor-saving machines and electronic devices which are beginning to replace workers and revolutionize the psychological and social character of work in American society. The replacement of human power by the processes of automation has decreased the number of jobs available in *both* blue-collar and white-collar occupations. Theoretically, some jobs will be created in the areas directly concerned with designing and servicing automated processes of production and record-keeping. A number of new occupations have been created, such as programming, key punching, and data

analysis in the field of computers. At the same time, the need for creating
new fields of employment goes undiminished. Retraining may provide employment for some people who suffer technological unemployment but who
is to provide the retraining? At present, employers have evinced little interest in establishing such programs, except when the federal government
provides funds and makes them profitable for corporations.

It has become increasingly evident that, at least for the foreseeable future,
employment will be less available than it was before the introduction of
automation. All but the most antediluvian social thinkers are in some sort
of general agreement that the resulting unemployment can be eliminated or
reduced only by public intervention on a massive scale. Primarily, this could
accomplish three things: (1) retrain the technologically unemployed, (2)
make work by shortening the work day and creating a more even distribution of work throughout the society, and (3) increase the number of occupations in the public sector. This last suggestion may be the most important
and most advantageous to all members of society.

Everything considered, there is a trememdous need to eliminate what
Galbraith has designated the public squalor amid private affluence. This
does not mean merely a general enhancement or upgrading of public facilities, such as parks and beaches, but also an increase in their number.
Moreover, it is in the less visible area of public services that increases in the
number of people employed in serving the public is required. Along these
lines, American society has vastly inadequate health services available to its
members, including both a dearth of medical personnel and those in ancil-
lary positions, such as nurses, orderlies, and technicians. The latter, traditionally ill-paid and held in low esteem, might also be regarded with the
dignity and given the rewards commensurate with their skills, their needs,
and their vital importance in the field of public and personal health. Finally,
there are new areas of occupations now required, particularly those related
to the life cycle and family living in an urban environment. Jobs in geron-
tology and child day-care centers are in urgent need of expansion.

A society which begins to eliminate some social problems by eliminating
others is a creative society. To make jobs available in the field of health care,
for example, is not the "make work" of public works projects, temporarily
created to keep people alive and active, but it is honest, human, purposeful
work from which one can develop a measure of self-respect. For what one
does in such an area is dramatic and important, being intrinsically more
interesting than tending a machine. Most important, one is directly serving
other members of the society, and the outcome of one's effort is directly
visible to the doer.

We Americans are now living in an advanced industrial society, an age of great productivity and much affluence. We are also, for the first time in the history of the world, at a point where most people do not have to work in primary production of those goods necessary for survival. In fact, most people do not have to work at all in order to supply the goods and services required by the American population. Indeed, it is possible to say that automation may eliminate much boring and repetitive work, perhaps eliminating a great deal of the "dirty work" and with it some of the creative work. In a society of this nature, each member can be guaranteed the means necessary to survive with respectability and dignity. Such conceptions of society go against the very work ethic which has created the social organization and technology that can now operate with much less human labor than in the past. It is possible, then, to understand the problems of poverty, unemployment, and automation as dimensions of governmental policy, rather than as the result of moral or educational failures among the poor, the unemployed, or the technologically dispossessed. These people are not the result of the unpredictable nature of the market place. In order for them to have some sense of control over their own lives, they must have guaranteed rights to income and employment, regardless of their morals and the whims of that market place.

Despite the possibility that alterations in government policies may eliminate not only the problems of poverty, unemployment, and automation, but also those related to inadequate health care and supportive services for families with working parents as well, it may at the same time create new troubles for members of society who cannot reconcile themselves to the prospect of greater leisure. This is an emerging problem because the compulsions of the market place are supported by an ideology of scarcity and its inner derivative—a learned need to attain security through continuous comparison of one's progress with others in the same situation. Freedom from this vision of scarcity and the ensuing status anxieties of modern living may not be possible only through political intervention in the way in which work is conducted and distributed. The guarantee of minimal standards of decency and the reduction of the work week require the concomitant ideology and set of values appropriate to those conditions.

To be at home with leisure requires that the members of society be capable of enjoying it: for its own sake, for the greater opportunity it provides us to respond to each other as human beings, and for the potential of becoming concerned with problems of who we are and what we can be in the presence of greater freedom. A stripping away of the rationalizations for avoiding these activities may not be a sufficient source for unrestricted involvement in leisure: we may still see it in utilitarian terms and, thereby, reduce its heady quality. It is precisely for this reason that new life styles

—the counterculture of communes, be-ins, rock music, drugs, and others —provide for some an alternative set of values. They further provide an alternative set of experiences to measure one's self-development against. Despite the modishness and slavishness of some of its doings and the destructive character of deep drug involvements, the hippie subculture gives the member or the ex-member this warrant—that having tried both the square and the hip styles of life, he can make a conscious choice, a decision of one over the other, without remorse or second thoughts about having failed to explore these alternative but interdependent pathways. For the rest of us, whether straight and square or marginal to the hippie world, we can only stand and wait until we are forced to make these choices when greater leisure is foisted upon us.

Major transformations in the meaning of work and leisure imply major transformations in the way we think about each other and ourselves. In turn, such reflexive thinking requires consideration of how the major institutions of American society control these visions of reality through their allocation of available goods and services, how the rewards for the performance of work influence our sense of who we are and on what that definition is based. A new valuation of labor may only be possible when there is a necessary reduction in the importance of property and competitiveness as motivational components in this institutional sphere. We cannot begin to deal with problems of policy if we think only in the language of corporate capitalism, i.e., by eliminating poverty and unemployment we will create more customers for the goods and services of our corporate enterprises. Therefore, at the foundation of the problems of policy is the compelling need to make corporate capitalism accountable to those whose fate is currently at the mercy of these institutions.

Shallow solutions, which seek to increase corporate profits by providing full employment and a guaranteed annual income, do not begin to eliminate those elements of our self-definition which are based upon real or psychic domination over others. The invidiousness of the forms and functions of an enlightened capitalism are revealed in our contempt for those who cannot work, regardless of their opportunities to do so; it is also found in the quest for possessions which make us feel secure and satisfied in a world ruled by social and economic scarcity.

Can anyone feel secure in such an infinite universe, one in which more and more must be accumulated? Can anyone feel satisfied by continued accumulation of standardized things? Is there not a limit to such pursuits when the rewards become meaningless and are used to hide our disgust with ourselves for having ever tried to acquire them? Are there not costs to the sense of self-regard that a person has when such a possessive individualism cuts us off from other persons who have entered into competitive relations with us, or who have less than we do?

These are the kinds of issues which may some day become the subject of a national debate on alternatives in living and what kinds of allocations are necessary to maintain them. Such a debate would be a sure way of knowing that the developing society is a possibility and that men may make choices to live free from the compulsions of scarcity, possessiveness, and competitiveness with other members of society. A debate of this kind would finally demonstrate the personal character of all policy questions in an interdependent society.

We start this section with a discussion by the late economist Ben B. Seligman, on the various ways in which poverty is measured in the United States. He poses the question: how many poor are there? In his discussion of the methods used to estimate the extent of poverty, Seligman notes the social concomitants of being poor: old age, female head of household, minority group membership, and others. He indicates that a sizable portion of the poverty group is passed on from generation to generation, implying that there is a permanent core of poor, trapped in hopeless deprivation which makes it impossible for even the next generation to "feel less oppressed, less tension in their lives, and able to acquire those little amenities that make material existence less desperate." In the numbers of poor, we find the grim statistics on the millions who may never have a minimum level of comfort and material decency.

John K. Galbraith, the noted economist and former ambassador, discusses the sources of unemployment in an advanced industrial society. He analyzes the cultural and economic sources of the discrepancy between the character of the labor force and the kinds and number of positions available. He argues that the presence of both an inadequately trained labor force and the failure of the society to generate a sufficient aggregate demand for products is now the responsibility of the state. The contradiction between the trends toward a highly educated labor force, greatly reduced in size, and the need to maintain demand of a great magnitude and constancy to keep those very workers employed, is implicit in his discussion. It is one of the central problems of policy in an advanced industrial society.

Ben B. Seligman, in a second selection we are using from this important social thinker, documents the impact of automation in reducing not only the number of manual occupations, but also the number of white-collar, middle-level managerial positions as well. The solution found in public and private retraining programs is inadequate, given the scope of the problem. The only solution that has wide-ranging ramifications is a shorter work week for labor. Despite the increased costs to the employer of such a scheme, the author notes that the implementation of reduced working hours in the past has always been accompanied by increased productivity. Such has been and still is the nature of the technological revolution.

Elliot Liebow, an urban anthropologist, in a trenchant article discusses the social-psychological consequences of unemployment, particularly for the black people of America, that segment of our society most directly affected by government policy decisions which seek to combat inflation by slowing down the growth of the economy. The resulting unemployment strikes at those who are least able to afford it—those at the bottom of American society. After discussing the meaning of work and its importance for the dignity of the members of society, he goes on to suggest that we upgrade menial jobs in society by increased pay (a suggestion that was forcefully made by Dr. King), by income supplement programs, and by making these jobs more dignified and respectable. The general premise that everyone who wants to work should be guaranteed a living wage would have to become part of our national commitments in order for poor people to feel that they have a stake in this society. Formal freedom, without the power to maintain minimum standards of decency and dignity, is no freedom at all.

Robert Coles, a psychiatrist, is a most sensitive observer of social change in America. Through his interviews with and observations on the disinherited black and white poor of America, he bears witness to the meaning of the connection between poverty and self-awareness. He illustrates dramatically the strengths and weaknesses of the poor during a period of transformation and hope. His analysis of the Child Development Group of Mississippi is not just a case study of the political pressures which brought this most creative of all poverty programs to a close. It is an eloquent testimony of how the consciousness of poor people can be raised when they are involved in running their own programs. Given the opportunity to take control over their own lives, they "may well be more capable of changing themselves than our nation is of changing itself." Implied in Coles' observation is a theory of social change—from the bottom up and from the grass roots—that might be the only viable program for the elimination of poverty in America. Perhaps the public policies that create, support, and sustain poverty and unemployment can only be removed by the demand and agitation of those who know too well the meaning of these programs. This is not to suggest a policy of "benign neglect" or non-involvement, but only that the poor are quite able to see through half-hearted schemes and political manipulation. It was the realization of their potential for social change that was feared in Jackson, Mississippi, and Washington, D. C., leading to the destruction of this most vital and involving program.

THE NUMBERS OF POOR
❧ Ben B. Seligman

Any social problem requires a definition of its boundaries. The limits of the condition presumably help to define the time and effort needed to work out a solution. When it comes to poverty, some definitions use consumption standards rather than money income. In other words, the limits of poverty are set by what a society believes is essential for minimal living. In effect, such a definition makes money income less significant, for it also includes non-money income, borrowing, gifts, and dissaving (using past savings for current consumption). A completely objective definition might begin with "disposable" or available personal income and then add or subtract, as the case may be, transfers of non-money income, public services, and the like. It is also possible, if one wishes, to add net assets to the definition, or to vary the standard of poverty by age, size of family, and type of head of family. To use all the variables involved in defining what poverty is becomes a highly statistical and complicated task.

Nevertheless, some sociologists and economists have deemed the effort worthwhile. Charles Booth, an English sociologist, defined poverty at the turn of the century as affecting those families with weekly incomes of less than 21 or 22 shillings a week. In essence, the definition depended on establishing some monetary dividing line. A similar procedure was employed by B. Seebohm Rowntree, who found in a classic study of York that some 28 per cent of the inhabitants were beneath the poverty line. Rowntree used budgetary and income concepts to establish his poverty line. In a similar manner, several University of Michigan economists, Morgan, Da-

SOURCE: Ben B. Seligman, *Permanent Poverty: An American Syndrome* (Chicago: Quadrangle Books, 1969), pp. 21–39. Copyright © 1968 by Ben Seligman. Reprinted by permission of the publisher.

vid, Brazer, and Cohen, insist that income, need, and "income adequacy" are all significant elements in a definition of poverty.[1] To measure income, these analysts start with "gross disposable income" and then adjust that figure to show the total cash flow of the family. Additions are made for imputed or estimated rental income on a home, and subtractions are made for income tax liabilities. Need itself is measured by standard family budgets, a rather knotty problem. Morgan, David, *et. al.,* make use of the New York Community Council budget for 1959 as a basis for estimating need; this budget analyzed various factors stemming from employment, the number of children and their ages, rental costs, and the like. For an employed head of family, housewife, and two children, aged eight and eleven, the Council budget was $4,330. Applying a variable income figure as a poverty line, based on the factors indicated, the authors estimated that the poor in the United States comprised a fifth of the nation's families.

This conclusion was confirmed two years later in the Report of the President's Council of Economic Advisers.[2] The War on Poverty had been declared in the State of the Union message in January 1964. The CEA then concluded that a fifth of the population of the United States was poor. It found that 22 per cent of the poor were Negroes, and that they compromised nearly half the Negro population of the country. Education was another significant factor in poverty: the heads of over 60 per cent of poor families had but a grade-school education; and of all Negro families headed by a person with eight years or less schooling, 57 per cent were poor. The CEA observed an inverse relationship between the extent of education of family heads and the incidence of poverty.

Discrimination was a powerful conditioning force, too, said the Council: a comparison of Negro and white families whose heads had similar educational attainments revealed that Negroes were likely to be poor about twice as often as whites. A third of poor families were headed by persons over the age of sixty-five; indeed, 50 per cent of such families could be classified as poor. The cities contained 54 per cent of the poor; 46 per cent could be found on farms. If a family lived in one of the southern states its chances of being poor were twice those of families living in other parts of the country. A fourth of poor families were headed by women; half of families headed by women were poor. In 1960 Texas had the largest number of poor; New York and California followed in close order. The facts were dreary and depressing.

How did the Council arrive at these measurements? CEA suggested in its 1964 report that the concept of poverty should refer to those persons and families whose basic needs exceeded the means to satisfy them. Presumably this would allow for such factors as size of family, age of its members, housing, and health requirements. The problem was to define the standard for basic needs: by present American levels of living, the rest of the world is clearly poor; by the same criteria, most Americans 150 years ago were poor. Yet such statistical difficulties did not prevent the Council from specifying 20 per cent of American families as poor—9.3 million families out of a total of approximately 43 million families. Included were eleven million children, or about one-sixth of all youth. The numbers had been derived by using a $3,000 yearly income cut-off.

Furthermore, said the Council, 5.4 million families had incomes of less than $2,000 a year. What of those persons who were living alone? The Council found that 45 per cent of such "unrelated" persons had incomes of less than $1,500 a year. The final estimate was that 33 to 35 million Americans were living at the poverty level, and the likelihood was that almost five million poor families would make no progress by 1980, even though the economy might continue its rapid expansion. Poverty had become endemic.

The poor were ubiquitous. They could be found in all parts of the population, in all sections of the nation, in all age groups. They were not necessarily unemployed; striking was the fact that almost 13 per cent of all families with an employed head were poor. Poverty was not merely a Negro problem, for 78 per cent of all poor families were white. Poverty, said the Council, could be traced to low earnings, low productivity, discrimination, low bargaining power, lack of mobility, and inadequate minimum wage protection.

Savings were not always available to help a poor family, and even if there were savings, they would not help very much to relieve the situation. On the average, the additional income that might accrue from savings on an annuity basis to a family with a head over age sixty-five would amount to about $135 a year.[3] An annuity of $1,500 a year would require a capital sum of $19,000 at age sixty-five; the average net worth for spending or consumption "units" with aged heads was $8,000, and most of this was frozen in home ownership. Thus property was no protection against poverty.

Yet the Council's estimates were considered by many economists and sociologists as either too conservative or too crude. Herman P. Miller, the Census Bureau's expert on income analysis, argued that the CEA choice of a $3,000 poverty cut-off line was much too arbitrary, for it did not take account of family size, the age of the family head, or geography.[4] The Council, said Miller, had made a quick choice of a poverty definition to provide a rationale for an impending political decision. Miller argued that a single poverty line distorts the analysis of poverty, overstating poverty among certain groups and understating it for others. A variable standard, or a "band" of poverty, centered around a figure of $3,000 for a family of four, might range from $1,800 a year for a young couple to $4,200 for a family with four or more children. Had CEA used such a standard, said Miller, the percentage of urban poor would have been 11 per cent less than the estimate in the Council's 1964 report.

The idea of a poverty band was also employed by Oscar Ornati in a study that relied mainly on data for the five decades prior to 1961. Ornati established lines described by the expressions "minimum subsistence," "minimum adequacy," and "minimum comfort," so that income requirements defined by these lines set the limits of the poverty band over the years. In current dollars the band moved from $413 to $726 in 1905, and from $2,662 to $5,609 in 1960. Since these figures were based on workers' family budgets, there seemed to be a measure of circularity in their computation, for, as Ornati observed, the budgets specify what people ought to buy but are derived from data based on what they actually do buy.[5]

Miller, in contrast to the CEA, argued that a single line overstated the number of aged among the poor, since they have smaller than average families and lower than average earnings. Furthermore, a band would have revealed many more children in the poverty strata. In the last analysis, the probability was that variable lines would have counted more persons among the poor, for as the economy changes, new demands and expectations develop, shifting the boundaries of poverty. As S. M. Miller and Martin Rein have argued, "Those not poor today may be poor in tomorrow's circumstances, though they have not suffered any absolute decline in their conditions."[6]

The notion of a band seems a reasonable way to measure the extent of poverty, because it is difficult to say that a family with an income of $3,010 is not as poor as one with an income of $2,090. The issue can be further complicated when consumption standards are considered. Take the problem of housing. Adequate housing may be defined as an apartment with direct access, a kitchen, cooking equipment, and hot water. On this basis, only 5 per cent of white families and 10 per cent of Negro families can be said to have had poor housing in 1963. If housing standards were employed as the sole measure, very few families would be classified as poor. Even when income is used to define poverty, one finds relatively high ownership of television sets and automobiles among the poor.

Yet to associate ownership or lack of ownership of such material objects with poverty would be quite misleading. In many instances, a television or radio is a relic of former affluence; or it may be a hand-me-down gift; and in fact, as Herman Miller concedes, such items contribute to poverty because they are bought at the expense of an adequate diet or adequate medical care. Perhaps the most important element in poverty is psychological—what aspirations do poor people have, what hope is there for them to break out of the cycle of poverty? Most of the evidence suggests there is little hope indeed without massive public programs to break the cycle.

Hence, where one places the poverty line or band sets the dimensions of the problem. When John Kenneth Galbraith suggested that poverty had been virtually eliminated in the United States, he was using a $1,000-a-year yardstick as a poverty cut-off.[7] With a low cut-off the poverty population would be dominated by rural families, the aged, and families with female heads. While farm families have some recourse to income-in-kind, their overall needs for material things appear to be less than for urban families. When one moves the poverty line higher, more low-paid workers and unskilled workers fall into the class of the poor. Yet such a movement of the poverty line does introduce statistical distortions: the increase in the proportion of aged among the poor from 1947 to 1962 may have been deceptive, for with an upward movement of the general income scale, a cut-off figure of $3,000 per annum would really have moved downward in the total scale. Such a poverty cut-off figure in 1947 was fairly close to the average or median income figure, so that the proportion of the aged was smaller. On the other hand, a definition of poverty in terms of the lower fifth of the income scale does not reveal much change in the composition of the poor over time.

Clearly, there is a measure of flexibility in defining poverty, especially if needs are taken into account. With needs representing an expression of social standards, poverty becomes an indication of the extent to which sectors of the population participate in the larger society. Electricity, automobiles, and television may appear to some sociologists to be luxuries, but today they do provide measures of involvement in the habits of Western civilization. To that extent poverty definitions express subjective evaluations from which there is no escape if realistic appraisals are to be made.

Michael Harrington tells in his important book how he arrived at his sizable estimate of fifty million poor.[8] He points out that in the late 1940's several congressional investigations had suggested $2,000 as a dividing line. Updating that figure to 1961 implied a line of $2,500 annual income. Subsequently, Robert Lampman of the University of Wisconsin related income to family size and came up with a poverty definition set at $2,500 for a family of four and $3,236 for a family of six. On this basis, 19 per cent of the population, or 32 million persons, were deemed to be poor. In 1963 a Joint Economic Committee study set standards of $1,261 for a single individual and $4,088 for a family of seven or more: this measure also included 32 million persons. AFL-CIO economists then estimated that poverty afflicted 24 per cent of Americans or 41.5 million persons. But, argued Harrington, if family budget data were taken into account, these estimates would be understatements, for the budgetary standard for a family of four in 1959 figures ranged from $5,370 in Houston to $6,567 in Chicago. Hence if half the budgetary standard were taken as a poverty cut-off, or around

$3,500, then, Harrington estimated, a count of fifty million poor would not be far off the mark.

Be that as it may, it was clear that consumption standards as well as income had to be incorporated into the analysis of poverty criteria. As Mollie Orshansky of the Department of Health, Education, and Welfare has said, a poverty profile ought to be based on accepted standards of consumption and should allow for different needs of families with varying numbers of adults and children.[9] Miss Orshansky developed a measure based on the amount of income remaining after allowing for adequate diets at minimum costs. She concluded that in 1963 there were 34.5 million poor in the United States, including fifteen million children and 5.2 million aged persons. These were the people who were compelled to choose between a minimum diet and other material needs of life, because they simply did not have enough for both. But, she added, if we include the "hidden poor"—2.8 million persons living with families—the total rises to 37.5 million. For the 34.5 million people there was a gap of some 40 per cent between what they had and what they required—in money, about $11.5 billion. "From data reported in the Bureau of the Census in March 1964, it can be inferred that one in seven of all families of two or more, and almost half of all persons living alone or with non-relatives, had incomes too low in 1963 to enable them to eat even the minimal diet that could be expected to provide adequate nutrition and still have enough left over to pay for all other living essentials."[10]

While Census data suggest that an income of $60 a week is characteristic of the poor, income, argued Miss Orshansky, cannot be considered as the sole factor. Food intake adequacy might be viewed as a supplementary guide in judging levels of living. Relying on the food plans devised by the Department of Agriculture, Miss Orshansky concluded that a poverty income cut-off would range from $1,580 for a single person in urban areas to $5,090 for a family of eight, with a pivot of $3,130 for a family of four. The food plans had long been used by welfare agencies to set public assistance budgets. The Department of Agriculture "economy" food plan provided 22 cents per meal per person in a four-person family. As of January 1964 the cost per person was $4.62 a week. It was obvious that a diet based on such estimates was extremely low and apt to be deficient in critical nutrients, such as calcium and proteins. After evaluating the relationship of income to the "economy" standard, Miss Orshansky suggested that poverty could be defined in terms of a family income less than three times the cost of an "economy" diet. This was applied to families of three or more persons. The income of families whose position in the economy was set in this manner was about 65 per cent of the required income necessary to remove them from poverty. The gap was quite substantial.

In a rapidly changing society, argued Miss Orshansky, there cannot be only one measure of poverty. A single line, such as advocated by the Council

of Economic Advisers, and which in fact established public policy for many
months, included some who did not belong in the poverty strata and excluded others who were decidedly poor. Any poverty measure ought to
reflect at least rough equivalency in levels of living for individuals and
families of different size. There might be an element of arbitrariness in the
resulting count of the poor, but the standards would at least be more
reasonable than a single income figure.

This line of thought underlay the "poverty index" of the Social Security
Administration.[11] The intent was to create a sensitive measure of poverty,
taking into account the different needs of different sorts of families. Following the Orshansky concept, the SSA Poverty Index specified the minimum
money income required to support an average family of given size at the
lowest level consistent with a decent standard of living. In essence, it
specified an acceptable level of consumption, thereby providing broad limits
to the relative incidence of poverty. A new poverty line was drawn separately for 124 different types of families. These were classified by sex of the
head of family, number of other adults, farm versus urban, and number of
children under the age of eighteen. Then the amount of income was determined that would buy an adequate diet based on Department of Agriculture
criteria, and excess income over this amount was used to set the various
poverty lines. While in the main the food bill was estimated at a third of
total income requirements, different ratios were used for different sizes of
families. The total sum necessary to meet the needs of a family headed by
a man, based on the "economy" diet, was $3,220 a year; for a family headed
by a woman, $2,960. The actual income medians were found to be $1,760
and $1,300 respectively. Again, the estimate of the number of poor persons
came to 35 million for 1963.

A clearer picture may be given from the following tabulation of possible
poverty lines:[12]

	Non-Farm		Farm	
Number of Persons in the Family	Male Head	Female Head	Male Head	Female Head
1 under 65 years of age	$1650	$1525	$ 990	$ 920
1 over 65	1480	1465	890	880
2 under 65	2065	1875	1240	1180
2 over 65	1855	1845	1110	1120
3	2455	2350	1410	1395
4	3130	3115	1925	1865
5	3685	3660	2210	2220
6	4135	4110	2495	2530
7 and more	5100	5000	3065	2985

These notions were also applied to counting the poor in specific areas. As a result, the Welfare Council of Chicago, for example, discovered in 1965 that the largest number of poor in its jurisdiction—more than 40 per cent —came from families of five or more persons. It found 55,600 children in families with annual incomes of less than $1,000, increasing its previous count of the poor by 62,000 to a new total of 762,000, one out of every eight persons in the Chicago metropolitan area. In fact, the sliding scale used, derived from the SSA Poverty Index, was low at all levels for families living in Chicago because the city was a high-cost living area, thus offsetting any improvements in economic conditions that had taken place since 1960. The new count underscored the fact that the special problems of large families had been receiving less attention than merited from poverty program officials.[13]

The significance of these figures was illustrated by Congress' attempt to employ poverty measures in various legislative programs. The major question was: should a family of four be considered poverty stricken, by federal standards, if its annual income falls below $3,130, the figure used by the Office of Economic Opportunity, or should the poverty cut-off be closer to $2,000, the figure used by the Office of Education in allocating aid to elementary and secondary schools? OEO was employing a flexible scale based on the Orshansky concept, but the Office of Education was bound by the school aid law passed in 1965, which defined families living in poverty as those with annual incomes of less than $2,000 a year or those receiving public assistance.

According to Leon Keyserling, all of the foregoing indices err grievously on the conservative side.[14] Using both single-line and "band" measurements, Keyserling came up with 38 million persons in poverty and 39 million in deprivation, a standard of living somewhat higher than poverty but still not affluent. The cut-off points for poverty were set at $4,000 a year for families and $2,000 a year for single persons. A range of $4,000 to $6,000 in income defined the "deprived" family, while a range of $2,000 to $3,000 was applied to single individuals. Why this seemingly more liberal definition? Keyserling relied on "modest but adequate" household budgets for 1959, then estimated the income required to sustain such budgets. Thus for large families the budgetary range was $6,216 to $9,607; for small families, $3,893 to $4,270; and for single individuals, $2,324 to $3,140. Nevertheless, continued Keyserling, such data failed to tell the whole story, for the average income of all families with incomes under $3,000 a year in 1962 was $1,778; and for all families with incomes under $2,000 the average was but $1,220.

Yet not all attempts to define the poverty spectrum were so liberal as Keyserling's. Some leaned quite the other way, seemingly anxious to dismiss the entire debate as irrelevant to the state of affluence in America. This point of view was stated most forcefully by Rose D. Friedman in a pamphlet written for the American Enterprise Institute.[15] According to Mrs. Friedman, the only objective basis for defining poverty is the nutritive sufficiency of the family's diet. With this standard, the cut-off point becomes $2,200 a year; the conclusion is that only 10 per cent of Americans may be said to live in condition of poverty.

How was this calculation achieved? The simple fact is that Americans enjoy a diet substantially greater than what the rest of the world gets. Half the people of other lands must live on 2,250 calories a day, and another 20 per cent are able to obtain 2,750 calories a day. But Americans not only have a superior diet, they also have radios, television, electricity, and plumbing. The latter, however, are non-quantitative elements: they cannot be measured, argued Mrs. Friedman, leaving only the caloric content of a family's food intake as the sole objective factor. And it is demonstrable, she continued, that Americans suffer from overweight. Moreover, the caloric content for the diets of the lowest third in the income scale increased 13 per cent between 1955 and 1956, from 2,580 calories a day to 2,910 calories a day. As the notion of "adequate nutrition" cannot be established in any genuinely scientific fashion, the estimation by Mrs. Friedman of such matters as protein requirements is little more than guesswork. As one sociologist, Peter Townsend, remarked, defining what one needs for adequate nutrition is like trying to define adequate height.[16]

Income or educational attainments were said by Mrs. Friedman to be irrelevant. She insisted that it was not true that any large segment of the American people had been left behind and had failed to share in the country's economic progress.[17] (We shall see later how well this assertion applies to Negroes and the aged.) As income could not be used to measure poverty, neither could housing standards or clothing consumption. For how many square feet of floor space, asked Mrs. Friedman, constitute adequate housing? Any effort to measure housing or clothing would be subjective and therefore not meaningful. The only way to define a housing standard would be to speak of protection from the elements, a function no doubt performed equally well by a ten-room heated home in suburbia and a tarpapered shack in Appalachia. Finally, Mrs. Friedman assumed that anyone with adequate nutrition would also have adequate clothing and shelter, a gratuitous assumption at best.

Such an approach, of course, would equate poverty with hunger, and since no one in his right mind would assert that hunger is rampant in the United States, *ergo* there is little or no poverty to be observed. At any rate, conversion of the nutrition adequacy definition into income provides for a flexible standard ranging from $1,295 a year for a two-person family to

$3,155 a year for a seven-person family. The average four-person family would require, on this basis, only $2,195 a year. Hence it is obvious to Mrs. Friedman, if not to many others, that grinding poverty in the United States does not exist, and in any case, only 4.8 million families in the country may be considered poor. Not unrelated to this view is that of the U.S. Chamber of Commerce, which defined poverty solely in case terms.[18] Since poverty involves only specific persons, families, and groups, it is not a serious issue, nor is it massive, said the Chamber. (To say that poverty affects only Negroes, families with female heads, or the uneducated, does not seem to make it less massive, however.)

A far more useful measure of poverty is the index developed by the Census Bureau, which combines five socioeconomic characteristics: low income, low education, unskilled men in the labor force, substandard housing, and children in broken homes. Such an index makes it possible to compare the characteristics of families residing in poverty areas with those living in non-poverty sections of metropolitan areas. Using this five-factor index, the Census Bureau discovered 193 poverty areas in the 101 Standard Metropolitan Statistical Areas (the official designation for large urban complexes). And within these 193 poverty areas were 57 per cent of urban and suburban Negro families, as compared to 10 per cent of white families. Moreover, Negro families comprised 42 per cent of all families in poverty areas. In contrast to the latter, the poverty areas had twice the percentage of families headed by a woman; the ratio of unskilled workers was three times as great; they had double the percentage of families with unemployed heads; and almost twice the percentage of families with five or more children.

While it is true that the poor can be classified into specific groups, the number of families involved total in the millions. Thus, Morgan, David, and their associates found that poor families with an aged head numbered 2.8 million; Negro heads of families totaled 2.9 million; single women with children comprised 1.2 million families; unemployed heads were 1.1 million; and families with disabled heads were 1.7 million.[19] In many instances, multiple factors accounted for poverty: thus 22 per cent of Negro heads were also aged, 26 per cent were disabled, 29 per cent were unemployed, and 43 per cent were single with children. Expected earnings of those families with inadequate income were set at $2,204 for 1959; the *actual* earnings per family head were $900. For many persons, the condition of poverty has been a long-term affair: the average highest income ever earned was $4,143 for the self-employed poor. For Negro heads of families it was $2,940; for the aged, $2,230 a year.

Whatever assets the poor have are likely to be used up quickly. They have little protection against illness: a third of poor families have some health coverage for the head, while 60 per cent have no health protection at all. This situation contrasts to hospitalization coverage for 63 per cent of the general population. In most cases the poor lack any sort of rights to either public or private retirement; for persons fifty-five or older this can become a critical matter.

These characteristics, in effect, condition the transmission of poverty from one generation to the next. They are reinforced by a lack of education. The Morgan-David study revealed that heads of poor families do not have much more education than their fathers had. Less than 40 per cent of poor family heads did better in school than the older generation, while in the general population 60 per cent of family heads whose parents had less than nine years of schooling went beyond that level. The consequence was that heads of poor families had skill attainments about on a par with those of their fathers. Expectations among the poor are low: only about a third of poor families would like to see their sons attend college, as compared to two-thirds of all families that express such desires. Poverty by no means is a short-run phenomenon; it is no accident; it is produced rather by an unprotected and unrewarded relationship of the poor to the rest of society.

Much of the problem may be attributed to the pattern of income distribution. While there has been some improvement as contrasted to pre-World War II periods, the fact remains that income distribution patterns are substantially unchanged since the mid-1940's. The lowest fifth of consumer units in 1965 had an average personal income of less than $2,900 and received only 4.6 per cent of total family personal income. In the main, reductions in income inequality have occurred only in the top half of the distribution scale; there are very few changes for families located in the lower half.[20] At the same time, the share of net worth that goes to the top 2 per cent of families increased (from 58 to 61 per cent between 1953 and 1962), while that going to the lowest fifth of income receivers fell from 11 to 7 per cent. Before 1950 Negroes had been closing the gap between themselves and whites, but in the mid-sixties that trend was reversed. And it was likely that the earnings of young men in the twenty-four age group were more unequally distributed in 1961 than in 1951. Superimposed on these factors is an overall tax system that is steadily losing its progressive character, placing a relatively heavier burden on low-income families. It seems that little can be done, for the poor are voiceless, without influence, and out of the mainstream of economic activity.

The poor consume very little and they produce very little. Lampman estimates that the poor account for about 3 per cent of the gross national product and consume about 5 per cent. The deficit is covered by transfer payments—social security, unemployment insurance, welfare payments— of which they obtain about 30 per cent. The total income of the lowest fifth in the distribution scale approximates $25 billion, including some $10 billion in transfer payments. Public assistance represents $4 billion of the latter, but half the poor receive no public aid at all. Those who argue that a more rapid rise in productivity would solve the problem forget that a third of poor families have no wage earners. To bring six million poor families and three million poor individuals just over a $3,000-a-year poverty line would cost about $10 billion. If this sum is to be in the form of wages, then GNP would have to be increased by $14 to $15 billion. Offsetting increased wages might be the loss of transfer payments, free public services, and high taxes for the poor. But against whatever net figure might result, there would be the qualitative gain of the involvement of the poor in the larger society, and it would be difficult to attach a price tag to that achievement.

Of course, the numbers of the poor vary with the vicissitudes of the business cycle. That is, there are exits from poverty as well as entrances. If one uses current standards measured in constant dollars, the conclusion is that poverty has dropped sharply. The Ornati "band" on this scale moves from a range of 39 to 88 million persons in 1941 to 20 to 71 million persons in 1960. However, an alternative calculation based on contemporary standards in current dollars—the actual situation in each year—shows much less "exiting" from poverty: the band in 1941 on this basis was 22 million to 63 million persons, compared with 20 million to 71 million in 1960.[21] Even if we focus only on the lower limit—minimum subsistence—the exits from poverty over a two-decade period appear to have been but two million persons (when contemporary standards are used).

In 1962, 9.3 million families were classified as poor; in 1963 the number had dropped to nine million families. But the outward movement is slow and may decelerate further, simply because the number of poor families with no head in the labor force increases proportionately. In 1950 such poor families represented 29 per cent of all poor families; by 1963 the ratio had increased to 48 per cent.[22] Not unexpectedly, the aged comprised the largest part of such families, but at 23 per cent Negro families were not far behind. In any case, the Johnson administration was elated at the outward movement of families from poverty: credit was given to "the general economic expansion and the anti-poverty, education, and health programs [which] had brought jobs, fuller work schedules, higher pay, job training, a lowering of the barriers of discrimination, and more adequate social insurance."[23] It was recognized, however, that much more had to be done for the aged, Negroes, rural areas, broken families, the uneducated, and the handicapped.

For it was evident that 70 per cent of poor families in 1962 were also poor in 1963. While 23 per cent moved up the income scale, to just above the poverty line, another 23 per cent dropped below that line. Whatever gains had been made seemed attributable to the dissolution of some 6 per cent of the poor families in excess of the creation of new poor families. Exits from poverty were highest for those families with a head of prime working age, but poverty persisted to a greater than average degree for Negroes, families headed by women, and the aged. Sometimes a family will climb out of the lowest income group when children come of working age and are able to add to its resources. The shifts do not take place evenly: demographic and geographic differences affect the changes. As the population grows older, there is an increase in aged poor; large families among the poor contribute to a further increase in the number of poor family units. And it is evident that richer states are able to reduce their poor more rapidly than poorer ones: in the decade from 1949 to 1959 Mississippi reduced the number of poor families within its borders from 70 per cent to 52 per cent, a one-fourth reduction, while Connecticut reduced its poor families from 20 per cent to 11 per cent, almost by half.

Can such a pace be maintained? After all, it is estimated that by 1975 the number of aged family heads will have increased by only 9 per cent as compared to 1962, while population will have increased by 21 per cent during the same period. But the variety and complexity of factors that press upon the poverty situation in America will in all probability leave the structure of poverty unchanged. And no matter what projections are employed—even a crude straight line—the long-term rate of decrease in the incidence of poverty will still leave 10 per cent of the population behind the rest of us. One assumes, of course, that high levels of economic activity will continue.

We ought not to feel complacent about exits from poverty and decreases in the numbers of poor stemming from prosperity. In 1964 there were still 34 million Americans below the poverty line, according to Mollie Orshansky.[24] The nation's poor may be fewer in number, but the gap between poverty and non-poverty has widened. In 1959 the median income of $6,070 for four-person families was twice the SSA poverty index. In 1964 the median income for such a family was $7,490, nearly two and a half times the index. But the income of the poor in 1964 totaled 59 per cent of estimated need, a mere 2 percentage points gain over 1959. Prices and living standards had moved with income, leaving the poor "outbid and outspent." The rapid expansion of the economy in 1964 proceeded about twice as fast as the rate by which deficits for the poor were being reduced.

Some will argue that the poor are simply a statistical category—people fall in and climb out in rapid succession. Stephen Thernstrom, a Harvard historian, cites the example of graduate students,[25] but at the same time he overlooks the larger and more significant situations of Appalachia and other permanent pockets of rural poverty, the fatherless family, the aged, and the urban Negro. Nor is he impressed by the fact that 40 per cent of parents receiving AFDC (Aid to Families with Dependent Children) were themselves raised in a home where public assistance was received. He does not see that this represents a condition of social entrapment for these families from which there is little escape.

Admittedly, the statistical definition of poverty is no simple matter. There are exits and there are entrances, even in an affluent society, but an increase in annual income of $50 or $100 a year over the official cut-off line does not make a family substantially less poor than it was before. Somewhere along the spectrum of income and family size, people begin to feel less oppressed, less tension in their lives, and able to acquire those little amenities that make material existence less desperate. But there are millions of persons in this country who have not yet made that passage, and there are millions who never will.

NOTES

1. Charles Booth, *Life and Labour of the People in London*, 1891–1903; B. S. Rowntree, *Poverty: A Study of Town Life*, London, 1922; J. N. Morgan, M. H. David, *et al.*, *Income and Welfare in the United States*, New York, 1962.

2. *Report of the Council of Economic Advisers*, Washington, D.C., 1964.

3. Morgan, David, *et al.*, *op. cit.*, p. 190.

4. H. P. Miller, "The Dimensions of Poverty," in B. B. Seligman, ed., *Poverty as a Public Issue*, New York, 1965, pp. 36ff.

5. *Ibid.*, p. 39; O. Ornati, *Poverty amid Affluence*, New York, 1966, pp. 10ff.

6. S. M. Miller and M. Rein, "The War on Poverty: Perspectives and Prospects," in Seligman, *op. cit.*, p. 281.

7. J. K. Galbraith, *The Affluent Society*, Boston, 1958.

8. M. Harrington, *The Other America*, New York, 1962, pp. 175ff.

9. M. Orshansky, "Consumption, Work, and Poverty," in Seligman, *op. cit.*, pp. 52ff.

10. M. Orshansky, "Counting the Poor: Another Look at the Poverty Profile," *Social Security Bulletin*, January 1965, p. 4.

11. *Idem*, "Who's Who Among the Poor," *ibid.*, July 1965. Cf. also E. G. Holmes, "Spending Patterns of Low Income Families," *Adult Leadership*, May 1965.

12. From Orshansky, *Social Security Bulletin*, January 1965.

13. *New York Times*, May 3, 1965; December 12, 1965.

14. L. Keyserling, *Poverty and Deprivation in the United States*, Washington, D.C., 1962.

15. R. D. Friedman, *Poverty: Definition and Perspective*, Washington, D.C., 1965.

16. P. Townsend, quoted in Ornati, *op. cit.*, p. 2.

17. Friedman, *op. cit.*, p. 12.

18. Chamber of Commerce, *The Concept of Poverty,* Washington, D.C., 1965.

19. Morgan, David, *et al., op. cit.,* p. 194.

20. R. J. Lampman, "Income Distribution and Poverty," in M. S. Gordon, ed., *Poverty in America,* San Francisco, 1965, pp. 102ff.

21. Ornati, *op. cit.,* pp. 28ff.

22. *Business Week,* July 17, 1965.

23. *New York Times,* January 28, 1966.

24. M. Orshansky, "Recounting the Poor—A Five Year Review," *Social Security Bulletin,* April 1966, pp. 20ff.

25. Stephen Thernstrom, "Poverty in Historical Perspective" in a forthcoming Harvard University Press book edited by D. P. Moynihan.

THE NATURE OF EMPLOYMENT AND UNEMPLOYMENT

John Kenneth Galbraith

"There is no rate of pay at which a United States pick-and-shovel laborer can live which is low enough to compete with the work of a steam shovel as an excavator."

NORBERT WIENER, *Control and Communication in the Animal and the Machine,* 1948.

On few matters is the image of industrial civilization so sharp as on that of its labor force. This is a great mass—the word itself is ubiquitous—which streams in at the beginning of the shift and out at the end. It consists of comparatively unskilled operatives who guide or attend the machines and a smaller aristocracy who have skills beyond the scope of the machine. When the system is functioning well, all or nearly all are at work. When it is not, the notices appear on the board, the men remain at home and the rising percentage of unemployed in the labor force as a whole measures the extent of failure of the economic system. Similarly, when labor relations are tranquil, men pass peacefully through the gates. When they are not, a picket line appears and the plant either shuts down or functions in face of the threats of the milling crowd outside. There are others in the enterprise—managers, engineers, designers, clerks, auditors and salesmen—but they are part of a shadowed background. The labor force, that which counts, is the great homogeneous blue-collared proletariat.

The image is not yet at odds with the reality of the industrial system. But it is strongly at odds with its trend. Within the system blue-collared proletarian is sharply in decline, both in relative numbers and in influence. And the notion of unemployment, as traditionally held, is coming year by year to have less meaning. More and more, the figures on unemployment enumerate those who are currently unemployable by the industrial system. This incapacity coexists with acute shortages of talent. The view of the system in the preceding chapters makes these tendencies predictable; and the statistics, which in this case are good, affirm the expectation or are consistent with it.

2

The industrial system, we have seen, has a strong technological orientation; indeed one of the subordinate goals of the technostructure is a showing of technical virtuosity. And the technostructure itself, among other things, is an apparatus that brings into conjunction the various branches of specialized scientific and engineering knowledge which bear on the solution of particular problems.

We have seen, also, that advanced technology in combination with high capital requirements make planning imperative. All planning seeks, so far as may be possible, to insure that what it assumes as regards the future will be what the future brings. This accords, too, with the concern of the technostructure for its own security, for such control minimizes the likelihood of developments which might jeopardize its earnings and thus its tenure.

These considerations tell with considerable precision the manpower requirements and labor policies of the industrial system and forecast virtually all of its principal tendencies.

That it will have a large and growing requirement for qualified talent is evident. Technology, planning and the coordination of the resulting organization all require such talent. This requirement, it is perhaps unnecessary to notice, is for *educationally* qualified, as distinct from skilled, manpower. Engineers, salesmen and sales managers, managers and management engineers, and the near infinity of other such specialists, though they are trained in their particular task, can only be so trained if they have prior preparatory education. This is not necessarily the case of the tool-and-die maker, carpenter, plasterer or other skilled craftsman. The engineer, sales manager, or personnel director applies specialized mental qualifications to a particular task. He must have, before learning his particular specialty, the requisite intellectual or mental preparation. The skilled journeyman brings manual dexterity and experience to bear. For this there is no minimum educational level.

At the same time the industrial system reduces relatively, and, it seems probable, absolutely, its requirement for bluecollared workers, both skilled and unskilled.

This situation arises partly from the nature of technology. Machines do easily and well what is done by repetitive physical effort unguided by significant intelligence. Accordingly they compete most effectively with physical labor, including that of no small dexterity and skill.[1]

But to see mechanization and automation purely as a problem in comparative cost is greatly to minimize their role—and to pay further for the error of confining economic goals, and economic calculation, to profit maximization.[2] The technostructure, as noted, seeks technical progressiveness for its own sake when this is not in conflict with other goals. More important, it seeks certainty in the supply and price of all the prime requisites of production. Labor is a prime requisite. And a large blue-collar labor force, especially if subject to the external authority of a union, introduces a major element of uncertainty and danger. Who can tell what wages will have to be paid to get the men? Who can assess the likelihood, the costs and consequences of a strike?

In contrast mechanization adds to certainty. Machines do not go on strike. Their prices are subject to the stability which, we have seen, is inherent in the contractual relationships between large firms. The capital by which the machinery is provided comes from the internal savings of the firm. Both its supply and costs are thus fully under the control of the firm. More white-collar workers and more members of the technostructure will be required with mechanization. But white-collar workers with rare exceptions do not join unions; they tend to identify themselves with the goals of the technostructure with which they are fused.[3] To add to the technostructure is to increase its power in the enterprise. Such is the result of replacing twenty blue-collar workers with two men who are knowledgeable on computers.

Thus the technostructure has strong incentives, going far beyond considerations of cost (which may themselves be important), to replace blue-collar workers.

In the thirteen years from 1951 to 1964, although the labor force in the United States grew by about 10 million—from 60.9 millions to 70.6 millions

—blue-collar employment did not increase at all, and during the earlier years of the period it declined. This includes blue-collar employment outside the industrial system, except for agriculture and the service industries. In basic steel, automobiles, petroleum, tobacco and much food processing —industries marked by a relatively small number of very large firms and thus strongly characteristic of the industrial system—blue-collar employment in 1964 remained well below (and in some instances far below) that of 1951[4] and continued so until more recently. In 1964, production of all goods was half again as great as in 1951. In 1960 the automobile industry had 172,000 fewer production workers than in 1953 and produced a half-million more passenger cars and about the same number of trucks and buses.[5] During the whole period there was a very large increase in white-collar employment.[6] Recent studies suggest, in general, that these trends will continue. There will be a rapid increase in professional and white-collar requirements, only a modest increase in blue-collar employment.[7]

3

As the relative demand for blue-collar workers declines, the requirement for those with higher educational qualification increases. These are needed by the technostructure. And, though with more modest educational qualification, they are required for the white-collar tasks.

It follows, further, that if the educational system does not keep abreast of these requirements there will be a shortage of those with a higher educational qualification and a surplus of those with less. This is the present situation.

It is the vanity of educators that they shape the educational system to their preferred image. They may not be without influence but the decisive force is the economic system. What the educator believes is latitude is usually latitude to respond to economic need.

In the early stages of industrialization, the educational requirement for industrial manpower was in the shape of a very squat pyramid. A few men of varying qualifications—managers, engineers, bookkeepers, timekeepers and clerks—were needed in the office. The wide base reflected the large requirement for repetitive labor power for which even literacy was something of a luxury. To this pyramid the educational system conformed. Elementary education was provided for the masses at minimum cost. Those who wanted more had to pay for it or to forgo income while getting it. This insured that it would be sought only by a minority. To this day the school systems of the older industrial communities in West Virginia, central and western Pennsylvania, northern New Jersey and upstate New York still manifest their ancient inferiority. It is assumed that an old mill town will have bad schools.[8]

By contrast the manpower requirements of the industrial system are in the shape of a tall urn. It widens out below the top to reflect the need of the technostructure for administrative, coordinating and planning talent, for scientists and engineers, for sales executives, salesmen, those learned in the other arts of persuasion and for those who program and command the computers. It widens further to reflect the need for white-collar talent. And it curves in sharply toward the base to reflect the more limited demand for those who are qualified only for muscular and repetitive tasks and who are readily replaced by machines.

This revision of educational requirements is progressive. The top of the urn continues to expand while the botton remains the same or contracts. To this change the educational system responds. It does so with a lag which is partly in the nature of any social response. But also the newly demanded education has required a sharp break with the social attitudes of the entrepreneurs. These, as noted, held the state to be an incubus; they sought to confine it to the provision of law and order, the protection of property and the common defense. Now the mature corporation must acknowledge dependence on the state for a factor of production more critical for its success than capital. Such a revision of attitudes takes time and so accordingly does the public response to it.

4

The effect of this delayed response is that when employment is comparatively high there will be numerous vacancies for those of higher qualification and most of the unemployed will be without educational qualification or without compensating work experience or seniority. This is the present situation—and as this is written in 1966, it has been so for a number of years. There are many openings for individuals with advanced educational qualification. The ardent recruitment efforts of the industrial system in universities and colleges and, even more, its newspaper advertising, attest the fact.[9] At the same time, since these vacancies are not yet fully recognized as the normal counterpart of unemployment, statistics thereon are meager.

The figures on the educational qualifications of the unemployed are better. In the spring of 1962, when the official unemployment rate was 6.0 per cent of the labor force it was 10.4 per cent for those with four years of schooling and 8.5 per cent for those with five to seven years of schooling. Those who are unemployable eventually become discouraged (as other workers do not) and withdraw from the labor market. When those not actively looking for work were added to the labor force the national unemployment rate was estimated at 7.8 per cent. For those with four years of schooling or less it was 17.2 per cent. For those with five to seven years of schooling it was 12.2 per cent. Among those with sixteen years of schooling or more, unemployment was only 1.4 per cent. Of all those officially counted as unemployed at the time, 40 per cent had eight years of schooling or (in most cases) much less.[10] Unemployment of teen-agers, reflecting the combined handicap of limited work experience and, in many cases, limited schooling, was 11.8 per cent. Adding those not in the labor force it was 25.6 per cent.[11] Additionally, the individual with a limited number of years of schooling will, ordinarily, have had poorer schooling than the person who has had more. Two principal reasons why he discontinues school are because the schools are bad and because he is doing badly. These suggest that his few years have been less good than the average. There can be no doubt, accordingly, that the unemployed include the predicted concentration of the uneducated.[12]

5

Lack of education is not the only disability of those who are rejected by the industrial system. A large proportion are Negroes or members of other racial minorities and it has anciently been observed that the Negro worker is the last to be hired when employment is expanding and the first to be fired when it is contracting. Negroes do suffer a special handicap. But a great deal must be attributed to the low level of educational qualification among Negroes, reflecting not discrimination, *per se,* by the industrial system but prior disadvantage in schools and environment. A well-educated Negro is not so necessarily the first fired or the last hired.[13]

Some unemployment is also associated with industrial change—with the decline of anthracite coal-mining in central Pennsylvania, the mechanization and consolidation of mining in the bituminous region, the loss of industry by mill towns in New York, New England or elsewhere. Here again, however, much must be attributed to the exiguous educational system which served the industries of these regions where, characteristically, a boy went into the mine or mill at the earliest age at which he was capable of manual labor. A well-educated population would not have remained stranded or it would have drawn industry to itself. An aeronautical engineer, with the decline in demand for manned military aircraft, may have trouble finding employment in his speciality. But with a little training and some slight loss of dignity he becomes an excellent appliance salesman.

The point is of much importance. Unemployment in the industrial system includes those who cannot find work in their particular craft or skill. It also includes qualified workers who are in the wrong place and who are reluctant to move. The number who fall in these categories will increase as demand presses less strongly on the capacity of the labor force and unemployment rises in consequence. But the increasing educational requirements of the industrial system add to the mobility of the working force both as between occupations and regions. The skilled craftsman of modest education does not easily learn a new skill. And the risks of movement are his own. So if he establishes himself as a tool-and-die-maker in Detroit there is a fair chance that he will remain there. The engineer or sales executive, though he is strongly specialized as to task, can acquire another perhaps less demanding qualification if he must. He is but little tied to his surroundings. If there is greater need for his specialty on the other side of the country he moves in response to a promise of employment, or is moved by his new employer as a matter of routine.

In recent years economists have debated whether unemployment in the modern economy is primarily structural, which is to say the result of a poor adaptation of the worker's qualification and skills to need, or whether it is the result of a general shortage of demand. Some blood has been spilled, for the argument has an important bearing on remedy. If unemployment is structural, the remedy is to retrain those who are out of work. But if the problem is merely a shortage of demand, then general action to increase spending or reduce taxes will suffice. The use of tax reduction as a remedy for insufficient demand has added a point to the debate. For it has been felt by advocates of structural causes and remedies that this may limit the spending on education, training and retraining which is the remedy for unemployment.

We now see the answer. Unemployment is both structural and the result of inadequate demand but also something more. It will appear with slackening of aggregate demand and it will be among those who are most inflexibly tied to particular occupations and locations. At the same time there will be vacancies in positions requiring high and specialized qualification. Employment would be higher both with stronger demand and with a better accommodation of qualification to need.

But unemployment will also be smaller, at any given level of demand, if there is a better *cultural* accomodation to the needs of the industrial system. There will then be a smaller core of functional illiterates who cannot be used at all. And there will be a larger number not only to fill the vacancies calling for higher qualification but also with the added mobility between occupations and regions that goes with education.[14] Modern unemployment is not only aggregate (in the sense that it results from a shortage of demand) and structural but also cultural.

It may be noted that unemployment, as a simple statistical concept, now has little relevance in the industrial system. This system requires a progressive accommodation of educated manpower to its needs. If this accommodation is imperfect, there will be a shortage of workers for specialized tasks. And there will, at the same time, be unemployment. Both measure the failure in the accommodation. Depending on the qualitative nature of the failure, the unemployed will consist of those who are unemployable because of insufficient education, or those who are occupationally or geographically immobile because of absence of education, or those who have a skill or specialty for which there is no demand and which, for reasons unrelated to education, they cannot exchange for one that is wanted. Or unemployment may have a quite different cause. It may be the result of an insufficiency of aggregate demand which reflects yet another accommodation of society to the needs of the industrial system. Simple statistics of unemployment reveal, it will be evident, almost nothing about the nature of the failure of accommodation at any given time. The crude steel capacity of a country was once a rather good indication of its ability to build railroads and meet its other needs for steel. It now tells nothing of the ability to provide special steels for the skin of supersonic aircraft or for similar uses. Technology has made the crude totals far less meaningful. One must now know the nature of the accommodation to the more refined, more specialized and constantly changing requirements for the metal. A surplus of steel could be combined with a severe shortage. So it is with labor. Here too one must look beyond the totals to the accommodation to educationally more refined, more specialized and constantly changing requirements. Here also totals have slight meaning. And here, as with steel, technology is one of the things that has made them so.

6

Much may be learned of the character of any society from its social conflicts and passions. When capital was the key to economic success, social conflict was between the rich and the poor. Money made the difference; possession or nonpossession justified contempt for, or resentment of, those oppositely situated. Sociology, economics, political science and fiction celebrated the war between the two sides of the tracks and the relation of the mansion on the hill to the tenement below.

In recent times education has become the difference that divides. All who have educational advantage, as with the moneyed of an earlier day, are reminded of their *noblesse oblige* and also of the advantages of reticence. They should help those who are less fortunate; they must avoid reflecting aloud on their advantage in knowledge. But this doesn't serve to paper over the conflict. It is visible in almost every community.

Thus the city with a high rate of accommodation to the requirements of the industrial system, i.e. a good educational system and a well-qualified working force, will attract industry and have a strong aspect of well-being. It will be the natural Canaan of the more energetic among those who were born in less favored communities. This explains the modern migration from the South, Southwest and border states to California, the upper Middle West and the eastern seaboard. Many of these migrants will be unqualified for employment in the industrial system. They thus contribute heavily to welfare and unemployment rolls in the communities to which they have moved. The nature of the opprobrium to which they are subject is indicated by the appellations that are applied to them—they are hillbillies, Okies or jungle-bunnies. It is not that they are poorer but that they are culturally inferior. It is such groups, not the working proletariat, that now react in resentment and violence to their subordination.

Politics also reflects the new division. In the United States suspicion or resentment is no longer directed to the capitalists or the merely rich. It is the intellectuals who are eyed with misgiving and alarm. This should surprise no one. Nor should it be a matter for surprise when semiliterate millionaires turn up leading or financing the ignorant in struggle against the intellectually privileged and content. This reflects the relevant class distinction in our time.

A further consequence of the new pattern of employment and unemployment is that full employment, though it remains an important test of successful performance of the economic system, can be approached only against increasing resistance. For, as noted, while the unemployed are reduced in number, they come to consist more and more of those, primarily the uneducated, who are unemployable in the industrial system. The counterpart of this resistant core is a growing number of vacancies for highly qualified workers and a strong bargaining position for those who are employed. This leads to the final source of instability in the industrial system and to yet a further resort to the state. This we now examine.

NOTES

1. This is a generalization. There are numerous operations—the sensory-manipulative operations that are involved in handling a power shovel for example —which have no appreciable educational requirements but which do not lend themselves to automatic processes.

2. For such an argument see Charles E. Silberman, "The Real News About Automation," *Fortune,* January, 1965. For an opposing and, I believe, more persuasive case see Ben B. Seligman, "Automation and the Unions" in *Dissent,* Winter, 1965. The word automation, narrowly construed, refers to an industrial process which provides data from its own operations and feeds this back usually through a computer to controls which fully govern the process. It thus dispenses with all direct manpower. But automatic machinery dispensing with much but not all human guidance, is, of course, very important. And this too is called automation. Because of this ambiguity I have used the phrase automation sparingly and mostly where paraphrasing popular argument.

3. I return to these matters in more detail in Chapters XXIII and XXIV of *The New Industrial State.*

4. *Manpower Report of the President and A Report on Manpower Requirements, Resources, Utilization and Training,* United States Department of Labor, March, 1966, pp. 164, 200.

5. The U.S. Labor Force, 1950–1960," *Population Bulletin,* Vol. XX, No. 3 (May, 1964), pp. 73–74.

6. I return to this in Chapter XXV of *The New Industrial State.*

7. National Commission on Technology, Automation and Economic Progress, *The Outlook for Technological Change and Employment,* Appendix Volume I (February, 1966), p. I–10. Here is the Commission's estimate of change between 1964 and 1975.

"The greatest increase in requirements will be for professional and technical workers; more than 4½ million additional personnel will be required, an increase of 54 percent. The white-collar group as a whole is expected to expand by nearly two-fifths, and to constitute 48 percent of all manpower requirements in 1975. The blue-collar occupations are expected to expand at less than half this rate, and will constitute 34 percent of all requirements. A rapid expansion in requirements for service workers [generally outside the industrial system] is anticipated—a 35 percent increase in employment, bringing this group to about 14 percent of the total."

8. Outside the industrial system, the same is true of the rural areas of the South. Here, too, the need was for crude, illiterate labor power and provision, accordingly, was made for nothing more. Northern agriculture was more demanding and the rural schools better. However, differences in income were a cause as well as a result of the difference.

9. A Boston newspaper editor noted in 1966 that his revenues from advertising of job opportunities had come to exceed that from department stores, with many fewer troublesome suggestions.

10. Charles C. Killingsworth, "Unemployment and the Tax Cut," Address before Conference on Economic Security, Michigan State University (October 26, 1963), Mimeographed.

By way of comparison, national unemployment was estimated at 25 per cent of the civilian labor force in 1933, the worst year of the Great Depression.

11. William G. Bowen, "Unemployment in the United States: Quantitative Dimensions," in *Unemployment in a Prosperous Economy,* William G. Bowen and Frederick Harbison, eds. A report of the Princeton Manpower Symposium, Princeton University, 1965, p. 36.

12. It must be kept in mind that the educational requirements and disqualifications discussed here are those of the industrial system while the educational characteristics of the unemployed are those of the labor force as a whole. And, without doubt, the opportunities for employment of those with minimal educational qualifications are better outside the industrial system. The service industries, construction and agriculture all have a substantial continuing requirement for common labor. In the case of migrant agricultural labor, one sees again how responsive the educational system is to context. No education is required for harvesting crops. And by more or less effectively denying education to the children of those who participate, further generations of such labor are assured.

13. Although earnings of educated Negroes remain well below those of white citizens of comparable qualification. *Population Bulletin,* p. 78.

14. In recent years, in much of western Europe unemployment has been consistently a smaller proportion of the labor force than in the United States. Something is to be attributed to a more persistent pressure of demand and to relatively larger employment opportunities outside the industrial system. But national educational standards and, in consequence, a more homogeneously qualified labor force have certainly been contributing factors. Foreign workers of lesser educational qualification have been added to the domestic labor force, but it has been possible for countries such as Germany, France and Switzerland to take these in the numbers needed and leave the unemployment associated with such lower qualification behind in Spain, Turkey or southern Italy.

MAN, WORK & THE AUTOMATED FEAST
Ben B. Seligman

Automation is said to have ancient beginnings. To be sure, the technology from which it stems goes back several centuries, at least. Automatic devices in the middle 18th century included a mechanical loom for the manufacture of figured silks; James Watt's steam engine utilized a fly-ball governor which controlled the speed at which his contrivance operated; and it has been suggested that automation's basic concept—the linkage of machines —is evident in the detachable harpoon head of the Eskimo. Yet to assert that automation is simply the latest link in a great chain of industrial history obscures what is patently a new phenomenon. In the old days, industrial change developed through fission: division of labor was the key to progress

SOURCE: Ben B. Seligman, "Man, Work and the Automated Feast," *Commentary* (July 1962), 9–19. Reprinted by permission of Mrs. Libby Seligman.

and work was made available to a huge pool of unskilled persons who in the main had been forced to migrate from farm to city. Today, it is precisely these unskilled, together with semi-skilled and even some of management's people, who are displaced and poured back into the pool. Furthermore, automation represents a marked acceleration of change with so cumulative a force that this alone spells a profound difference from what went on before.

Automation is already moving with a rapidity that threatens to tear apart existing social and organizational structures; according to some observers, it will even alter the habits of thought that men have up to now prided themselves on. Such a prospect is perhaps not surprising when we consider the cataclysmic results of the 18th century's Industrial Revolution: the changes then were so swift as to constitute a whole new phenomenon. And Marx and Weber and Sombart had shown convincingly how human and social transformation accompanied technological transformation.

Now, new industrial functions, new economic forms, new work habits, and new social headaches are being created in ways that signify a kind of dialectic leap. Even John Diebold, who claims to have invented the word "automation" and whose ebullient advocacy of computer technology has done much to spread the gospel, confesses: "I believe that [automation] marks a break with past trends, a qualitative departure from the more conventional advance of technology that began with jagged pieces of flint and progressed up to the steam engine."

Why is this so? Up to recent times, technology simply sought to substitute natural force for animal or human force. In the early days, primacy of place was given to windmills and waterfalls. Then came metallurgical discoveries; and the screw and the lathe made possible the machine, essentially a contrivance which man could watch in action. But man remained at the center of the whole business, essential to both operation and control, still more or less the maker and master of materials. With automation, man not only loses irrevocably his function as *homo faber;* he no longer even possesses the character of *animal laborans.* At best, he is a sometime supervisor of a flow process. Actual control is removed from him and given to an electronic contraption whose feedbacks and servomechanisms make it possible to produce goods and manipulate information in a continuous system, without human participation.

To realize what automation implies, we must examine the kinds of machines employed and see what they do to people and organizations. Essentially, today's scientific upheaval comprises four aspects: the conversion of industrial materials into a flow; the setting of uniform standards so that output can be treated as a flow; the utilization of electronic computers with built-in feedbacks to enable the exercise of automatic control; and the application of new energy sources to the whole process. Thus, raw materials, which represent the "input" of an industry, must be handled without human hands, as in a modern meat-packing plant. Production, at one time a series of discrete steps, is completely integrated by means of transfer machines. In some cases, computers tied to cams or templates can make the producing machine follow a predetermined pattern with greater accuracy and sharper tolerances than were dreamed possible in the heyday of the skilled machinist. Computers, into which all sorts of complex information can be fed by "programmers," automatically correct errors. A wide range of goods is now produced in this startling manner—chemicals, automobiles, steel, glassware, electric bulbs, television sets, beverages, and drugs, to name a few. Factories are able to function 24 hours a day, 365 days a year, while manpower needs are reduced dramatically. And with the development of nuclear energy for industrial power, manufacturers no longer need to be near their source of raw materials; they can set up their plants closer to markets, or—if they are seeking to escape the union organizer—in the most isolated of places. Yet one industry necessarily must relate itself more intimately with the next; a seamless web envelops all the entrepreneurs and their works.

There is no lack of Panglossian attempt to assuage our concern. In the long run, we are told (who lives that long?), natural economic forces will work out the necessary adjustments. A shorter work week might stem from automation, suggest some experts; but at the thought that men might work less than the ordained forty hours a week, all kinds of people, from Secretary of Labor Arthur Goldberg down, immediately explode with great cries of anguish. Or we are told that human desires are insatiable: demand will grow, enough to reabsorb men displaced by machines—which calls to mind an apocryphal conversation between Henry Ford II and Walter Reuther. "How," said Ford, as he revealed his automatic factory, "are these machines going to pay you dues, Walter?" "How," replied Reuther, "will they buy your autos?"

We are assured that more jobs will be created by new industry, that higher skills will be required, that economic stability will be guaranteed by automation. There are pitifully few facts available to support these euphoric hopes. More likely a vast trauma awaits us all, to use Irving Howe's phrase. Then why automate? The underlying motives were exposed with unaccustomed bluntness in one of the trade journals recently when an automation advocate wrote: "[Machines] don't call in sick; they don't talk back; they work early and late and without overtime; they don't get tired; and last, but far from least, they don't line up at the cashier's window every week for a slice of the operating funds."

The automobile industry illustrates how an integrated set of machines can function. There the engine production line, for example, consists of a series of drilling, boring, and milling operations connected by transfer machines which move the engine blocks from one point to the next. Tolerances are checked automatically; if something is awry, the whole line is stopped by an electronic device. Or one can see an automatic assembly machine put the components of a television set on a printed board and then solder them into place. These are repetitive operations and their economic justification stems from the replacement market. There is not much of a style factor here and such model changes as do occur can be handled with relative ease. Yet even where variation in the product is essential, as in machine tools, the operation still can be made automatic.

The machine tool industry, mainly a congeries of small shops employing highly skilled labor, has notoriously resisted innovation. But since it is now so closely allied to Air Force and Space technology, it has been impelled willy-nilly by the needs of the armed forces to the adoption of newer techniques. Formerly, a human operator worked from blueprints, controlling his equipment with a variety of jigs and templates. To avoid waste, and perhaps because he was concerned with craftsmanship, he worked slowly. But now, all the variables can be "programmed" into computers, and with the technique known as "numerical control" these electronic brains direct the same cutting tools, handle the same jigs and templates once operated by the machinist. Most important of all, this sort of automation is economically feasible for small lots in which there are changes in product design.

The key here is feedback, the simplest case of which is the home thermostat turning a furnace on and off in order to maintain a constant room temperature. In essence, signals are sent from one part of the automated line to another, correcting errors, shifting power loads, or modifying the speed of the line. No human need adjust gauges or read thermometers or press buttons. Feedback or servomechanisms do a better control job than humans, especially when many elements are involved. Whereas the human eye can follow the motion of a gauge at about two cycles a second, a servomechanism does about 100 a second. Now, marry feedback to a computer and automation is complete. The computers, really giant adding machines and calculators, receive information from the gauges and thermometers, analyze the data, and then transmit new instructions to other gauges and instruments.

Computers, whose basic concept goes back to Blaise Pascal, were developed in their electronic form during World War II to help guns hit their targets more efficiently. There are two basic types—the analog and digital computer. The former operates much as the desk calculator, adding, subtracting, multiplying, dividing, and even integrating. It is a kind of electronic slide rule able to apply higher mathematics to problems of rates of change in various flows. However fast it might have been, for the engineer, mathematician, and operations researcher it was not fast enough. So the digital computer was devised, a machine that employs the binary number system and consequently can only add and subtract. This is no impediment, for like an electronic abacus, the digital computer sends its impulses forward at an unbelievable speed, giving it a marked advantage over the analog machine. Moreover, digital computers have "memory" drums in which data can be stored for future use. The electrical pulses in a digital computer last less than one-millionth of a second. Information can be extracted from the memory drum in about ten-millionths of a second.

Of course, a considerable amount of human brain power is expended before the computer can be put to work. This is the science of programming. Instructions are written on a process sheet, then coded and entered on tape. That is, English is translated into machine language. The control unit of the system then "reads" the tape, gives forth with the appropriate electrical impulses, and sets the servomechanisms to work. One writer compared the operation to an old-fashioned player piano in which the punched holes in the roller actuate the hammers to bank out either the "Basin Street Blues" or a Beethoven sonata.

Lending a nightmarish quality to these developments is the current scientific talk about artificial intelligence. Machines, it is said, can be built to recognize certain patterns and can learn to plan simple tasks. While the computer may be something of a moron, awaiting instructions from a human Ph.D., the fact that an electrical contrivance can be made to learn anything is astonishing enough. If a heuristic or generalized solution is sufficient, then a thinking computer is no longer science fiction. Chess playing machines are at least feasible: the only problem seems to be that they would have to review the outcomes of all possible plays and that might take centuries. Perhaps that is what makes them morons.

The names one often sees bandied about—PERT, ALGOL, COBOL GECOM, SURE—are merely abbreviations for specific programming methods, each utilizing one or more computer installations constructed by Burroughs, Bendix, Rand, or IBM. PERT, for example—Program Evaluation and Review Technique—is based on the concept of a tree network with alternatives to be considered at each node of the tree. Since the computer works so much faster than the human mind and also uses stored information, it can review the accumulating cost of a flow process at each step and then direct the sequence of decisions along the critical or least-cost pathway. PERT originated in the Polaris Missile Project when it became essential to keep track of some 11,000 contractors and subcontractors. Again, military need provided the research motive. So complex can these matters become that the Defense Department had to work out a standardized pidgin English to coordinate programming.

It is sometimes said that the considerable investment in these systems precludes all but the largest firms from employing them. This is not so. Any number of consulting services are available for smaller concerns to meet data-processing needs, and some firms have set up cooperative research centers. Span, Inc. is one such co-op doing the bookkeeping for a number of insurance companies in Hartford; Tamcor maintains brokerage records in New York, and IBM, the biggest of them all, makes its equipment available to all comers through 70 locations around the country. In fact, the latter is now compiling tape libraries, dubbed by one journal "computer laundromats." Thus, the new technology is available to anyone who wants to make use of it.

All this must be worthwhile, for rental costs run from $12,000 a year up and outright purchase of computer equipment can cost millions. Some $2 billion has been invested in computers by private companies since 1950, and this does not include what the government has spent. It is estimated that by 1970 computer sales will hit $500 million a year or about 2½ times present outlays. When the Pennsylvania Railroad automated its Conway, Pa. yards, it expected to recoup its $34 million cost within three years. At Ford, 9 workers at 3 machines putting holes into crankshafts replaced 39 workers at 39 machines. A Philco plant reduced its work force by 25 per cent by using printed circuitry. A computer engineer once remarked that he could cut one man off the payroll for every $5,000 spent on automated equipment. And finally, the initial cost of installing a computer system, according to Wassily Leontief, comes to no more than 6 per cent of total plant investment. The value of the new technology seems undeniable.

By now "Detroit" automation is quite well known. Automatic machines, linked by transfer equipment, move engine blocks through a complete manufacturing process, performing 530 precision cutting and drilling operations in 14½ minutes as compared to 9 hours in a conventional plant. The Chrysler Corporation's recent breakthrough on computer "balancing" of assembly lines, essentially a "combinatorial" problem, now defines each job so rigidly that little liberties like a worker's taking a few minutes out for a smoke become serious impediments to the smooth flow of cars. An automated power plant in Louisiana saved $175,000 in fuel, $100,000 in maintenance, $1.5 million in eliminating delays and mishaps, and $500,000 in labor. A Jones & Laughlin sheet-plate mill turns out strip at the speed of 70 miles an hour with no labor other than the supervision of engineers. Punch-card systems in a reversing roughing mill modify ingot shapes, and the computer even "remembers" what to do when the forms have to be changed. Foundry work, traditionally a hand operation, is now being tied to the computer. In petroleum and chemicals, the story is almost ancient: as far back as 1949 catalytic cracking plants were turning out 41,000 barrels a day with instruments and only a few workers to watch gauges. In a Texaco refinery the computer controls 26 flow rates, 72 temperatures, 3 pressure levels, and 3 gas combinations. General Electric uses segmented "automation," that is, batch production, for motors of varying models up to 30 horsepower. Ribbon machines make 800 electric bulb blanks a minute, running without end, and requiring only one worker who stands by to make an occasional adjustment.

Even in the office and retail store, one finds evidence of the new technology. Although office work has expanded tremendously since 1910 (today 17 per cent of the labor force is found in the office as compared to 5 per cent fifty years ago), it is precisely the enormous quantity of paper work and routine operation that makes automation feasible here. Banks, utilities, insurance companies, and government bureaus have eagerly made room for yards of the new equipment—so much faster is the computer than the old-fashioned bookkeeper and clerk. As a result, office work no longer is the growth industry it was—at least in terms of jobs. One California firm, studied by Mrs. Ida R. Hoos, put only two accounting operations on a computer and promptly eliminated 300 out of 3,200 office jobs and drastically altered the functions of some 980 others.

In retailing, automation starts with inventory and accounting records. Sales data are transmitted to control centers where billing, inventory, and credit information is stored. Bad credit risks are automatically checked and information returned to the sales clerk before the package can be wrapped. Sylvania and IBM have been working on automatic check-out counters for supermarkets—the number of cash registers would be reduced, as well as the number of workers. Ferris wheels, conveyor belts, chutes, and slides, all controlled by electronic computers, deliver garments from receiving platforms to stockrooms and even return the merchandise to the ground floor if necessary. Eventually we will pay our traffic penalties to a computer: in Illinois, records of driver violations are stored in a computer and the fines calculated by machine.

This, then, is the automated feast. Tasks are accomplished with unimaginable speed. Decisions are made by coded instructions and errors quickly detected. Facts are stored and extracted from memory drums. The machines learn and "perceive": they analyze stock market conditions; establish rock flight patterns before the shot is fired into space; write television script that compare favorably with what is now available; compose music; translate; and play games. They combine high technical competence with just enough of an I.Q. to keep them tractable. They do precisely the kind of work to which junior executives and semi-skilled employees are usually assigned.

No slur is intended here, for in addition to the ordinary worker it is the middle manager, the backbone of the average corporation, who will be most affected by automation. He has a bleak future indeed, when computers relay information to each other, do all the scheduling, and control manufacturing from inception to the point at which the product is packaged and rolled onto a box car. It is rather the archon of industry—as Edward Ziegler has dubbed him—who ultimately wins out, for with the elimination of both plant and office staff, this man at the very top gains even tighter control over the decision-making process. The sort of organizational looseness that prevailed prior to the advent of the computer is eliminated, and corporate structure becomes more formal, more "integrated," since with the computer there must be greater "cooperation." The number of links in the chain of command is reduced drastically; vice-presidents are soon out of a job. No less an authority than Herbert A. Simon of Carnegie Tech has said that by 1985 machines can dispense with all middle echelons in business. Production planning is handed over to the digital demon, while both the middle manager and the displaced worker drive taxicabs. The sociologist may very well ask, whither the American dream of status and success?

Quite often, the computer engineer tries to build his own empire within the corporation. Fresh to the ways of business life, he has unabashedly played havoc with established relations. He and his programmer cohorts, cutting across all divisions, have often ignored and undermined the authority of department heads and vice-presidents. Many middle management people in automated companies now report that they are awaiting the ax, or, if more fortunate, retirement. Bright young men leave for non-automated firms, hoping to reach the top elsewhere before the computer catches up with them. Sometimes the new elite does lose out: it has not been unknown for a computer installation to be yanked as a result of corporate internecine warfare.

Usually though, archon and engineers are in complete accord. With the computer creating certain expectations, the firm must operate through a series of highly rigid sequences. Flexibility has been dispensed with, for the whole plant is now a single technical structure in which total performance must be "optimized." The engineer examines each step in the process solely in terms of efficiency—industrial logic of the most unremitting kind takes primacy of place. Under automation, the engineer or mathematician is *the* skilled man in the plant, while workers, those who remain and those who do not, are expected to adjust with equanimity to a situation for which they have had no responsibility. In fact, the engineer's attitude quite often is tough and hard, too much so for ordinary men: what the worker doesn't know, says he, won't hurt him. The scientists appreciate only "facts": the human problems of an industrial system frequently have little meaning for them. Unlike the organization men of the 50's, they are usually "inner directed," disturbers of the corporate peace, free-booters in pursuit of the idols of efficiency. Since the latter is measured by high profit and low cost, such scientific ruthlessness meets the approval of the archon. The latter really doesn't know what the scientist is doing: top management merely voices a faith based on payoff. Thus the programmer, who often assumes the aspect of a medieval alchemist, runs his own show, designing projects, cutting corporate red tape with abandon, and advising the industrial relations department that labor displacement is "none of your business." At best, the engineer can parrot some devotee of the conventional economic wisdom by repeating that automation creates new demand and new jobs, upgrades the worker and inspires everyone with its challenge. There must be a certain glory in the marvels of automation: but the men who once worked in the chemical plants, oil refineries, and steel mills are now out of sight and out of mind.

Between 1953 and 1960, a million and a half jobs disappeared. In one plant, studied by Floyd Mann of Michigan State University, automation reduced the work force by half. In the electrical industry, output increased 21 per cent between 1953 and 1961, while employment declined 10 per cent. There was a loss of 80,000 production jobs in steel during the decade of the 50's. In the shift from aircraft to missiles, 200,000 jobs went down the technological drain. For the 5-year period 1955–1960, production workers in automobile factories were down 21 per cent. All this displacement occurred in an affluent society that itself went through four postwar recessions each of which left behind an increasingly hard-core residue of unemployment—3 per cent in 1951–53; 4 per cent in 1955–57; and 5 per cent in 1959–60.

Full employment for the next 10 years means creating 12 million new jobs —25,000 a week, or almost double the number of new openings in the 1947–57 decade. Extending the period to 1961, we find that output rose 65 per cent while the number of production and maintenance jobs declined. True, white collar workers increased 7 per cent, but now automation is making them just as insecure. If we assume that demand in the 60's will expand at the same rate as it did in 1947–57, then output by 1970 may very well be 50 per cent greater. However, if the present rate of productivity is maintained, then the number of required man-hours will have increased by 12 per cent, providing only 75 million jobs at the end of the decade. Thus, about 8 million persons, 10 per cent of the labor force, will have no work. And this is a moderate forecast, for should the secular growth rate fall below 3 per cent per annum, as is conceivable, output will have gone up about 40 per cent. Add to this the effects of automation, and the job increase by 1970 may be only 2 million, leaving a residue of perhaps 10 million persons without jobs.

Is this so weird a tale? The ever optimistic Bureau of Labor Statistics' chief, Ewan Clague, recently admitted to an Arden House conclave that

200,000 jobs a year would be lost through "disemployment by automation." He found that in 70 per cent of manufacturing industries such "disemployment" comprised four-fifths of the jobs lost. And his estimate did not include computer displacement among white collar workers.

The unions now know what automation can do to them. No matter how strong the security clause in a collective bargaining agreement, the serious drop in membership for most internationals is a harbinger of approaching catastrophe. Further, it is so much easier now for plants to escape to communities where unionism seems to represent little threat. And in such towns, management does not worry about a labor supply, for under automation what need is there for workers? There are also related problems for the unions: What happens to seniority? How about pension rights? Can traditional unionism with its roots in craft concepts cope with an industry whose shape has assumed the form of a process? Is the programmer a part of the bargaining unit? Or does his role in decision-making place him in management's ranks? And how effective is the strike when a handful of engineers can operate the whole works? This last question was answered in Port Arthur, Texas, where about 3,700 production workers walked off the job at an oil refinery, leaving 600 white collar employees and supervisors behind to run the plant at 65 per cent of capacity. One labor relations man was reported to have said: "Maybe they ought to have removed a couple of transistors."

Some have argued that the displaced can be directed to jobs in the service and white collar fields. What jobs? Automation, as we have already noted, has been moving into these fields in the last three years just as rapidly as elsewhere. In 1960, at the Census Bureau, 50 technicians plus a battery of computers did the work that it had taken over 4,000 statisticians to do in 1950. The little black code numbers now appearing on bank checks inform us that our accounts are debited, credited, and cleared by a scanning device hooked into a computer. It is poor consolation, moreover, to be told that employment adjustments will be made via the A & P route—attrition and pregnancy—for this is an admission that there really are no jobs for those who want to work.

The notion that all who have been displaced by machines will quickly find new employment is a cheerful thought, something like whistling while walking through a cemetery. Some years ago, such cheerfulness was quite common, even among labor leaders. Walter Reuther's early speeches all but embraced the computer, so high was the regard for technology, so powerful the belief in growth and progress. The Joint Economic Committee's 1955 report on automation urged laissez-faire, for no serious problems were envisioned. In the short space of seven years, hesitation and doubt have cropped up. There is no longer the ancient and well-regarded optimism that more machines mean expanded employment elsewhere or that automation will upgrade workers. It is evident, rather, that the new technology enforces a deterioration of skills for the great mass of workers and offers only the social junk pile for the unskilled and untutored.

What is the solution? Frankly, there is none, at least none of a definitive character. The numerous suggestions for dealing with the pressing problems that stem from automation are all piecemeal, pecking at a spot here and a point there. No amount of federal fiscal tinkering will meet the immediate needs of those who are attached to a dying industry. Economic growth, while essential, will not of itself put to work again the idle coal miner, ex-machinist, and troubled bookkeeper whose jobs have vanished like the first atom bomb tower. Administration economists believe that automated unemployment can be solved by turning on ordinary Keynesian tap valves: it's all a matter of failing effective demand, they assert. There seems little awareness in important circles that the American economy is undergoing deep-rooted and subtle structural changes and that it will take massive economic and social therapy to assuage the hurt.

The AFL-CIO has been advocating a series of measures, including meaningful retraining programs, especially for workers over forty, area redevelopment, better unemployment insurance, an improved national placement service, special help to relocate the "disemployed," higher pensions, and even shorter hours. But will we—American management, American unions, Congress, the administration—really expend the necessary hard thought? Don Michael doubts it, for it is unlikely, says he, that ". . . our style of pragmatic making-do and frantic crash programs can radically change in the next few years. . . ." It is hard to disagree.

Consider the retraining effort. A case of too little, if not too late, it is hardly a roaring success. In West Virginia, the federal pilot scheme plus the state's own 22-month-old program had been able to uncover new jobs for only half the 3,000 "graduates." Most of the others simply returned to the ranks of the unemployed. In Pennsylvania, 1,760 persons enrolled in retraining classes in 1957. Of these, 884 completed their re-education, 741 obtained new jobs. The state had a half million unemployed at the time.

Where private enterprise undertakes some corrective steps, it is usually found that a labor union had been doing the prodding, as in the meatpacking industry. Yet when 433 workers were laid off in Armour's Oklahoma City plant, only 60 could qualify for retraining and those who did secure new employment had to accept a lower rate of pay. Some firms are genuinely disturbed about the effects of automation. For example, U. S. Industries, a manufacturer of electronic equipment, and the machinists' union have agreed upon a jointly managed fund to study the entire question. The company's president, John Snyder, at least acknowledges that each one of his machines sends 60 workers scurrying to the unemployment insurance offices. Incidentally, one of U. S. Industries' contributions is the invention of automatic equipment to train displaced workers for typing and similar tasks.

There have been other experiments in adjustment. Some take the form of liberal severance-pay allowances. One of the earliest such schemes, though not related to automation per se, was the famous 1936 Washington Agreement between the railroad companies and the unions. Displaced workers receive 60 per cent of their average pay as severance compensation for periods as long as five years whenever mergers occur. In cases of relocation, moving expenses are paid and losses resulting from forced sale of homes reimbursed. More recently, another generous plan was agreed upon by TWA and its navigators, who if replaced by automatic instruments will receive $25,000 plus $400 a month for three years as severance. In addition, the now foot-loose navigators will be given free lifetime travel passes on the airline. Thus they will have at least acquired mobility and will be able to search for jobs in all corners of the globe. Yet such measures offer no genuine solution: they are mere palliatives, for they fail to confront the fundamental question—what does a man do with his time, either during the temporary period of affluence, or when the windfall resources will have given out, or for that matter, even when he has not been detached from industry?

Not every arrangement exhibits a handsome concern for the displaced. In the coal fields a contemptible alliance between John L. Lewis and the operators has cast adrift almost 300,000 miners. The coal industry, caught between the grinders of competitive fuels and high operating costs, was thoroughly run-down by the mid-40's. Deciding not to worry any more about the unemployed at the pits, Lewis acquiesced in rapid technological change. Output per day rose from 6.4 tons in 1949 to 14.4 tons in 1961; one ton of coal now requires less than half the labor it did a decade ago. At the Paradise, Kentucky coal field an automatic shovel larger than the Statue of Liberty strips 200 tons of material in one scoop. In Harvey Swados' words, Lewis decided to trust to time and mortality to resolve the problem of the unemployed. And so the coal industry no longer suffers from economic decay. With a return on investment of 7.5 per cent, it compares favorably with steel and oil. To hasten the day when his union can depend upon a healthy industry for its 40-cent per ton royalty, Lewis directed the mine workers to invest in sundry mine operations and even lent $35 million to Cyrus Eaton, whose interests include peace movements as well as coal. Of course, it would have been troublesome to apprise the membership of these transactions, so all the deals were carried through with great secrecy, only to be smoked out last year in a Tennessee lawsuit. At a recent convention of the union, an innocent delegate who suggested that perhaps something

might be done for the unemployed was ". . . verbally torn to pieces by a
buckshot charge of oratory from John L. Lewis himself." Declining dues
are amply compensated for by investment returns in banks, mines, railroads, and power plants. Meanwhile, 300,000 miners continue to rot in the
idle towns of Pennsylvania and West Virginia.

This sort of cooperation could set a strange trend if other unions were
to adopt the Lewis formula. One that did is Harry Bridge's West Coast
Longshoremen's International. Several years ago, the ILWU signed an
agreement with the Shipping Association that was hailed as a reply to
automation. Indeed, the retirement benefits are quite munificent and the pay
scale was increased somewhat, but at the same time the employers were
given the go-ahead signal to install a whole range of technological improvements which will virtually exclude entire blocs of workers not yet ready to
retire. Moreover, the new work rules, extracted by the employers as a price
for the higher pay and liberalized pensions, have intensified work loads on
the docks virtually to the human breaking point.

Thus, one comes back to an immediate step, which though not by any
means a "solution," nevertheless offers a practicable way for mitigating
some of the effects of automation—the shorter work week. Mere mention
of this is apt to send a shudder down the backs of administration economists
and devotees of the conventional wisdom. Expressing their horror at the
thought that man should have even more leisure than he now enjoys, the
latter urge that a shorter work week means less production and higher costs.
And in the present context of growthmanship, this is unthinkable. Arthur
Goldberg, whose grasp of legal subtleties contrasts sharply with his simplistic formulations of economic issues, warned the International Ladies' Gar-
ment Workers' Union recently that fewer hours per week would ". . . impair
adversely our present stable price structure [and] make our goods less
competitive both at home and abroad. . . ." The enormous productive
capacity of America's industry was conveniently forgotten, a capacity so
enhanced by automation that it can more than compensate for the alleged
loss of output. And this is to say nothing about the quality and content of
contemporary "production"—that would require another essay. The point
to observe now is the curious inner tension of an industrial system whose
fundamental Puritan outlook demands an incessant, unremitting outpour-
ing of goods (for what?) while at the same time it imposes dreary idleness
and dismal futures on those to whom the cornucopia is directed. We may
well ask, what is the feedback in this insane circle?

But to return to the shorter work week—a cursory review of its history
would demonstrate how completely reasonable it is. Prior to 1860, the rule
was dawn to dusk with as much as 72 hours as the weekly standard.
Demands for a shorter span were met with the contention that 12 hours a
day, 6 days a week had been divinely ordained in order to strengthen worker

morality. Three decades later the work week had been shortened by 12 hours. In 1910, the average ranged from 51 to 55 hours, and at that time a work force of 34 million produced a Gross National Product of about $37 billion. The work week continued to shrink: in 1920, it was 48 hours; in 1929, 44 hours; and since 1946, 40 hours. By 1955, the labor force had almost doubled while GNP increased 10-fold as compared to 1910. And all the time the work week kept declining, about 13 hours in a 45-year span, or roughly 15 minutes a year.

Was anyone hurt? Did productivity lag? Has technology been impeded? The depression years aside, whatever unemployment did occur would have been unquestionably greater without the steady drop in hours. A continuation of this secular decline would cut back the normal work week by one hour every four years. According to one estimate, this might create about a million jobs a year which, together with the normal increase in job openings, could really begin to cut into the displacement caused by automation. When Harry van Arsdale of the New York electricians' union obtained a 5-hour day, he was savagely flayed for selfishness and lack of patriotism. Even the labor movement felt embarrassed. Arsdale insisted that he was only seeking to "spread the work." Now it seems, according to Theodore Kheel, the industry's arbitrator, that well over 1,000 new jobs will be made available as a result of the union's action.

What has happened in agriculture presents, in a sense, an object lesson we ought to heed. As W. H. Ferry remarked in a perceptive paper on affluence and plenty, the farm is technology's most notorious victory. Here abundance has become an economic catastrophe. So advanced is our agricultural establishment that even the 10 per cent of the labor force it now employs is too much. Farm output increased 77 per cent between 1910 and 1954, while land used for crops went up only 15 per cent. During the same period, labor on farms as measured by man-hours dropped over 30 per cent. This suggests an almost threefold rise in productivity. According to the late John D. Black, a leading farm expert, the major element in this change unquestionably was the substitution of machine power for muscle power. Yet the economic and political thrust of our system is such that 70 to 80 per cent of the federal government's spending on agriculture goes to counteract the price impact of an ever accumulating surplus.

The parallel between farm and industry is startling. There is enough grain in storage to feed everyone from Maine to Hawaii, but some 50 million Americans, barely manage to subsist, even today. The steel industry functions at 65 per cent of capacity, or thereabouts, while thousands of able-bodied men are shoved aside by automation. Strategic curtailment of production is employed, like the farm parity program, to distort the genuine capacities of our economy. Technology, rather than man, becomes the central focus of existence, and at the same time that it destroys, for example, the belief in the family farm, it seemingly ought to compel a desiccated concept of resource allocation and optimum production to retire in favor of a philosophy of distribution. But we really have no adequate social theory to deal with the latter. The ideas of a Galbraith, a C. Wright Mills, a Paul Goodman, or a Harvey Swados deal only with aspects of the problem. We await to be told what is happening to us, what we need to do. And even then we shall not listen.

It is of course a common cliché that scientific advances have outrun our capacity to deal with them. Technology, the practical and material basis of life, has acquired a tidal force of its own which threatens to inundate human thought. Moreover, modern technology, as evidenced by automation, manifests no orderly growth. Its leads and lags, its uneven development, create new power centers that result in unaccustomed strains. To be sure, this has happened before, but always at immense human cost. It is this that the high priests of automation fail to grasp, while those of us who are merely bystanders can only hope that society will eventually catch up with the engineers and scientists and archons of industry who see only a handsome profit in what the machine can do.

NO MAN CAN LIVE WITH THE TERRIBLE KNOWLEDGE THAT HE IS NOT NEEDED
⚜ Elliot Liebow

Now that we have, in effect, seized upon unemployment as a weapon of choice in the battle against inflation, we face the prospect of a 1970 unem-

SOURCE: Elliot Liebow, "No Man Can Live With The Terrible Knowledge That He Is Not Needed," *The New York Times Magazine* (April 5, 1970), 28–29, 129–133. Copyright © 1970 by The New York Times Company. Reprinted by permission of *The New York Times*.

ployment rate of 5 per cent (4 million persons) or more. And as the unemployment rate goes up, economists and public policy makers debate the question: How much unemployment can the country stand?

Strictly speaking, it is not "the country" that is being asked to "stand unemployment." Unemployment does not, like air pollution or God's gentle rain, fall uniformly upon everyone, nor does it strike randomly at our labor force of 80 million. Unemployment is directional and selective; it strikes particularly at those at the bottom of our society. Managers, professional people, scientists, technicians and others with special skills and training are generally secure in their jobs whatever the unemployment rate. Indeed, even with a 5 per cent unemployment rate, there would continue to be a labor shortage at many of these occupational levels. When we talk about unemployment, then, we are talking mainly about those at the bottom of society: the day worker, the unskilled and semiskilled laborer, the Job Corps and the on-the-job trainee, those with little or no seniority in the labor unions and those making their first try at breaking into the labor force.

Since there is little unemployment at the upper and middle occupational level, a 5 per cent *average* rate means unemployment rates of 10 per cent and 20 per cent in our ghettos and other hard-core areas. And among certain groups, such as black and other minority-group youths and women, it means an unemployment rate as high as 25 or 30 per cent. Increased unemployment, then, means not only more people out of work, it means mainly more black people, more young people and more poor people out of work. The question is not simply how much more unemployment we can stand, but whether we can stand, through deepening unemployment, a deepening of the race and class divisions that are already threatening to tear our society apart.

We could, of course, deal with the newcomers to the ranks of the unemployed and the poor in the same way that we deal with those who are already there, but this would be to make believe that we don't know the destructive and self-defeating consequences of our public-welfare programs, whose positive effects are largely limited to the simple maintenance of life at bare subsistence levels.

One difficulty in generating alternative solutions comes from our looking at unemployment too narrowly. We tend to see unemployment as a kind of inevitable exhaust of our economic engine. We fail to see that it is also a social process powered by the values we hold and the choices we make.

It might be useful, for example, to look closely at work and unemployment without regard to poverty. There are, after all, many people who work very hard and yet live in poverty, and there are others who do not work at all and are very rich. For the moment, then, let us ignore poverty and look only at work, in the ordinary, day-to-day meaning of the word as having to do with a job, with earning a living.

From the very beginning of human history, it is through work that man has provided himself with the necessities of life. So closely is work tied in with the social and psychological development of man that it is almost impossible to think of what it means to be human without thinking of work. Indeed, the connection is so strong, so close and so obvious that attempts to talk about the importance of work often sound banal. Work is the fundamental condition of human existence, said Karl Marx; work is man's strongest tie to reality, said Freud.

It is also through work, as a producer of socially useful goods or services, that the individual—especially the adult male—carries out those social roles (husband, father, family head) that define him as a full and valued member of his society.

That work becomes, in effect, a kind of admission ticket to society is not something invented by white middle-class Americans, although many of us often act as if it is. There is nothing especially white or middle-class about wanting to earn a living and support one's family. That is what the working-class man wants, and the Eskimo hunter and the Chinese peasant and the African herdsman—all of them want it, too. "In every known human society," Margaret Mead tells us, "everywhere in the world, the young male learns that when he grows up one of the things he must do in order to be a full member of society is to provide food for some female and her young."

The centrality of work, then, is not new to human experience, and it did not arrive only with the appearance of capitalism and the Protestant ethic, although each of these did add its own embellishments to the meaning and importance of work. What does seem to be relatively new, however, is the appearance of widespread, systematic nonwork—unemployment—as an integral part or by-product of the ordinary functioning of society, an appearance which seems to date from the introduction of market economies and wage labor typically associated with the rise of capitalism.

In subsistence economies, the entire population has to work to produce the goods and services necessary to survival, and there is always work to be done. In such societies, people are not recognizable as being in or out of the work force—the work force is synonymous with the total population.

In industrial societies, unemployment strikes deep at the man, as well as at the way he fits into his family, his community, and the larger society. It can put a man "out of it," and can turn him into a caricature of himself, giving him the appearance of being stupid and lazy with no concern for the future. Some of this can be seen in Marie Jahoda's description of what happened to the workers in the Austrian village of Marienthal when its only factory was shut down in the nineteen-thirties:

The unemployed men lost their sense of time. When asked at the end of a day what they had done during it, they were unable to describe their activities. "Real" time . . . was vague and nebulous. Activities such as fetching wood from the shed, which could not have consumed more than 10 minutes, were recorded as if they had filled a morning . . . The men's waking day was shortened to 12 or 13 hours. Rational budget planning . . . was abandoned in favor of expenditure on trinkets, while essentials could not be paid for.

Edward Wight Bakke's study of white Americans thrown out of work in those same Depression years makes it equally clear that there is more going on here than a simple lack of money to live on. He found that public assistance for the unemployed was initially effective. After a few months, however, public assistance, by itself, could no longer hold back the destructive consequences of not working, and the man's relationships with his family, friends and neighbors, indeed, with the whole community, degenerated dramatically. Once this degenerative process established itself, only work could halt it, and only through work could the man gain again his position as a valued member of society.

Bakke also found that the man cannot wait forever for a job. Being unemployed quickly reaches a point of no return. The man learns to live with his failure by lowering his life goals and by other rationalizing measures which effectively remove him from ordinary society. No longer a producer, a contributor to the commonweal, and no longer the bread-winning husband and father, he is also, in his own eyes and in the eyes of society, no longer a man. Faced with nothing to do, he has no place to go. He hangs around. He is superfluous, and he knows it.

Moreover, if we now widen our view of work and unemployment to include money and poverty, we see that unemployment is only the tip of the iceberg. The unemployed man is just a special case of the man who cannot support himself and his family. For every man who is looking for a job, there are dozens more who have jobs and are still unable to support themselves and their dependents. The effects are, perhaps, no less disastrous for the man who works than for the man who does not, nor are they any less disastrous for their families, their communities or the whole society.

We can see the general problem most clearly by narrowing our focus to black people and other racial minorities in our society, for they are the principal victims. Black people suffer more from unemployment not only because more of them, proportionately, are unemployed, but because they are more likely than their white counterparts to have been unemployed in the past and to remain unemployed or underemployed in the future. This circumstance of life—a major thread in the collective history and present experience of black people as a group—shapes the way the black man sees himself and is seen by others as fitting into the larger community. It also gives meaning to the assertion that we are a racist society, a racism that is intimately bound up with work and productivity and individual worth.

Let me give an example. The 6-year-old son of a woman on welfare was struck and killed by an automobile as he tried to run across the street. The insurance company's initial offer of $800 to settle out of court was rejected. In consultation with her lawyer, the mother accepted the second and final offer of $2,000. When I learned of the settlement, I called the lawyer to protest, arguing that the sum was far less than what I assumed to be the usual settlement in such cases, even if the child was mainly at fault. "You've got to face the facts," he said. "Insurance companies and juries just don't pay as much for a Negro child." Especially, he might have added, a Negro child on welfare.

If the relative worth of human life must be measured in dollars and cents, why should the cash surrender value of a black child's life be less than that for a white child's life? The answer clearly has nothing to do with private prejudice and discrimination. Insurance companies and our legal system take an actuarial perspective. Damage awards are based primarily on the projected life-time earnings of the individual; they are statements about his probable productivity, not about his skin color.

But this child, this Anthony Davis, was only 6 years old. On what basis do they make lowered projections of earnings for a 6-year-old child, before he has acquired or rejected an education, before he has demonstrated any talents or lack of them, before he has selected an occupation or, indeed, before he has made a single life choice of his own?

There can be only one answer. The answer is, simply, on the basis of skin color and social class. And what is most important for us to know and admit is this: the insurance company was *absolutely right*. Anthony was more likely than his white, middle-class counterpart to go to an inferior school, to get an inferior education, to be sick, to get an inferior job, to be last hired and first fired, to be passed over for promotion, and to live a shorter life. In all probability, then, Anthony *would* be less productive over his lifetime than his white middle-class counterpart. And we are a racist society because we know this to be true before the fact, when Anthony is only 6 years old.

Typically, we admit the problem but we place the cause in the Negro (Puerto Rican, Mexican-American, American Indian, Appalachian white) himself. We say that because of their history, or their subculture or their family structure, these minorities are lazy, irresponsible and don't want to work. Then, in the midst of an affluence never before achieved by any society, we offer them the most menial, the dullest, the poorest paid jobs in our society, and sure enough, some of them don't want to work.

But the one most important fact is often overlooked. Most Negroes (Puerto Ricans, etc.), like everyone else in our society, do want to work.

Indeed, most of them have been working all along. In Washington, for example, the garbage does get picked up, the streets get swept, hotel beds are made, school and office-building floors and halls get mopped and polished, cars and restaurant dishes get washed, ditches get dug, deliveries are made, orderlies attend the aged, the sick, the mentally ill, and so on. And most of the people whose job it is to do those things are black.

But if most Negroes do have jobs, what is the problem? It is mainly that most of those jobs pay from $50 to $80 or $90 a week. In 1966, for example, 25 per cent of all non-white, *full-time, year-round* male workers earned less than $3,000, and this in a year when the Bureau of Labor Statistics said that it required $9,200 to maintain a modest standard of living for a family of four in an urban area. The man with a wife and one or two children who takes such a job can be certain he will live in poverty so long as he keeps it. The longer he works, the longer he cannot live on what he makes.

This situation makes for a curious paradox: the man who works hard may be little or no better off than the man who does not look for a job at all. In a sense, he may even be worse off. The man who works hard but cannot earn a living has put himself on the scales and been found wanting. He says to society, "I have done what needed doing. Now, what am I worth?" and society answers, "Not much, not even enough to support yourself and your dependents." But the man who does not seek out or accept such a job may, for a while at least, fool himself or his fellows into thinking that he has not climbed onto the scales at all.

By itself, then, work alone does not guarantee full and valued participation in society. Participation requires not only an opportunity to contribute to the day-to-day life of that society, but it requires, reciprocally, an acknowledgment by society that the contribution is of value. That acknowledgment, typically in the form of wages, lets the man know that he is somebody, that he is important, useful and even necessary.

But the man who cannot find a job, or the man who finds one but is still unable to support himself and his family, is being told in clear and simple language, and loud enough for his wife and children and friends and neighbors and everyone else to hear, that he is not needed, that there is no place for him.

No man can live with this terrible self-knowledge for long. Both the youth who has never worked but who sees this situation as his probable future, and the man who has experienced it, retreat to the street corner where others like themselves, in self-defense, have constructed a world which gives them that minimum sense of belonging and being useful without which human life is perhaps impossible and which the larger society gives up so very grudgingly or not at all. And after we tell a man that he cannot earn enough to support himself and his family, that he is not a full and valued member of society, what claims have we on his loyalty and goodwill? I strongly suspect that we have none. From his point of view, if we deny his claim on us, he does not owe us a thing, not loyalty, not goodwill, not "responsible" protest.

From this perspective, the problem is how can we change our society so that all who belong to it can become full and valued participants in it?

For a beginning, we must make the poor less poor. We must get money into their hands. We must choose one or a combination of the many income-supplement programs that have been proposed and put them into practice.

Another beginning step might be to focus our concerns on the low-paying, menial jobs that have to be done in every society. Since these jobs have to be done by someone, it makes little sense to keep insisting that we must always and only upgrade the person. At some point we are going to have to upgrade the job.

For systematically upgrading jobs such as these, we might use the airline stewardess as a model. Casual observation suggests that, for the most part, her job is that of a waitress. But the airlines, through adroit public relations, through the use of smartly designed uniforms, by setting performance standards and by paying a decent salary, have upgraded the job of the airborne waitress to a much higher level of respectability and desirability than that enjoyed by her ground-based counterpart.

Not all menial jobs can be upgraded so easily and so far. Many menial jobs are dirty jobs, and there is not a lot we can do at this time to make them less dirty. But that is not the only reason they are despised and among the lowest status jobs in our society. They are also among the lowest paying jobs. They are the kind of job a man can work at full time, year round, and still earn less than $3,000 and both the job and the man are despised for this reason, too.

It is very easy to overestimate the extent to which such jobs are despised because they are dirty or hard and to underestimate the extent to which they are despised because they pay so little money. There is little that is intrinsically bad about being a janitor or trash collector. What is so bad about them is that in such jobs you cannot earn a living. Where the pay for garbage and trash collectors approaches a living wage, as in New York City, there is intense competition for the work that is elsewhere shunned and accepted only as a last resort.

That these jobs tend also to be dead-end jobs is probably true, but perhaps we make too much of this also. The job of the lathe operator, the assembly-line worker, the truck driver, the secretary, these tend to be dead-end jobs too, but they are not bad jobs because of it. Not everyone in our society is career-oriented. We have a large and relatively stable working-class population which does not aspire to moving up a career ladder. The working man who earns a living and supports his family by doing work that everyone agrees is socially useful does not necessarily want to become a foreman, or plant manager, or office executive. If he is dissatisfied, it is probably because he wants more of what he has, and wants to be more certain of keeping what he has, not because he wants something different. So would it be, perhaps, with jobs that are presently considered menial, dead-end jobs. If a man could earn a living at these jobs, they would not be dead-end. They would be much like other jobs—a job.

I do not mean to suggest that all unemployed and underemployed men and youths want nothing more than jobs that pay a living wage. Many do want careers, and an opportunity to use their brains and their strengths to take them as high and as far as they can go, and they must have these opportunities. The point here is that not everyone wants to scratch his way to the top of something. Most people, black and white, want the creature comforts and the psychic rewards that come with having jobs that enable them and their families to live like most other people in our society.

This brings us to my final proposal. It has been suggested many times by many people, but because it has been labeled unrealistic or too expensive or destructive of free enterprise, it does not seem to be getting the serious attention I think it deserves. Too long have we geared our national domestic policies to what we say we can afford, rather than to our needs. We are faced with massive alienation and growing hostility of the poor and the non-white, especially of black youth in the cities—the "underclass" that Presidential counselor Daniel Moynihan and others believe to be the principal victims of our social system and the principal threat to it. One problem is that we do not know the nature of this underclass, to what extent it is now a self-sustaining, self-perpetuating class or to what extent it is simply an artifact of present policies and lower-class life circumstances.

We do know, however, that the young, black member of this underclass is no longer responsive to mere promises and to subminimal opportunities for a better life. Promises are no longer enough. We have lost his confidence and trust, and before we can regain them, we must change the reality for the young black man and let him experience the change.

Without that confidence and trust, the system simply does not work. He will continue to do poorly in school, to drop out or be pushed out, to pass from the wary eye of the teacher to the wary eye of the policeman on the street. Then he or his friends will join the ranks of the unemployed or underemployed, add to the number of dependent women and children, further load the court and jail facilities, and so on and so on until the National Guard and the Army are called in.

How do we change the reality and let him experience it? If having a job and earning a living is, as I believe it is, the linchpin of full and valued participation in our society, then every able-bodied man must have a right —a legal, statutory right—to a job doing socially useful work which pays a decent wage.

To do this would probably require that government—Federal, state and local—already the largest employer, become also the employer of last resort. At the Federal level, there are many different employment models to choose from: Civil Service, the Tennessee Valley Authority, and Public Health Service, contract, grant and draft mechanisms, the old WPA and CCC, etc.

The crucial thing here is not the mechanism but the avoidance of contemptible make-work by matching a wide range of job skills and aspirations to tasks that are clearly of a high order of social usefulness, such as construction of public and low-cost housing, restoration of cities, expansion and improvement of mail service, and a host of other programs and projects directed at the unmet public need in the areas of health, education, child care, urban mass transit, conservation, pollution and so on. Where appropriate, the Federal Government could subcontract such projects or parts of them to state and local governments through a revenue-sharing system, thereby insuring that national programs and policies were matched to local needs.

We have already seen that by themselves, neither money nor a job is sufficient to guarantee full and valued participation. The two must be linked together. A man must have the right to a job that pays a decent wage. Thus, though income-assistance plans are needed for the immediate future, and indeed always will be needed for those persons—the aged, the sick, the handicapped and women with dependent children—who cannot or should not work, such plans should be viewed for the working poor as stop-gap emergency measures rather than long-range solutions.

In general, income assistance plans for the man who works but does not earn a living wage are focused on the wrong end of the employer-employee relationship. We are probably all agreed that, given a wage-labor system, a man who does an honest day's work, whether it be sweeping the floor or simply guarding a gate, is entitled to an honest day's pay. An honest day's pay must mean, at the minimum, enough for the man to support himself and an average number of dependents. If it means anything less, it means nothing at all.

If a business or industry cannot afford to pay the worker enough to live on, the failure lies with the company, not the employee, and it is the employer who needs welfare, not the worker. Enterprises which through inefficiency or other reasons cannot afford to pay their workers enough to live on must leave the field or, if they are deemed socially useful and necessary, must be subsidized by the Government—let's call it cost-sharing —so they can pay their workers a living wage. In this way, the stigma, the badge of dependency that goes with being a recipient of public assistance, is removed from the worker (where it did not really belong in the first place) and placed on the employer (where it does belong). Moreover, business and industry have already demonstrated that they carry very lightly the burden of receiving public assistance.

The adoption of a program coupling a guaranteed job to a living wage would produce a flow of far-reaching consequences, including perhaps, wage and price controls and a redefinition of work and free enterprise. But the principle that lies behind it is not at all radical. It is consistent with our history and our national purpose. In 1945, the United States Government pledged itself to take action toward the goal of full employment as set forth in Article 55 of the United Nations Charter. The original draft of the Employment Act of 1945 guaranteed jobs at a decent wage to all those able and willing to work. As finally passed, the watered-down version still acknowledges the right of every citizen to such a job, although it takes it all back in the same breath with qualifying phrases about free enterprise and the common good. Similarly, every Administration in recent times has restated the national commitment to the individual's right to work and earn a living wage. What has been lacking is the will to put into practice what we preach.

Acknowledgement of every citizen's uncompromised right to earn a living is not proposed as a solution to all of our social problems. It would, however, be an important first step toward dealing with many of them: behind much of what presents itself to us as family instability, dependent women and children, violence, crime and retreatist life styles, stand men and women, black and white, who cannot support themselves and their families. In addition, raising the social and economic status of its members is the surest and safest way for a society to reduce its rate of population growth.

Most immediately and directly, however, the right to a job at a decent wage would go a long way toward removing simple, brutal poverty from our national life. And unlike variations on the welfare theme, it would do this in a way that would help reorder the relationship between citizen and society so that everyone could enjoy that minimum sense of security and self-respect without which talk of freedom and equality and opportunity does not mean very much.

RURAL UPHEAVAL: CONFRONTATION AND ACCOMMODATION

❧ Robert Coles

The rural South and Appalachia have exerted enormous influence on our nation's political climate, an unjustifiable influence if only the total number of people in both regions is considered. It was in Little Rock and New Orleans that schoolchildren faced mobs, and through television did so before millions of Americans in California, Illinois, and in New York. It was in Montgomery, Alabama, that Rosa Parks said she would not move to the rear of a bus. And it was in that same city that Martin Luther King —a young Negro Baptist minister "out of Atlanta"—came to her side. It was in Greensboro, North Carolina, that four students staged a sit-in; and if they failed to get any of Woolworth's coffee for their effort, they had the eventual satisfaction of seeing a random act of theirs in 1960 become an example to thousands of other nonviolent demonstrators. Freedom rides, marches, state-wide summer projects—the South experienced them all; and so did the rest of the country when newspapers and cameras covered the news that was made.

In 1960 John F. Kennedy went before Appalachia's poor rural Protestant people to ask their help in his quest for the Presidency. They said yes to him, those "hillbillies" did, with their long bodies and craggy faces and their

SOURCE: Robert Coles, "Rural Upheaval: Confrontation and Accommodation," from *On Fighting Poverty* ed. James L. Sundquist with the assistance of Corinne/Saposs Schelling (New York: Basic Books, 1969), pp. 103–126. Copyright © 1969 by The American Academy of Arts and Sciences, Basic Books, Inc. Reprinted by permission of the publisher.

Protestant Anglo-Saxon heritage. The young Catholic aspirant, out of Boston and Harvard, drew them down in large numbers from the hollows. Each one of them seemed at first glance shy and sad, perhaps members of Lincoln's family still in mourning. At first glance, they also seemed impossibly unwilling to commit themselves, content merely to stand and watch, listen and on occasion faintly smile. They nevertheless knew a winner, and they knew that they needed him to be *their* winner. John Kennedy worked hard in West Virginia and never quite knew while there to what avail. From what I have heard these recent years from people in the region, he was the prototypal "community organizer" from the "outside." He came in to offer help and, admittedly, to be helped himself. He was "different," a stranger. He didn't talk the right way: in every promise of assistance, a prickly, oversensitive ear could detect an implied criticism. Still, the mountain people were in trouble, and this man from "over there in Massachusetts" offered help. Despite any misgivings the Applachian people may have had and any mistakes in their dealings with a "special subculture" made by John Kennedy and his aides, an alliance was forged. To this day, I find the former President's picture on the walls of cabins that lie in the remotest hollows imaginable.

It is possible, then, for isolated rural people to reach and be reached; it is possible for them to affect significantly, even momentously, the populous cities and to respond more quickly to urban influences than some observers would seem to think. It can be argued that the South's villages and small towns provided the atmosphere of clear-cut contrast, of total black exile and total white control, that made the civil rights struggle so appealing to the entire nation. (I fear the word "appealing" may be just right in its implication of something that calls for an almost self-serving kind of sympathy rather than active, dedicated, and sacrificial involvement.) Yet, something contagious happened in the South, something that for a while began—and only began—to make a difference elsewhere, in more ambiguous situations. It is possible to see the War on Poverty as a direct aftermath of conflict in the South and of the "new" interest in Applachia that developed after 1960 (and perhaps culminated so far as the public is concerned in the famous CBS documentary "Christmas in Appalachia").

Nor is it stretching a point to call many of our present urban problems in essence rural ones that have been exported. The sharecroppers and tenant farmers, the migrant farmers and Appalachian people I have studied these past years all have their kin in Chicago, New York, or Detroit. Some of them have gone North and stayed, so that I now am studying not their rural lives but their lives in transition, their lives as immigrants—from two very distant regions that both, perhaps, qualify as nations within a nation. We in the cities are beginning to learn about what life *was* like in the Delta or in the mountain hollows of Kentucky and West Virginia. The presence among "us" of thousands of confused and virtually penniless exiles from "the land" makes the problems of, say, McCormick County, South Carolina, the very real problems of New York City. For example, I am appalled at the poor health I find among ghetto children, and I am also puzzled when a Negro mother I know refuses to avail herself of the medical services of a "city hospital" that was built and is run to provide people like her and her children free medical care. Yet that mother has only recently come to Boston from McCormick County, South Carolina. She is thirty-five and has seven children. Except for the three times she was taken to Augusta, Georgia, to have her baby in a hospital, she has never seen a doctor in her life. (Her other children were born at home.)

Here are the "facts," the raw medical information that might be called the "background" to her current "attitudes" toward doctors and hospitals. (The welfare woman who visits the mother has asked me to look into her client's "fears" and "anxieties," so that four boys and three girls will receive the attention and care they need, the inoculations and vitamin supplements, the corrective surgery and eyeglasses, the dental care.) There are exactly two (white) physicians in McCormick County, South Carolina. When they are called for help, they ask for a fee, and that is known by the mothers and fathers who are farm hands, occasional harvesters, or out of work altogether. In 1961, the infant-mortality rates in McCormick County were as follows: for white children, 208 per 10,000; and for Negro children, 1,073 per 10,000.[1] Those terrible numbers, comparable to what comes forth from government bureaus in New Delhi,[2] have a far wider, greater, and more persistent "meaning" than the most covetous statistician could ever wish or dream. "In McCormick County we learned to do without doctors, because there just wasn't none around," said our welfare worker's troubled Negro mother recently. Then she went on:

Now up here, they tell us they're here, waiting. But I get the shakes every time I think of going near the hospital, and I don't know how to stop them, the shakes. If you're brought up to have them, you can't just stop because you're moved up the road, no matter how far.

Actually, several months later she did go to the Boston City Hospital, and since then she has overcome her childhood inhibitions, perhaps more directly and easily than some of us. I mention her experience not only to make the obvious point that lives in their continuity transcend abstractions like "rural" or "urban" but also in order to introduce her younger brother, whose activities I believe have helped make poor people all over America more bothersome—if that is the word—to the rest of us.

He is twenty-six, Peter, and it is hard to know what to "call" him. There are words, but none of them quite fit. In the early sixties he was "simply" a civil rights worker, a young Negro college student who worked with Dr. Martin Luther King's organization. He worked in rural Georgia, not too far from his home county of McCormick, South Carolina. In 1965, he became a "community organizer" for a brief period. The work was in Washington, D.C., where he hoped to gain some "techniques" and "skills" that he could put to use in what he then called "the rural situation." (He had already learned a good deal of jargon when he arrived in Washington.) He lasted three months in the city, then went "home"—his way of describing the return South. And he went South with a vengeance—to the Mississippi Delta, where he became involved in the now-rather-famous Child Development Group of Mississippi (CDGM). Without enumerating the historical and political details of the group's brief existence,[3] I can say that the "operation" is designed to reach the poorest children of that very poor state and begin to educate them (through Headstart programs) in such a way that they learn not only their "letters and numbers" but something about *themselves*—children of the Delta, poor Negro boys and girls who need better food, a doctor, clothes, and perhaps most of all a sense of what a future can be, one that is not an endless repetition of the past. CDGM was started in 1965 and funded by the Office of Economic Opportunity (OEO). Many of its leaders were white "outsiders," though fairly soon Negroes from Mississippi became not only recipients of the "benefits" of Headstart programs but by design active in planning the organization's purposes and activities. Peter was one of the early "organizers" who helped shape the philosophy of what might be called, with no exaggeration, the nation's most forceful and unusual preschool "program."

"I think of myself when I'm with these kids," he says repeatedly. He even tells the children about his own life and does so in a direct, open way that commands the extraordinary gift of silent attention from five-year-old boys and girls:

I come from nothing, the way white people would call it, and black men, too, the few of us that have got a lot of money and put on airs like the white man. No one in my family ever went to school except a few weeks here and there, you know, when there was no work to do in the fields or around the house. The white people, they didn't care—they didn't even want us to take school too seriously. And our colored teachers, they wanted us all white and starchy, neat and obedient. They knew they couldn't get what they wanted—us to be little angels for them—so they called us all kinds of names, right to our faces, and pushed us around. We felt lousy before them—afraid and no good, no damn good. I recall when I was about five or six I'd hear from them that niggers were no good, most of them, and they were poor because they didn't know how to take care of themselves. So, I'd go home and tell that to my mother, and she got so nervous she didn't know what to say. Sometimes she would shake her head, but agree. Sometimes she would say it wasn't so, but tell me to mind the teachers and try to follow what she says, so that I wouldn't have to work the white man's land. Most of the time, though, she didn't say a word. Nor did my daddy. They were too tired, and maybe too confused. I don't know the truth, even today.

Well, actually, I owe a lot to one teacher. She gave me a test when I was in the third grade, or the fourth—it didn't make any difference, it was just a one-room school. She said I was a genius or something from the results and I must have cheated somehow. (How's that for building up a guy's confidence about himself!) So they sent me over to Columbia, South Carolina, or someplace for another test, and they watched me like hawks and police dogs and everything. And I broke the bank again.

So, they gave me a special plan, they called it. They asked my parents to keep me in school all the time, no matter what, and they said they'd even send me over to Greenwood, South Carolina, for a special class they had for smart little colored children who knew how to behave and had a lot of brains. They even brought in white teachers every once in a while to give us a special talk. As I recall, we'd spend most of *that* hour or so just looking, not listening. If they had asked me what I learned after a white lady's talk I'd have had to tell them nothing, except what she wore, and how she was made up, and how her hair looked, and the way she talked, and the jewelry she had on, and all that. I'd go home and tell my mother about all that, and she'd tell me that "white folks sure can look pretty"—meaning *we* can't. I remember learning that over and over again when I was five or six—how pretty white people are and how useless and hopeless it is for us to try to be pretty or good-looking, or whatever. (It's not the words, it's the feeling, you know. My parents never came out and told us that "white" meant "beautiful," or "black" meant "ugly" or "menial." They made us *feel* all that—and you never forget it that way.)

That's what CDGM is about. We want to help these kids, the poorest kids in America, feel some self-respect, feel that there's a chance for them, on their own, as black kids from the Black Belt, as farm kids, the sons and daughters of sharecroppers. We want them to feel they can stay here, as well as go North to Chicago—and be *men* and *women,* wherever they go, wherever they live. You talk about poverty; you could give a lot of these people here—maybe a lot of Negroes everywhere—a million dollars and they'd still feel so low and scared before the white man that they'd feel poor, even with color television in every room of a 25-room house.

We try to show them that we respect them, as children, as human beings. We aren't forever comparing them to some white face in a white child's book. We show them the strength and value of their *own* words, their own tradition—they are the children of workers, who built this whole state, with their sweat and tears and shortened lives. We tell the kids that, and they listen.[4]

In 1965 I heard him tell children just that, and they did listen, much more attentively than I might have believed had I not seen them do so again and again. He would stand before them and talk, much as he did with me and then show them pictures of white suburban homes near Jackson, of words and illustrations from books used in both the Negro and white schools of Mississippi, of their own homes. He would emphasize the *reality* of their condition, but insist on the possibilities that nevertheless exist: "We have to learn not because the white man is embarrassed if we can't sign our name to prove we owe him everything. We have to learn *who* we are and *where* we're going and *what* we want." He would say it over and over to the children, that last sentence, and I would later hear them reciting their who's, where's, and what's to one another. They would also carry the message home, to the cabins and huts, up the alleys of the small towns, or alongside the cotton fields.

In one home that I had been visiting for years before CDGM came into existence, I heard this from the mother of one of Peter's students:

That teacher must be sent down here from Someone Big, I'll say. If I didn't think all the Disciples were white, I'd begin to wonder. He talks like he knows everything, and isn't one bit scared. He talks different from those civil rights ones, too. They'll tell you not to be afraid to follow them, their lead. He says go be yourself and don't be afraid of that, being who you are. I tell my boy I don't understand it, to be honest, but it sure sounds different, I'll have to admit. Of course, what should we do next, that's what I'd like to know, and that's what I'd like to ask him, Mr. Peter.

Mr. Peter, like all good modern teachers, wants to bring the home into the school, the school into the home. After he had figured out what he was going to say to his young students, how he was going to hold their interest, he did indeed visit their parents and get them to ask him the questions he knew they had in mind anyway:

I try to tell them that we've got to stick together and *do* something. At first a lot of them would give me that blank stare, or the sly look, and some still do; but a lot of them have changed. Especially they pay attention when I remind them that the only way to change things is *acting*—even when it seems hopeless. I must have told the story of Rosa Parks in Montgomery a million times in the past few months. She reaches them, and the story of the Freedom Rides. I tell them that everyone said they were wrong, the Freedom Riders, or they were foolish, or they weren't doing the right thing in the right way at the right time. Even our "friends," I tell them, said we should "take it easy," and not do too much marching, and too much demonstrating, and too much protesting. "You have to pace youselves," we'd hear from the conservative Negroes, and "not so fast you don't bring along the rest of the country" from the liberal whites.

Then I tell them what *happened*—because we didn't do the "right" thing, the "sensible" thing, the "smart" thing, the "practical" thing. They *know* what happened, but I remind them, about five times each visit. And before I leave I tell them what *they* can do: support us, CDGM; send their children to a Headstart center that means business; go register to vote; tell the "bossman" they want more money. I know the last thing isn't likely to happen—they'll be thrown off the land first. But they're going to be thrown off anyway—and even *they* know there's no point going North now. All that's up there is welfare and rats; and what happens in Watts is what they'll be traveling two thousand miles to see. So, we've got to stay here, and organize here, and make it work down here. It's our state, as much as whitey's, and we'd better let him know it, and let the people in Washington know it. They can invest in dams and conservation and foreign countries; let them invest in us, right in this place, and they'll be helping their cities in the bargain, I'll tell you.

They nod, the people he visits, and I've seen some of them give him an unbelieving smile that I suppose someone like me has to call "hostile." They sometimes escort him to the door as if he were a white insurance salesman; it's an ingratiating "yes" and "yes" and "yes" until he has left—when you know that they will laugh scornfully and bitterly. The mother in the family I knew best put it this way:

I don't see what they're talking about. There's nothing, absolutely nothing, we can do, except be as always—and hope somehow it'll change. He can't fool me, that man Peter, he can't even fool himself. I can tell that he doesn't know what to do any more than I do.

Yet, her children were excited by what they learned, and they were getting the best meals they ever had—and all at government expense. What is more, she and other parents were coming together and talking—about their children, yes, but about other matters, too. From visit to visit I could watch a federal anti-poverty program—a unique one in a uniquely difficult situation—take root in the mind of an individual mother. Coming together with others prompted this observation from her: "I've never done that, sat and talked about anything with people. At first you don't know what there is to say, and then you find you've been thinking about this and that and the other thing, and you start in."

She would come home and talk to her husband and to her neighbors about the meetings. She began to tell her older children that there were other ways to learn, other things to learn, than those provided by the state of Mississippi and their county's board of education. She would also become downcast and have no reply to make when her husband pointed out that good ideas were useless in the face of a sheriff's gun. But she would go to the next meeting and bring up *that* subject for discussion:

My husband says for me to think about the sheriff and the policemen and what they'll do when we start getting more and more ideas in our head, and then talk out loud about them in front of the courthouse. There won't be one of us left here, he says. We won't have a job among us; we won't have a cent in welfare money; we won't have our homes; we'll have to run for our lives, clear out of the state. And my brother tried that, and went up to Cleveland, Ohio. Now he sits all day in a store to keep from the snow, and he hides from the welfare lady, so that his wife Martha can collect her check. He says it's like a real good job down here, being on welfare is, because they gives you enough to pay the rent and eat. But he says there's not a thing for him to do, and he gets tired, and he thinks he's getting sick from sitting around all day. Sometimes he wishes he could just do some chopping and go get the water like in the old days down here—but he'd never want to come back, you can be sure, just to do that. So, if we're going to leave, all of us, then O.K. But if we plan to stay we'd best be careful, that's what my husband says. And isn't he right?

They weren't at all sure her husband was right. One or two mothers nodded their heads, and another one paid her recognition to the length and ardor of the statement she had heard by saying, as if in church, "Yes, you're right." Peter was there as an observer and a teacher. He wanted to know what "others" thought. For a minute and ten seconds there was silence, and the chairs squeaked with shifting bodies. I used the movement in my watch as an excuse to avoid looking around, and all the while I expected *Peter* to come up with something, to break the impasse and send us along a more hopeful road. Suddenly, one of those enormous women I have sometimes seen at such meetings stood up. I had seen her at several earlier gatherings. She always wore large printed dresses full of flowers and bold colors as if she long ago had decided to enjoy her fat. She regularly sat in the rear, on a long bench, for which she seemed grateful. She had a habit of putting her right hand through her hair as if she were looking for something, then inspecting her palm and fingers when she was through, and finally resting the entire arm on the back of the bench—where no one else sat. The fingers would soon be moving again and one could safely bet everything in the world that the hand would soon be raised again, the fingers soon be weaving and scratching their way on the top of her head.

She had immediately commanded everyone's attention by her move. They heard her get up and move two steps forward. She hesitated. She seemed voiceless. She seemed ready to sit down again. Peter stood up, nervous and ready to have his say. Suddenly the woman spoke:

I have two children here in Headstart. I have older ones, and they're not eligible for anything as I see it. I have three of them younger, and God knows if the government up there in Washington will desert us after a while. But I plan to stay here, and if for no other reason just to hear my boy, he's five, and my girl, she's six, come home and talk to me the way they do. They say I'm a fool and I've been a fool all these years putting up with things. I ask them what "things," and they can't answer except to show me that they can fill in the picture books they're given at school—and the pictures show us with our heads looking up and real proud-like.

So I think we should stay right here and keep our poverty program going the way it is, and if the state police come and try to break it up, and scare us to death, then we might as well fight them over this than anything else. To me it don't matter if we vote or not, because we can't seem to win even if we do vote, from what I hear, like up there in the North. But the children, they're learning how to spell right and speak right, and most of all, learning about themselves and us, the colored people and what we've gone through these past ten thousand years (and every year is a century to you and me), and what we've done for the country—build all that's important, I think, if you would ask me.

She opened her left hand and released, for her own use, a small handkerchief. It was a child's. She didn't wipe her brow, but patted it. She moved back to the bench without turning her back on the others; and then she sat down. The impact of her body on the bench could be heard and so could the sound of the wood accommodating to the new weight. Peter looked around, curious about what would happen next. I thought to myself that the woman had succeeded in triggering off a series of similar exhortations that would come one after another for at least an hour. And to myself I made a reassuring analysis: They were nervous, and they felt stymied; there was just so far they could go, and they knew it; they were becoming "organized," but they were also becoming afraid—and aware of their own weakness; they were now "supporting" one another with brave speeches, but they were also ready to run, and they knew it, and Peter knew it.

In point of fact, it was the state of Mississippi that became afraid; eventually, the Federal Goverment began to look very warily at the workings of CDGM, to investigate it from top to bottom. Its "management" was declared poor by Washington; its purposes and goals obviously offended the Governor's Mansion in Jackson. In 1965, I was asked by officials of OEO to evaluate and help improve the medical program that had to be a significant part of a rural Mississippi Headstart program. My impressions were welcomed and later that year submitted to the Senate as it prepared to finance the War on Poverty for yet another year. In 1966, quite another set of circumstances prevailed. A beleagured CDGM had to fight what seemed like a hopeless battle; the state of Mississippi was its avowed enemy, and as for the federal agencies—well, I'll let another mother I heard speak out at a meeting make her summary:

The government people up there in Washington, D.C.—they're more afraid than we are. We must have gone through a lot down here when the day comes that the people representing the United States are more scared than we are. It used to be they'd come down here and tell us *we* shouldn't be afraid. "There's *nothing* to be afraid of," I heard one of them government lawyers tell the NAACP man. "This is still America, and if they go too far, we can take them all into *court.*" I was standing there on the street, and they were coming out of the Church they burned down that he was referring to, but I came home and said to my mother that it was the biggest joke I'd heard in 37 years of living—as if the white man doesn't own the courts! And my mother is 64, and she said it wasn't so special, that kind of talk. She said they're always doing that, the outsiders: They come here and tell us to stand up and do this and do that, and then they go away. And who's left? Who's here to have "nothing to be afraid of"? It's us, and we have nothing; and with nothing yours, there's a lot to be afraid of. That's the way my mother saw it, truly, and she never went to school a day in her life. That's the truth. But she knows about things, everything there is to know, I believe.

And now it's changing. It must be when I have to go tell my mother that *we're* not scared, but *they* are, in Washington, D.C. I guess they gave up on us a long time ago; so when they gave us the Headstart program they thought it would be a real quiet-like thing. But we have some real good people teaching our children, and they give us food for them, and a woman like me, they've given me a job, not sweeping after Mrs. Charley for five dollars a week and maybe a piece of donut I'd get to share with the dog and the coffee that otherwise would be spilled out, but a *real job* and one that pays me good *to do what's important for me and my family.* I never believed there were jobs like that, where you could get paid a good salary to spend your time helping your own children and your people's children, instead of the white man's kids. (I help serve cookies and juice; and I arrange things, and clean up after the kids, and help them go take a nap and wake up and things like that. They call me an "aide" and pay me, but I'll tell you I'd do it for nothing, the way I feel.)

It didn't take them long to figure out we was up to no good, no good at all. We was being "uppity." And we're scaring the colored as well as the white. "An uppity nigger will get shot sooner or later, and mostly sooner"—that's what I used to hear my grandaddy say. Well, his daddy was a slave, I think, or the son of one, so you could understand his thinking. But here ,I am, and born only 37 years ago, and I believed the same thing until last year. Now isn't that something! And if you had known me five years ago—well you couldn't, because I'd have been afraid to look you in the eye, or let you get within a mile of our house, for fear of being shot dead talking to a man from Massachusetts who is white.

It was the way they went about doing this that got us feeling drawn to it, I'd say. They made us feel it was *ours,* and we were somebody, and not people they'd throw us something, so that they could go home and feel better. (And I mean the colored as well as the white. Have you ever seen a rich colored man telling his "brothers" how bad off they are, and how he's going to give them five dollars, not one but five United States dollars—if they'll be real good and nice?)

They probably saw that they got us going too fast, and that we'd be real, honest-to-goodness practicing citizens of the U.S.A., and they never have allowed that here, and maybe up in Washington they're not ready for it either.

What has surprised not only me, but even a veteran civil rights activist like Peter, comes across in that woman's words, and even more in the insistent, assertive, defiantly wry quality to the delivery of those words. Peter and I both remember the apathy and fear that one met in Delta Negroes, without exception. Whether the "projects" were limited and conservative in aim, or far-reaching and "radical," they invariably came to a slow, familiar halt when ideas planned in New York or Atlanta or even

Jackson had to face the "reality" of a sharecropper's life or a tenant farmer's life in Itta Bena, Louise, or Sidon, Mississippi. No matter how clever and persuasive the "field worker" was, the "people" shunned him or accepted him with fear and open distrust. Nor in many cases was "time" the answer. In time, the outsider—dark-skinned, sincere, earnest, full of ideas and plans —can become familiar and likable. What else can he become, though? Does he bring bread, or enough men and guns, to change things, really change them? Does he bring work or land that he owns and wants worked? Does he bring anything but trouble? And trouble for what? So that I, James, called a "boy" all my fifty-eight years, can go put my "X" by some politician's name—and of all crazy things, go get some coffee in one of those Holiday Inns in Greenwood or someplace like that? Even if he laughs with me about all those *other* organizer types, what has *he* got to offer, really? Well, he's got plenty of talk about how bad every white man is, and we've always known that even if we don't tell the white man so. He's got his idea that we should all be like him and be together, and that would create new power, black power, and change things. But when and how would it change things, down here, where there are a lot of Negroes, a lot, but still more whites, and all of them determined to hold on to what they have? And what about the beginning, the dangerous, terrible, awesome first steps when we're so naked and weak, so exposed to those gruff, stocky, beefy, red-faced sheriffs, with the *two* guns they carry around their waists, and the cars they drive with the lights whirling about on top of them? And what are we supposed to do when the plantation owner or his managers—they do the "dirty-work" and they're often the real mean ones—come around and tell us to "get away," to "move on" real fast—if we want to stay alive, that is? And then there would be the storekeeper who'd be after us for all we owe. What do we tell him—that we're together, the poor black people of Mississippi, and let him try to bother us or let the Mississippi Highway Patrol try?

Those are the questions that aren't asked right away. In a stare, a long silence, a gesture, they can be conveyed to the visitor. It is true: In "time" they are put to words—finally, and, in my experience, eloquently, vividly, pointedly. By then it is perhaps harder for the visitor, the organizer, the "worker" in this or that cause, to reply. Some day, when all the accounts are settled and regions like the South or Appalachia have at last achieved the kind of democracy we assume America is all about, a historian or two will need to know about the despair of "outsiders" like Peter, as it emerged —point, counterpoint—in the face of the apathy felt by the "insider," the isolated, lonely farm hand who knew all too concretely about abstractions like "power" or "class" or the "meaning" of race.[5]

In 1966, more than a year after CDGM had proved it could work, proved it could miraculously fit into and inspire the lives of the most "backward" and "remote" farm people—who still live by the thousands in Mississippi and the millions in the exile of our cities—I heard this look backward spoken by Peter:

I never would have believed we could have done it. The whole thing doesn't make sense according to every idea and slogan we believe in these days. Here was a program devised by white liberals from New York and a few civil rights people. We were looking for the *real* poor, and the ones way out in the countryside as well as in the towns. We were running nursery schools, mind you—of all things to go out to people and offer them. I would have laughed at the idea a few years ago.

But we had money, enough money to give people who need food, need clothes, need all kinds of advice, some real, tangible help. That was one thing that made a difference, and the other was our approach. We wanted them to feel it was theirs, their program to do something with and feel proud of. If they owned nothing else, they could own those Headstart centers. They could see that the books were specially designed for them and their kids, that they were the staff, that the "experts" admitted how much they had to learn and didn't know. We could offer them doctors for their kids and good food. We could bring them together to talk about something real, something that *went on* every weekday morning from 8:30 to noon, or whatever. The checks came to the centers, and poor people who never had seen a check in their lives got them—for working as "aides," for cooking and cleaning and "minding" their *own* children, for a change.

That's what got to them, money and a chance to join in together. But the third thing that glued this operation together, if you ask me, was opposition. We never had it easy, even when the War on Poverty was going strong nationally and they were sending all sorts of visitors down here to see how even Mississippi was in the "war." The state caught on to us right away, even if Washington didn't. They knew we were interested in the families of children, not only in five-year-old children, and they knew we considered the words "health" and "preschool education" to be much broader than a lot of politicians would like. So a federal agency was giving us money, and we were trying to let people know—as many as we could afford to let know— that they were actually a little free, to come together and speak out and have their children taught what mattered to *them* and what *they* thought important and desirable. How subversive could you get?

Now no one in power in this state and no one representing this state in Washington can afford to ignore something like that, a program like that; and they didn't. The more they attacked, the stronger we became with the people. It was beautiful: they couldn't really burn down our centers as if they were churches, and it was like in the old days. We were connected to the federal government, and anyway the state of Mississippi has learned it can't let that kind of thing happen too often any more. They couldn't stop us from functioning either. We had the money, for at least a year we did. Talk about "education," it was the greatest education these parents—apart from their little children—ever had. They saw their own strength, their own power, in daily operation—against the white man's opposition. They never had gone through anything like that before, and I doubt they can ever be the same afterwards.

You should see the letters they sent up to Washington, and the petitions they wrote, and the statements they issued—to one another. And when we thought that we were through, that we had had it, that we were getting no more money—well, they knew about it, and they stuck together. They were fighting for *theirs*, for a pay check, against the bosses—like in the old days of the labor-union movement. From isolated, unorganized people—at the mercy of every sheriff, every plantation owner, every redneck in the state—they became tied together as "members of CDGM," that's what a lot of them called themselves, spontaneously, "members."

You know there were a dozen or more critical moments when the whole thing could have collapsed. From the very beginning Washington and Jackson pushed us here and there. They'd want a compromise on this issue, a little ground given on something else. Sometimes they seemed to want to bribe us to surrender! If we'd only move our headquarters, or fire so-and-so, who is too "radical," or too much an "open civil rights type"—like me! If we'd only stop letting the children and their parents know that just about all other Americans are richer; that is they have more money and don't want to share it with a few million Negroes. If we'd only use those nice, sweet middle-class "farm books" and stop telling it like it is, which is called being "inflammatory." We say to a woman who practically never sees money at all that she is being exploited by the white plantation owner and the white political system that won't let her vote and won't give her the kind of food and medicine and education her kids need; and for that we're accused of turning a pre-school program into a "political" program. We're called agitators. And when they call us agitators in Jackson—when the governor does and *his* representatives in the Congress do—then believe me the bureaucrats in Washington listen, even in the "flexible" agencies, the ones full of imagination, like the OEO.

So we'd go tell the people *that*, as if they didn't know in their own way. During one bad time, when they had inspectors all over the place and they were telling us in Washington we'd have to "slow down," cleanse house, and—really—stop being so successful at organizing poor people and helping them get a beginning of what they want and need, I heard a woman get up at a meeting of Headstart parents and say: "If we do like they want us to, we'll turn into nothing. If we make a fight of it, we'll win even if they cut off the money, because for the first time we'll stick together and stand up to them. And maybe when they see we're doing that, it'll be them who'll back down. They won't know what to do with us behaving that way."

She was right. Even *we* were surprised, the so-called "leaders." Those people were determined to have their kind of Headstart program, and if we wavered because we knew "the facts," they kept on telling us that they knew everything *had* to turn out right, even when the checks stopped coming, and we reminded them about the threats coming down upon us.

Yes, I suppose they were "naïve." But they also were "involved," really so. And I agree—their attitude gave us strength even when we didn't admit it. You can persuade yourself to be "realistic"—in fact, to sell out a good and decent program that is working beautifully—when the people in it are only halfhearted members. It's a little harder to do so with a really emotional and enthusiastic group—who talk a lot about the Bible and God and make you feel like a two-bit Judas for entertaining ideas of being "practical" and "realistic" and giving in to the politicians, and I don't only mean the state ones, but the federal ones, too.

The encounter of rural "innocence" and American *realpolitik* had been stated rather well. It was an encounter that to some extent took place inside him as well as one he watched. Yes, he was for "the people," for CDGM, and against the whole social and political system that keeps those people in their present circumstances; but he was also part of that system, perhaps more than he cared to realize. I was myself awakened and stunned at some of the introspection and self-scrutiny that emerged in those moments of "struggle" with the state and federal governments. We had the same all-night "soul sessions" I had once heard civil rights workers "conduct"[6] or unwittingly slip into—always with a later sense of incredulity. ("Like, man, we've spent the whole night talking and taking ourselves down until there's nothing left, and no one knows how it all got started.") A young man like Peter—of the people, for the people, with the people—had to face his own "distance" from "them." It wasn't only that he had gone to college, or even that he had worked at "community organization" or in a protest movement. It wasn't only his "savvy," his political shrewdness, his canny understanding of what in the news was "really" significant—his "worldliness" it used to be called by cloistered men and women. What separated him, finally, from the ranks of the "poor"—so he began to believe and say—were the assumptions he took for granted and ordinarily never questioned or indeed thought about. When he was literally penniless these past years, he had not been "poor"; and when he was fighting hardest alongside the tenant farmers or the abandoned mothers and their children, he was not struggling the way they were. Even when he tried to forget everything he knew, everything he had ever learned, he could not achieve their ignorance, their vulnerability, their concrete, earthy vision—both idealistic, shattered, pitiful, foolish, and at times enormously, powerfully convincing. "You look at me, at my life, someone like you could, and you'd think I could really 'make it' with these people." So he started one night when we were trying to distinguish between the leader and the led—in a "movement" and in an organization that were both doing their best to blur the distinction, or at the very least be embarrassed by it, and call it a temporary, unavoidable "fact of life" or of the "society," a grim necessity. Then Peter went on:

The truth is that I'm miles from the very people I'm "from" and now working "for." It's not my education, and it certainly isn't my "background." It's hard to put into words, but I think something happens to you, no matter how "radical" you are, when you work to change a political system. Some of the system's values rub off on you—you can't help it—even when you're fighting them. It happens to all of us. In fact, in a way the *more* you fight, the more you become entangled in what you're fighting, and the more it all becomes part of you. I remember when I was in SNCC, I'd go up to Washington—in 1962 or 1963. We'd meet all those government people. I remember the time I went into Bobby Kennedy's office. I thought to myself, here I am Peter Woods, from McCormick County, South Carolina, a southern nigger from the back country if ever there is back country, and I'm standing in the office of the Attorney General of the United States. Of course I said to myself, "watch yourself" or "beware," as my mother used to say it, "beware of evil." Well, you know what the greatest evil is? Maybe you don't. Every little colored boy in McCormick County knows that the sin of pride is the worst of them all, them all. My mother used to tell me it didn't matter what the white man had, the property and cash and everything; he has pride, too—the sinful kind, and so he'll burn while we stand by and watch. Later on, of course, is when he'll burn, the time will be later on, and it won't be here on this earth. Our bones will be lying around, tired as usual, but at least getting a rest; and the white man's will be lying comfortable in a satin coffin. But up there it will get reversed—because of pride and its temptations.

Well, you can only be tempted so many times, and even if you resist it every time, you've tasted it and smelled it and felt it and learned about it. We'd leave Washington all heady and walking on air. Each of us knew enough not to show how we felt to the other. We'd try to be real suspicious and angry—and we *were* suspicious and angry. I'm not telling you that we "sold out" or were "conned" or "had," nothing like that. It's not even that we were so impressed and excited; if that was all, we'd just be ordinary tourists. The point is that we were fighting something, and we left still fighting it, but we also left just a little more a part of what we were against. *We* began to think about this group and that one, and the pressures here and there, and what might happen if we did one thing or another one. *We* began to worry about what one group would do, or another. *We* began to realize how difficult everything was, and complicated, and involved, and hard to solve. We'd leave Washington telling one another how unmoved we were, how unimpressed we were with all the people there, and the offices they had and the flunkies around them—United States power! Then we'd get home and the next thing you'd hear, when we were talking about *our* strategies, *our* tactics, we'd begin sounding like *them* when we spoke to one another. I remember a guy saying to me "What's got into you?" when I said something to the effect that we had to "think our options through carefully," and "not inflame the rednecks into starting their own kind of movement." Then the guy said: "If we thought like you during the last three years, there wouldn't be *any* movement, not ours and not a hypothetical one of theirs to worry about. We wouldn't have had the sit-ins, or the freedom rides, or the projects in Alabama or Mississippi, certainly not the Mississippi one. We'd have had nothing but a lot of talk, a lot of conferences and meetings and discussions and plans that are so well 'thought out' that they lead you nowhere, which is exactly where they're supposed to lead you." I blew up at him and told him it was easy to demonstrate and much harder to figure out what was happening in the country. But as soon as I said that I knew I was a fool, and I apologized to him. The fact was that we were *making* things happen, and the more we sat around and worried about a lot of "effects" and "potential reactions" or "responses" to what we did—well, the less we would do and the less there would be to worry about, though there are a lot of people who can always find something to keep themselves busy, and "worried" too, I guess.

What I mean is that we were trying to change things, but in this country it's hard to keep your momentum going. You try to change things and the first thing you know you're being wined and dined, and the TV people are hanging around you, listening to your every word, and people write newspaper columns about you, and kids come from every campus in America to "help" you, and a million journalists and political scientists and sociologists and psychologists (cats like you) try to figure us out and study us and write about us—and make their living off us, make money from what we *do*. Pretty soon *we're* making money, too. There's plenty of it around, and people will give it to you. Then *we* become worried about our "image," and *we* become interested in the "larger picture"—until that's about *all* we're doing: trying to "mobilize public opinion" by saying things that "get across" or doing things *because* they'll "get across"; worrying about our telephone lines, our lines to the "power structure," rather than what's going on between us and the people in the Delta. (And we can always defend ourselves for that "approach" by saying we're doing the people in the Delta the most good possible this way.)

So, that's it. You're with the people here, a guy like me; but you're somewhere else, too—even if you're Negro, even if you're a poor farm boy yourself. That's all right though, so long as you don't forget the difference, and so long as you stay here and do what you can. I believe a lot of my friends have left because they're further removed from life down here than they can allow themselves to admit. So they find excuses, and they leave. I'm not criticizing them. I'm not. They're—a lot of them —city boys, black boys from the ghetto. They want to go back. I may want to leave, too; but for me to go "back" means McCormick County, South Carolina. So, I'm removed from the scene here because I'm "wise" to a lot of things, but I'm also close to the scene—out of my life, man. You know?

I think I know, a little. I think that in Appalachia I have seen the very same struggle take place among those who "work" there with the poor and among the poor.[7] Peter's struggle comes to my mind often when I hear an Appalachian Volunteer,[8] a middle-class college student, talking about his effort to "reach" the "people" in a particular hollow and "do" something for them—teach their children, take stock of their medical problems, join them in their battle with a county courthouse or a strip-mining company that wants to devour their land. In eastern Kentucky, western North Carolina, and West Virginia I have once again seen myths exploded—only to reveal new sorts of "problems." Like sharecroppers of the Delta, the people of Appalachia have been called a lot of discouraging things: backward, disadvantaged, primitive, deprived, parochial, isolated, unreachable, a subculture, fundamentally different in their values and goals.[9] Those who would dare try to live among them and work alongside them have usually heard all those words and then had to face the inevitable warnings: Mountain people suspect outsiders, distrust them, find them of little interest, pay no attention to them, want no help from them—in fact, have so little in common with them that the years outsiders put into sharing time and space with "hollow folk" and into making gestures of conciliatory self-abasement at the feet of "mountain culture" eventually prove futile.

Yet, the War on Poverty (insofar as it has brought on a number of skirmishes in the Appalachian mountains during the mid-sixties) has been remarkably able to "penetrate" all those cultural "resistances" and demonstrate one more time that loyalty to a particular kind of past can live side by side with a willing and even eager acceptance of new opportunities and possibilities. The terribly private, solitary man of the hollows—so out of the world, so out of the way—feels the lure of bread and medicine, work and money. He does more; he abandons in their wake some of the social and psychological characteristics that people like me take pains to observe, analyze, and fit into one or another "frame of reference." He does so almost unnervingly, but only when the "change" makes real sense for him. Here is a man in Wolfe County, Kentucky, speaking:

I don't know about all these college kids coming in here, wanting to do things, all kinds of things—you wonder how they think up so many ideas at the same time. They tell us they want to be here with us and be our friends, and I wonder what about their friends back home where they come from. Do you think they don't have any there? But I don't care. They say they'll go fix our bridge and help us with the road we've been meaning to lay down for—I'd say ten years, I guess. There's enough of them to go do it, too. They'll hurt themselves a little, I think (some of them don't look too strong to me), but they'll do the work, I can tell. And they're good with the kids. The kids like them. My wife says they tickle my son and my daughters, and they're real nice with them.

They've got some money to bring here, and that's welcome, let me tell you. The kids get a good lunch, and if we put up a volunteer, they pay us out of the government's pocket. The one with us, his name is Richard, and he comes from someplace near New York, I think outside the city there. His mother writes him these letters and tells him to be real careful and not to get sick. You'd think he was someplace over in China. But he's O.K. We've never before met anyone from where he comes, or like him, but he's good to have around. I think he's taken to my wife's food pretty good, and he likes the singing we do. He's a little jittery we notice. He can't sit for too long. He has to be doing something or moving about. I guess that's his way. A while back I never thought we'd see people like him hereabouts—ever. But I've lived to see them. First it was in the army, where you meet all types, and we got sent over there to England and France. Yes, and it's television, too. I've never seen so much in all my life as TV brings into your home. It's the thing that my kids pay most attention to—more than to me or their mother, even. Nowadays they've seen everything before a father has a chance to talk.

Of course Richard is in the flesh, not on a program. My daughter Jeanne, she said he's really cute, and she was sure he was like two or three people she'd seen on TV.

He talks like them, and he wears the same kind of clothes. I can't figure why he came all the way down here to be with us, even for a summer. And now I hear him talking about staying here for a while and working with us on a couple projects they have in mind, the AV's.

There's plenty for them to do. They say we can fight the mine-strippers. I think they'll find out different, but let them go try. I don't mind someone coming in here so long as he tries to do what needs doing and not what *he* wants. You know some of the people who used to come through, back in my daddy's day and way before, too, they'd be a certain kind of minister or a teacher maybe—for a disguise—and they'd want to change *us*, not the things that these kids do. They'd preach at us; but these kids, they don't say a bad word about us, and it's pretty clear that they're trying to be of some help, and they want to do some building or clearing or whatever there is. Now that's a difference. Of course you don't really give yourself over to them. Why should you? Some are a little too one-sided for me. You know what I mean? They're so all-fired serious, and they want to make over the hollow and the county and the whole state of Kentucky, for all I know. I told one the other night to just relax and not lose so much sleep on things, the "poverty" as she keeps calling it. Sure it's bad down here, and elsewhere from what you hear, but these mountains have been here for a long time, and so have we, and you can't just dissolve the world's misery in your own time.

I'm glad they're here, though—on the whole. One or two may be a nuisance to us, but they're workers, and that's what counts. And they have money to bring in here, and that's the scarcest thing around. And they don't hand it out, they ask us for help, for their room and food, and to work with them, so it's not something that's welfare and charity. We have to take *that,* too—but no man like me wants it. If there were jobs around here, I'll tell you, none of us would be sitting around trying to get a handout here and there from anyone he can. Not our people. We want work.

A year later, he and others were more wrought up than I ever thought possible. Those "kids"—some of them were well into their twenties—had done a quiet, respectful, but clear-cut job of bringing together people whom tradition, geography, and a sense of futility had long kept apart. Moreover, the volunteers were increasingly coming from within the region, even from local people who were not students but unemployed men whose sharp, well-articulated sense of what is "wrong" with the Appalachian region often surprises the well-meaning and arrogant outside observer. While "we"— student activists and people like me who "observe" them—have come to accept the "wisdom" that relatively uneducated poor people have, it still comes as a surprise to hear an unemployed former coal miner, or even a "dirt farmer" from one of the Kentucky hills, give a sharp and comprehensive analysis of the social and economic system in the United States.

As a matter of fact the repeated irony has been inescapable: It is not due to the reluctance of the hidebound, the "hillbillies" of the backwoods, that the War on Poverty in Appalachia has been a limited one; rather, the issue has been resources. How much can come into the region, after all, to a people largely willing to take what they can get, what they need, and be grateful? "Yes, we get annoyed at some of these people who come in here," I heard one man from near Beckley, West Virginia, say to a group of "outsiders," some of whom, I knew, did indeed annoy him. "But if they bring the bacon in with them, well that's what counts."

In Kentucky and West Virginia both I have seen virtual mob scenes unheard of in "mountain history." That is, "community organization" has worked. People have come together because they have been led to believe that it pays to do so, that jobs and various "improvements" will result. Even more interesting and potentially significant, once a number of people have "organized" themselves, they are newly sensitive and newly prepared to act when confronted with an insult, a rebuff, an assault of one kind or another. "The best thing that can happen to bring one of these mountain communities *really* together is a strip-miner coming along." The owner of a gas station in a small West Virginia town told me that—as a criticism, actually, of the federal government's community-action program. He went on, though:

People around here are to themselves, mostly; they know their kin, and they don't have much to do with others. Maybe it's that way in the city, too—except you notice it more here. Actually, they're friendly to one another here, but they don't work together. Why should they? In the city, they probably do—one man by the other on the assembly line, I guess. Now all this "community action" they talk about, I don't think it means much. I guess the people down here will go along, of course. They'll go along with practically *anything* if it means more food and money and a new road put in and some water from the hills brought under control. But I have noticed that if a stripper comes along now, they'll be in a better position to fight him, the people in the "action program"; and they do so much talking when they meet that I think they're all primed up and *looking* for trouble, for something to go fight and win, if you ask me. I admit we have plenty of things to fight about down here, but it's not so easy to find who the enemy is. From what I see, if they can't find a mine-stripper, they turn on the school people or the mayor, or on the federal government who's paying to "organize" them in the first place. It all goes round and round from what we can figure out. Now they're talking about marching on the state capital, and Washington, and letting the country know about conditions down here. So, you see, they don't just sit together and talk; they look for trouble and go out and make it when they can't find it, and they won't adjust themselves to the real situation around here, but they have to go find someone to have a duel with.

In his "community" he is rather well-to-do. His gas station is also a grocery store, and he has the local post office in his quarters, too. In other words, he is a shopkeeper, a member of the bourgeoisie if there ever was one. I think he deserves to be credited with assets. He has a keen eye for the principles of "group psychology," though he denies himself and his listeners any "formulation" of what he sees. He knows that Appalachia, *his* Appalachia by virtue of property as well as birth, is not for long going to "stay put." Ironically, the region is "backward"—in the case of the hollows unbelievably so to an outsider—but also plagued with the "post-technological" unemployment that comes with automated (mining) industry. The new roads will bring in outsiders—and for a gas-station owner like him, more money. Television sets have already brought him and his neighbors face to face with the rest of the country. Most unsettling of all, however, are "those VISTA types" and "the people who are always talking about organizing, organizing, organizing." He thinks they are looking for trouble, the organizers, volunteers, and activists of all descriptions. He knows there is trouble to be found. He is afraid they will persist long enough to make more trouble for him and for the order of things he has always taken for granted. He once put the whole issue very clearly:

I believe you have to bend with the wind and give way sometimes. But there's just so much giving you can do and still have something yourself. If they keep on telling us this is wrong, and that, and something else, we'll have to *draw the line*, draw it firm, and say: "What you trying to do, change the whole society on us?"

It would seem that those who give and those who demand, those who accommodate and those who confront, may yet have to find out whether in fact there has to be a line drawn, a decisive struggle waged, or whether in America, somehow, the blurred limits of our enormous, confusingly disparate but nonetheless real "middle class" will be yet again stretched, reluctantly or hospitably. I don't frankly know whether this nation at this particular stage in its history will choose to make the political choices, the social and economic changes, that are needed if a vulnerable and relatively powerless and isolated minority is to be made—in essence—wealthier and stronger. In the thirties, the poor, the downtrodden, were all over—visible victims of a "system" that clearly was in trouble. Today, the country as a whole is prospering, as people in the Delta or in Appalachia know better than we may suppose. Yes, some exceptional and highly publicized atrocity —to a civil rights worker, to mountain land by a strip-mining company— can command a certain sympathy from the rest of us. Is that kind of response enough, though, to get a national legislature to initiate the kind of planned economic investment that will reach our rural areas and make them reasonably self-sufficient and capable of keeping people who don't *want* to go to urban ghettos but feel they *must* go? Right now we seem committed to a patchwork of doles, to commodity food programs that leave children on the brink of serious malnutrition, to "happy pappy" programs that are susceptible to the worst sort of political control and, in addition, are humiliating, to welfare checks that are disgracefully inadequate and given or held back in the most inhumane and arbitrary way.

If I have learned anything from the work I've done with migrant farmers, sharecroppers or tenant farmers, and mountain families, it is that the people "we" consider so distant, removed, backward, illiterate, passive—and whatever—may well be more capable of changing themselves than our nation is of changing itself. Of course, people cower and appear dumb, stony, impassive, inert when they face (in the clutch) gun-wielding sheriffs with implied and covert power. Of course, "outsiders" and their "help" are spurned by people who are shrewd enough to appraise that help, to take stock of it, and in an unnervingly brief time see it for what it is and isn't. Of course, despair and "hostility" appear regularly among people who are hungry or have no significant work. Yet, given a chance, "they" don't have to be that way. I have seen enough to know *that*. Perhaps one of America's achievements is that its rural "proletariat" is not, in psychological and social fact, a *"lumpen proletariat,"* a truly and fatally disorganized "mass." There is hope in that "observation" or "conclusion," but also the makings of a historical scandal and a great tragedy for a rich and powerful nation. The next few years will probably give us the answer: whether or not this country will be persuaded (and led) to concern itself with people all too easily and conveniently kept out of sight, out of mind, deprived of just about everything the rest of us enjoy, pride ourselves on having, and ask the rest of the world to emulate.

NOTES

1. Those were the figures given in a report on rural medical problems to OEO by the Tufts University Department of Medicine in 1966.

2. The infant-mortality rate in India in 1966 was 831 per 10,000 according to The United Nations Demographic Yearbook.

3. Excellent historical accounts of CDGM have been written by Pat Watters, Director of Information at the Southern Regional Council. See "CDGM: Who Really Won," *Dissent* (May–June 1967) and *New South* (Spring 1967). Mr. Watters make quite clear what the political and economic stakes were (and are) in the struggle between an exceptional Headstart program and the "local authorities" in Mississippi.

4. The quotations in this essay have been taken from a number of tape-recorded interviews. As always, for the sake of clarity and force, I have edited them and, in some instances, drawn fragments from different interviews together.

5. In 1964 I tried to describe some of the weariness and despair felt by youths like Peter in a paper called "Social Struggle and Weariness," *Psychiatry* (November

1964). See also the discussion of the civil rights workers I have known in *Children of Crisis: A Study of Courage and Fear* (Boston: Little, Brown, 1967).

6. See R. Coles and J. Brenner, "American Youth in a Social Struggle: The Mississippi Summer Project," *American Journal of Orthopsychiatry* (October 1965).

7. See R. Coles, "Mountain Thinking," *Appalachian Review* (Summer 1966).

8. For an extended analysis of the work done by The Appalachian Volunteers see R. Coles and J. Brenner, "American Youth in a Social Struggle (II): The Appalachian Volunteers." Presented at the Annual Meeting of the American Orthopsychiatric Association, Washington, D.C., April 1967, and published in *American Journal of Orthopsychiatry* (January 1968).

9. There is an extensive literature on the Appalachian "subculture," much of it discussed and listed in the paper mentioned in the preceding footnote. See also R. Coles, "Childhood in Appalachia," *Appalachian Review* (Summer 1967). In this regard, Harry Caudill's book *Night Comes to the Cumberlands* (Boston: Little, Brown, 1962) is indispensable. Also, see John Fetterman's *Stinking Creek* (New York: Dutton, 1967).

SUGGESTED READINGS

Daniel Bell, "Work and Its Discontents," in *The End of Ideology,* rev. ed. (New York: Collier Books, 1961).

Norman Birnbaum, *The Crisis of Industrial Society* (New York: Oxford University Press, 1969).

Robert Blauner, *Alienation and Freedom: The Factory Worker and His Industry* (Chicago: Univ. of Chicago Press, 1964).

David Caplovitz, *The Poor Pay More* (New York: Free Press, 1963).

Harry M. Caudill, *Night Comes to the Cumberlands* (Boston: Little, Brown, 1963).

Richard M. Elman, *The Poorhouse State* (New York: Pantheon, 1966).

Georges Friedmann, *Industrial Society* (Glencoe, Ill.: Free Press, 1955).

John Kenneth Galbraith, *The New Industrial State* (Boston: Houghton Mifflin, 1967).

Todd Gitlin and Nanci Hollander, *Uptown: Poor Whites in Chicago* (New York: Harper & Row, 1970).

Michael Harrington, *The Other America* (New York: Macmillan, 1962; Baltimore: Penguin Books, 1966).

Gabriel Kolko, *Wealth and Power in America* (New York: Praeger, 1962).

C. Wright Mills, *White Collar* (New York: Oxford University Press, 1951).

Arthur Pearl and Frank Riessman, *New Careers for the Poor* (New York: Free Press, 1965).

Edward B. Shils, *Automation and Industrial Relations* (New York: Free Press, 1965).

John R. Seely, "Progress from Poverty?" *Liberation,* August 1966.

Studs Turkel, *Hard Times* (New York: Pantheon, 1969).

III

PROBLEMS OF WORLD POWER ❦ ❦

MILITARISM, ANTI-COMMUNISM, AND NEO-COLONIALISM ✺

America is the most powerful nation on earth. The foundation for what may be the most dominant state ever conceived underlies and directs this Behemoth with a modicum of coercive force upon the majority of its citizens. Yet, we know that it can come down heavily upon rebellious minorities within and outside its borders. It is difficult to comprehend that the very strength of a society is regarded as a major source of its weakness and as a serious threat for the members of that society as well as for other inhabitants on earth. How is it possible that the might of America may emerge as a major danger to its survival?

It is our task to comprehend America's enormous destructive capacities, its overextension of world commitments, and its worldwide domination of other societies via control of their economic resources, sometimes their governments, and often the education and propaganda reaching their people. In such an overview we see the aim of the social analyst as showing what the institutional arrangements and beliefs are doing to others in terms of the alternative priorities and rewards foregone, and to ourselves, and our capacities to choose, and change, and realize our identities as autonomous human beings, open to experience, communion with others and purposeful development.

Of all societies ours has come perhaps the closest to achieving a freedom from developing the necessities for sustaining life as well as a freedom to develop and realize ourselves as distinct individuals. While this potential exists, various institutions and a common ideology which underlies them work to deny this emancipation, and if they continue to remain unchanged, it can only mean further divorcement from the possibilities of social diversity, equality, and community. In our own and the following essays, we critically examine and call into question the ideology and the institutions

173

which dominate the contemporary scene in America: militarism, neo-colonialism, and anti-communism.

The three "isms" we speak of here are inextricably related and mutually supportive of each other. They are expressed here as ideologies, belief systems, or ways of looking at the world. Moreover, while they are all of relatively recent origin, they are buttressed by the aggregation of material wealth in the hands of a small number of corporations. Many of these corporations have been able to avoid bankruptcy and have remained solvent only by virtue of the enormous expansion and development of the federal government, particularly through weapons contracts from the Department of Defense. On another level, the prosperity of the country is now very much dependent upon the government's purchases which maintain an effective demand of the magnitude and constancy necessary to sustain full production and employment. In a way, the ideology of anti-communism has contributed to the collectivization of the American economy.

Already in the origins of corporate capitalism one finds the institutional support and the social bases of certain ways of responding to world politics. The modern corporation began growing in late nineteenth-century America. The inner logic of these giant private bureaucracies was and is growth, dependent upon the constant development of more mechanized means of production, the more efficient use of labor as a means of production, heavy reinvestment, particularly in research on technological innovation, internal coordination via refinements in management practices and organizational arrangement, and access to continuously expanding markets which provide the demand necessary for growth. These arrangements also depend upon the acquisition of cheap raw materials, foreign markets in which to sell goods, and foreign locations for investments of surplus capital at high profits because of the use of cheaper labor.

Any system of production so organized cannot stagnate, for if it should, the result would be not a mere diminution in size or importance, but expiration. As the competition between corporations becomes reduced when large concerns buy out or force out smaller ones, and as fewer remain, growth becomes even more important since the remaining producers are basically producing similar standardized products. Profit-making is based on reducing costs and having predictable outlets for goods, rather than on the production of a superior product. Moreover, the rate of profit is continuously being reduced, as more and more capital is required to be reinvested as a necessity for continuous development of innovative technological and organizational means of production.

In order to maintain the optimal conditions for the continuous development of corporate capitalism, decision-making must be both long range in its consequences and highly coordinated with other institutions that can guarantee such conditions. Those who make decisions about foreign and domestic policy in the federal government often share the same view of reality as those who man the strategic positions in large corporations. Indeed, this is no accident or even the result of a recognition of common interests. They are generally from the same social class as big business leaders, have been trained at the same schools, know the same people, and face similar problems of management. In addition, it is indicative of this situation that they are able to move easily from top-level positions in governmental bureaucracies to similar positions in industry and commerce. Moreover, ex-military men are able to secure such positions with equal ease with the large producers of weapons systems. Finally, every major decision of the federal government since the end of World War II has extended our military, economic, and political domination over the rest of the world, and has, in turn, benefitted the continued growth of corporate capitalism. Most interestingly, these decisions have been made in the name of national security and the defense of freedom around the world.

Americans do not regard themselves as a militaristic or colonialistic people, but admittedly they are strongly anti-communist. Without this ideological component, militarism and neo-colonialism might have made fewer inroads in our national consciousness and policies. Although most Americans agree that they are anti-communist, there is much confusion over exactly what they are against. The full consequences of this ideology are still unknown to us, but it has made us inflexible with regard to seeing the necessity for major power transformations at home and less capable of understanding the non-western world in all its complexity.

Communism has never been viewed as a variety of competing political and economic arrangements, competing as much within its own world as with our version of capitalist democracy. Instead, the public view of this belief system has been manipulated by the economic, political, and military elites of America to justify extraordinary expenditures on armaments, the maintenance of military bases around the world, the subversion of foreign governments, the support of reactionary regimes, and an almost endless war in Indochina. The very freedom we seek to guarantee abroad can be systematically denied at home, and denied in the name of enhancing the struggle for its maintenance abroad. The techniques of repression used by our troops and agents on several continents in the name of our freedom is being introduced as the institutionalized means of maintaining the political status quo at home.

To say that we have gained nothing from our military and colonialist ventures would not be true. We now have a large number of young people at home who have learned to kill with impunity and have never been able to understand why they had to do this. Accordingly, some of the most eloquent testimony against the war comes from these young men who served in Indochina. Along with college students, hippie dropouts, and blacks who reject white supremacy in Asia and many of their elders, we now have a new contingent of disaffected Americans—the veterans of that very war, who now express their moral revulsion at the wanton murder committed in the name of democracy. A colonialist war is always brutal, and it is also brutalizing, especially when it is fought as an impersonal exercise in what becomes, even if it did not start as such, the genocide of another race.

We have become conditioned to responding to the third world and its revolutions in this way because militarism and neo-colonialism are institutionalized solutions to political and economic problems in America. We cannot reconcile ourselves to the price of enormous power, the willingness to limit it, to continue it, to transform it so that all benefit from it. It is the solution to the specific problem of maintaining our economic and political institutions that has let loose the problems of militarism, neo-colonialism and anti-communism.

Implicit in this analysis are some fundamental questions concerning the direction of American society in the future and the quality of life available to us and to the rest of the world. Are democracy and political freedom possible in a society dominated by corporate capitalism and its supportive institutions and ideologies? Can the human potential of our technology ever be realized so long as those who control the inputs for this engine are unwilling to recognize their responsibility for maintaining a vast military-industrial complex which endangers the very survival of the species? Can the underdeveloped nations of the world modernize on their own terms, without becoming Americanized? Are other social problems in America, such as infant mortality and health care for the aged, resolvable, so long as our view of social reality is dominated by militarism, colonialism and anti-communism? How much of our view of the world is an extension of our racist views at home, or, alternatively, how much of our racism at home is a result of or is perpetuated by our domination of the underdeveloped world? The readings in this section not only outline the dimensions of militarism, neo-colonialism and anti-Communism and show their interrelations, they also shed light upon the social sources of these problems.

Ralph Lapp, a noted physicist, concerns himself with the way in which weapons dominate our thinking, reacting, and responding to world problems. In this selection from his book *The Weapons Culture,* he analyzes the ways in which weapons' production is an indispensable part of our economy and how the belief in the need for national security beyond adequate preparedness is sustained, thereby, increasing the dangers of world security rather than reducing them. Moreover, he ably shows that the armament makers in American society have an inordinate amount of influence with the military, Congress, and the various branches of the federal government responsible for overseeing the military. He points out the enormous difficulty that even elected officials have in evaluating critically the merits of the weapons-systems being considered for implementation. The dangers pointed to by President Eisenhower in his famous warning to the American people as he left office are clear in Lapp's careful documentation of the defense establishment.

I. F. Stone, an independent journalist-publisher based in Washington, D.C., provides a detailed case study of the promotion and implementation of one such weapons-system, the F-lll all-purpose fighter-bomber. The implications are clear here that the needs for many new weapons-systems are based on irrational considerations related to political pandering for votes and the need to keep defense industries alive for the sake of maintaining aggregate demand, i.e., keeping purchases and purchasing power high. As is shown by Ralph Lapp in the previous selection, the production of weapons in the United States goes beyond maintaining the capacity to deter aggression from the other side, but is based on the dynamics of anti-communism and the continuous growth of corporate capitalism.

David M. Shoup knows the military from the inside. An American war hero and a former Commandant of the United States Marine corps, this retired general argues that the posture of America has changed from being a "typically isolationist, pacifist and generally anti-military" country to being a "militaristic and aggressive nation." He documents this change as beginning with our massive involvement in World War II and the residual effect this had on about one-fifth of the contemporary adult population, creating a nation of veterans and filling the ranks of the various militaristic veterans' organizations. In addition, the weapons' industries provide a great deal of financial support for the various armed forces. In turn, the armed services and their career officers know how to reward their friends in industry with lucrative contracts. Professional military men, according to Shoup, by virtue of their training and recruitment, are better able to dominate organizations than civilians; indeed, they measure their worth by the amount of responsibility they are able to acquire. Also their interservice rivalries precipitate the use of military solutions to political problems, since each branch of the armed services wishes to demonstrate its preparedness at a moment's notice. Thus, militarism is regarded by this military man as a dangerous part of our social, political, and economic activities.

The problems of American power are reflected in our fears and aspirations concerning the state of the world and the nature of our adversaries. Most significantly, they mirror our anxieties concerning the major transformations occurring in American life, particularly the growth of corporate capitalism, with its handmaiden, organized labor, and the increased militancy of oppressed minorities. Some American centers of power wish to recreate the world in their own image, yet it is an older more traditional version of a free enterprise system that no longer exists which they find exemplary. Ronald Steel, a political scientist, examines these fundamental social-psychological bases of our view of the world at large as well as the political conditions which made us the possessors of a universal responsibility that cannot be fulfilled, given the changing character of the world. The evangelical nature of American foreign policy, despite the good intentions which may generate it, is just another way of patronizing other nations. In some ways, old-fashioned territorial imperialism was more genuinely dominating but less penetrating, for native nationalists knew better what they were fighting against. American imperialism is more elusive but still does not allow poorer nations to determine their own destinies.

Carl Oglesby and Richard Shaull, in contrast, directly connect the problems of international empire with the nature of corporate capitalism. The "Free World Empire" is no accident of post-World War II international changes and controversies, but a direct result of the inner necessity of these industrial and financial giants to find new sources of raw materials, labor, markets, and outlets for investments. Despite the fact that foreign investments constitute a relatively small percentage of all American investments, the domination of entire economies of small, less economically developed countries is obviously great. Oglesby and Shaull ably document the way in which the Brazilian economy and others are taken over by American capital, thus draining out the investment capital necessary for economic growth. In addition, the Americanization of these economies has tremendous social, cultural, and political ramifications, often culminating in wars of national liberation or revolutions against the native ruling elites who are dependent upon American capital, weapons and sometimes troops as ways of maintaining their regimes. Thus, in order to protect our interests, we permit the destruction of democratic elements, generally in the name of anti-communism and resistance to internal subversion.

Americans claim to be interested in making the world a better place in which to live. A generic condition of that desire is the economic development of the underdeveloped world of Latin America, Asia, and Africa. Robert Heilbroner, an economist, argues that the problem of economic change is one of modernization of social relationships and ways of viewing the world, rather than one of exploiting natural resources and building factories. He claims that one way to get modernization going, before it is too late for many countries, is through a mobilizing ideology, often a fusion of nationalism and communism. By virtue of our rigid anti-communist stance, we may, then, be impeding economic development, thus reinforcing a continued backwardness for much of the world. In "Counterrevolutionary America," the author joins the three problems of domination—militarism, neo-colonialism, and anti-communism—and ascertains the costs and rewards of the continuation of policies which emanate from them.

THE EISENHOWER WARNING
Ralph Lapp

In framing a government which is to be administered by men over men, the great difficulty lies in this: you must first enable the government to control the governed; and in the next place oblige it to control itself.

—The Federalist Papers

President Dwight D. Eisenhower's Farewell Address in 1961 contained a barbed admonition: "In the councils of government we must guard against the acquisition of unwarranted influence, whether sought or unsought, by the military-industrial complex. The potential for the disastrous rise of misplaced power exists and will persist."

Less well known than the "military-industrial complex" is the fact that in his stinging indictment-prophecy, Eisenhower added: "In holding scientific research and discovery in respect, as we should, we must also be alert to the equal and opposite danger that public policy could itself become the captive of a scientific-technological elite."

President Eisenhower did not take the Congress to task for its involvement in defense contracting, but he was well aware of ties linking together the Pentagon and defense industry. We may think of this as a geometrical figure—a defense-based triangle—in which industry and the Congress form two sides. Within this defense triangle reside the fortunes of millions of Americans who depend on Pentagon-disbursed paychecks. The postwar rise of the arms industry, especially in the past decade, is an innovation without precedent in American history.

It is no exaggeration to say that the United States has spawned a weapons culture which has fastened an insidious grip upon the entire nation. This book inquires into the evolution of this new culture and seeks to explore its

SOURCE: Ralph Lapp, *The Weapons Culture* (New York: W. W. Norton & Company, Inc. 1968), pp. 11–30. Copyright © 1968 W.W. Norton & Company, Inc. Reprinted by permission of the publisher. Certain appendices have been omitted from this reprinting. —Eds.

impact on our democracy. We shall be concerned with the deadliest game man has ever invented—deterring war by threat of nuclear attack.

Huge defense spending has become a fixed feature of our national budget. As the chart (Appendix X) shows rather dramatically, the military expenditures have loomed large ever since Korea. There was no letdown after Korea; instead, high priority was assigned to research and development, and costly new weapons systems emerged. Never once has the U.S. Congress failed to fund a single major weapons system that was proposed to it and, more often than not, it has championed new arms while they were still in prospect. All in all, our nation has spent about one trillion dollars on its postwar armaments.

Our massive commitment to weapons development and deployment in time of peace is quite new to the American experience. Equally novel is the emergence of techno-military industries which depend for their existence upon winning prime military contracts for missiles, aircraft, and complex electronic equipment. An aerospace industry has undergone a heady growth primarily as a result of federal funding to a point where its single customer, the U.S. Government, becomes its captive. Pressures exerted by powerful corporations are felt in the Pentagon, in the White House, and are reflected in the Congress. Illustrative of the stakes involved in this defense industry is the fact that the Lockheed Aircraft Corporation has won a total of $10 billion in the prime military contracts in the first seven years of this decade.

It is not just the formidable size of these government contracts that is impressive, it is also the fact that 88 percent of Lockheed's sales are purely military. Appendix II on page 195 lists the major U.S. defense contractors and tabulates their annual prime military-contract awards. Appendix I shows how defense-contract awards are distributed by state and pinpoints the military and civilian payrolls. Here we sense the impact of military spending on a geopolitical basis. Defense corporations employ workers who form part of a constituency that acts to perpetuate and accelerate the arms business. According to the Bureau of Labor Statistics, "The total employment generated by these expenditures, including military personnel and Defense Department civilian employees, is estimated at about 5.7 million persons in fiscal year 1965 and 7.4 million in 1967." The fact that the latter figure represents only a tenth of the total employed civilian labor force is often used as an argument against defense domination of the U.S. economy. However, it is a much greater fraction of the U.S. *manufacturing* labor force; and its geographic localization, together with the special political nature of defense contracting, makes it a highly significant sector of the national economy.

The United States has institutionalized its arms-making to a point where there is grave doubt that it can control this far-flung apparatus. The machinery of defense is lubricated by politics so that it has become a juggernaut in our modern society. Few Congressmen care to challenge defense expenditures, even if they possess the technical competence to appraise techno-military issues. "We are always afraid," Sen. Paul Douglas once remarked, "that if we vote for a reduction in a given expenditure not only will our friends in the Defense Department criticize us, but our opponents in our states and Congressional Districts back home will say: 'When you voted to cut back the appropriation, you voted to weaken the preparedness program of the United States.' " If this battle-scarred Marine, who at age 50 enlisted as a private, could express such a fear, imagine how Congressmen with no war record might feel about tilting with the Pentagon.

During the past 10 years the U.S. aerospace industry has steadily grown in military sales and in political influence. Total sales for 1967 approached $25 billion, and 70 percent of these were paid for by the Federal Government. A total of 1,300,000 workers are employed by aerospace contractors, and about half of these employees are salaried. So far the rambunctious aircraft-missile industry has boomed, but cutbacks in military contracts could inflict serious economic hardships on Southern California and parts of Washington, Texas, and Georgia where new defense technology has its industrial base. To be sure, there have been a number of academic analyses of this problem, and these studies tend to minimize the economic impact of defense cutbacks. But it should be borne in mind that analysts, who cite the ability of the United States to deploy its defense plants to civilian markets at the end of World War II as evidence pointing to optimism for converting defense industry to peacetime products, neglect the significance of pent-up civilian demand for consumer goods. A rocket company that attempts to penetrate a civilian market already well served by existing consumer-oriented businesses has a severe conversion problem. Switching from the U.S. Government as its sole customer to the competitive market-place means that the defense contractor must produce a line of consumer goods on a competitive basis and be able to market them. General Dynamics Corporation, for example, would not be tempted to risk producing motor-cars to compete with General Motors, Ford, and Chrysler.

Given the stiff competition of companies long used to producing, selling, and servicing consumer goods, aerospace firms prefer to garner as much defense business as possible. One well-established principle of private enter-prise is that of constant growth. While many aerospace firms are quaint cousins in the family of private enterprises, they too worship growth and corporate expansion of their plant. Some try to diversify, but others like Lockheed, General Dynamics, and McDonnell Douglas continue to depend on federal sales as their principal source of corporate income. This depend-ency has come to involve them in advocacy of arms and in promotion of increased defense spending. Herein lies a great danger: that the United States will be unable to break out of an upward spiral of armaments.

Defense industry today is turning out products that were little dreamed of a decade or two ago. To understand the origin of this new arms technology it is useful to look back to prewar days when science and the military were strangers. It is true that during World War I a shotgun marriage had brought scientists into an uneasy union with the War Department. But this soon broke up, and scientists returned to the serenity of their academic posts. The United States Government engaged in only a relatively little research and development, largely in agriculture, and had no R&D budget as such prior to World War II.

In the late 1930's Hitler's warlike intentions energized some U.S. leaders in science to leave the sanctity of the ivory tower and to think of applying the power of science to weapons of war. When a few nuclear scientists, all foreign-born, traveled to Washington, D.C., in 1939, they met with a very cool military reception to their proposal for an atomic-bomb project. The professor-physicists might have been men from another planet so far as the U.S. Army was concerned. Unabashed, but fearful of the consequences if Hitler's scientists developed an A-bomb first, Drs. Eugene P. Wigner and Leo Szilard, both from Hungary, seized the initiative via another channel. The two physicists persuaded their colleague Albert Einstein to write a letter to President Franlkin D. Roosevelt, urging him to authorize work on the A-bomb. By going to the top, Wigner and Szilard succeeded in getting a go-ahead for the atomic project, and six years later the A-bomb was a reality.

America's $2 billion wartime A-project did more than birth the bomb and multiply a million-fold the explosive power that could be released from a lump of matter. It sowed the seeds of a weapons culture that blossomed forth in the postwar years. Thereafter science was never to be divorced from weaponry. Moreover, science was transformed in the process and mushroomed to unimagined size and affluence. Scientists tasted the intoxicating elixir of power, and they were profoundly changed. U.S. industry was also deeply influenced by its wartime experience with research and development. It soon linked science and technology as a vital component of weapons development and eagerly sought out federal contracts for researching and developing new weapons systems. Without the all-important additive of science, the "military-industrial complex" would be a humdrum affair devoted to tanks, guns, armor, and World War II-type vehicles.

Although the wartime atomic project and similar efforts in radar and electronics triggered the unleashing of American science, the spectacular technological developments of the past two decades have been largely reactions to Soviet threats. In this sense, U.S. research and development have been masterminded by the Cold War leaders, Joseph Stalin and Nikita Krushchev. For example, Soviet ballistic successes and Sputnik I, which went into orbit on October 4, 1957, catapulted the United States into a crash program to develop rockets.

When President Eisenhower entered the White House, U.S. funds for research and development added up to $2 billion per year. But when he left, the R&D budget had shot up to $9 billion per year. The upward course of the R&D budget is clearly shown in the graph in Appendix X.

Khrushchev continued to dominate the research and development scene during the Kennedy years. Although Defense Secretary Robert S. McNamara managed to hold defense R&D budgets to a level of about $7 billion per year, space spending triggered a great surge in funds for science and technology. Much of the congressional support and national psychology underlining the civilian space effort to land men on the moon had a military basis. The great boost in federal funds for research and development could not be sustained at the rate of growth it exhibited in the early '60's. When he took office, President Lyndon B. Johnson was confronted with the necessity for bringing the rampaging R&D budget under control for the simple reason that if it continued to grow, then by 1978 it would consume all federal funds. It was at this point in time that science and technology came into collision with the competing demands of veterans' benefits, health, education, and welfare, as well as all the other slices of the national budget.

Under President Johnson, funds for science and technology tapered off and reached a plateau of $17 billion in fiscal year 1968. Khrushchev's retirement and the public disaffection with the U.S. space program were contributing factors in the leveling off of the R&D funds from the federal treasury. No colorful successor to Khrushchev appeared to act as a provocative ogre in stimulating the flow of R&D money. Then, too, the United States became heavily involved in jungle fighting, where high technology was little match for the primitive mode of conflict in Vietnam.

Paralleling the spectacular federal underwriting of American research and development, and as a consequence of it, the apparatus of war was profoundly modified. Highly complex weapons systems using sophisticated microelectronics and computer control came into being, introducing a new technology quite foreign to the tradition of the Military Establishment. Generals and admirals felt uneasy in the new scheme of things, which seemed quite at odds with their classical training. Emphasis was placed on the concept of deterring war and, at the same time, the concept of victory seemed elusive in a contest where nuclear weapons could lay waste to much of civilization. Military planners were confronted with levels of destructive potential beyond the wildest dreams of strategists who were trained in pre-Hiroshima days. The military-industrial-political complex was beset with doubts that the weapons business could prosper by growing larger when so much destruction was at hand.

But if the generals and admirals were set somewhat adrift by the innovations in military technology, they could always hark back to the familiar world of men, guns, tanks, and ships. Initially the mere fact that a single B-29 bomber carrying one A-bomb could destroy a whole city presented air-power enthusiasts with a terrifying prospect. With such weapons in existence, not to mention even more powerful ones in the offing, might not force levels for bombers be severely restricted? The prospect of a small strategic bomber force worried men like Gen. Curtis LeMay of the U.S. Air Force. Air power advocates longed for the massed formations of World War II and the power that such massiveness conferred upon the Air Force.

Gradually the U.S. Air Force discovered it could escalate its force levels, especially after the Korean emergency took the lid off the defense budget. The latter had been pegged at $13 billion for 1950, but it quickly doubled and almost doubled again within a period of three years. Before Korea the Air Force had run into trouble pressing for a 70-wing air-power complex, which included 20 medium and heavy bomber groups. But afterward it raised its sights to 143 wings and unleashed a nationwide campaign of high-powered public relations to sell air power to the American people. Even radio-TV star Arthur Godfrey was pressed into service to drum up support for the huge air force.

President Eisenhower attempted to keep his defense budget within reasonable limits, but he found that powerful exponents of air power, both within industry and in Congress, skillfully built up pressure for more armaments. Although the President-General did succeed in leveling out the arms spending, he could not cut it back, and it was during his Administration that the weapons octopus grew and embraced the fortunes of millions of Americans. But it is only fair to trace the origins of this weapons build-up to the Democratic Administration that had preceded the Republicans in office. Eisenhower's defense spending did not satisfy many Democratic critics, and the Republican President was subjected to bitter attacks for allowing, first, a bomber gap, and then a missile gap, to develop. As we shall see, not even the President's military authority sufficed to protect him from charges of short-changing the national security.

The advent of ballistic missiles was an anathema to the U.S. Air Force. Air Force generals looked at the prospective manless vehicles as sorry substitutes for aircraft that required huge bases, constant operational missions and sky-blue glamour of heroic dimensions. In a very real sense missiles took the sex out of air power. The thought of burying Minuteman intercontinental missiles deep under the earth and stationing officers at underground consoles was abhorrent to the U.S. Air Force. There was even the chilling doubt that this inland artillery was more properly the function of the U.S. Army.

Another and deep-rooted reason why the Air Force disliked being saddled with ballistic responsibilities was the fact that the long-term implications of intercontinental missilery might eclipse the future of air power. One basis on which air enthusiasts had been able to sell the concept of huge bomber armadas was that losses near the enemy target zones would be heavy, and this attrition could be compensated by building more bombers. Since the alternative meant busy production lines, this pleased certain influential legislators. But the intercontinental ballistic missiles as compared to lumbering aircraft seemed unstoppable. If an ICBM could be made accurate in seeking its target, then a missile launch was the same as an assured hit. This kind of reckoning inevitably meant that the numbers of strategic ICBM's would be subject to rational assessment. Furthermore, ICBM's were almost cold-storage items—they could be built and stored away without the requirement for "spares" and replacements. All in all, the Air Force was unhappy about the long-range future if it converted from bombers to missiles. By the same token, legislators with an eye on defense-plant employment in their states viewed the ICBM as a dubious national investment—but a necessary one since a "gap" had to be filled.

Elsewhere in this book we shall trace the evolution of nuclear firepower, but it is sufficient at this point to interject that the combination of an ICBM and a superpowerful nuclear warhead rated at a million tons of TNT equivalent was a deadly package. Sooner or later an alert and conscientious Defense Secretary would add up these packages and then the U.S. Air Force would be in trouble. But at the time that ICBM's poked their terrifying noses over the technological horizon, Mr. Robert S. McNamara was still an automobile executive, and the Air Force decided to follow a double track, amassing both bombers and missiles.

In point of fact, the fundamental issue underlying the question of "how many missiles?" had been raised in 1953 by the late J. Robert Oppenheimer. Writing in the July issue of *Foreign Affairs,* the scientist who had headed up the nation's A-bomb laboratory at Los Alamos, N. Mex., took issue with the strategic doctrine of the U.S. Air Force. "The very least we can say is that, looking ten years ahead," wrote the weapons expert, "it is likely to be small comfort that the Soviet Union is four years behind us, and small comfort that they are only half as big as we are. The very least we can conclude is that our twenty-thousandth bomb, useful as it may be in filling the vast munitions pipeline of a great war, will not in any deep strategic sense offset their two-thousandth." Dr. Oppenheimer was giving voice to a deep concern over the nature of the arms race and enunciating the folly of strategic superiority. This, more than any other offense he may have committed in the eyes of defense officials, was an assault upon strategic doctrine, and for it he paid dearly.

Once a nation possesses the strategic power to "kill" another nation, however the degree of this devastation may be defined, then the addition of higher degrees of kill fails to alter the strategic situation. Ultimately the other power achieves its own degree of kill power or strategic sufficiency, and a state of parity exists. The word "parity" rubs raw the nerves of Americans who reckon strength in preatomic measure. They prefer superiority, for it connotes the ability to win in war or to prevail in international contests of power. Superiority is translated into outproducing an enemy in weapons—in building more and more powerful arms. Thus America, which in the past slumbered between periods of war, overreacted to the threat of foreign competition and escalated its arms spending. Part of this over-reaction—and it will remain for historians to dig out the facts, if they can —was due to the self-interest of the military-industrial-political complex. Once the defense plants were built they could be abandoned only at great political risk. As Senator Douglas so well phrased it, the Congress was not equipped to do battle with the Pentagon. Furthermore, the economic impact of defense expenditures on the various states grew greater with each passing year.

The degree of economic impact of defense spending on the various states is shown statistically in Appendix I. Here are presented the annual defense outlays for the past 10 years ending with fiscal year 1967. California, of course, heads the list with a decade total of $54.4 billion, accounting for over a fifth of the $252 billion for all states. During the past decade 15 states have done a total of more than $5 billion worth of business with the Defense Department. Ranked on a per capita basis, the states having the highest defense funds are, respectively, Connecticut, California, Washington, Utah, Kansas and Massachusetts.

During the course of a 1967 hearing on disarmament, Vermont's Sen. George D. Aiken looked at the flow of federal funds to the various states and observed, "I think we are overlooking one important phase of this whole program. That is the growing dependence of areas and states on Government orders until they get to where they are almost helpless. For example, for the state of Washington, over 50 percent of their gross national product is from Government orders." The state of Washington is far from "helpless" because it has defense facilities galore and it is well represented by its congressional delegation in keeping funds moving to support them. The U.S. Air Force and the National Aeronautics and Space Administration have awarded Boeing Company of Seattle huge contracts for military aircraft and spacecraft. The U.S. Navy provides funds for a huge complex of shore facilities and naval bases. The Atomic Energy Commission has built nuclear production facilities with a total cost of $1.2 billion along the banks of the Columbia River. This air-sea-space-atomic orientation of Washington's economy is capably managed by strong congressional support. Sen. Henry M. Jackson, Democrat from Everett, Wash., is highly placed on the Senate Armed Services Committee as well as on the Joint Committee on Atomic Energy. Senator Jackson has consistently championed increased defense spending and is regarded as a leading spokesman for the military-industrial complex. Sen. Warren G. Magnuson, Democrat of Seattle, is a prominent member of the Commerce, Appropriations, and Aeronautical and Space Sciences committees—well placed to protect the vital interests of his constituency.

Senator Aiken's observations regarding the state of Washington are equally applicable to other states where the dependence on defense is less visible. Utah, for example, might at first glance seem far removed from the clutches of the weapons culture. Yet the state of the Mormons has strong economic ties to the Pentagon, especially in the area of ballistic missiles. When Khrushchev's Sputnik added thrust to the U.S. missile program, it quite literally made deserts bloom in Utah. In the span of seven years, Utah won over $2 billion in prime military contracts. Defense plants have sprung up in the vicinty of Salt Lake City, Ogden, and Logan. Solid propellants are manufactured by Thiokol Chemical Corporation, which has built an aerospace complex in Utah amounting to an investment of almost $100 million, much of it an Air Force commitment. Hercules Powder Company built a plant at Bacchus which had a peak employment of 5,700 workers in the early 1960's. The Sperry Utah Company's $18 million factory attained a maximum labor force of 3,500, while Marquardt Corporation's work force ran about half that figure. Electronics firms like Litton Industries, Inc., built plants in Utah for making missile guidance systems. In addition to these industrial plants, the Air Force constructed defense facilities for fabrication of missiles like Minuteman. Utah's dependence on the Defense Department also includes the Tooele Army Depot with more than 3,600 workers and the Hill Air Force Base—the third-ranking base as measured by volume of air traffic. An annual payroll of $140 million keeps 17,000 workers employed at the mammoth air base. Utah also has other less important military posts, depots, training centers, test facilities, laboratories, and weapons ranges. One of every seven workers employed in Utah owes his job to defense. The ratio jumps to one in three if we consider only manufacturing employees.

Two Utah State University economists surveyed the significance of Utah's defense industry in 1965 and concluded: "The defense industry, as a whole, has proved itself to be one of the state's most stable industries. At least defense employment has not been sensitive to the 'business cycle,' which was true of those major industries of past years." That the defense-missile boost to Utah's economy should be reckoned as a stabilizing influence is indeed a commentary on our weapons culture. No one has suggested erecting a statue of Khrushchev in Salt Lake City, but nonetheless the Soviet leader brought prosperity and new affluence to the land of the Mormons.

When a state has a considerable fraction of its manufacturing labor force working on defense or other federal contracts, the danger exists that a temporary contractual arrangement will harden into a permanent feature of the economy. Here we find the cruelest expression of the weapons culture —its perpetuation for reasons other than national security. Indeed, since continued hostility is essential to maintaining a high defense budget, feedback from defense industry may act to accentuate the rift between the Cold War opponents. It is no accident that leaders of the military-industrial-political complex are often hard-line anti-Communists. Do they act out of conviction or are their views colored by a vested interest in the arms race?

What happens when the Defense Department comes to the brink of decision on the award of a weapons-system contract that must go to a single prime contractor? The question is even more acute and pertinent to the weapons culture when that contract may involve a total of $12 billion. Such a question was posed—but never fully answered—when the Pentagon faced the run-off between General Dynamics and Boeing in the award of the TFX contract. The latter is now known as the F-111 aircraft; it is a multipurpose plane originally designed to satisfy both U.S. Navy and Air Force requirements for a fighter-bomber and recently adapted in an FB-111 version as an Air Force strategic bomber.

It was generally considered that Boeing was the more technically qualified to win the TFX contract, but the decision went the other way and it has since been roundly criticized, especially by Sen. John L. McClellan (Democrat from Arkansas), chairman of the Government Operations Committee. It was alleged that the politics of defense had weighted the decision in favor of General Dynamics. Clearly, California stood to benefit handsomely from the TFX award, and that state could be pivotal in an election. But over and above this factor was the dilemma of what the Government should do with a firm, predominantly a defense contractor, when it faced financial difficulties and might suffer serious reverses if it did not win a contract for a billion-dollar defense system. The issue was politely phrased in a question put to President John F. Kennedy in a press conference held April 3, 1963:

QUESTION: Is it valid, sir, for the Government to give a defense contract to a firm in order to keep that firm as part of the production arsenal of this country? And, two, did that happen in the case of the TFX award to General Dynamics?

THE PRESIDENT: No, to the last part. In the first case, if it is a hypothetical case, I would say it would depend on the circumstances, how great the need is. Is it for particular kinds of tools which we might need in case of an emergency? I can think of cases where it would be valid. It has nothing to do with the TFX.

Despite President Kennedy's denial in the instance of the TFX award, much acrimony and skepticism still surround the issue. Indeed, there have even been allegations, unproved to date, that some contributions were made to the Democratic campaign chest in 1960 in order to influence the TFX award.

When a multibillion-dollar defense contract is involved, it is not unthinkable that corporations might make substantial political contributions, especially when relatively small lump-sum—and unaccounted—payments can be highly influential in a given state. Even if untrue in the case of TFX, the financial stakes involved in modern defense contracts are so high that they may well tempt business executives to seek a privileged position in contracting through political activity. This is all the more feasible because of the close association of personalities in the military-industrial-political complex. There is, of course, the common tie of military service and Reserve status. For example, Strom Thurmond, Republican senator from South Carolina, is a major general in the U.S. Army Reserve and a past national president of the Reserve Officers Association and Military Government Association. An outspoken member of the Senate Armed Services Committee, Thurmond generally comports himself as though he is still on active duty in the armed services. The line of congressional "friendship" to the Pentagon extends from elected legislators down to key members of committee staffs. In effect, the Department of Defense has a "built-in" lobby on Capitol Hill ready and willing to support almost any conceivable defense appropriation.

Industry, in its zeal to establish good relations with the Pentagon and to get on the inside track in contract bidding, uses the well-known "wining and dining" techniques of public relations, but this is rather superficial. More to the point is the fact that private industry locks itself into the Military Establishment by hiring large numbers of retired military officers. The possibility of a conflict of interest led the House Committee on Armed Services under Louisiana's Representative F. Edward Hébert to hold a special investigation in 1959. It was then revealed that 72 defense contractors employed 1,426 retired military officers. Of 251 flag rank and general officers employed by these companies, Lockheed and General Dynamics topped the list, each having 27 admirals and generals on its payroll. No up-to-date statistics on the industrial employment of retired officers are available because the Congress has not subsequently looked into this problem, but it is likely that the booming defense business now employs far more ex-military men than it did in 1959.

Defense funds flow not only to industry; they also go out to the nation's most respected educational institutions. In fiscal year 1966, U.S. colleges and universities received a total of $385 million from the Pentagon; 54 of these institutions were awarded contracts in excess of $1 million each. Johns Hopkins University and the Massachusetts Institute of Technology are both to be found on the list of the Defense Department's top 100 prime contractors, with awards amounting to about $50 million apiece. Appendix IV lists the Federal Government's payments to the leading 100 educational institutions. It should be noted that the National Aeronautics and Space Administration provided $126 million in funds; while these are presumably meant for scientific purposes, there is a military basis of support in Congress for NASA. The same is true for the $97 million of Atomic Energy Commission funds dispensed to colleges and universities. In this connection the AEC paid the University of California over $100 million in 1966 for running its Los Alamos weapons facility and an additional $169 million for operating the Lawrence Radiation Laboratory and associated facilities in the state of California. During the emergency of World War II there was a reason for having the University of California manage the affairs of atomic weapons laboratories, but a quarter century has passed and these facilities should more properly come under the administration of the Department of Defense. All in all the Federal agencies call upon the universities to handle more than $1 billion in funds each year for operation of federal contract research centers (see Appendix VI).

Since the United States has a priceless resource in its institutions of higher education, there is a great risk involved in contaminating the campus with military research. Our colleges and universities have a cherished tradition of being oases of independence where freedom of inquiry and unfettered research are practiced. But the inflow of federal funds, especially when they are tagged for secret research, can disrupt the pattern of academic life. When a professor has to keep a triple-locked filesafe in his office for classified work, he courts a conflict of interest on campus. His responsibility to the university, to his colleagues, and to his students is brought into jeopardy by dependence on funds from an interested off-campus source. The very integrity of the educational institution may be compromised by enlisting its scholars in *sub rosa* activities of the type funded by the Central Intelligence Agency, where even top university officials are kept in the dark about the nature of the work done for CIA.

Even with this brief survey we can sense the spread of the weapons culture through our society, extending to almost every phase of our life. Because this impact is not felt as a flash flood but more like the gradual rise of a swollen river, the American people are as yet only imperfectly aware of how far the infection has spread in our society. But a recent development, so to speak—a clinical manifestation of the disease—illustrates how the forces of military, industrial, political, and scientific elements are conspiring to plunge the nation into a new phase of the arms race. In July, 1967, L. Mendel Rivers, chairman of the House Armed Services Committee, released a report titled, "The Changing Strategic Military Balance—U.S.A. vs. U.S.S.R." It turns out that this is not a committee report at all, but rather a private paper which is given the committee's imprimatur. The report is actually the work of a Cold War institution called the American Security Council whose chairman, Robert W. Galvin, is chief executive officer and chairman of the board of Motorola, Inc. The American Security Council describes one of its major functions as "the mobilization of U.S. business in the continuing Cold War."

The American Security Council's task force for its comparison of U.S. and Soviet military strength included eight retired generals, six retired admirals, two professors and Dr. Edward Teller. Gen. Curtis E. LeMay, Gen. Thomas S. Power, and Gen. Albert C. Wedemeyer were three of the task-force members who illustrate the complexion of the group as being unalloyed air-power advocates and champions of the political right wing. "The stock in trade of almost all these individuals" writes Daniel Bell in *The Radical Right:* "is the argument, reinforced by references to their experiences, that negotiation or coexistence with Communists is impossible, that anyone who discusses the possibility of such negotiation is a tool of the Communists, and that a 'tough policy'—by which, *sotto voce,* is meant a preventive war of a first strike—is the only means of forestalling an eventual Communist victory."

The overt alliance of scientific, technical, and military men under the aegis of a congressional committee to promote a step-up in the arms race is an ugly excrescence in our weapons culture. The committee report is a blatant attempt to increase U.S. armaments by preaching the gospel of a "megaton gap." It trumpets a cry for more nuclear warheads, more ballistic missiles, more strategic bombers, and pleads for a stout defense against ballistic missiles. We shall return to the issue of the "megaton gap" after examining the "bomber gap" and the "missile gap." For the moment, it is important to focus on the critical issue of ballistic-missile defense.

The U.S. Army, the service with primary responsibility for missile defense, began applying pressure for deploying an antiballistic-missile system (ABM) during the second term of President Eisenhower. Powerful industrial and congressional forces merged to promote the ABM system, which became known as Nike-X, the Army's project named after the winged Greek goddess of victory. Both Presidents Eisenhower and Kennedy resisted development of the Nike-X system but authorized continued research and development of ABM defenses. By 1967 about $3 billion had been expended on the development of ballistic-missile defense, and the military-industrial-political complex pulled out all stops in an effort to win approval for deploying the system. A sidelight on the issue reveals how this complex appealed to the speculative interest of many Americans. The following advertisement appeared in *The New York Times:*

Nike-X
$30 Billion for Whom?

f the U.S. deploys its Nike-X defense, $30 billion could flow into certain electronics, missile, and computer companies. The impact would be enormous.

About $2.4 billion has already been spent on Nike-X development. Some companies are benefiting from this spending now, are likely to continue benefiting even if the program remains in the R&D stage, and could profit handsomely if a full-scale program is approved.

Arthur Wiesenberger & Co., stockbrokers who paid for the ad, invited readers to mail in five dollars for a 24-page special report on nine U.S. companies apt to reap the most profits from Nike-X. Investments in defense stocks thus bring even more Americans into the embrace of the weapons culture than the number of aerospace employees.

No sooner had Defense Secretary McNamara announced that he had capitulated to the Nike-X pressure groups, by deciding to deploy a "thin" ABM defense ($5 billion), than the weapons cultists began demanding a "thick" ($40 billion) system. We shall in due course examine the merits of ballistic-missile defense, but here we stress the significance of venturing into a whole new domain of weaponry and accelerating the arms race. In pressing for greater national defense efforts, the military-industrial-political complex takes advantage of the fact that military technology is today largely incomprehensible to the average, or even not-so-average, layman. As University of Chicago's Prof. Hans J. Morgenthau observed shortly after the Nike-X decision, "The great issues of nuclear strategy, for instance, cannot even be the object of meaningful debate, whether in Congress or among the people at large, because there can be no competent judgment without meaningful knowledge. Thus the great national decisions of life and death are rendered by technological elites, and both the Congress and the people at large retain little more than the illusion of making the decisions which the theory of democracy supposes them to make." Professor Morgenthau's observation would subordinate democratic decision-making to elitist circles, and it is therefore of the greatest importance that national decisions on such matters as a $40 billion Nike-X system be made on the basis of public discussion.

The tragedy of the U.S. decision to deploy a "thin" Nike-X system is that it jeopardizes the treaty that the United States was attempting to get with other nations in restraining the proliferation of nuclear weapons to nonnuclear powers. It was well summed up by presidential assistant Walt W. Rostow in remarks he made early in 1967: "We are all actively trying to find the terms for a non-proliferation agreement; and the emergence of an anti-ballistic-missile defense for Moscow has posed for the United States and the Soviet Union the question of whether the nuclear arms race shall be brought under control or go into a vast and expensive round of escalation on both sides with respect to both offensive and defensive weapons."

If the United States is incapable of applying restraints to its own weapons industry, then what hope is there that other nations will be less aggressive in pursuit of national security? As will be shown in subsequent chapters the United States has overreacted to foreign threats, building up military strength to fill fictitious "gaps" and in the process creating a weapons culture that threatens to encage the nation.

APPENDIX I

Military Prime Contract Awards by State
NET VALUE OF MILITARY PROCUREMENT ACTIONS
FOR SUPPLIES, SERVICES AND CONSTRUCTION[a]
Fiscal Years 1958–1967
Source: Dept. of Defense
(Amounts in Thousands)

State		1958	1959	1960	1961	1962
TOTAL U. S.	Rank	$22,752,260	$23,902,014	$22,462,217	$25,304,677	$27,800,407
NOT DISTRIBUTED BY STATE		1,743,447	1,925,278	2,055,411	2,192,231	2,761,717
STATE TOTALS		21,008,813	21,976,736	20,406,806	22,112,446	25,038,690
Alabama	28	163,220	138,175	103,371	105,564	154,419
Alaska	33	105,931	121,714	78,649	91,797	63,320
Arizona	26	189,314	23,8989	168,974	244,837	152,951
Arkansas	43	31,562	16,012	10,891	46,586	84,798
California	1	4,457,666	5,282,659	4,839,252	5,276,760	5,993,244
Colorado	19	205,470	252,476	246,749	465,904	565,279
Connecticut	4	897,283	920,309	838,535	1,018,500	1,213,067
Delaware	41	127,021	62,136	53,352	28,180	47,197
District of Columbia	27	84,573	98,477	95,499	149,551	181,954
Florida	13	308,891	404,663	489,803	492,654	645,478
Georgia	16	323,086	270,821	177,924	300,529	337,478
Hawaii	44	35,821	36,742	48,971	26,916	31,875
Idaho	50	12,050	9,270	46,630	14,131	26,121
Illinois	14	577,329	490,760	385,053	437,250	531,008
Indiana	15	421,046	388,990	310,632	353,202	571,184
Iowa	29	106,199	155,423	147,443	126,819	179,153
Kansas	17	1,169,464	450,204	573,563	538,687	393,507
Kentucky	42	34,422	39,411	32,741	45,778	43,510
Louisiana	22	141,863	151,486	197,157	139,336	244,036
Maine	37	87,237	116,751	32,216	96,977	79,585
Maryland	12	472,275	509,160	515,887	527,591	469,491
Massachusetts	6	734,514	1,150,522	1,070,436	1,072,370	1,310,055
Michigan	11	531,791	782,914	600,947	590,480	677,786
Minnesota	21	155,891	238,400	192,984	188,652	297,306
Mississippi	31	42,589	86,724	46,946	69,395	100,220
Missouri	9	498,744	571,505	336,668	337,500	545,553
Montana	45	35,184	27,712	27,058	94,538	31,264
Nebraska	39	47,025	62,589	71,034	51,123	53,172
Nevada	51	10,533	10,828	8,965	8,850	8,246
New Hampshire	35	33,634	41,313	72,272	104,589	58,926
New Jersey	7	884,589	918,916	1,274,664	949,737	1,063,096
New Mexico	36	77,397	72,743	77,707	63,540	60,729
New York	2	2,424,043	2,408,734	2,377,522	2,642,803	2,668,744
North Carolina	20	329,537	321,272	172,899	237,196	268,990
North Dakota	40	19,558	17,416	8,683	12,980	99,627
Ohio	5	1,007,230	1,303,556	907,068	1,004,245	1,129,017
Oklahoma	30	173,880	134,562	146,519	123,433	135,825
Oregon	46	27,917	31,486	23,963	27,626	46,129
Pennsylvania	8	700,262	684,331	671,314	804,389	952,058
Rhode Island	38	24,174	27,478	26,081	25,292	57,966
South Carolina	34	57,654	38,323	31,314	40,804	65,212
South Dakota	47	13,099	12,315	43,591	27,626	112,682
Tennessee	25	80,489	106,096	109,396	144,069	183,794
Texas	3	1,446,482	1,304,740	1,138,026	1,138,471	1,006,253
Utah	23	76,391	174,550	176,394	349,611	298,596
Vermont	49	17,895	13,645	18,746	16,176	16,421
Virginia	18	220,947	292,576	422,164	505,158	446,183
Washington	10	1,202,354	961,238	715,087	646,359	921,115
West Virginia	32	15,997	89,154	36,098	61,884	133,782
Wisconsin	24	161,190	168,221	167,214	221,749	258,735
Wyoming	48	6,100	41,239	41,754	24,252	22,252

1963	1964	1965	1966	1967	10-Yr. Total	
$28,107,882	$27,470,379	$26,631,132	$35,713,061	$41,817,093	$280,961,122	PERCENTAGE STATE TO U.S.A. (STATE TOTAL)
2,874,642	3,053,272	3,363,052	3,999,758	4,435,530	28,404,238	
25,233,240	24,417,107	23,268,080	31,713,303	37,381,663	252,568,248	
194,990	190,681	165,176	281,549	297,049	1,794,194	0.7
103,476	101,545	74,175	71,666	85,648	897,931	0.4
285,751	173,825	176,857	248,228	249,559	2,129,285	0.8
39,114	29,731	39,284	95,701	127,180	520,859	0.2
5,835,670	5,100,650	5,153,639	5,813,078	6,688,851	54,441,469	21.5
444,196	389,511	249,151	255,893	210,409	3,285,038	1.3
1,048,449	1,126,054	1,180,111	2,051,560	1,935,895	12,229,763	4.9
67,035	30,424	38,239	37,445	51,672	542,701	0.8
238,120	222,947	247,576	328,111	357,666	2,004,474	0.8
593,237	782,591	633,332	766,955	799,022	5,906,626	2.3
423,290	520,169	662,417	799,362	1,148,354	4,973,430	2.0
45,206	52,112	72,213	64,170	65,445	479,471	0.2
8,634	7,804	11,724	20,004	14,772	171,140	0.1
486,067	429,201	421,899	919,779	1,063,776	5,742,699	2.3
486,759	537,940	604,925	1,068,259	898,247	5,641,184	2.2
130,406	103,392	133,951	247,619	279,328	1,609,733	0.6
331,687	289,045	229,051	312,629	398,899	4,686,736	1.9
55,725	40,476	42,749	70,057	124,294	529,163	0.2
195,341	181,427	255,834	302,906	656,031	2,465,417	1.0
58,409	31,531	68,771	51,340	56,558	679,375	0.3
606,365	547,936	584,333	842,527	869,808	5,945,373	2.4
1,060,165	1,032,062	1,178,729	1,335,952	1,422,272	11,367,077	4.5
633,047	591,290	532,897	918,426	1,033,706	6,893,284	2.7
273,757	217,941	259,500	497,994	650,584	2,973,009	1.2
186,039	155,911	152,188	162,305	114,800	1,117,117	0.4
686,111	1,349,071	1,060,781	1,112,665	2,277,616	8,776,214	3.5
79,349	16,422	69,375	13,779	78,452	473,133	0.2
33,559	33,921	42,708	80,478	103,522	579,131	0.2
13,143	6,361	19,142	32,028	29,315	147,411	0.1
51,174	64,857	52,400	109,591	162,551	751,307	0.3
1,251,608	917,561	820,309	1,090,122	1,234,768	10,405,370	4.1
61,642	71,486	84,137	86,230	80,472	736,855	0.3
2,500,146	2,496,438	2,229,473	2,819,153	3,261,750	25,828,806	10.2
258,987	273,516	288,408	449,331	447,608	3,047,744	1.2
64,855	192,025	48,997	83,113	16,729	563,983	0.2
1,345,686	1,028,946	863,113	1,588,955	1,602,593	11,507,409	7.3
111,204	122,489	119,803	158,492	157,350	1,383,566	0.5
41,777	29,104	39,624	89,983	99,319	456,928	0.2
887,452	883,065	988,811	1,665,087	1,649,142	9,885,911	3.9
46,970	38,173	86,323	131,722	198,030	662,209	0.3
57,747	51,621	81,580	176,424	180,777	781,456	0.3
80,630	23,308	21,062	23,315	9,486	367,114	0.1
183,478	193,364	197,283	502,168	538,225	2,238,570	0.9
1,203,123	1,294,431	1,446,769	2,291,454	3,546,978	15,816,727	6.7
408,127	340,040	191,173	169,681	178,850	2,363,413	0.9
12,258	14,012	32,202	81,066	100,157	322,578	0.1
484,989	690,852	469,097	425,487	665,240	4,622,693	1.8
1,041,581	1,085,696	545,607	444,368	606,114	8,169,519	3.2
162,201	87,327	90,312	149,300	140,324	966,379	0.4
219,427	177,217	203,003	364,684	383,602	2,325,042	0.9
125,081	49,408	7,867	11,112	32,868	362,232	0.1

APPENDIX II

Prime Military Contracts Awards 1960–1967 to U.S. Companies
For firms totaling more than $1 billion in this 7-year period.

(Amounts in millions of dollars)

FISCAL YEAR	1961	1962	1963	1964	1965	1966	1967	7-yr. TOTAL	PERCENT OF TOTAL SALES
1 Lockheed Aircraft	1,175	1,419	1,517	1,455	1,715	1,531	1,807	10,619	88%
2 General Dynamics	1,460	1,197	1,033	987	1,179	1,136	1,832	8,824	67
3 McDonnell Douglas	527	779	863	1,360	1,026	1,001	2,125	7,681	75
4 Boeing Co.	920	1,133	1,356	1,365	583	914	912	7,183	54
5 General Electric	875	976	1,021	893	824	1,187	1,290	7,066	19
6 No. American-Rockwell	1,197	1,032	1,062	1,019	746	520	689	6,265	57
7 United Aircraft	625	663	530	625	632	1,139	1,097	5,311	57
8 American Tel & Tel.	551	468	579	636	588	672	673	4,167	9
9 Martin-Marietta	692	803	767	476	316	338	290	3,682	62
10 Sperry-Rand	408	466	446	374	318	427	484	2,923	35
11 General Motors	282	449	444	256	254	508	625	2,818	2
12 Grumman Aircraft	238	304	390	396	353	323	488	2,492	67
13 General Tire	290	366	425	364	302	327	273	2,347	37
14 Raytheon	305	407	295	253	293	368	403	2,324	55
15 AVCO	251	323	253	279	234	506	449	2,295	75
16 Hughes	331	234	312	289	278	337	419	2,200	u
17 Westinghouse Electric	308	246	323	237	261	349	453	2,177	13
18 Ford (Philco)	200	269	228	211	312	440	404	2,064	3
19 RCA	392	340	329	234	214	242	268	2,019	16
20 Bendix	269	286	290	257	235	282	296	1,915	42
21 Textron	66	117	151	216	196	555	497	1,798	36
22 Ling-Temco-Vought	47	133	206	247	265	311	535	1,744	70
23 Internat. Tel. & Tel.	202	244	266	256	207	220	255	1,650	19
24 I.B.M.	330	155	203	332	186	182	195	1,583	7
25 Raymond International*	46	61	84	196	71	548	462	1,568	u
26 Newport News Shipbuilding	290	185	221	400	185	51	188	1,520	90+
27 Northrop	156	152	223	165	256	276	306	1,434	61
28 Thiokol	210	178	239	254	136	111	173	1,301	96
29 Std. Oil of N.J.	168	180	155	161	164	214	235	1,277	2
30 Kaiser Industries	—	87	49	152	219	441	306	1,255	45
31 Honeywell	86	127	170	107	82	251	306	1,129	24
32 General Tel.	61	116	162	229	232	196	138	1,124	25
33 Collins Radio	94	150	144	129	141	245	202	1,105	65
34 Chrysler	158	181	186	170	81	150	165	1,091	4
35 Litton	—	88	198	210	190	219	180	1,085	25
36 Pan. Am. World Air.	127	147	155	164	158	170	115	1,046	44
37 F.M.C.	88	160	199	141	124	163	170	1,045	21
38 Hercules	117	182	183	137	101	120	195	1,035	31

u—unavailable.
* Includes Morrison-Knudsen, Brown & Root, and J .A. Jones Construction Co.
Source: Dept. of Defense, Directorate for Statistical Services.

APPENDIX VI
Total Federal Obligations to Federal Contract Research Centers Administered by Universities and Colleges, 1966

[Dollar amounts in thousands]

LOCATION AND NAME	Total Federal obligations 1966	Sponsoring agency	ADMINISTERED BY
Total	$931,402		
Alaska: Naval Arctic Research Laboratory	1,411	DOD	University of Alaska.
Arizona: Kitt Peak National Observatory	5,791	NSF	Association of Universities for Research in Astronomy, Inc.
California:			
Jet Propulsion Laboratory	230,091	NASA	California Institute of Technology.
Stanford Linear Accelerator Laboratory	50,969	AEC	Stanford University.
Navy Biological Laboratory	1,766	DOD	University of California.
Lawrence Radiation Laboratory	169,870	AEC	University of California.
Colorado: National Center for Atmospheric Research	11,791	NSF	University Corporation for Atmospheric Research.
District of Columbia:			
Center for Research in Social Sciences	1,808	DOD	American University.
Human Resources Research Office	2,752	DOD	George Washington University.
Illinois: Argonne National Laboratory	87,255	AEC	University of Chicago.
Iowa: Ames Laboratory	9,089	AEC	Iowa State University.
Maryland: Applied Physics Laboratory	52,491	DOD	Johns Hopkins University.
Massachusetts:			
Apollo Guidance Project	16,019	NASA	Massachusetts Institute of Technology.
Cambridge Electron Accelerator	6,130 / 3,517	AEC	Harvard University. / Massachusetts Institute of Technology.
Lincoln Laboratory	64,060	DOD	Massachusetts Institute of Technology.
New Jersey:			
Princeton Stellerator	6,556	AEC	Princeton University.
Princeton-Penn. Proton Accelerator	8,825	AEC	Princeton University. / University of Pennsylvania.
New Mexico: Los Alamos Scientific Laboratory	103,311	AEC	University of California.
New York:			
Brookhaven National Laboratory	64,407	AEC	Associated Universities, Inc.
Hudson Laboratory	4,673	DOD	Columbia University.
Pennsylvania: Ordnance Research Laboratory	9,597	DOD	Pennsylvania State University.
Tennessee: Oak Ridge Associated Universities	6,168	AEC	Oak Ridge Associated Universities.
Washington: Applied Physics Laboratory	5,145	DOD	University of Washington.
West Virginia: National Radio Astronomy Observatory	4,719	NSF	Associated Universities, Inc.
Wisconsin: Army Mathematics Center	1,390	DOD	University of Wisconsin.

Source: Adapted from NSF-67-14.

APPENDIX VII

Obligations by the Department of Defense for Research and Development at 100 Universities and Colleges Receiving the Largest Amounts, 1964

(Dollar Amounts in Thousands)

INSTITUTION NAME	STATE	RANK	DOD	ARMY	NAVY	AIR FORCE	DEF. AGENCY
Mass. Inst. of Technology	Mass.	1	46,819	3,965	18,807	21,928	2,119
University of Michigan	Mich.	2	14,736	5,413	1,284	4,966	3,073
Stanford University	Cal.	3	12,815	1,824	5,214	4,573	1,204
Columbia University	N.Y.	4	9,194	1,489	4,459	3,184	36
University of Illinois	Ill.	5	7,612	2,524	1,704	1,343	2,041
U. of Cal. Los Angeles	Cal.	6	6,871	397	5,221	1,106	147
U. of Cal. Berkeley	Cal	7	5,424	439	3,140	1,592	253
Univ. of Pennsylvania	Pa.	8	5,304	1,473	673	961	2,197
University of Texas	Tex.	9	5,281	571	3,502	1,208	0
Ohio State University	Ohio	10	5,256	466	253	4,185	0
University of Chicago	Ill.	11	4,615	774	1,702	1,374	765
Harvard University	Mass.	12	4,539	705	1,425	1,010	1,399
Carnegie Inst. Technology	Pa.	13	4,519	130	334	340	3,668
Cornell University	N.Y.	14	4,358	510	680	452	2,570
California Inst. of Tech.	Cal.	15	4,232	348	1,673	2,211	0
New York University	N.Y.	16	4,019	1,750	1,239	1,030	0
Illinois Inst. of Tech.	Ill.	17	3,852	2,069	352	1,431	0
University of Denver	Colo.	18	3,773	488	81	3,204	0
Johns Hopkins University	Md.	19	3,732	1,098	757	1,867	0
Princeton University	N.J.	20	3,709	561	1,863	1,285	0
Northwestern University	Ill.	21	3,461	332	843	722	1,564
Polytechnic Inst. Brooklyn	N.Y.	22	3,254	113	1,411	1,730	0
University of Maryland	Md.	23	3,089	1,001	210	1,324	514
Duke University	N.C.	24	2,946	2,341	169	436	0
Brown University	R.I.	25	2,746	325	647	389	1,385
University of Colorado	Colo.	26	2,709	2,163	152	394	0
University of Dayton	Ohio	27	2,643	0	0	2,643	0
U. of Cal. San Diego	Cal.	28	2,455	0	29	2,426	0
University of Miami	Fla.	29	2,174	467	1,605	102	0
New Mexico State Univ.	N.M.	30	2,157	1,546	343	268	0
University of Pittsburgh	Pa.	31	2,080	886	340	680	100
Syracuse University	N.Y.	32	2,046	337	382	2,327	0
University of Washington	Wash.	33	1,986	199	1,381	406	0
Purdue University	Ind.	34	1,981	477	10	694	800
Yale University	Conn.	35	1,813	274	530	1,009	0
Northeastern University	Mass.	36	1,685	98	12	1,575	0
Univ. of Southern California	Cal.	37	1,617	121	462	1,034	0
George Washington Univ.	D.C.	38	1,526	395	926	205	0
Univ. of N.C. at Chapel Hill	N.C.	39	1,441	211	74	605	551
Pennsylvania State Univ.	Pa.	40	1,214	381	89	744	0
Texas A. & M. University	Tex.	41	1,204	233	808	163	0
University of New Mexico	N.M.	42	1,199	0	150	1,049	0
University of Oklahoma	Okla.	43	1,193	533	36	624	0
U. of Wis. Madison	Wisc.	44	1,102	358	278	466	0
University of Iowa	Iowa	45	1,077	0	947	55	75
U. of Minn. Mnpls.-St. Paul	Minn.	46	1,076	0	764	312	0
Indiana University	Ind.	47	1,075	153	342	580	0
University of Virginia	Va.	48	1,030	295	643	92	0
Tufts University	Mass.	49	1,021	303	88	630	0

INSTITUTION NAME	STATE	RANK	DOD	ARMY	NAVY	AIR FORCE	DEF. AGENCY
University of Utah	Utah	50	1,020	333	69	618	0
Wentworth Institute	Mass.	51	979	0	0	979	0
Univ. of Minn. All Campuses	Minn.	52	967	0	0	967	0
University of Florida	Fla.	53	958	352	143	308	0
Okla. St. U. Agric. & App. Sci.	Okla.	54	924	119	111	694	0
Oregon State University	Oreg.	55	887	46	453	388	0
University of Rochester	N.Y.	56	877	314	152	411	0
Univ. of Rhode Island	R.I.	57	857	1	751	105	0
Texas Western College	Tex.	58	846	781	0	65	0
Stevens Institute of Tech.	N.J.	59	839	247	350	242	0
American University	D.C.	60	834	780	54	0	0
Lowell Technological Inst.	Mass.	61	748	79	0	669	0
University of Arizona	Ariz.	62	725	213	199	172	27
Western Reserve Univ.	Ohio	63	720	417	126	177	0
Utah State University	Utah	64	713	100	0	613	0
Georgia Institute of Tech.	Ga.	65	710	419	214	77	0
Catholic Univ. of America	D.C.	66	679	110	228	155	186
Boston College	Mass.	67	661	25	0	636	0
Georgetown University	D.C.	68	658	550	33	75	0
University of Cincinnati	Ohio	69	648	134	0	474	40
University of Hawaii	Hawaii	70	612	103	253	256	0
Florida State University	Fla.	71	607	81	134	392	0
Case Inst. of Technology	Ohio	72	594	71	197	326	0
N. Mex. Inst. Mining & Tech.	N.M.	73	554	0	540	14	0
Washington University	Mo.	74	552	235	160	157	0
Arizona State University	Ariz.	75	532	65	54	413	0
University of Puerto Rico	P.R.	76	531	502	29	0	0
University of Delaware	Del.	77	502	198	109	195	0
Rensselaer Poly. Institute	N.Y.	78	500	149	212	139	0
University of Missouri	Mo.	79	494	369	76	49	0
University of Connecticut	Conn.	80	469	340	0	129	0
Colorado State University	Colo.	81	446	297	95	54	0
Michigan State University	Mich.	82	428	145	71	89	0
Iowa St. U. of Sci. & Tech.	Iowa	83	424	213	0	151	0
Brandeis University	Mass.	84	422	253	30	139	0
University of Alaska	Alaska	85	402	80	74	248	0
Medical Col. of Virginia	Va.	86	386	157	45	0	184
Boston University	Mass.	87	383	150	32	201	0
Rutgers—The State Univ.	N.J.	88	379	158	89	132	0
St. Univ. N.Y. All Inst.	N.Y.	89	370	0	0	370	0
Tulane Univ. of Louisiana	La.	90	369	248	30	75	0
Ohio University	Ohio	91	368	0	15	353	0
Dartmouth College	N.H.	92	364	173	76	115	0
Yeshiva University	N.Y.	93	364	115	10	239	0
St. Louis University	Mo.	94	361	114	15	232	0
Univ. of N.C. St. at Raleigh	N.C.	95	344	113	67	164	0
U. of Cal. San Francisco	Cal.	96	343	297	46	0	0
University of Georgia	Ga.	97	327	0	13	134	0
University of Louisville	Ky.	98	325	315	10	0	0
U. of Cal. Riverside	Cal.	99	319	62	0	257	0
Emmanuel College	Mass.	100	312	0	0	312	0

Source: National Science Foundation Report 67-14 (July 1967).

APPPENDIX IX

Major U.S. Military and Foreign Assistance Programs*
*Data from Statistical Abstract of U.S. 1967 and Congr. Rec. pp. S14297-99 (1967).

AREA	NATION	Military Aid (1950–1967)	Foreign Aid (1946–1966)	TOTAL
		(in millions)		
Far East				
	Australia	$ 126	$ 37	$ 163
	Cambodia	87	256	343
	China, Republic of	2,492	2,150	4,642
	Indochina	710	*	710
	Indonesia	64	708	772
	Japan	898	2,587	3,485
	Korea	2,524	4,037	6,561
	Malaysia	24	35	59
	Philippines	378	1,151	1,529
	Thailand	667	384	1,051
	Vietnam	1,512	2,831	4,343
	Other	251	1,323	1,574
	Totals	$ 9,733	$15,499	$ 25,233
Near East				
	Greece	$ 1,489	$ 1,656	$ 3,145
	India	*	5,901	5,901
	Iran	1,037	687	1,724
	Iraq	47	47	94
	Israel	28	908	936
	Jordan	68	525	593
	Lebanon	30	86	116
	Pakistan	#	2,804	2,804
	Saudi Arabia	242	12	254
	Turkey	2,703	1,888	4,591
	United Arab Republic	—	1,106	1,106
	Other	23	1,191	1,214
	Totals	$ 5,667	$16,811	$ 22,478
Europe				
	Austria	#	$ 1,089	$ 1,089
	Belgium	$ 1,248	680	1,928
	Denmark	618	263	881
	France	4,233	4,042	8,275
	Germany	901	2,849	3,750
	Italy	2,290	2,793	5,083
	Luxembourg	8	—	8
	Netherlands	1,219	828	2,047
	Norway	897	236	1,133
	Portugal	323	162	485
	Spain	573	910	1,483
	United Kingdom	1,034	6,450	7,484
	Yugoslavia	696	2,009	2,705
	Other	209	1,193	1,402
	Totals	$14,249	$23,504	$ 37,753

AREA	NATION	Military Aid (1950–1967)	Foreign Aid (1946–1966)	TOTAL
		(in millions)		
Africa				
	Congo	$ 22	$ 277	$ 299
	Liberia	7	184	191
	Libya	32	208	204
	Morocco	41	497	538
	Other	12	1,459	1,471
	Totals	$ 114	$ 2,627	$ 2,740
Latin America				
	Argentina	$ 71	$ 377	$ 448
	Bolivia	19	374	393
	Brazil	271	1,892	2,163
	Chile	96	822	918
	Colombia	83	474	557
	Cuba	11	41	52
	Dominican Republic	19	224	243
	Ecuador	38	144	182
	Guatemala	12	165	177
	Mexico	7	457	464
	Nicaragua	10	78	88
	Paraguay	7	71	78
	Peru	107	282	389
	Uruguay	39	64	103
	Venezuela	97	189	286
	Other	38	597	635
	Totals	$ 925	$ 6,251	$ 7,176
Worldwide (Other)		$ 4,684	$ 2,595	$ 7,279
Grand Total		$35,372	$67,287	$102,659

* Not available, listed under other. # Classified.

APPENDIX X: Federal Expenditures for National Defense and Research & Development 1940–1968

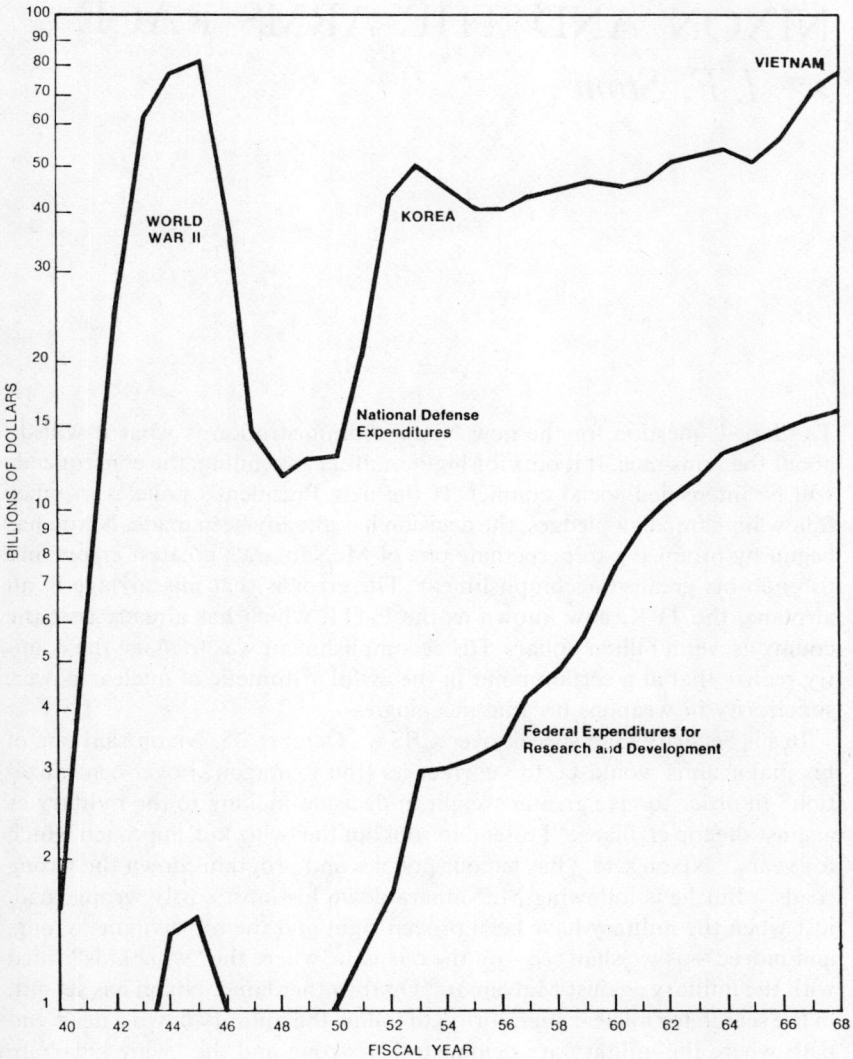

BILLIONS OF DOLLARS

VIETNAM

WORLD WAR II

KOREA

National Defense Expenditures

Federal Expenditures for Research and Development

FISCAL YEAR

NIXON AND THE ARMS RACE
✿ *I. F. Stone*

I

The No. 1 question for the new Nixon Administration is what it will do about the arms race. If it opts for higher military spending, the consequence will be intensified social conflict. If the new President's policies in office follow his campaign pledges, the decision has already been made. Nixon has begun by promising to perpetuate one of McNamara's greatest errors and to undo his greatest accomplishment. The error is that miscarriage of an airplane, the TFX, now known as the F-111, which has already cost the country several billion dollars. His accomplishment was to make the country realize that at a certain point in the awful arithmetic of nuclear power, superiority in weapons became meaningless.

In his Security Gap speech over CBS on October 25, Nixon said one of his major aims would be to "correct its [the Pentagon's] over-centralization" in order to give greater weight in decision-making to the military as against the top civilians. "I intend to root out the 'whiz kid' approach which for years," Nixon said, "has led our policies and programs down the wrong roads." But he is following McNamara down his most costly wrong road, just when the military have been proven right and the top civilians wrong, and indeed—as we shall see—on the one issue where the "whiz kids" sided with the military against McNamara. On the other hand, Nixon has set out, in the search for nuclear superiority, to follow the military down a dead-end path where the military are demonstrably wrong and the "whiz kids" are

SOURCE: I.F. Stone, "Nixon and the Arms Race: The Bomber Boondoggle," *The New York Review of Books* (January 2, 1969). Reprinted with permission from *The New York Review of Books.* Copyright © *The New York Review of Books.*

demonstrably right. To examine these two divergent courses is to see the trouble which lies ahead, on many different levels, for the new Administration and the country.

Let us begin with the TFX and with the speech Nixon made November 2 at Fort Worth, Texas. Fort Worth is where General Dynamics builds the TFX or F-111, the plane that was the focus of the longest and bitterest controversy of McNamara's years in the Pentagon. "The F-111 in a Nixon Administration," the candidate said at Fort Worth that day, "will be made into one of the foundations of our air supremacy." This pledge, which received too little attention, may prove to be the biggest blooper of the campaign, and the beginning—if Nixon tries to keep that pledge—of the biggest fight between the Nixon Administration and the very forces he might have counted on for a honeymoon, the Senate conservatives who specialize in military policy and who were most critical of McNamara in the TFX affair.

This Nixon pledge at Fort Worth will repay patient examination. It is startling that a man as cautious as Nixon should have made so unqualified a pledge to a plane which has become a tragic joke.

Last May, when the Senate Appropriations subcommittee on the Department of Defense was holding hearings on the budget for the fiscal year 1969, the Chairman, Senator Russell of Georgia, booby-trapped the Air Force Chief of Staff, General McConnell, with what appeared to be an innocent question on this plane, the F-111:

SENATOR RUSSELL: Would it be a very serious matter if one of these planes were recovered by any potential enemy in a reasonably good condition?

GENERAL MCCONNELL: Yes, we have quite a few things in it that we would not want the enemy to get.

SENATOR RUSSELL: That is mainly electronic devices.

GENERAL MCCONNELL: That is true of practically all the aircraft we have.

SENATOR RUSSELL: Of course the Russians got a B-29 when they were one of our allies. They fabricated a great many of them as nearly comparable to the B-29's as they could. I was hoping if they got a F-111 they would fabricate some of them as near ours as they could and see if they had as much trouble as we did. It would put their Air Force out of business.[1]

Neither General McConnell nor his civilian superior Air Force Secretary Harold Brown dared say one word in reply to Senator Russell's cruel jibe.

Russell's sardonic view of the F-111 is shared on both sides of the aisle in the Senate. On October 3, Senator Curtis of Kansas, a senior Republican, a member of the Aeronautical and Space Sciences Committee, delivered a devastating attack on the F-111 in the Senate, in which he said McNamara's "obstinacy" in producing the F-111, "will be a major problem that the new

Administration must face." Just one month later Nixon began to face it by pledging himself at Fort Worth to make this plane "one of the foundations of our air supremacy."

Either Nixon and his staff do not read the newspapers, much less the *Congressional Record* and the hearings, or Nixon like McNamara is determined to override military judgment and keep the billions flowing into General Dynamics for this jinxed plane. The difference is that when McNamara overrode the military, it was difficult for outsiders to judge so complex a technological controversy; especially when so many of the facts were still classified. Newspapermen like myself, who start with a strong bias against the military, assumed that McNamara was probably right. But 1968 is the year when the F-111 finally went into combat; the results have led many people inside and outside Congress to look at the old controversy with a fresh eye.

Nixon's reckless pledge was the only bright spot for the F-111 in the year 1968. The latest, 1969, edition of *Jane's Aircraft*[2] says succinctly,

> The 474th Tactical Fighter Wing at Nellis [Air Force Base, Nevada] was the first to be equipped with the F-111As [the Air Force version of the F-111]. Six aircraft from Nellis arrived at the Takhli base in Thailand on 17 March 1968 and made their first operational sorties over Vietnam on 25 March. Two were lost in the next five days.

The Forward, which went to press later, says "Three of the first 8 F-111A's dispatched to Vietnam were lost in a matter of weeks and the type was grounded shortly afterwards." No mention was made of these losses by Secretary of the Air Force Brown when he read his prepared statement to the Senate appropriations defense subcommittee in executive session last May 6. On the contrary he said the F-111 "is proving, in its tests and operational units, to be an outstanding aircraft." By then three of the original six had been lost, as may be seen from the following colloquy, where the reader will notice Secretary Brown's squeamish reluctance to use the word "lost."

> SENATOR RUSSELL: How many of these have we sent over to Southeast Asia?
> SECRETARY BROWN: We sent six and have sent two replacements.
> SENATOR RUSSELL: You have lost three, so you have five?
> SECRETARY BROWN: There are five there now.
> SENATOR RUSSELL: Do you have any information on these three that were lost? Do you know whether any of them fell into the hands of the North Vietnamese to be sent to Moscow along with all the secret equipment of the Pueblo?
> GENERAL MCCONNELL [Air Force Chief of Staff]: No, sir.[3]

In his Senate speech of October 3, Senator Curtis disclosed, "Thus far, 11 F-111 aircraft have crashed with a number of fatalities." He revealed that the wings were broken off one plane during a "static ground test" just six weeks before the first six planes were deployed to Southeast Asia, and that the week before his Senate speech another F-111A had crashed during a training flight owing to "a fatigue failure in the wing carrythrough structure."

If rightists treated Nixon and the Defense Department the way he treated the State Department in the days when he was a practicing witch-hunter, a proposal to make such a plane, with such a record, a foundation stone of American air supremacy would have been adduced as proof positive that the Pentagon had been infiltrated with Red and pinko saboteurs.

Last January the British Royal Air Force cancelled its order for fifty F-111K's. In March Congress ordered work stopped on the F-111B's, the version for the US Navy. On October 7, Senator Symington followed Senator Curtis with a speech suggesting that production of the F-111's for the Air Force also be stopped: He said "the series of crashes in the past five months" makes it doubtful that it will ever prove to be "a truly reliable airplane" and declared that its future should "receive highest priority upon convening of the new Congress."

The strangest discovery which turns up in studying Nixon's pledge at Fort Worth is that he and his staff were either unaware of, or ignored, his own famous "position papers." The one on "Research and Development: Our Neglected Weapon,"[4] which was made public in May, 1968, says of the F-111:

> The effort to transform the TFX (F-111) into an all-purpose all-service aircraft has created serious problems. Against military advice, the F-111 was selected as a superior, yet economical, weapons system . . . The aircraft were to cost approximately $2.4 million each. Now they are priced at more than $6 million each . . . In view of the recent decision that the F111B, the Navy version, is unacceptable, and a substitute aircraft be initiated, the final cost of the program will increase enormously coupled with years of delay. The program has resulted in the Air Force having a new aircraft that does not meet the original requirements . . . The F111B has been found unacceptable and the F111 Bomber version does not meet Air Force requirements for an advanced bomber in the 1970 time frame.

Nixon devoted one of his main campaign speeches to "the research gap." The Fort Worth speech showed his own research gap. Did he and his staff fail to read their position papers? Another of these papers, "Decisions on National Security: Patchwork or Policy?" is also in conflict with his Fort Worth speech. That paper says "a notable example" of how the top civilians overrode military judgment in the McNamara years was the original award of the contract for the F-111. "The contractor unanimously recommended by both the military analysts and the Weapons Evaluation Systems Group,"

it says, "was rejected." The rejected bidder was Boeing. The contractor
McNamara chose was General Dynamics. Nixon at Fort Worth affirmed
the same choice.

II

We are not dealing here with a minor item. General Dynamics is the
country's biggest weapons producer. A Defense Department press release
of November 18 on the nation's top ten defense contractors showed General
Dynamics as No. 1. In the fiscal year ending last June 30, it received $2.2
billion in arms contracts, or 5.8 percent of the total awarded in those twelve
months. More than 80 percent of the firm's business comes from the government.
The TFX represented the biggest single plum in military procurement.
The original contract was for 1,700 planes at a total cost of $5.8
billion, or about $3 million per plane. These figures have since skyrocketed.
This year, before the Navy contract was cancelled, the Pentagon admitted
the cost of the Navy version would be $8 million apiece and of the Air Force
version $6.5 million. As usual these, too, were understatements. Senator
Curtis disclosed that the contractor's cost information reports put the average
cost of the Navy plane at $9.5 million and that internal budgeting
projections at the Pentagon put the Air Force plane at $9.1 million each.
The original contract would have run up in the neighborhood of $15 billion.

Even with the cutbacks, more than $6 billion has already been spent and
at least between $3 and $4 billion more "will be added in succeeding years,"
Senator Curtis said, "if present Defense Department plans are carried to
completion." If Nixon keeps his word, they *will* be completed, perhaps
expanded. But if he tries to do so, he will almost certainly find himself
embattled with the Air Force buffs in Congress. For Curtis, Symington,
Russell, and McClellan speak for a group of Senators who feel that the Air
Force has been starved and stunted while all this money has been wasted
on the TFX. We are in the presence of a wide-open split not only between
the proponents of General Dynamics and Boeing respectively but within the
Air Force and the whole military-industrial complex.

History is repeating itself and it is the history of subordinating military
efficiency to moneyed and political pressures. The only difference is that
Nixon will find it harder than did McNamara to hide the realities, now that
the F-111 has finally begun to fly—and fall. When the Kennedy Administration
took over, General Dynamics was drifting close to receivership. It
lost $27 million in 1960 and $143 million in 1961. *Fortune* Magazine in
January and February of 1962 published a fascinating two-part study of its
misjudgments and its business losses by Richard Austin Smith. Smith said
its losses on its civilian plane business had been so disastrous that its
working capital had dropped below the minimum required by its agreement

with its bankers and that if the bankers had not reduced the minimum this "technically could have started the company down the road to receivership." Smith wrote that the output of the General Dynamics plant at Fort Worth in 1962 would be half what it was in 1961. *Fortune* said in its strangulated prose that General Dynamics would have to shut down its facilities "unless it gets contract for joint Navy-Air Force fighter." This was the TFX.

The TFX contract saved General Dynamics in 1962. The cancellation of the F-111 could ruin it in 1969. The effect of cancelling the Navy version of the plan was already reflected in a third quarter deficit, as of September 30, 1968, amounting to $1.51 a share compared with a net profit of $1.13 a share in the third quarter of 1967. *Moody's News* showed General Dynamics had to write off $39.6 million in contracts in 1968 as against only $12 million in 1967. Its net after taxes for the first nine months of 1968, after allowing for sales of assets which made the accounts look better than they otherwise would have, was only $9 million as compared with $36 million for the same period the previous year.

Standard & Poor's Outlook, October 7, 1968, said the stock of General Dynamics was "a speculation in the success of this F-111 program" and that "the most important price determinant over the near term will be developments in this trouble-plagued F-111 program." *The Value Line* October 18 said, "Since our July review the ever sensitive stock market has sold these shares down to a two-year low." It said that if the problems of the F-111 were not soon resolved, it was "vulnerable to further procurement cutbacks." This was the bleak outlook two weeks before Nixon's speech at Fort Worth. McNamara saved General Dynamics in 1962. Nixon promised on November 2 to save it again.

III

McNamara's error on the TFX, which Nixon is now taking over, is worth close study because it shows the diminishing relationship between military procurement and genuine considerations of defense. It demonstrates the growing extent to which procurement is determined by military-bureaucratic and industrial considerations. The prime determinants were to save the largest company in the military-industrial complex financially and to appease the bomber generals, who simply will not admit that their expensive toys have grown obsolete. Billions which could do so much for poverty are squandered to maintain these favorite Pentagon clients on the military relief rolls in the lush style to which they have become accustomed.

General Dynamics, behind its glamorous front, is almost as much a creature of the government as the Air Force. In 1967 some 83 percent of its sales were to the government. *Moody's* observes of the huge Fort Worth establishment, where Nixon gave so much solace to this peculiar form of free and private enterprise, that the "plant, including most machinery and equipment, is leased from the US government." The chief asset of General Dynamics seems to be its ability to wangle contracts out of the Pentagon.

The error in the TFX affair occurred on three levels, which have had varying degrees of attention, in inverse ratio to their importance. McNamara was wrong—so events seem to have proven—(1) in giving the TFX contract to General Dynamics instead of Boeing, (2) in insisting that the same basic plane be adopted for the diverse needs of the Air Force and Navy, and (3) in surrendering to the pressure of the Air Force for a new bomber and the Navy for a new missile weapons system to meet a non-existent Soviet bomber threat just so they could go on with their expensive bomber game.

The first, the least important, got the most attention in earlier years since it promised Republican and conservative Democratic critics of the Kennedy and Johnson Administrations a scandal. But the shock of the Kennedy assassination cut short the McClellan committee investigation. A key figure was Roswell Gilpatric, a corporation lawyer who has done two tours of duty at the Pentagon, the first as Under Secretary of the Air Force in 1951–3 and again as Deputy Secretary of Defense in 1961–64, returning on each occasion to the famous Wall Street law firm of Cravath, Swaine and Moore with which he has been associated since 1931. Through Gilpatric's efforts the firm became counsel for General Dynamics in the late Fifties and Gilpatric has combined his law work with activity in foreign and military policy in the Council on Foreign Relations and as a member of the Rockefeller Brothers Special Study project, which called for a sharp increase in military expenditures in January, 1958. In 1960 he was named as adviser on national security affairs by Kennedy during his campaign for the Presidency and after the election became Deputy Secretary of Defense, No. 2 man to McNamara at the Pentagon. There he played a major role in awarding the TFX contract. (See the Supplement to this article "Gilpatric and General Dynamics: Some Unanswered Questions.")

General Dynamics has always been adept at having friends at court. It chose for its president in the Fifties a former Secretary of the Army, Frank Pace. The $400-million losses of its Convair division during his incumbency make one wonder whether his chief qualification for the job was that he knew his way around Washington. Similarly it did not hurt General Dynamics to have its ex-counsel as No. 2 man in the Pentagon while it was fighting for the contract which could alone save it from receivership. Nor was General Dynamics hurt by the fact that Fred Korth, whom the Kennedy Administration had for some unfathomable reason made Secretary of the Navy, was a Fort Worth, Texas, banker, a past president of the

Continental Bank which had loaned money to General Dynamics, "and that Korth had kept an active, though not a financial, interest in the activities of this bank"[5] while in public office.

Korth told the McClellan committee "that because of his peculiar position he had deliberately refrained from taking a directing hand in this decision [within the Navy] until the last possible moment."[6] But it was "the last possible moment" which counted. Three times the Pentagon's Source Selection Board found that Boeing's bid was better and cheaper than that of General Dynamics and three times the bids were sent back for fresh submissions by the two bidders and fresh reviews. On the fourth round, the military still held that Boeing was better but found at last that the General Dynamics bid was also acceptable.

It was at this last moment that the award was made to General Dynamics. The only document the McClellan committee investigators were able to find in the Pentagon in favor of that award, according to their testimony, was a five-page memorandum signed by McNamara, Korth, and Eugene Zuckert, then Secretary of the Air Force, but not—interestingly enough— by Gilpatric. Senator Curtis charged in his Senate speech, October 3, that some months after the contract was announced in November, 1962, "a team of experts was assembled in the Pentagon to review the designs . . . The experts were directed to find strong points for General Dynamics and weak points for Boeing so the decision could be defended in Senate hearings."

During the McClellan committee hearings in 1963, Senator Ervin of North Carolina focused on another angle to this contract when he said to McNamara, "I would like to ask you whether or not there was any connection whatever between your selection of General Dynamics, and the fact that the Vice President of the United States happens to be a resident of the state in which that company has one of its principal, if not its principal office." The reference of course was to Lyndon Johnson, to Texas, and to Fort Worth. McNamara answered, "Absolutely not."[7] In the dissolute atmosphere of Washington there were few to believe such political virginity possible. When General Accounting Office investigators asked McNamara how he came to override military judgment, "The Secretary said that, after finding the Air Force estimates inadequate for judging the cost implications of the two proposals [i.e., General Dynamics' and Boeing's], he had made rough judgments of the kind he had made for many years with the Ford Motor Company." The most charitable comment is that the TFX, then, proved to be the Edsel of his Pentagon years.

Under normal circumstances one would have expected all this to be aired in the 1968 campaign. But the military-industrial complex plays both sides of the political fence, and the defense contractors are an easy source of campaign funds. Nixon not only kept silent but pledged himself to the very same plane. The same cynical charges made behind the scenes about the original TFX contract will no doubt be made again about Nixon's reaffirmation of it. The first point in favor of General Dynamics was and is its financial weakness. Boeing, with a better record for engineering and on costs, is in good shape; half its business is commercial, a testimony to its reputation. Why let the weaker company go down the drain? The TFX affair illustrates the survival of the unfittest in the military corporate jungle.

The second point in favor of General Dynamics was and remains political. General Dynamics is in Texas, a swing State with twenty-four electoral votes, and its biggest subcontractor on the F-111, Grumman, is in New York with forty-five electoral votes. Boeing would have produced the plane in Kansas with eight votes, which go Republican anyway, and in the State of Washington with nine. Nixon's November 2 pledge shows that any major new plane must show it can fly successfully through the electoral college. Its aerodynamics must be designed for a maximum number of votes. Nixon's pre-election speech at Fort Worth recalls two other comparable appearances there, one *opera buffa,* one tragic. The former occurred on December 11, 1962, a month after General Dynamics won the TFX contract, when Johnson made a triumphant visit to the plant at Fort Worth and was greeted by union members waving banners which said "LBJ Saved the Day" and "We're Here to Say Thanks to LBJ."[8] The other was the morning of November 22, 1963, a few hours before he was assassinated, when President Kennedy addressed a rally in Fort Worth and paid tribute to the TFX as "the best fighter system in the world."[9] For Johnson and Kennedy, as for Nixon, in the TFX contract electioneering and defense were inextricably mingled.

A key word in the TFX controversy was "commonalty." McNamara wanted a plane which could be used by the Air Force and the Navy in common. With the cancellation of the contract for the Navy's version of the F-111, the battle for commonalty between the two services was lost. But Nixon's pledge on the F-111 shows that commonalty still exists in defense politics. For Republican as well as Democratic administrations, what is best for General Dynamics is best for the country.

IV

This mention of "commonalty" brings us to the other two misjudgments involved in the TFX decision. One was to try to build one plane for many diverse Air Force and Navy missions. The other was to counter a Soviet bomber threat which does not now exist and is unlikely ever to come into being. With these misjudgments[10] we come to technological details which must become part of public knowledge if we are to understand the expensive and nightmarish nonsense in which the arms race has engulfed us.

President-elect Nixon, as we have seen, pledged himself to "root out 'the whiz kid' approach" to national defense. As it happens the "whiz kids" were as opposed to the TFX as Generals and Admirals to the idea of trying to build a common plane for both services. "Pressure within the Defense Department for a single sophisticated multimission aircraft [using the new swing-wing design] came from the Office of Defense Research and Engineering which was headed in the early 1960s by Harold Brown, the present Secretary of the Air Force," *Congressional Quarterly* reported last February 16. "Although the concept was opposed by the young systems analysts that Defense Secretary McNamara had brought with him to the Pentagon, they were not then in a position to conduct a running battle with Brown. At the time the Office of Systems Analysis was subordinate to the Pentagon comptroller, which was one level below Brown." Nixon to the contrary, this mistake might not have been made if the "whiz kids" had had more influence.

McNamara had been trying to cut down duplication in supplies among the three services, a source of enormous waste, and he accomplished substantial savings in this field. His critics in Congress say privately that to an automobile man, accustomed to mounting various kinds of cars on much the same chassis, the idea of using the same "chassis" in military planes must have seemed a natural. Indeed to an outsider there seems to be little reason why the same plane should not be used by the various services for the same type of mission. Why—for example—can't the Air Force and the Navy use the same dogfighter?

The trouble in the case of the TFX or F-111 is that the Air Force and the Navy had such diverse missions to be performed by the common plane on which McNamara insisted. It is being built for a tactical fighter, a long-range strategic bomber, a reconnaissance plane, and—until the Navy contract was cancelled—a new weapons system, a plane carrying a new type of missile.

The Navy wanted the plane to be light enough for a carrier but big enough to carry a special missile—the Phoenix—and a big load of radar equipment. Its Naval mission would be to loiter hour after hour over the fleet to protect it from a nuclear supersonic bomber attack; the radar would enable the plane to detect an incoming plane and hit it with the missile far enough away so that the fleet would be safe from nuclear blast and radiation. The Air Force wanted the plane to be able to fulfill a very different mission. It was to be able to fly at supersonic speed under the radar defenses around the Soviet Union and then, after unloading its nuclear bombs on target, make altitude swiftly enought to elude not only enemy ack-ack or fighter planes but the effects of the nuclear blast it had set off. To fit one plane to two such diverse purposes would seem to require the ingenuity of a Rube Goldberg. This particular mistake has been thoroughly debated, since it serves intra-service animosity. There's nothing the Navy hates worse than losing a battle to the Air Force.

A second level of misjudgment, the most basic of all, has hardly been discussed at all, at least in public. Here one is led to question the good sense of both the Air Force and the Navy. The Navy is still as full of bomber Admirals as the Air Force is of bomber Generals. They started the bomber gap nonsense in the Fifties and still suffer from the obsessions which the arms lobby exploits so skillfully. "In the early 1950s we were told the Russians were going to build thousands of supersonic bombers," Senator Symington commented ruefully last May during the Senate hearings on the 1969 defense budget. "They did not build any longe-range bombers of that type."[11] Symington was himself once the captive and spokesman of those inflated fears, as he was several years later of the "missile gap" campaign which he later helped to expose as fraudulent.

In the hearings last April on "The Status of US Strategic Power," which reflected the views and fears of those who favor a bigger arms budget, Chairman Stennis said of the present Soviet bomber fleet, "I have never looked upon these bombers as a serious threat to the US unless we just let our guard down completely. They are the same old bombers, the Bear and the Bison." There are the subsonic bombers whose appearance in Moscow in the Fifties set off the bomber gap scare. The Russians just aren't spending money on long-range supersonic nuclear bombers when the same delivery job can be done so much more cheaply and quickly by missiles.

When Stennis's Preparedness Subcommittee of Senate Armed Services filed its report October 4 on the US Tactical Air Power Program, it said "The F-111B [i.e., the Navy version of the F-111 armed with the Phoenix missile—IFS] was designed primarily for fleet air defense against a Soviet supersonic bomber. But that threat is either limited or does not exist." Yet the Navy, having got rid of the F-111B, is planning its new VFX-1 to carry a Phoenix missile for use against the same non-existent supersonic Soviet bomber attack. The Navy insisted in the fiscal 1969 hearings that the Phoenix-armed plane "is the only system that provides the Navy with an acceptable level of Fleet Air Defense for the 1970–80 era, particularly for any missile threat against the fleet."[12]

This assumes that the Soviets will play the game our way and build the supersonic nuclear bombers the Phoenix is designed to counter. In chess, when one sees the other side concentrating his forces in one sector, one attacks in another. But our Joint Chiefs of Staff do not seem to play chess. *Congressional Quarterly,* which has good sources in the Pentagon, reported last May 3 that many Navy aviators were hostile to both the F-111B and its successor, the VFX-1 project, for a Phoenix-armed plane. It quoted a

Pentagon source as saying the whole program was based on a false premise. It said Soviet doctrine envisioned the use of fighters, submarines, and missile-launching patrol boats instead of nuclear supersonic bombers for attacks on carriers and battleships. Obviously an attack would come where the other side can see we are least prepared. The Phoenix is likely to prove not only a waste of funds but an impediment to genuine defense by concentrating on a threat which does not exist now and is not likely to exist later.

V

The main Air Force mission for the F-111 is a reflection of the same bomber delusions, but on a larger scale. To see this in perspective one must step back and observe that we now have three major ways of destroying the Soviet Union. One is the ICBM, the intercontinental ballistic missile. The second is the submarine-launched nuclear missile, the Polaris. The third is the intercontinental bomber force of the Strategic Air Command. Any one of these three forces can itself deliver much more than the 400 megatons which McNamara estimates would destroy three-fourths of the Soviet Union's industrial capacity and 64 million people or one-third its population.

Of the three mega-murder machines, the only one which can be stopped is the bomber fleet. It's an expensive luxury, a toy on which the bomber Generals dote, and which the aircraft industry is only too happy to supply. High-flying bombers cannot get through the Soviet's radar and SAM (surface-to-air) missile defenses. So the F-111 is designed to duck low under Soviet radar defenses, drop nuclear bombs, and make a high fast getaway, all at supersonic speeds. The basic argument against the F-111 is that if we ever want to hit major targets in the Soviet Union, we would do so with missiles which can reach their targets in thirty minutes with fifteen-minute warning time instead of planes whose flight and warning time would be measured in hours. If we tried to use bombers first, they would only warn the enemy and provide plenty of time for retaliatory missile strikes against our cities. If these bombers were to be used for a second strike *after* a Russian attack on us, the bombers (if any were left) would arrive hours after the missiles, and there would be little if anything left to destroy anyway. The intercontinental bomber is a surplus and obsolete deterrent but $1 ⅓ billions is allocated to the F-111 in the fiscal 1969 budget, much of it for these bombers.

But this is not the end of this expensive nonsense. The military always assumes that the enemy will do what we do, that anything *we* produce *they* will produce. This is sometimes but not always true. The geographical and strategic situation of the Soviet Union is not the same as that of the United States; this dictates differences in weapons systems. In addition—no small consideration—the country which is poorer and has fewer resources to waste will be more careful in its expenditures. But we always estimate that the enemy will spend as prodigally as we do. This is how the bomber and missile gap scares originated. So we are spending billions to "keep ahead" of Soviet bombers and bomber defenses. We are also assuming that the Soviets will be as silly as we are and also build a fleet of F-111's to "get under" our radar defenses. So Congress has already embarked on another multi-billion-dollar program of building new radar "fences" and new types of interceptor planes to deal with these hypothetical Soviet F-111's.

To make all this plausible, the Air Force does its best to hide from the Congress the true facts about the Soviet air force. Twice during the past year Senator Symington, who feels that the billions spent on this bomber are diverting funds which could more sensibly be spent on new fighter planes, has asked Pentagon witnesses for the numbers of the various Soviet bombers. "Do you believe," he asked Dr. John S. Foster, Jr., director of Defense Research and Development, "that the Soviet Union poses a serious bomber threat to the United States today?" The answer was "Yes, Senator Symington, I do." Symington replied incredulously, "The Soviets have not built a bomber for years, except the Blinder—and the latter's performance is not as good as the B-58 which we abandoned. In spite of that we now have to spend billions of dollars defending against bombers also."

He then asked Dr. Foster to supply the Appropriations Committee with the numbers of each type of Soviet bomber. The numbers were deleted by the censor.[13] But if one turns to McNamara's final statement in the same hearings[14] he gives the number of Soviet intercontinental bombers as 155 as compared with our 697. These Soviet bombers are mostly the old subsonic Bear and Bison bombers, neither of which could possibly duck under US radar defenses in the way the F-111 is supposed to duck under the Soviet Union's.

Even the report on *The Status of US Strategic Power* filed last September 27 by the Senate's Preparedness Subcommittee under Senator Stennis, which argues for larger arms expenditures, says, "There is no evidence that the Soviets are proceeding with the development of a new heavy bomber and, should they elect to develop one, it is probable we would see indications of the program 3 to 4 years before the aircraft becomes operational."

To counter this, the Air Force sophists have come up with a new argument. When Senator Symington asked Dr. Foster, as head of Pentagon research and development, why they were planning new types of bomber defense against non-existent types of Soviet planes, Dr. Foster replied, "discouragement of Soviet aspirations to develop a more advanced bomber."[15] But why spend billions to discourage the Soviets from building a bomber they show no signs of building anyway?

Another favorite reason often used by the Air Force may be found in Air

Force Chief of Staff General McConnell's presentation to the Stennis hearings on strategic power last April. "A bomber force," the General said, "causes the Soviets to continue to develop bomber defenses rather than concentrating their expenditures just on missile defenses."[16] *So we waste money to make them waste money.* Though we are richer, this may be worse for us than them, because our planes are far more elaborate and expensive.

Since the Air Force thus admits that there is no sign as yet of a new supersonic Soviet bomber able to penetrate our existing defenses, why does it go on talking of a Soviet bomber "threat"? As usual, it turns out that this simple word has an unexpected meaning in the special language developed at the Pentagon. This prize item of military semantics may be found in the testimony of Air Force Secretary Brown to these same Stennis committee hearings. Dr. Brown was explaining to the committee that if Soviet anti-aircraft defenses were improved and we had to build in additional "penetration aids" to get past more efficient radar devices, we would have to build bigger bombs than we now have. "Otherwise," he said, "we will find ourselves carrying many penetration aids and comparatively few weapons." Dr. Brown went on to say there was "general agreement" at the Pentagon that such an advanced US bomber "probably will be needed at some time in the future" but just when would depend on "how fast and far the Soviet threat is likely to evolve." Then he explained, "By threat here we are principally talking about Soviet defenses against bombers."[17]

The threat, in other words, is not that they might be able successfully to attack us with their bombers but that they might build up their anti-bomber defenses to the point where we might not be able to attack them successfully with *our* bombers! It would be only a short step from this to defining aggression as the building of defenses to discourage an enemy attack.

The reductio ad absurdum is in a passage I found in the fiscal 1969 defense budget hearings before the House Appropriations Committee. Mahon of Texas, the able chairman of the defense subcommittee, was questioning Air Force officials about the Soviet bomber menace. Here is the colloquy which spills the whole and final truth about this costly nightmare:

MR. MAHON: Officials of the Department of Defense have not indicated to this committee that they think the Soviets will go very strong on the manned bomber. They will rely principally on the ICBM. Is that right?

GENERAL MCCONNELL [Air Force Chief of Staff]: That is the consensus.

MR. MAHON: The Air Force has a little different view?

GENERAL MCCONNELL: [Deleted by censor].

MR. MAHON: [Deleted by censor].

GENERAL MCCONNELL: [Deleted by censor].

MR. MAHON : How long have the Soviets had, Secretary [of the Air Force] Brown, to develop a follow-on[18] bomber?

SECRETARY BROWN: They have had ten years.

MR. MAHON: Have you seen any evidence?

SECRETARY BROWN: I see no evidence of it, Mr. Chairman. The Air Force view is at least as much a view that "they ought to have one" as it is "they will have one."[19]

Billions in contracts for new bombers and new bomber defense are threatened should the Russians stubbornly persist in not building a new bomber force. In extremity perhaps Congress might be persuaded to add the Soviet Union to our foreign aid clients and give them an advanced bomber force to keep the US aircraft business strong and prosperous. Or General Dynamics and the other big companies in the military-industrial complex might pass the hat among themselves and buy Moscow a new bomber. Should those old obsolete subsonic Bears and Bisons stop flying altogether, it would be a catastrophe for Fort Worth, a form of economic aggression in reverse. Ours—the rich man's strategy—is to make the Russians waste their resources by wasting ours. Theirs—the poor man's strategy—might be to strike a mortal blow at the arms business here by cutting their own expenditures to the minimum the balance of terror requires.

Nothing so terrifies the military-industrial complex as this notion of a *minimum* deterrent, as we shall see in our next installment, when we analyze Nixon's pledge to restore that crucial notion of "nuclear superiority," about which McNamara had finally succeeded in making the country see a little sense.

NOTES

1. Senate Appropriations Committee Hearings on the 1969 Defense Department budget, Part I, Department of the Air Force, p. 103. Released September 19, 1968.

2. *Jane's All the World's Aircraft, 1968–69,* edited by John W. R. Taylor, McGraw-Hill, p. 279.

3. Senate 1969 Defense Appropriations Hearings, *op. cit.,* pp. 102–3.

4. All these position papers have been reprinted in a one-volume compilation, *Choice for America: Republican Answers to the Challenge of Now,* published July, 1968, by the Republican National Committee, 1625 Eye St. N.W., Washington 20006.

5. *The TFX Decision,* by Robert J. Art, Little, Brown, p. 4.

6. *Ibid.,* p. 5.

7. *Ibid.*

8. Fort Worth *Star-Telegram,* December 12, 1962, quoted in McClellan Committee hearings on the TFX, Part X, p. 2658.

9. *Public Papers of the Presidents: John F. Kennedy 1963,* p. 887.

10. I venture to speak so dogmatically not only because of what has happened

this year to the F-111, but because among men at the Pentagon devoted to McNamara I have found no one who does not feel the TFX was a mistake.

11. 1969 Senate Defense Appropriations Hearings, Part V, p. 2664.
12. *Ibid.*, Part IV, p. 1426.
13. See p. 2362, 1969 Defense Department Budget Hearings, Part IV.
14. *Ibid.*, Part V, p. 2718.
15. *Ibid.*, p. 2719.
16. "Status of US Strategic Power," Preparedness Investigating Subcommittee of the Senate Committee on Armed Services, 90th Congress, 2nd Session, April 30, 1968, Part II, p. 169.
17. *Ibid.*, p. 179.
18. Air Force lingo for a new bomber.
19. House Appropriations Committee Hearings on the Fiscal 1969 Defense budget, Executive Session, February 26, 1968, Part I, p. 751.

THE NEW AMERICAN MILITARISM
General David M. Shoup

America has become a militaristic and aggressive nation. Our massive and swift invasion of the Dominican Republic in 1965, concurrent with the rapid buildup of U.S. military power in Vietnam, constituted an impressive demonstration of America's readiness to execute military contingency plans and to seek military solutions to problems of political disorder and potential Communist threats in the areas of our interest.

This "military task force" type of diplomacy is in the tradition of our

SOURCE: David M. Shoup, "The New American Militarism," *The Atlantic Monthly* (April 1969), 51–56. Copyright © 1969 by The Atlantic Monthly Company. Reprinted by permission of the publisher. This essay was written in collaboration with Col. James A. Donovan.

more primitive, pre-World War II "gunboat diplomacy," in which we landed small forces of Marines to protect American lives and property from the perils of native bandits and revolutionaries. In those days the U.S. Navy and its Marine landing forces were our chief means, short of war, for showing the flag, exercising American power, and protecting U.S. interests abroad. The Navy, enjoying the freedom of the seas, was a visible and effective representative of the nation's sovereign power. The Marines could be employed ashore "on such other duties as the President might direct" without congressional approval or a declaration of war. The U.S. Army was not then used so freely because it was rarely ready for expeditionary service without some degree of mobilization, and its use overseas normally required a declaration of emergency or war. Now, however, we have numerous contingency plans involving large joint Air Force-Army-Navy-Marine task forces to defend U.S. interests and to safeguard our allies wherever and whenever we suspect Communist aggression. We maintain more than 1,-517,000 Americans in uniform overseas in 119 countries. We have 8 treaties to help defend 48 nations if they ask us to—or if we choose to intervene in their affairs. We have an immense and expensive military establishment, fueled by a gigantic defense industry, and millions of proud, patriotic, and frequently bellicose and militaristic citizens. How did this militarist culture evolve? How did this militarism steer us into the tragic military and political morass of Vietnam?

Prior to World War II, American attitudes were typically isolationist, pacifist, and generally anti-military. The regular peacetime military establishment enjoyed small prestige and limited influence upon national affairs. The public knew little about the armed forces, and only a few thousand men were attracted to military service and careers. In 1940 there were but 428,000 officers and enlisted men in the Army and Navy. The scale of the war, and the world's power relationships which resulted, created the American military giant. Today the active armed forces contain over 3.4 million men and women, with an additional 1.6 million ready reserves and National Guardsmen.

America's vastly expanded world role after World War II hinged upon military power. The voice and views of the professional military people became increasingly prominent. During the post-war period, distinguished military leaders from the war years filled many top positions in government. Generals Marshall, Eisenhower, MacArthur, Taylor, Ridgeway, LeMay, and others were not only popular heroes but respected opinion-makers. It was a time of international readjustment; military minds offered the benefits of firm views and problem-solving experience to the management of the nation's affairs. Military procedures—including the general staff system, briefings, estimates of the situation, and the organizational and operational techniques of the highly schooled, confident military professionals—spread throughout American culture.

World War II had been a long war. Millions of young American men had matured, been educated, and gained rank and stature during their years in uniform. In spite of themselves, many returned to civilian life as indoctrinated, combat-experienced military professionals. They were veterans, and for better or worse would never be the same again. America will never be the same either. We are now a nation of veterans. To the 14.9 million veterans of World War II, Korea added another 5.7 million five years later, and ever since, the large peacetime military establishment has been training and releasing draftees, enlistees, and short-term reservists by the hundreds of thousands each year. In 1968 the total living veterans of U.S. military service numbered over 23 million, or about 20 percent of the adult population.

Today most middle-aged men, most business, government, civic, and professional leaders, have served some time in uniform. Whether they liked it or not, their military training and experience have affected them, for the creeds and attitudes of the armed forces are powerful medicine, and can become habit-forming. The military codes include all the virtues and beliefs used to motivate men of high principle: patriotism, duty and service to country, honor among fellowmen, courage in the face of danger, loyalty to organization and leaders, self-sacrifice for comrades, leadership, discipline, and physical fitness. For many veterans the military's efforts to train and indoctrinate them may well be the most impressive and influential experience they have ever had—especially so for the young and less educated.

In addition, each of the armed forces has its own special doctrinal beliefs and well-catalogued customs, traditions, rituals, and folklore upon which it strives to build a fiercely loyal military character and esprit de corps. All ranks are taught that their unit and their branch of the military service are the most elite, important, efficient, or effective in the military establishment. By believing in the superiority and importance of their own service they also provide themselves a degree of personal status, pride, and self-confidence.

As they get older, many veterans seem to romanticize and exaggerate their own military experience and loyalties. The policies, attitudes, and positions of the powerful veterans' organizations such as the American Legion, Veterans of Foreign Wars, and AMVETS, totaling over 4 million men, frequently reflect this pugnacious and chauvinistic tendency. Their memberships generally favor military solutions to world problems in the pattern of their own earlier experience, and often assert that their military service and sacrifice should be repeated by the younger generations.

Closely related to the attitudes and influence of America's millions of veterans is the vast and powerful complex of the defense industries, which have been described in detail many times in the eight years since General Eisenhower first warned of the military-industrial power complex in his farewell address as President. The relationship between the defense industry and the military establishment is closer than many citizens realize. Together they form a powerful public opinion lobby. The several military service associations provide both a forum and a meeting ground for the military and its industries. The associations also provide each of the armed services with a means of fostering their respective roles, objectives, and propaganda.

Each of the four services has its own association, and there are also additional military function associations, for ordnance, management, defense industry, and defense transportation, to name some of the more prominent. The Air Force Association and the Association of the U.S. Army are the largest, best organized, and most effective of the service associations. The Navy League, typical of the "silent service" traditions, is not as well coordinated in its public relations efforts, and the small Marine Corps Association is not even in the same arena with the other contenders, the Marine Association's main activity being the publication of a semi-official monthly magazine. Actually, the service associations' respective magazines, with an estimated combined circulation of over 270,000 are the primary medium serving the several associations' purposes.

Air Force and Space Digest, to cite one example, is the magazine of the Air Force Association and the unofficial mouthpiece of the U.S. Air Force doctrine, "party line," and propaganda. It frequently promotes Air Force policy that has been officially frustrated or suppressed within the Department of Defense. It beats the tub for strength through aerospace power, interprets diplomatic, strategic, and tactical problems in terms of air power, stresses the requirements for quantities of every type of aircraft, and frequently perpetuates the extravagant fictions about the effectiveness of bombing. This, of course, is well coordinated with and supported by the multibillion-dollar aerospace industry, which thrives upon the boundless desires of the Air Force. They reciprocate with lavish and expensive ads in every issue of *Air Force.* Over 96,000 members of the Air Force Association receive the magazine. Members include active, reserve, retired personnel, and veterans of the U.S. Air Force. Additional thousands of copies go to people engaged in the defense industry. The thick mixture of advertising, propaganda, and Air Force doctrine continuously repeated in this publication provides its readers and writers with a form of intellectual hypnosis, and they are prone to believe their own propaganda because they read it in *Air Force.*

The American people have also become more and more accustomed to militarism, to uniforms, to the cult of the gun, and to the violence of combat. Whole generations have been brought up on war news and wartime propaganda; the few years of peace since 1939 have seen a steady stream of war novels, war movies, comic strips, and television programs with war or military settings. To many Americans, military training, expeditionary service, and warfare are merely extensions of the entertainment and games of childhood. Even the weaponry and hardware they use at war are similar to the highly realistic toys of their youth. Soldiering loses appeal for some of the relatively few who experience the blood, terror, and filth of battle; for many, however, including far too many senior professional officers, war and combat are an exciting adventure, a competitive game, and an escape from the dull routines of peacetime.

It is this influential nucleus of aggressive, ambitious professional military leaders who are the root of America's evolving militarism. There are over 410,000 commissioned officers on active duty in the four armed services. Of these, well over half are junior ranking reserve officers on temporary active duty. Of the 150,000 or so regular career officers, only a portion are senior ranking colonels, generals, and admirals, but it is they who constitute the elite core of the military establishment. It is these few thousand top-ranking professionals who command and manage the armed forces and plan and formulate military policy and opinion. How is it, then, that in spite of civilian controls and the national desire for peace, this small group of men exert so much martial influence upon the government and life of the American people?

The military will disclaim any excess of power or influence on their part. They will point to their small numbers, low pay, and subordination to civilian masters as proof of their modest status and innocence. Nevertheless, the professional military, as a group, is probably one of the best organized and most influential of the various segments of the American scene. Three wars and six major contingencies since 1940 have forced the American people to become abnormally aware of the armed forces and their leaders. In turn the military services have produced an unending supply of distinguished, capable, articulate, and effective leaders. The sheer skill, energy, and dedication of America's military officers make them dominant in almost every government or civic organization they may inhabit, from the federal Cabinet to the local PTA.

The hard core of high-ranking professionals are, first of all, mostly service academy graduates: they had to be physically and intellectually above average among their peers just to gain entrance to an academy. Thereafter for the rest of their careers they are exposed to constant competition for selection and promotion. Attrition is high, and only the most capable survive to reach the elite senior ranks. Few other professions have such rigorous selection systems; as a result, the top military leaders are top-caliber men.

Not many industries, institutions, or civilian branches of government have the resources, techniques, or experience in training leaders such as are now employed by the armed forces in their excellent and elaborate school systems. Military leaders are taught to command large organizations and to plan big operations. They learn the techniques of influencing others. Their education is not, however, liberal or cultural. It stresses the tactics, doctrines, traditions, and codes of the military trade. It produces technicians and disciples, not philosophers.

The men who rise to the top of the military hierarchy have usually demonstrated their effectiveness as leaders, planners, and organization managers. They have perhaps performed heroically in combat, but most of all they have demonstrated their loyalty as proponents of their own service's doctrine and their dedication to the defense establishment. The paramount sense of duty to follow orders is at the root of the military professional's performance. As a result the military often operate more efficiently and effectively in the arena of defense policy planning than do their civilian counterparts in the State Department. The military planners have their doctrinal beliefs, their loyalties, their discipline—and their typical desire to compete and win. The civilians in government can scarcely play the same policy-planning game. In general the military are better organized, they work harder, they think straighter, and they keep their eyes on the objective, which is to be instantly ready to solve the problem through military action while ensuring that their respective service gets its proper mission, role, and recognition in the operation. In an emergency the military usually have a ready plan; if not, their numerous doctrinal manuals provide firm guidelines for action. Politicians, civilian appointees, and diplomats do not normally have the same confidence about how to react to threats and violence as do the military.

The motivations behind these endeavors are difficult for civilians to understand. For example, military professionals cannot measure the success of their indivudual efforts in terms of personal financial gain. The armed forces are not profit-making organizations, and the rewards for excellence in the military profession are acquired in less tangible forms. Thus it is that promotion and the responsibilities of higher command, with the related fringe benefits of quarters, servants, privileges, and prestige, motivate most career officers. Promotions and choice job opportunities are attained by constantly performing well, conforming to the expected patterns, and pleasing the senior officers. Promotions and awards also frequently result from heroic and distinguished performance in combat, and it takes a war to become a military hero. Civilians can scarcely understand or even believe that many ambitious military professionals truly yearn for wars and the opportunities for glory and distinction afforded only in combat. A career of peacetime duty is a dull and frustrating prospect for the normal regular officer to contemplate.

The professional military leaders of the U.S. Armed Forces have some additional motivations which influence their readiness to involve their country in military ventures. Unlike some of the civilian policy-makers, the military has not been obsessed with the threat of Communism per se. Most military people know very little about Communism either as a doctrine or as a form of government. But they have been given reason enough to presume that it is bad and represents the force of evil. When they can identify "Communist aggression," however, the matter then becomes of direct concern to the armed forces. Aggressors are the enemy in the war games, the "bad guys," the "Reds." Defeating aggression is a gigantic combat-area competition rather than a crusade to save the world from Communism. In the military view, all "Communist aggression" is certain to be interpreted as a threat to the United States.

The armed forces' role in performing its part of the national security policy—in addition to defense against actual direct attack on the United States and to maintaining the strategic atomic deterrent forces—is to be prepared to employ its *General Purpose Forces* in support of our collective security policy and the related treaties and alliances. To do this it deploys certain forces to forward zones in the Unified Commands, and maintains an up-to-date file of scores of detailed contingency plans which have been thrashed out and approved by the Joint Chiefs of Staff. Important features of these are the movement or deployment schedules of task forces assigned to each plan. The various details of these plans continue to create intense rivalries between the Navy-Marine sea-lift forces and the Army-Air Force team of air-mobility proponents. At the senior command levels parochial pride in service, personal ambitions, and old Army-Navy game rivalry stemming back to academy loyalties can influence strategic planning far more than most civilians would care to believe. The game is to be ready for deployment sooner than the other elements of the joint task force and to be so disposed as to be the "first to fight." The danger presented by this practice is that readiness and deployment speed become ends in themselves. This was clearly revealed in the massive and rapid intervention in the Dominican Republic in 1965 when the contingency plans and interservice rivalry appeared to supersede diplomacy. Before the world realized what was happening, the momentum and velocity of the military plans propelled almost 20,000 U.S. soldiers and Marines into the small turbulent republic in an impressive race to test the respective mobility of the Army and the Marines, and to attain overall command of "U.S. Forces Dom. Rep." Only a fraction of the force deployed was needed or justified. A small 1935-model Marine landing force could probably have handled the situation. But the

Army airlifted much of the 82nd Airborne Division to the scene, included a lieutenant general, and took charge of the operation.

Simultaneously, in Vietnam during 1965 the four services were racing to build up combat strength in that hapless country. This effort was ostensibly to save South Vietnam from Viet Cong and North Vietnamese aggression. It should also be noted that it was motivated in part by the same old inter-service rivalry to demonstrate respective importance and combat effectiveness.

The punitive air strikes immediately following the Tonkin Gulf incident in late 1964 revealed the readiness of naval air forces to bomb North Vietnam. (It now appears that the Navy actually had attack plans ready even before the alleged incident took place!) So by early 1965 the Navy carrier people and the Air Force initiated a contest of comparative strikes, sorties, tonnages dropped, "Killed by Air" claims, and target grabbing which continued up to the 1968 bombing pause. Much of the reporting on air action has consisted of misleading data or propaganda to serve Air Force and Navy purposes. In fact, it became increasingly apparent that the U.S. bombing effort in both North and South Vietnam has been one of the most wasteful and expensive hoaxes ever to be put over on the American people. Tactical and close air support of ground operations is essential, but air power use in general has to a large degree been a contest for the operations planners, "fine experience" for young pilots, and opportunity for career officers.

The highly trained professional and aggressive career officers of the Army and Marine Corps played a similar game. Prior to the decision to send combat units to South Vietnam in early 1965, both services were striving to increase their involvement. The Army already had over 16,000 military aid personnel serving in South Vietnam in the military adviser role, in training missions, logistic services, supporting helicopter companies, and in Special Forces teams. This investment of men and matériel justified a requirement for additional U.S. combat units to provide local security and to help protect our growing commitment of aid to the South Vietnam regime.

There were also top-ranking Army officers who wanted to project Army ground combat units into the Vietnam struggle for a variety of other reasons; to test plans and new equipment, to test the new air-mobile theories and tactics, to try the tactics and techniques of counterinsurgency, and to gain combat experience for young officers and noncommissioned officers. It also appeared to be a case of the military's duty to stop "Communist aggression" in Vietnam.

The Marines had somewhat similar motivations, the least of which was any real concern about the political or social problems of the Vietnamese people. In early 1965 there was a shooting war going on and the Marines were being left out of it, contrary to all their traditions. The Army's military advisory people were hogging American participation—except for a Marine Corps transport helicopter squadron at Danang which was helping the Army of the Republic of Vietnam. For several years young Marine officers had been going to South Vietnam from the 3rd Marine Division on Okinawa for short tours of "on-the-job training" with the small South Vietnam Marine Corps. There was a growing concern, however, among some senior Marines that the Corps should get involved on a larger scale and be the "first to fight" in keeping with the Corps's traditions. This would help justify the Corps's continued existence, which many Marines seem to consider to be in constant jeopardy.

The Corps had also spent several years exploring the theories of counterinsurgency and as early as 1961 had developed an elaborate lecture-demonstration called OPERATION CORMORANT, for school and Marine Corps promotion purposes, which depicted the Marines conducting a large-scale amphibious operation on the coast of Vietnam and thereby helping resolve a hypothetical aggressor-insurgency problem. As always it was important to Marine planners and doctrinaires to apply an amphibious operation to the Vietnam situation and provide justification for this special Marine functional responsibility. So Marine planners were seeking an acceptable excuse to thrust a landing force over the beaches of Vietnam when the Viet Cong attacked the U.S. Army Special Forces camp at Pleiku in February, 1965. It was considered unacceptable aggression, and the President was thereby prompted to put U.S. ground combat units into the war. Elements of the 3rd Marine Division at Okinawa were already aboard ship and eager to go, for the Marines also intended to get to Vietnam before their neighbor on Okinawa, the Army's 173rd Airborne Brigade, arrived. (Actually the initial Marine unit to deploy was an airlifted antiaircraft missile battalion which arrived to protect the Danang air base.) With these initial deployments the Army-Marine race to build forces in Vietnam began in earnest and did not slow down until both became overextended, overcommitted, and depleted at home.

For years up to 1964 the chiefs of the armed services, of whom the author was then one, deemed it unnecessary and unwise for U.S. forces to become involved in any ground war in Southeast Asia. In 1964 there were changes in the composition of the Joint Chiefs of Staff, and in a matter of a few months the Johnson Administration, encouraged by the aggressive military, hastened into what has become the quagmire of Vietnam. The intention at the time was that the war effort be kept small and "limited." But as the momentum and involvement built up, the military leaders rationalized a case that this was not a limited-objective exercise, but was a proper war in defense of the United States against "Communist aggression" and in honor of our area commitments.

The battle successes and heroic exploits of America's fine young fighting men have added to the military's traditions which extol service, bravery, and sacrifice, and so it has somehow become unpatriotic to question our military strategy and tactics or the motives of military leaders. Actually, however, the military commanders have directed the war in Vietnam, they have managed the details of its conduct; and more than most civilian officials, the top military planners were initially ready to become involved in Vietnam combat and have the opportunity to practice their trade. It has been popular to blame the civilian administration for the conduct and failures of the war rather than to question the motives of the military. But some of the generals and admirals are by no means without responsibility for the Vietnam miscalculations.

Some of the credibility difficulties experienced by the Johnson Administration over its war situation reports and Vietnam policy can also be blamed in part upon the military advisers. By its very nature most military activity falls under various degrees of security classification. Much that the military plans or does must be kept from the enemy. Thus the military is indoctrinated to be secretive, devious, and misleading in its plans and operations. It does not, however, always confine its security restrictions to purely military operations. Each of the services and all of the major commands practice techniques of controlling the news and the release of self-serving propaganda: in "the interests of national defense," to make the service look good, to cover up mistakes, to build up and publicize a distinguished military personality, or to win a round in the continuous gamesmanship of the interservice contest. If the Johnson Administration suffered from lack of credibility in its reporting of the war, the truth would reveal that much of the hocus-pocus stemmed from schemers in the military services, both at home and abroad.

Our militaristic culture was born of the necessities of World War II, nurtured by the Korean War, and became an accepted aspect of American life during the years of cold war emergencies and real or imagined threats from the Communist bloc. Both the philosophy and the institutions of militarism grew during these years because of the momentum of their own dynamism, the vigor of their ideas, their large size and scope, and because of the dedicated concentration of the emergent military leaders upon their doctrinal objectives. The dynamism of the defense establishment and its culture is also inspired and stimulated by vast amounts of money, by the new creations of military research and matériel development, and by the concepts of the Defense Department-supported "think factories." These latter are extravagantly funded civilian organizations of scientists, analysts, and retired military strategists who feed new militaristic philosophies into the Defense Department to help broaden the views of the single service doctrinaires, to create fresh policies and new requirements for ever larger, more expensive defense forces.

Somewhat like a religion, the basic appeals of anti-Communism, national defense, and patriotism provide the foundation for a powerful creed upon which the defense establishment can build, grow, and justify its cost. More so than many large bureaucratic organizations, the defense establishment now devotes a large share of its efforts to self-perpetuation, to justifying its organizations, to preaching its doctrines, and to self-maintenance and management. Warfare becomes an extension of war games and field tests. War justifies the existence of the establishment, provides experience for the military novice and challenges for the senior officer. Wars and emergencies put the military and their leaders on the front pages and give status and prestige to the professionals. Wars add to the military traditions, the self-nourishment of heroic deeds, and provide a new crop of military leaders who become the rededicated disciples of the code of service and military action. Being recognized public figures in a nation always seeking folk heroes, the military leaders have been largely exempt from the criticism experienced by the more plebeian politician. Flag officers are considered "experts," and their views are often accepted by press and Congress as the gospel. In turn, the distinguished military leader feels obliged not only to perpetuate loyally the doctrine of his service but to comply with the stereotyped military characteristics by being tough, aggressive, and firm in his resistance to Communist aggression and his belief in the military solutions to world problems. Standing closely behind these leaders, encouraging and prompting them, are the rich and powerful defense industries. Standing in front, adorned with service caps, ribbons, and lapel emblems, is a nation of veterans—patriotic, belligerent, romantic, and well intentioned, finding a certain sublimation and excitement in their country's latest military venture. Militarism in America is in full bloom and promises a future of vigorous self-pollination—unless the blight of Vietnam reveals that militarism is more a poisonous weed than a glorious blossom.

The opinions contained herein are the private ones of the author and are not to be construed as official or reflecting the views of the Navy Department or the naval service at large.

THE AMERICAN EMPIRE
❧ Ronald Steel

A great empire and little minds go ill together.
—EDMUND BURKE

If the British Empire, as Macaulay once said, was acquired in a fit of absent-mindedness, the American empire came into being without the intention or the knowledge of the American people. We are a people on whom the mantle of empire fits uneasily, who are not particularly adept at running colonies. Yet, by any conventional standards for judging such things, we are indeed an imperial power, possessed of an empire on which the sun truly never sets, an empire that embraces the entire western hemisphere, the world's two great oceans, and virtually all of the Eurasian land mass that is not in communist hands.

We are the strongest and most politically active nation in the world. Our impact reaches everywhere and affects everything it touches. We have the means to destroy whole societies and rebuild them, to topple governments and create others, to impede social change or to stimulate it, to protect our friends and devastate those who oppose us. We have a capacity for action, and a restless, driving compulsion to exercise it, such as the world has never seen. We have a technology that is the wonder of the world, an energy that compels us to challenge the obdurate forces of man and nature, and an affluence that could support whole nations with its waste. We also have a taunting sense of insecurity that makes it difficult for us to accept the limitations of our own remarkable power.

Although our adventure in empire-building may have begun without

SOURCE: Ronald Steel, "The American Empire," *Pax Americana* (New York: Viking Press, 1967), pp. 15–27. Copyright © 1967, 1970 The Viking Press, Inc. Reprinted by permission of the publisher.

regard to its consequences, it could not have occured at all had it not appealed to a deep-rooted instinct in our national character—an instinct to help those less fortunate and permit them to emulate and perhaps one day achieve the virtues of our own society. There was nothing arrogant in this attitude; indeed, it was heavily tinged with altruism. But it did rest upon the belief that it was America's role to make the world a happier, more orderly place, one more nearly reflecting our own image. We saw this as a special responsibility fate had thrust upon us. Standing alone as the defender of Europe, the guardian of Latin America, the protector of weak and dependent nations released from the bondage of colonialism, possessing the mightiest military force in history, an economy productive beyond any man had ever known, and a standard of living the envy of the world—we naturally became persuaded of the universal validity of our institutions, and of our obligation to help those threatened by disorder, aggression, and poverty.

We acquired our empire belatedly and have maintained, and even expanded, it because we found ourselves engaged in a global struggle with an ideology. When we picked up the ruins of the German and Japanese Empires in 1945, we discovered that we could not let them go without seeing them fall under the influence of our ideological adversaries. Struggling against communism, we created a counter-empire of anti-communism. This counter-empire was built upon the idealism enshrined in the charter of the United Nations, the altruism exemplified by the Marshall Plan, the cautious improvisation of the Truman Doctrine, and the military arithmetic of the NATO pact. It spread to Korea and the Congo, to Pakistan and Vietnam, and to a hundred troubled spots where inequality bred grievances, disorder, and instability. We came to see the world as a great stage on which we choreographed an inspiring design for peace, progress, and prosperity. Through American interventionism—benignly where possible, in the form of foreign aid; surgically where necessary, in the form of American soldiers —we hoped to contain the evil forces from the East and provide a measure of hope and security for the rest of mankind. We engaged in a kind of welfare imperialism, empire-building for noble ends rather than for such base motives as profit and influence. We saw ourselves engaged, as Under Secretary of State George Ball declared shortly after we began bombing North Vietnam, in "something new and unique in world history—a role of world responsibility divorced from territorial or narrow national interests."[1]

While it is true that we did not acquire our empire as spoils of war or from a desire for economic profits, "history," as Arnold Toynbee has observed, tells us that conquest and annexation are not the only means, or indeed the most frequent and most effective means, by which empires have been built up in the past. The history of the Roman Empire's growth, for instance, is instructive when one is considering the present-day American Empire's structure and prospects. The principal method by which Rome established her political supremacy in her world was by taking her weaker neighbors under her wing and protecting them against her and their stronger neighbors; Rome's relation with these protégées of hers was a treaty relation. Juridically they retained their previous status of sovereign independence. The most that Rome asked of them in terms of territory was the cession, here and there, of a patch of ground for the plantation of a Roman fortress to provide for the common security of Rome's allies and Rome herself.[2]

Unlike Rome, we have not consciously exploited our empire. In fact, our empire has exploited us, making enormous drains on our resources and our energies. It has not been the most efficient or the most profitable of empires. But then, unlike most empires of the past, ours was not acquired for efficiency or profit. It was acquired because we believe we have a responsibility to defend nations everywhere against communism. This is not an imperial ambition, but it has led us to use imperial methods: establishment of military garrisons around the globe, granting of subsidies to client governments and politicians, application of economic sanctions and even military force against recalcitrant states, and employment of a veritable army of colonial administrators working through such organizations as the State Department, the Agency for International Development, the United States Information Agency, and the Central Intelligence Agency. Having grown accustomed to our empire and having found it pleasing, we have come to take its institutions and its assumptions for granted. Indeed, this is the mark of a convinced imperial power: its advocates never question the virtues of empire, although they may dispute the way in which it is administered, and they do not for a moment doubt that it is in the best interests of those over whom it rules. A basically anti-colonial people, we tolerate, and even cherish, our empire because it seems so benevolent, so designed to serve those embraced by it.

But, many will ask, have we not been generous with our clients and allies, sending them vast amounts of money, and even sacrificing the lives of our own soldiers on their behalf? Of course we have. But this is the role of an imperial power. If it is to enjoy influence and command obedience, it must be prepared to distribute some of its riches throughout its empire and, when necessary, to fight rival powers for the loyalty of vulnerable client states. Empires may be acquired by accident, but they can be held together only by cash, power, and even blood. We learned this in Korea, in Berlin, and in Cuba; and we are learning it again in Vietnam. Whatever the resolution of that tragic conflict, it has once again shattered the recurrent illusion that empires can be maintained on the cheap.

Our empire has not been cheap to maintain, but we have never conceived of it as an empire. Rather, we saw it as a means of containing communism, and thereby permitting other nations to enjoy the benefits of freedom, democracy, and self-determination. This was particularly true in the vast perimeter of colonial and ex-colonial states which offered an enticing field for communist exploitation—and also for our own benevolent intervention. With the European colonial powers weakened and discredited, we were in a position to implement our long-standing sentiments of anti-colonialism. Opposed to the efforts of France, Britain, and Holland to regain control of their Asian colonies, we actively encouraged the efforts of such nationalists as Nehru, Sukarno, and Ho Chi Minh to win the independence of their countries.

However, once the war-weakened European powers finally did leave their colonies, we discovered that most of the newly independent nations had neither the resources nor the ability to stand on their own. With a very few exceptions, they were untrained for independence and unable, or unwilling, to exercise it in ways we approved of. Having proclaimed self-determination as a moral principle valid on every continent and in every country, we found ourselves saddled with the responsibility for some of its consequences. As a result, we stepped into the role left vacant by the departed European powers. In many of the new states we performed the tasks of an imperial power without enjoying the economic or territorial advantages of empire. We chose politicians, paid their salaries, subsidized national budgets, equipped and trained armies, built soccer stadiums and airports, and where possible instructed the new nations in the proper principles of foreign policy. We did this with good intentions, because we really did believe in self-determination for everybody as a guiding moral principle, and because we thought it was our obligation to help the less fortunate "modernize" their societies by making them more like ours. This was our welfare imperialism, and it found its roots in our most basic and generous national instincts.

But we also plunged into the economic primitiveness and political immaturity of the new nations because we saw them as a testing-ground in the struggle between freedom and communism, the cataclysmic duel that was to determine the fate of the world. Carried away by the vocabulary of the cold war, we sought to combat communism and preserve "freedom" in whatever area, however unpromising or unlikely, the battle seemed to be joined. Confusing communism as a social doctrine with communism as a form of Soviet imperialism, we assumed that any advance of communist doctrine anywhere was an automatic gain for the Soviet Union. Thus we believed it essential to combat communism in any part of the globe, as though it were a direct threat to our security, even in cases where it was not allied to Soviet power. Our methods were foreign aid, military assistance, and, where all else failed, our own soldiers.

But while this policy was a reasonable one in Europe, where there was a real threat of a Soviet take-over and where our allies shared our feelings about the danger facing them, it was less reasonable throughout most of the ex-colonial world. There the ruling elites were worried not so much by communism as by the real or imagined "imperialism" of the Western powers. They were not particularly committed to our advocacy of free speech and democracy, having never experienced it themselves, and they were totally mystified by our praises of capitalism, which in their experience was associated with exploitation, bondage, and misery. Insofar as they thought about communism at all, they could not help being drawn to a doctrine to which the Western powers were opposed. Western antipathy in itself was a major recommendation.

Most of these new nations have genuinely tried to keep out of the struggles among the great powers. They are anti-colonial and suspicious of the West by training and instinct. But they also have not wanted to compromise their neutrality by too close an association with the communists. Insofar as communist doctrine has seemed to offer a solution for their problems of political authority and economic development, they have been receptive to it—as a doctrine. But where it has been allied with Soviet power, they have uniformly resisted it, because it represents a threat to their independence. Most of the new nations, therefore, have tried to tread a path between the conflicting demands of East and West.

Some of them, of course, have been led by clever men who learned to take advantage of our phobias. They found that a threat to "go communist" would usually win large infusions of American foreign-aid funds, just as a threat to "join the imperialists" would inspire Russian counter-bribes. They learned, with the agility of Ben Franklin at the court of Louis XVI, how to manipulate our obsessions, seek out sympathetic ears in Congress and the Pentagon, and conjure up terrible happenings that were about to befall them. The twin doctrines of communism and anti-communism became tools by which they could secure outside help to build up their feeble economies and gain a larger voice in world affairs.

These nations cannot really be blamed for any of this. Being poor, they naturally wanted to secure as much outside assistance as they could, and played upon the anxieties of the great powers to do so. They thus served their own interests and pursued legitimate objectives of their foreign policy. What was less natural, however, was that we permitted ourselves to be manipulated by those who had so little to offer us. We allowed this because we feared that the new nations would fall under the influence of communism. Just as they were inspired by sentiments of anti-colonialism, so we were inspired by an equally powerful anti-communism. It provided the stimulus which led the United States to a massive postwar interventionism and to the creation of an empire that rests upon the pledge to use American military power to combat communism not only as a form of imperialism, but even as a social doctrine in the underdeveloped states. The foundation of this American empire can be traced back to the threat to Europe as it existed more than twenty years ago.

The American empire came into being as a result of the Second World War, when the struggle against Nazi Germany and imperial Japan brought us to the center of Europe and the offshore islands of Asia. With Russian troops on the Elbe and with the governments of Western Europe tottering under the strain of reconstruction, it seemed that only American power could halt the spread of communism. Consequently, the United States intervened to meet this new European danger, first with economic aid under the Marshall Plan, and then with direct military support under NATO. This was a necessary and proper response to a potential threat, although the emphasis on military over economic support has been sharply debated by historians. However, even before the Marshall Plan was announced, and two years before the NATO pact was signed, the United States laid down the guidelines for its intervention in Europe—and ultimately throughout the world—in the Truman Doctrine of March 12, 1947. Urging Congress to grant $400 million to help the Greek royalists fight the communist rebels, and to enable the Turks to defend themselves against Russia, President Truman declared: "It must be the policy of the United States to support free peoples who are resisting attempted subjugation by armed minorities or by outside pressure."

While such military aid may have been necessary to prevent Greece and Turkey from falling into the communist camp, the language in which the Truman Doctrine was cast implied a commitment far beyond the communist threat to those nations. Had it been confined to the containment of Soviet power, the Truman Doctrine would have expressed a legitimate American security interest. But by a vocabulary which pledged the United States to oppose armed minorities and outside pressure, it involved us in the containment of an ideology. In so doing, it provided the rationale for a policy of global intervention against communism, even in areas where American security was not involved. What was, as Kenneth Thompson has written, "a national and expedient act designed to replace British with American power in Central Europe, was presented as the defense of free democratic nations everywhere in the world against 'direct or indirect aggression.' It translated a concrete American interest for a limited area of the world into a general principle of worldwide validity, to be applied regardless of the limits of American interests and power."[3]

President Truman probably did not envisage the extreme ends toward which this policy would eventually be applied. While he argued that the United States could not permit communism to overturn the status quo by aggression or armed subversion, he put the emphasis on economic assistance and self-help. And he assumed that our efforts would be made in conjunction with our allies. What he did not intend, at least at the time, was unilateral American military intervention in support of client states threatened from within by communist-inspired insurgents. He did not suggest that the Greek civil war should be fought by American troops, nor did he seriously contemplate the bombardment of Yugoslavia, from whose territory the Greek communist rebels were being supplied. The language of the Truman Doctrine was sweeping, but its application was limited. It grew into a policy of global interventionism only with the later acknowledgment of America's imperial responsibilities.

Historically speaking, the Truman Doctrine was essentially an extension of the Monroe Doctrine across the Atlantic to non-communist Europe. Just as the Monroe Doctrine was designed to maintain the nineteenth-century balance of power between the New World and the Old, so its twentieth-century counterpart was meant to prevent communism from upsetting the political balance between East and West. Where the former used British sea-power to serve the security interests of the United States, the latter used American economic and military power to protect non-communist Europe and thereby defend American interests. The implied limitations of the Truman Doctrine were, however, swept aside by the communist attack on South Korea and the resulting assumption that the Russians were prepared to resort to a policy of open aggression. The extension of the Truman Doctrine to cover the Korean war set the stage for its expansion into a general commitment to resist communism everywhere, not only by economic and military support, but by direct American military intervention where necessary. The alliances forged by Dulles were based upon this premise, and even the war in Vietnam is a logical corollary of the Truman Doctrine.

The old limitations of spheres of influence, treaty obligations, and Congressional consent are no longer relevant in cases where the President should deem it necessary to launch a military intervention. As Dean Rusk told a Senate committee: "No would-be aggressor should suppose that the absence of a defense treaty, Congressional declaration, or United States military presence grants immunity to aggression."[4] As a hands-off warning by an imperial power, this statement is eminently logical. It does, however, take us into waters a good deal deeper than those chartered by the Truman

Doctrine. By indicating that the United States would not feel itself restricted even to the military treaties it has with more than forty nations, the Secretary of State implicitly removed all inhibitions upon a Presidential decision to intervene against communism wherever, whenever, and however it is deemed necessary.

Behind the warning of Secretary Rusk lies the belief that American military power is so great that the old considerations of national interest—which confined a nation's military interventions to areas deemed vital to its security—are no longer necessary. The growth of American military power —the enormous array of weapons, the awesome nuclear deterrent, the largest peacetime standing army in our history, and an economy that dominates the world—has apparently convinced many in Washington that "the illusion of American omnipotence," in D.W. Brogan's famous phrase, may not be an illusion. The old feeling of being locked in a closet with Russia appears to have vanished and to have been replaced by the conviction that America alone has world responsibilities, that these are "unique in world history" and justify a policy of global interventionism. If this is not an illusion of omnipotence, it might at least be described as intoxication with power.

Although we consciously seek no empire, we are experiencing all the frustrations and insecurities of an imperial power. Having assumed a position of world leadership because of the abstinence of others, America has not been able to evolve a coherent concept of what she wants and what she may reasonably expect to attain in the world. She has not been able to relate her vision of a universal order on the American model to the more limited imperatives of her own national interests. She is a territorially satiated power, yet plagued by terrible insecurities over her global responsibilities and even over her own identity. America has rejected the old tradition of abstinence and isolationism without having been able to find a new tradition that can bring her interests into line with her ideals.

One of the expressions of this insecurity has been the emergence of anti-communism *as an ideology,* rather than as a reaction to the imperial policies followed by the Soviet Union and other communist powers. This counter-ideology of anti-communism has been both internal and external, reflecting our anxieties about ourselves and about our position in the world at large. As an external anxiety, anti-communism arose from the frustrations of the early postwar period and the disappointments of a terrible war which brought a terrible peace. To possess a military power unequaled in human history, to have marshaled an atomic arsenal capable of eradicating an enemy in a matter of hours, to have no conscious political ambitions other than to spread the virtues of American democracy to less fortunate peoples—to experience all this and still not be able to achieve more than stalemate in the cold war has been difficult for many Americans to accept.

The transformation of adversaries into demons followed almost inevitably. Anti-communism as an ideology was a response not only to stalemate abroad, but also to the insecurities of life at home, where traditional values had been uprooted. To those whose sense of security had been destroyed by the extreme mobility of American life, who felt threatened by the demands of racial minorities for equality, and who were humiliated by the impersonality of an increasingly bureaucratized society, ideological anti-communism served as a focal point of discontent. It could not allay these anxieties, but it could explain them in a form that was acceptable to those who saw as many enemies within the gates as they did outside. The McCarthyism and the witch-hunts of the 1950s, which so debased American intellectual life and spread a blanket of conformity over the government, were a reaction to this insecurity, acts of self-exorcism by a people tormented by demons.

Plagued by domestic anxieties and faced with external dangers that defy the traditional virtues of the American character—an ability to organize, to solve problems, to get things done by sustained energy and determination —the American people have been deeply shaken throughout the whole postwar period. They have had to accept the frustrations of stalemate with Soviet Russia and learn to live in the shadow of atomic annihilation, where the very survival of America is threatened for the first time in her history. This is a situation which, after the traumas of the 1950s, we have now learned to accept with resignation, and even with a certain equanimity. But it is one which breeds deep-rooted anxieties of the kind expressed on the radical right. These frustrations conflict with the most basic elements of Americanism as a secular faith. To challenge this faith is to commit a kind of heresy, and it is as a heretical doctrine that communism has been treated in this country. This is comprehensible only if we accept the fact that Americanism is a creed, that, as a British commentator has observed,

America is not just a place but an idea, producing a particular kind of society. When immigrants choose to become Americans they are expected to accept the political values of this society, associated with the egalitarian and democratic traditions of the American revolution. As an immigrant country, perhaps only Israel is comparable in the demands it makes for the acceptance of an ideology as well as a territorial nationality. Consequently American patriotism is more readily identified with loyalty to traditional political values; . . . the reverence paid to the American Constitution and the basic political principles of the American revolution encourages the tendency to believe that all failures of the political system must be blamed on corruption, conspiracy or some external enemy. Communism has uniquely provided both an internal and external threat.[5]

Pampered by a continent of extraordinary riches, insulated from political responsibility in the world for longer than was healthy, her soil untouched by war for more than a century, spoiled by an economy which produces a seemingly inexhaustible wealth, flattered by an unnatural dominion over temporarily indigent allies, America has found it difficult to bring her political desires into line with her real needs. We think of solving problems rather than of living with them, and we find compromise an unnatural alternative to "victory." These attitudes are a reflection of our frontier mentality, of the cult of individualism, and of a national experience where success is usually the ultimate result of a major effort.

We have fought every war on the assumption that it was the final war that would usher in universal peace. We believed that every adversary was the architect of a global conspiracy, and that once he was overcome there would be "no more war." But every time we overcame an adversary, conflict continued, and we found ourselves confronted with a new adversary to take his place. The change of adversaries has not persuaded us to re-examine the theory, and we still remain chained to the belief in a global conspiracy (now directed from Peking) and the war to end all wars (now being decided in the jungles of Vietnam). We have become the victims of our own mythology: the myth of American omnipotence and the myth of a global communist conspiracy. In combination they have made it exceedingly difficult for us to evolve a foreign policy responsive to the real world we live in.

The decline of political ideology, the rise of a new Europe, the disintegration of the colonial system, the resurgence of China, the technological revolution, the population explosion, the break-up of the cold-war military blocs—these are the central realities of our time. Yet our diplomacy remains frozen in the posture of two decades ago and mesmerized by a ritual anti-communism that has become peripheral to the real conflict of power in today's world. We are in an age of nationalism, in which both communism and capitalism are ceasing to be ideologically significant, and in which the preoccupations of our diplomacy are often irrelevant. We are the last of the ideologues, clinging to political assumptions that have been buried by changing time and circumstance, a nation possessed of an empire it did not want, does not know how to administer, and fears to relinquish. We live in a time of dying ideologies and obsolete slogans, where much of what we have taken for granted is now outdated, and where even the political condition that has dominated our lives—the cold war—may now be over.

NOTES

1. George Ball, "The Dangers of Nostalgia," *Department of State Bulletin,* April 12, 1965, pp. 535–36.

2. Arnold Toynbee, *America and the World Revolution.* London: Oxford University Press, 1962, pp. 29–30.

3. Kenneth Thompson, *Political Realism and the Crisis of World Politics: An American Approach to Foreign Policy.* Princeton: Princeton University Press, 1960, p. 124.

4. Dean Rusk, statement to the Senate Preparedness Subcommittee, *The Washington Post,* August 26, 1966.

FREE WORLD EMPIRE

✤ Carl Oglesby and Richard Shaull

Even anti-Imperialists welcome an Imperial policy which contemplates no conquests but those of commerce.

—LONDON *Times,* 1900[1]

We [Americans] shall run the world's business whether the world likes it or not. The world can't help it—and neither can we, I guess.

—HOLROYD, IN CONRAD'S *Nostromo,* 1904

Neither America nor the Western tradition which America has brought to maturity will be rightly understood until one understands that free enterprise is ultimately a political theory, that it bases itself upon an ethical premise of conflict, and that its virtue system appropriately confers esteem and privilege not upon the humane (although humanity is not precluded) but upon the willful and relentless—the powerful.

Applied to international politics, these virtues demand imperialism, imperialism being most basically the forcible (however indirect) management of one state's political economy by another state.

But imperialism has many operational modes. The American world businessman may very well think of himself as a liberal, a liberator, a hardened anti-imperialist *cum* anticommunist. He points out to us that he has no flag of commerce and arms, assures us that he wants only the chance to do business, and feels no contradiction when he at once repledges his support for the holding and extending of the Free World.

It is the word "free," of course, which is so misleading. One supposes off hand that the Free World must be that part of the earth in which men enjoy civil rights and liberties. That these rights and liberties are of the Western liberal tradition more than of any other, that they are both more practiced and more practical in the West than elsewhere, and that their existence is intimately connected to the development of Western capitalism are all historically indisputable truths. The Free World is freer in this sense than the non-Western world. But we also observe that this Free World is considered to include more than the Western democracies. It includes Spain and Portugal, Mozambique and South Africa, Paraguay and Argentina, Thailand and Formosa. So, whatever its connotation, the freedom denoted by this term "Free World" must be different. It can only mean freedom of capital access: The Free World is the world economic area in which the American businessman enjoys greatest freedom of commercial maneuver. Simply add to this the observation that America is the *leader* of the Free World, and one has grasped the essentials of America's Free World imperialism. The Free World, full of special situations, un-uniform and continually in flux, is nevertheless at root the basically integrated zone of American economic hegemony. The Free World itself is the American Empire.

America's contribution to the steadily evolving art of Western empire is simple but profound. Almost haphazardly, America built an efficiency case against colonial imperialism. Colonies created a host of ugly and unnecessary problems—centrally, the problem of colonial nationalism, which always threatened to culminate in riot and rebellion and thus impaired the security of the economic control mechanisms. Much better than the idea of the imperial colony (defined by earth coordinates, rivers, mountain ranges, and racial and ethnic discontinuities) was the idea of the open market (defined by real and potential wealth, labor reserves, shipping and distribution networks, and so on). This idea relocates the center of imperial impulse (shutting off such fustian as "the white man's burden") and more sharply defines the dimensions of imperial victory. It sees cultures in terms of their systemic economic components and pays less attention to their political habits and geographical shapes. An imperfect example (imperfect because it finally worked itself out in nearly ritual militarism) is Japan's prewar doctrine of the Greater East Asia Coprosperity Sphere, in which China was seen not as a unitary geopolitical entity to be conquered whole, devoured by destiny, but rather as a specific uneven pattern of economic resources and potentials whose most strategic relationship was with other such systems. Economies were to be organized horizontally with other economies instead of vertically with their national cultural environment. Transnational economics replaces national politics.

In America's pragmatic and opportunistic revision of the forms of empire, the old-fashioned European colony or sphere of influence becomes a materials source and a market to be developed in concert with other sources and markets, often along the lines of a global specialization of labor. In an old and famous instance, China makes silk, Turkey opium; American traders monopolize Turkish opium, barter it for Chinese silk, and bring the silk to America.* Of the local political position of Turkey or China, it is important only that it not obstruct the orderly development of the systemized whole. The colony, an economic sphere whose boundaries are no longer seen as mainly territorial, becomes the site of an open, free-enterprise competition—which of course will be won by the leading economic power. For the idea of the nation, Free World imperialism substitutes the idea of the integrated global economic system. For the conqueror's idea of territorial boundaries, it substitutes the engineer's idea of interwoven economic components.†

America produced such a theory at least in part because she had come last to the table to find the bountiful places already occupied. Our half-century-old anticolonialism may have originated as a somewhat resentful demand for access to the imperial spheres already established (notably in China) by the European and Asian powers. The Open Door Policy affirmed the priority of our economics over their politics, a specific to American commercial requirements.‡

Free World imperialism responds to the problem of small-state nationalism by arguing in effect that collaborative native government is more stable than foreign overlordship, and that through the sophisticated use of economic pressure and inducement (sometimes called "education"), native

---

* Comecon, the East European response to the Common Market, is a bloc attempt to "rationalize" an international economy along these lines, one country producing the food, another mining the ore, a third refining the steel. This departed from the more autarkic model employed up to about 1955, and that departure is one of the reasons for Romania's difficulties with the U.S.S.R.: Romania has voiced a basic preference for national self-sufficiency over bloc interdependency.[2]

† Thorstein Vebelen's *The Engineers and the Price System* (Harbinger, 1963), first published in 1921, is an interesting and wieldy elaboration on the theme of economic systems engineering.

‡ And during World War II, as America continued to push for access to Europe's colonies, justifying this with the same open-doorist rhetoric, Roosevelt policy-maker William L. Clayton said: "As a matter of fact, if we want to be honest with ourselves, we will find that many of the sins that we freely criticize other countries for practicing [i.e., colonial protectionism] have their counterparts in the United States."[3]

governments can be persuaded to make all the correct decisions. The colonial governor and the Foreign Legion become simultaneously obsolete, there remaining no need to debase and infuriate native peoples with colonial status. That is, one of the saddest features of America's open-door, free-market, anticolonial, Wilsonian, Free World imperialism is that it preferred not to be imperialism. Like the wasp that masters but does not mutilate its prey with one well-placed paralyzing sting, America wanted the substance without the show, the riches without the act of overt plunder. Her wild anti-communism is some kind of evidence that she failed. The colonial governor is back, calling himself now an ambassador, and our Foreign Legionnaires wear green berets. But whether from naïveté or a very tall guile, we seem to have wanted a different outcome, an expansion confined to commerce, culturally unintrusive, even helpful to the host. That was a new idea. Compare it with the French attempt to Frenchify their colonies, to transplant French cultural forms at whatever expense to the native culture, with unsurprisingly disastrous results to the life of the colonized and the composure of the *colon*. As French Indochina's first civilian governor confessed in 1885, "We have destroyed the past and nothing has taken its place."[4] What France got for her trouble was a great deal of rubber at a very good price and a handful of superb Asian scholars; and transported back to that time, a modern American consultant might have pointed out that these prizes were available without the misguided effort to turn Hanoi into a kind of Paris.

But for all its pretenses of cultural and political nonintervention, American Free World imperialism has been fully as damaging and fully as predatory. The economic life of a culture cannot be changed without consequence to every other aspect of the culture. Money propagates. Western economic systems need Westernized economic infrastructures, a Westernized legal apparatus, a Westernized labor force, and ultimately a Western political bias. Commercial impact is total impact.

It is this same impact of West on East, so often a mauling of sophisticated but undynamic cultures, which the explainers of Free World imperialism represent as at root a healthy phenomenon. They explain over and again to the good American people, whom they apparently suspect of retaining a residual antipathy for injustice, that such social fissures as may agonize the "developing" countries are the entirely natural by-products of the "revolution of modernization" (or "rising expectations"), which is depicted as basically independent of external causes: a historical process which unwinds of itself as slumbering peoples come awake. It could hardly be clearer that this "modernization" is only a polite name for the rude, concussive impact of technological cultures upon the nontechnological. But official theories gloss over American responsibility for the dislocations induced by

American expansion, and the idea that the nearly ubiquitous traumatizing of the Third World might have something to do with a specific American cash profit is rarely even entertained. A representative expression of this viewpoint, the following passages are from Walt Whitman Rostow's famous address to the 1961 graduating class of the Army's Fort Bragg Special Warfare School (Rostow is President Johnson's chief foreign-policy adviser and probably America's leading Cold War theoretician):

> What is happening throughout Latin America, Africa, the Middle East, and Asia is this: Old societies are changing their ways in order to create and maintain a national personality on the world scene and to bring to their peoples the benefits modern technology can offer. This process is truly revolutionary. . . .
>
> Like all revolutions, the revolution of modernization is disturbing. . . . Men and women in the villages and the cities, feeling that the old ways of life are shaken and that new possibilities are open to them, express old resentments and new hopes. . . .
>
> This is the grand arena of revolutionary change which the Communists are exploiting with such great energy. . . . We Americans are confident that, if the independence of this process can be maintained over the coming years and decades, these societies will choose their own version of what we would recognize as a democratic, open society. . . .
>
> Thus, our central task in the underdeveloped areas . . . is to protect the independence of the revolutionary process now going forward. . . .
>
> The diffusion of power is the basis for freedom within our own society, and we have no reason to fear it on the world scene. But this outcome would be a defeat for communism. . . . [Communists] are driven in the end, by the nature of their system, to violate the independence of nations. . . . We are struggling to maintain an environment on the world scene which will permit our open society to survive and to flourish.[5]

The key elements of Rostow's thoroughly mainline vision are the following:

1. Tacit disavowal of Western responsibility for that "turbulence" that is caused primarily by the Western intrusion—commercial, ideological, military—into the East and South.

2. The claim that America's purpose is the creation of free, independent, and (what is not so obvious) *technological* societies. This is, of course, an inherently contradictory claim.

3. Repudiation of the possibility that "communism" (which, for Rostow, probably stands for any oppositionist political violence) can also be a nationalism. That is, Rostow's language presents us with that old familiar image of the Communist as a man without a country, someone who has always appeared from some other place, and whose allegiance always lies elsewhere. (Communists, he says, are "scavengers," and communism is "a

disease of transition.") What such a description has on its side is the theory of some Bolshevik ideologues, mostly the Trotskyists, that the proletarian revolution would be international (class above flag) and would have to result in the decomposition of the nation-state, a bourgeois institution. What it has going against it is about two hundred years of history. With the variously resolved American, French, Russian, Chinese, and Cuban revolutions behind us, we are obliged to conclude that popular revolutions, whatever their opening fusillade of rhetoric, are unfailingly nationalistic. The only genuinely internationalist (better, transnationalist) group in the modern world is what Marx called the ruling class; Veblen, the captains of finance; Mill, the power elite; and the organs of our popular culture, the jet set. Rostow pays attention to none of this. He is an inverted Trotskyist.*

4. Virtually explicit declaration that America shall be the sole judge of the permissibility of social change everywhere, that America confers upon herself (as Free World leader) all rights of preemptory intervention in the change process, and that America requires the ultimate emergence of "independent, modern" societies. Both American practice and ideology require us to assume that this means open-door economies. Thus, America demands and will only tolerate such "revolutions" as widen the Free World empire.

5. Insistence (a traditional theme) that the final emergence of open-door societies *is required for America's survival.*

The Holy Roman arrogance of this will grow only more suffocating if one reflects upon the harrowing inability of this judge, jury, and executioner America to solve her own internal problems. Worsening American racism, poverty, Big Brotherhood, and militaristic oligarchism confer upon the world a right to wonder about us. How can an America which cannot develop east Kentucky or pacify Harlem develop India and pacify Vietnam?

But we should push the question harder. The Rostovian thesis can be boiled down to two large claims; namely, that what he calls our "protecting the independence of revolutionary modernization" and what I call our Free World imperialism

---

* In his *Prospects for Communist China* (M.I.T. Press, Cambridge, 1954, pp. 27–28), Rostow takes on the problem, Why did the Chinese Communists prefer military coalition with Chiang's Nationalist forces against the Japanese invaders? Why did they not prefer continued civil war? With stroke after stroke, in an intellectual performance that strikes me as no less brilliant than bizarre, Rostow lays bare an immense Red dissimulation: They wanted coalition because Russia wanted Japan stopped, because they wanted Chiang to spend himself against the Japanese, because they wanted to seem patriotic to the people, because coalition offered propaganda channels, because it would allow them to extend their civil administration. For Rostow, it is not even a possibility to be named and dismissed that these Reds may also have been Chinese people who cared about China, and who for ordinary patriotic reasons wanted to hit the invaders with everything China could muster. For him, the Communist is a political Martian. Rostow is my favorite Cold Warrior.

1. develops the underdeveloped; and
2. promotes their freedom, meaning
    a) that their governments are independent, and
    b) that their people enjoy basic civil rights and liberties.

These are concrete claims and they can be concretely examined. What follows is, first, a pointillistic statistical sketch of the American corporation whose impact, for good or bad, is being felt by the underdeveloped countries; next, looking at a few of the countries considered to lie in the domain of the rescued and protected, we shall ask: Are their economies developing? Are their governments independent of other governments? Does the freedom of their people prosper, and is its growth being stimulated?

The American supercorporation is no longer defined mainly by its product. It combines in itself the basic functions that once distinguished finance and industry as separate spheres. It pulls together and coordinates the economic acts of capital accumulation and dispersion (banking), technological innovation ("inventors"), production (plant construction and management), distribution (middleman enterprise), and demand management (the free market). By persuasion and purchase, it has won the cooperation of the labor bureaucracies, whose corporate responsibility is to guarantee the stability of the nation's labor force. Between management and organized labor, there are no fundamentally divisive questions of values or aims; they are unequal members of the same corporate entity. With the active or passive support of labor and government, management coordinates centrally all operations in the source-to-user product stream, vertical integration being crucial for efficiency. Decision-making is scientific and centralized.

The supercorporation's immensity and power may be suggested by the following passage from *In Few Hands* (Penguin, 1965), Estes Kefauver's posthumously published record of his Senate committee's antitrust investigations:

In 1962 the 20 largest manufacturing corporations alone had $73.8 billion in assets, or about one quarter of the total assets of the United States manufacturing companies. In turn, the 50 largest companies held 36 per cent; the 100 largest, 46 per cent; the 200 largest, 56 per cent; and the 1000 largest, nearly 75 per cent.

Geared in directly or indirectly with the major financial and industrial centers of Europe, these giants inspired Development and Resources Corporation Chairman David E. Lilienthal (TVA director for Roosevelt, AEC director for Truman) to coin the now standard term "multinational corporation."[6] With the equally globalized big banks with which they are interlocked, the multinational corporations are the chief sources of American overseas investment capital.

The value of direct U.S. investment abroad, less than $25 billion in 1955, was about $50 billion a decade later and increasing at a rate of about $10 million a day.[7] Total U.S. foreign investment, direct and portfolio,* was about $130 billion in 1965, of which more than 30 percent was in oil.[8] Of the $50 billion total direct foreign investment, 60 percent invested in Canada and Europe; of the 40 percent invested in the underdeveloped countries, half is in Latin America.[9]

The multinational corporation does not merely export its products and money; it transplants itself. In 1965 about 2000 American firms were doing business abroad, and of their net foreign sales of $110 billion, only one fifth of that amount came from sale of goods and products shipped from the United States. Extreme instances of transplant occur in the automobile industry. In 1965 General Motors built 20 percent of its cars outside the United States, Chrysler 30 percent, and Ford 40 percent.[10]

Europe is apprehensive. The aggregate sales of Volkswagen, Fiat, Daimler-Benz, British Motors, and Renault are only two thirds of Ford's sales, only one third of GM's. U.S. firms control almost the entire electronics industry of France, produce 90 percent of her synthetic rubber, distribute 65 percent of her petroleum, and manufacture 65 percent of her farm machinery.[11] Louis Armand has said, "Unless Europe reacts and gets organized, we are condemning ourselves to industrial colonization."[12] He is echoed by Gaston Defferre: "The economic invasion by the United States is a clear and present danger. American economic power, the dynamic power of its big businesses and the size of their investments in Europe . . . are the beginning of the colonization of our economy."[13] German officials of government and industry react by urging the merger of European firms, especially in steel and cars, both on a national and continental basis.

The direction of the growth of American corporate control abroad is no easier to predict than its inner process is to describe, but Richard J. Barber, special counsel for the Senate Subcommittee on Antitrust and Monopoly, offers an expert's guess:

By functioning multinationally, American and other business corporations have effectively avoided the reach of the antitrust laws of any single country in which they produce or sell their wares. . . . Based on recent experience, 300 corporations will by 1975 control more than 75 per cent of all industrial assets.[14]

The overseas expansion of corporate America has the ardent support of the American government, if not of the French. The U.S. government cooperates in many different ways. For one, it operates the Agency for International Development, which *Forbes* calls "the principal agency

---

* Direct investments give the investor a voice, sometimes controlling, in the management of the enterprise. Portfolio investments usually do not.

through which the U.S. government finances business abroad. . . . AID distributes about $2 billion a year. Of this, 85 percent is spent in the U.S. for American products and raw materials."[15]* For another, the U.S. government helps capitalize and manage such Free World financial institutions as the International Bank for Reconstruction and Development (the World Bank), the International Finance Corporation, the Export-Import Bank, the Inter-American Development Bank, the Overseas Development Fund, and the International Development Association, all of which (but notably the World Bank and the Ex-Im Bank) exist to serve the international interest of the American-dominated multinational corporation either by the direct financing of certain ventures or, more importantly, by financing the development of that infrastructure—roads, railroads, dock, power plants—which private capital feels it cannot afford to build, cannot live without, and deserves to have.[18]

This expansionary corporation may or may not stimulate the growth of material prosperity and the advance of democratic values in the host countries; we shall look into that shortly. But there is no question that this expansion is highly profitable to the corporations themselves. Chase Manhattan Bank Chairman David Rockefeller insists that U.S. profits in Latin America are not usually great: "The United States investment in Latin America has fortunately been moderately successful [he puts it at about 13 percent], but it can hardly be called 'exploitative.' "[19] This is not an entirely lame dissimulation. Figures can be produced to serve his point. It is not at all easy to determine the absolute profitability of our overseas operations. One reason for this is that a variety of concealing accounting techniques are available to the imperial clerk. For a simple and basic example, imagine a corporation in which the home-based production unit buys its materials from the foreign-based extractive unit. Corporate management may direct the latter to keep its prices low since low book profits will result in local tax advantages, and in any case will be recouped at the production end.

But it is still possible to get a good general sense of the immense cash value of our corporations' foreign adventures. "In industry after industry," said *Business Week* in 1963, "U.S. companies found that their overseas

---

* For a different but complementary view of AID, consider this statement by D. A. Fitzgerald, former deputy director of the United States International Cooperation Administration: "A lot of criticism of foreign aid is because the critic thought the objective was to get economic growth, and this wasn't the objective at all. . . . The objective may have been to buy a lease, or to get a favorable vote in the UN, or to keep a nation from falling apart, or to keep some country from giving the Russians airbase rights, or any one of many other reasons."[16] AID also uses the public money to ensure American companies' overseas operations. Toward the end of 1965, AID issued its biggest single policy, $179 million, to guarantee International Telephone & Telegraph's Chilean expansion against losses from inconvertible currency, expropriation, war, and revolution.[17]

earnings were soaring, and that their return on investment abroad was frequently much higher than in the U.S. As earnings abroad began to rise, profit margins from domestic operations started to shrink. . . . This is the combination that forced development of the multinational company."[20] Department of Commerce figures show that in the period 1950–61 there was a direct American foreign investment outflow of $13.7 billion. In the same period, returned income was $23.2 billion, a profit of $9.5 billion.[21] A survey made by the First National City Bank concluded that "remitted income [i.e., repatriated profit] on private investment abroad is actually the largest single item of our international receipts apart from merchandise exports."[22] A British survey in 1961 showed that American companies doing business in England averaged a 17 percent return on their investment, twice as high as the average return in the United States.[23]

For profitability, the underdeveloped world is at least Europe's equal, more probably its superior. Standard Oil of New Jersey *reports* a 17.6 percent return on its Latin American investment and a 15 percent return on Eastern Hemisphere investments for 1962, compared with a 7.4 percent return on domestic.[24] Commerce Department figures show Americans putting $516 million (new investment and unreturned earnings) into Europe in 1956 and taking home $280 million. By 1961 the nearly 2-to-1 investments-earnings ratio had dropped toward 3 to 1: $1.5 billion new investment, $525 million returned earnings. Compare the figures for Latin America, remembering that the stakes here are the real wealth and real labor of Latin American people, not just so many numbers in a book: In 1956 we invested $500 million and returned a profit almost half again as big, $770 million, for a net capital loss to Latin America of $270 million.[25]

That cold, still statistic of profit and loss is a statement about someone's happiness and someone else's pain, the uneven qualities of the lives of men and women. It needs to be worked, mined, laid open. With some general sense of what the multinational American corporation is doing for itself, we move now to examine the condition of its hosts. Does the global expansion of the American commercial state develop the underdeveloped? Does it democratize the public life of man? Does it make for nations which, in Rostow's words, "stand up straight" and are "strong, assertive, and independent"?

Some cases.

Brazil stands first among Latin American recipients of U.S. military aid ($206 million through 1963), third in U.S. economic assistance ($172.6 million plus $1.4 billion in World Bank and Ex-Im Bank loans), and is only second to Venezuela in direct U.S. investment (more than $1 billion).[26] It is the biggest, most populated, and potentially richest of all the South American countries; in any long-term sense, the key to the economic and political development of the continent. It deserves more than a glance. Brazil's revolution has been fitfully pulsing since 1930, when Getulio D. Vargas of the Labor Party came to power, first as provisional president (1930–33), then as elected president (1933).[27] Attacked once from the left and three times from the right, he was finally overthrown in 1945 by a right-wing military junta which called itself democratic and revolutionary, reversed his moderate reformist policies, and brought on depressed wages, high joblessness, rising inflation—and more U.S. corporations. The 1950 elections returned Vargas to power, convinced more than ever of the need for national management of national resources, Brazilian ownership of Brazil. He created Petrobras (national oil) and Electrobras (power), and in August 1954, despairing of the struggle against what his farewell note called "the looting by international economic and finance groups," he killed himself.

After one year of routine dictatorship under Café Filho (more social decay, more foreign money) came the presidency of Juscelino Kubitschek, who founded the interior capital of Brasilia, a visionary's act, but who could not resist the further penetration of Brazil's economy by the strong northern interests. He was followed in 1961 by Janio Quadros, winner of the largest majority vote ever received by a Brazilian president. Quadros was a ramrod conservative. He put down hunger riots in the agony-rich northeast with the Fourth Army and student agitation with the police. But he was also a nationalist. He saw a Brazil which led the world in coffee exports, had more arable land than all of Europe, 15 percent of the world's forests, 35 percent of its iron deposits, and one of its highest hydroelectric potentials. That such a country was poor was a disgrace. That it should remain poor was a crime. Quadros moved to change Brazil. "Why should the United States trade with Russia and her satellites," he said, "but insist that Brazil trade only with the United States?"[28] He renewed relations with the U.S.S.R., made trade agreements with Communist countries, and treated Castro as that nationalist revolutionary whose motive was so easy to grasp from the vantage of the slums of Rio. The right-wing barons Adhemar de Barros and Carlos Lacerda were observed to cast dark intimate glances to the north.

In August 1961, Quadros went too far: a show of independence at the Punte del Este founding of the Alliance for Progress; the *Cruzeiro do Sul* for Che Guevara; vice president João Goulart in Peking on a trade mission; worst of all, a new tax proposal designed to strengthen the federal budget, stimulate investment in the northeast, and retain for Brazil's uses a larger share of the profits being removed from the country.

Within days the army held Quadros' "resignation" in its hands. But the Barros-Lacerda plans for an old-fashioned junta rule were resisted by the people, who demanded that succession of office be maintained and that

Goulart succeed to the presidency. Some now contend that at that moment the liberal millionaire Goulart might have broken the hold of the plutocrats once and for all. The army was divided and the people were behind him, peasants and workers, students and the middle class, leftists and nationalists together in the constitutionalist resistance called the *Legalidade*. But Goulart was indecisive. He chose to negotiate with the rightists and accept their demand for a weakened presidential office. After a year and a half of stagnation, a plebiscite restored full presidential power by a vote of 6 to 1. Goulart, however, ignored the mandate. His speeches blazed with the promise of social change, but not one of his reform proposals even reached the congress. The Bank of Brazil continued to print the watered money with which the monopolies financed their inefficiency; expensive coffee price supports were never touched. General Peri Belacuva used troops to break up popular demonstrations that called for nothing more than implementation of Goulart's own program; Belacuva was made chief of staff. More concessions were granted to American oil and mineral firms. Having tightened to 600 to the dollar at the time of the plebiscite, the cruzeiro fell to 1700 to 1.

Exasperated progressives and nationalists began to press harder for action, and perhaps Goulart was at last beginning to respond. Suddenly he was defying America on the Cuba question, disarmament, and trade. He spoke of suffrage for illiterates (half the people) and legal relief for the bedraggled and conservative Communist party. He revealed his socialist tendencies by expropriating some oil holdings (Brazilian, not American). On January 17, 1964, he committed again the most criminal crime of attacking American profits. "The new regulations," wrote Juan de Onis from Rio, "limit the legal remittance of profits abroad to 10 percent a year of the real foreign investment of a company in equipment and capital." "Regarded as hostile to foreign capital," the new profit-restriction rules were a response "to nationalist demands for higher controls on foreign investors." (*NYT*, January 18, 1964.)

This finally triggered a response from an intriguing São Paulo group, which *Fortune*'s Philip Siekman ("When Executives Turned Revolutionaries," September 1964) says had been growing since the middle fifties. Known either as the Paulistas (after their city) or the Mesquitas (after their leader Júlio de Mesquita Filho, owner of São Paulo's conservative newspaper, *O Estado de São Paulo*), the group consisted of important São Paulo businessmen like Paulo Ayres Filho (its founder and one-time head of the Bank of Brazil), Flavio Galvão, Luis Warneck, and João-Adelino Prado Neto (editor of the Mesquita paper). By 1964 the group had won the support of Adhemar de Barros, governor of São Paulo and commander of that state's forty-thousand-man militia; Carlos Lacerda, governor of

Guanabara; and the (World War II) Brazilian Expeditionary Force, which gave it access to important members of the military elite. Early in 1964, writes Siekman—perhaps spurred by Goulart's last-minute reformist vigor —the Mesquita group sent an emissary to ask U.S. Ambassador Lincoln Gordon what the U.S. position would be if civil war broke out. The emissary reported back that Gordon was cautious and diplomatic, but he left the impression that if the Paulistas could hold out for forty-eight hours they would get U.S. recognition and help.[29]

Event chased event. On March 14 the Brazilian right wing met to plan impeachment proceedings against Goulart (*NYT*, March 16, 1964). On March 15 Goulart called for new constitutional amendments to "free national energies crushed by the narrowness of an outdated economic structure that serves the interests of the privileged groups only" (*NYT*, March 16, 1964). On the same day, Latin delegates to the third-anniversary conference of the Alliance for Progress assembled in Washington. In the air were the still-unsettled Panama dispute, de Gaulle's triumphant trip to Mexico, rumblings of unrest in Colombia, new leftist electoral gains in Chile, China's about-to-be-announced major grain deal with Argentina, and, above all, what Tad Szulc called "the pre-revolutionary state" of Brazil (*NYT*, March 15, 1964)—pro-Goulart rioting in Brasilia, anti-Goulart demonstrations in São Paulo, and presidential candidate Kubitschek's promise to make the Alliance "wilt like a flower" (*NYT*, March 19, 1964). On March 16 President Johnson addressed the Alliance delegates: "But I now today assure you that the full power of the United States is ready to assist any country whose freedom is threatened by force dictated from beyond the shores of this [sic!] continent." On March 18 Assistant Secretary of State for Inter-American Affairs Thomas C. Mann conferred privately with U.S. Latin American diplomats, and Tad Szulc's front-page *Times* story the next day was headlined: "U.S. May Abandon Effort to Deter Latin Dictators." Szulc wrote, "Mr. Mann's views were considered as representing a radical modification of the policies of the Kennedy administration" (*NYT*, March 19, 1964). On March 19 State Department spokesman Richard I. Phillips came forward to deny a policy change, but seemed in fact to confirm it. Alluding to the Estrado Doctrine (diplomatic recognition based on control, not on politics), Phillips explained that "United States policy toward unconstitutional governments will, as in the past, be guided by the national interest and the circumstances peculiar to each situation as it arises"* (*NYT*, March 20, 1964).

---

* In fact, this had not been United States policy "in the past." At various times and for varying durations, Kennedy had suspended aid to and broken diplomatically with undemocratic governments in Argentina, Haiti, Peru, Guatemala, Ecuador, the Dominican Republic, and Honduras (*NYT*, March 19, 1964). Nor was Brazil the first instance of the Johnson turnabout. *The New York Times* reported on March 21 that the United States had renewed

It appears that all of Latin America immediately understood what it had heard. Brazilian Communists left for Mexico City; the idealistic governor of Rio Grande do Sul, Leonel Brizola (then a JFK admirer, today in exile), called on the people to prepare for a new *Legalidade*; and two weeks after the Johnson speech, on April 1, Goulart was almost ritualistically removed from office by the Barros-Lacerda-Mesquita combine. Less than twenty-four hours after the news of the *golpe* reached Washington, before it was even known that Goulart had left the capital, President Johnson wired "America's warmest good wishes" to the new government, which was shortly to consolidate around General Humberto Castelo Branco (elected president, April 11, 1964) and to proclaim its love of democracy and revolution.† On July 22 the Congress voted to extend Branco's term to March 15, 1967.

By November 1964, the United States had dramatized its enthusiasm for the new regime by a loan of $400 million over and above already programmed Alliance for Progress funds.[30]* Castelo Branco was quick to reveal his understanding and gratitude. On November 25, 1964, the government imprisoned one hundred former aides of the governor of Goias on a vague charge of subversion. Four months later, a new law made possible the lengthy imprisonment of individuals without declaration of offense or pressing of charges. During the same period, the government announced a new tax proposal designed to finance a 35 percent increase in military salaries. On October 27, 1965, Institutional Act. No. 2 was promulgated, banning all thirteen existing political parties and creating two new ones, one to serve as "loyal opposition."[31] Around the same time, government attempts to sanitize the faculty of the University of Brasilia provoked student-faculty protests, mass faculty resignations, and finally the virtual closing of

---

aid to Haiti, which Kennedy had suspended in 1962 (see discussion of Haiti). The new loan had been approved on March 9. To avoid an open policy reversal, the loan had been placed through the Inter-American Bank.

† Castelo Branco plays an intriguing game with the generals of the so-called hard-line right. In this game, the generals demand fascism, Castelo Branco answers that they go too far, everyone is impressed with Castelo Branco's courageous stand, and Castelo Branco proceeds to do essentially what the hard-liners wanted in the first place. As this is written, the Brazilian people are showing a surprisingly solid resistance; the activist students are beginning to enjoy more and more popular support; and within this turbulence other surprises unfold: The formerly reactionary Catholic hierarchy takes an advanced antigovernment stand, and Carlos Lacerda, of all people, comes out for land reform, nationalizations, democracy, and so on. Perhaps the ecclesiastical elite has really been converted to Christianity and perhaps they have saved Lacerda. But perhaps the oligarchic fugue only adds a new variation, orchestrates itself with new brass. There is at the moment no reason to believe that hard-liner General Costa e Silva's "election" will not take place as planned. (Since the forgoing was written, he has been named to a four-year term.)

* For the way $400 million can be shrunk to $40 million and then advertised as a cool billion, see note, page 255.

the university. On January 27, 1966, all ports were declared national security zones, which automatically made all dock strikes and slowdowns military crimes.[32]

A month after that, speaking in Belo Horizonte, Branco defended his government against the charge that it was dictatorial. "Say what they will," he declared, "the adversaries of the revolution . . . cannot negate the fact that here in Brazil we have in full force the two greatest and most basic expressions of a real democracy: the National Congress and freedom of the press."* Four months earlier, the day after the Second Institutional Act was decreed, Minister of Justice Juraci Magalhães is supposed to have met in Rio with a select group of Brazilian editors and publishers to explain the act's provisions and "complementary decrees." The meeting was private, if not secret, and certainly off the record; but a verbatim transcript was made and smuggled out, later to be printed in the organ of the Brazilian Christian underground movement, *Revolution.* Portions of the transcript follow.

Magalhães informed the press that the government would no longer permit:

(a) the publication of interviews with those who have had their mandates in office curtailed or their political rights annulled . . . ; *(b)* any threats to or provocations of the revolutionary government, such as referring to it as a dictatorship . . . ; *(c)* aid to subversion by any means or the publication of news that causes the people to oppose the government; *(d)* the publication of articles written by newsmen who have lost their political rights.

That last point provoked the following conversation:

DANTON JOBIM (of the *Última Hora*): Your excellency means that we cannot publish any pronouncements whatsoever made by people who have had their political rights suspended?

MAGALHAES: That's exactly what I said. You are an old friend of mine, but you'll be punished if you disobey. Is that clear?

JOBIM: Very clear.

ROBERTO MARINHO *(Globo)*: I do not agree that a newsman who has lost his political rights should be punished. I assume the responsibility—the full responsibility for everything that is published in my newspaper. And I shall vehemently protest if you try to make me fire some of the newsmen that work for me who have lost their political rights.

MAGALHAES: The law will be enforced. You and the newsman will be punished. You are both responsible.

MARINHO: Even if the article is not signed?

* This quotation and the material that follows are from the English-language edition of *Revolution,* the newspaper (mimeo) of the Brazilian Christian underground. Verification of the Magalhães dialogue is impossible for the obvious reason that those supposedly taking part in it would condemn themselves by confirming that it took place.

MAGALHAES: No. It is obvious that if he writes an unsigned article, we wouldn't know about it. The law means that these newsmen who have lost their political rights cannot use the press to provoke or threaten the government or to spread subversion. It's simply that.

MARINHO: Oh! Okay.

NASCIMENTO BRITO *(Jornal do Brasil):* How can we know if we're threatening the government? Does this mean we cannot comment on the acts of the government?

MAGALHAES: No. The government does not have the intention of restricting your liberty, but of preventing subversion. We have a criterion by which to decide what constitutes provocation, and we will adhere to it strictly.

JOAO DANTAS *(Diario do Notícias):* How do you expect us to know if someone is the spokesman of someone who has lost his political rights? How are we supposed to guard against this?

MAGALHAES: You will be able to know this by reading the material the spokesman gives you. In any case, the majority of these spokesmen are well known to all of us.

AN UNIDENTIFIED PERSON: I would like to take this opportunity to ask a few questions. Is there a new list of people who will lose their political rights?

MAGALHAES: This is a good example of the kind of question we consider provocative. If you ask it again, you will be punished according to law.

SAME PERSON: Don't misunderstand me. I'm only asking a question.

MAGALHAES: And if you ask it again, you will be punished.

So much for the promoting of Rostow's Free World democracy. What about developing the underdeveloped?

Within the year, the Mann-Gordon-Branco government had passed a set of bills cutting short the construction of new steel mills and authorizing Castelo Branco to sell a majority interest in any national industry. Consultec, the government's technical advisory board, announced that Brazil should abandon or indefinitely postpone its independent industrialization efforts and concentrate on the production of foodstuffs and the extraction of raw materials for export. Steel and iron works nationalized under Kubitschek were returned to their private owners.[33]

The most poignant of these success stories features Cleveland's Hanna Mining Company.[34] Back in 1935, Hanna had bought control of a British mining firm, St. John d'el Rey, and from that time forward had cultivated an epicure's interest in Brazil's immense iron deposits, situated principally in the state of Minas Gerais. In 1958, during the presidency of Juscelino Kubitschek, Minister of Mines Gabriel Passos canceled three of Hanna's concessions on reserves estimated at four billion tons of exceptionally high-assay (65 percent iron) hematite. Hanna pulled out the stops in an effort to reverse this cancellation and to acquire as well the rights to develop new rail and port facilities at Sepetiba Bay, a few miles south of Rio. Hanna's big guns were its president, former Secretary of the Treasury George Humphrey, Herbert Hoover, Jr. (like his father, a mining engineer), and John Dulles, son of the late Secretary of State (*NYT*, June 16, 1966). Kubitschek and Passos were unyielding, however, and Hanna's attempted recovery foundered in Brazil's courts. Into the early sixties, with most of its concessionary rights still enjoined, Hanna was shipping about 400,000 tons of iron ore a year through Rio and claiming that it was not making money.

The April 1964 *golpe* changed the picture. Step by step, with the deliberateness proper to momentous events, Hanna came back into its own. In June 1964, the Paulista-Mesquitas were in New York to explain the new Brazil's friendliness to foreign capital, and Robert Campos, the new finance minister, announced that the government was reconsidering its profit-repatriation regulations in light of the foreign businessman's "realistic" needs (*NYT*, June 18, 1964). Moved by this realism, the Hague-Paris Club* was disbanding, creditor states were generously preparing to refinance Brazil's debt, and the World Bank was about to end its fourteen-year-long virtual boycott of Brazil by sending a twenty-man ("largest-ever") mission on a seven-week tour of the Redeemed Potential's interior (*NYT*, October 2, 1964). Most moving to the new realists perhaps was Brazil's willingness to discuss legislation under which the Brazilian government would guarantee foreign investments.

On November 6, 1964, President Castelo Branco received a call from two famous gentlemen. One was the U.S. Ambassador Lincoln Gordon. The other was John J. McCloy, former U.S. High Commissioner in Germany, but at this time employed as a representative of the Hanna Mining Company. They had come, reported *The New York Times* dispatch of November 7, "to discuss company plans to develop iron ore deposits totaling an estimated four billion tons" and Hanna's "long-standing proposal to build an iron-ore shipping port at Sepetiba Bay." "After presenting Mr. McCloy," said *The New York Times* story, "Ambassador Gordon paid President Castelo Branco a second visit, outlining the United States' financial and economic mission to Brazil."

Castelo Branco's position must not have been an easy one. Clearly, the United States was pressuring for release of Hanna's concessions (then under litigation in Brazil's Federal Court of Appeals, where Hanna's claim was

---

* President Goulart had abruptly informed Brazil's foreign creditors that Brazil would be from $350 to $400 million short over the 1964–65 period in foreign-exchange needs. The United States, Britain, France, West Germany, Italy, and Japan had therefore met at the Hague (hence, "the Hague Club") apparently to determine on a collective policy toward their common debtor. Later meetings took place at Paris (hence, "the Hague-Paris club") and were attended also by Austria, Belgium, the Netherlands, Switzerland, the International Monetary Fund, and the World Bank. After the April *golpe*, evidently on the sound principle that Castelo Branco was no Goulart, the club members decided to treat individually with Brazil in refinancing her debt (*NYT*, July 2, 1964).

about to be denied). But at the same time, Castelo Branco was being pressured domestically by at least two strongman Mesquitas *not* to accede to Hanna's demands. One was the fiery Governor Carlos Lacerda, who had plans to construct a state-owned steel mill in his state of Guanabara and who wanted all iron-ore shipping in the area to keep going through Rio, Guanabara's chief city. The other heavyweight opponent was Jose Magalh ães Pinto, governor of Minas Gerais, where the disputed concessions lay. General Peri Bevilacqua, army commander of São Paulo, was also opposed to Hanna's proposition (NYT, December 24, 1964).

One does not know what Gordon told Castelo Branco on his second visit that day. But within two weeks, *The New York Times* (November 23, 1964) told of unconfirmed United States aid plans for $400 million "to rebuild the country's deteriorated economic position." The money would be used to support Brazil's monetary stabilization program and to finance imports (financing of American sales abroad, as noted above, is AID's basic function). A month later (NYT, December 15, 1964), the happy story broke: "U.S. Gives Brazil a Billion in Aid."* And little more than a week thereafter (NYT, December 24, 1964), Castelo Branco promulgated "a Presidential decree [which] called . . . for private competitive development of Brazil's vast iron ore reserves and ordered discouragement of any monopoly by the state or other enterprises." Within two months (*NYT*, February 27, 1965) the World Bank had put up $80 million for the development of hydroelectric power in the south-central region—that is, the region which (a) is already most developed, and (b) is the site of Hanna's claims. Lacerda and Co., it seemed, were losing out.

But Hanna still faced the hurdle of Brazil's supreme court, which would

---

*Here is how to invent a billion dollars: According to the cited *Times* story, AID "gives" $150 million in budgetary investments—that is, U.S. dollars are banked in Brazil (where they earn interest) in order to help harden the inflated cruzeiro. An un-named source (probably the World Bank) "gives" $100 million to develop the economic infrastructure needed by business —a "gift" that is, of course, merely a loan that Brazil must repay with rent. The U.S. Treasury "gives" $50 million to meet exchange requirements—which amounts to a credit extension. Next, this breathless Brazil is "given" the right to buy $90 million worth of surplus U.S. commodities—the price is no doubt right, but it is still a price. The Export-Import Bank "gives" Brazil $30 million—in the form of rescheduled 1965 debt. The same sort of "gift" comes in the amount of $90 million from European countries and Japan—which may be amused to find their favors counted as American beneficence. Finally, the *Times* story itemizes a $25-million food donation and $15 million in grants earmarked for "agriculture and education." The real market value of the food donation is anyone's guess, but we may assume that the grants are good honest grants. Thus, we have here a total of $40 million in goods and services that may properly be termed "gifts." That puts us, with the other items named, at a paper level of $550 million. "The remaining $450 million," continues the *Times* story, "*estimated for next year* [ital. added]," will come from the World Bank (which only lends, does not give), the International Monetary Fund (ditto), the Inter-American Development Bank (ditto), and private investors (who tend to make big profits in poor countries). Look again at the *Times'* good gray headline: "U.S. Gives Brazil a Billion in Aid."

have to decide its concessions claim and which was still dominated by "leftist" judges appointed by Goulart. By August 1965, Finance Minister Campos was complaining that U.S. investors were not exactly flying down to Rio. He had hoped for $150 million in U.S. investment and had seen less than $20 million (*NYT,* August 10, 1965). Senator William Fulbright, in Brazil with an American "fact-finding" mission, explained that American investors were waiting to see if Brazil would really become the democracy its officials vowed they were making it; that is, would the elections schedules for October really take place? But Thomas Mann, who was along on the same mission, seems to have suggested quite another, less frivolous, theory. Said *The New York Times (ibid.),* "The impression is that political uncertainty over the continuation of present policies by an elected Government is holding back potential investors."

American businessmen's fears of the Brazilian people proved generally well founded. The October election resulted in important victories for the left opposition. But their faith in the resourceful Castelo Branco should have been tougher. On October 27 he responded to the crisis of the "revolution" by issuing Institutional Act No. 2 . . ., which not only had the effect of nullifying the election but which also provided him with the (self-conferred, army-backed) right to pack the supreme court, which was proving such a nuisance to Hanna. On November 2 five new "revolutionaries" were admitted to the bench (*NYT,* November 3, 1965). Seven months later (the mills of the gods!), on June 15, 1966, the supreme court gave Hanna its four billion tons of iron ore back and the go-ahead for the Sepetiba Bay project (*NYT,* June 16, 1966).

Nationalist resentment over Hanna's privileged position was perhaps somewhat blurred by Hanna's agreement to go junior partners (49 percent of the stock) with Brazilian steel baron Auguste Antunes, who holds 51 percent of the stock in the new development company, United Brazilian Mining (*ibid.*).

Antunes is also a 51 percenter with Rockefeller's Bethlehem Steel, which owns 49 percent of the Industria e Comercio de Minerios (ICOMI). For more than fifteen years, ICOMI has been mining manganese in the Amapa Territory near the mouth of the Amazon and more recently has been taking niobium, a rich atomic ore, in the same area. This firm was godfathered ir 1949 through railroad-building loans from the World Bank and the Ex-In Bank. Since its first manganese shipments in 1957, it has been turning ar annual profit of $12 to $15 million.*

*So says David Rockefeller of Chase Manhattan in his *Foreign Affairs* article of April 196("What Free Enterprise Means to Latin America." In this same piece he discusses the questior Are American profits too high in Latin America? His answer is in character, and he cites study that showed North American profits in Latin America to be about 13 or 14 percent. Hig enough, one might think. But perhaps—who really knows!—they are even higher. In *Fortune*

The production of fertilizers, formerly the preserved domain of Petrobras, has been penetrated by Gulf and Esso, which have been allowed to make a $250-million foray into the petrochemicals industry (*Time,* October 15, 1965, p. 104). According to the underground Brazilian newspaper *Revolution,* Petrobras was essentially squeezed out of refining and sales by mid-1963 and found itself limited to exploration and extraction, the least profitable operations in the oil industry.

Crucial to this "development" of Brazil's underdeveloped economy was the National Congress's rubber-stamp approval of the Guarantee of Investments Agreement, which certain cynical Brazilians claim was drafted in Washington, D.C. By this act, the Brazilian government committed itself (1) never to expropriate an American firm except with that firm's "full and complete agreement"; (2) to pay any damages caused to American enterprises by "war, revolution, insurrection, strikes, and sabotage"; and (3) to allow American firms to invest in Brazil under the regulations of American laws (*NYT,* February 13, 1965; December 28, 1965).

There is, of course, an argument for these democratic, revolutionary, and patriotic derangements of the Brazilian economy: Inflation had to be stopped. That indeed was the argument by which the April 1964 *golpe* announced and explained itself. Brazil's economy was paralyzed in chaos and extreme correctives were required, and (so it was explained) it was all for the sake of fiscal stability that strikes were outlawed, dissent crushed, national Brazilian industries decimated, northeastern reform abandoned, the army's pay increased, schools closed, courts packed, unemployment allowed to move past 15 percent, wages frozen, doors thrown wide to foreign capital. It is therefore only doubly poignant that inflation is worse than ever. The government, having predicted a cost-of-living increase of 25 percent for 1965, confessed to an actual increase of more than 45 percent.* But it is not dismayed; indeed, it pursues its democratic revolution with unbewildered confidence.

A final Brazilian-American story. It is about two coastal villages in

---

April 1966 profile on Antunes, this same ICOMI is named. *Fortune* says, "Since shipments started in 1957, the venture has grossed $235 million." Rockefeller's above-quoted figures are annual *net.* If we assume that both Rockefeller and *Fortune* had access to figures through most of 1965, then the time span is roughly eight years. If ICOMI has netted an average of $13.5 million per year for eight years, its total profit through 1965 is $108 million. Given *Fortune's* figure for an eight-year gross of $235 million, ICOMI's profit is thus not a merely robust 14 percent, but a towering—and perhaps "exploitative"?—46 percent.

*NYT, February 3, 1966. This figure compares favorably, of course, with the 80 percent increase in 1964. But it is probably a low estimate. *Business Week* of March 13, 1965 ("When Cruzeiros Spiral, Think Dollars") reports that many Brazilian businesses were automatically boosting their prices by 7 percent every month. From January to June of 1966, the cost of living had already increased 25 percent (*NYT,* July 11, 1966), and *The New York Times* of October ?, 1966, was heading its Brazil story, "prices soar, imports decline."

Brazil's northeast, a region notorious for its poverty even in impoverished
Latin America. One village is Ponta de Carvelhos; the other, Pontezinha.
Near them flow two rivers, the Pirapanga and the Vaboatão, which are
connected by the high tides. Both villages, mostly Negro, at one time could
barely subsist on the two rivers' sweetwater fish and crabs. Then one day
not long ago, in Castelo Branco's time, America's Union Carbide Company
came to the banks of the Pirapanga and built for itself a gleaming chemicals
plant. It was explained to the people that this plant represented "development" and "progress."

But what American chemical plants do in America to American rivers,
they do doubly in Brazil to Brazilian rivers; so the plant's pollutions very
soon killed the fish and the crabs of the Pirapanga and the Vaboatão.

Since the villagers now faced death straight ahead, they felt they should
do something. They sent spokesmen to appeal to the authorities. The authorities commiserated with them, but explained that they had no authority.
Then the villagers decided they would have to make a demonstration. The
police would not hear of it. But desperation makes ingenuity, and two
priests asked, What about a religious procession? That was different, said
the police.

No one knew whether or not the procession would be understood and
joined, there never having been such a thing in either of these two obscure
fishing villages in the backward northeast. But on August 16, 1965, more
than 2000 fishermen and their wives and children marched twenty miles
over the blistering highway in equatorial summer heat, all the way down
to the softly gleaming fenced-in aluminum tanks and pipes, giant retorts and
vials, of the Union Carbide Company's Pirapanga River chemical plant.
Marching in the lead was a man who carried a large wooden cross. Over
the cross was draped a fishing net. Behind him, the people carried signs
whose slogans told their story very well. *O rio é vosso pao.* (The river is our
bread.) *Homens é peixes vivem é morrem juntos.* (Men and fish die together.)
O desenvolvimento é a favor ou contra nos? (Development: Is it for us or
against us?) *Progresso que traez miseria nao presta.* (Progress that brings
misery is not worth a damn.) *Eis a horo em que viemos pedir a soluçao.*
(Behold the hour in which we demand a solution.)

They came to the plant, gathered together, and some made speeches,
priests and fishermen, each hearing the others say what each knew each one
already knew. Besides the police who had come to guard against trouble
there were no onlookers. The Union Carbide Company's Pirapanga River
chemical plant quietly continued making chemicals for someone, heaving
back to the river poisoned what it had taken unpoisoned from the earth, for
it was automated.

This plant is not alone in its quietude. The people of the two villages are dying quietly, or quietly joining the revolutionary priest Padre Alepio de Freitas, who is working quietly in the country, a fugitive from Castelo Branco's unquiet, other-directed revolution.

Or consider South Africa, where some twelve million black people are the culture slaves of the growing Afrikaaner fascism of some three and a half million whites. Said J. G. Strijdorm, the second Prime Minister of South Africa, "If we reject the *Herenvolk* [i.e., master-race] idea and . . . if the franchise is to be extended to non-Europeans . . . and the non-Europeans are developed on the same basis as the Europeans, how can the European remain *Baas* [master]?"[35] Said the late H. F. Verwoerd, his successor: "There is no place for him [the African] in the European community above the level of certain forms of labor."[36]

American statesmen affirm their concern for the material advance of all men and the prosperity of democratic values. There is no clearer case of the blockade of that advance and the spoilation of those values than the case of South Africa, where whites have the fourth highest standard of living in the world but where every third black child dies of undernourishment before it is a year old and 60 percent of all blacks live below the bread line.[37] American statesmen periodically make strong speeches—in the UN, on commencement days at great universities—against this apartheid South Africa. But everyone understands that speeches are not actions. So we ask: In this least ambiguous of all cases, what is the material nature of the American response?

The Sharpeville massacre occured on March 21, 1960. Fears were at once aroused among some foreign investors that a South African rebellion might be brewing; and when the government subsequently declared itself a republic and abandoned the sterling standard, European capital became sufficiently nervous to threaten the regime's economic stability. At that time about eighty American firms had substantial investments in South Africa.[38] They had to decide to pull out or push in. Some meetings were apparently held in certain financial centers, because when action came in 1961 it was concerted and direct. American firms increased their investments by $23 million (to about $442 million in 1962[39]), and an *ad hoc* financial consortium advanced a $150 million loan to the government, the First National City Bank putting up $5 million, the Chase Manhattan Bank $10 million, the International Monetary Fund $38 million, the World Bank $28 million, and "U.S. lenders not publicly identified" $70 million.[40] The situation was saved. Since that crisis, the number of American companies investing in South Africa's future has nearly tripled.

The giants are there, the Babe Ruths, the Horsemen of the Dollar Apocalypse. One is the investment banking firm of Dillon, Read & Co., whose chairman until 1953, C. Douglas Dillon, was Secretary of the Treasury under Kennedy and Johnson and who has since moved to the board of the Chase Manhattan.[41] Another is American Metal Climax, which owns the largest mine in South West Africa (which South Africa regards as its "fifth province"). A huge consumer of South Africa's uranium (which accounted for close to 40 percent of our South African imports in 1961), AMC supplies about 10 percent of the total U.S. production. (Former AMC vice president and current board member Arthur H. Dean is a leading figure in the shaping of American nuclear-weapons control policy.[42]) Another is the Atomic Energy Commission itself, which is collaborating with Allis-Chalmers to bring the boon of nuclear power to South Africa.[43] Another is the formal consortium of American banks which has made available to South Africa a revolving credit fund (principal automatically replenished upon rent payment) which stands now at about $50 million. The participants in this consortium include the powerhouses of corporatized American finance: Chase Manhattan, First National City, Morgan Guaranty Trust, Bank of America, Bankers Trust, First National of Chicago, Irving Trust, and Continental Bank and Trust.[44]

The supergiants are Harry Oppenheimer's twin empires, Consolidated Gold Fields of South Africa Ltd. and the Anglo American Corporation, entities so immense as to scale, global as to extent, intricate as to operations, and absolute as to power as to humble the imagination of a Dante. Paradise for hundreds, Purgatory for thousands, Inferno for millions, these two corporations wholly dominate the economic life of sub-Saharan Africa. Now and then, a fragment of this cosmos may be forced to yield to some impious African.* But in the long term, it is simply not subject to the whims, bright ideas, or anger of any tribe or nation, because it transcends all peoples and all leagues. There is not one legislative or judicial body that can confront it. By itself and in Africa alone, Anglo American is 8 diamond mines, 17 coal mines, 5 copper mines, 15 gold mines, 11 "other" mines, 11 prospecting operations, 22 industrial firms, 7 land and estate centers, and 31 finance and investment houses.[46]

America's ambassador to Oppenheimerdom is Charles Englehard of Englehard Industries and the domestic Anglo American, whose 1965 stock-

---

*Until 1955, for example, one element of Anglo American, Sierre Leone Selection Trust, had exclusive diamond rights throughout Sierre Leone. In that year, a nationalist protest led the government to reduce SLST's concession area to the 209 square miles then being worked (including the rich Konor area). The victory was, of course, not complete, SLST retaining unlimited rights on deep deposits and collecting $4 million from Sierre Leone as compensation for its "lost opportunities." Again, in 1963, Sierre Leone required a service fee from Consolidated African Selection Trust Ltd., SLST's parent organization. (CAST itself is only a fourth-tier body in the Anglo American hierarchy.) CAST paid under protest, but in spite of the tax still returned a 70 percent dividend for that year, not one point under the previous year's return.[45]

holders' report devotes one sentence to African operations. Involved also in Canadian, Australian, and Colombian mining industries, and with distributing houses in Paris, Rome, and London, Englehard holds directorships in 23 South African companies, is a director of the government's Witwatersrand Native Labour Association and the Native Recruiting Corporation (which import black labor for mine work), a director of the Chamber of Mines (which sets standards for mine wages and working conditions), and is a member of the even more exclusive United States Foreign Policy Association.[47]

The claim of the liberal imperialist—Englehard, a close friend of Hubert Humphrey, is a good specimen [48]—is that the expansion of industry and the resulting transformation of society which this expansion accelerates are in the long haul liberating forces. If he means that these forces induce revolutionary violence, the liberal imperialist seems to be horribly correct. If he means that the imperialist process is itself progressive, he is baldly wrong. The stronger Afrikaaner fascism grows, the more uninhibited grow its racial mutilations. In 1953, 47.3 percent of Africans taking the college entrance examination passed it. In that year, the hypersegregationist Bantu Education Act went into effect. In 1960, the figure having steadily declined over the intervening years, the test was passed by only 17.9 percent. In 1954, one of the apartheid "bush colleges," Fort Hare, had an enrollment of 374 students. Ten years later enrollment had dropped by a hundred, and the previous yearly average of 60 B.A. degrees had fallen to 13. In 1965, out of 3.4 million whites, 33,000 attended universities; out of 12 million blacks, 946.[49] In 1935, the average annual income of a white mineworker was $2,264. By 1964, this had increased to $3,214. The average African miner made $203 in 1935, $196 in 1960.[50] Mining profits were close to $400 million.

At the end of 1964, direct American investments in South Africa were $467 million, concentrated in manufacturing ($192 million) and mining ($68 million). Net earnings on this investment were $87 million, $41 million in manufacturing and $20 million in mining. The rate of return was thus 20 percent over all, 24 percent in manufacturing, and 31 percent in mining.[51]

Publicly, our government deplores Afrikaaner racism. It imposed an arms embargo at the beginning of 1964 (under pressure to do so from the independent African countries) and is no doubt appalled to know that the poison gases soman, sarin, and tabun are being manufactured in large quantities in South Africa.[52] But embargo or not, the South African armed forces fly in 36 F-86 Sabrejet interceptors (to intercept whom?), C-47 and C-130B transports (to supply what front?), and about 30 Sikorsky helicopters (to leap to the scene of whose insurgency?). This is not only an American game, however; it is a Free World game. France, whose policy is not to supply arms "which can be used in defense of apartheid," supplied 16 Mirage IIIC (Mach 2) jet fighters with AS-30 air-to-surface missiles, about 30 Aloutte helicopters, and license for the production of Panhard armored cars. Britain, whose policy is "not to export arms to South Africa which would enable the policy of apartheid to be enforced," has supplied 16 Buccaneer light bombers, 16 Canberra B-12 light bombers, seven Shackleton long-range reconnaissance bombers, 30 subsonic Vampire jets, and about 500 Harvard light aircraft with a per-plane payload of eight 19-pound antipersonnel fragmentation bombs.[53]

But maintaining the peace and quiet, no matter at whose expense or what the cause of anger, may very well be worth a few scruples in a country which absorbs an extremely profitable $4 billion in U.S., British, French, and German direct investment, which offers nearly twice the world average investment return rate,[54] and which produces 70 percent of the Free World's gold.[55]

Consider the Free World's Paraguay, where the per capita income is $95 and 25 families own land equal in area to Denmark, Belgium, and Holland combined.[56] Alfredo Stroessner has held absolute dictatorial power since 1954, and probably the best single symbol of his regime's evolving democracy is Peña Hermosa, the Chaco Island prison camp where his unluckier political opponents are being permanently rehabilitated. Has this totalitarianism at least been materially efficient? In 1940, Paraguay had over 2500 industrial firms; there were 700 in 1965. In 1955, the agricultural index was 113.5; in 1965, only one percent of the land was cultivated and the index was 77.6. Three quarters of the land is timber forest, and wood exports in 1956 were 229,000 tons; in 1961, although demand had increased, exports were little more than half that.[57] The Liberal party's President Carlos Pastore, a wealthy pro-American self-exiled in Uruguay, told John Gerassi: "If all United States aid to Stroessner stopped today, democracy might still be salvageable tomorrow." Gerassi writes:

When I repeated this to United States Embassy officials in Asunción, they answered, "But Stroessner is anti-Communist." The argument that anti-Communist butchers accelerate Communist takeovers seemed to carry no weight. "In the last analysis," I was told, "our policy is one of survival. Thus, a sure anti-Communist, no matter how despicable, is better than a reformer, no matter how honest, who might turn against us."[58]

Or Free World Haiti. Duvalier has received more than $57 million in AID support and nearly as much in loans from the likes of the World Bank and the Ex-Im Bank;[59] a very few Haitians are very rich, Duvalier is bodily secured by a 20,000-man palace guard trained by the U.S. Marines, and for their part the Haitian people have the lowest school attendance in the hemisphere (5.7 percent, the next lowest, Bolivia's, being 20.9 percent), the fewest hospital beds and doctors per inhabitant, and the lowest per capita income ($70) in Latin America.[60] Democratic Americans might prefer their financial support to show better social results than tyrant Duvalier seems able to produce; but American Cold Warriors, on the other hand, might fear that a Haiti without its dollar would be a Haiti without its Duvalier; and without its Duvalier, yet another segment of the Greater Antilles archipelago that shields the strategic Panama Canal Zone might go the way of Cuba.

Jamaica ought to be for Jamaicans that island paradise which the travel advertisements claim it is for others. It has fewer than two million people on 4500 square miles; it is a major exporter of sugar; it does a strong tourist business; and, most importantly, it is the world's leading supplier of bauxite, from which all aluminum blessings flow. How is it that on the base of such wealth this country is in debt to outsiders, with 93 percent of its people earning less than $480 a year? Jamaica should be the Switzerland of the Caribbean—at least. But it is not, nor is it moving in that direction. It is moving in the direction of deeper debt to outsiders. And as Jamaica's poverty gets worse, Alcan, Alcoa, Kaiser, and Reynolds continue to ship to the north the Jamaican bauxite which is owned not by Jamaica but by Alcan, Alcoa, Kaiser, and Reynolds.[61]

Venezuela belongs to the same camp. Venezuelan oil and iron have an annual average dockside value of about $4 billion—a solid economic base, it might seem, for a country of some eight million people (three percent of whom, however, own 90 percent of the land). But Venezuela's annual income on the $3 billion in oil she ships each year is only $800 million—revenues collected from the outsiders who control the oil. Rockefeller's Creole Petroleum Corporation accounts for more than 40 percent of the total production and sales volume, Mellon's Mene Grande Oil for 15 percent, Mobil for 5 percent, and Royal-Dutch Shell for most of the remainder[62]. The government-owned Venezuelan group has "concessionary rights" on less than one percent of the oil reserve and is too underfinanced for profitable operations.

If the claim that American free enterprise collaborates with the revolution of rising expectations is ever going to be valid, then it ought to be valid for Venezuela, which has absorbed well over $3 billion in direct U.S. investment (behind only Canada, Britain, and Germany), and which has been a favorite territory of the Rockefeller modernizers since the turn of the century. It is indeed true that Venezuela's per capita income is the highest in Latin America; but it is unfortunately also true that it is only $800, that per capita figures by no means represent real national wealth or its distribution,* and that of the gross national product figure upon which this is calculated, well over one third is in exports, more than 90 percent of that third is in oil alone, and that oil income is effectively monopolized by American and European interests.[64]

Moreover, Venezuela's long-term prospects seem still darker: known oil reserves will be exhausted in about fifteen years. Especially since the world oil market is in a protracted glut, it would seem prudent for Venezuela to slow down oil extraction and concentrate now on developing a diversified, balanced, and essentially self-sufficient urban-rural economy. But oil extractions are far from being curtailed. Of the five major oil exporters among the underdeveloped countries (the others are Kuwait, Saudi Arabia, Iran, and Iraq), Venezuela has both the smallest reserves and the highest annual production rate. Kuwait, with reserves of 62 billion barrels in 1960, produced 601 million barrels; Venezuela, with reserves of 17 billion barrels, produced one billion.[65] The fact is that the decision is not Venezuela's to make. Production rates are determined by the outside firms holding the concessionary rights—*rights which are scheduled to expire in 1984.* One may certainly say that Venezuela is being "developed." One then asks: By whom? And to serve whose needs?

The roll is long. We might as well have looked at Iran, where in 1953 the CIA and British intelligence conspired to overthrow Premier Mohammed Mossadeq because he advocated Cold War neutralism for Iran and threatened to nationalize foreign oil-holdings. We might have pursued the career of the James Bond of that operation, the CIA's Kermit Roosevelt, through the time of the coup itself, the subsequent reallocation of Iranian oil rights to the advantage of American companies (Standard and Gulf), on up through 1958 when Gulf made him its "government relations" man and to 1960 when he became a vice president.[66]

Or we might have looked at Guatemala of 1954, where the CIA helped overthrow democratically elected President Arbenz because his modest agrarian reform program threatened unused United Fruit Company plantation land. We might have combed for the implications of the facts that then-Secretary of State John Foster Dulles' law office had written the United Fruit Company's 1930 and 1936 agreements with Guatemala; that

---

*From per capita income figures, for example, one could conclude that the second loveliest place in the world to live is Kuwait, whose per capita income is $1800—ahead of Canada ($1600), Switzerland ($1400), Sweden ($1300), and Britain ($1100), and not very far behind the United States ($2300).[63] The more revealing figure, much harder to calculate for any country and close to impossible for the underdeveloped, would be the distribution of income, the mean. A huge part of most underdeveloped-country populations is not even in the money economy.

then-Assistant Secretary of State for Inter-American Affairs John Moors Cabot was a major United Fruit Company shareholder; that then-CIA Director Allan Dulles had been president of the United Fruit Company; that Dulles' predecessor in the CIA directorship, General Walter Beddell Smith, was to become a United Fruit Company vice president in 1955.[67]

Or we might have looked at our Dominican Republic intervention of 1965 and probed the facts that its chief architect, Organization of American States Ambassador Ellsworth Bunker, Jr., is a board member of the National Sugar Refining Company, which depends upon privileged access to Dominican sugar; that roving ambassador Averell Harriman's private investment house (Brown Bros. Harriman) owns about 10 percent of National Sugar; that President Johnson's close friend Supreme Court Justice Abe Fortas and a leading rhetorician of corporate liberalism, Adolf Berle, Jr., have sat since 1946 on the board of the Sucrest Company, which imports black-strap molasses from the Dominican Republic; and that former ambassador to the Dominican Republic Joseph Farland is on the board of the South Puerto Rico Sugar Company, which owns 275,000 acres of the best plantation land in the Dominican Republic and is the largest employer on the island (average wage to Dominicans, about a dollar a day). [68]

Or we might have looked at the Philippines, favored child of American anticolonialism, whose "national" constitution's U.S.-drafted "parity amendment" prohibits Filipinos from protecting their internal markets and resources against American commercial penetration—that is, effectively obstructs the development of an independent Filipino entrepreneurial class.[69]

Or at Liberia, another child of American humanism, whose rubber plantations have netted Firestone an average net profit three times the amount of the entire Liberian national revenue, and whose rich iron deposits in the Nimba range have been conceded to private European and American (Bethlehem Steel) interests.[70]

Or at hapless Ghana, whose anti-Nkrumah coup of February 1966 appears to have had CIA support, and which in any case led at once to the explicit opening of the Ghanaian door to U.S. business and the collapse of Ghanaian efforts to achieve diversified self-sufficiency. As E. N. Omaboe, the new regime's chief economic official, told a New York meeting of the African-American Chamber of Commerce on May 20, 1966: "We want New England and Californian fishermen to fish our coasts and set up canneries." As enticements, Omaboe offered ten-year tax exemption, duty-free import of materials, and a guarantee that on the outside chance of an expropriation the settlement would be arbitrated by the World Bank.[71]

Or at India, two thirds of whose currency is controlled by the United States government, which used this leverage to help persuade Madam

Gandhi that fertilizer plants run by expensive Rockefeller oil were better for India than fertilizer plants run by cheap Iranian gas.[72]

Or at Indonesia, where history's most appalling bloodbath and the new government's return or "purchase" of formerly nationalized American rubber and oil holdings led directly to the resumption of U.S. aid.[73] But the list is endless. We should attempt a generalization.

The United States has shown in Europe that it knows how to reconstruct bombed-out capitalist economies. But it has not shown in the Third World that it can develop Western-style political economies: in preindustrial countries where there is no capitalist class structure, no entrepreneurial tradition, no skilled urbanized work force, and no internalized commitment to capitalist life-styles, the arrival of the American corporatist is in fact a disaster. Preoccupied with the extraction of resources for export and the immediate exploitation of all opportunities without regard to the damage this does to others, our business statesmanship may justly claim to have excited the underdeveloped world's growing revolutionary demands. But it is nothing but double talk for this same statesmanship to pretend that it assents to those demands—the demands for unobstructed opportunity to develop the natural wealth of the nation, for time and freedom to cultivate a national economic style, for exemption from the Cold War, for political independence.

America is not baby-simple, and her imperialism has other moods. There is, for example, the apparently genuine effort of some AID (and even some CIA) people to foster social reform under frustrating and often dangerous conditions; there is the Peace Corps, which, as badly as it has been abused, no doubt embodies a popular American willingness to be of help to other people; there is the Asian Rice Institute in the Philippines, a joint effort of the Rockefeller and Ford foundations which may prove very valuable to the people of Asia. If these represented the behavioral core, the main driving force of American foreign policy, a political humanist could throw his efforts behind that policy without much hesitation. But all imperialisms have produced their mercy angels; and one has to conclude that the good people of AID, the Peace Corps, the Rice Institute, are performing only marginal and auxiliary roles. The America which the rising world most deeply experiences is the America of United Fruit and the U.S. Marines, cool plunder, and the napalm fist. One may wish that the Peace Corps were the State Department. It is not even a match for the CIA's third string. America is not the friend but the enemy of that deformed, uneven, frustrated, and frightening revolution whose fundamental motives seem so compelling and whose fundamental claims seem so just.

It is hard to see how it could be otherwise with the corporate state. Adolf Berle, Jr., who has been a sympathetically insightful analyst of American corporatism, has himself recognized that "preachments about the value of private enterprise and investment and the usefulness of foreign capital [in the underdeveloped countries] were . . . a little silly. . . . Foreign and/or private investment may industrialize, may even increase production, and still leave the masses in as bad a shape as ever."[74] It may seem strange to hear as much from Berle. But worried corporate capitalists are not at all hard to find. It is often from them, in fact, that we get the most perceptive and realistic descriptions of Free World imperialism's effects on the backward. Gerassi quotes the 1958 statement of J. P. Grace, Jr., President of Grace & Co., whose Latin American profits are immense: "Chile, Peru, Mexico and Bolivia," said Grace, "have seen the export prices of their metals drop from 40 percent to 50 percent during the last several years. At the same time, since 1951, the average price that Latin America pays for its imports from the United States has risen about 11 percent."[75]

The editors of *Fortune* have pointed out that the long-term debt of the underdeveloped countries, some $40 billion in 1966, costs $4.5 billion annually in interest charges and consumes one eighth of all their foreign-trade earnings. "To get enough foreign exchange for what they import, [underdeveloped countries] have to borrow more, which in turn means they will have to meet greater servicing costs."[76] Sanz de Santamaria, chairman of the Inter-American Committee of the Alliance for Progress, has made the same point: "[Latin American] debt amortization alone will require $1.7 billion this year [1966], thus pre-empting 16 percent of all export earnings."[77] Josué de Castro, one of Brazil's foremost economists and a former president of the United Nations Food and Agriculture Organization, has written of the Alliance for Progress that it "is nothing but pure colonialism. . . . Colonialism is the only cause of hunger in Latin America."[78]

That might seem a bitter exaggeration. But there is only a difference of tone, not of substance, between that statement and the following passages from the editorial page of the *Wall Street Journal:*

The industrial nations have added nearly $2 billion to their reserves, which now total $52 billion. At the same time, the reserves of the less-developed group not only have stopped rising, but have declined some $200 million. To analysts such as Britain's [Barbara] Ward, the significance of such statistics is clear: the economic gap is rapidly widening "between a white, complacent, highly bourgeois, very wealthy, very small North Atlantic elite and everybody else, and this is not a very comfortable heritage to leave to one's children." "Everybody else" includes approximately two thirds of the population of the earth, spread through about 100 nations. . . . Many diplomats and economists view the implications as overwhelmingly—and dangerously—political. Unless the present decline can be reversed, these analysts fear, the United States and other wealthy industrial powers of the West face the distinct possibility, in the words of Miss Ward, "of a sort of international class war."[79]

But there is rarely any indication that this problem is *caused* by someone, that it is in preponderant part caused by American corporations, that this problem (instead of communism) is what lies behind Third-World revolution. Indeed, there is always an implicit suggestion that the man who can solve this problem best is none other than the Free World capitalist himself. It seems to be certainly true that many aspects of the development problem could be solved by that figure—if he would just remove himself from the picture. But how will he be persuaded to do that? To surrender in someone else's name the immense profits which he considers it his main business to make? Further, how is his disengagement to be achieved by a government which has always considered his foreign successes to be America's domestic successes, and which is unalterably committed to the political ideology of free enterprise?

Consider that the capitalist's commitment to capitalism does not entail a commitment to other capitalists. The ideology obliges him only to *compete*, and the interwoven morality obliges him to win *as much as he can*. If his dominance is to be restricted, his victories contained, that will only happen through the independent competitive action of other capitalists. In theory, this is indeed how the system is supposed to operate: New entrepreneurs, new capitalists, steadily emerge to create and wield new power, and thus continuously reconstitute the dynamics of the open, free market. But we have noticed a problem: Even in our own supposedly model economy, there is an accelerating breakout from this theoretically internalized and permanent system of competition-based limits. The competition is won, and the winner gets stronger; lost, and the loser gets weaker. Power condenses in the hands of steadily smaller, steadily more integrated and collaborative victor groups. And the federal government, not so very long ago the American businessman's arch enemy, now becomes his delighted and delightful partner. Without the federal government's Special Forces and Marines, United Fruit could not dominate Guatemala. Without AID and the World Bank and the supportive hands of the Commerce and State Departments, the corporations could not multinationalize themselves. Without the federal government's sugar subsidies, the sugar companies could not maintain their lethal grip on the economies of small states from the Caribbean to the Central Pacific. Without the State Department's Cold War sales campaign and the active support of the Defense Department's weapon hucksters, General Dynamics could not continue to fatten on arms sales to Europe. Without big government, big business would be lost.

One sees in America the emergence (maybe it is too late for such a word) of what we can only describe as a somewhat permissive, domestically benign fascist state. *Fascism*—an extravagant term? *Webster's* definition: "a centralized autocratic national regime with severely nationalistic policies, exercising regimentation of industry, commerce, and finance, rigid censorship, and forcible suppression of opposition." On the last two counts, I hope not too hopefully, I defer judgment. And in any case, there is no need to suppress an already harmless dissent. But centralization of the basic economic and political decisions, the sophisticated nationalism of our foreign policy, the *de facto* top-down "regimentation" (our word for it is "rationalization") of industry, commerce, and finance—these are very clearly the dominant features of our system. Big government and big business are essentially one and the same. And the normative act of competition that now takes place does not occur between independent entrepreneurial groups and is apparently not fought out in terms of the superiority of one man's product over another's (product "superiority" now being purchasable, all but prepackaged, from any advertising agency). Rather, the crucial competition takes place on the inside of a homogeneous, informal, but very real and very bureaucratic commercial monolith, and the paramount issue of that competition is the internal succession of power and authority: not where power will be moved to, but who will win occupancy of power's present seats; not the rearrangement of power in the market place, but the acquisition of power within the closed system that commands it.

Will someone claim that the appetite for dominance which stimulated the growth of this corporate state will restrain itself when it goes on foreign cruises? David Rockefeller may very well exhort his fellow businessmen to "demonstrate [to Latin Americans] that a new brand of capitalism has evolved, based on the concept of a fair profit for free enterprise combined with social responsibility to the community as a whole."[80] And he may very well hope that someone takes his advice, for the businessman who does so, this same Rockefeller will crush. The idea of capitalism is that the "fair profit" will not have to be determined by a Christian capitalist alone with his morality. It will be set through his act of competing with *other* capitalists. Then where are the competitive capitalists of the Third World? And how are they to be produced? And who is to produce them?

Nothing the American businessman can see in past, present, or future will persuade him to forgo whatever commercial advantages may come to hand. *And for him, the Third World is a commercial advantage.* The Third World is that exposed, unprotected gold mine where his investment dollars fare better than anywhere else. Why should he want to change that? The United Fruit Company may be "enlightened," may (sometimes does, sometimes does not) build roads, houses, schools, and hospitals in model company towns on its plantations in the "banana republics." But why should it want to surrender its privileged position there, all in the name of some fuzzy humanitarian ideal? Or why should it rejoice to see the emergence of local capitalists who may some day get strong enough to give it some competition? Since when is the capitalist his colleague's keeper?

As ordinary, intelligent men giving the rest of the world a look, the American corporatists can see the truth as well as anyone else. They can even be concerned about the bloody implications of what they see, and they might even have an ideological, impersonal preference for a Third World, in the best sense, Americanized. But to build that "American" Vietnam, that dynamic, free-enterprising Brazil, that middle-class Guatemala—if that indeed is what these countries want—that is the job of independent, unharassed, unmanipulated Vietnamese, Brazilians, and Guatemalans; it can no more be the job of American capitalists than the building of the American nation could have been the job of British mercantilists. For matters to stand otherwise, the Yankee free-enterpriser would for the first time in his life have to work for his competition. He would have to recognize a difference of interest, a dual economic good, and take sides against himself. He would have to supplant his money ethic with a social ethic. He would have to change entirely his style of thought and action. In a word, he would have to become a revolutionary socialist whose aim was the destruction of the present American hegemony. I see no reason to suppose that such a metamorphosis is about to transfigure this Yankee.

The agents of change in this world are today, as they have always been, those whose battered lives stand most in need of change. The entrepreneurs of social progress are those whose condition requires it. And at bottom, this revolution is nothing but the emergence of competitors who employ the only means of competition available to them. Revolution is the collective free enterprise of the collectively dispossessed.

NOTES

1. *Tragedy*, p. 18.

2. Frederic L. Pryor, *The Communist Foreign Trade System*, MIT Press, Cambridge, Mass., 1963.

3. *Tragedy*, p. 234.

4. *In* Edmund Stillman and William Pfaff, *The Politics of Hysteria*, Harper & Row (Colophon book), New York, 1964, p. 97.

5. W. W. Rostow, "Guerrilla Warfare in Underdeveloped Areas," in Raskin and Fall, eds., *The Viet Nam Reader*, Random House (Vintage Books), New York, 1965, pp. 110–112.

6. David E. Lilienthal, "The Multinational Corporation," paper delivered at the Carnegie Institute of Technology, April 1960.

7. Richard J. Barber, "Big, Bigger, Biggest: American Business Goes Global," *New Republic*, April 30, 1966.

8. *Wall Street Journal*, February 8, 1966.

9. Barber, *loc. cit.*

10. *Ibid.*

11. *Newsweek*, March 8, 1965.

12. Barber.

13. *Quoted in* Marshall Windmiller "Viet-Nam and the Power Elite," *The Commentary of Marshall Windmiller*, TLD Press, Berkeley, Calif., March 31, 1966. The quotation is from Defferre's article in the April 1966 *Foreign Affairs*.

14. Barber.

15. *Forbes*, April 1, 1966.

16. Seymour Melman, *Our Depleted Society*, Holt, Rinehart & Winston, New York, 1965, p. 150.

17. "What U.S. Companies Are Doing Abroad," *U. S. News & World Report*, January 24, 1966.

18. For a good short review of these institutions and their shortcomings, see the memorandum "A Bank for Economic Acceleration of Backward Countries," by Morris Forgash, president of the United States Freight Company, published as Appendix D *in* Melman, pp. 342–352.

19. David Rockefeller, "What Free Enterprise Means to Latin America," *Foreign Affairs*, April 1966.

20. "Special Report on Multinational Companies," *Business Week*, April 20, 1963.

21. Paul Baran and Paul Sweezy, "Notes on the Theory of Imperialism," *Monthly Review*, March 1966.

22. John Gerassi, *The Great Fear in Latin America*, The Macmillan Company (Collier book), New York, 1965, p. 276.

23. *Ibid.*, p. 354.

24. Baran and Sweezy cite Standard's *1962 Annual Report*.

25. Gerassi, p. 355.

26. *The Economic Almanac 1964*, National Industrial Conference Board and *Newsweek*, New York, 1964, pp. 477, 480, 490, 511. (Referred to hereafter as *Almanac*.)

27. Gerassi, pp. 76–99.

28. *Ibid.*, p. 83.

29. Philip Siekman, "When Executives Turned Revolutionaries," *Fortune*, September 1964.

30. *NYT*, November 23, 1964.

31. *NYT*, November 25, 1964; March 21, 1965; October 11, 1965; October 28, 1965; November 8, 1965.

32. *NYT*, January 28, 1966.

33. *NYT*, October 2, 1964; December 24, 1964.

34. Besides the *NYT* citations in the text, the following magazine articles provide

good immediate and general background on the Hanna Mining affair: *Fortune,* "Brazil: Hanna's Immovable Mountains," April 1965; *Fortune,* "Brazil's Battle with Inflation," December 1965; *Fortune,* "Brazil's Chief Miner," April 1966; *International Commerce,* "U.S.-Brazilian Guaranty Pact to Stimulate Private Investment," February 22, 1965; *Business Week,* "Harsh Curbs Generate Growing Discontent," March 27, 1965; *Business Week,* "Brazil: Some Success, Much Work to Do," January 22, 1966; Lincoln Gordon, "Brazil-United States: Partners in Progress," *U.S. Department of State Bulletin,* April 18, 1966.

35. Franz Lee, *Anatomy of Apartheid in Southern Africa,* Alexander Defense Committee, New York, 1966, p. 32. Lee is a South African political refugee.

36. *Ibid.*

37. *Ibid.,* p. 14.

38. Paul Booth and Christopher Z. Hobson, "Information on Involvement of U.S. Corporations in South Africa," Students for a Democratic Society, Chicago, 1966. This fact sheet summarizes continuing primary research on American corporate interests in South Africa being carried out by members of SDS and the American Committee on Africa. Data is continually accumulated at the SDS National Office in Chicago and is available on request. However, the best single, most convenient source on the subject is the January 1966 issue of *Africa Today,* "A Special Report on American Involvement in the South African Economy." Copies of this issue are available from the American Committee on Africa, 211 East 43rd Street, New York, N.Y. 10017.

39. *Ibid.*

40. *Ibid.* See also *New Republic,* "South Africa," August 13, 1966.

41. Booth and Hobson, *Africa Today.*

42. Kwame Nkrumah, *Neo-Colonialism, The Last Stage of Imperialism,* International Publishers Co., New York, 1965, p. 104. This book's cold, fine-grain research was surely conducted by the scholars of the Ideological Institute at Winneba, which was closed after the coup of February 1966.

43. *U. S. News & World Report,* November 22, 1965.

44. Booth and Hobson, *Africa Today.*

45. Nkrumah, pp. 147–149.

46. *Ibid.,* pp. 127–136.

47. *Ibid.,* p. 122; Booth and Hobson, *Africa Today.*

48. *Forbes,* "The Englehard Touch," August 1, 1965.

49. Lee, pp. 27–28.

50. *Ibid.,* p. 12.

51. *Ibid.,* p. 17. See also *New Republic,* August 13, 1966.

52. Lee, p. 19.

53. *The Military Balance, 1965–1966,* The Institute for Strategic Studies, London, 1965, p. 36. M. J. V. Bell, "Military Assistance to Independent African States," *Adelphi Papers,* The Institute for Strategic Studies, London, December 1964, p. 14.

54. Lee, p. 42.

55. *Almanac,* p. 505.

56. Gerassi, pp. 125–126.

57. *Ibid.*, p. 126.

58. *Ibid.*, p. 127.

59. *Almanac,* pp. 488, 490.

60. Gerassi, p. 192.

61. *Ibid.,* 191.

62. *Ibid.*, pp. 367–372.

63. *Almanac,* p. 492.

64. Gerassi, pp. 20, 32, 155–166.

65. *Ibid.*, p. 368.

66. Ross and Wise, *The Invisible Government,* Bantam ed., New York, 1965, pp. 116–121.

67. *Ibid.* Paul W. Blackstock, *The Strategy of Subversion,* Quadrangle Books, Chicago, 1964, p. 185. Gerassi, p. 241.

68. On Bunker and National Sugar's Dominican interests, see Joseph P. Lash, "Bunker Hits the Trail Again," New York *Post,* January 27, 1957; *Standard and Poor's* "Sugar—Basic Survey" and "Sugar—Company Survey" for 1963–1965; *Commodity Year Book* (annual) and *International Sugar Journal* (monthly); and Dana L. Thomas, "Richer Sweet," *Barron's,* September 27, 1965. On Harriman and National, see *Standard and Poor's Register of Directors and Officers* (annual) and any recent National *Annual Report.* On Fortas, Berle, and Sucrest, see Charles B. Seib and Alan I. Otten, "Abe, Help—LBJ," *Esquire,* June 1965; *Who's Who in America;* Sucrest *Annual Report.* On Farland, see South Puerto Rico's 1965 *Annual Report.* I am indebted for this data to Michael Locker of SDS.

69. A. Orlov, "The Philippines," *International Affairs,* November 1965.

70. Nkrumah, pp. 60, 66.

71. *NYT,* May 21, 1966.

72. *NYT,* June 19, 1966.

73. *NYT,* April 8, 1966.

74. Gerassi, p. 275.

75. *Ibid.*, p. 28.

76. *Fortune,* June 1966.

77. *Economic Affairs,* June 1, 1966.

78. Gerassi, p. 263.

79. *Wall Street Journal,* May 12, 1965.

80. Rockefeller, *loc. cit.*

COUNTERREVOLUTIONARY
AMERICA ✒ *Robert L. Heilbroner*

Is the United States fundamentally opposed to economic development? The question is outrageous. Did we not coin the phrase, "the revolution of rising expectations"? Have we not supported the cause of development more generously than any nation on earth, spent our intellectual energy on the problems of development, offered our expertise freely to the backward nations of the world? How can it possibly be suggested that the United States might be opposed to economic development?

The answer is that we are not at all opposed to what we conceive economic development to be. The process depicted by the "revolution of rising expectations" is a deeply attractive one. It conjures up the image of a peasant in some primitive land, leaning on his crude plow and looking to the horizon, where he sees dimly, but for the *first time* (and that is what is so revolutionary about it), the vision of a better life. From this electrifying vision comes the necessary catalysis to change an old and stagnant way of life. The pace of work quickens. Innovations, formerly feared and resisted, are now eagerly accepted. The obstacles are admittedly very great—whence the need for foreign assistance—but under the impetus of new hopes the economic mechanism begins to turn faster, to gain traction against the environment. Slowly, but surely, the Great Ascent begins.

There is much that is admirable about this well-intentioned popular view of "the revolution of rising expectations." Unfortunately, there is more that is delusive about it. For the buoyant appeal of its rhetoric conceals or passes in silence over by far the larger part of the spectrum of realities of the

SOURCE: Robert Heilbroner, "Counterrevolutionary America," *Commentary* (April 1967), 31–38. Copyright © 1967 by the American Jewish Committee. Reprinted by permission of the author and publisher.

development process. One of these is the certainty that the revolutionary aspect of development will not be limited to the realm of ideas, but will vent its fury on institutions, social classes, and innocent men and women. Another is the great likelihood that the ideas needed to guide the revolution will not only be affirmative and reasonable, but also destructive and fanatic. A third is the realization that revolutionary efforts cannot be made, and certainly cannot be sustained, by voluntary effort alone, but require an iron hand, in the spheres both of economic direction and political control. And the fourth and most difficult of these realities to face is the probability that the political force most likely to succeed in carrying through the gigantic historical transformation of development is some form of extreme national collectivism or Communism.

In a word, what our rhetoric fails to bring to our attention is the likelihood that development will require policies and programs repugnant to our "way of life," that it will bring to the fore governments hostile to our international objectives, and that its regnant ideology will bitterly oppose capitalism as a system of world economic power. If that is the case, we would have to think twice before denying that the United States was fundamentally opposed to economic development.

But is it the case? Must development lead in directions that go counter to the present American political philosophy? Let me try to indicate, albeit much too briefly and summarily, the reasons that lead me to answer that question as I do.

I begin with the cardinal point, often noted but still insufficiently appreciated, that the process called "economic development" is not primarily economic at all. We think of development as a campaign of production to be fought with budgets and monetary policies and measured with indices of output and income. But the development process is much wider and deeper than can be indicated by such statistics. To be sure, in the end what is hoped for is a tremendous rise in output. But this will not come to pass until a series of tasks, at once cruder and more delicate, simpler and infinitely more difficult, has been commenced and carried along a certain distance.

In most of the new nations of Africa, these tasks consist in establishing the very underpinnings of nationhood itself—in determining national borders, establishing national languages, arousing a basic national (as distinguished from tribal) self-consciousness. Before these steps have been taken, the African states will remain no more than names insecurely affixed to the map, not social entities capable of undertaking an enormous collective venture in economic change. In Asia, nationhood is generally much further advanced than in Africa, but here the main impediment to development is the miasma of apathy and fatalism, superstition and distrust that vitiates every attempt to improve hopelessly inefficient modes of work and patterns of resource use: while India starves, a quarter of the world's cow population devours Indian crops, exempt either from effective employment or slaughter because of sacred taboos. In still other areas, mainly Latin America, the principal handicap to development is not an absence of national identity or the presence of suffocating cultures (although the latter certainly plays its part), but the cramping and crippling inhibitions of obsolete social institutions and reactionary social classes. Where landholding rather than industrial activity is still the basis for social and economic power, and where land is held essentially in fiefdoms rather than as productive real estate, it is not surprising that so much of society retains a medieval cast.

Thus, development is much more than a matter of encouraging economic growth within a given social structure. It is rather the *modernization* of that structure, a process of ideational, social, economic, and political change that requires the remaking of society in its most intimate as well as its most public attributes.[1] When we speak of the revolutionary nature of economic development, it is this kind of deeply penetrative change that we mean— change that reorganizes "normal" ways of thought, established patterns of family life, and structures of village authority as well as class and caste privilege.

What is so egregiously lacking in the great majority of the societies that are now attempting to make the Great Ascent is precisely this pervasive modernization. The trouble with India and Pakistan, with Brazil and Ecuador, with the Philippines and Ethiopia, is not merely that economic growth lags, or proceeds at some pitiable pace. This is only a symptom of deeper-lying ills. The trouble is that the social physiology of these nations remains so depressingly unchanged despite the flurry of economic planning on top. The all-encompassing ignorance and poverty of the rural regions, the unbridgeable gulf between the peasant and the urban elites, the resistive conservatism of the village elders, the unyielding traditionalism of family life —all these remain obdurately, maddeningly, disastrously unchanged. In the cities, a few modern buildings, sometimes brilliantly executed, give a deceptive patina of modernity, but once one journeys into the immense countryside, the terrible stasis overwhelms all.

To this vast landscape of apathy and ignorance one must now make an exception of the very greatest importance. It is the fact that a very few nations, all of them Communist, have succeeded in reaching into the lives and stirring the minds of precisely that body of the peasantry which constitutes the insuperable problem elsewhere. In our concentration on the politics, the betrayals, the successes and failures of the Russian, Chinese, and Cuban revolutions, we forget that their central motivation has been just such a war *á l'outrance* against the arch-enemy of backwardness—not alone

the backwardness of outmoded social superstructures but even more critically that of private inertia and traditionalism.

That the present is irreversibly and unqualifiedly freed from the dead
hand of the past is, I think, beyond argument in the case of Russia. By this
I do not only mean that Russia has made enormous economic strides. I refer
rather to the gradual emancipation of its people from the "idiocy of rural
life," their gradual entrance upon the stage of contemporary existence. This
is not to hide in the smallest degree the continuing backwardness of the
Russian countryside where now almost fifty—*and formerly perhaps eighty*
—per cent of the population lives. But even at its worst I do not think that
life could now be described in the despairing terms that run through the
Russian literature of our grandfathers' time. Here is Chekhov:

During the summer and the winter there had been hours and days when it seemed
as if these people [the peasants] lived worse than cattle, and it was terrible to be with
them. They were coarse, dishonest, dirty, and drunken; they did not live at peace
with one another but quarreled continually, because they feared, suspected, and
despised one another. . . . Crushing labor that made the whole body ache at night,
cruel winters, scanty crops, overcrowding, and no help, and nowhere to look for
help.

It is less certain that the vise of the past has been loosened in China or
Cuba. It may well be that Cuba has suffered a considerable economic
decline, in part due to absurd planning, in part to our refusal to buy her
main crop. The economic record of China is nearly as inscrutable as its
political turmoil, and we may not know for many years whether the Chinese
peasant is today better or worse off than before the revolution. Yet what
strikes me as significant in both countries is something else. In Cuba it is
the educational effort that, according to the New York *Times,* has constituted a major effort of the Castro regime. In China it is the unmistakable
evidence—and here I lean not alone on the sympathetic account of Edgar
Snow but on the most horrified descriptions of the rampages of the Red
Guards—that the younger generation is no longer fettered by the traditional
view of things. The very fact that the Red Guards now revile their elders,
an unthinkable defiance of age-old Chinese custom, is testimony of how
deeply change has penetrated into the texture of Chinese life.

It is this herculean effort to reach and rally the great anonymous mass
of the population that is *the* great accomplishment of Communism—even
though it is an accomplishment that is still only partially accomplished. For
if the areas of the world afflicted with the self-perpetuating disease of
backwardness are ever to rid themselves of its debilitating effects, I think
it is likely to be not merely because antiquated social structures have been
dismantled (although this is an essential precondition), but because some

shock treatment like that of Communism has been administered to them. By way of contrast to this all-out effort, however short it may have fallen of its goal, we must place the timidity of the effort to bring modernization to the peoples of the non-Communist world. Here again I do not merely speak of lagging rates of growth. I refer to the fact that illiteracy in the non-Communist countries of Asia and Central America is increasing (by some 200 million in the last decade) because it has been "impossible" to mount an educational effort that will keep pace with population growth. I refer to the absence of substantial land reform in Latin America, despite how many years of promises. I refer to the indifference or incompetence or corruption of governing elites: the incredible sheiks with their oildoms; the vague, well-meaning leaders of India unable to break the caste system, kill the cows, control the birthrate, reach the villages, house or employ the labor rotting on the streets; the cynical governments of South America, not one of which, according to Lleras Camargo, former president of Colombia, has ever prosecuted a single politician or industralist for evasion of taxes. And not least, I refer to the fact that every movement that arises to correct these conditions is instantly identified as "Communist" and put down with every means at hand, while the United States clucks or nods approval.

To be sure, even in the most petrified societies, the modernization process is at work. If there were time, the solvent acids of the 20th century would work their way on the ideas and institutions of the most inert or resistant countries. But what lacks in the 20th century is time. The multitudes of the underdeveloped world have only in the past two decades been summoned to their reveille. The one thing that is certain about the revolution of rising expectations is that it is only in its inception, and that its pressures for justice and action will steadily mount as the voice of the 20th century penetrates to villages and slums where it is still almost inaudible. It is not surprising that Princeton historian C. E. Black, surveying this labile world, estimates that we must anticipate "ten to fifteen revolutions a year for the foreseeable future in the less developed societies."

In itself, this prospect of mounting political restiveness enjoins the speediest possible time schedule for development. But this political urgency is many times compounded by that of the population problem. Like an immense river in flood, the number of human beings rises each year to wash away the levees of the preceding year's labors and to pose future requirements of monstrous proportions. To provide shelter for the three billion human beings who will arrive on earth in the next forty years will require as many dwellings as have been constructed since recorded history began. To feed them will take double the world's present output of food. To cope with the mass exodus from the overcrowded countryside will necessitate cities of grotesque size—Calcutta, now a cesspool of three to five millions, threatens us by the year 2000 with a prospective population of from thirty to sixty millions.

These horrific figures spell one importunate message: haste. That is the *mene mene, tekel upharsin* written on the walls of government planning offices around the world. Even if the miracle of the loop is realized—the new contraceptive device that promises the first real breakthrough in population control—we must set ourselves for at least another generation of rampant increase.

But how to achieve haste? How to convince the silent and disbelieving men, how to break through the distrustful glances of women in black shawls, how to overcome the overt hostility of landlords, the opposition of the Church, the petty bickerings of military cliques, the black-marketeering of commercial dealers? I suspect there is only one way. The conditions of backwardness must be attacked with the passion, the ruthlessness, and the messianic fury of a jehad, a Holy War. Only a campaign of an intensity and single-mindedness that must approach the ludicrous and the unbearable offers the chance to ride roughshod over the resistance of the rich and the poor alike and to open the way for the forcible implantation of those modern attitudes and techniques without which there will be no escape from the misery of underdevelopment.

I need hardly add that the cost of this modernization process has been and will be horrendous. If Communism is the great modernizer, it is certainly not a benign agent of change. Stalin may well have exceeded Hitler as a mass executioner. Free inquiry in China has been supplanted by dogma and catechism; even in Russia nothing like freedom of criticism or of personal expression is allowed. Furthermore, the economic cost of industrialization in both countries has been at least as severe as that imposed by primitive capitalism.

Yet one must count the gains as well as the losses. Hundreds of millions who would have been confined to the narrow cells of changeless lives have been liberated from prisons they did not even know existed. Class structures that elevated the flighty or irresponsible have been supplanted by others that have promoted the ambitious and the dedicated. Economic systems that gave rise to luxury and poverty have given way to systems that provide a rough distributional justice. Above all, the prospect of a new future has been opened. It is this that lifts the current ordeal in China above the level of pure horror. The number of human beings in that country who have perished over the past centuries from hunger or neglect, is beyond computation. The present revolution may add its dreadful increment to this number. But it also holds out the hope that China may finally have been galvanized into social, political, and economic attitudes that for the first time make its modernization a possibility.

Two questions must be answered when we dare to risk so favorable a verdict on Communism as a modernizing agency. The first is whether the result is worth the cost, whether the possible—by no means assured— escape from underdevelopment is worth the lives that will be squandered to achieve it.

I do not know how one measures the moral price of historical victories or how one can ever decide that a diffuse gain is worth a sharp and particular loss. I only know that the way in which we ordinarily keep the books of history is wrong. No one is now toting up the balance of the wretches who starve in India, or the peasants of Northeastern Brazil who live in the swamps on crabs, or the undernourished and permanently stunted children of Hong Kong or Honduras. Their sufferings go unrecorded, and are not present to counterbalance the scales when the furies of revolution strike down their victims. Barrington Moore has made a nice calculation that bears on this problem. Taking as the weight in one pan the 35,000 to 40,000 persons who lost their lives—mainly for no fault of theirs—as a result of the Terror during the French Revolution, he asks what would have been the death rate from preventable starvation and injustice under the *ancien regime* to balance the scales. "Offhand," he writes, "it seems unlikely that this would be very much below the proportion of .0010 which [the] figure of 40,000 yields when set against an estimated population of 24 million."[2]

Is it unjust to charge the *ancien regime* in Russia with ten million preventable deaths? I think it not unreasonable. To charge the authorities in pre-revolutionary China with equally vast and preventable degradations? Theodore White, writing in 1946, had this to say: . . . "some scholars think that China is perhaps the only country in the world where the people eat less, live more bitterly, and are clothed worse than they were five hundred years ago."[3]

I do not recommend such a calculus of corpses—indeed, I am aware of the license it gives to the unscrupulous—but I raise it to show the onesidedness of our protestations against the brutality and violence of revolutions. In this regard, it is chastening to recall the multitudes who have been killed or mutilated by the Church which is now the first to protest against the excesses of Communism.

But there is an even more terrible second question to be asked. It is clear beyond doubt, however awkward it may be for our moralizing propensities, that historians excuse horror that succeeds; and that we write our comfortable books of moral philosophy, seated atop a mound of victims—slaves, serfs, laboring men and women, heretics, dissenters—who were crushed in the course of preparing the way for our triumphal entry into existence. But at least we are here to vindicate the carnage. What if we were not? What if the revolutions grind flesh and blood and produce nothing, if the end of the convulsion is not exhilaration but exhaustion, not triumph but defeat? Before this possibility—which has been realized more than once in history—one stands mute. Mute, but not paralyzed. For there is the necessity of calculating what is likely to happen in the absence of the revolution whose prospective excesses hold us back. Here one must weigh what has been done to remedy underdevelopment—and what has not been done—in the past twenty years; how much time there remains before the population flood enforces its own ultimate solution; what is the likelihood of bringing modernization without the frenzied assault that Communism seems most capable of mounting. As I make this mental calculation I arrive at an answer which is even more painful than that of revolution. I see the alternative as the continuation, without the substantial relief—and indeed with a substantial chance of deterioration—of the misery and meanness of life as it is now lived in the sinkhole of the world's backward regions.

I have put the case for the necessity of revolution as strongly as possible, but I must now widen the options beyond the stark alternatives I have posed. To begin with, there are areas of the world where the immediate tasks are so far-reaching that little more can be expected for some decades than the primary missions of national identification and unification. Most of the new African states fall into this category. These states may suffer capitalist, Communist, Fascist, or other kinds of regimes during the remainder of this century, but whatever the nominal ideology in the saddle, the job at hand will be that of military and political nation-making.

There is another group of nations, less easy to identify, but much more important in the scale of events, where my analysis also does not apply. These are countries where the pressures of population growth seem sufficiently mild, or the existing political and social framework sufficiently adaptable, to allow for the hope of considerable progress without resort to violence. Greece, Turkey, Chile, Argentina, Mexico may be representatives of nations in this precarious but enviable situation. Some of them, incidentally, have already had revolutions of modernizing intent—fortunately for them in a day when the United States was not so frightened or so powerful as to be able to repress them.

In other words, the great arena of desperation to which the revolutionizing impetus of Communism seems most applicable is primarily the crowded and masses and archipelagoes of Southeast Asia and the impoverished areas of Central and South America. But even here, there is the possibility that the task of modernization may be undertaken by non-Communist lites. There is always the example of indigenous, independent leaders who ise up out of nowhere to overturn the established framework and to galvanize the masses—a Gandhi, a Marti, a pre–1958 Castro. Or there is that fertile ground for the breeding of national leaders—the army, as witness Ataturk or Nasser, among many.[4]

Thus there is certainly no inherent necessity that the revolutions of modernization be led by Communists. But it is well to bear two thoughts in mind when we consider the likely course of non-Communist revolutionary sweeps. The first is the nature of the mobilizing appeal of any successful revolutionary elite. Is it the austere banner of saving and investment that waves over the heads of the shouting marchers in Jakarta and Bombay, Cairo and Havana? It most certainly is not. The banner of economic development is that of nationalism, with its promise of personal immortality and collective majesty. It seems beyond question that a feverish nationalism will charge the atmosphere of any nation, Communist or not, that tries to make the Great Ascent—and as a result we must expect the symptoms of nationalism along with the disease: exaggerated xenophobia, a thin-skinned national sensitivity, a search for enemies as well as a glorification of the state.

These symptoms, which we have already seen in every quarter of the globe, make it impossible to expect easy and amicable relations between the developing states and the colossi of the developed world. No conceivable response on the part of America or Europe or, for that matter, Russia, will be able to play up to the vanities or salve the irritations of the emerging nations, much less satisfy their demands for help. Thus, we must anticipate an anti-American, or anti-Western, possibly even anti-white animus from any nation in the throes of modernization, even if it is not parroting Communist dogma.

Then there is a second caution as to the prospects for non-Communist revolutions. This is the question of what ideas and policies will guide their revolutionary efforts. Revolutions, especially if their whole orientation is to the future, require philosophy equally as much as force. It is here, of course, that Communism finds its special strength. The vocabulary in which it speaks—a vocabulary of class domination, of domestic and international exploitation—is rich in meaning to the backward nations. The view of history it espouses provides the support of historical inevitability to the fallible efforts of struggling leaders. Not least, the very dogmatic certitude and ritualistic repetition that stick in the craw of the Western observer offer the psychological assurances on which an unquestioning faith can be maintained.

If a non-Communist elite is to persevere in tasks that will prove Sisyphean in difficulty, it will also have to offer a philosophical interpretation of its role as convincing and elevating, and a diagnosis of social and economic requirements as sharp and simplistic, as that of Communism. Further, its will to succeed at whatever cost must be as firm as that of the Marxists. It is no impossible that such a philosophy can be developed, more or less independent of formal Marxian conceptions. It is likely, however, to resemble the creed of Communism far more than that of the West. Political liberty, economic freedom, and constitutional law may be the great achievements and the great issues of the most advanced nations, but to the least developed lands they are only dim abstractions, or worse, rationalizations behind which the great powers play their imperialist tricks or protect the privileges of their monied classes.

Thus, even if for many reasons we should prefer the advent of non-Communist modernizing elites, we must realize that they too will present the United States with programs and policies antipathetic to much that America "believes in" and hostile to America as a world power. The leadership needed to mount a jehad against backwardness—and it is my main premise that only a Holy War will begin modernization in our time—will be forced to expound a philosophy that approves authoritarian and collectivist measures at home and that utilizes as the target for its national resentment abroad the towering villains of the world, of which the United States is now Number One.

All this confronts American policymakers and public opinion with a dilemma of a totally unforeseen kind. On the one hand we are eager to assist in the rescue of the great majority of mankind from conditions that we recognize as dreadful and ultimately dangerous. On the other hand, we seem to be committed, especially in the underdeveloped areas, to a policy of defeating Communism wherever it is within our military capacity to do so, and of repressing movements that might become Communist if they were allowed to follow their internal dynamics. Thus, we have on the one side the record of Point Four, the Peace Corps, and foreign aid generally; and on the other, Guatemala, Cuba, the Dominican Republic, and now Vietnam.

That these two policies might be in any way mutually incompatible, that economic development might contain revolutionary implications infinitely more far-reaching than those we have so blandly endorsed in the name of rising expectations, that Communism or a radical national collectivism might be the only vehicles for modernization in many key areas of the world —these are dilemmas we have never faced. Now I suggest that we do face them, and that we begin to examine in a serious way ideas that have hitherto been considered blasphemous, if not near-traitorous.

Suppose that most of Southeast Asia and much of Latin America were to go Communist, or to become controlled by revolutionary governments that espoused collectivist ideologies and vented extreme anti-American sentiments. Would this constitute a mortal threat to the United States?

I think it fair to claim that the purely *military* danger posed by such an eventuality would be slight. Given the present and prospective capabilities of the backward world, the addition of hundreds of millions of citizens to the potential armies of Communism would mean nothing when there was no way of deploying them against us. The prospect of an invasion by Communist hordes—the specter that frightened Europe after World War II with some (although retrospectively, not too much) realism—would be no more than a phantasm when applied to Asia or South America or Africa.

More important, the nuclear or conventional military power of Communism would not be materially increased by the armaments capacities of these areas for many years. By way of indication, the total consumption of energy of all kinds (in terms of coal equivalent) for Afghanistan, Bolivia, Brazil, Burma, Ceylon, Colombia, Costa Rica, Dominican Republic, Ecuador, El Salvador, Ethiopia, Guatemala, Haiti, Honduras, India, Indonesia, Iran, Iraq, Korea, Lebanon, Nicaragua, Pakistan, Paraguay, Peru, Philippines, U.A.R., Uruguay, and Venezuela is less than that annually consumed by West Germany alone. The total steel output of these countries is one-tenth of U.S annual production. Thus, even the total communization of the backward world would not effectively alter the present balance of military strength in the world.

However small the military threat, it is undeniably true that a Communist or radical collectivist engulfment of these countries would cost us the loss of billions of dollars of capital invested there. Of our roughly $50 billions in overseas investment, some $10 billions are in mining, oil, utility, and manufacturing facilities in Latin America, some $4 billions in Asia including the Near East, and about $2 billions in Africa. To lose these assets would deal a heavy blow to a number of large corporations, particularly in oil, and would cost the nation as a whole the loss of some $3 to $4 billions a year in earnings from those areas.

A Marxist might conclude that the economic interests of a capitalist nation would find such a prospective loss insupportable, and that it would be "forced" to go to war. I do not think this is a warranted assumption, although it is undoubtedly a risk. Against a Gross National Product that is approaching ¾ of a trillion dollars and with total corporate assets over $1.3 trillions, the loss of even the whole $16 billions in the vulnerable areas should be manageable economically. Whether such a takeover could be resisted politically—that is, whether the red flag of Communism could be successfully waved by the corporate interests—is another question. I do not myself believe that the corporate elite is particularly war-minded—not nearly so much so as the military or the congressional—or that corporate seizures would be a suitable issue for purposes of drumming up interventionist sentiment.

By these remarks I do not wish airily to dismiss the dangers of a Communist avalanche in the backward nations. There would be dangers, not least those of an American hysteria. Rather, I want only to assert that the threats of a military or economic kind would not be insuperable, as they might well be if Europe were to succumb to a hostile regime.

But is that not the very point?, it will be asked. Would not a Communist success in a few backward nations lead to successes in others, and thus by degrees engulf the entire world, until the United States and perhaps Europe were fortresses besieged on a hostile planet?

I think the answer to this fear is twofold. First, as many beside myself have argued, it is now clear that Communism, far from constituting a single unified movement with a common aim and dovetailing interests, is a movement in which similarities of economic and political structure and ideology are more than outweighed by divergencies of national interest and character. Two bloody wars have demonstrated that in the case of capitalism, structural similarities between nations do not prevent mortal combat. As with capitalism, so with Communism. Russian Communists have already been engaged in skirmishes with Polish and Hungarian Communists, have nearly come to blows with Yugoslavia, and now stand poised at the threshold of open fighting with China. Only in the mind of the *Daily News* (and perhaps still the State Department) does it seem possible, in the face of this spectacle, to refer to the unified machinations of "international Communism" or the "Sino-Soviet bloc."

The realities, I believe, point in a very different direction. A world in which Communist governments were engaged in the enormous task of trying to modernize the worst areas of Asia, Latin America, and Africa would be a world in which sharp differences of national interest were certain to arise within these continental areas. The outlook would be for frictions and conflicts to develop among Communist nations with equal frequency as they developed between those nations and their non-Communist neighbors. A long period of jockeying for power and command over resources, rather than anything like a unified sharing of power and resources, seems unavoidable in the developing continents. This would not preclude a continuous barrage of anti-American propaganda, but it would certanly impede a movement to exert a coordinated Communist influence over these areas.

Second, it seems essential to distinguish among the causes of dangerous national and international behavior those that can be traced to the tenets of Communism and those that must be located elsewhere. "Do not talk to me about Communism and capitalism," said a Hungarian economist with whom I had lunch this winter. "Talk to me about rich nations and poor ones."

I think it *is* wealth and poverty, and not Communism or capitalism, that establishes much of the tone and tension of international relations. For that reason I would expect Communism in the backward nations (or national collectivism, if that emerges in the place of Communism) to be strident, belligerent, and insecure. If these regimes fail—as they may—their rhetoric may become hysterical and their behavior uncontrolled, although of small consequence. But if they succeed, which I believe they can, many of these traits should recede. Russia, Yugoslavia, or Poland are simply not to be compared, either by way of internal pronouncement or external behavior, with China, or, on a smaller scale, Cuba. Modernization brings, among other things, a waning of the stereotypes, commandments, and flagellations so characteristic of (and so necessary to) a nation engaged in the effort to alter itself from top to bottom. The idiom of ceaseless revolution becomes less relevant—even faintly embarrassing—to a nation that begins to be pleased with itself. Then, too, it seems reasonable to suppose that the vituperative quality of Communist invective would show some signs of abating were the United States to modify its own dogmatic attitude and to forego its own wearisome clichés about the nature of Communism.

I doubt there are many who will find these arguments wholly reassuring. They are not. It would be folly to imagine that the next generation or two, when Communism or national collectivism in the underdeveloped areas passes through its jehad stage, will be a time of international safety. But as always in these matters, it is only by a comparison with the alternatives that one can choose the preferable course. The prospect that I have offered as a plausible scenario of the future must be placed against that which results from a pursuit of our present course. And here I see two dangers of even greater magnitude: (1) the prospect of many more Vietnams, as radical movements assert themselves in other areas of the world; and (2) a continuation of the present inability of the most impoverished areas to modernize, with the prospect of an eventual human catastrophe on an unimaginable scale.

Nevertheless, there *is* a threat in the specter of a Communist or near-Communist supremacy in the underdeveloped world. It is that the rise of Communism would signal the end of capitalism as the dominant world order, and would force the acknowledgement that America no longer constituted the model on which the future of world civilization would be mainly based. In this way, as I have written before, the existence of Communism frightens American capitalism as the rise of Protestantism frightened the Catholic Church, or the French Revolution the English aristocracy.

It is, I think, the fear of losing our place in the sun, of finding ourselves at bay, that motivates a great deal of the anti-Communism on which so much of American foreign policy seems to be founded. In this regard I note that the nations of Europe, most of them profoundly more conservative than America in their social and economic dispositions, have made their peace with Communism far more intelligently and easily than we, and I conclude that this is in no small part due to their admission that they are no longer the leaders of the world.

The great question in our own nation is whether we can accept a similar scaling-down of our position in history. This would entail many profound changes in outlook and policy. It would mean the recognition that Communism, which may indeed represent a retrogressive movement in the West, where it should continue to be resisted with full energies, may nonetheless represent a progressive movement in the backward areas, where its advent may be the only chance these areas have of escaping misery. Collaterally, it means the recognition that "our side" has neither the political will, nor the ideological wish, nor the stomach for directing those changes that the backward world must make if it is ever to cease being backward. It would undoubtedly entail a more isolationist policy for the United States *vis-á-vis* the developing continents, and a greater willingness to permit revolutions there to work their way without our interference. It would mean in our daily political life the admission that the ideological battle of capitalism and Communism had passed its point of usefulness or relevance, and that religious diatribe must give way to the pragmatic dialogue of the age of science and technology.

I do not know how to estimate the chances of affecting such deepseated changes in the American outlook. It may be that the pull of vested interests, the inertia of bureaucracy, plus a certain lurking fundamentalism that regards Communism as an evil which admits of no discussion—the antichrist—will maintain America on its present course, with consequences that I find frightening to contemplate. But I believe that our attitudes are not hopelessly frozen. I detect, both above and below, signs that our present view of Communism is no longer wholly tenable and that it must be replaced with a new assessment if we are to remain maneuverable in action and cogent in discourse.

Two actions may help speed along this long overdue modernization of our own thought. The first is a continuation of the gradual thawing and convergence of American and Russian views and interests—a rapprochement that is proceeding slowly and hesitantly, but with a discernible momentum. Here the initiative must come from Russia as well as from ourselves.

The other action is for us alone to take. It is the public airing of the consequences of our blind anti-Communism for the underdeveloped world. It must be said aloud that our present policy prefers the absence of development to the chance for Communism—which is to say, that we prefer hunger and want and the existing inadequate assaults against the causes of hunger and want to any regime that declares its hostility to capitalism. There are

SOCIAL PROBLEMS

strong American currents of humanitarianism that can be directed as a counterforce to this profoundly anti-humanitarian view. But for this counterforce to become mobilized it will be necessary to put fearlessly the outrageous question with which I began: is the United States fundamentally opposed to economic development?

NOTES

1. See C. E. Black, *The Dynamics of Modernization.*
2. *Social Origins of Dictatorship and Democracy,* p. 104.
3. *Thunder Out of China,* p. 32.
4. What are the chances for modernizing revolutions of the Right, such as those of the Meiji Restoration or of Germany under Bismarck? I think they are small. The changes to be wrought in the areas of greatest backwardness are much more socially subversive than those of the 19th century, and the timespan allotted to the revolutionists is much smaller. Bourgeois revolutions are not apt to go far enough, particularly in changing property ownership. Still, one could imagine such revolutions with armed support and no doubt Fascistic ideologies. I doubt that they would be any less of a threat than revolutions of the Left.

SUGGESTED READINGS

N. S. Adams and A. W. McCoy, eds., *Laos: War and Revolution* (New York: Harper & Row, 1971).

Gar Alperovitz, *Atomic Diplomacy* (New York: Simon & Schuster, 1965).

Paul A. Baran and Paul M. Sweezy, *Monopoly Capital* (New York: Monthly Review Press, 1966).

Noam Chomsky, *At War with Asia* (New York: Pantheon, 1970).

G. William Domhoff, *Who Rules America?* (Englewood Cliffs, N. J.: Prentice-Hall, 1967).

Bernard Fall, *The Two Viet Nams* (New York: Praeger, 1965).

Philip Green, *Deadly Logic: The Theory of Nuclear Deterrence* (Columbus: Ohio State University Press, 1966).

Harry Magdoff, *The Age of Imperialism* (New York: Monthly Review Press, 1969).

C. Wright Mills, *The Power Elite* (New York: Oxford University Press, 1959).

I. F. Stone, *Polemics and Prophecies: 1967–1970* (New York: Random House, 1970).

IV

PROBLEMS OF RACE, CONFLICT, AND CONFRONTATION ✤ ✤

THE DYNAMICS OF RACE AND RACISM IN AMERICA ✦

America is a land populated by strangers who came here to realize opportunities not available or allowed in their native lands. Coupled with the desire to create a new way of life was the need to find a new self-dignity, a self-respect, to be somebody.

No longer needed to work the land or to engage in crafts, migrants came first to the newly emerging commercial and industrial towns of Europe only to find stiff competition from their fellow cast-offs from agriculture for the jobs in the factories and mills. Not needed there, they came to America as colonizers to provide what their native countries lacked: cheap foodstuffs to feed the factory workers and raw materials to feed the factories, particularly those items which could not be grown, cut down, or dug up at home. The new land was rich in these natural resources: fertile soil for raising cotton, wheat, and sugar, large tracts of virgin lumber, and ores and other forms of mineral wealth that were found later.

Aside from the plentifulness of the land's vast riches, it was easy to organize the American colonies for commercialized exploitation, especially in agriculture. America was a traditionless society, unfettered by the often inefficient practices of groups which impede innovation and foster fixed relationships and fixed earnings to maintain their way of life, namely, a landed aristocracy and a peasantry, insulated from alternative life styles. Despite this advantage, the colonizers were neither sufficient in number nor motivated to do the backbreaking labor of commercialized agriculture, for they had not come to America to become even less than peasants, at least not while there was a chance of starting careers open to talent. They sought to improve their status by managing the large estates and commercial enterprises.

Yet, a labor supply was needed to pick the cotton, grow the rice, and cut the sugar cane. Others from Europe would not provide the labor so long

291

as the opportunity for entrepreneurial activity was great, and they continued in the same dream as the newly emerging commercial and agrarian elites of America. The major need of the agrarian capitalists was for a disciplined labor force, not particularly skilled, that need not be highly motivated to do the work, so long as it was reliable enough to meet the demands of the market for these products. These demands had to be fulfilled if the factories were to turn out their goods and the workers were to eat. The labor force had to be readily available, but it could not be too costly. In this way the basis was being laid for a system that would be dependent on indentured servants and slaves, and soon only the latter for the labor necessary for large-scale agriculture.

Slavery worked best in the South where the products needed in Europe were most easily grown. The cotton produced in America provided the raw material for the very first factories, the textile mills of England. Through the Islamic, Portuguese, and Dutch slavetraders, the captains of Southern agriculture acquired a labor force which was not motivated by the same search to be somebody. This was mainly because they already had established identities as members of tribes or even as slaves to those tribes, for it was possible to earn membership in the tribe as a captive. Commercial penetration into Africa made the Africans dependent upon exchange with the slavetraders while resulting in the domination of large areas of sub-Saharan Africa by Islamic people. The possession of advanced weaponry in the form of firearms by the traders helped in no small part to encourage the trade in human lives.

It did not require any long period of time for American slaveholders to learn that disciplined labor could not just be bought but had to be created out of independent people. It worked much in the same way that the factory owners in England in the days of early industrialization sought to create a disciplined work force by avoiding the hiring of independent artisans. Through a process of desocialization and resocialization (concepts referring to the ways in which old roles and identities are destroyed and concomitantly, replacements for them are learned or acquired) a new class of people was created, without any identity independent of their being slaves except for the few African cultural traits they managed to maintain. The slavemaster referred to this process as one of "seasoning": a systematic program of conditioning independent people to be docile and obedient.

All sources of prior identity were considered threats to this end so that constant dispersal of prior associates was enforced in a regular way; members of the same tribes, parents and children, husbands and wives were forcibly separated. No mistake should be made about these practices as being accidental offshoots of an unsettled situation; they were deliberate policies introduced to weaken ties among the slaves and replace the possibility of dependence upon each other with a dependence on the slaveholder. The practice continued during much of the slave era, the task being made much easier by the fact that the children of slaves had no direct knowledge of their African heritage.

How much of the brutality of the slave system was based upon the need to create a docile rather than a highly motivated labor force to meet the schedules imposed by the demands of the cotton mills of England and how much was imposed by the needs of the new agrarian capitalists to dominate others in order to become regarded as a legitimate class is a difficult assessment to make. One thing is clear—slavery in North America was one of the cruelest labor systems found anywhere in the world. To justify the treatment of black people or any people in that manner requires an extreme negation of the others' humanity and, at the same time, an extreme dependency upon them for a sense of one's identity. The master could only measure his worth in accordance with the number of slaves he held and the flattery he received from them as to his merits. Surely he could not justify his success by any other means. He took no risks in investing capital in new industry, he showed no ingenuity in the creation of new technologies or skill in managing his enterprise. Indeed, he did his best to demonstrate his separation from the very class upon which he was dependent by cultivating a life of leisure and gentility.

To justify this dependency upon the slave for his very being, the slave master propagated the myth of racial inferiority, an ideology which turned his own dependency into its very opposite. In this new ideology, the slave needed the slavemaster to tell him what to do because he (the slave) was innately inferior, childlike, irresponsible, lazy, shiftless, and promiscuous. Accordingly, he needed paternalism in the form of a combination of harsh treatment and rewards for loyalty and obedience. Although the reconstruction of this era in American history is fraught with extraordinary difficulties, it appears that slaves were able to see through this projection and were able to discover an almost transparent formula for success. This consisted in behavior in a docile and obedient manner in the presence of the master, which would validate his view of reality and make it possible to gain favor with him; and at the same time, the concealment of one's true feeling from the master in order to maintain better respect among one's own.

This duality would seem to be illustrated by the way in which care and competency in work went unrewarded, while wanton destructiveness was treated with satisfied responses of resignation to the terrible responsibility of being the all-powerful father. To some extent, slaves may have also identified with their masters, treating animals in contemptible ways since they were at the same time the master's property; yet they could not retaliate for the cruel treatment they received. The racist ideology was reinforced by the master's perceptions of the actions of the slaves as destructive and irresponsible.

Nevertheless, a master race does not rest easily in the beliefs that it holds about those it oppresses, and so it was with the American slaveholders. They were in great fear of a servile rebellion, and when occasional insurrections occurred (e.g., the Nat Turner rebellion), a wave of indiscriminate killings of black people followed. Had the masters really believed in the Negro's inferiority, then the system of domination would not have been preserved by the gun, the whip, and the rope, but by free competition. For how can innately inferior people succeed against superior ones in an open marketplace?

While the origins of racism in America are part of the historical experience of slavery, its acceptance in the North was accomplished easily and at quite an early date. The same ideology of racial inferiority was used by whites to justify the exclusion and oppression of blacks, even when the former were not slaveholders and the latter were not slaves. For slave labor and black labor were regarded as one and the same—a threat to the incomes and social standing of the free artisan and laborer, and so it continued, perhaps even intensified, when the struggle to abolish slavery had been won. Seen as similar threats were the hordes of unassimilated immigrants from southern and eastern Europe, who came to this country in large numbers, starting in the 1880s. Forces in American society saw their Anglo-Saxon domination of America endangered by the influx of these masses who often brought with them ways alien to American respectability.

Today it can be seen, but few saw then, that this anxiety of the white Anglo-Saxon Protestant majority over the arrival of newcomers was a misplaced attack upon the sources of their displacement. Their way of life was indeed being threatened by the large-scale structural changes in the American economy and technology. Small-scale, pluralistic capitalism, an economic system in which many people owned property, and the possibility of becoming a small businessman was great was being replaced during the late nineteenth century by large, centrally organized industrial corporations, which made it increasingly difficult for small property holders to remain independent, self-employed people. Many native Americans confounded the effect of these structural changes—the need for cheap labor—with the cause of their problems.

The reduction of the independent owner-artisan to a wage earner, or to dependence upon large firms, divorced from control over the means of production, created a problem in defining and redefining who they were in society. As a reaction to the need to repress their prior identities and their failure to preserve this small-town way of life, they embraced the doctrines of racial inferiority to justify their own feelings of being threatened, and they turned upon those who were oppressed and who cast them in the role of the oppressors. They were confirmed in these views by the success of American imperialism abroad, in which dark-skinned people were coming under American domination.

More importantly, so long as they did not regard themselves at the bottom of the heap at home, the white wage earners did not attempt to challenge the newly emerging industrial elite above them. Indeed, they allowed the big entrepreneurs to run wild by not forming a coalition with the poor, the unskilled, the blacks, and the recent immigrants. In some ways, populism was a feeble attempt to regain independence, without developing new coalitions with those at the bottom. The recent immigrants from Europe were in turn assimilated into the newly developing white working classes and middle classes, validating their claims to membership in these groups by giving up much of their prior identities and by becoming more racist and exclusionist than the older Americans. The solution to the problem of repression of one's prior social identity is to adopt the style of the oppressor. In a land of strangers, where all men have come down the same road, the problem of establishing new identities is made easy by the exemplary tales about how inferior one once was and extolling the virtues of submission and deracination.

How, then, did the black people respond to the racist traits in American society? One basic model was already presented in the prior discussion of slavery: to have two social selves, one for the white man and one for one's own. The end of slavery in the South did not materially change the need for this kind of adaptation. "Freedom" came without power to control one's own life, an outline of liberation rather than its substance. The plantation system was replaced by the sharecropping system, which provided even less material security than existed during the days of slavery. What was created by the abolition of slavery was a new set of social relationships in the form of a caste system, which rigidly separated the races into fixed economic and social roles, complete with a racial etiquette to reinforce these relationships in situations where they might break down, such as might result from the close cooperation often found in work groups. In line with the establishment of new rules for social comportment between the races, there developed an ideology of contamination which ensued from interracial contacts. To make such incidents less frequent, a segregation of the races, more complete than any that had existed while "free men of color" resided in a land in which their brethren were slaves, was developed, spread into all sectors of American life, and became formally codified into law and institutionalized.

The most profitable services needed by the formally free black communities were provided by white entrepreneurs, often without black employees. At the same time, fed by illusions of the benefits of the caste system, there came into being a new but small class of black professionals, businessmen (almost always small businessmen) and even some middlemen. This new middle class, later to be devastatingly described in a critique by E. Franklin Frazier, was composed of those blacks who were most desirous of emulating the life style of the white middle class. They were, therefore, often contemptuous of their own people and sought to disidentify from them. In so doing, they rarely earned the trust of the black masses in small Southern towns. However, they were not accepted as brethren by the white middle class, but were used by whites to show blacks and whites alike that education or moderate wealth would not mean emancipation from the burdens of race.

A few of these newly educated blacks caught on to their dilemma of being marginal in Southern society. They sought to improve their situation by leaving for the North in hope of avoiding the burdens of race and pursuing their professional or business aspirations. Many stayed in the South and became the upholders of a strict work ethic that preached the nobility of toil, humility, suffering, and endurance. In our own time, if the events of the 1950s and 1960s can be considered our own time in a fast-moving society, Martin Luther King, Jr., came out of this tradition of quiet dignity and inner grace.

With the dawn of the twentieth century, the black migration to the cities began, spurred on by the decline in the demand for their agricultural labor in the South and the possibility for unskilled or semiskilled work in the North. The coherent world view provided by the ideology of the established black churches in the South did not serve its members well in the North. New, more militant, and more ethnically oriented solutions were required. No longer constrained by the encapsulated Southern towns, and at the same time no longer protected by the certainty of its harsh rules, black people came in large numbers in search of that very American dream—to be somebody. Having lost an identity when the African was converted to a slave, the black person in America could not help but acquire the promise to realize an identity. Yet, he acquired much more from the American experience, a realization that the quest for identity is self-actualizing. In this way, the black people are truly the most American people of all, not because their identities were taken from them, but because they have had to face the harsh reality that one must establish an identity for oneself.

This is nowhere better illustrated than in the search for freedom in the ambiguous, elusive North, a place which ultimately revealed the recondite character of racism in America. The push for integration and legal equality, spurred on by the momentous Supreme Court decision in *Brown* vs. *Board of Education* (1954), showed just how little was to be given up and transferred to black people and how much they were expected to give up if they were to be assimilated into American society. For the exponents of integration in the white world, the cost of becoming part of that world would have to be the renunciation of whatever identities had been created independently of the oppressor's vision of how the oppressed ought to act. The irony of this lesson, still being learned at great travail by millions in America, is that liberation of the black person is not possible until white people liberate themselves from their dependencies on notions that they can be autonomous only at the expense of others and only through the repression of their prior identities.

Liberation begins with the self-consciousness created in oppression, a recognition of the external conditions which shape our being and our destiny. The great refusal of black people to give up the sources of their strength—their autonomous institutions, culture, and experiences—provided the coherence necessary for their survival in America as an ethnic group. The persistence of this black world has opened up the possibility for white America to free itself. The avoidance of the American syndrome of repression of prior social identities is based on alternatives to adopting the style of the oppressor. The black experience, as represented in its artistic manifestations, provides one such model. Once again, as always, Americans are dependent upon the disrespectable for their self-respect.

The impressions of the dynamics of race and racism in America presented here do not deal with the dimensions of the problem in conventional sociological ways. Nor do we offer any solutions to ending racism in America. In this respect, we are in good company, for no contemporary thinker on the problem has any happy predictions or suggestions to make. At best we have begun to examine critically the sources of our condition, why we remain as we began, strangers to each other and ourselves. For the millions of poor, blacks, Puerto Ricans, Chicanos, and Indians, the quest for success and recognition—the American dream—has been their nightmare of destruction and despair.

Just as relations between blacks and whites are one aspect, and probably the most significant for the survival of American society, of the wider problem of interethnic relationships, so the latter have become one phase of the growing problem of intergroup confrontation that sometimes takes on the form of violence and disorder. While blacks in the city, as a group outside of the mainstream of American life, challenge our existing institutional arrangements, college youth expresses its revulsion with society as seen from the inside. Interestingly, it has been those closest to freedom from necessity who have become most disaffiliated in their ideology from the social conditions which produced this freedom. The young of suburbia, products of this cultural and social dynamic, are often in the vanguard of the challenge to this order.

What are we to make of expressions of violence and disruption, in the streets and on the campuses? How can it be that black people burn down their very neighborhoods, and college students bring institutions of higher learning to a "grinding halt"? We know that violence can never, in itself, produce far-reaching social changes in society; yet it can make visible the sources of oppression. It can also make for a counterviolence by those who have already lost much in the form of moral authority with those they are to represent. Otherwise, why the need for violence as a source of social control?

In many ways the violence of the ghetto and the campus has already started a new consciousness about modern society via such establishment documents as the Cox report on the Columbia University rebellion and the Kerner Commission report on civil disorders. At this time, the advocates of technology and bureaucracy are on the defensive, and the premature "American Celebrations" of the 1950s cannot be taken seriously. The outcome of the turbulence of the 1960s is still indeterminate. We may face a repression based on counterviolence or more appeals for reason to those who have found talk to be irrational in the face of continued and increasing indifference to their plight. In either event, an increasing delegitimation of modern culture and institutions will continue unless a renewal of moral authority occurs, through which individuals work to build a new world in which creative men and their dreams prevail over their creations. Violence arises when institutions lose their moral authority, and the latter can never be recreated by violence in itself.

Throughout American history violence and race have been interwoven themes. Violence was effective in subduing blacks, Indians, and other racial minorities, and it was often not even clothed in the robes of legitimation. In the era of intergroup confrontation that marked the decade of the 1960s and seems to be continuing into the 1970s, many groups—hippies, students, antiwar demonstrators, militant feminists—embraced tactics that went beyond the bounds of nonviolent civil disobedience.

Despite its limitations and its dangers, violence reveals much about the nature of modern society, its constituent problems and prospects. Lewis Coser has written extensively on the functions of social conflict in society. In contrast to sociologists of the functional school, Coser does see conflict as having important positive consequences for group and societal integration. In his theoretical treatise on violence, which appears in this section, he argues (1) that violence has positive value for individuals denied access to legitimate channels of expression, self-fulfillment, and social recognition; (2) that it is a means by which the agencies of control in society can respond in anticipation of greater polarization and conflict; and (3) that it can serve to unite into a single moral community a public whose sentiments are violated, whether against those defined as criminals or by excessive law enforcement.

Turning from violence to the nature of racism, we find the latter built into our institutions and constructed anew and reaffirmed in interaction in everyday life. C. Eric Lincoln discusses the various meanings of color in intergroup and interpersonal relations in American society. Skin color is used as a measure of the other's social standing and consequently one's own in a very pervasive way. This standard has been readily adopted by black people themselves in relations among their own. Where in the past light-skinned blacks were regarded as more desirable marital partners, friends, or associates, this pattern of affiliation among blacks is changing, reflecting some change in the meaning of color in the larger society. In their rejection of white society, black people are now rejecting the adoption of white standards but are still using color as the basis for group identity and group cohesion. Lincoln, himself a black man, wonders whether this persistence of consciousness of color can provide the moral basis for group cohesion.

Institutionalized racism is reflected in the differences in social status, economic opportunity, and participation in the larger society. St. Clair Drake, in an exhaustive examination of these dimensions of race, points out clearly how these structures affect the life chances of those who are born black. In this careful documentation, he shows how the "victimization" process operates similarly and differently upon poor and middle-class black people. Moreover, he suggests that the vast technological changes already being introduced into the American economy may well turn the black people in America into a permanent underclass, misaligned with the opportunities for employment or advanced education. In some ways the recent demands for "forced inclusion" of black youth in larger numbers and proportion at our universities is a response to this fear of becoming obsolete in an advanced industrial society.

The demographic study of the National Advisory Commission on Civil Disorders focuses on the ways in which our cities are becoming the repositories for this newly forming permanent underclass of black people. It demonstrates the need for vast transformations in our institutions if we are to reverse the social separation produced by racism. In order to make this society whole, we must begin to think of ways which would provide the means to make each person feel that society has a moral claim to make upon him and that he can receive respect and support from that society as a right, precisely because he is a member. The piecemeal solutions or benign neglect of the problems of the poor practiced during the period of the great migrations from Europe, may have been tolerable at a time when the opportunity structure was quite different. The commission's comparison of the immigrant experience to the black experience is instructive because it dispels the notion that the two periods are analogous.

In the search for solutions to racial and other intergroup relations, violence may be seen as creating the possibility for people to develop new ways of viewing each other. E. L. Quarantelli and Russell R. Dynes, in their discussion of looting, demonstrate that a new definition of the situation for blacks and whites in the cities may be imminent. Old shared definitions of property rights are being challenged. An individual in modern society has the right to dispose or use his property as he sees fit. Looting, because of its socially approved and shared character within a dispossessed group, could become the engine by which property is redefined as something which involves enforced social obligations as well as socially protected rights. In this way, violence enables a new shared definition of the situation to arise.

Finally, Robert Blauner uses the model derived from the colonization experience of Africa and Asia in a modified way to examine how colonization of the ghetto has created the conditions for a transformation of social relationships and identities of black people. The three major manifestations of the change in identity—urban riots, cultural nationalism, and ghetto control politics—are regarded as positive signs of an attempt by black people to gain control over their own lives, starting with their own communities and the institutions and organizations constituent to them. This movement for recognition and autonomy should not be dismissed lightly as black chauvinism or racism, nor should it be considered as alternatives to enlarging economic and educational opportunities in the wider society. Ghetto revolt is a direct result of the ambiguous position that black people are in, when freedom and power are not coequal.

Neither racism, on the one hand, nor minority group problems in the ordinary ethnic sense of that expression, on the other, can properly be confined to the black experience in America. The politics of protest, of urban revolt, or the search to control one's own life while being a part of the society (and hence the lives) of others, the search for self-respect, dignity, and identity—these are all matters of deep concern to the first Americans, the Indians, and to many immigrant groups that came after, Puerto Ricans, Orientals, Mexicans, among others. Probably in no other country of the world are the social problems of intergroup relations so central to the entire struggle of the society to survive as an ongoing system as in America. We choose to focus on the black experience, not in exclusion of the others, but because it so clearly illustrates and delineates the significance of racism and racial oppression; because by dint of its history it has left a mark on America which is inescapable; because it presents both to Americans and to the entire world the sharpest contrast between dream and reality, ideology and truth; because demography itself makes it a social problem demanding answers; and because in the study of the black experience one can find in prototypical fashion something that will illustrate the world of all other oppressed groups.

SOME SOCIAL FUNCTIONS OF VIOLENCE ✿ Lewis A. Coser

The folklore of psychology has it that animals in experimental studies display systematically different behavioral characteristics depending on the investigator. Rats described by American observers are seen as frenetically active, given to a great deal of motor activity, forever dashing in and out of mazes, always trying to get somewhere—though not always certain of exactly where. In contrast, experimental animals seen through the lens of German investigators, apes, for example, seem given to long and intense periods of pensive deliberation and musing cogitation.

This jest highlights an important truth. There *are* systematic differences in the ways a particular scholarly community at a given moment in time chooses to approach the manifold data with which it is confronted. In sociology, for example, even if most American social theorists would readily agree in the abstract that conflict as well as order, tension as well as harmony, violence as well as peaceful adjustment characterize all social systems in varying degrees, social theory actually has settled mainly for a remarkably tame and domesticated view of the social world. This is so despite the fact that European social thinkers such as Marx, Weber, and Simmel, upon whose works so much of American theorizing depends for its inspiration, had an entirely different orientation.

It seems as if American social science, developing in a society which, its birth through revolution notwithstanding, has only known one major internal upheaval throughout its history, has failed to be sensitized to the pervasive effects of violence, conflict, and disorder which to the European thinker

SOURCE: Lewis A Coser, "Some Social Functions of Violence," *The Annals,* 364 (March 1966), 8–18. Reprinted by permission of the author and the publisher.

were facts that they could not but be acquainted with intimately. While to the European thinker the fragility of the social fabric and the brittleness of social bonds seemed self-evident experiences, American social science proceeded from a world view in which social violence was at best seen as a pathological phenomenon. As Arnold Feldman has recently argued:

Violence is conceived as being *incidental* to the basic character of social structures and processes. Indeed the very conception of social structure ordinarily excludes the source of structural destruction.[1]

As long as American sociology confined its attention mainly to a limited view of the contemporary American scene, its neglect of conflict and violence was, perhaps, none too disabling, at least until recently. But at present, when sociology has happily awakened to the need of doing comparative studies of social structures in both geographical space and historical time, this domesticated vision of the social world can be severely hampering. In addition, it seems that even the proper study of American society can no longer profit from exclusive emphasis on models and constructs in which conflict and violence are deliberately or unwittingly minimized. Just as analyses of, say, contemporary South Africa, Latin America, or Southeast Asia, or of seventeenth-century England or nineteenth-century France, would be patently unrealistic if they ignored the functions of political violence, so it has become increasingly evident that such ignoring would be just as unrealistic in the study of the current racial scene in the United States.

For a number of years I have urged a correcting of the traditional balance in theoretical and empirical emphasis in studies of social conflict and social order and have suggested that it is high time to tilt the scale in the direction of greater attention to social conflict.[2] Though much of my work was more generally concerned with the wider topic of social conflict rather than with the somewhat narrower area of social violence, a number of propositions previously advanced apply to violence as well. There is no need, therefore, to reiterate them in this paper. Instead, I shall focus selectively on but a few functions of social violence: violence as a form of achievement, violence as a danger signal, and violence as a catalyst. It is to be understood that this is by no means an exhaustive list of the functions of violence, nor will its dysfunctions be dealt with in this paper.

Violence as Achievement

Certain categories of individuals are so located in the social structure that they are barred from legitimate access to the ladder of achievement, as

Merton has argued in convincing detail.[3] Moreover, as Cloward and Ohlin[4] have shown more recently, certain categories of persons may find themselves in structural positions which effectively prevent them from utilizing not only legitimate channels of opportunity but criminal and illegitimate channels as well. I shall argue that when all such channels are barred, violence may offer alternate roads to achievement.

Cloward and Ohlin take as a case in point adolescents in disorganized urban areas who are oriented toward achieving higher positions and yet lack access to either conventional or criminal opportunity structures. "These adolescents," they argue, seize upon the manipulation of violence as a route to status not only because it provides a way of expressing pent-up angers and frustrations but also because they are not cut off from access to violent means by vicissitudes of birth. In the world of violence, such attributes as race, socio-economic position, age, and the like are irrelevent; personal worth is judged on the basis of qualities that are available to all who would cultivate them. The acquisition of status is not simply a consequence of skill in the use of violence or of physical strength but depends, rather, on one's willingness to risk injury or death in the search for "rep."[5]

In the area of violence, then, ascriptive status considerations become irrelevant. Here, the vaunted equal opportunity, which had been experienced as a sham and a lure everywhere else, turns out to be effective. In the wilderness of cities, just as in the wilderness of the frontier, the gun becomes an effective equalizer. Within the status structure of the gang, through a true transvaluation of middle-class values, success in defense of the "turf" brings deference and "rep" which are unavailable anywhere else. Here the successful exercise of violence is a road to achievement.

Nor need we rest consideration with the case of juvenile delinquency. One can make the more general assertion that in all those situations in which both legitimate and illegitimate socioeconomic achievement seems blocked, recourse to aggressive and violent behavior may be perceived as a significant area of "achievement." This may help to explain the ideal of *machismo* in the lower classes of Latin America. Here, as in the otherwise very different violence in disorganized urban areas of American cities, men tend to feel that only prowess in interpersonal violence or in aggressive sexual encounters allows the achievement of personal identity and permits gaining otherwise unavailable deference. Where no social status can be achieved through socioeconomic channels it may yet be achieved in the show of violence among equally deprived peers.

Somewhat similar mechanisms may be at work in the intrafamilial aggression and violence of American lower-class fathers. These men tend to compensate for inadequate rewards in the occupational world at large by an aggressive assertion of male superiority within the little world of the family—as Donald McKinley has recently argued with much cogency.[6] The disproportionately high rate of interpersonal violence among Negro males may yield to a similar explanation. Since Negroes are assigned lowest position in all three major dimensions of the American status system—ethnicity, class, and education—and since their mobility chances are nil in the first and minimal in the second and third, it stands to reason that achievement in the area of interpersonal violence might be seen as a channel leading to self-regard and self-enhancement—at least as long as conflict with the dominant white majority seems socially unavailable as a means of collective action. This does not preclude that violent acting out may not also at the same time call forth a feeling of self-hatred for acting in the stereotypical manner in which the Negro is accused of acting by the dominant white.

Revolutionary violence, both in the classical revolutions of the past and in the anticolonialist liberation movements of the present, can also be understood in this manner. Participation in such violence offers opportunity to the oppressed and down-trodden for affirming identity and for claiming full manhood hitherto denied to them by the powers that be. Participation in revolutionary violence offers the chance for the first act of participation in the polity, for entry into the world of active citizenship. In addition, participation in acts of violence symbolizes commitment to the revolutionary cause. It marks to the actor, but also to his circle, the irrevocable decision to reject the *ancien régime* and to claim allegiance to the revolutionary movement. This has been well described by the late Frantz Fanon, an active participant in the Algerian movement of liberation and one of its most powerful ideological spokesmen. "For colonial man," he writes,

violence incarnates absolute *praxis*. . . . The questions asked of militants by the organization are marked by this vision of things. "Where did you work? With whom? What have you done?" The group demands that the individual commit an irreversible deed. In Algeria, for example, where almost all of the men who called for the struggle of national liberation were condemned to death or pursued by the French police, confidence in a man was proportional to the degree of severity of his [police] case. A new militant was considered reliable when he could no longer return to the colonial system. It seems that this mechanism was at play among the Mau Mau in Kenya where it was required that each member of the group strike the victim. Hence everyone was personally responsible for the victim's death. . . . Violence once assumed permits those who have left the group to return to their place and to be reintegrated. Colonial man liberates himself in and through violence.[7]

The act of violence, in other words, commits a man symbolically to the revolutionary movement and breaks his ties with his previous life and its commitments. He is reborn, so to speak, through the act of violence and is now in a position to assume his rightful place in the revolutionary world of new men.

Similar considerations may also account for the otherwise puzzling fact that women, normally much less given to violence than men, have played leading roles in classical revolutionary movements and in such modern liberation movements as that of Algeria. Here one may suggest that situations where the old norms have broken down differ significantly from normatively stable situations. In the latter, women, having internalized the acceptance of their lower status relative to men, tend to have low rates of active violence. Their suicide as well as their homicide rates are much lower than those of men. Being more sheltered in their lower status positions, women tend to have less motivation for aggression whether directed toward self or toward others. The situation is different, however, when the old norms are challenged, as in revolutions. Here many observers have noted high female participation rates in violent crowds and in street riots. In certain key revolutionary events, such as the March to Versailles of October 1790, and in later food riots, women were predominant. Writes the foremost student of revolutionary crowds, George Rudé, "On the morning of October 5 the revolt started simultaneously in the central markets and the Faubourg Saint-Antoine; in both cases women were the leading spirits."[8]

Revolutionary situations topple the status order and allow underdogs to aspire to equal participation. They provide the occasion for women to act like men. It is as if women were to say to themselves:

If all these extraordinary actions have become possible, then it is perhaps permissible to entertain the extraordinary idea that women need no longer accept their inferior status and can aspire to achieve a hitherto unattainable equality.

Here, as in all the other cases considered, violence equalizes and opens to the participants access to hitherto denied areas of achievements.[9]

Violence as a Danger Signal

The late Norbert Wiener once remarked that cancer is so peculiarly dangerous a disease because it typically develops through its early stages without causing pain. Most other diseases, by eliciting painful sensations in the body, bring forth bodily signals which allow early detection of the illness and its subsequent treatment. Pain serves as an important mechanism of defense, permitting the medical readjustment of bodily balance which has been attacked by disease. It seems hardly farfetched to apply this reasoning to the body social as well.

A social dysfunction can, of course, be attended to only if it becomes visible, if not to the total community, at least to certain more sensitive and powerful sectors of it. But the sensitive usually lack power, and the powerful often lack sensitivity. As Merton has phrased the issue, there are latent social problems, "conditions which are . . . at odds with values of the group but are not recognized as being so,"[10] which can become manifest, and hence subject to treatment, only when particular groups or individuals choose to take cognizance of them. Merton urges that it is the task of the sociologist to make latent social problems manifest; at the same time he stresses that

those occupying strategic positions of authority and power of course carry more weight than others in deciding social policy and so . . . in identifying for the rest what are to be taken as significant departures from social standards.[11]

Granted that the social perceptions of those in power and authority may be influenced by social scientists calling attention to previously neglected problems, it would be an indulgence in unwarranted Comtean optimism to assume that such enlightenment will at all times be sufficient to alert them. It is at this point that the signaling functions of social violence assume importance.

Although there are individual, subcultural, and class variations in the internalized management and control of anger in response to frustration, I take it to be axiomatic that human beings—other than those systematically trained to use legitimate or illegitimate violence—will resort to violent action only under extremely frustrating, ego-damaging, and anxiety-producing conditions. It follows that if the incidence of violence increases rapidly, be it in the society at large or within specific sectors of it, this can be taken as a signal of severe maladjustment. I would further suggest that this signal is so drastic, so extremely loud, that it cannot fail to be perceived by men in power and authority otherwise not noted for peculiar sensitivity to social ills. This is not to say, of course, that they will necessarily respond with types of social therapy that will effectively remove the sources of infection. But I suggest that outbreaks of social violence are more apt than other less visible or sensitive indicators at least to lead them to perceive the problem.

To be sure, outbreaks of violence can be seen as mere manifestations of underlying conditions. Yet, perhaps because of this, they may lead powerholders to effect a change in these conditions. Two illustrations will have to suffice. Conventional historical and sociological wisdom has it that the British Chartist movement of the first half of the last century and the often violent and destructive popular movements which preceded it were but manifestations of temporary imbalances brought by the Industrial Revolution upon the British social and political scene. These imbalances, it is argued, were progressively eliminated through a variety of social-structural differentiation which gradually provided the homeostatic forces that led to the restabilization of British society in the second part of the nineteenth century.[12] In this view, Chartism was a symptom of a temporary pathological condition, and its defeat highlighted the return to equilibrium and stability.

This view seems to be seriously deficient, if for no other reason than that it ignores the impact of Chartism and related movements on the political decision-makers. It ignores, in other words, the determining contribution of this movement. Far from being but an epiphenomenal manifestation of temporary maladjustment, Chartism had a direct impact by leading to a series of reform measures alleviating the conditions against which it had reacted. Violence and riots were not merely protests: they were claims to be considered. Those involved in them assumed that the authorities would be sensitive to demands and would make concessions. And it turned out that they were right.[13]

Historians will hardly deny that the condition of the laboring poor, and more particularly the industrial working class, between the beginning of the Industrial Revolution and the middle of the nineteenth century was appalling. Nor is it subject to debate that for a long time these conditions were barely perceived by those in power. Finally, it is not to be doubted that legislative remedies, from factory legislation to the successive widening of the franchise and the attendant granting of other citizenship rights to members of the lower classes,[14] came, at least in part, in response to the widespread disorders and violent outbreaks that marked the British social scene for over half a century. Let me quote from Mark Hovell, one of the earliest, and still one of the best, of the historians of the Chartist movement. "The Chartists," he writes:

first compelled attention to the hardness of the workmen's lot, and forced thoughtful minds to appreciate the deep gulf between the two nations which lived side by side without knowledge of or care for each other. Though remedy came slowly and imperfectly, and was seldom directly from Chartist hands, there was always the Chartist impulse behind the first timid steps toward social and economic betterment. The cry of the Chartists did much to force public opinion to adopt the policy of factory legislation in the teeth of the opposition of the manufacturing interests. It compelled the administrative mitigation of the harshness of the New Poor Law. It swelled both the demand and necessity for popular education. It prevented the unqualified victory of the economic gospel of the Utilitarians . . . The whole trend of modern social legislation must well have gladdened the hearts of the ancient survivors of Chartism.[15]

The often violent forms of rebellion of the laboring poor, the destructiveness of the city mobs, and other forms of popular disturbances which mark English social history from the 1760's to the middle of the nineteenth century, helped to educate the governing elite of England, Whig and Tory alike, to the recognition that they could ignore the plight of the poor only at their own peril. These social movements constituted among other things an effective signaling device which sensitized the upper classes to the need for social reconstruction in defense of a social edifice over which they wished to continue to have over-all command.[16]

My second example concerning violence as a danger signal will be brief since it deals with recent experiences still vivid in social memory: the civil rights movement and the war against poverty. The plight of the American Negro and of the urban poor until recently had a very low degree of visibility for the bulk of the white population and the decision-makers on the American scene. Much of it was physically not visible in the sense that it took place in segregated areas not customarily visited by "good people." Much of it, on the other hand, though physically visible, was yet not socially perceived. The sociology of social perception, a sociology elucidating why people sometimes look and why they sometimes look away, it may be remarked in passing, still is to be written. Be that as it may, the shock of recognition, the jolt to conscience, occurred only when the Negroes, through by-and-large nonviolent action in the South and through increasingly violent demonstrations and even riots in the North, brought the problem forcibly to the attention of white public opinion and the white power structure. To be sure, a whole library of books has been written on the dehumanizing consequences of the racial caste system. Yet all this became a public issue only after a number of large-scale social conflicts, beginning in Montgomery, Alabama, helped to highlight the issue. No doubt, the slow process of structural differentiation might have taken care of the problem some time in the indeterminate future. In fact, something was done about it here and now mainly because Negroes, no longer satisfied with promises and having gained some advances, now raised their level of expectations, indicating in quite drastic a manner that they were no longer prepared to wait, that they wanted *Freedom Now*. (I shall return to the topic in the last part of this paper.) Much as one might deplore the often senseless violence displayed in such racial riots as those in Los Angeles, one cannot help feeling that they, too, constituted quite effective signaling devices, perhaps desperate cries for help after other appeals had been unavailing. They indicated a sickness not in the body social which demands immediate remedy if it is not to undermine social order altogether.

Violence as a Catalyst

Marx once remarked: "The criminal produces an impression now moral, now tragic, and hence renders a 'service' by arousing the moral and aesthetic sentiments of the public." Marx here anticipated by many years similar formulations by Durkheim and Mead stressing the unanticipated functions of crime in creating a sense of solidarity within the community.[17] Here I shall argue a related idea, namely, that not only criminals, but law-enforcing agents also, may call forth a sense of solidarity against their behavior. More particularly, the use of extralegal violence by these officers may, under certain circumstances, lead to the arousal of the community and to a revulsion from societal arrangements that rest upon such enforcement methods.

It is common knowledge that the violence used by sheriffs and other Southern officers of the law against Southern Negroes engaged in protest activities and voting-registration drives has had a major impact upon public opinion and federal legislation. The fact is that such methods had been relied upon by Southern police for a very long time without any marked reaction against them. Why, then, did they suddenly become counterproductive? Two major factors seem to account for this reversal. First, modes of control involving the extralegal uses of violence worked well as long as the acts in question could be committed with a minimum of publicity and visibility. They became suicidal when they were performed under the glare of television cameras and under the observation of reporters for national newspapers and magazines.

Everett Hughes, in discussing the Nazi case, has argued that all societies depend for their maintenance on a certain amount of "dirty work" by shady agents of the powers that be, and he added that such dirty work is usually performed far from the sight of "good people."[18] Indeed, the usefulness of those doing the "dirty work" may well come to an end when it must be performed in full view of "good people." If, as Hughes argues, those who do the dirty work "show a sort of concentrate of those impulses of which we are or wish to be less aware," then it stands to reason that they cease to be useful if they have to operate in full view. The solid middle-class citizen of Nazi Germany seems, by and large, to have been unconcerned with what was being done to the Jews; even the early public degradation of Jews in city streets seems to have left them unaffected. But the Hitler regime showed very good judgment indeed in carefully hiding and camouflaging its later murderous methods. One may doubt that the death camps could have been operated except in secret. Similarly, solid middle-class citizens in both North and South may have been aware of the extralegal uses of violence habitually resorted to by Southern sheriffs and police. Yet as long as such knowledge did not intrude too much in their visual field, they remained unconcerned. Matters changed drastically when these inhuman methods were fully exposed to the public at large. Now visibility could no longer be denied. Had these officials become conscious of the changed circumstances under which they were now forced to operate, they might well have abandoned these methods in favor of more subtle means of intimidation. As it turned out, they were subject to the "trained incapacity" upon which Veblen and Kenneth Burke have commented. They adopted measures in keeping with their past training—and the very soundness of this training led them to adopt the wrong measures. Their past training caused them to misjudge their present situation.[19] The very exercise of violence which had been productive of "order" in the past now produced a wave of public indignation which undermined the very practice.

The matter of publicity, powerfully aided by the recent "communication revolution," though crucially important, is not the only one to be considered here. It is equally relevant to observe that violent tactics of suppression tend to be much less successful when used against people who are publicly committed to the principle of nonviolence. Violence by the police, even extralegal violence, may be approved, or at least condoned, when it can be justified by reference to the supposed actual or potential violence of the offending criminal. That is, such behavior seems to be justified or condoned when there exists, or seems to exist, a rough equivalence between the means used by both sides. A tooth for a tooth tends to be a maxim popularly applicable in these cases. But the matter is very different when the presumed offender is committed in principle to a politics of nonviolence. The nonviolent resisters in the South, as distinct from other cases where nonviolence was not based on principle, had consciously assumed the burden of nonviolence. That is, they had made a commitment to the public not to have recourse to violence. When violence was used against them, this hence came to be seen as a breach of a tacit reciprocal commitment on the part of those they opposed. What is ordinarily perceived as a multilateral relationship in which both sides actually or potentially use violence, came now to be perceived as unilateral violence. This impression was still accentuated when acts of official or semiofficial violence were being directed against ministers that is, against men who enjoy specific mandates and immunities as men of peace.

For these reasons, extralegal violence habitually used in the South to maintain the caste system turned out to be a most effective triggering device for measures to abolish it. One need, perhaps, not go so far as to argue, a Jan Howard has recently done,[20] that the very effectiveness of the nonviolent methods used depended on the assumption or expectation that it would encounter violent reactions that would arouse the public conscience. The violent reactions did not have to be anticipated. But it was nevertheless one of the latent functions of Southern violent response to the nonviolent tactic used to lead to the arousal of a previously lethargic community to a sense of indignation and revulsion.

Nor is the Southern case unique. Even in earlier periods extralegal violence on the part of law-enforcement agencies has often been suicidal. The Peterloo Massacre of 1819 in Manchester, when a crowd of listeners to speeches on parliamentary reform and the repeal of the Corn Laws was charged by soldiers who killed ten and injured hundreds, became a rallying cry for the reformers and radicals. The wholesale massacre of participants in the French Commune of 1871 created a sense of intimate solidarity, but also of alienation from society at large, among large sectors of the French working class. In these latter cases the impact was not on the total society but only on particular sectors of it, but in all of them the show of violence on the part of officialdom was suicidal in so far as it transformed victims into martyrs who became symbols of the iniquity and callousness of the rulers.

Lest it be understood that I argue that unanticipated and suicidal uses of violence are limited to cases involving law-enforcement agents alone, let me remark, even if only in passing, that there are clearly other groups within society whose resort to violence may under specifiable circumstances bring forth similar suicidal consequences. In particular, when minority groups appeal to the public conscience and attempt to dramatize the fact that they are treated with less than justice and equity, their resort to violence may effectively hamper their cause. They must depend in their appeal on winning to their side previously indifferent and unconcerned sectors of the public. Resort to violence, however, even though it may serve as a danger signal, is also likely to alienate precisely those who are potential recruits for their cause. Hence groups such as the Black Muslims and other extremist Negro organizations may, if they resort to violence, bring about suicidal results by turning previously indifferent or potentially sympathetic bystanders into hostile antagonists.

Conclusion

The preceding discussion has identified and examined a series of cases in which violence may perform latent or manifest functions. The approach was meant to be exploratory and tentative rather than exhaustive and systematic. It is hoped, however, that enough has been said to show that the curiously tender-minded view of the social structure which has generally predominated in American social theory is seriously deficient and needs to be complemented by a more tough-minded approach.

NOTES

1. Arnold S. Feldman, "Violence and Volatility: The Likelihood of Revolution," *Internal War*, ed. Harry Eckstein (New York: Free Press of Glencoe, 1964), p. 111. See also, Ralf Dahrendorf, *Class and Class Conflict in Industrial Society* (Stanford, Calif.: Stanford University Press, 1959) and a series of later papers collected in the author's *Gesellschaft und Freiheit* (Munich: R. Piper, 1961).

2. Lewis A. Coser, *The Functions of Social Conflict* (Glencoe, Ill.: Free Press, 1956); Lewis A. Coser, "Social Conflict and the Theory of Social Change," *British Journal of Sociology*, VIII, 3 (September 1957), pp. 197–207; Lewis A. Coser, "Some Functions of Deviant Behavior and Normative Flexibility," *American Journal of Sociology*, LXVIII, 2 (September 1962), pp. 172–181; Lewis A. Coser, "Violence and the Social Structure," *Violence and War*, Vol. VI of *Science and Psychoanalysis*, ed. Jules Masserman (New York: Grune and Stratton, 1963).

3. Robert K. Merton, *Social Theory and Social Structure* (rev. ed.; Glencoe, Ill.: Free Press, 1957), chaps. 4 and 5.

4. Richard A. Cloward and Lloyd E. Ohlin, *Delinquency and Opportunity* (Glencoe, Ill.: Free Press, 1960).

5. *Ibid.*, p. 175.

6. Donald G. McKinley, *Social Class and Family Life* (New York: Free Press of Glencoe, 1964).

7. Frantz Fanon, *Les Damnés de la Terre* (Paris: Francis Maspero, 1961), pp. 63–64.

8. George Rudé, *The Crowd in the French Revolution* (Oxford: Clarendon Press, 1959), p. 73.

9. I have dealt with this in a somewhat different framework in "Violence and the Social Structure," *op. cit.*

10. Robert K. Merton, "Social Problems and Social Theory," *Contemporary Social Problems*, ed. Robert K. Merton and Robert A. Nisbet (New York: Harcourt, Brace, 1962), p. 709.

11. *Ibid.*, p. 706.

12. Cf. Neil J. Smelser, *Social Change in the Industrial Revolution* (Chicago: University of Chicago Press, 1959) and the same author's *Theory of Collective Behavior* (New York: Free Press of Glencoe, 1963). In the latter work, social movements are seen as always involving the "action of the impatient" who "short-circuit" the press of social readjustment by "exaggerating reality," see pp. 72–73. In this perspective one might be justified in concluding that had impatient Christians not shortcircuited the adjustment process in ancient Israel, the Jews would have readjusted in time—and spared the world the spectacle of much later impatient religious action.

13. Eric J. Hobsbawm, *The Age of Revolution* (London: Weidenfeld and Nicholson, 1962), p. 111.

14. Cf T. H. Marshall, *Class, Citizenship and Social Development* (New York: Doubleday Anchor Books, 1965).

15. Mark Hovell, *The Chartist Movement* (London: Longmans, Green, 1918), pp. 210–211. See also Edouard Dolléans, *Le Chartisme* (Paris: Marcel Riveère, 1949).

16. On the politics of rioting and crowd action see, among others, George Rudé, *The Crowd in History* (New York: John Wiley & Sons, 1964); and *Liberty* (Oxford: Clarendon Press, 1962); Eric J. Hobsbawm, *Labouring Men* (London: Weidenfeld and Nicholson, 1964) and his earlier *Social Bandits and Primitive Rebels* (Glencoe, Ill.: Free Press, 1959).

17. For the relevant quotations from Marx, Durkheim, and Mead, see Coser, "Some Functions of Deviant Behavior," *op. cit.*

18. Everett C. Hughes, "Good People and Dirty Work," *Social Problems,* X, 1 (Summer 1962), pp. 3–11.

19. Kenneth Burke, *Permanence and Change* (New York: New Republic, 1936), p. 18.

20. In *Dissent* (January–February 1966).

COLOR AND GROUP IDENTITY IN THE UNITED STATES

C. Eric Lincoln

Mary had a little lamb
Its fleece was white as snow
And everywhere that Mary went
That little white lamb could go.

Mary had another lamb
Its fleece was black, you see

SOURCE: C. Eric Lincoln, "Color and Group Identity in the United States," *Daedalus,* 96, No. 3 (Spring 1967), 527–541. Reprinted by permission of *Daedalus,* Journal of the American Academy of Arts and Sciences.

They thought he was a "you-know-what"
And hung him from a tree.[1]

In the United States where the enduring problem in social relations is between whites and Negroes, skin color is probably the most important single index for uncritical human evaluation. It is paradoxical that this is so, for color is notoriously unreliable as a tool for determining any substantial qualities of an individual, particularly his "race." And it is with race that the question of color is ultimately concerned. Despite this obvious unreliability, color is made to function as a cultural index for racial determination whenever it is conceived of as a valid external symbol of supposedly intrinsic qualities. The presence or absence of these qualities determines whether a person belongs to an "inferior" or "superior" social group, and whether his life chances are circumscribed or maximized in terms of his group membership.

In social relations in the United States, color is often read as a signal to denigrate, to discriminate, to segregate. It takes on the characteristics of a cultural norm, so much so that a complex of rewards, punishments, and the strictest taboos have grown up around it. American children, both Negro and white, very early develop behavior patterns and adopt value systems based on color, and American adults are seldom free from its connotations. That a racial determination on the basis of color can only be approximate and for a limited spectrum of individuals at best does not seem to impair its credibility as a legitimate index for human evaluation. Nor does it seem to diminish the apparent *need* for identifying persons by race. On the surface this would seem to indicate that America's cultural concern about color is essentially nominal. The need to make decisions on a racial basis is perhaps psychologically atavistic, a tribal anachronism rooted in the dim past when everyone not a member of the tribe threatened its well-being.

Thousands of Negroes "pass" permanently into the white race each year. This cannot be effectively prevented so long as there are interracial unions, with or without benefit of law or clergy. Thousands of others pass whenever it provides social or economic opportunities not readily available outside the majority group. Reliable estimates on the basis of three hundred and fifty years of miscegenation and passing suggest that there are several million "caucasians" in this country who are part Negro insofar as they have Negro blood or Negro ancestry.[2] Since there are few Negro Americans who do not have some white blood, the continuing preoccupation with racial identification by color would seem to be of little reward—the more crucial facts having already been established by a countervailing proclivity.

Nonetheless, American society has troubled itself considerably to detect by various supplementary devices—sometimes refined, but more often of a cruder sort—what may be undetectable to the uncritical eye. It thus reaffirms its apparent need (and the quality of its commitment) for the establishment of racial identity as a crucial factor in social intercourse. A generation ago when strict segregation followed identification, some of the night clubs, hotels, and other places of entertainment and public accommodation in Chicago and other cities hired "spotters" to point out light-skinned Negroes who sought to pass for white and enter the segregated establishments. Since the operating premise of the white proprietors was that "one coon can recognize another," the spotters were always Negroes, some of whom were themselves light enough to pass. The system broke down during the depression years when few Negroes, light-skinned or otherwise, had enough money to bother about trying to spend it in places where they had to run a color gantlet. Having nobody to spot, the "spotters" felt their jobs in jeopardy and began to ask their friends to come by occasionally in the interest of the survival of the profession. The whole sordid arrangement collapsed when the supply of friends of "passable" skin color ran low, and the ersatz "Caucasians" became darker and darker with hair that was fuzzier and fuzzier. Reduced to spotting the obvious, the spotters were soon dispensed with.

This absurd practice demonstrates the near pathological obsession with race and color Americans have exhibited. It is *e pluribus unum*—one out of a multitude. In the illustration given, those most anxious about color and identity were Caucasian, which is to say, white. But in a well-known southern city a leading Negro church for years discouraged the attendance of would-be worshippers who were darker than a *café au lait* stripe painted conveniently on the doorjamb of the sanctuary.

In its American manifestations, the fundamental problem of color and group identity derives in large measure from the desire of the established white hegemony, particularly the former slave-owning class, to distinguish itself by all means available from the blacks, who, whether as slaves or freedmen, had little status and no power.[3] As long as the vast majority of the blacks were of unmixed African descent, the problem was minimized. Their distinctive visibility made their racial origins unmistakable. In fact, the very first significance of color was the early development of a rationale in the colonies that made it possible to hold a black bondservant for life, to make him a slave, while a white bondservant could be held only for a term of years.[4]

From the date that blacks could, as a matter of course, be held in legal servitude for life, color became an important index of race and, hence, of prestige and status.[5] A ban against intermarriage was immediately instituted. Theretofore, intermarriage between black bondsmen from Africa and white bondswomen from England and Ireland had been common.

Social acceptability was measured in terms of class, which could be transcended, rather then in terms of race, which was immutable. In the context of a distribution of status and power that implied the freedom of all white men and the susceptibility to chattel slavery of all Negroes, color became the visual rule of thumb for the assignment of "place" or status.

It is no less ironic for all its inevitability that Negroes, who were (and who remain) the prime subjects of color discrimination, adopted color as an index of social worth. They made the evaluative modifications necessary to suit their peculiar condition as a color caste undergirding an otherwise class-oriented society.

In the process of establishing a "democracy" in the New World, colonial Europeans did not contemplate the inclusion of Negroes (nor Indians for that matter) in the ruling caste. As American social and moral philosophy evolved through an agonizing assessment of economic preferments and political demands, consensus arose that the issue of color and caste implied in Negro slavery should be excluded from the founding documents of the emergent democracy.[6] For the British founders and the succeeding generations of Euro-Americans, the issue of color was without complication once Negro slavery had become institutionalized. Indeed, the issue of political status transcended the issue of color. All white men were free; all black men were slaves (with the exception of "free" Negroes who were in a sort of limbo in between).[7] Unlike the complicated experiments of slaveholding countries that sought to match a hierarchy of privileges with a spectrum of color, America's color-caste arrangement was inflexible. There were but two recognized categories of color: "white" and "colored." "Colored" was the common designation for any person having any Negro ancestry whatever—no matter how "light" or how "dark" his skin color, and irrespective of any quantity of "white blood" less than 100 per cent. The term *mulatto* was loosely used in commercial parlance to refer to a slave of mixed blood in any degree, but it had no political, social, or legal meaning. From the perspective of the white ruling caste, all Negroes of any color were of a lower caste. The question of color as a matter of identity was to have substantial meaning only to Negroes.

In search for an identity based on color, the Negro reacted (and perhaps is still reacting) to a status first ascribed to him by the white man and then perpetuated in a self-fulfilling prophecy. The white man rationalized the Negro's peculiar fitness, even his God-willed destiny, to be a slave and then enslaved him. The Negro in his yearnings to be free and equal, and everywhere observing that blacks were in servitude and whites were free, mistakenly equated whiteness as a necessary corollary to freedom, and blackness as the inevitable concomitant to bondage.

Aught's de aught
Figger's de figger. . .
All fo' de white man
And none fo' de nigger.

Even the experience of emancipation, a rather qualified freedom, did not significantly change the black man's awe of the mystery of whiteness.

There is not, to my knowledge, any history of pre-colonial color-consciousness among the various African tribes whose descendants make up the Negro population in America. If color-consciousness was *not* a factor in their social relations, two hundred and fifty years of slavery, and another hundred years of marginal involvement in the pervasive, ubiquitous culture of a white, European society have created a color-consciousness that has become such a factor. In a sub-society alienated so completely and with such finality from its parent culture and its traditional spectrum of values, a modified adoption of the cultural values of the host society would seem to be predictable.

At the uncritical stage of their yearning for equivalence, the powerless and the disinherited find attractive whatever is associated with the peculiar mystique of the group in power. This was true of the Jews, the American colonists, and probably of every other subject people. The slave affects the style of his master; the student, the language of his teacher. Whether the quality affected or yearned after is germane to the status associated with it is unimportant so long as it is *thought* to be by those impressed by it. In America, the white man was unchallenged in his power. His grand style bespoke wealth and learning. Negroes were powerless, poor, and ignorant. Indeed, both races commonly supposed that an unmixed Negro was incapable of education, to say nothing of mastering the intricacies of politics or economics.

If the secret of the white man's success lay in his color, it stood to reason that the closer to being "white" a black man was, the more likely he was to have power and status. This reasoning reinforced by the slave-era tradition of making household servants of the slave master's mulatto offspring, thus securing them in positions of relative privilege *vis à vis* the unmixed field hands. Frequently, the law permitting, a conscience-stricken master would free the half-white fruit of his cabin dalliances when they reached majority, or he would provide for their freedom in his will.

Thus, a substantial proportion of free Negroes were mulattoes. The various literary and mutual-aid societies, and sometimes churches formed by 'free persons of color"[8] often disdained the admission of free Negroes with dark skin. When the slavocracy was destroyed and all Negroes were elevated to a single legal status, the Negro group—as a sub-society—already had an emerging class arrangement based on color within a nether caste also defined by color. The mulattoes were at the top of the lowly heap. They maintained their position as a class within the caste until after World War II when values like wealth, education, and profession reduced the mere possession of a light skin to relative insignificance.

Yet to say that color is dead as an aspect of racial psychosis would be to lay prematurely to rest a troublesome syndrome likely to defy interment. Quite apart from its elemental concern with status and power, color as a cultural value has continuing significance for aesthetics and for personal identity. The prevailing conceptions of what or who is beautiful vary widely between native Africans and their Afro-American counterparts. The white ideal of feminine pulchritude, though less stressed than formerly, is still the archetype for the overwhelming majority of Negro American women and the persistent choice of Negro men. Cosmetic preparations for lightening skin and straightening hair represent a multi-million-dollar market among Negroes not favored with Caucasoid features. Among the less affluent and more credulous, urine rinses for the face and "mammy-leg"[9] presses for the hair contribute to the unending search for some approximation of the white ideal.

To the intense delight of a street-corner gathering, a Negro punster described the ideal woman in exaggerated terms reflecting the Negro's preoccupation with color:

> She got to be *white*, Jack—
> 'Cause white is right
> Both day and night!
> She got to be *old* and white,
> 'Cause if she's old
> She's been white *longer!*
> She got to be *big* and white,
> Cause if she's big
> She's much *more* white!
> But listen, Jack—
> If she just can't be *white*
> Then let her be real *light brown!*[10]

A college jester put it this way: "A light woman is your passport to Negro society. I'd rather give a light woman plane fare to St. Louis than to tell a tack head[11] what time the train leaves!"

During the uncertain years of World War II, "passport parties" were actually held as pranks on some college campuses. To attend such a party male escorts were made to pay (unknown to their dates) a color tax based on the complexion of the girls they escorted; the money thus raised made up a pot to buy refreshments. Any girl as fair as a secretly agreed upon

"Fairy Queen" was designated a "Natural Passport"; she and her escort were admitted without charge. The color of the male was inconsequential. That college youths could face the color issue squarely enough to joke about it is probably indicative of its declining importance as early as two decades ago, but is no less indicative of its pervasiveness.

The problem of negative associations with blackness goes deeper than aesthetics. American culture associates Negroes with darkness, an extremely negative quality. In the innocent and painful prattle of Negro children heard a scant generation ago, *"Black is evil!"* was a retort intended to account for behavior one disapproved of in a playmate.[12] In the rural areas, black people were frequently associated with sorcery and voodoo.[13] Everywhere black people were pitied, for deep in the soul of even the whitest Negro was an erosive *self*-pity, even a self-hatred that gnawed at his vitals, questioned his manhood, and excused his failures in a way he did not want them to be excused. There was something inherent in being black that marked a man; something sinister that mocked a man.

The crucial question has always been the question of identity. Who *is* this Negro whose identifying characteristic is his color and what is his status in the world? *Whence does that status derive!* Is he African—an involuntary expatriate? Is he, in fact, "just a nigger"—a monster, blackened by God, broken in servitude, and inherently incapable of human excellence? How should he designate himself? By what name should he identify himself before the world and serve notice of what he conceives himself to be?

There has been little unanimity in the Negro's search for his identity. The Negro slaves came from many tribes and many cultures. Even though the experience of slavery reduced them all to a common denominator, it did not fuse them into an ideological unit. Only attractive ideas and persuasive leadership could do that; the nature of slavery in America left little room for the development of either.

The confusion of identity is vividly expressed in the names by which Negroes have chosen at various times to designate themselves: "persons of color," "colored people," "Negroes," "colored Americans," "Black Anglo-Saxons," "Americans," "Afro-Americans," "Afra-Americans," "Negro Americans"; and, more recently: "black men," "black Americans," "black people." Widely used by white writers, but commonly rejected by Negro intellectuals and black nationalists is the term *American Negroes.* This eristic term allegedly carries the stamp of something "made in America" and is the inverse of the designations commonly applied to other ethnic groups—"German Americans," for instance.[14] "That we are called 'American Negroes,' " a prominent Negro writer has said, "is a concession of courtesy on the part of our Caucasian brothers. In translation, 'the American Negro' can only mean 'our nigger'. "

Despite some improvements in the Negroes' position as a major ethnic group pressing for a larger share of the common values of the society, the question of color and identity has in some sense become more involved and more intricate than before. There have been changes in the way Caucasians and Negroes see each other, and profound changes in the way Negroes see themselves. These newly developing attitudes have not always found mutual acceptance, nor are they necessarily consistent with one another. The de-escalation of color as an index of social standing in the Negro sub-society immeasurably strengthened and unified the factions previously contending for leadership and prestige. Forced to more diligently prepare themselves, the descendants of the less-favored field hands of plantation days have at least caught up. Today, education, wealth, high social status, and leadership are distributed fairly evenly across the color spectrum of the Negro community.

If anything, the light-skinned Negro is at a disadvantage. In the old days, color meant (at least nominal) privilege, for it bespoke the presence of the master's blood. Today, as the Negro develops an increasing appreciation of his own accomplishments and shares vicariously the accomplishments of other non-whites, the premium on "the master's blood" is signally diminished. Anyone whose light skin color is thought to be of recent derivation is exposed to a degree of censure and disapproval not known in former times.

As far as the larger society is concerned, the presence of white blood in a Negro does not bridge the chasm between castes any more today than it did formerly. In personal relations, Caucasians have, since the plantation days, usually been less threatened by blacks who were thought of as "knowing their places" than by mulattoes or "yellow niggers" who were always suspect. This white attitude can be explained in part, of course, by guilt feelings deriving from a covert recognition of kinship, which could never be openly admitted without violating the strictest taboos. But there was also the deep-seated belief that too much white blood transformed the stereo-typed docile, accommodating Negro into a dissatisfied, potential trouble-maker. Hence, enduring bonds of affection and qualified respect frequently developed between whites and darker Negroes, a felicitous relationship from which light-skinned Negroes were generally excluded. In quite recent times, this tradition has undergone some interesting changes that reflect the inconsistencies of a color differential.

When civil rights legislation first required the employment of Negroes in major industry, wherever possible the "instant Negroes"[15] hired were of very fair complexions. Negroes serving as clerks and saleswomen in depart-ment stores or as route salesmen were frequently mistaken for white by their customers and sometimes by their co-workers. This was, of course, precisely what their employers had hoped for. In hiring Negroes who could "pass," they complied with the law without appearing to have done so. They thus reduced the supposed threat of customer and white employee reaction against being served by or working with Negroes. This policy was discontinued in favor of hiring highly visible Negroes and placing them in the most conspicuous assignments when compliance officials could discover no change in hiring policies, and Negro leaders protested that their followers wanted to "see their people on the job without having to look for them."

There are signs that the civil rights movement as a supporting thrust to a certain degree of Negro "readiness" in terms of education, accomplishment, and demonstrated potential has successfully breached the wall separating Negroes and whites into two castes. The breach is certainly not general, but for the first time in American history, Negroes enjoy some degree of lateral mobility. There is *some* social movement across color lines. Perhaps the sudden recognition of this fact contributed in no small degree to the amazing "pull-back" on the part of large numbers of whites who had been heavily involved in the civil rights movement so long as it was limited to civil rights—and concentrated in the South. The white retreat would seem to buttress other evidence that white America in general, despite some fits and starts, is not yet ready to accept Negroes on equal terms so long as they remain Negroes. Arnold Toynbee's observations of thirty years ago are still valid:

The . . . [Negro] may have found spiritual salvation in the White Man's faith; he may have acquired the White Man's culture and learnt to speak his language with the tongue of an angel; he may have become adept in the White Man's economic technique, and yet it profits him nothing if he has not changed his skin.[16]

A few, select, individual Negroes have been able to approach the American main stream with varying degrees of marginality. In doing so, they run the inevitable risk of becoming as alienated from the nether culture from which they came as they are likely to remain in reference to the culture they seek to enter. But change *is* occurring.

Even as the machinery of caste is being dismantled and discarded, the color-caste psychology persists. It is not difficult to understand the continuing frustrations of the black masses. A universal system of *apartheid* has, in effect, been exchanged for a selective system of *apartheid*. This may be progress, but it is not progressive enough to satisfy the present-day needs of the black millions who are still beyond the pale. The color computer has been programmed to extend to selected Negroes of high accomplishment selected categories of privileges previously withheld from all Negroes. An "integrated" society in which the common values of that society will be freely accessible to the general population regardless of color has not been realized, nor does it seem to be rapidly approaching.

Taking no comfort from what they perceive as an *entente cordiale* between the white establishment and the Negro leadership class, the black *lumpen proletariat* seethes with hostility and resentment. Despite modifications of law and practice produced by the efforts of the civil rights movement, the black masses are unimpressed because they are unaffected. Critical selectivity functions at the top; the tortured masses at the bottom feel no tremor of change.

The Great Society has spent millions of dollars in the interest of the poor and the disinherited. In doing so, the government created yet another clique of petty bureaucrats and interposed them between the people and the help they need. By day the black ghetto is resplendent with sleek, fat professionals—Negro and white—striving mightily to re-mold the people in images they reject and despise; by night—the professionals having fled home to the suburbs—the people gather on the street corners to contemplate the probabilities of black power, or the ecstasy of long, hot summers. Despite the ministrations of the professionals, the people are as hungry, as unemployed, and as hostile as before.

As their frustrations multiply, the black masses become more and more alienated from the larger society and from the tiny Negro middle class that hopes to cross the chasm eventually and to enter the American main stream. The problem of color and identity takes on crucial meaning in this context. The term *Negro,* which has for so long aroused mixed emotions even among those who accepted it, has for the militant[17] masses become an epithet reserved for the Negro middle class, particularly those suspected of desiring to be integrated into the white society.

Neither the traditional black nationalists nor the advocates of "black power," which is a new form of militant black nationalism, accept integration as being either possible or desirable under existing conditions. Integration is interpreted as a one-way street. It means to those not impressed by its possibilities the abandonment of traditional values and styles of life on the off-chance of being accepted by a group "which never appreciated you for what you were, and resents you for what you are trying to become." Stokely Carmichael declares:

Integration . . . speaks to the problem of blackness in a despicable way. As a goal it has been based on complete acceptance of the fact [sic] that in order to have a decent house or education, blacks must move into a white neighborhood or send their children to a white school.

This reinforces, among both black and white, the idea that "white" is automatically better and "black" is by definition inferior. This is why integration is a subterfuge for the maintenance of white supremacy.[18]

To the black masses, the Negro integrationists and integrationist leaders seem to take on the characteristics of "collaborators with the enemy," and need to be labeled distinctly as such. Hence, the black militants have resurrected the connotation of "Negro" as being a thing, a puppet, a creation of the white man, finding it peculiarly applicable to the Negro middle class and its leadership.[19]

Like the Garveyites and the Black Muslims before them, the new black militants—particularly those in the Student Non-Violent Coordinating Committee—do not see themselves in the image of the white American. They dress unaffectedly and wear their hair *á la mode Africaine*—combed, but unstraightened. They refer to themselves and to all other non-integrationist-minded black Americans as "black people." The term is deliberately chosen as a symbol of racial polarization. It intends to imply the solidarity of the black masses, here and abroad; to disavow any necessary commitment to white values or deference to the white establishment; to distinguish the masses from the integrationist; and to exploit new feelings of black nationalism and *négritude* that have taken hold in the Negro community since World War II. It answers, at least for the time being, all the important questions of identity and color. Many middle-class Negroes, remembering the negative stereotypes formerly associated with blackness, cannot bring themselves to speak of Negroes as "black people." Neither can many whites for that matter.[20] The stereotypes die too hard.

The new SNCC strategy aims at organizing a power base from which black people can influence decisions within the existing political arrangement without being subject to review by white monitors. Implied is a fundamental rejection of reliance upon the white man's integrity, a point to which all black nationalist groups must come by definition. The synonym for black nationalism is black ethnocentrism, and ethnocentrism always implies a suspicion of some other peoples' integrity, their values, and their truth.

In the conventional interpretation of human confrontation, belief is always preceded by doubt. Not so with the Negro in America. He believed first and has but lately learned to doubt. It is a tragedy that doubt was even necessary, since the faith he had required so little to fulfill. But America is now forever beyond the point of naïveté and innocence, and is unlikely to pass that way again. The lessons that have been learned cannot be forgotten, and there are new teachers to interpret old experiences. Elijah Muhammad justifies his all-black Muslim organization on the grounds that "You can't whip a man when he's helping you," thus surreptitiously but unequivocally identifying the enemy as the white man. The SNCC rationale is more adroit. SNCC wants its white supporters to work among prejudiced whites "who are not accessible" to its Negro agents. The net result is the same: the effective removal of white individuals, however well-intentioned, from sensitive strategy and policy-making areas where racial loyalties may jeopardize the pursuit of the black man's program.

Traditional black nationalism has been oriented toward separatism—or, at best, toward a pluralistic society. The "black-power" syndrome recognizes the substantial existence of a plural society already and intends to capitalize on it. Like the integrationists, SNCC wants power within the existing political structure, but unlike more moderate organizations, SNCC is impatient with indirect power and suspicious of contingent or shared power. "Black power" is conceived as palpable, manipulatable, black-controlled power that carries with it a sense of dignity for black people and a feeling of security from white caprice. An organized, voting black minority with a substantially unified ideological orientation could conceivably produce such power. Whether it can be produced on the basis of color alone is debatable.[21]

The question is not whether black people are capable of leadership and self-direction or of making the sacrifices that may be needed. They have demonstrated their capabilities in all these areas, and more. The more fundamental question is whether color alone is a unifying force sufficient to weld together in a monolithic (or, better, monochromatic) sociopolitical movement a black minority exhibiting an immense spectrum of needs, wants, desires, and intentions based on conflicting systems of value. The question of identity has not been resolved. Color alone does not answer satisfactorily the questions about the self one needs to have answered as the basis for intelligent decision-making about oneself and others. Negroes in America still do not know who they are. Not having resolved this elemental problem, they approach all other problems in human relations with predictable ambivalence and uncertainty. That is why they fight bravely in the far off places of the world, march peacefully in Washington, and die cravenly in Mississippi and Alabama. This, too, is why they sing "Black and White Together" by day, and "Burn! Baby, Burn!" by night.

The Negro's experiences in America have produced in him a mass social neurosis that can only become more morbid as the frustrations of trying to cope with the problem of color and identity are intensified by education and increased marginality at the top of the social pyramid, and by increasing poverty and the concomitant loss of personhood at the bottom. Involuntary servitude did not shatter the psyche of the Negro. He could overcome servitude—slavery if you insist—just as countless other peoples of different races and cultures had. Slavery was not a unique experience. Still, although it existed for centuries in Africa as well as elsewhere, nowhere but in America was it accompanied by such devastation of personality. It was not the slavery *per se,* but the pitiless obliteration of the history and the culture of a people, the deliberate distortion of that history and culture. It was the casual pollution of a race without the compassion and responsibility of acknowledgment. It was, above all, the snide rejection of the Negro's claim to be "American." Less deserving people from all over the world could come to America and claim that identity so long as they were white. The Negro could never claim it because he was black.

The trauma of this rejection polarizes the color crisis between the races and keeps alive the anxieties of identification and color within the Negro sub-group. Charles Silberman is probably right: "Consciousness of color is not likely to disappear unless color itself disappears, or unless men lose their eyesight."[22] But consciousness of color, like consciousness of kind, is not a reasonable basis upon which to project a system of group relations. Nor has it ever been.

NOTES

1. From "Joe Jipson," *The Autobiography of a Southern Town;* an unpublished manuscript by C. Eric Lincoln.

2. Sociologist Robert P. Stuckert of Ohio State University estimates: "Over 28 million white persons are descendants of persons of African origins"—about 21 per cent of the Caucasian population of the United States.

3. In a larger sense, the problem of color and identity in America is related to the general ascendancy of the West, which is to say white Europeans, since the fifteenth century, and the subsequent colonization of Asia, Africa, and the New World. In his book, *Caste, Class and Race* ([Garden City, N. Y., 1948], p. 346), Oliver Cox makes the signal observation that "since the belief in white superiority —that is to say white nationalism—began to move over the world, no people of color have been able to develop race prejudice independent of whites."

4. See John Hope Franklin, *From Slavery to Freedom* (New York, 1947), p. 70ff.

5. This was first practiced in Virginia in 1661; Maryland followed in 1663. A Virginia law of 1670 fixed the status of Negroes and Indians respectively by decreeing that "all servants not being Christians" (that is, not being "white") coming into the colony by sea, "shall be slaves for their lives." Those "coming by land" (Indians) could be bound for a term of years.

6. The Continental Congress refused to accept Thomas Jefferson's draft of the Declaration of Independence which included a strong indictment of Negro slavery and of the English Crown which was allegedly responsible for the establishment and continuation of slavery in the colonies. It is significant that once free of British rule, the colonies continued slavery on their own, although there was always dissent against the practice.

7. "His color" says, Wade, "suggested servitude, but his national status secured

a portion of freedom." Richard C. Wade, *Slavery in the Cities* (New York, 1964), p. 249.

8. A term normally meaning "colored"—that is, "Negro."

9. A sort of cap made from a woman's stocking, the "mammy-leg" is much used by males and females to hold the hair in place during informal hours at home. They are sometimes seen on children and teen-agers on neighborhood streets.

10. Lincoln, "Joe Jipson." *The Autobiography of a Southern Town.*

11. A slang term for a dark woman with crimpy hair.

12. In Boston, the author was once physically attacked by a white child with no other explanation than, "I don't like you because you're black!"

13. A belief possibly reinforced by once popular "jungle" films and stories; but possibly in recollection of a fragmentary cultural experience having to do with tribal religious rites or witchcraft.

14. The implication, say the critics, is that the Negro has no prior nationality or culture, that he is in fact a creation of the white man, "something made in America." Only the Indian should have "American" placed before his ethnic name, it is argued.

15. Negroes hired in token numbers merely to comply with the law.

16. Arnold J. Toynbee, *A Study of History*, Vol. 1 (London, 1935), p. 224.

17. The greater portion of the black masses can still be classified as "quiescent," although they are certainly more susceptible to sporadic activities than ever before.

18. Stokely Carmichael, "What We Want," *The Boston Sunday Herald,* October 2, 1966.

19. In conversation, the word may be sarcastically pronounced with excessive stress on the first syllable ("NEE-gro"), recalling readily to the ingroup mind the slurred pronunciation of some Southerners that renders the word "Negra," which to sensitive ears is a covert way of saying "nigger."

20. In a graduate seminar on minority relations, a young white student protested to a Negro classmate: "Why do you call yourself 'black'? I could never call you black. There is something not right about it. Besides, I think you're a nice guy." "You can't call me 'black,' " the Negro student answered, "and that is your guilt. I can call myself 'black,' and that is my freedom."

21. Malcolm X saw color as the only possible basis of unification. He attempted to eclipse the problem of white ancestry so obvious in many Negroes, himself included, by declaring: "We are all black, different shades of black, and not one of us means any more to a white cracker than any other one."

22. Charles E. Silberman, *Crisis in Black and White* (New York, 1964), p. 166.

THE SOCIAL AND ECONOMIC STATUS OF THE NEGRO IN THE UNITED STATES ✿ *St. Clair Drake*

Caste, Class, and "Victimization"

During the 1930's, W. Lloyd Warner and Allison Davis developed and popularized a conceptual scheme for analyzing race relations in the Southern region of the United States which viewed Negro-white relations as organized by a color-caste system that shaped economic and political relations as well as family and kinship structures, and which was reinforced by the legal system. Within each of the two castes (superordinate white and subordinate Negro), social classes existed, status being based upon possession of money, education, and family background as reflected in distinctive styles of behavior. "Exploitation" in the Marxist sense was present within this caste-class system, but also much more; for an entire socio-cultural system, not just the economic order, functioned to distribute power and prestige unevenly between whites and Negroes and to punish any individuals who questioned the system by word or behavior.[1]

Students of the situation in the North rarely conceptualized race relations in terms of caste, but tended rather to view specific communities as areas in which *ethnic* groups were involved in continuous competition and conflict, resulting in a hierarchy persisting through time, with now one, and again another, ethnic group at the bottom as previous newcomers moved "up." Each ethnic group developed a social class structure within it, but as individuals acquired better jobs, more education, and some sophistication,

SOURCE: St. Clair Drake, "The Social and Economic Status of the Negro in the United States," *Daedalus,* 96, No. 3 (Spring 1967), 771–814. Reprinted by permission of *Daedalus,* Journal of the American Academy of Arts and Sciences.

they and their families often detached themselves from immigrant colonies (usually located in slum areas) and sometimes from all ethnic institutions as well. They tended to become a part of the middle class. The Negroes who migrated North in large numbers during World War I were the latest arrivals in this fluid and highly competitive situation, but their high visibility became a crucial factor limiting their upward mobility. Upwardly mobile Negroes could not "disappear" into the middle class of the larger society as did European ethnics.[2]

Thus, on the eve of World War II, students of race relations in the United States generally described the status of Negroes as one in which they played subordinate roles in a caste system in the South and an ethnic-class system in the North. The actions of persons toward those of another race were explained not in terms of some vaguely defined emotions connected with "prejudice," but rather in terms of the behavior they felt was expected of them by others in various positions within the social structure, and as attempts to protect and maximize whatever power and prestige accrued to them at their locus in the system. John Dollard, a psychologist, in his *Caste and Class in a Southern Town*, added an additional dimension. He analyzes the situation in terms of the "gains" and "losses"—sexual, psychological, economic, and political—which both Negroes and whites sustained at different levels in the Southern caste-class system.[3]

The caste-class analysis still provides a useful frame of reference for studying the behavior of individuals and groups located at various positions in the social structure. It can also serve as a starting point for viewing the *processes* of race relations in terms of their consequences. Of the racial and ethnic groups in America only Negroes have been subjected to caste-deprivations; and the ethnic-class system has operated to their disadvantage as compared with European immigrants. In other words, Negroes in America have been subject to "victimization" in the sense that a system of social relations operates in such a way as to deprive them of a chance to share in the more desirable material and non-material products of a society which is dependent, in part, upon their labor and loyalty. They are "victimized," also, because they do not have the same degree of access which others have to the attributes needed for rising in the general class system—money, education, "contacts," and "know-how."

The concept of "victimization" implies, too, that some people are used as means to other people's ends—without their consent—and that the social system is so structured that it can be deliberately manipulated to the disadvantage of some groups by the clever, the vicious, and the cynical, as well as by the powerful. The callous and indifferent unconsciously and unintentionally reinforce the system by their inaction or inertia. The "victims," their autonomy curtailed and their self-esteem weakened by the operation of the caste-class system, are confronted with "identity problems." Their social condition is essentially one of "powerlessness."

Individual "victims" may or may not accept the rationalizations given for the denial to them of power and prestige. They may or may not be aware of and concerned about their position in the system, but, when they do become concerned, victimization takes on important social psychological dimensions. Individuals then suffer feelings of "relative deprivation" which give rise to reactions ranging from despair, apathy, and withdrawal to covert and overt aggression. An effective analysis of the position of the Negro in these terms (although the word "victimization" is never used) may be found in Thomas F. Pettigrew's *A Profile of the Negro American* (1964).

Concepts developed by Max Weber are useful for assessing the degree of victimization existing within the American caste-class system.[4] Individuals and groups can be compared by examining what he refers to as "life chances," that is, the extent to which people have access to economic and political power. *Direct victimization* might be defined as the operation of sanctions which deny access to power, which limit the franchise, sustain job discrimination, permit unequal pay for similar work, or provide inferior training or no training at all. *Indirect victimization* is revealed in the consequences which flow from a social structure which decreases *"life chances,"* such as high morbidity and mortality rates, low longevity rates, a high incidence of psychopathology, or the persistence of personality traits and attitudes which impose disadvantages in competition or excite derogatory and invidious comparisons with other groups. Max Weber also compared individuals and groups in terms of differences in *"life styles,"* those ways of behaving which vary in the amount of esteem, honor, and prestige attached to them. Differences in "life chances" may make it impossible to acquire the money or education (or may limit the contacts) necessary for adopting and maintaining prestigious life styles. The key to understanding many aspects of race relations may be found in the fact that, in American society, the protection of their familiar and cherished life styles is a dominating concern of the white middle classes, who, because many Negroes have life styles differing from their own, have tried to segregate them into all-Negro neighborhoods, voluntary associations, and churches.[5] (Marxist sociologists tend to overemphasize protection of economic interests as a dynamic factor in American race relations, important though it is.)

The "Ghettoization" of Negro Life

Pressure upon Negroes to live within all-Negro neighborhoods has resulted in those massive concentrations of Negro population in Northern metropolitan areas which bitter critics call "concentration camps" or "plantations" and which some social scientists refer to as "Black Ghettos."[6] Small town replicas exist everywhere throughout the nation, for the roots of residential segregation lie deep in American history. In older Southern towns slave quarters were transformed into Negro residential areas after Emancipation—a few blocks here, a whole neighborhood there, often adjacent to white homes. In newer Southern towns and cities a less secure upwardly mobile white population usually demanded a greater degree of segregation from ex-slaves and their descendants. Prior to World War I, the residential patterns did not vary greatly between North and South, but the great northward migration of Negroes between 1914 and 1920 expanded the small Negro neighborhoods into massive Black Belts. Middle-class white neighbors used "restrictive-covenants" as their main device for slowing down and "containing" the expansion of Negro neighborhoods. Thus, with continued in-migration and restricted access to housing in "white neighborhoods," the overcrowded Black Ghetto emerged with its substandard structures, poor public services, and high crime and juvenile delinquency rates.

Scholars know from careful research, and increasingly wider circles are becoming aware of the fact, that Negroes do not depress property values, but that middle-class white attitudes toward Negroes do.[7] As long as Negroes, as a group, are a symbol of lower social status, proximity to them will be considered undesirable and such social attitudes will be reflected in the market place. The problem is complicated by the fact that a very high proportion of Negro Americans actually does have lower-class attributes and behavior patterns. The upward mobility of white Americans, as well as their comfort and personal safety, is facilitated by spatial segregation. (Older cities in the South have been an exception.) The white middle class could protect its values by acting solely in terms of class, letting middle-class Negro families scatter into white neighborhoods irrespective of race. Instead, the white middle class in American cities protects its own neighborhoods from behavior patterns it disapproves of and from chronic social disorganization by "ghettoizing" the Negro. Real-estate operators, black and white, have exploited the fears of the white middle class from the beginning of the northern migration by "block busting," that is, by buying property for less than its normal market value and reselling it at a higher price to Negroes barred from the open market or by charging them higher rentals. Eventually the profit-potential in residential segregation was maximized by the institutions which controlled mortgage money and refused to finance property for Negro residence outside of the Black Belts except under conditions approved by them.

In 1948, the Supreme Court declared racial restrictive covenants unenforceable in the courts, but this action tended to accelerate rather than reverse the process of ghettoization, for many whites proceeded to sell to Negroes at inflated prices and then moved to the suburbs, or they retained their properties, moved away, and raised the rents. The Court's decision was based partly upon a reevaluation of the concept of civil rights and partly upon a recognition of the fact that serious economic injustice was a by-product of residential segregation, a situation summed up by Thomas Petti-grew:

While some housing gains occurred in the 1950's, the quality of Negro housing remains vastly inferior relative to that of whites. For example, in Chicago in 1960, Negroes paid as much for housing as whites, despite their lower incomes. . . . This situation exists because of essentially two separate housing markets; and the residen-tial segregation that creates these dual markets has increased steadily over past decades until it has reached universally high levels in cities throughout the United States, despite significant advances in the socio-economic status.of Negroes. . . .[8]

The trend has not yet been reversed despite F.H.A. administrative regula-tions and Supreme Court decisions.

The spatial isolation of Negroes from whites created Negro "communi-ties." Within these Negro neighborhoods, church and school became the basic integrative institutions, and Negro entrepreneurs developed a variety of service enterprises—barbershops and beauty parlors, funeral homes and restaurants, pool parlors, taverns, and hotels—all selling to what came to be called "The Negro Market." Successful banking and insurance busi-nesses also grew up within some Negro communities. A Negro "subculture" gradually emerged, national in scope, with distinctive variations upon the general American culture in the fields of literature, art, music, and dance, as well as in religious ritual and church polity.

The spatial isolation of Negroes from whites in "Black Belts" also in-creased consciousness of their separate subordinate position, for no whites were available to them as neighbors, schoolmates, or friends, but were present only in such roles as school teachers, policemen, and social workers, flat janitors and real-estate agents, merchants and bill collectors, skilled laborers involved in maintenance, and even a few white dentists and doctors with offices in the Black Belt. Such a situation inevitably generated anti-white sentiments (often with anti-Semitic overtones), and the pent-up feel-ings have occasionally erupted in anti-white riots. Normally, however, this intense racial consciousness finds expression in non-violent forms of social protest and is utilized by Negro leaders to sanction and reinforce Negro institutions and their own personal welfare. It has also lent powerful sup-port to the segments of municipal political machines existing within Negro neighborhoods. As long as ghettos remain, race consciousness will be strong.

Residential segregation created the demographic and ecological basis for "balance of power" politics, since the possibility of a Negro bloc vote had to be recognized by both political parties. Northern Black Belt voters are not only occasionally the decisive factor in municipal elections, but have also sent a half-dozen Negroes to Congress. Indeed, it is ironic that one of the most effective weapons against segregation and discrimination in the South has been the political power generated in Negro precincts and wards of Northern Black Ghettos, thus reinforcing the direct action tactics of the civil rights movement. In the South, too, with the passage of the Civil Rights Act of 1964 and subsequent legislation, the political strength of newly enfranchised voters lies in their spatial concentration. There is some evidence that fear of this strength may operate as a factor in Northern cities to support "open occupancy," desegregation being considered preferable to Negro dominance.[9]

While the development of machine politics has brought some gains to Negro communities, it has also resulted in various forms of indirect victimization. Local Negro leaders often co-operate with the city-wide machine in the protection of "the rackets"—policy, dope, and prostitution—and sacrifice group welfare to personal gain for self and party. They have not hesitated, in some places, even to drag their heels in the fight for residential desegregation rather than risk wiping out the base of their power. Being saddled with a "bought leadership" is one of the greatest burdens Black Ghettos have had to bear. Economic victimization is widespread, too. In the "affluent society" of the sixties, consumption-oriented and given to the "hard sell," Negroes like other Americans are under social pressure to spend beyond their means. Given the lack of sophistication of many recent migrants and the very low median income of those with less than a high-school education, it is not surprising that loan sharks and dubious credit merchants (of all races) make the Black Ghetto a prime target. Negroes pay a high price for "protection" of the white middle-class way of life, since those who aspire to leave the ghetto are trapped, and those who are content to stay develop a limited and restricted view of the world in which they live.

Folkways and Classways Within the Black Ghetto

Black Ghettos in America are, on the whole, "run down" in appearance and overcrowded, and their inhabitants bear the physical and psychological scars of those whose "life chances" are not equal to those of other Americans. Like the European immigrants before them, they inherited the worst housing in the city. Within the past decade, the white "flight to the suburbs" has released relatively new and well-kept property on the margins of some of the old Black Belts. Here, "gilded ghettos" have grown up, indistinguishable from any other middle-class neighborhoods except by the color of the residents' skin.[10] The power mower in the yard, the steak grill on the rear lawn, a well stocked library and equally well stocked bar in the rumpus room—these mark the homes of well-to-do Negroes living in the more desirable portions of the Black Belt. Many of them would flee to suburbia, too, if housing were available to Negroes there.

But the character of the Black Ghetto is not set by the newer "gilded," not-yet run down portions of it, but by the older sections where unemployment rates are high and the masses of people work with their hands—where the median level of education is just above graduation from grade school and many of the people are likely to be recent migrants from rural areas.[11]

The "ghettoization" of the Negro has resulted in the emergence of a ghetto subculture with a distinctive ethos, most pronounced, perhaps, in Harlem, but recognizable in all Negro neighborhoods. For the average Negro who walks the streets of any American Black Ghetto, the smell of barbecued ribs, fried shrimps, and chicken emanating from numerous restaurants gives olfactory reinforcement to a feeling of "at-homeness." The beat of "gut music" spilling into the street from ubiquitous tavern juke boxes and the sound of tambourines and rich harmony behind the crude folk art on the windows of store-front churches give auditory confirmation to the universal belief that "We Negroes have 'soul.' " The bedlam of an occasional brawl, the shouted obscenities of street corner "foul mouths," and the whine of police sirens break the monotony of waiting for the number that never "falls," the horses that neither win, place, nor show, and the "good job" that never materializes. The insouciant swagger of teen-age drop-outs (the "cats") masks the hurt of their aimless existence and contrasts sharply with the ragged clothing and dejected demeanor of "skid-row" types who have long since stopped trying to keep up appearances and who escape it all by becoming "winoes." The spontaneous vigor of the children who crowd streets and playgrounds (with Cassius Clay, Ernie Banks, the Harlem Globe Trotters, and black stars of stage, screen, and television as their role models) and the cheerful rushing about of adults, free from the occupational pressures of the "white world" in which they work, create an atmosphere of warmth and superficial intimacy which obscures the unpleasant facts of life in the overcrowded rooms behind the doors, the lack of adequate maintenance standards, and the too prevalent vermin and rats.

This is a world whose urban "folkways" the upwardly mobile Negro middle class deplores as a "drag" on "The Race," which the upper class wince at as an embarassment, and which race leaders point to as proof that Negroes have been victimized. But for the masses of the ghetto dwellers this is a warm and familiar milieu, preferable to the sanitary coldness of middle-class neighborhoods and a counterpart of the communities of the foreign-born, each of which has its own distinctive subcultural flavor. The arguments in the barbershop, the gossip in the beauty parlors, the "jiving" of bar girls and waitresses, the click of the poolroom balls, the stomping of feet in the dance halls, the shouting in the churches are all *theirs*—and the white men who run the pawnshops, supermarts, drug stores, and grocery stores, the policemen on horseback, the teachers in blackboard jungles—all these are aliens, conceptualized collectively as "The Man," intruders on the Black Man's "turf." When an occasional riot breaks out, "The Man" and his property become targets of aggression upon which pent-up frustrations are vented. When someone during the Harlem riots of 1964 begged the street crowds to go home, the cry came back, "Baby, we *are* home!"

But the inhabitants of the Black Ghetto are not a homogeneous mass. Although, in Marxian terms, nearly all of them are "proletarians," with nothing to sell but their labor, variations in "life style" differentiate them into social classes based more upon differences in education and basic values (crystallized, in part, around occupational differences) than in meaningful differences in income. The American caste-class system has served, over the years, to concentrate the Negro population in the low-income sector of the economy. In 1961, six out of every ten Negro families had an income of less than $4000.00 per year. This situation among whites was just the reverse: six out of every ten white families had *over* $4000.00 a year at their disposal. (In the South, eight out of ten Negro families were below the $4000.00 level.) This is the income gap. Discrimination in employment creates a job ceiling, most Negroes being in blue-collar jobs.

With 60 per cent of America's Negro families earning less than $4000.00 a year, social strata emerge between the upper and lower boundaries of "no earned income" and $4000.00. Some families live a "middle-class style of life," placing heavy emphasis upon decorous public behavior and general respectability, insisting that their children "get an education" and "make something out of themselves." They prize family stability, and an unwed mother is something much more serious than "just a girl who had an accident"; pre-marital and extra-marital sexual relations, if indulged in at all, must be discreet. Social life is organized around churches and a welter of voluntary associations of all types, and, for women, "the cult of clothes" is so important that fashion shows are a popular fund raising activity even in churches. For both men and women, owning a home and going into business are highly desired goals, the former often being a realistic one, the latter a mere fantasy.

Within the same income range, and not always at the lower margin of it, other families live a "lower-class life-style" being part of the "organized" lower class, while at the lowest income levels an "unorganized" lower class exists whose members tend always to become *dis*organized—functioning in an anomic situation where gambling, excessive drinking, the use of narcotics, and sexual promiscuity are prevalent forms of behavior, and violent interpersonal relations reflect an ethos of suspicion and resentment which suffuses this deviant subculture. It is within this milieu that criminal and semi-criminal activities burgeon.

The "organized" lower class is oriented primarily around churches whose preachers, often semi-literate, exhort them to "be in the 'world' but not of it." Conventional middle-class morality and Pauline Puritanism are preached, although a general attitude of "the spirit is willing but the flesh is weak" prevails except among a minority fully committed to the Pentecostal sects. They boast, "We *live* the life"—a way of life that has been portrayed with great insight by James Baldwin in *Go Tell it on the Mountain* and *The Fire Next Time*.

Young people with talent find wide scope for expressing it in choirs, quartets, and sextets which travel from church to church (often bearing colorful names like The Four Heavenly Trumpets or the Six Singing Stars of Zion) and sometimes traveling from city to city. Such groups channel their aggressions in widely advertised "Battles of Song" and develop their talent in church pageants such as "Heaven Bound" or "Queen Esther" and fund-raising events where winners are crowned King and Queen. These activities provide fun as well as a testing ground for talent. Some lucky young church people eventually find their fortune in the secular world as did singers Sam Cooke and Nat King Cole, while others remain in the church world as nationally known gospel singers or famous evangelists.

Adults as well as young people find satisfaction and prestige in serving as ushers and deacons, "mothers," and deaconesses, Sunday-school teachers and choir leaders. National conventions of Negro denominations and national societies of ushers and gospel singers not only develop a continent-wide nexus of associations within the organized lower class, but also throw the more ambitious and capable individuals into meaningful contact with middle-class church members who operate as role models for those talented persons who seek to move upward. That prestige and sometimes money come so easily in these circles may be a factor militating against a pattern of delaying gratifications and seeking mobility into professional and semi-professional pursuits through higher education.

Lower-class families and institutions are constantly on the move, for in recent years the Negro lower class has suffered from projects to redevelop the inner city. By historic accident, the decision to check the expansion of physical deterioration in metropolitan areas came at a time when Negroes were the main inhabitants of substandard housing. (If urban redevelopment had been necessary sixty years ago immigrants, not Negroes, would have suffered.) In protest against large-scale demolition of areas where they live, Negroes have coined a slogan, "Slum clearance is Negro clearance." They resent the price in terms of the inconvenience thrust upon them in order to redevelop American cities[12] and the evidence shows that, in some cities, there is no net gain in improved housing after relocation.

At the opposite pole from the Negro lower class in both life styles and life chances is the small Negro upper class whose solid core is a group in the professions, along with well-to-do businessmen who have had some higher education, but including, also, a scattering of individuals who have had college training but do not have a job commensurate with their education. These men and their spouses and children form a cohesive upper-class stratum in most Negro communities. Within this group are individuals who maintain some type of contact—though seldom any social relations—with members of the local white power élite; but whether or not they participate in occupational associations with their white peers depends upon the region of the country in which they live. (It is from this group that Negro "Exhibit A's" are recruited when white liberals are carrying on campaigns to "increase interracial understanding.") They must always think of themselves as symbols of racial advancement as well as individuals, and they often provide the basic leadership at local levels for organizations such as the N.A.A.C.P. and the Urban League. They must lend sympathetic support to the more militant civil rights organizations, too, by financial contributions, if not action.[13]

The life styles of the Negro upper class are similar to those of the white upper *middle* class, but it is only in rare instances that Negroes have been incorporated into the clique and associational life of this group or have intermarried into it. (Their participation in activities of the white upper class occurs more often than with those whites who have similar life styles because of Negro upper-class participation as members of various civic boards and interracial associations to which wealthy white people contribute.) Living "well" with highly developed skills, having enough money to travel, Negroes at this social level do not experience vicitimization in the same fashion as do the members of the lower class. Their vicitimization flows primarily from the fact that the social system keeps them "half in and half out," preventing the free and easy contact with their occupational peers which they need; and it often keeps them from making the kind of significant intellectual and social contributions to the national welfare that they might make if they were white. (They are also forced to experience various types of nervous strain and dissipation of energy over petty annoyances and deprivations which only the sensitive and the cultivated feel. Most barbershops, for instance, are not yet desegregated, and taxi drivers, even in the North, sometimes refuse Negro passengers.)

The Negro upper class has created a social world of its own in which a universe of discourse and uniformity of behavior and outlook are maintained by the interaction on national and local levels of members of Negro

Greek-letter fraternities and sororities, college and alumni associations, professional associations, and civic and social clubs. It is probable that if all caste barriers were dropped, a large proportion of the Negro upper class would welcome complete social integration, and that these all-Negro institutions would be left in the hands of the Negro middle-class, as the most capable and sophisticated Negroes moved into the orbit of the general society. Their sense of pride and dignity does not even allow them to imagine such a fate, and they pursue their social activities and play their roles as "race leaders" with little feeling of inferiority or deprivation, but always with a tragic sense of the irony of it all.

The Negro middle class covers a very wide income range, and whatever cohesion it has comes from the network of churches and social clubs to which many of its members devote a great deal of time and money. What sociologists call the Negro middle class is merely a collection of people who have similar life styles and aspirations, whose basic goals are "living well," being "respectable," and not being crude. Middle-class Negroes, by and large, are not concerned about mobility into the Negro upper class or integration with whites. They want their "rights" and "good jobs," as well as enough money to get those goods and services which make life comfortable. They want to expand continuously their level of consumption. But they also desire "decent" schools for their children, and here the degree of victimization experienced by Negroes is most clear and the ambivalence toward policies of change most sharp. Ghetto schools are, on the whole, inferior. In fact, some of the most convincing evidence that residential segregation perpetuates inequality can be found by comparing data on school districts in Northern urban areas where *de facto* school segregation exists. (Table 1 presents such data for Chicago in 1962.)

TABLE 1. *Comparison of White, Integrated and Negro Schools in Chicago: 1962*

Indices of Comparison	Type of School		
	White	*Integrated*	*Negro*
Total appropriation per pupil	$342.00	$320.00	$269.00
Annual teachers' salary per pupil	256.00	231.00	220.00
Per cent uncertified teachers	12.00	23.00	49.00
No. of pupils per classroom	30.95	34.95	46.80
Library resource books per pupil	5.00	3.50	2.50
Expenditures per pupil other than teachers' salaries.	86.00	90.00	49.00

Adapted from a table in the U. S. Commission on Civil Rights report, *Public Schools, Negro and White* (Washington, D.C., 1962), pp. 241–248.

Awareness of the poor quality of education grew as the protest movement against *de facto* school segregation in the North gathered momentum. But while the fight was going on, doubt about the desirability of forcing the issue was always present within some sections of the broad Negro middle class. Those in opposition asked, "Are we not saying that our teachers can't teach our own children as well as whites can, or that our children can't learn unless they're around whites? Aren't we insulting ourselves?" Those who want to stress Negro history and achievement and to use the schools to build race pride also express doubts about the value of mixed schools. In fact, the desirability of race consciousness and racial solidarity seems to be taken for granted in this stratum, and sometimes there is an expression of contempt for the behavior of whites of their own and lower income levels. In the present period one even occasionally hears a remark such as "Who'd want to be integrated with *those* awful white people?"

Marxist critics would dismiss the whole configuration of Negro folkways and classways as a subculture which reinforces "false consciousness," which prevents Negroes from facing the full extent of their victimization, which keeps them from ever focusing upon what they could be because they are so busy enjoying what they are—or rationalizing their subordination and exclusion. Gunnar Myrdal, in *An American Dilemma,* goes so far as to refer to the Negro community as a "pathological" growth within American society.[14] Some novelists and poets, on the other hand, romanticize it, and some Black Nationalists glorify it. A sober analysis of the civil rights movement would suggest, however, that the striking fact about all levels of the Negro community is the absence of "false consciousness," and the presence of a keen awareness of the extent of their victimization, as well as knowledge of the forces which maintain it. Not lack of knowledge but a sense of powerlessness is the key to the Negro reaction to the caste-class system.

Few Negroes believe that Black Ghettos will disappear within the next two decades despite much talk about "open occupancy" and "freedom of residence." There is an increasing tendency among Negroes to discuss what the quality of life could be within Negro communities as they grow larger and larger. At one extreme this interest slides over into Black Nationalist reactions such as the statement by a Chicago Negro leader who said, "Let all of the white people flee to the suburbs. We'll show them that the Black Man can run the second largest city in America better than the white man. Let them go. If any of them want to come back and integrate with *us* we'll accept them."

It is probable that the Black Belts of America will increase in size rather than decrease during the next decade, for no city seems likely to commit itself to "open occupancy" (although a committee in New York has been discussing a ten-year plan for dismantling Harlem).[15] And even if a race-free market were to appear Negroes would remain segregated unless drastic changes took place in the job ceiling and income gap. Controlled integration will probably continue, with a few upper- and upper-middle class Negroes trickling into the suburbs and into carefully regulated mixed neighborhoods and mixed buildings within the city limits.[16] The basic problem of the next decade will be how to change Black Ghettos into relatively stable and attractive "colored communities." Here the social implications of low incomes become decisive.

Social Implications of the Job Ceiling and the Income Gap

Nowhere is direct victimization of Negroes more apparent than with respect to the job ceiling and the income gap; but indirect victimization which is a consequence of direct victimization is often less obvious. For instance, it has been mentioned that family incomes for Negroes are lower than for whites; but family income figures are inadequate tools for careful sociological analysis unless we know which, and how many, members of a family labor to earn a given income. In 1960, half of the white families were being supported by a husband only, while just a few more than a third of the Negro families could depend solely upon the earnings of one male breadwinner. In six out of ten nonwhite families where both a husband and wife were present, two or more persons worked; yet less than half of the white families had both husband and wife working. But even in those families which commanded an income of over $7,000.00 a year, twice as many nonwhite wives had to help earn it as white.[17] One not unimportant consequence is that a smaller proportion of Negro than white wives at this income level can play roles of unpaid volunteers in civic and social work, a fact which should be remembered by those who criticize Negroes in these income brackets for not doing more to "elevate their own people."

One of the most important effects of the income gap and the job ceiling has been the shaping of social class systems within Negro communities which differ markedly in their profiles from those of the surrounding white society. Negro class structure is "pyramidal," with a large lower class, a somewhat smaller middle class, and a tiny upper class (made up of people whose income and occupations would make them only middle class in the white society). White class profiles tend to be "diamond shaped," with small lower and upper classes and a large middle class. Unpromising "life chances" are reflected in inferior "life styles," and Black Ghettos are on the whole "rougher" and exhibit a higher degree of social disorganization than do white communities.

The job ceiling and the income gap do not create classways—for these reflect educational levels and cultural values, as well as the economic situation—but job ceiling and income gap do set the limits for realization of class values. It is a fact of American life (whether one approves of it or not) that as long as Negroes are predominantly lower-class they will, as a group, have low esteem. Yet, Negroes are victimized in the sense that the job ceiling and the income gap make it more difficult for them than for whites to maintain middle-class standards equivalent to those obtaining among whites. A given life style demands a minimum level of income, but it is evident that Negroes are victimized in the sense that their effort as reflected in the acquisition of an education does not bring equal rewards in terms of purchasing power, for they have less to spend than their white counterparts at any given educational level. Nonwhite family heads in 1960 had a smaller median income than whites for every educational level. (See Table 2.)[18]

In a sense, getting an education "pays off" for Negroes as for all other Americans; but while some individuals "get ahead" of other Negroes, education has not yet raised their earning power to the level of whites with equivalent training. In fact, the average income for a nonwhite family with a male head who had finished high school was less than that of a white male

TABLE 2. *White and Nonwhite Median Family Income by Educational Level, 1960: U.S.A.*

Amount of Education in Yrs. of School Completed	White	Nonwhite
Elementary School		
Less than 8 years	$3,656	$2,294
8 years	4,911	3,338
High School		
1–3 years	5,882	3,449
4 years	6,370	4,559
College		
1–3 years	7,344	5,525
4 or more years	9,315	7,875

head who had finished only the eighth grade. Since any aspects of the caste-class system which make it more difficult for Negroes than for whites to achieve middle-class norms of family behavior retard the process of eventual "integration," the income differential and the necessity for more members of the family to work operate in this negative fashion. Even more serious in determining deviations from general middle-class family norms is the manner in which both income distribution and the occupational structure function to reinforce the number of families without fathers and to lower the prestige of Negro males *vis-à-vis* their mates, prospective mates, and children. Thus a pattern of male insecurity which originated under slavery persists into the present. In fact, the struggle of Negro men, viewed as a group, to attain economic parity with Negro women has, up to the present, been a losing fight. Norval Glenn, in an exhaustive study of this problem,[19] has concluded that "Among full-time workers, non-white females were, in 1959, less disadvantaged relative to whites than were non-white males." Women were obtaining employment at a relatively faster rate than men and sustained a more rapid proportionate increase in income between 1939 and 1959. According to Glenn, there was an actual reversal in the income growth pattern of Negro males and females during a twenty-year period, and he notes that if their respective rates remain the same it will take twice as long for Negro males to catch up with white males as for Negro women to catch up with white women (93 years to achieve occupational equality and 219 to achieve equality of income). This is a case of *relative* deprivation, of course, but is significant nevertheless. An impressive body of evidence indicates that rather serious personality distortions result from the female dominance so prevalent in the Negro subculture, since the general norms of the larger society stress the opposite pattern as more desirable.

The interplay between caste and evaluations and economic and ecological factors has tended not only to concentrate a low-income Negro population within ghettos, but has also concentrated a significant proportion of them in vast public housing projects—sometimes "high rise." In the 1930's public housing projects were often exciting experiments in interracial living, but here has been a tendency in many cities for them to become ghettos within ghettos. Within housing projects as well as out, a small hard core of mothers without husbands and a larger group of youth without jobs are developing a pattern which social psychologist Frederick Strodtbeck has called "the poverty-dependency syndrome." Here and there an integrated program of professional family services has proved its usefulness, but, in general, family ase-work becomes a mere "holding operation."

Only the future will tell whether a large-scale "Poverty Program" coordinated through federally sponsored agencies will break the interlocking vicious circles which now victimize urban Negro populations. The dominant pattern in the American economic system has never been one of racial segregation. In fact, the racial division of labor has always involved considerable close personal contact, while demanding that Negroes play subordinate occupational roles carrying the lesser rewards in terms of economic power and social prestige. Doctrines of racial inferiority originated as dogmas to defend the use of African slave labor and were later used by white workers to defend their own privileged position against Negro competition. Trade union restrictionism reinforces employer preference in maintaining a job ceiling. Often, even when an employer decided it was profitable to use Negro labor, white workers used intimidation or violence against both white employer and black employee.

Access to new roles in the economic structure has occurred during periods of a great shortage of labor, as in the North during both world wars. Negroes entered at the bottom of the hierarchy, but were "last hired and first fired." Yet the job ceiling *was* raised, and, beginning with the organization of industrial unions in the 1930's and reaching a climax in the civil rights movement of the 1960's, ideological factors have reinforced economic interest in breaking the job ceiling. Now, for the first time in American history the full weight of top leadership in labor, industry, and government has been thrown in the direction of "fair employment practices," and public opinion is tolerating an all-out drive against job discrimination (partly because the economy is still expanding). Yet so drastic are the effects of the past victimization of the Negro that any decisive alteration in the caste-class structure without more drastic measures seems remote. Thomas Pettigrew, after an analysis of recent changes, concludes:

At the creeping 1950–1960 rate of change, non-whites in the United States would not attain equal proportional representation among clerical workers until 1992, among skilled workers until 2005, among professionals until 2017, among sales workers until 2114, and among business managers and proprietors until 2730![20]

"In Sickness and in Death"

The consequences of being at the bottom in a caste-class system are revealed clearly in comparative studies of morbidity, mortality, and longevity, the later being a particularly sensitive index to the physical well-being o groups. Comparing Negroes and whites with respect to longevity, Thoma Pettigrew notes that:

At the turn of this century, the average non-white American at birth had a li expectancy between 32 and 35 years, 16 years less than that of the average whi American. By 1960, this life expectancy had risen from 61 to 66 years. . . . But whi the percentage gain in life expectancy for Negroes over these sixty odd years h; been twice that of whites, there is still a discrepancy of six to eight years. . . .[21]

In other words, Negroes were "catching up," but, as a Department of Lab study pointed out in 1962, they ". . . had arrived by 1959 at about tl longevity average attained by whites in 1940."[22] They were twenty yea behind in the race toward equality of longevity.

Differences in longevity reflect differences in morbidity rates. Among tl communicable diseases, for instance, the Negro tuberculosis rate is thr times greater than that of whites, and the rates for pneumonia and influenza are also higher. The incidence of venereal disease is substantially higher among Negroes, although the Public Health Service figure of a syphilis rate ten times larger than that for whites has been questioned in Dr. Ann Pettigrew's study.[23] Twice as many Negro children per thousand as white children suffer from measles, meningitis, diphtheria, and scarlet fever. Given such differences between Negroes and whites in the incidence of specific diseases, it is not surprising to find that the *death* rate from childhood diseases is six times higher among Negroes than whites and that the tuberculosis death rate is four times higher in all age-groups.[24]

The analysis of mortality rates provides one tool for studying the effects of the caste-class system which victimizes the Negro population. A United States government report for the year 1963 noted that "The age pattern of mortality . . . as in previous years, is similar for each of the color-sex groups —high rates in infancy, lower rates until the minimum is reached during grade-school age, then rising for the older age-groups."[25] Although the *pattern* was the same, there were racial differentials in the actual rates; for instance, "The relative increases in the 1963 death rates over the prior years were slightly greater for non-white persons than for white. . . ." There were other differentials too.

The death rate among mothers at childbirth in 1963 was four times greater for nonwhites than for whites (96.9 deaths per 100,000 live births to 24.0). The death rate of nonwhite babies during the first year after birth was almost double the rate for white babies (46.6 per thousand to 25.3 per thousand for males and 36.7 to 19.0 for females.) Prenatal hazards were, as in previous years, greater for nonwhites than for whites. Up to the age of five the nonwhite death rate was twice that for whites, and for older age-groups varied from two to four times the white rate.

Using broad categories of classification, the U.S. National Center for Health Statistics reported in 1963 that "the three chief causes of death— diseases of heart, malignant neoplasms [Cancer], and vascular lesions affecting central nervous system account for three fifths of all deaths. They are also the chief causes of death for each color-sex group."[26] Here, too, racial differentials exist, the nonwhite to white death ratios being: (a) diseases of heart (333.9/100,000 to 277.9); (b) malignant neoplasms (145.2/100,000 to 123.7); (c) vascular lesions of central nervous system (133.4/100,000 to 71.3). A comparison of deaths from specific diseases and from other causes also reveals racial differentials and the pattern of indifferences suggests a relationship between high rates and low socio-economic status.

If the ten leading causes of death in 1963 for nonwhites and whites are compared by sex, the results of indirect victimization of Negroes are apparent: Those diseases which rate highest as causes of death are found disproportionately among lower-class families, those who suffer from poor nutrition, overcrowded housing, hazardous occupations, and inadequate medical care. Table 3 presents rates for ten leading causes of death for males:

TABLE 3. *The Ten Leading Causes of Death: Males, U.S.A., 1963*

| | Nonwhite | | White | |
Causes of Death	*Rate*	*Rank*	*Rate*	*Rank*
Diseases of the heart	330.6	1	444.8	1
Vascular lesions of Central Nervous System	116.8	2	100.5	2
Certain diseases of early infancy	81.8	3	34.3	7
Influenza and pneumonia	70.6	4	39.3	5
Hypertensive heart disease	61.1	5	24.1	9
Accidents other than motor vehicle	57.9	6	37.8	6
Cancer of digestive organs	51.1	7	54.1	3
Symptoms-senility and ill-defined conditions	42.1	8	10.9†	—
Motor vehicle accidents	36.7	9	34.4	8
Homicide	35.7	10	3.9†	—
Cancer of respiratory system	34.5*	—	43.7	4
Diabetes mellitus	13.9*	—	14.2	10

*Not among first ten for nonwhites
†Not among first ten for whites

Among males, certain causes of death directly related to standard of living affect nonwhites two to four times more frequently than whites: (a) certain diseases of early infancy (2.38×); (b) influenza and pneumonia (1.79 ×); and (c) "symptoms-senility and ill-defined conditions" (3.86×). The last named "cause" does not even appear among the first ten for whites. (See Table 4.)

Two causes of death on the list for nonwhite males are probably directly related to the caste situation. The death rate for hypertensive heart disease is over twice that for whites and ranks fifth as a cause of death, compared to ninth for whites. Thomas Pettigrew, commenting on all types of hypertension, notes that some students feel that it is related to "psychosocial influences" and that, with regard to the high rates for Negroes, ". . . the problem of repressing hostility against whites . . . may be an important factor."[27] A homicide death rate nine times higher than that for whites, and appearing among the ten leading causes of death for nonwhite males, reflects the overt terror in the Black Belt, the explosions of in-caste aggression, and the anomic lower-class situation, as well as the distinctive ethos of the Negro subculture where crimes of passion among the lower-class are not condemned to the extent that they are in some other segments of American society.

Of the ten leading causes of death among nonwhite males, eight are also leading causes of death for white males, but in the case of six of these the nonwhite rate is higher (diseases of the heart and cancer of digestive organs being the exceptions). The extent of the difference is indicated in Table 4.

TABLE 4. *Comparison of Death Rates for Nonwhites and Whites, by Sex, for the Ten Leading Causes of Death for Each Color-Sex Group*

	Males		Females	
DEGREE OF DIFFERENCE BETWEEN RATES	CAUSE OF DEATH	RATIO OF NONWHITE TO WHITE RATES	CAUSE OF DEATH	RATIO OF NONWHITE TO WHITE RATES
Very much higher for Nonwhites	Homicide†	9.14	None	
Considerably higher for Nonwhites	Symptoms— Senility, and ill-defined conditions†	3.86	Symptoms— Senility, and ill-defined conditions†	4.35
	Certain diseases of early infancy	2.38	Certain diseases of early infancy	2.56
	Hypertensive heart disease	2.12	Hypertensive heart disease	2.09
Somewhat higher for Nonwhites	Influenza and pneumonia (except pneumonia of newborn)	1.79	Influenza and pneumonia (except pneumonia of newborn)	1.68
	Accidents other than motor vehicle accidents	1.37	Diabetes mellitus	1.38
	Vascular lesions affecting central nervous system	1.16	Cancer of genital organs	1.17
	Motor vehicle accident	1.07	Accidents*	1.15
			Vascular lesions affecting central nervous system	1.08
Lower for Nonwhites	Diabetes mellitus*	.97	Diseases of the heart	.84
	Cancer of digestive organs	.94	Cancer of digestive organs†	.71
	Cancer of respiratory system*	.78	Cancer of the breast	.67
	Diseases of the heart	.73		

*Among ten top-ranking causes for whites but not for nonwhites
†Among ten top-ranking causes for nonwhites but not for whites

The prenatal period is much more serious for nonwhite male babies than white, death rates for "certain diseases of infancy" (birth injuries, infections, and so forth) ranking seventh as a cause of death for white males, but only third for nonwhites.

The section of Table 4 dealing with females indicates that nonwhite women are also more vulnerable to death from pneumonia and influenza, hypertension, diseases of early infancy, and "senility and ill-defined conditions" than are white women and to the same degree as nonwhite males. Deaths from "deliveries and complications of pregnancy, childbirth, and the puerperium" are not a major cause of death for any American women but for the 1,466 cases reported for 1963 the nonwhite rate was over five times that for whites (5.6 to 1.0). Anemias, too, are not prime killers, but nonwhite women have more than their share of death from this cause (3.0/1,000 to 1.7), with the same situation obtaining from asthma (3.2 to 1.8), and gastric ailments (7.2 to 3.9). Table 5 summarizes the data for the ten leading causes of death among women. The diseases of infancy rank fourth as a cause of death among nonwhite women and ninth among white women, a similar situation to that involving males. On the other hand, while the nonwhite female hypertension rate is twice that of whites, the rank order as a cause of death is not very different.

TABLE 5. *The Ten Leading Causes of Death: Females, U.S.A., 1963*

	Nonwhite		White	
Causes of Death	*Rate*	*Rank*	*Rate*	*Rank*
Diseases of the heart	262.2	1	312.1	1
Vascular lesions of central nervous system	120.4	2	110.9	2
Hypertensive heart disease	67.0	3	32.0	5
Certain diseases of early infancy	58.1	4	22.7	9
Influenza and pneumonia	51.0	5	30.3	6
Accidents	38.1	6	33.0	4
Cancer of digestive organs	32.1	7	45.5	3
Symptoms-Senility, and ill-defined conditions	30.9	8	7.1†	—
Cancer of genital organs	28.2	9	24.0	8
Diabetes mellitus	25.4	10	19.2	10
Cancer of the breast	18.2	—*	27.0	7

*Not among first ten for nonwhites
†Not among first ten for whites

In addition to an analysis of the ten leading causes of death, other 1963 death rates reflect the low socio-economic status and the influences of the Negro subculture. Of the 6,835 who died from tuberculosis, three and one-half times as many nonwhites as whites succumbed. Only about 2,000 deaths from syphilis occurred, but nonwhites were over-represented four to one.

As for a group of deaths from children's diseases, the pattern of over-representation for nonwhites also prevails. (See Table 6.)

Problems of Race and Confrontation 347

TABLE 6. *Number of Deaths and Rates for Whites and Nonwhites,
for Certain Children's Diseases: U.S.A., 1963*

Diseases	Cases	Nonwhite	White
Whooping Cough	115	.3	.0
Scarlet Fever	102	.1	.0
Diptheria	45	.1	.0
Measles	364	.4	.2

It was once both fashionable and scientifically respectable to explain these differences in terms of differential racial susceptibility to various diseases, but as Thomas Pettigrew points out:

The many improvements in his situation since 1900 rendered a dramatic increment in the Negro's health, providing solid evidence that corrosive poverty and inadequate medical care were the reasons for his short life span in the past. . . . this difference [between Negro and white rates] can be traced to the diseases which are treatable, preventable and unnecessary.[28]

This is now the generally accepted view among serious students of the problem, and "corrosive poverty" and "inadequate medical care" are aspects of the victimization to which Negroes have been subjected. Further improvement in the health status of Negroes depends upon the eradication of poverty and all its accompanying side effects as well as upon access to adequate medical care.

Much of the "corrosive poverty" has been associated with life in the cotton fields, the logging camps, the mines, and the small-town slums of a poverty-stricken South. Conditions were bad for most people, and the caste-system made them worse for the Negro. Dr. Ann Pettigrew has presented convincing evidence that the massive shift of Negro population into Northern and Western cities during the past two decades has resulted in some health gains for the Negro, and these gains have been due largely to greater access to medical advice and medical care.[29] But, the differentials are still large, even in the North, especially for tuberculosis, pneumonia, and venereal diseases. "Ghettoization," with its associated overcrowding, has been one important factor in keeping these rates high; but for these, as well as for other ailments, hospital discrimination is a primary factor limiting access to adequate medical care.

Patterns of discrimination and segregation by hospitals are prevalent throughout the country. A report prepared in 1962 for circulation to members of the National Medical Association (an organization of Negro physicians)[30] summarized the hospital situation in a sentence, "Things are bad all over," and the report included the bitter comment that "Hospitals under religious auspices have been the most vicious in discrimination." Conditions were worst in the South where the caste-system has not yet been shattered. In Birmingham, Alabama, for instance, a city of 750,000 people half of whom are Negro, only 1,100 beds were available for whites, and only 500 for Negroes. In Atlanta, Georgia, the South's most progressive city, 4,000 beds were available for whites, but only 600 for Negroes. (Nonwhites were 22.8 per cent of the population of the metropolitan area.) In Augusta, Georgia, a smaller city, twelve beds were set aside for Negroes in the basement of the white hospital but there were no beds for Negro pediatrics or obstetrics patients. The Hill-Burton Act under which federal funds may be secured for aid in building hospitals has a non-discrimination clause, but, generally, it has been evaded or ignored in the South. In one large Texas city a new $6,000,000 hospital constructed with federal aid refused to admit any Negroes until threatened with a suit. (The National Medical Association report emphasized that it was a Catholic hospital.) In Richmond, Virginia, a new "treatment center" accepted Negroes only as out-patients. By 1962, about 2,000 hospitals had been built in the South with federal assistance, and of these 98 would accept no Negroes, while the others stayed within the letter of the law by providing as little space for them as possible. In the few places where Negro physicians are practicing, they usually find it impossible to have their patients hospitalized under their own care since they cannot become members of hospital staffs. (In Elizabeth City, North Carolina, a Negro physician was recently taken on a staff after thirty-two annual applications.) Most Southern local medical societies bar Negroes from membership. (In South Carolina, however, twenty-five of the sixty-five Negro doctors belong to the state medical association, but must hold separate sessions. They can join local societies only if they will agree in advance to stay away from social functions.)

In the more fluid ethnic-class system in the North, patterns of discrimination and segregation vary from city to city. At one extreme is Pittsburgh, Pennsylvania, of which the National Medical Association report simply says, "No hospital problems." A similar assessment is made of Philadelphia. In Gary, Indiana, after a prolonged fight, 85 per cent of the Negro physicians were placed on the staff of some formerly all-white hospitals. When the National Medical Association says that "There is no hospital problem" in these cities, what it really means is that Negro physicians no longer find it difficult to have their patients hospitalized. But the Negro masses still face other problems; for, insofar as they are disproportionately represented in low-income groups, more of them are "charity" patients and must face the more subtle forms of victimization which the poor face everywhere in American hospitals—less careful attention to their needs psychological and physical, than private patients receive. There is substantial evidence from studies made in one Northern city that such patients are more frequently handled by medical students and interns than by fully trained doctors, and there is reliable statistical evidence indicating that more infants die on the wards than in the rooms of private patients. As important as it is to insist upon the right of Negro doctors to take their patients into hospitals which formerly barred them, other aspects of the Negro health problem must be dealt with, too.

The city of Chicago, with its 900,000 Negroes rigidly segregated into ghettos, reveals the full dimensions of the problem. As recently as 1960 there were no more than 500 beds available to Negroes in private hospitals —one-half bed per 1000 Negroes as compared with 4.5 beds per 1000 whites. A distinguished Negro physician serving as Chairman of a Committee to End Discrimination in Medical Institutions released a statement to the press in October, 1963, in which he said that only thirty-three out of eighty private hospitals admitted Negroes and that:

Many of these do so on a segregated and discriminating basis . . . Some hospitals which do admit Negroes place them in the oldest rooms, in basements, in all-Negro wings and often have a quota system limiting the number of Negro patients they will accept. . . . when a Negro becomes ill, he knows he will be accepted at County hospital and is in no mood to have to fight to gain admittance to a private hospital where he will be discriminated against.[31]

The Negro physicians, however, did take up the issue by insisting upon staff appointments so they could take their own patients into these hospitals and insure adequate care for them.

The fight began seriously in 1955 with the passage of an anti-discrimination bill in the City Council and a plea for compliance by Cardinal Stritch. In 1960, after five years of publicity and pleading, only twenty-one of the two hundred fifteen Negro physicians in Chicago held appointments on any private hospital staff outside of the Black Belt, these being at twenty-one of the sixty-eight hospitals of this type. At this point the Mayor appointed a special committee to work on the problem, and a group of ten Negro doctors filed suit under the Sherman and Clayton anti-trust acts against fifty-six hospitals, the Illinois Hospital Association, the Chicago Medical Society, the Chicago Hospital Council, and the Illinois Corporations operating Blue Cross and Blue Shield medical prepayment plans. They took this action, they said, "to thwart the more subtle and sophisticated techniques" being used to evade the issue.[32]

In response to these pressures (and to the general atmosphere regarding civil rights), forty-two of the sixty-eight hospitals in the city had given one hundred two staff appointments to sixty-four of the city's two hundred twenty-five Negro doctors by 1965. (Only eighty-eight of these, however, "permit the physician to admit his private patients.") The downward trend in the number of Negro physicians choosing to practice in Chicago was arrested. For a city which ranked only fourth from the bottom among fourteen cities on degree of hospital integration, the breakthrough has been a major victory.[33] One measure of the extent of the Negro's victimization is the fact that scores of physicians had to spend their money and invest time which could have been devoted to research or professional development in fighting for access to hospital facilities.

The victory of the Chicago Negro doctors has alleviated the plight of paying patients who now have a wider choice of hospitals, though not necessarily closer to their homes. (Because of the fear of being "swamped" by Negro patients, some hospitals near the Black Belt have interposed stronger barriers against Negro doctors than have those farther away.) As early as 1949, a health survey of Chicago pointed out that "A serious problem faced by the Blue Cross Plan for hospital care in this area is its inability to fulfil its obligations to the 50,000 Negro subscribers, since they are not accepted by all the member hospitals. . . . Many of the subscribers must be admitted to Cook County Hospital under the guise of emergencies. . . ." Six years later, the Packinghouse Workers Civic and Community Committee complained that "Our union has struggled and won hospital benefits for all our members, but a great number of UPWA-CIO members who are Negroes are being cheated out of those benefits. . . ." With over 100,000 insured Negroes and less than 1,000 beds available to them in private hospitals they are still being cheated, and not they alone.[34]

Chicago Negroes have been forced by hospital discrimination to use the facilities of four or five hospitals within the Black Belt and the large but overcrowded Cook County Hospital which should be serving only those who cannot pay and emergency cases. By 1960, almost two-thirds of all the Negro babies delivered in a hospital were being born at Cook County. Some white hospitals near the Black Ghetto closed down their maternity wards rather than serve Negroes. A prominent white physician delivering an address in 1960 in favor of widening access to hospital care stressed that this was unfair both to the paying patients who were denied the right to choose and to the indigent who were being deprived of space at the Cook County Hospital by Negroes who could pay. He said:

Cook County Hospital is even being used to absorb a large number of Negro patients unwanted by the voluntary hospitals even though they may be able and willing to pay . . . the Chicago public would not tolerate this misuse of a tax-supported hospital. . . . for an equivalent number of non-Negro patients. . . .[35]

Placing Negroes on the hospital staffs has not solved the fundamental problem of the shortage of beds available to a rapidly expanding Negro

population. To build new hospital facilities in the Black Belt *before* eliminating segregation in *all* hospitals would be considered bad strategy by most
Negro leaders and a "sell-out" by the militants. The Chicago paradigm has
general relevance and is not applicable only to the local scene.

Hospital discrimination is only one facet of a complex process involving
both direct and indirect victimization which leads to a lower level of physical and mental well-being among Negroes and which is reflected in morbidity and mortality rates. Health hazards for most of the Negro population
begin even before birth, and they affect both mother and child. These
hazards are greatest in the rural South, but they exist in urban situations
as well, both Northern and Southern. Premature births occurred 50 per cent
more frequently among Negroes than among whites during 1958–1959 and
maternal mortality rates among Negroes were four times higher.[36] A higher
proportion of Negro mothers failed to receive prenatal care, and a higher
proportion died in childbirth. The most authoritative testimony on the
disadvantaged position of the Negro expectant mother has been supplied by
an eminent obstetrician, Dr. Philip F. Williams, who has called attention
to the fact that "one survey of maternal mortality is cited which found
errors in judgment and technique as well as neglect on the part of the
physician, as much as fifty per cent more frequently in the case of Negro
than white mothers." He pointed out, too, that Negro women who were
pregnant and those who had babies were victims of a set of interlocking
conditions which included a lack of concern by husbands and putative
fathers, a relatively high exposure to gonorrhea and syphilis, and, in the
South ". . . a scarcity of physicians that has resulted in an inferior grade
of attendance at birth (the untrained mid-wife). . . ."[37] In both North and
South, hospital facilities are still inadequate and all of these factors combine
to create a situation ". . . more or less adversely affecting the chances of
survival of the Negro mother at childbirth." They affect the chances of the
baby's surviving, too. Studies made soon after World War II revealed that,
for Negroes as compared with whites, fewer Negro babies were delivered
in hospitals and therefore more of them died at birth or during the first year
after (and more died before they could be born, too). Immunization of
children was less common among Negroes and childhood diseases more
prevalent and more often fatal.[38] Negro children, on the average, received
fewer of the benefits of deliberately planned feeding, and fewer parents, in
proportion, ate according to the more advanced nutritional standards.

Insofar as the job ceiling, the income gap, and Ghettoization preserve and
reinforce lower-class behavior patterns among Negroes to a greater extent
than in the general society, the general health status of the Negro will be
affected. For instance, a less adequate nutritional level than is found among
whites is one factor often cited in accounting for the poorer average health

status of Negroes. It is conceivable that Negroes could improve their nutritional status immediately by altering their present patterns of food consumption, but this is likely to occur less as a result of education and propaganda than as a by-product of changes in the caste-class situation. Except in wartime or during depressions, food habits are among the most difficult to change, unless change is related to mobility strivings. Maximizing the opportunity for Negroes to achieve the values and norms of the general American middle class is likely to do more to change the eating habits of the Negro population than all of the written or spoken exhortations of home economists or the most seductive of television commercials. A shift in social class supplies the motivation to change, and such a shift is dependent upon an increase in the number and proportion of Negroes entering white-collar occupations.

Maintaining a style of living consonant with any occupational roles demands a minimum level of income. Success in improving the health status of the Negro population may ultimately depend upon an indirect rather than a frontal assault. One student of the problem gives us a clue to the strategy when he observes that ". . . the much lower income level of the American Negro, to the extent that it is a measure of standard of living, explains, in part at least, the differences in health status and longevity between whites and non-whites in the United States."[39] Carefully controlled studies "point up the intimate relationship between physical illness and economic . . ."[40] to use Dr. Ann Pettigrew's expression. Economic factors not only partially explain, or serve as indices of, the causes of divergent morbidity and mortality rates, but they also give us the clues to a strategy for change, namely, working toward a continuously rising standard of living. Whether hope or pessimism is warranted depends upon the possibility of drastically changing the economic status of the Negro over the next decade, of eliminating economic "victimization."

Closing the income gap is crucial, or alternatively, the provision of a subsidy for medical services. Large masses of Negroes will never become members of the white-collar class, but better job opportunities in commerce and industry will place many of them in a position to benefit from privately sponsored health and insurance plans. These will be of maximum benefit, however, only if hospital discrimination is eliminated. Also, the wider extension of adequate medical care to all citizens through the use of public funds, and the more effective use of social workers and educators, will automatically benefit those Negroes who are not upwardly mobile.

Chronic illness, as well as frequent periods of sickness, not only results in loss of man-hours of production, but also increases stress and strain in interpersonal relations and deprives individuals of the maximum amount of pleasure to be derived from a sense of physical well-being and from recreation and pleasurable interaction with other human beings. Insofar as the general health level of Negroes is lower than that of whites they suffer more from these deprivations. Tendencies to escape from pain and its consequences by habitual use of alcohol and drugs, or the anodyne of excessive preoccupation with the supernatural world, may be related to the general health situation within the Negro lower class. These less tangible and immeasurable disabilities are as real as the financial burdens imposed by sickness.

The Identification Problem

Some of the most damaging forms of indirect victimization manifest themselves at the psychological level. The Black Ghetto and the job ceiling are the key variables in accounting for differences in morbidity and mortality rates, and for the persistence of subcultural behavior patterns which deviate from middle-class norms. At the subjective level they also determine the crucial points of social reference for the individual Negro when answering the questions "Who am I today?" and "What will I be tomorrow?" The Black Ghetto forces him to identify as a Negro first, an American second, and it gives him geographical "roots." The job ceiling is an ever present reminder that there are forces at work which make him a second-class American. But the Black Ghetto and the job ceiling are only two components of a caste-class system now undergoing revolutionary transformation —an institutional complex which includes the courts, schools, churches, voluntary associations, media of mass communication, and a network of family units. Like all other persons the individual Negro receives his orientation to this social nexus first from his family and later from his peer group. Exposure to schools and the mass media continues the process of socialization and personality formation while membership in voluntary associations provides a tie to the class system and constitutes an aid to upward mobility.

The white middle class is the reference group for those who are mobile; yet the entire system operates to emphasize identity with "The Race," since defensive solidarity must be maintained against the white world. Inner conflicts are inevitable; and conventional, as well as idiosyncratic, adjustments to this situation have been thoroughly studied. Ann Pettigrew suggests that ". . . the perception of relative deprivation, the discrepancy between high aspirations and actual attainments . . . is a critical psychological determinant of mental disorder. And certainly racial discrimination acts to bar the very achievements which the society encourages individuals to attempt."[41] A disparity in psychosis rates reflects this discrepancy, but for most Negroes the reaction to oppression is less severe. Neither insanity nor suicide is a *typical* Negro reaction.

Both Negroes and whites are "victims" of one persisting legacy of the slave trade—the derogation of "negroidness." The idea that a dark skin indicates intellectual inferiority is rapidly passing, but at the esthetic level derogatory appraisal of thick lips, kinky hair, and very dark skin is still prevalent. That many Negroes reject their own body image is evident from advertisements for skin lighteners in the major Negro publications,[42] and Negro children in experimental situations begin to reject brown dolls for white ones before the age of five.[43] The ever present knowledge that one's negroid physiognomy is evaluated as "ugly" lowers self-esteem and, therefore, weakens self-confidence. The rise of the new African states has given a psychological "lift" to those American Negroes who still look more African than *metis,* but extreme Negro physical traits are still a source of inner disquiet—especially for women. (There is no equivalent in America of the African cult of *negritude* whose poets idealize the black woman.) These negative esthetic appraisals are part of a larger stereotype-complex which equates Africa with primitiveness and savagery and considers Negro ancestry a "taint." A frontal assault on a world-wide scale is necessary to undo this propaganda of the slave era which still exists as a form of cultural lag which has lost even the excuse of the functional utility it once had in rationalizing an integral part of the Western economic system—Negro slavery.[44]

Negroes in America, as a numerical minority, always have a feeling of being "on the outside looking in," of not being "in the main stream." Yet, the mere fact of being only one in ten does not automatically generate this feeling; the "victimization" flows, rather, from the values of the majority who refuse to accept every individual upon his own merit, but insist upon ascription of status on the basis of membership in a racial group. (Bahia, Brazil, presents an interesting case where the opposite is true, where individual achievement can almost completely over-ride racial origin.)[45] This sense of alienation is reinforced by traditional or deliberate omission of Negroes from the decision-making process. That they are absent from the boards of major corporations is not surprising; but it is surprising that they are virtually absent from the boards of foundations and professional associations. Only in the realm of public administration and the world of sports and entertainment are Negroes present in sufficient numbers to be "visible," and to serve as role models for Negro youth.

These omissions are particularly crucial in a society where numerous illustrated publications function as the image-makers. A Negro child seldom sees a person like himself in an advertisement or in illustrations accompanying fiction. The children in the textbooks are all white. The image of the powerful, the desirable, the admirable is set very early as "white." There is an increasing awareness of the seriousness of this problem, and by 1964 the television industry was making a half-hearted attempt to use a few Negroes in commercials, and one or two Northern cities were experimenting with "integrated textbooks." But still, Negro newspapers and magazines alone cater to this hunger to see the Negro image in print. These publications also give prominence to whatever interracial participation is taking place, but they cannot eliminate the feeling of resentment over exclusion from the collective representations of the larger society.

Leaders in the civil rights movement frequently refer to the process of desegregation and integration as having the goal of "bringing Negroes into the main stream." This sense of isolation from "the main stream" was given poetic expression by the late Dr. W. E. B. Du Bois in the 1890's when he spoke of living behind, or within, "The Veil." This isolation not only generates distorted perceptions of the total society and occasionally bizarre definitions of situations, but it also results in cognitive crippling. The communication flow needed to provide data for rational decision making is often impeded. Incomplete information is available for "playing the game" the way it is played in various segments of the larger society, and in a highly mobile society it is all-important to know "who is who" and "what is what." There is some evidence, for instance, to indicate that lower-middle-class and lower-class Negro parents often have high aspirations for their children but have no clear idea how to realize them. Negro students in segregated colleges and high schools are also often woefully ignorant of opportunities and techniques for succeeding.[46]

One cannot be mobile without learning the professional codes and the folkways of other social strata. It was this which the Supreme Court had in mind when it ruled some years ago that a separate law school for Negroes cut the student off from those contacts which were necessary to make a person a first-class lawyer and therefore could not meet the criterion of equality. It is this contact which most Negro physicians are denied. Also, in a society where the social ritual is so much a part of the business world, Negroes are generally not in a position to secure the cues and tips needed for competition on a basis of complete equality. If they cannot meet their peers at professional meetings and in the informal gatherings of persons who pursue similar occupations and professions, they, of necessity, will see only "through a glass darkly." Very clever and ambitious individuals (and persistent ones) sometimes rip aside "The Veil," but such persons are rare within any ethnic group. Most individuals remain victims of the communication blockage, and special efforts will be necessary to open the channels of communication. Participation across race lines with persons in similar occupations is the first step toward structural integration.

In a social system which forces Negroes to think of themselves *first* as Negroes and only second as Americans, a problem of "double identification" is posed for those who are partially integrated. Guilt feelings sometimes arise over the charge hurled by others that they are "running away from the Race." Negroes who represent the country abroad are exposed to the criticism of Africans and Asians as being "the tool of the white man." Personnel officers, political leaders, and work-supervisors are always open to the charge that they are "Uncle Toms," have "sold out," or have "forgotten the Race." This problem will be intensified if the process of integration at upper levels of power and prestige is not accompanied by the complete disappearance of racial barriers to upward mobility, or if the masses of Negroes are doomed to be America's permanent lower class. In the meanwhile, the rise of Malcolm X and the appeal of the Black Muslims and various local Black Nationalist groups suggest that the lower classes and lower middle classes can work their way out of the problem of double identification by rejecting "white" values and by proudly proclaiming their psychological independence. Such a solution is not available to the more sophisticated Negroes, but the possibility is not to be excluded that, since America insists upon limited integration rather than complete acceptance, increased identification of educated Negroes with some aspects of the Negro subculture and with the cultural renaissance taking place in Africa may become the norm.[47]

The Condition of Powerlessness

The problem of "identification" is crucial, but Charles Silberman, in *Crisis in Black and White*, puts his finger upon the most critical aspect of Negro-white relations in the United States when he stresses the psychological effect of being "powerless." Negroes realize that, as a minority in "the white man's country," they do not set the rules of the game. Unlike Negroes in Africa and the West Indies they do not fight for national independence, but rather for "desegregation" and "integration," and they can attain these goals only if the white majority sanctions them as legitimate and desirable. "Integration," in the final analysis, also means that the Negro community must increasingly become more middle-class in values and behavior if it is to win respect and approval. Negroes do not determine the ends for which they struggle, nor the means. The most they can expect is an increasingly greater share in the *joint* determination of their future. The problem of maintaining dignity and some autonomy in such a situation is, for sensitive personalities, a continuous one, even within the civil rights movement, for white friends, even in liberal-left circles, often strive to bend Negroes to their will and not to ask their advice as co-workers.

In the past, this sense of "powerlessness" to determine their own destiny or to change their position in the caste-class system has been one important factor in accentuating in-group aggression among lower-class Negroes, in the diversion of energy and financial resources into the over-elaboration of the church-voluntary association complex, and in the development of those styles of life which E. Franklin Frazier portrayed so unsympathetically in *Black Bourgeoisie*. Black Belt crime, juvenile delinquency, and cynical exploitation have also been interpreted by some sociologists as one reaction to a state of "powerlessness." Within the lower class and lower middle class, hostility and resentment become "socialized" for a few in the form of Black Nationalism and take organized form in movements such as the Black Muslims.[48] Among the rootless masses, the anger flowing from frustration bursts forth periodically in verbal abuse and violent assault, in arson and looting, in attacks upon policemen and property—thus the tragedy of Harlem, Rochester, and Philadelphia in 1964 and of Los Angeles and Chicago in 1965. The feeling of having made the conquest of power, of being in control of their own fate, if only for a moment, is symbolized in a widely circulated photograph of jubilant Negroes in Los Angeles. But these Black Belt explosions underscore a basic fact—that no revolution can follow the storming of the Bastille by Negroes in America. Camus and Sartre, not Marx, provide the key for understanding these events.

Conventional politics has been the most realistic approach to gaining at least the semblance of power. Recent demographic trends, including the flight of whites to the suburbs, have placed some Negro communities in a strategic position to play "balance of power" politics more effectively, and the civil rights movement may result in increased political power for Negroes in the South. Yet, all Negro leaders know the limits of their ability to wield decisive political influence. (And in the world of "big business" their influence is even less.) Silberman has suggested the importance— cathartic and practical—of grass-roots movements, with "middle-level" leadership, fighting for limited goals where results can be achieved, and Thomas Pettigrew has stressed the psychological liberating effect of participation in the civil rights movement.[49] The feed-back in terms of an increased incentive to secure more education or to get better jobs can be sustained only if society actually provides the rewards in terms of expanded occupational mobility. The sense of being powerless can disappear, however, only if the social system eventually changes to the extent that Negroes will not need to organize *as Negroes* to defend their interests and if color ceases to be a factor in membership in the "power structure." Riots will cease only when Americans allow Black Ghettos to dissolve.

The Myth of "Separate but Equal"

Negroes have been "victimized" throughout the three hundred fifty years of their presence on the North American continent. The types of social systems which have organized their relations with whites have been varied —over two hundred years of slavery and indenture, ten years of post-Civil War Reconstruction in the South, and eighty years of experimentation with a theory of "separate but equal" ostensibly designed to replace caste relations with those of class. The "separate but equal" doctrine has now been repudiated by the federal government and a broad section of public opinion as unjust and inimical to the national welfare. The period of desegregation has begun. Yet, the legacy of the past remains. As a transition to some new, and still undefined system of race relations takes place, it is relevant to examine the extent to which victimization persists, probing for its more subtle and covert manifestations. An estimate, too, should be made of whether or not what Merton has called "the unintended consequences of purposive social action" carry a potential for new forms of victimization.

By 1900 the doctrine had become firmly established that it was desirable for Negroes and whites to be members of two functionally related segments of a bi-racial society in which families, intimate friendship groups, and voluntary associations (including churches) would be separate, although members of both races were participating in a common economic system and political order. Both Negro and white leaders emphasized the point that "social equality" was not a Negro aspiration, and Booker T. Washington's famous Atlanta Compromise address delivered in 1895 made this point very explicit with his symbolism of the five fingers, separate and distinct, but joined together at the palm.

The theory of "separate but equal" visualized a future in which Negroes would gradually acquire wealth and education on such a scale as to develop a social-class system within the Negro community paralleling that of the white community. Then, as the sociologist Robert Park once phrased it, Negroes and whites would "look over and across" at each other, not "up and down." Defenders of "biracialism" believed that although institutional life—including schools and neighborhoods—should remain separate, Negroes should be allowed to compete freely for jobs and should gradually acquire the full voting rights which they had lost in the South after 1875. It was considered unwise, however, to make a frontal assault upon segregation in public places since the key to the ultimate dissolution or transformation of the caste system lay in the acquisition of education and economic well-being—not in protest. The "correct" behavior of an enlarged Negro middle class would eventually win acceptance by the white middle class. The doctrine of "separate but equal" was given legal sanction in a number of Supreme Court decisions, the most famous being that of *Plessy vs. Ferguson*, and it became the operating ideology among Southern white liberals between the two world wars.

During the first decade after World War II the doctrine of "separate but equal" was abandoned as a guide to the formulation of public policy insofar as the armed forces, public transportation, public accommodations, and public schools were concerned. Experience between the two world wars had demonstrated that, while it might be theoretically possible to achieve equality within the framework of a segregated school system in the South, it seemed impossible in actual practice. In the field of public transportation, no matter how many shiny new coaches replaced the old rickety "Jim Crow" coaches, Negroes did not consider them "equal," and they never ceased to be resentful that there were two American armies instead of one. The cost of duplicating facilities to make public accommodations and schools truly equal would have been exorbitant even if Negroes welcomed the idea. Thus, a demand for change was in the air when the historic 1954 decision requiring school desegregation was taken, and the Court cut through to a fundamental question which had often been evaded: whether or not it was possible to maintain any kind of *forced* segregation in an open society without pejorative implications. Did not the very insistence upon separation imply inferiority? The caste-class system organizing race relations was recognized for what it really was—a system which, irrespective of the intent of individuals, resulted in the victimization of Negroes. Makers of national policy have now embarked upon a thoroughgoing program of desegregation coupled with an assault upon all institutionalized forms of racial discrimination. But the white public has not accepted the concept of "total integration."

Some Paradoxes of Progress

The abandonment of the doctrine of "separate but equal" has forced consideration of many provocative questions, such as: "Can the victimization resulting from unequal treatment of Negroes in the past be eliminated without preferential treatment for present-day victims?" There are those who contend that justice demands more than equality, that it requires a "revolutionary break-through" in the form of preferential hiring, distinctive programs of education, and special scholarship schemes. The existence of entrenched patterns of residential segregation also raises the question of the desirability and probability of the persistence of Negro neighborhoods and institutions. If *forced* separation eventually disappeared would separateness cease to be an index of victimization? Would it then lose its pejorative implications? Would the right to choose, if it ever came, mean that some Negroes will choose *not* to be "integrated" except in the economic and political order?

New types of victimization are emerging which are not only indirect but are also unintended consequences of actions designed to eliminate victimization. For instance, in several Northern cities an earnest effort is being made to facilitate and speed up the process of residential desegregation at the middle-class level. Negroes whose incomes and life styles approximate those of the white middle class are accepted into neighborhoods and apartment buildings in limited numbers in order not to excite fear and panic among white residents. The goal, as one Chicago neighborhood association states it, is "an integrated neighborhood with high community standards," to reverse the process of ghettoization. However, without a commitment to "open occupancy" at the city level, attainment of this goal demands a neighborhood-by-neighborhood approach, which calls for studying "tipping points" and setting up "benign quotas" in order to maintain a "racial balance." It may also involve a program which forces all lower-class residents to leave irrespective of their color, while integrating a small number of middle-class Negroes into neighborhoods or specific apartment buildings. One effective technique has been clearance of slums followed by rebuilding at a high enough rent level to keep the proportion of Negroes automatically very low. This process is frequently called "controlled integration."[50] Actions such as these often result in the concentration of many lower-class Negroes into almost completely segregated public housing projects. What is gained for some in terms of better physical surroundings is lost in increased "ghettoization." Other displaced persons increase the degree of overcrowding in already overcrowded neighborhoods or filter into middle-class Negro neighborhoods and disorganize them.

Serious problems also arise within the middle class at the psychological level. Insofar as Negro families have to cooperate actively in setting and maintaining quotas on the number of Negroes who enter, and in eliminating lower-class Negroes from the neighborhood, they become vulnerable to attack by other Negroes. Some sensitive individuals suffer from a feeling of guilt over manipulating the situation to maintain exclusiveness; others feel a loss of dignity in carrying on continuous discussion about race with white people. They dislike dealing with themselves as "a problem." A few people simply withdraw from such "integrated" situations into the comfort of the middle-class "gilded ghetto." This situation is only a special case of a more general problem confronting some Negroes in this Era of Integration—how to reconcile being a "loyal Negro" or a "Race Man" with new middle-class interracial relations or new occupational roles.

Rapid and fairly complete "integration" of middle-class Negroes into neighborhoods, churches, educational, and voluntary associations could have a profound effect upon Negro institutional life, "skimming off the cream" of the Negro élites to the disadvantage of the larger Negro community. This would result in a kind of victimization of the Negro masses which would be permanent unless the conditions of life for the lower classes were drastically changed.

Unfortunately there are few signs of hope that the Negro masses will profit from current economic changes, for at the very moment when the civil rights movement has been most successful, and when access to training is being made more widely available to Negroes, forces are at work which could render these gains meaningless. Whitney Young, Jr., of the National Urban League, emphasizing economic problems facing Negroes, stated upon one occasion: "Unless we identify these problems and take steps to meet them, we will find the masses of Negroes five years from today with a mouthful of rights, living in hovels with empty stomachs."[51] About 12 per cent of the nonwhite labor force were unemployed in 1960, twice the rate for white workers.[52] In some urban areas it was between 15 and 20 per cent. It was higher for Negro men than for women. Unemployment rates are particularly high for Negro youth. In 1961, nonwhite boys and girls between fourteen and nineteen had the highest unemployment rate of any age-color group in the nation, while the unemployment rate for Negro high-school graduates between the ages of sixteen and twenty-one was twice that for white youth and higher than the rate for whites who had *not* attended high school. One out of five Negro high-school graduates were unable to find jobs.[53] If high-school graduates face such a situation, the plight of the untrained Negro is likely to be even worse. It was estimated in 1964 that automation was wiping out about 40,000 unskilled jobs a week, the sector of industry where Negro workers are concentrated. This trend is likely to continue for some time.[54]

If Negroes are not to become a permanent *lumpen-proletariat* within American society as a result of social forces already at work and increased automation, deliberate planning by governmental and private agencies will be necessary. Continued emphasis upon "merit hiring" will benefit a few individuals, but, in the final analysis, structural transformations will have to take place.[55] There are those who feel that only a radical shift in American values and simultaneous adjustments of economy and society will wipe out, forever, the victimization of the Negro. If such a situation does occur it is not likely to be the result of any cataclysmic proletarian upheaval, but rather through drift and piece-meal pragmatic decisions. One straw in the wind has been raised to test the temper of the time. Gunnar Myrdal and twenty-nine other scholars, writers, and political scientists have released a statement on "The Cybernation Revolution, the Weaponry Revolution, and the Human Rights Revolution." In discussing the need for adjustment to the effects of largescale automation, they made a revolutionary suggestion:

We urge, therefore, that society, through its appropriate legal and governmental institutions, undertake an unqualified commitment to provide every individual and every family with an adequate income as a matter of right. . . .

Should this ever happen, Negroes would, of course, profit even more than whites, but demands for radical reforms of this type have not arisen from within the Civil Rights Movement whose leaders generally accept a middle-class work ethic which is incompatible with such a solution.

The author wishes to acknowledge with gratitude the assistance of Miss Odessa D. Thompson.

NOTES

1. The first systematic formulation of a caste-class hypothesis to explain American race relations appeared in an article by W. Lloyd Warner and Allison Davis, "A Comparative Study of American Caste," one of several contributions to a volume edited by Edgar Thompson, *Race Relations and The Race Problem* (Raleigh, N. C., 1939). The field research upon which much of the article was based was published later as Allison Davis, Burleigh Gardner, and Mary Gardner, *Deep South* (Chicago, 1941). For a Marxist criticism of the caste-class interpretation of American race relations see Oliver Cromwell Cox, *Caste, Class and Race* (New York, 1948).

2. Analysis of inter-ethnic mobility in terms of conflict, accommodation, and assimilation characterized the work of "The Chicago School" of Sociology during the 1920's and early 1930's. For more sophisticated analysis, note W. L. Warner and Leo Srole, *The Social Systems of American Ethnic Groups* (New Haven, Conn., 1946), in which studies of comparative mobility rates of various ethnic groups are made. Nathan Glazer and Patrick D. Moynihan, in *Beyond The Melting Pot* (Cambridge, Mass., 1963), have recently suggested that ethnic solidarities are much more enduring than earlier sociologists had expected them to be.

3. John Dollard, in association with Allison Davis, has added other dimensions to his analysis in *Children of Bondage* (Washington, D. C., 1940).

4. For a discussion of these concepts see Hans Gerth and C. Wright Mills, *From Max Weber: Essays in Sociology* (New York, 1946), chapter on "Caste, Class and Party."

5. The distinguished psychotherapist, Bruno Bettelheim, of the Orthogenic School of the University of Chicago, in a provocative and perceptive article in *The Nation*, October 19, 1963 ("Class, Color and Prejudice"), contends that protection of social class values is a more important variable than race prejudice in structuring relations between Negroes and whites in the North of the U.S.A.

6. St. Clair Drake and Horace R. Clayton, in *Black Metropolis* (New York, 1962), use the term "Black Ghetto" to refer to the involuntary and exploitative aspect of

the all-Negro community and "Bronzeville" to symbolize the more pleasant aspects of the segregated community. Robert C. Weaver, another Negro scholar, called his first book *The Negro Ghetto* (New York, 1948). The term is widely used by contemporary Negro leaders with pejorative implications. See also Kenneth Clark, *Dark Ghetto* (New York, 1965).

7. The most careful study of the effect of Negro entry into all-white neighborhoods is to be found in a book published by the University of California Press in 1961 which reports upon the results of research in Detroit, Chicago, Kansas City, Oakland, San Francisco, Philadelphia, and Portland, Oregon—Luigi Laurenti's *Property Values and Race* (Berkeley, Calif., 1961).

8. Thomas F. Pettigrew, *A Profile of the Negro American* (Princeton, N. J., 1964), p. 190. His wife, Dr. Ann Pettigrew, M.D., collaborated with him on the chapter dealing with health.

9. Though based upon only one community in Chicago, *The Politics of Urban Renewal,* by Peter Rossi and Robert A. Dentler (Glencoe, Ill., 1961) analyzes basic processes to be found in all Northern cities.

10. Professor Everett C. Hughes makes some original and highly pertinent remarks about new Negro middle-class communities in his introduction to the 1962 edition of Drake and Cayton's *Black Metropolis.*

11. Pettigrew, *op. cit.,* pp. 180–181.

12. The issue of the extent to which Negroes have been victimized by urban redevelopment is discussed briefly by Robert C. Weaver in *The Urban Complex: Human Values in Urban Life* (New York, 1964). See also Martin Anderson, *The Federal Bulldozer: A Critical Analysis of Urban Renewal: 1949–1962* (Cambridge, Mass., 1964).

13. Drake and Cayton, *op. cit.,* Chap. 23, "Advancing the Race."

14. See section on "The Negro Community as a Pathological Form of an American Community," Chap. 43 of Gunnar Myrdal, *An American Dilemma* (New York, 1944), p. 927.

15. A report appeared on the front page of *The New York Times,* April 5, 1965, stating that a commission was at work trying to elaborate plans for "integrating" Harlem by 1975. Columbia University was said to be co-operating in the research aspects of the project.

16. A successful experiment in "controlled integration" has been described by Julia Abrahamson in *A Neighborhood Finds Itself* (New York, 1959).

17. Jacob Schiffman, "Marital and Family Characteristics of Workers, March, 1962," in *Monthly Labor Review,* U. S. Department of Labor, Bureau of Labor Statistics, Special Labor Force Report No. 26, January 1963.

18. *Ibid.*

19. Norval D. Glenn, "Some Changes in the Relative Status of American Non-whites: 1940–1960," *Phylon,* Vol. 24, No. 2 (Summer 1963).

20. Pettigrew, *op. cit.,* p. 188.

21. *Ibid.,* p. 99; see also Marcus S. Goldstein, "Longevity and Health Status of Whites and Non-Whites in the United States," *Journal of the National Medical*

Association, Vol. 46, No. 2 (March 1954), p. 83. Among other factors, the author emphasizes the relationship between nutrition and racial mortality differentials.

22. Marion Haynes, "A Century of Change: Negroes in the U. S. Economy, 1860–1960," *Monthly Labor Review,* U. S. Department of Labor, Bureau of Labor Statistics, December 1962.

23. Pettigrew (*op. cit.,* p. 87) comments that some research indicates that ". . . these group differences are inflated through disproportionate under-reporting of whites. . . ."

24. The rates cited are from Pettigrew, *op. cit.,* Chap. 4, "Negro American Health."

25. *Monthly Vital Statistics Report,* National Center for Health Statistics, U. S. Department of Health, Education and Welfare, Public Health Service, Vol. 13 (November 2, 1964), p. 8.

26. *Ibid.,* p. 7.

27. Pettigrew, *op. cit.,* p. 96.

28. *Ibid.,* p. 99.

29. *Ibid.,* pp. 82–94, "Communicable Diseases," and pp. 97–98, "Economics and Physical Health."

30. It has been demonstrated with data drawn from six Southern states that Negro mothers occupying private rooms in hospitals had a lower death rate among their infants than white mothers on the wards. See H. Bloch, H. Lippett, B. Redner, and D. Hirsch, "Reduction of Mortality in the Premature Nursery," *Journal of Pediatrics,* Vol. 41, No. 3 (September 1952), pp. 300–304.

31. Dr. Arthur G. Falls' statement was released through the Chicago Urban League on October 20, 1963, having been sent out on October 16th with a "hold." (Copy in files of Chicago Urban League, C.E.D.)

32. These actions are discussed in the Presidential Address delivered to the Institute of Medicine of Chicago, January 14, 1960, by Dr. Franklin C. McLean, "Negroes and Medicine in Chicago." (Mimeographed copy in files of Chicago Urban League).

33. The 1965 assessment is from a statement by Dr. Robert G. Morris, circulated in mimeographed form by the Chicago Urban League. The standard work on the problems facing Negro physicians in Dietrich C. Reitzes, *Negroes and Medicine* (Cambridge, Mass., 1958).

34. Summarized from documents on file with Chicago Urban League.

35. Dr. F. C. McLean, cited in 32 *supra.*

36. Note Pettigrew, *op. cit.,* p. 97, which cites "lack of prenatal care, poor family health education, inadequate diet and inexpert delivery" as factors.

37. Philip F. Williams, "Material Welfare and the Negro," *Journal of American Medical Association,* Vol. 132, No. 11 (November 16, 1946), pp. 611–614.

38. M. Gover and J. B. Yaukey, "Physical Impairments of Members of Low-Income Farm Families," *Public Health Reports,* Vol. 61, No. 4 (January 25, 1946), and Marion E. Altenderfer and Beatrice Crowther, "Relationship Between Infant Mortality and Socio-economic Factors in Urban Areas," *Public Health Reports,* Vol. 64, No. 11 (March 18, 1949), pp.331–339.

39. Marcus S. Goldstein, *op. cit.*, p. 93.

40. Dr. Ann Pettigrew cites a study carried out in Chicago, using 1950 data, in which, when Negroes and whites of the same economic level were compared, mortality rates were about the same although the rates for Negroes as a group when compared with those for whites as a group were higher. Other studies using the same body of data indicate sharp differences in mortality rates as between laborers and skilled workers among Negroes, a situation similar to that found among whites (Pettigrew, *op. cit.*, p. 98).

41. *Ibid.*, p. 80.

42. *Ebony*, a well-edited, widely circulated, popular weekly magazine which concentrates upon the display of what its editor calls "Negro achievement" carries skin-lightener advertisements routinely. *Ebony's* African imitator, *Drum*, also carries such advertisements.

43. The classical study in this field is Kenneth B. Clark and Mamie P. Clark, "Racial Identification and Preference in Negro Children," which has been made widely accessible through T. M. Newcomb and E. L. Hartley's *Readings in Social Psychology* (New York, 1947), pp. 169–178.

44. Analyses of the genesis of the derogatory stereotypes of Africa and Africans may be found in Kenneth Little, *Negroes in Britain* (London, 1948), and Philip Curtin, *The Image of Africa* (Madison, Wisc., 1964). See also "Toward an Evaluation of African Societies," by St. Clair Drake, in *Africa Seen by American Negro Scholars* (New York, 1958).

45. The extent to which the pattern in Bahia, Brazil, differs from that in the United States is analyzed by Donald Pierson in *Negroes in Brazil* (Chicago, 1942).

46. Wilson Record, "Counseling and Communication," *Journal of Negro Education*, Vol. 30, No. 4 (Fall 1961).

47. Note Harold Isaacs, *The New World of Negro Americans* (New York, 1963), and St. Clair Drake, "To Hide My Face? An Essay on Pan Africanism and Negritude," in Herbert Hill (ed.), *Soon One Morning* (New York, 1963).

48. See Essien-Udom, *Black Nationalism: A Search for an Identity in America* (Chicago, 1962); and Charles Eric Lincoln's *The Black Muslims in America* (Boston, 1961). Reactions to the deaths of Patrice Lumumba and Malcolm X among a segment of the Negro American lower-class reveal the not-to-be-ignored depth of Black Nationalist feeling in the U.S.A.

49. Pettigrew, *op. cit.*, pp. 161–168, "The New Role of the Equal Citizen."

50. Peter Rossi, *op. cit.*

51. Quoted by James Reston in a column, "The Ironies of History and the American Negro," *The New York Times*, May 15, 1964.

52. See Glenn, *op. cit.*, and Haynes, *op. cit.*

53. See Schiffman, *op. cit.*

54. Pettigrew, *op. cit.*, p. 169.

55. *Ibid.*, "Some Needed Societal Reforms," pp. 168–176.

THE FORMATION OF RACIAL GHETTOS ⚑

⚑ ⚑ National Advisory Commission on Civil Disorders

Major Trends in Negro Population

Throughout the 20th century, and particularly in the last three decades, the Negro population of the United States has been steadily moving from rural areas to urban, from South to North and West.

In 1910, 2.6 million Negroes lived in American cities—27 percent of the nation's Negro population of 9.8 million. Today, about 15 million Negro Americans live in metropolitan areas, or 69 percent of the Negro population of 21.5 million. In 1910, 800,000 Negroes—9 percent—lived outside the South. Now, almost 10 million, about 45 percent, live in the North or West.

These shifts in population have resulted from three basic trends:

- A rapid increase in the size of the Negro population.
- A continuous flow of Negroes from Southern rural areas, partly to large cities in the South, but primarily to large cities in the North and West.
- An increasing concentration of those Negroes in large metropolitan areas within racially segregated neighborhoods.

Taken together, these trends have produced large and constantly growing concentrations of Negro population within big cities in all parts of the nation. Because most major civil disorders of recent years occurred in all-Negro neighborhoods, we have examined the causes of this concentration.

SOURCE: Report of the National Advisory Commission on Civil Disorders, *The Formation of Racial Ghettos* (Washington, D. C., 1968), pp. 236–250.

The Growth Rate of the Negro Population

During the first half of this century, the white population of the United States grew at a slightly faster rate than the Negro population. Because fertility rates[1] among Negro women were more than offset by death rates among Negroes and by large-scale immigration of whites from Europe, the proportion of Negroes in the country declined from 12 percent in 1900 to 10 percent in 1940.

By the end of World War II—and increasingly since then—major advances in medicine and medical care, together with the increasing youth of the Negro population resulting from higher fertility rates, caused death rates among Negroes to fall much faster than among whites. This is shown in the following table:

	Death Rate/1,000 Population		RATIO OF NONWHITE RATE
YEAR	WHITES	NONWHITES	TO WHITE RATE
1900	17.0	25.0	1.47
1940	10.4	13.8	1.33
1965	9.4	9.6	1.02

In addition, white immigration from outside the United States dropped dramatically after stringent restrictions were adopted in the 1920's.

TWENTY YEAR PERIOD	TOTAL IMMIGRATION (MILLIONS)
1901–1920	14.5
1921–1940	4.6
1941–1960	3.6

Thus, by mid-century, both factors which previously had offset higher fertility rates among Negro women no longer were in effect.

While Negro fertility rates, after rising rapidly to 1957, have declined sharply in the past decade, white fertility rates have dropped even more, leaving Negro rates much higher in comparison.

	LIVE BIRTHS PER 1,000 WOMEN AGED 15–44		RATIO OF NONWHITE
YEAR	WHITE	NONWHITE	TO WHITE
1940	77.1	102.4	1.33
1957	117.4	163.4	1.39
1965	91.4	133.9	1.46

The result is that Negro population is now growing significantly faster than white population. From 1940 to 1960, the white population rose 34.0

percent, but the Negro population rose 46.6 percent. From 1960 to 1966, the white population grew 7.4 percent; whereas Negro population jumped 14.4 percent, almost twice as much.

Consequently, the proportion of Negroes in the total population has risen from 10.0 percent in 1950 to 10.5 percent in 1960, and 11.1 percent in 1966.[2]

In 1950, at least one of every ten Americans was Negro; in 1966, one of nine. If this trend continues, one of every eight Americans will be Negro by 1972.

Another consequence of higher birth rates among Negroes is that the Negro population is considerably younger than the white population. In 1966, the median age among whites was 29.1 years, as compared to 21.1 among Negroes. About 35 percent of the white population was under 18 years of age, compared with 45 percent for Negroes. About one of every six children under five and one of every six new babies are Negro.

Negro-white fertility rates bear an interesting relationship to educational experience. Negro women with low levels of education have more children than white women with similar schooling, while Negro women with four years or more of college education have fewer children than white women similarly educated. The following table illustrates this:

EDUCATION LEVEL ATTAINED	NUMBER OF CHILDREN EVER BORN TO ALL WOMEN (MARRIED OR UNMARRIED) 35–39 YEARS OLD BY LEVEL OF EDUCATION (BASED ON 1960 CENSUS)	
	NONWHITE	WHITE
Completed elementary school	3.0	2.8
Four years of high school	2.3	2.3
Four years of college	1.7	2.2
Five years or more of college	1.2	1.6

This suggests that the difference between Negro and white fertility rates may decline in the future if Negro educational attainment compares more closely with that of whites, and if a rising proportion of members of both groups complete college.

The Migration of Negroes From the South

THE MAGNITUDE OF THIS MIGRATION

In 1910, 91 percent of the nation's 9.8 million Negroes lived in the South. Twenty-seven percent of American Negroes lived in cities of 2,500 persons or more, as compared to 48 percent of the nation's white population.

By 1966, the Negro population had increased to 21.5 million, and two significant geographic shifts had taken place. The proportion of Negroes living in the South had dropped to 55 percent and about 69 percent of all Negroes lived in metropolitan areas compared to 64 percent for whites. While the total Negro population more than doubled from 1910 to 1966, the number living in cities rose five-fold (from 2.6 million to 14.8 million) and the number outside the South rose eleven-fold (from 880,000 to 9.7 million).

Negro migration from the South began after the Civil War. By the turn of the century, sizeable Negro populations lived in many large Northern cities—Philadelphia, for example, had 63,400 Negro residents in 1900. The movement of Negroes out of the rural South accelerated during World War I, when floods and boll weevils hurt farming in the South, and the industrial demands of the war created thousands of new jobs for unskilled workers in the North. After the war, the shift to mechanized farming spurred the continuing movement of Negroes from rural Southern areas.

The Depression slowed this migratory flow, but World War II set it in motion again. More recently, continuing mechanization of agriculture and the expansion of industrial employment in Northern and Western cities have served to sustain the movement of Negroes out of the South, although at a slightly lower rate.

PERIOD	NET NEGRO OUT-MIGRATION FROM THE SOUTH	ANNUAL AVERAGE RATE
1910–1920	454,000	45,400
1920–1930	749,000	74,900
1930–1940	348,000	34,800
1940–1950	1,597,000	159,700
1950–1960	1,457,000	145,700
1960–1966	613,000	102,000

From 1960 to 1963, annual Negro out-migration actually dropped to 78,000 but then rose to over 125,000 from 1963 to 1966.

IMPORTANT CHARACTERISTICS OF THIS MIGRATION

It is useful to recall that even the latest scale of Negro migration is relatively small when compared to the earlier waves of European immigrants. A total of 8.8 million immigrants entered the United States between 1901 and 1911, and another 5.7 million arrived during the following decade. Even during the years from 1960 through 1966, the 1.8 million immigrants from abroad vastly outnumbered the 613,000 Negroes who departed the

South. In these same six years, California alone gained over 1.5 million new residents from internal shifts of American population.

Three major routes of Negro migration from the South have developed. One runs north along the Atlantic Seaboard toward Boston, another north from Mississippi toward Chicago, and the third west from Texas and Louisiana toward California. Between 1955 and 1960, 50 percent of the nonwhite migrants to the New York metropolitan area came from North Carolina, South Carolina, Virginia, Georgia, and Alabama; North Carolina alone supplied 20 percent of all New York's nonwhite immigrants. During the same period, almost 60 percent of the nonwhite migrants to Chicago came from Mississippi, Tennessee, Arkansas, Alabama, and Louisiana; Mississippi accounted for almost one-third. During these years, three-fourths of the nonwhite migrants to Los Angeles came from Texas, Louisiana, Mississippi, Arkansas, and Alabama.

The flow of Negroes from the South has caused the Negro population to grow more rapidly in the North and West, as indicated below.

TOTAL NEGRO POPULATION GAINS (MILLIONS)

PERIOD	NORTH & WEST	SOUTH	PERCENT OF GAIN IN NORTH & WEST
1940–1950	1.855	0.321	85.2%
1950–1960	2.732	1.086	71.5%
1960–1966	2.147	0.517	80.6%

As a result, although a much higher proportion of Negroes still reside in the South, the distribution of Negroes throughout the United States is beginning to approximate that of whites, as the following tables show.

Percent Distribution of the Population By
Region—1950, 1960 and 1966

	NEGRO			WHITE		
	1950	1960	1966	1950	1960[3]	1966
United States	100	100	100	100	100	100
South	68	60	55	27	27	28
North	28	34	37	59	56	55
Northeast	13	16	17	28	26	26
North-central	15	18	20	31	30	29
West	4	6	8	14	16	17

Negroes as a Percentage of the Total Population
in the United States and Each Region
1950, 1960, and 1966

	1950	1960	1966
United States	10	11	11
South	22	21	20
North	5	7	8
West	3	4	5

Negroes in the North and West are now so numerous that natural increase rather than migration provides the greater part of Negro population gains there. And even though Negro migration has risen steadily, it comprises a constantly declining proportion of Negro growth in these regions.

PERIOD	PERCENTAGE OF TOTAL NORTH & WEST NEGRO GAIN FROM SOUTHERN IN-MIGRATION
1940–1950	85.9%
1950–1960	53.1%
1960–1966	28.9%

In other words, we have reached the point where the Negro populations of the North and West will continue to expand significantly even if migration from the South drops substantially.

FUTURE MIGRATION

Despite accelerating Negro migration from the South, the Negro population there has continued to rise.

DATE	NEGRO POPULATION IN THE SOUTH (MILLIONS)	CHANGE FROM PRECEDING DATE TOTAL	ANNUAL AVERAGE
1940	9.9	—	—
1950	10.2	321,000	32,100
1960	11.3	1,086,000	108,600
1966	11.8	517,000	86,200

Nor is it likely to halt. Negro birth rates in the South, as elsewhere, have fallen sharply since 1957, but so far, this decline has been offset by the rising Negro population base remaining in the South. From 1950 to 1960, Southern Negro births generated an average net increase of 254,000 per year, and from 1960 to 1966, an almost identical 188,000 per year. Even if Negro birth rates continue to fall, they are likely to remain high enough to support significant migration to other regions for some time to come.

The Negro population in the South is becoming increasingly urbanized. In 1950, there were 5.4 million Southern rural Negroes; by 1960, 4.8 million. But this decline has·been more than offset by increases in the urban population. A rising proportion of inter-regional migration now consists of persons moving from one city to another. From 1960 to 1966, rural Negro population in the South was far below its peak, but the annual average migration of Negroes from the South was still substantial.

These facts demonstrate that Negro migration from the South, which has moved at an accelerating rate for the past 60 years, will continue, unless economic conditions change dramatically in either the South or the North and West. This conclusion is reinforced by the fact that most Southern states (including the District of Columbia) "exported" white population— as compared to 13 which "exported" Negro population. Excluding Florida's net gain by migration of 1.5 million, the other 16 Southern states together had a net loss by migration of 1.46 million whites.

The Concentration of Negro Population in Large Cities

WHERE NEGRO URBANIZATION HAS OCCURRED

Statistically, the Negro population in America has become more urbanized, and more metropolitan, than the white population. According to Census Bureau estimates, almost 70 percent of all Negroes in 1966 lived in metropolitan areas, compared to 64 percent of all whites. In the South, more than half the Negro population now lives in cities. Rural Negroes outnumber urban Negroes in only four states: Arkansas, Mississippi, North Carolina, and South Carolina.

Basic data concerning Negro urbanization trends, presented in tables at the conclusion of this chapter, indicate that:

• Almost all Negro population growth is occurring within metropolitan areas, primarily within central cities. From 1950 to 1966, the U. S. Negro population rose 6.5 million. Over 98 percent of that increase took place in metropolitan areas— 86 percent within central cities, 12 percent in the urban fringe.

• The vast majority of white population growth is occurring in suburban portions of metropolitan areas. From 1950 to 1966, 77.8 percent of the white population increase of 35.6 million took place in the suburbs. Central cities received only 2.5 percent of this total white increase. Since 1960, white central-city population has actually declined by 1.3 million.

• As a result, central cities are steadily becoming more heavily Negro, while the urban fringes around them remain almost entirely white. The proportion of Negroes in all central cities rose steadily from 12 percent in 1950, to 17 percent in 1960, and became 96 percent white by 1966.

• The Negro population is growing faster, both absolutely and relatively, in the larger metropolitan areas than in the smaller ones. From 1950 to 1966, the proportion of nonwhites in the central cities of metropolitan areas with one million or more persons doubled, reaching 26 percent, as compared with 20 percent in the central cities of metropolitan areas containing from 250,000 to one million persons, and 12 percent in the central cities of metropolitan areas containing under 250,000 persons.

• The 12 largest central cities (New York, Chicago, Los Angeles, Philadelphia,

Detroit, Baltimore, Houston, Cleveland, Washington, D. C., St. Louis, Milwaukee, and San Francisco) now contain over two-thirds of the Negro population outside the South, and one-third of the Negro total in the United States. All these cities have experienced rapid increases in Negro population since 1950. In six (Chicago, Detroit, Cleveland, St. Louis, Milwaukee, and San Francisco), the proportion of Negroes at least doubled. In two others (New York and Los Angeles), it probably doubled. In 1968, seven of these cities are over 30 percent Negro, and one (Washington, D. C.) is two-thirds Negro.

FACTORS CAUSING RESIDENTIAL SEGREGATION IN METROPOLITAN AREAS

The early pattern of Negro settlement within each metropolitan area followed that of immigrant groups. Migrants converged on the older sections of the central city because the lowest cost housing was there, friends and relatives were likely to be there; and the older neighborhoods then often had good public transportation.

But the later phases of Negro settlement and expansion in metropolitan areas diverge sharply from those typical of white immigrants. As the whites were absorbed by the larger society, many left their predominantly ethnic neighborhoods and moved to outlying areas to obtain newer housing and better schools. Some scattered randomly over the suburban area. Others established new ethnic clusters in the suburbs, but even these rarely contained solely members of a single ethnic group. As a result, most middle-class neighborhoods—both in the suburbs and within central cities—have no distinctive ethnic character, except that they are white.

Nowhere has the expansion of America's urban Negro population followed this pattern of dispersal. Thousands of Negro families have attained incomes, living standards, and cultural levels matching or surpassing those of whites who have "upgraded" themselves from distinctly ethnic neighborhoods. Yet most Negro families have remained within predominantly Negro neighborhoods, primarily because they have been effectively excluded from white residential areas.

Their exclusion has been accomplished through various discriminatory practices, some obvious and overt, others subtle and hidden. Deliberate efforts are sometimes made to discourage Negro families from purchasing or renting homes in all-white neighborhoods. Intimidation and threats of violence have ranged from throwing garbage on lawns and making threatening phone calls to burning crosses in yards and even dynamiting property. More often, real estate agents simply refuse to show homes to Negro buyers.

Many middle-class Negro families, therefore, cease looking for homes beyond all-Negro areas or nearby "changing" neighborhoods. For them, trying to move into all-white neighborhoods is not worth the psychological efforts and costs required.

Another form of discrimination just as significant is "white flight"—withdrawal from, or refusal to enter neighborhoods where large numbers of Negroes are moving or already residing. Normal population turnover causes about 20 percent of the residents of average United States neighborhoods to move out every year because of income changes, job transfers, shifts in life-cycle position or deaths. This normal turnover rate is even higher in apartment areas. The refusal of whites to move into "changing" areas when vacancies occur there from normal turnover means that most vacancies are eventually occupied by Negroes. An inexorable shift toward heavy Negro occupancy results.

Once this happens, the remaining whites seek to leave, and this seems to confirm the existing belief among whites that complete transformation of a neighborhood is inevitable once Negroes begin to enter. Since the belief itself is one of the major causes of the transformation, it becomes a self-fulfilling prophecy, which inhibits the development of racially integrated neighborhoods.

Thus, Negro settlements expand almost entirely through "massive racial transition" at the edges of existing all-Negro neighborhoods, rather than by a gradual dispersion of population throughout the metropolitan area.

Two important points to note about this phenomenon are that:

• "Massive transition" requires no panic or flight by the original white residents of a neighborhood into which Negroes begin moving. All it requires is the failure or refusal of other whites to fill the vacancies resulting from normal turnover.
• Thus, efforts to stop massive transition by persuading present white residents to remain will ultimately fail unless whites outside the neighborhood can be persuaded to move in.

Some residential separation of whites and Negroes would occur even without discriminatory practices by whites. Separation would result from the desires of some Negroes to live in predominantly Negro neighborhoods like many other groups, and from differences in meaningful social variables, such as income and educational levels, between many Negroes and many whites. But these factors would not lead to the almost complete segregation of whites and Negroes, which has developed in our metropolitan areas.

THE EXODUS OF WHITES FROM CENTRAL CITIES

The process of racial transition in central-city neighborhoods has been only one factor among many others causing millions of whites to move out of central cities as the Negro populations there expanded. More basic perhaps have been the rising mobility and affluence of middle-class families and the more attractive living conditions—particularly better schools—in the suburbs.

Whatever the reason, the result is clear. In 1950, 45.5 million whites lived in central cities. If this population had grown from 1950 to 1960 at the same rate as the nation's white population as a whole, it would have increased by eight million. It actually rose only 2.2 million, indicating an outflow of 5.8 million.[4]

From 1960 to 1966, the white outflow appears to have been even more rapid. White population of central cities declined 1.3 million instead of rising 3.6 million as it would if it had grown at the same rate as the entire white population. In theory, therefore, 4.9 million whites left central cities during these six years.

Statistics for all central cities as a group understate the relationship between Negro population growth and white outflow in individual central cities. The fact is, many cities with relatively few Negroes experienced rapid white-population growth, thereby obscuring the size of white out-migration that took place out of cities having big increases in Negro population. For example, from 1950 to 1960, the 10 largest cities in the United States had a total Negro population increase of 1.8 million, or 58 percent, while the white population there declined 1.5 million. If we remove the two cities where the white population increased (Los Angeles and Houston), the nonwhite population in the remaining eight rose 1.4 million; whereas their white population declined 2.1 million. If the white population in these cities had increased at only half the rate of the white population in the United States as a whole from 1950 to 1960, it would have risen by 1.4 million. Thus, these eight cities actually experienced a white out-migration of at least 3.5 million, while gaining 1.4 million nonwhites.

THE EXTENT OF RESIDENTIAL SEGREGATION

The rapid expansion of all-Negro residential areas in central cities and large-scale white withdrawal from them have continued a pattern of residential segregation that has existed in American cities for decades. A recent study[5] reveals that this pattern is present to a high degree in every large city in America. The authors devised an index to measure the degree of residential segregation. The index indicates for each city the percentage of Negroes who would have to move from the blocks where they now live to other blocks in order to provide a perfectly proportional, unsegregated distribution of population.

According to their findings, the average segregation index for 207 of the largest United States cities was 86.2 in 1960. This means that an average of over 86 percent of all Negroes would have had to change blocks to create an unsegregated population distribution. Southern cities had a higher average index (90.9) than cities in the Northeast (79.2), the North Central (87.7), or the West (79.3). Only eight cities had index values below 70, whereas over 50 had values above 91.7.

The degrees of residential segregation for all 207 cities has been relatively stable, averaging 85.2 in 1940, 87.3 in 1950, and 86.2 in 1960. Variations within individual regions were only slightly larger. However, a recent Census Bureau study shows that in most of the 12 large cities where special censuses were taken in the mid-1960's, the proportions of Negroes living in neighborhoods of greatest Negro concentration had increased since 1960.

Residential segregation is generally more prevalent with respect to Negroes than for any other minority group, including Puerto Ricans, Orientals, and Mexican Americans. Moreover, it varies little between central city and suburb. This nearly universal pattern cannot be explained in terms of economic discrimination against all low-income groups. Analysis of 15 representative cities indicates that white upper- and middle-income households are far more segregated from Negro upper- and middle-income households than from white lower-income households.

In summary, the concentration of Negroes in central cities results from a combination of forces. Some of these forces, such as migration and initial settlement patterns in older neighborhoods, are similar to those which affected previous ethnic minorities. Others—particularly discrimination in employment and segregation in housing and schools—are a result of white attitudes based on race and color. These forces continue to shape the future of the central city.

Proportion of Negroes in Each of the 30 Largest Cities,
1950, 1960, and Estimated 1965

	1950	1960	(Estimate)[6] 1965
New York, N.Y.	10	14	18
Chicago, Ill.	14	23	28
Los Angeles, Calif.	9	14	17
Philadelphia, Pa.	18	26	31
Detroit, Michigan	16	29	34
Baltimore, Md.	24	35	38
Houston, Texas	21	23	23
Cleveland, Ohio	16	29	34
Washington, D.C.	35	54	66
St. Louis, Mo.	18	29	36
Milwaukee, Wis.	3	8	11
San Francisco, Calif.	6	10	12
Boston, Mass.	5	9	13
Dallas, Texas	13	19	21
New Orleans, La.	32	37	41
Pittsburgh, Pa.	12	17	20
San Antonio, Tex.	7	7	8
San Diego, Calif.	5	6	7
Seattle, Wash.	3	5	7
Buffalo, N.Y.	6	13	17
Cincinnati, Ohio	16	22	24
Memphis, Tenn.	37	37	40
Denver, Colo.	4	6	9
Atlanta, Ga.	37	38	44
Minneapolis, Minn.	1	2	4
Indianapolis, Ind.	15	21	23
Kansas City, Mo.	12	18	22
Columbus, Ohio	12	16	18
Phoenix, Ariz.	5	5	5
Newark, N.J.	17	34	47

SOURCE: U. S. Department of Commerce, Bureau of the Census.

Percent of All Negroes in Selected Cities Living in Census Tracts
Grouped According to Proportion Negro in 1960 and 1964–1966[7]

	YEAR	ALL CENSUS TRACTS	75 PERCENT OR MORE NEGRO	50 TO 74 PERCENT NEGRO	25 TO 49 PERCENT NEGRO	LESS THAN 25 PERCENT NEGRO
Cleveland,	1960	100	72	16	8	4
Ohio	1965	100	80	12	4	4
Phoenix,	1960	100	19	36	24	21
Ariz.	1965	100	18	23	42	17
Buffalo,	1960	100	35	47	6	12
N.Y.	1966	100	69	10	13	8
Louisville,	1960	100	57	13	17	13
Ky.	1964	100	67	13	10	10
Rochester,	1960	100	8	43	17	32
N.Y.	1964	100	16	45	24	15
Sacramento,	1960	100	9	—	14	77
Calif.	1964	100	8	14	28	50
Des Moines,	1960	100	—	28	31	41
Iowa	1966	100	—	42	19	39
Providence,	1960	100	—	23	2	75
R.I.	1965	100	—	16	46	38
Shreveport,	1960	100	79	10	7	4
La.	1966	100	90	—	6	4
Evansville,	1960	100	34	27	9	30
Ind.	1966	100	59	14	—	27
Little Rock,	1960	100	33	33	19	15
Ark.	1964	100	41	18	22	19
Raleigh,	1960	100	86	—	7	7
N.C.	1966	100	88	4	2	6

SOURCE: U. S. Department of Commerce, Bureau of Census.

Population Change by Location, Inside and Outside
Metropolitan Areas, 1950–1966 (numbers in millions)
Population

	NEGRO			WHITE		
	1950	*1960*	*1966*	*1950*	*1960*	*1966*
United States	15.0	18.8	21.5	135.2	158.8	170.8
Metropolitan areas	8.4	12.2	14.8	80.3	99.7	109.0
Central cities	6.5	9.7	12.1	45.5	47.7	46.4
Urban fringe	1.9	2.5	2.7	34.8	52.0	62.5
Small cities, towns and rural	6.7	6.7	6.7	54.8	59.2	61.8

Change, 1950–1966

	Negro		White	
	NUMBER	PERCENT	NUMBER	PERCENT
United States	6.5	43	35.6	26
Metropolitan areas	6.4	77	28.7	36
Central cities	5.6	87	.9	2
Urban fringe	.8	42	27.7	79
Smaller cities, towns and rural	—8	1	7.0	12

Percent Distribution of Population by Location, Inside
and Outside Metropolitan Areas, 1950, 1960 and 1966

	NEGRO			WHITE		
	1950	*1960*	*1966*	*1950*	*1960*	*1966*
United States	100	100	100	100	100	100
Metropolitan areas	56	65	69	59	63	64
Central cities	43	51	56	34	30	27
Urban fringe	13	13	13	26	33	38
Smaller cities, towns and rural	44	35	31	41	37	36

Negroes as a Percentage of Total Population by Location,
Inside and Outside Metropolitan Areas, and by Size of
Metropolitan Areas—1950, 1960 and 1966

	PERCENT NEGRO		
	1950	*1960*	*1966*
United States	10	11	11
Metropolitan areas	9	11	12
Central cities	12	17	20
Central cities in metropolitan areas[9] of—			
1,000,000 or more	13	19	26[10]
250,000 to 1,000,000	12	15	20[10]
Under 250,000	12	12	12[10]
Urban fringe	5	5	4
Smaller cities, towns and rural	11	10	10

SOURCE: U.S. Department of Commerce, Bureau of the Census

NOTES

1. The "fertility rate" is the number of live births per year per 1,000 women age 15 to 44 in the group concerned.

2. These proportions are undoubtedly too low because the Census Bureau has consistently undercounted the number of Negroes in the U.S. by as much as 10 percent.

3. Rounds to 99.

4. The outflow of whites may be somewhat smaller than the 5.8 million difference between these figures, because the ages of the whites in many central cities are higher than in the nation as a whole, and therefore the population would have grown somewhat more slowly.

5. *Negroes in Cities,* Karl and Alma Taeuber, Aldine Publishing Co., Chicago (1965).

6. Except for Cleveland, Buffalo, Memphis, and Phoenix, for which a special census has been made in recent years, these are very rough estimations computed on the basis of the change in relative proportions of Negro births and deaths since 1960.

7. Selected cities of 100,000 or more in which a special census was taken in any of the years 1964–1966. Ranked according to total population at latest census.

8. Rounds to less than 500,000.

9. In metropolitan areas of population shown as of 1960.

10. Percent nonwhite; data for Negroes are not available. The figures used are estimated to be closely comparable to those for Negroes alone, using a check for Negro and nonwhite percentages in earlier years.

COMPARING THE IMMIGRANT AND NEGRO EXPERIENCE 🎺

🎺 🎺 National Advisory Commission on Civil Disorders

We have in the preceding chapters surveyed the historical background of racial discrimination and traced its effects on Negro employment, on the social structure of the ghetto community, and on the conditions of life that surround the urban Negro poor. Here we address a fundamental question that many white Americans are asking today: why has the Negro been unable to escape from poverty and the ghetto like the European immigrants?

The Maturing Economy

The changing nature of the American economy is one major reason. When the European immigrants were arriving in large numbers, America was becoming an urban-industrial society. To build its major cities and industries, America needed great pools of unskilled labor. The immigrants provided the labor, gained an economic foothold, and thereby enabled their children and grandchildren to move up to skilled, white collar, and professional employment.

Since World War II, especially, America's urban-industrial society has matured; unskilled labor is far less essential than before, and blue-collar jobs of all kinds are decreasing in number and importance as a source of new employment. The Negroes who migrated to the great urban centers lacked the skills essential to the new economy; and the schools of the ghetto have

SOURCE: Report of the National Advisory Commission on Civil Disorders, *Comparing the Immigrant and Negro Experience* (Washington, D. C., 1968), pp. 278–282.

been unable to provide the education that can qualify them for decent jobs. The Negro migrant, unlike the immigrant, found little opportunity in the city; he had arrived too late, and the unskilled labor he had to offer was no longer needed.

The Disability of Race

Racial discrimination is undoubtedly the second major reason why the Negro has been unable to escape from poverty. The structure of discrimination has persistently narrowed his opportunities and restricted his prospects. Well before the high tide of immigration from overseas, Negroes were already relegated to the poorly paid, low status occupations. Had it not been for racial discrimination, the North might well have recruited Southern Negroes after the Civil War to provide the labor for building the burgeoning urban-industrial economy. Instead, Northern employers looked to Europe for their sources of unskilled labor. Upon the arrival of the immigrants, the Negroes were dislodged from the few urban occupations they had dominated. Not until World War II were Negroes generally hired for industrial jobs, and by that time the decline in the need for unskilled labor had already begun. European immigrants, too, suffered from discrimination, but never was it so pervasive as the prejudice against color in America, which has formed a bar to advancement, unlike any other.

Entry into the Political System

Political opportunities also played an important role in enabling the European immigrants to escape from poverty. The immigrants settled for the most part in rapidly growing cities that had powerful and expanding political machines, which gave them economic advantages in exchange for political support. The political machines were decentralized; and ward-level grievance machinery, as well as personal representation, enabled the immigrant to make his voice heard and his power felt. Since the local political organizations exercised considerable influence over public building in the cities, they provided employment in construction jobs for their immigrant voters. Ethnic groups often dominated one or more of the municipal services—police and fire protection, sanitation, and even public education.

By the time the Negroes arrived, the situation had altered dramatically. The great wave of public building had virtually come to an end; reform groups were beginning to attack the political machines; the machines were no longer so powerful or so well equipped to provide jobs and other favors. Although the political machines retained their hold over the areas settled by Negroes, the scarcity of patronage jobs made them unwilling to share with the Negroes the political positions they had created in these neighborhoods. For example, Harlem was dominated by white politicans for many years after it had become a Negro ghetto; even today, New York's Lower East Side, which is now predominantly Puerto Rican, is strongly influenced by politicians of the older immigrant groups.

This pattern exists in many other American cities. Negroes are still underrepresented in city councils and in most city agencies.

Segregation played a role here too. The immigrants and their descendants felt threatened by the arrival of the Negro and prevented a Negro-immigrant coalition that might have saved the old political machines. Reform groups, nominally more liberal on the face issue, were often dominated by businessmen and middle-class city residents who usually opposed coalition with any low-income group, white or black.

Cultural Factors

Cultural factors also made it easier for the immigrants to escape from poverty. They came to America from much poorer societies, with a low standard of living, and they came at a time when job aspirations were low. When most jobs in the American economy were unskilled, they sensed little deprivation in being forced to take the dirty and poorly paid jobs. Moreover, their families were large, and many breadwinners, some of whom never married, contributed to the total family income. As a result, family units managed to live even from the lowest paid jobs and still put some money aside for savings or investment, for example, to purchase a house or tenement, or to open a store or factory. Since the immigrants spoke little English and had their own ethnic culture, they needed stores to supply them with ethnic foods and other services. Since their family structures were patriarchal, men found satisfactions in family life that helped compensate for the bad jobs they had to take and the hard work they had to endure.

Negroes came to the city under quite different circumstances. Generally relegated to jobs that others would not take, they were paid too little to be able to put money in savings for new enterprises. Since they spoke English, they had no need for their own stores; besides, the areas they occupied were already filled with stores. In addition, Negroes lacked the extended family characteristic of certain European groups—each household usually had only one or two breadwinners. Moreover, Negro men had fewer cultural incentives to work in a dirty job for the sake of the family. As a result of slavery and of long periods of male unemployment afterwards, the Negro family structure had become matriarchal; the man played a secondary and marginal role in his family. For many Negro men, then, there were few of the cultural and psychological rewards of family life. A marginal figure in the family, particularly when unemployed, Negro men were often rejected by their wives or often abandoned their homes because they felt themselves useless to their families.

Although most Negro men worked as hard as the immigrants to support their families, their rewards were less. The jobs did not pay enough to enable them to support their families, for prices and living standards had risen since the immigrants had come, and the entrepreneurial opportunities that had allowed some immigrants to become independent, even rich, had vanished. Above all, Negroes suffered from segregation, which denied them access to the good jobs and the right unions, and which deprived them of the opportunity to buy real estate or obtain business loans or move out of the ghetto and bring up their children in middle-class neighborhoods. Immigrants were able to leave their ghettos as soon as they had the money; segregation has denied Negroes the opportunity to live elsewhere.

The Vital Element of Time

Finally, nostalgia makes it easy to exaggerate the ease of escape of the white immigrants from the ghettos. When the immigrants were immersed in poverty, they too lived in slums, and these neighborhoods exhibited fearfully high rates of alcoholism, desertion, illegitimacy, and the other pathologies associated with poverty. Just as some Negro men desert their families when they are unemployed and their wives can get jobs, so did the men of other ethnic groups, even though time and affluence has clouded white memories of the past.

Today, whites tend to exaggerate how well and how quickly they escaped from poverty, and contrast their experience with poverty-stricken Negroes. The fact is, among many of the Southern and Eastern Europeans who came to America in the last great wave of immigration, those who came already urbanized were the first to escape from poverty. The others who came to America from rural backgrounds, as Negroes did, are only now, after three generations, in the final stages of escaping from poverty. Until the last 10 years or so, most of these were employed in blue-collar jobs, and only a small porportion of their children were able or willing to attend college. In other words, only the third, and in many cases, only the fourth generation has been able to achieve the kind of middle-class income and status that allows it to send its children to college. Because of favorable economic and political conditions, these ethnic groups were able to escape from lower-class status to working class and lower middle-class status, but it has taken them three generations.

Negroes have been concentrated in the city for only two generations, and they have been there under much less favorable conditions. Moreover, their escape from poverty has been blocked in part by the resistance of the European ethnic groups; they have been unable to enter some unions and to move into some neighborhoods outside the ghetto because descendants of the European immigrants who control these unions and neighborhoods have not yet abandoned them for middle-class occupations and areas.

Even so, some Negroes have escaped poverty, and they have done so in only two generations; their success is less visible than that of the immigrants in many cases, for residential segregation has forced them to remain in the ghetto. Still, the proportion of nonwhites employed in white-collar, techni-cal, and professional jobs has risen from 10.2 percent in 1950 to 20.8 percent in 1966, and the proportion attending college has risen an equal amount. Indeed, the development of a small but steadily increasing Negro middle class while the greater part of the Negro population is stagnating economi-cally is creating a growing gap between Negro haves and have-nots.

This gap, as well as the awareness of its existence by those left behind, undoubtedly adds to the feelings of desperation and anger which breed civil disorders. Low-income Negroes realize that segregation and lack of job opportunities have made it possible for only a small proportion of all Negroes to escape poverty and the summer disorders are at least in part a protest against being left behind and left out.

The immigrant who labored long hours at hard and often menial work had the hope of a better future, if not for himself then for his children. This was the promise of the "American dream"—the society offered to all a future that was open-ended; with hard work and perseverance, a man and his family could in time achieve not only material well-being but "position" and status.

For the Negro family in the urban ghetto, there is a different vision—the future seems to lead only to a dead-end.

What the American economy of the late 19th and early 20th century was able to do to help the European immigrants escape from poverty is now largely impossible. New methods of escape must be found for the majority of today's poor.

LOOTING IN CIVIL DISORDERS:
AN INDEX OF SOCIAL CHANGE
✢ E. L. Quarantelli and Russell R. Dynes

Outbreaks of looting have increasingly become one of the core concerns of communities which have undergone large-scale civil disorders in America within the past several years. Most current press reports of such outbreaks have as one of their central themes the occurrence of looting, and frequently depict looters in action. Even after-accounts of the civil disturbances or editorial polemics often emphasize stories of plunder to illustrate the "breakdown of law and order."

Part of the intensified popular attention to looting undoubtedly stems from actual increases of incidents. In one of the very first large-scale disturbances, that in Harlem in 1964, 112 stores were looted.[1] However, about 600 establishments were plundered or burned during the 1965 Watts outbreak.[2] A peak was reached in Detroit in July, 1967, when, according to unofficial accounts, around 2,700 stores were raided by looters.

The explanation commonly given for such "anti-social" behavior is that, in periods of social stress, the thin veneer of civilization is stripped off the human animal, revealing man's basest nature.[3] Under more normal circumstances, these base tendencies are somehow held in check. However, under the pressure of crisis situations, man is revealed not as Rousseau's "noble savage," but as Hobbes' "creature," at war with all. Anticipating that

SOURCE: E. L. Quarantelli and Russell R. Dynes, "Looting in Civil Disorders: An Index of Social Change," *American Behavioral Scientist*, 11, no. 4 (March–April 1968), 7–10, and *Riots and Rebellion: Civil Violence in the Urban Community*, eds. Louis H. Masotti and Don R. Bowen (Beverly Hills, Calif., Sage Publications, Inc., 1968), pp. 131–141. Reprinted by permission of Sage Publications, Inc.

certain kinds of large-scale emergencies activate this depravity, community officials often request additional law enforcement officers. The National Guard is alerted or mobilized, and a wide variety of supplementary security measures are undertaken. Such steps are frequently initiated on first reports of the beginnings of a civil disturbance. Often, expressions of concern that looting will occur, and the steps being taken to prevent it, are among the first stories circulated by radio and television after reporting the event itself. In the absence of any actual information about what is occurring, mass media outlets often report that which is expected to happen.

As a consequence of this common interpretation of looting as being a manifestation of man's irrationality in periods of social disorganization, punitive control measures are most frequently advocated as befitting the situation. In addition, such behavior tends to reinforce both manifest and latent conceptions which many whites have of Negroes, or at least his inherent anti-social nature. Such views tend to reinforce calls for action which are repressive in nature.

While there is no doubt that much behavior in current urban civil disorders is illegal, we suggest that the spiraling outbreaks of looting are also indicative of the end of a particular era of accommodation between American Negroes and whites. In effect, the plundering and looting increasingly signal the end of a period of time when existing "rights" in a community will be automatically accepted by a significant proportion of Negroes therein as being given. These signals, of course, can be read as an invitation to institute strong repressive measures, as they seemingly have been in most recent civil disturbances. (That the potential for highly repressive actions lies not far below the surface of American society is suggested by the herding of most Japanese-Americans into detention camps at the start of World War II.)[4] However, looting can also be seen as a rather violent beginning to a new process of "collective bargaining" concerning rights and responsibilities of various groups in most American communities. The behavior, defined as anti-social by the larger community and unlawful according to legal norms, actually marks the end of one era and the beginning of a new one in racial intergroup relations in American society. In short, looting is an index of social change. (From another perspective it is also an *instrument* for societal change, but we will not develop that point in this article.)[5]

The reasons for seeing looting as the end of one era and the start of another are perhaps not self-evident. The same difficulty probably applies also to the meaning of looting and its implication. An understanding of both requires an analysis of existing definitions of property within a community. As Kingsley Davis notes: "So ingrained in human thought is the fallacy of misplaced concreteness that property is often regarded as the thing owned rather than the rights which constitute the ownership."[6] In popular parlance, property is generally equated with material goods or physical objects. Even the United States Supreme Court did not recognize that property refers to rights, rather than a tangible object, until the end of the nineteenth century.[7] Rights and obligations are not tangible in a physical sense, nor is the tangibility or intangibility of what is owned of great consequence. What is important are the rights and obligations with respect to something scarce but valuable.

Property thus is a set of cultural norms that regulates the relations of persons to items with economic value. "It consists of the rights and duties of one person or group (the owner) as against all other persons and groups with respect to some scarce good. It is thus exclusive, for it sets off what is mine from thine; but it is also social, being rooted in custom and protected by law."[8] In effect, property is a shared understanding about who can do what with the valued resources within a community.

The norms or rules, the legal ones in particular, specify the legitimate forms of use, control, and disposal of economically valued objects. These norms, besides defining the rights and responsibilities of owners, also delineate social relationships among other individuals, because the "right" of any person in relation to an object entails at the very least the "obligations" of others to respect that right. There is obviously considerable variation in what the norms specify in different time periods and different societies, but at any given point they are normally widely shared and accepted in a community.

In contrast, civil disturbances such as American communities have recently witnessed are *situations of temporary and localized redefinitions of property rights.* The urban disorders we are discussing represent conflict on community goals and manifest differences of opinion in the community regarding economically valued objects. In these situations, rights to the use of existing resources become problematical, and in many instances there are open challenges to prior ownership.[9] If property is thought of as the shared understanding of who can do what with the valued resources within a community, in civil disorders there occurs a breakdown in this understanding. What was previously taken for granted now becomes a matter of open dispute, expressed concretely in a redefinition of existing property rights.

The problematic nature of property in urban disorders can be seen by noting the pattern of looting in such situations. Two aspects of the pattern are particularly important. First, the looting is highly selective, focusing almost exclusively on certain kinds of goods or possessions. Second, instead of being negatively sanctioned, looters receive strong although localized social support for their actions.

The degree of selectivity can be seen in the fact that particular types of stores have been the prime focus of looting. In Detroit, 47 grocery stores were attacked, more than in any other category.[10] Furniture, apparel, and liquor stores are also frequent objects of looters, with more than a million dollars' worth of stocks of each being plundered during the Newark disorder.[11] In contrast, banks, schools, plants, and private residences are generally ignored, although some of the latter have been inadvertently damaged as a result of being close to burned business establishments. Looting, contrary to many initial press reports of such situations, has not been indiscriminate; in fact, certain kinds of consumer goods have been the only foci of attention.

In addition to the selective pattern it assumes, looting at its peak is almost always if not exclusively engaged in by local residents who receive support from segments of their local community. This appearance of normative support can be seen in the almost spiraling pattern that occurs in situations of civil disorder and which reveals cumulative shifts in redefinitions of property rights. The pattern appears to proceed roughly through three stages: (1) A primarily symbolic looting stage, where destruction rather than plunder appears to be the intent. It often seems initiated by alienated adolescents or ideologically motivated agitators in an area. (2) A stage of conscious and deliberate looting, in which the taking of goods is organized and systematic. It frequently appears spurred by the involvement of omnipresent delinquent gangs and theft groups operating on pragmatic rather than ideological considerations. (3) A stage of widespread and nonsystematic seizing and taking of goods. At this point, plundering becomes the normative, the socially supported thing to do. Property rights become so redefined that it becomes permissible if not mandatory to transfer to different private ownership the possession of certain material goods. The legal right does not change, but the group consensus supporting the prerogative to appropriate valued resources in the community does shift, among a segment of the population.

In the first phase, little looting, if by that is meant the taking of goods, occurs. Instead, destructive attacks are most often directed at objects symbolic of the underlying sources of conflict. Police cars and stores operated by white merchants are attacked. These attacks signal the start of the redefinitions of property rights. Illegal use is made of possessions normally and generally accepted as being under the control of formal community representatives (e.g., police and fire department equipment) or "extra-community" agents (e.g., stores in urban black ghetto areas owned by whites). In actual fact, many outbreaks of civil disorders up to the present have not progressed beyond this initial phase of window breaking, car burning, tossing of isolated fire bombs, and the like.

In the second stage, there is a definite change. Looting of goods rather than destruction of equipment or facilities becomes the mode. White merchants dealing with consumer goods particularly become the object of attack. However, that the white merchants have goods which are readily moved probably makes them the focus of looters as much as the fact that the owners are white. Negro-owned stores of the same general type are not always spared by the marauding bands operating during this time period. There are some indications that a "soul brother" designation has become less and less of a protecting device as the disturbances have increased in intensity over the last several years. The racial dimension, while not absent, appears to be secondary to the economic factor in the behavior of the looters.

In the third stage there is a full redefinition of certain property rights. The "carnival spirit," particularly commented upon in the Newark and Detroit disturbances, does not represent anarchy. It is, instead, an overt manifestation of widespread localized social support for the new definition of the situation. The new consensus that emerges in such situations is suggested by the almost total absence of competition or conflict by looters over plundered goods. In fact, in contrast to looting in other situations such as disasters,[12] such behavior in civil disorders is quite open and often collective. Goods are openly taken, not by stealth. Looting is often undertaken by people working together in pairs, as family units or small groups; seldom is it carried out by solitary individuals. The availability of potential loot is frequently called to the attention of bystanders, and in some cases, strangers are handed goods by looters coming out of stores.

Not only is most looting in large-scale civil disorders by "insiders" (i.e., local community members) and not outsiders, but there is evidence suggesting that participants are from all segments of the population. Looters do not come only from the lowest socioeconomic levels or from neighborhood delinquent gangs. Arrested looters are, typically, employed persons, and roughly similar to persons generally participating in the disturbances. There is definite evidence that the latter are from all segments of the community. Thus, a statistically random sample revealed that all participants in the Detroit outbreak were, in about the same proportion, across all income brackets.[13] A U.C.L.A. survey in Watts discovered that those active in the disorders there—perhaps a fourth of the residents—along certain dimensions, represented a cross section of the younger male population in that ghetto area.[14]

This type of phenomenon is not new in history. Rudé has analyzed nineteenth-century demonstrating mobs in England and France.[15] He found that they were typically composed of local residents, respectable and employed persons, rather than the pauperized, the unemployed, or the "rabble" of the slums. As in the instance of current disturbances, the more privileged classes of those times defined these popular agitations as criminal, i.e., as fundamentally and unconditionally illegitimate.

Certainly most contemporary community authorities see looting as essentially a legal problem and consequently as a matter largely of law enforcement. Many segments of American society, particularly middle-class persons with their almost sacred conception of private property, also tend to define the problem in the same way. Legislators, in response to pressures generated by such perceptions, move to strengthen "anti-riot" laws and other repressive measures.

There is, of course, no question that looting is criminal behavior, violating in various ways numerous statutes and ordinances. Viewed primarily in this context, looting, as well as the civil disorder, can be seen—as stated in FBI and other reports—as "meaningless" behavior.[16] However, such a view obscures something more fundamental.

The laws themselves are based on certain dominant conceptions of property rights. The legal framework is the residue of the past consensus regarding the distribution of property. It reflects an accommodation arrived at sometime before the present.

We suggest that the current civil disorders in American cities are communicating a message about the society. A time of social change, particularly with regard to the distribution of valued resources in communities, is at hand. The old accommodative order defining certain limits to property rights of American Negroes is being directly challenged to the point of collapse, although this seems presently more recognized by the subordinate rather than the superordinate group involved.

Perhaps the current situation has many parallels to the situation in the United States over a hundred years ago. The Civil War symbolized a period of time of disagreement about human beings as property, and the rights of their owners. The reluctance to redefine in a peaceful manner the legal structure which supported these property rights resulted in tremendous social costs to the society. Some of these costs were immediate, while others are still being collected today.

Viewed in this context, the attack against existing property rights is neither "irrational" nor "senseless." This is particularly so if it leads to a more institutionalized system of articulating demands and responses in which the rights and obligations of the contending parties become a matter of general community consensus. If this is the case, the current looting will mark the initial steps in the evolution of a social system in which certain heretofore urban segments of the society can nonviolently express their views, and in which the more favored groups and the elites will listen.

If more responsive and representative institutions cannot be established, certain groups in American urban communities will continue to engage in disorder and violence or, in our earlier terminology, to indicate their racial discontent and economic aspirations in periodic and increasingly costly redefinitions of property rights. There have been incidents of looting in earlier outbreaks in urban ghettos, some as early as two decades ago, as in Harlem in 1943.[17] However, the scope and intensity of current attacks indicate that increasingly larger number of persons no longer share the consensus about property rights held by the larger community. If property is seen not just as physical goods, but as a shared understanding about the allocation of valued resources within a society, a growing lack of consensus will progressively manifest itself in open conflict.

In actual fact, a point of no return may already have been reached. Lambert, in his study of communal violence in India,[18] found that a breakdown in the formal means of social control accompanied broad changes in the social organization of Indian society in the decades immediately preceding independence. Police officers there came to be viewed, not as impartial arbiters of social disputes and as operating within a system of legal redress for grievances; rather they were seen as armed representatives of their socio-ethnic groups. This interpretation of the policemen's role was accepted by members of the opposing group, by their own groups, and, increasingly, by the police officers themselves. "When this occurred the usefulness of the police in social control was sharply reduced and, in some cases, police activities contributed to further disruption of social organization."[19]

Much of this reads as if it were written of local police actions in American ghettos. A typical popular interpretation is to see all of this as a breakdown of "law and order." In one sense, it is that. However, in another more fundamental sense, as in Indian society, the failure or inability of the police in a community to prevent looting (apart from those instances where their own actions may initiate such behavior) can be seen as marking the end of an era. The psychological controls which really are the bases of police control in a community no longer suffice. The sheer power of National Guard or regular military units, when disorders reach a peak, is the only formal control left to communities.

Given any foreseeable combination of circumstances, military forces will prevail. However, it would seem that American society, if it wishes to insure domestic tranquility, should move to institutionalize nonviolent means for redistributing certain property rights. Looting can only be a temporary and localized redefinition of property rights. But if no other solution is found, the pattern itself may become routine across more and more American communities. If that is the case, instead of being an index of social change, the looting that has increasingly appeared in recent civil disorders may establish itself as a major structural device for change in the American social system.

Similar patterns of behavior have so established themselves in the past. Rudé, in the analysis mentioned earlier, notes that the disorderly demonstrations became a means of protest that in time enabled a segment of the urban population to communicate to the elite.[20] Hobsbawn, in his similar analysis of the pre-industrial "city mob," states the point even more strongly. He observes that the mobs did not just riot to protest, but because they expected to achieve something by their disorder. They assumed that the local authorities would be sensitive to the disturbances and make attempts to deal with the implicit demands of the mobs. According to Hobsbawn, "this mechanism was perfectly understood by both sides."[21]

A similar situation could develop in American communities. Some militant Negro ghetto leaders have almost been explicit about such a possibility. However, the cost to the society would be high and would not really settle the underlying bases of the conflict.

Furthermore, an even greater threat to the society may develop in such a direction. Signs of it have already appeared. The participation of poor white looters in the Detroit outbreak hints at the possibility that the broader middle-class-lower-class consensus about property rights may also become subject to attack, if the more immediate problem is not solved. The development of such an open class conflict would make the current racial conflict a highly desirable alternative state of affairs.

Thus, a failure to see looting in current disorders as something more than "meaningless" or "criminal" behavior may eventually fragment the social consensus far more than it has been up to the present. This perspective upon looting as an index of social change may suggest alternative ways of dealing with property rights.[22] In fact, if nonviolent ways are to be found, there may be no choice on how to think about the current disturbances sweeping American cities.

NOTES

1. James Jones and Linda Bailey, "A Report on Race Riots" (unpublished paper), p. 37.

2. This and all other information not later footnoted has been acquired in field work on civil disturbances by members of the Disaster Research Center at Ohio State University. Data have been obtained primarily through personal interviews with organizational officials, supplemented by systematic observations and analyses of unpublished agency reports.

3. See Anselm Strauss, *Mirrors and Masks* (Glencoe, Ill.: Free Press, 1959), for a criticism of this point of view.

4. Morton Grodzins, *The Loyal and Disloyal* (Univ. of Chicago Press, 1956).

5. This is a point of view also expressed in Kurt and Gladys Lang, "The Significance of Recent Racial Disturbances for Theories of Collective Behavior," in *Proceedings of the Seventh Annual Intergroup Relations Conference*, Houston, Texas, 1966, pp. 2–15.

6. Kingsley Davis, *Human Society* (N. Y.: Macmillan, 1949), p. 452.

7. John Commons, *Legal Foundations of Capitalism* (N. Y.: Macmillan, 1924), p. 14.

8. Davis, *op. cit.*, p. 452.

9. As Davis observes, there is an important distinction between ownership and possession, since property rights in an object do not necessarily imply actual use and enjoyment of the object by the owner. *Op. cit.*, p. 454.

10. *Detroit Free Press*, August 20, 1967, p. 4B.

11. These figures were given in an AP dispatch of August 17, 1967, citing a report issued by the mayor's office.

12. See Quarantelli and Dynes, "Looting in Civil Disturbances and Disasters" (unpublished paper).

13. This is from a study by University of Michigan social scientists, reported in the *Detroit Free Press*, August 20, 1967, p. 1B.

14. Raymond Murphey and James Watson, *The Structure of Discontent: The Relationship Between Social Structure, Grievance, and Support For The Los Angeles Riot* (Institute of Government and Public Affairs, U.C.L.A., 1967).

15. George Rudé, *The Crowd in History* (N.Y.: Wiley, 1964).

16. *Report on the Nature of the City Riots* (U. S. Dept. of Justice, 1964).

17. Allen D. Grimshaw, "Urban Racial Violence in the United States: Changing Ecological Considerations," Am. J. Sociol., LXVI (Sept., 1960), p. 112.

18. Richard D. Lambert, "Hindu-Muslim Riots" (unpublished Ph.D. dissertation, Univ. of Pennsylvania, 1951).

19. Allen D. Grimshaw, "Actions of Police and the Military in American Race Riots," *Phylon*, XXIV (Fall, 1963), p. 271.

20. E. J. Hobsbawn, *Social Bandits and Primitive Rebels* (Glencoe, Ill.: Free Press, 1959).

21. *Ibid.*, p. 116.

22. The acceptance of the problem of the Negroes as basically a labor-market problem is set forth in Norbert Wiley, "America's Unique Class Politics: The Interplay of the Labor, Credit and Commodity Markets," Am. Sociol. Rev., XXXII (August, 1967), 529–541.

INTERNAL COLONIALISM AND GHETTO REVOLT
𝕩 *Robert Blauner*

It is becoming almost fashionable to analyze American racial conflict today in terms of the colonial analogy. I shall argue in this paper that the utility of this perspective depends upon a distinction between colonization as a process and colonialism as a social, economic, and political system. It is the experience of colonization that Afro-Americans share with many of the non-white people of the world. But this subjugation has taken place in a societal context that differs in important respects from the situation of "classical colonialism." In the body of this essay I shall look at some major developments in Black protest—the urban riots, cultural nationalism, and the movement for ghetto control—as collective responses to colonized status. Viewing our domestic situation as a special form of colonization outside a context of a colonial system will help explain some of the dilemmas and ambiguities within these movements.

The present crisis in American life has brought about changes in social perspectives and the questioning of long accepted frameworks. Intellectuals and social scientists have been forced by the pressure of events to look at old definitions of the character of our society, the role of racism, and the workings of basic institutions. The depth and volatility of contemporary racial conflict challenge sociologists in particular to question the adequacy of theoretical models by which we have explained American race relations in the past.

For a long time the distinctiveness of the Negro situation among the

SOURCE: Robert Blauner, "International Colonialism and Ghetto Revolt," *Social Problems,* 16, no. 4 (Spring 1969), 393–408. Reprinted by permission of the publisher and author.

ethnic minorities was placed in terms of color, and the systematic discrimination that follows from our deep-seated racial prejudices. This was sometimes called the caste theory, and while provocative, it missed essential and dynamic features of American race relations. In the past ten years there has been a tendency to view Afro-Americans as another ethnic group not basically different in experience from previous ethnics and whose "immigration" condition in the North would in time follow their upward course. The inadequacy of this model is now clear—even the Kerner Report devotes a chapter to criticizing this analogy. A more recent (though hardly new) approach views the essence of racial subordination in economic class terms: Black people as an underclass are to a degree specially exploited and to a degree economically dispensable in an automating society. Important as are economic factors, the power of race and racism in America cannot be sufficiently explained through class analysis. Into this theory vacuum steps the model of internal colonialism. Problematic and imprecise as it is, it gives hope of becoming a framework that can integrate the insights of caste and racism, ethnicity, culture, and economic exploitation into an overall conceptual scheme. At the same time, the danger of the colonial model is the imposition of an artificial analogy which might keep us from facing up to the fact (to quote Harold Cruse) that "the American black and white social phenomenon is a uniquely new world thing."[2]

During the late 1950's, identification with African nations and other colonial or formerly colonized peoples grew in importance among Black militants.[3] As a result the U.S. was increasingly seen as a colonial power and the concept of domestic colonialism was introduced into the political analysis and rhetoric of militant nationalists. During the same period Black social theorists began developing this frame of reference for explaining American realities. As early as 1962, Cruse characterized race relations in this country as "domestic colonialism."[4] Three years later in *Dark Ghetto,* Kenneth Clark demonstrated how the political, economic, and social structure of Harlem was essentially that of a colony.[5] Finally in 1967, a full-blown elaboration of "internal colonialism" provided the theoretical framework for Carmichael and Hamilton's widely read *Black Power.*[6] The following year the colonial analogy gained currency and new "respectability" when Senator McCarthy habitually referred to Black Americans as a colonized people during his campaign. While the rhetoric of internal colonialism was catching on, other social scientists began to raise questions about its appropriateness as a scheme of analysis.

The colonial analysis has been rejected as obscurantist and misleading by scholars who point to the significant differences in history and social-political conditions between our domestic patterns and what took place in Africa and India. Colonialism traditionally refers to the establishment of domination over a geographically external political unit, most often inhabited by people of a different race and culture, where this domination is political and economic, and the colony exists subordinated to and dependent upon the mother country. Typically the colonizers exploit the land, the raw materials, the labor, and other resources of the colonized nation; in addition a formal recognition is given to the difference in power, autonomy, and political status, and various agencies are set up to maintain this subordination. Seemingly the analogy must be stretched beyond usefulness if the American version is to be forced into this model. For here we are talking about group relations within a society; the mother country—colony separation in geography is absent. Though whites certainly colonized the territory of the original Americans, internal colonization of Afro-Americans did not involve the settlement of whites in any land that was unequivocally Black. And unlike the colonial situation, there has been no formal recognition of differing power since slavery was abolished outside the South. Classic colonialism involved the control and exploitation of the majority of a nation by a minority of outsiders. Whereas in America the people who are oppressed were themselves originally outsiders and are a numerical minority.

This conventional critique of "internal colonialism" is useful in pointing to the differences between our domestic patterns and the overseas situation. But in its bold attack it tends to lose sight of common experiences that have been historically shared by the most subjugated racial minorities in America and non-white peoples in some other parts of the world. For understanding the most dramatic recent developments on the race scene, this common core element—which I shall call colonization—may be more important than the undeniable divergences between the two contexts.

The common features ultimately relate to the fact that the classical colonialism of the imperialist era and American racism developed out of the same historical situation and reflected a common world economic and power stratification. The slave trade for the most part preceded the imperialist partition and economic exploitation of Africa, and in fact may have been a necessary prerequisite for colonial conquest—since it helped deplete and pacify Africa, undermining the resistance to direct occupation. Slavery contributed one of the basic raw materials for the textile industry which provided much of the capital for the West's industrial development and need for economic expansionism. The essential condition for both American slavery and European colonialism was the power domination and the technological superiority of the Western world in its relation to peoples of non-Western and non-white origins. This objective supremacy in technology and military power buttressed the West's sense of cultural superiority, laying the basis for racist ideologies that were elaborated to justify control and exploitation of non-white people. Thus because classical colonialism and America's internal version developed out of a similar balance of technological, cultural, and power relations, a common *process* of social oppression characterized the racial patterns in the two contexts—despite the variation in political and social structure.

There appear to be four basic components of the colonization complex. The first refers to how the racial group enters into the dominant society (whether colonial power or not). Colonization begins with a forced, involuntary entry. Second, there is an impact on the culture and social organization of the colonized people which is more than just a result of such "natural" processes as contact and acculturation. The colonizing power carries out a policy which constrains, transforms, or destroys indigenous values, orientations, and ways of life. Third, colonization involves a relationship by which members of the colonized group tend to be administered by representatives of the dominant power. There is an experience of being managed and manipulated by outsiders in terms of ethnic status.

A final fundament of colonization is racism. Racism is a principle of social domination by which a group seen as inferior or different in terms of alleged biological characteristics is exploited, controlled, and oppressed socially and psychically by a superordinate group. Except for the marginal case of Japanese imperialism, the major examples of colonialism have involved the subjugation of non-white Asian, African, and Latin American peoples by white European powers. Thus racism has generally accompanied colonialism. Race prejudice can exist without colonization—the experience of Asian-American minorities is a case in point—but racism as a system of domination is part of the complex of colonization.

The concept of colonization stresses the enormous fatefulness of the historical factor, namely the manner in which a minority group becomes a part of the dominant society.[7] The crucial difference between the colonized Americans and the ethnic immigrant minorities is that the latter have always been able to operate fairly competitively within that relatively open section of the social and economic order because these groups came voluntarily in search of a better life, because their movements in society were not administratively controlled, and because they transformed their culture at their own pace—giving up ethnic values and institutions when it was seen as a desirable exchange for improvements in social position.

In present-day America, a major device of Black colonization is the powerless ghetto. As Kenneth Clark describes the situation:

> Ghettoes are the consequence of the imposition of external power and the institutionalization of powerlessness. In this respect, they are in fact social, political, educational, and above all—economic colonies. Those confined within the ghetto walls are subject peoples. They are victims of the greed, cruelty, insensitivity, guilt and fear of their masters. . . .
>
> The community can best be described in terms of the analogy of a powerless colony. Its political leadership is divided, and all but one or two of its political

leaders are shortsighted and dependent upon the larger political power structure. Its social agencies are financially precarious and dependent upon sources of support outside the community. Its churches are isolated or dependent. Its economy is dominated by small businesses which are largely owned by absentee owners, and its tenements and other real property are also owned by absentee landlords.

Under a system of centralization, Harlem's schools are controlled by forces outside of the community. Programs and policies are supervised and determined by individuals who do not live in the community . . .[8]

Of course many ethnic groups in America have lived in ghettoes. What make the Black ghettoes an expression of colonized status are three special features. First, the ethnic ghettoes arose more from voluntary choice, both in the sense of the choice to immigrate to America and the decision to live among one's fellow ethnics. Second, the immigrant ghettoes tended to be a one and two generation phenomenon; they were actually way-stations in the process of acculturation and assimilation. When they continue to persist as in the case of San Francisco's Chinatown, it is because they are big business for the ethnics themselves and there is a new stream of immigrants. The Black ghetto on the other hand has been a more permanent phenomenon, although some individuals do escape it. But most relevant is the third point. European ethnic groups like the Poles, Italians, and Jews generally only experienced a brief period, often less than a generation, during which their residential buildings, commercial stores, and other enterprises were owned by outsiders. The Chinese and Japanese faced handicaps of color prejudice that were almost as strong as the Blacks faced, but very soon gained control of their internal communities, because their traditional ethnic culture and social organization had not been destroyed by slavery and internal colonization. But Afro-Americans are distinct in the extent to which their segregated communities have remained controlled economically, politically, and administratively from the outside. One indicator of this difference is the estimate that the "income of Chinese-Americans from Chinese-owned businesses is in proportion to their numbers 45 times as great as the income of Negroes from Negro owned businesses."[9] But what is true of business is also true for the other social institutions that operate within the ghetto. The educators, policemen, social workers, politicians, and others who administer the affairs of ghetto residents are typically whites who live outside the Black community. Thus the ghetto plays a strategic role as the focus for the administration by outsiders which is also essential to the structure of overseas colonialism.[10]

The colonial status of the Negro community goes beyond the issue of ownership and decision-making within Black neighborhoods. The Afro-American population in most cities has very little influence on the power structure and institutions of the larger metropolis, despite the fact that in numerical terms, Blacks tend to be the most sizeable of the various interest groups. A recent analysis of policy-making in Chicago estimates that "Negroes really hold less than 1 percent of the effective power in the Chicago metropolitan area. [Negroes are 20 percent of Cook County's population.] Realistically the power structure of Chicago is hardly less white than that of Mississippi."[11]

Colonization outside of a traditional colonial structure has its own special conditions. The group culture and social structure of the colonized in America is less developed; it is also less autonomous. In addition, the colonized are a numerical minority, and furthermore they are ghettoized more totally and are more dispersed than people under classic colonialism. Though these realities affect the magnitude and direction of response, it is my basic thesis that the most important expressions of protest in the Black community during the recent years reflect the colonized status of Afro-America. Riots, programs of separation, politics of community control, the Black revolutionary movements, and cultural nationalism each represent a different strategy of attack on domestic colonialism in America. Let us now examine some of these movements.

Riot or Revolt?

The so-called riots are being increasingly recognized as a preliminary if primitive form of mass rebellion against a colonial status. There is still a tendency to absorb their meaning within the conventional scope of assimilation-integration politics: some commentators stress the material motives involved in looting as a sign that the rioters want to join America's middle-class affluence just like everyone else. That motives are mixed and often unconscious, that Black people want good furniture and television sets like whites is beside the point. The guiding impulse in most major outbreaks has not been integration with American society, but an attempt to stake out a sphere of control by moving against that society and destroying the symbols of its oppression.

In my critique of the McCone report I observed that the rioters were asserting a claim to territoriality, an unorganized and rather inchoate attempt to gain control over their community or "turf."[12] In succeeding disorders also the thrust of the action has been the attempt to clear out an alien presence, white men and officials, rather than a drive to kill whites as in a conventional race riot. The main attacks have been directed at the property of white business men and at the police who operate in the Black community "like an army of occupation" protecting the interests of outside exploiters and maintaining the domination over the ghetto by the central metropolitan power structure.[13] The Kerner report misleads when it attempts to explain riots in terms of integration: "What the rioters appear to be seeking was fuller participation in the social order and the material benefits enjoyed by the majority of American citizens. Rather than rejecting the American system, they were anxious to obtain a place for themselves in it."[14] More accurately, the revolts pointed to alienation from this system on the part of many poor and also not-so-poor Blacks. The sacredness of private property, that unconsciously accepted bulwark of our social arrangements, was rejected; people who looted apparently without guilt generally remarked that they were taking things that "really belonged" to them anyway.[15] Obviously the society's bases of legitimacy and authority have been attacked. Law and order has long been viewed as the white man's law and order by Afro-Americans; but now this perspective characteristic of a colonized people is out in the open. And the Kerner Report's own data question how well ghetto rebels are buying the system: In Newark only 33 percent of self-reported rioters said they thought this country was worth fighting for in the event of a major war; in the Detroit sample the figure was 55 percent.[16]

One of the most significant consequences of the process of colonization is a weakening of the colonized's individual and collective will to resist his oppression. It has been easier to contain and control Black ghettoes because communal bonds and group solidarity have been weakened through divisions among leadership, failures of organization, and a general disspiritment that accompanies social oppression. The riots are a signal that the will to resist has broken the mold of accommodation. In some cities as in Watts they also represented nascent movements toward community identity. In several riot-torn ghettoes the outbursts have stimulated new organizations and movements. If it is true that the riot phenomenon of 1964–68 has passed its peak, its historical import may be more for the "internal" organizing momentum generated than for any profound "external" response of the larger society facing up to underlying causes.

Despite the appeal of Frantz Fanon to young Black revolutionaries, America is not Algeria. It is difficult to foresee how riots in our cities can play a role equivalent to rioting in the colonial situation as an integral phase in a movement for national liberation. In 1968 some militant groups (for example, the Black Panther Party in Oakland) had concluded that ghetto riots were self-defeating of the lives and interests of Black people in the present balance of organization and gunpower, though they had served a role to stimulate both Black consciousness and white awareness of the depths of racial crisis. Such militants have been influential in "cooling" their communities during periods of high riot potential. Theoretically oriented Black radicals see riots as spontaneous mass behavior which must be replaced by a revolutionary organization and consciousness. But despite the differences in objective conditions, the violence of the 1960's seems to serve the same psychic function, assertions of dignity and manhood for young Blacks in urban ghettoes, as it did for the colonized of North Africa described by Fanon and Memmi.[17]

Cultural Nationalism

Cultural conflict is generic to the colonial relation because colonization involves the domination of Western technological values over the more communal cultures of non-Western peoples. Colonialism played havoc with the national integrity of the peoples it brought under its sway. Of course, all traditional cultures are threatened by industrialism, the city, and modernization in communication, transportation, health, and education. What is special are the political and administrative decisions of colonizers in managing and controlling colonized peoples. The boundaries of African colonies, for example, were drawn to suit the political conveniences of the European nations without regard to the social organization and cultures of African tribes and kingdoms. Thus Nigeria as blocked out by the British included the Yorubas and the Ibos, whose civil war today is a residuum of the colonialist's disrespect for the integrity of indigenous cultures.

The most total destruction of culture in the colonization process took place not in traditional colonialism but in America. As Frazier stressed, the integral cultures of the diverse African peoples who furnished the slave trade were destroyed because slaves from different tribes, kingdoms, and linguistic groups were purposely separated to maximize domination and control. Thus language, religion, and national loyalties were lost in North America much more completely than in the Caribbean and Brazil where slavery developed somewhat differently. Thus on this key point America's internal colonization has been more total and extreme than situations of classic colonialism. For the British in India and the European powers in Africa were not able—as outnumbered minorities—to destroy the national and tribal cultures of the colonized. Recall that American slavery lasted 250 years and its racist aftermath another 100. Colonial dependency in the case of British Kenya and French Algeria lasted only 77 and 125 years respectively. In the wake of this more drastic uprooting and destruction of culture and social organization, much more powerful agencies of social, political, and psychological domination developed in the American case.

Colonial control of many peoples inhabiting the colonies was more a goal than a fact, and at Independence there were undoubtedly fairly large numbers of Africans who had never seen a colonial administrator. The gradual process of extension of control from the administrative center on the African coast contrasts sharply with the total uprooting involved in the slave trade and the totalitarian aspects of slavery in the United States. Whether or not Elkins is correct in treating slavery as a total institution, it undoubtedly had a far more radical and pervasive impact on American slaves than did colonialism on the vast majority of Africans.[18]

Yet a similar cultural process unfolds in both contexts of colonialism. To the extent that they are involved in the larger society and economy, the colonized are caught up in a conflict between two cultures. Fanon has described how the assimilation-oriented schools of Martinique taught him to reject his own culture and Blackness in favor of Westernized, French, and white values.[19] Both the colonized elites under traditional colonialism and perhaps the majority of Afro-Americans today experience a parallel split in identity, cultural loyalty, and political orientation.[20]

The colonizers use their culture to socialize the colonized elites (intellectuals, politicians, and middle class) into an identification with the colonial system. Because Western culture has the prestige, the power, and the key to open the limited opportunity that a minority of the colonized may achieve, the first reaction seems to be an acceptance of the dominant values. Call it brainwashing as the Black Muslims put it; call it identifying with the aggressor if you prefer Freudian terminology; call it a natural response to the hope and belief that integration and democratization can really take place if you favor a more commonsense explanation, this initial acceptance in time crumbles on the realities of racism and colonialism. The colonized, seeing that his success within colonialism is at the expense of his group and his own inner identity, moves radically toward a rejection of the Western culture and develops a nationalist outlook that celebrates his people and their traditions. As Memmi describes it:

Assimilation being abandoned, the colonized's liberation must be carried out through a recovery of self and of autonomous dignity. Attempts at imitating the colonizer required self-denial; the colonizer's rejection is the indispensible prelude to self-discovery. That accusing and annihilating image must be shaken off; oppression must be attacked boldly since it is impossible to go around it. After having been rejected for so long by the colonizer, the day has come when it is the colonized who must refuse the colonizer.[21]

Memmi's book, *The Colonizer and the Colonized*, is based on his experience as a Tunisian Jew in a marginal position between the French and the colonized Arab majority. The uncanny parallels between the North African situation he describes and the course of Black-white relations in our society is the best impressionist argument I know for the thesis that we have a colonized group and a colonizing system in America. His discussion of why even the most radical French anti-colonialist cannot participate in the struggle of the colonized is directly applicable to the situation of the white liberal and radical vis-à-vis the Black movement. His portrait of the colonized is as good an analysis of the psychology behind Black Power and Black nationalism as anything that has been written in the U.S. Consider for example:

Considered *en bloc* as *them, they,* or *those,* different from every point of view, homogeneous in a radical heterogeneity, the colonized reacts by rejecting all the colonizers *en bloc.* The distinction between deed and intent has no great significance in the colonial situation. In the eyes of the colonized, all Europeans in the colonies are de facto colonizers, and whether they want to be or not, they are colonizers in some ways. By their privileged economic position, by belonging to the political system of oppression, or by participating in an effectively negative complex toward the colonized, they are colonizers. . . . They are supporters or at least unconscious accomplices of that great collective aggression of Europe.[22]

The same passion which made him admire and absorb Europe shall make him assert his differences; since those differences, after all, are within him and correctly constitute his true self.[23]

The important thing now is to rebuild his people, whatever be their authentic nature; to reforge their unity, communicate with it, and to feel that they belong.[24]

Cultural revitalization movements play a key role in anti-colonial movements. They follow an inner necessity and logic of their own that comes from the consequences of colonialism on groups and personal identities; they are also essential to provide the solidarity which the political or military phase of the anti-colonial revolution requires. In the U.S. an Afro-American culture has been developing since slavery out of the ingredients of African world-views, the experience of bondage, Southern values and customs, migration and the Northern lower-class ghettoes, and most importantly, the political history of the Black population in its struggle against racism.[25] That Afro-Americans are moving toward cultural nationalism in a period when ethnic loyalties tend to be weak (and perhaps on the decline) in this country is another confirmation of the unique colonized position of the Black group. (A similar nationalism seems to be growing among American Indians and Mexican-Americans.)

The Movement for Ghetto Control

The call for Black Power unites a number of varied movements and tendencies.[26] Though no clear-cut program has yet emerged, the most important emphasis seems to be the movement for control of the ghetto. Black leaders and organizations are increasingly concerned with owning and controlling those institutions that exist within or impinge upon their community. The colonial model provides a key to the understanding of this movement, and indeed ghetto control advocates have increasingly invoked the language of colonialism in pressing for local home rule. The framework of anti-colonialism explains why the struggle for poor people's or community control of poverty programs has been more central in many cities than the content of these programs and why it has been crucial to exclude whites from leadership positions in Black organizations.

The key institutions that anti-colonialists want to take over or control are business, social services, schools, and the police. Though many spokesmen have advocated the exclusion of white landlords and small businessmen from the ghetto, this program has evidently not struck fire with the Black population and little concrete movement toward economic expropriation has yet developed. Welfare recipients have organized in many cities to protect their rights and gain a greater voice in the decisions that affect them, but whole communities have not yet been able to mount direct action against welfare colonialism. Thus schools and the police seem now to be the burning issues of ghetto control politics.

During the past few years there has been a dramatic shift from educational integration as the primary goal to that of community control of the schools. Afro-Americans are demanding their own school boards, with the power to hire and fire principals and teachers and to construct a curriculum which would be relevant to the special needs and culture style of ghetto youth. Especially active in high schools and colleges have been Black students, whose protests have centered on the incorporation of Black Power and Black culture into the educational system. Consider how similar is the spirit behind these developments to the attitude of the colonized North African toward European education:

He will prefer a long period of educational mistakes to the continuance of the colonizer's school organization. He will choose institutional disorder in order to destroy the institutions built by the colonizer as soon as possible. There we will see indeed a reactive drive of profound protest. He will no longer owe anything to the colonizer and will have definitely broken with him.[27]

Protest and institutional disorder over the issue of school control came to a head in 1968 in New York City. The procrastination in the Albany State legislature, the several crippling strikes called by the teachers union and the almost frenzied response of Jewish organizations makes it clear that decolonization of education faces the resistance of powerful vested interests.[28] The situation is too dynamic at present to assess probable future results. However, it can be safely predicted that some form of school decentralization will be institutionalized in New York, and the movement for community control of education will spread to more cities.

This movement reflects some of the problems and ambiguities that stem from the situation of colonization outside an immediate colonial context. The Afro-American community is not parallel in structure to the communities of colonized nations under traditional colonialism. The significant difference here is the lack of fully developed indigenous institutions besides the church. Outside of some areas of the South there is really no Black economy, and most Afro-Americans are inevitably caught up in the larger society's structure of occupations, education, and mass communication. Thus the ethnic nationalist orientation which reflects the reality of colonization exists alongside an integrationist orientation which corresponds to the reality that the institutions of the larger society are much more developed than those of the incipient nation.[29] As would be expected the movement for school control reflects both tendencies. The militant leaders who spearhead such local movements may be primarily motivated by the desire to gain control over the community's institutions—they are anti-colonialists first and foremost. Many parents who support them may share this goal also, but the majority are probably more concerned about creating a new education that will enable their children to "make it" in the society and the economy as a whole—they know that the present school system fails ghetto children and does not prepare them for participation in American life.

There is a growing recognition that the police are the most crucial institution maintaining the colonized status of Black Americans. And of all establishment institutions, police departments probably include the highest proportion of individual racists. This is no accident since central to the workings of racism (an essential component of colonization) are attacks on the humanity and dignity of the subject group. Through their normal routines the police constrict Afro-Americans to Black neighborhoods by harassing and questioning them when found outside the ghetto; they break up groups of youth congregating on corners or in cars without any provocation; and they continue to use offensive and racist language no matter how many intergroup understanding seminars have been built into the police academy. They also shoot to kill ghetto residents for alleged crimes such as car thefts and running from police officers.[30]

Police are key agents in the power equation as well as the drama of dehumanization. In the final analysis they do the dirty work for the larger system by restricting the striking back of Black rebels to skirmishes inside the ghetto, thus deflecting energies and attacks from the communities and institutions of the larger power structure. In a historical review, Gary Marx notes that since the French revolution, police and other authorities have killed large numbers of demonstrators and rioters; the rebellious "rabble" rarely destroys human life. The same pattern has been repeated in America's recent revolts.[31] Journalistic accounts appearing in the press recently suggest that police see themselves as defending the interests of white people against a tide of Black insurgence; furthermore the majority of whites appear to view "blue power" in this light. There is probably no other opinion on which the races are as far apart today as they are on the question of attitudes toward the police.

In many cases set off by a confrontation between a policeman and a Black citizen, the ghetto uprisings have dramatized the role of law enforcement and the issue of police brutality. In their aftermath, movements have arisen to contain police activity. One of the first was the Community Alert Patrol in Los Angeles, a method of policing the police in order to keep them honest and constrain their violations of personal dignity. This was the first tactic of the Black Panther Party which originated in Oakland, perhaps the most significant group to challenge the police role in maintaining the ghetto as a colony. The Panther's later policy of openly carrying guns (a legally protected right) and their intention of defending themselves against police aggression has brought on a series of confrontations with the Oakland police department. All indications are that the authorities intend to destroy the Panthers by shooting, framing up, or legally harassing their leadership— diverting the group's energies away from its primary purpose of self-defense and organization of the Black community to that of legal defense and gaining support in the white community.

There are three major approaches to "police colonialism" that correspond to reformist and revolutionary readings of the situation. The most elementary and also superficial sees colonialism in the fact that ghettoes are overwhelmingly patrolled by white rather than by Black officers. The proposal—supported today by many police departments—to increase the number of Blacks on local forces to something like their distribution in the city would then make it possible to reduce the use of white cops in the ghetto. This reform should be supported, for a variety of obvious reasons, but it does not get to the heart of the police role as agents of colonization.

The Kerner Report documents the fact that in some cases Black policemen can be as brutal as their white counterparts. The Report does not tell us who polices the ghetto, but they have compiled the proportion of Negroes on the forces of the major cities. In some cities the disparity is so striking that white police inevitably dominate ghetto patrols. (In Oakland 31 percent of the population and only 4 percent of the police are Black; in Detroit the figures are 39 percent and 5 percent; and in New Orleans 41 and 4.) In other cities, however, the proportion of Black cops is approaching the distribution in the city: Philadelphia 29 percent and 20 percent; Chicago 27 percent and

17 percent.[32] These figures also suggest that both the extent and the pattern of colonization may vary from one city to another. It would be useful to study how Black communities differ in degree of control over internal institutions as well as in economic and political power in the metropolitan area.

A second demand which gets more to the issue is that police should live in the communities they patrol. The idea here is that Black cops who lived in the ghetto would have to be accountable to the community; if they came on like white cops then "the brothers would take care of business" and make their lives miserable. The third or maximalist position is based on the premise that the police play no positive role in the ghettoes. It calls for the withdrawal of metropolitan officers from Black communities and the substitution of an autonomous indigenous force that would maintain order without oppressing the population. The precise relationship between such an independent police, the city and county law enforcement agencies, a ghetto governing body that would supervise and finance it, and especially the law itself is yet unclear. It is unlikely that we will soon face these problems directly as they have arisen in the case of New York's schools. Of all the programs of decolonization, police autonomy will be most resisted. It gets to the heart of how the state functions to control and contain the Black community through delegating the legitimate use of violence to police authority.

The various "Black Power" programs that are aimed at gaining control of individual ghettoes—buying up property and businesses, running the schools through community boards, taking over anti-poverty programs and other social agencies, diminishing the arbitrary power of the police—can serve to revitalize the institutions of the ghetto and build up an economic, professional, and political power base. These programs seem limited; we do not know at present if they are enough in themselves to end colonized status.[33] But they are certainly a necessary first step.

The Role of Whites

What makes the Kerner Report a less-than-radical document is its superficial treatment of racism and its reluctance to confront the colonized relationship between Black people and the larger society. The Report emphasizes the attitudes and feelings that make up white racism, rather than the system of privilege and control which is the heart of the matter.[34] With all its discussion of the ghetto and its problems, it never faces the question of the stake that white Americans have in racism and ghettoization.

This is not a simple question, but this paper should not end with the impression that police are the major villains. All white Americans gain some privileges and advantage from the colonization of Black communities.[35] The majority of whites also lose something from this oppression and division in society. Serious research should be directed to the ways in which white individuals and institutions are tied into the ghetto. In closing let me suggest some possible parameters.

1. It is my guess that only a small minority of whites make a direct economic profit from ghetto colonization. This is hopeful in that the ouster of white businessmen may become politically feasible. Much more significant, however, are the private and corporate interests in the land and residential property of the Black community; their holdings and influence on urban decision-making must be exposed and combated.

2. A much larger minority have occupational and professional interests in the present arrangements. The Kerner Commission reports that 1.3 million non-white men would have to be upgraded occupationally in order to make the Black job distribution roughly similar to the white. They advocate this without mentioning that 1.3 million specially privileged white workers would lose in the bargain.[36] In addition there are those professionals who carry out what Lee Rainwater has called the "dirty work" of administering the lives of the ghetto poor: the social workers, the school teachers, the urban development people, and of course the police.[37] The social problems of the Black community will ultimately be solved only by people and organizations from that community; thus the emphasis within these professions must shift toward training such a cadre of minority personnel. Social scientists who teach and study problems of race and poverty likewise have an obligation to replace themselves by bringing into the graduate schools and college faculties men of color who will become the future experts in these areas. For cultural and intellectual imperialism is as real as welfare colonialism, though it is currently screened behind such unassailable shibboleths as universalism and the objectivity of scientific inquiry.

3. Without downgrading the vested interests of profit and profession, the real nitty-gritty elements of the white stake are political power and bureaucratic security. Whereas few whites have much understanding of the realities of race relations and ghetto life, I think most give tacit or at least subconscious support for the containment and control of the Black population. Whereas most whites have extremely distorted images of Black Power, many—if not most—would still be frightened by actual Black political power. Racial groups and identities are real in American life; white Americans sense they are on top, and they fear possible reprisals or disruptions were power to be more equalized. There seems to be a paranoid fear in the

white psyche of Black dominance; the belief that Black autonomy would mean unbridled license is so ingrained that such reasonable outcomes as Black political majorities and independent Black police forces will be bitterly resisted.

On this level the major mass bulwark of colonization is the administrative need for bureaucratic security so that the middle classes can go about their life and business in peace and quiet. The Black militant movement is a threat to the orderly procedures by which bureaucracies and suburbs manage their existence, and I think today there are more people who feel a stake in conventional procedures than there are those who gain directly from racism. For in their fight for institutional control, the colonized will not play by the white rules of the game. These administrative rules have kept them down and out of the system; therefore they have no necessary intention of running institutions in the image of the white middle class.

The liberal, humanist value that violence is the worst sin cannot be defended today if one is committed squarely against racism and for self-determination. For some violence is almost inevitable in the decolonization process; unfortunately racism in America has been so effective that the greatest power Afro-Americans (and perhaps also Mexican-Americans) wield today is the power to disrupt. If we are going to swing with these revolutionary times and at least respond positively to the anti-colonial movement, we will have to learn to live with conflict, confrontation, constant change, and what may be real or apparent chaos and disorder.

A positive response from the white majority needs to be in two major directions at the same time. First, community liberation movements should be supported in every way by pulling out white instruments of direct control and exploitation and substituting technical assistance to the community when this is asked for. But it is not enough to relate affirmatively to the nationalist movement for ghetto control without at the same time radically opening doors for full participation in the institutions of the mainstream. Otherwise the liberal and radical position is little different than the traditional segregationist. Freedom in the special conditions of American colonization means that the colonized must have the choice between participation in the larger society and in their own independent structures.

NOTES

1. This is a revised version of a paper delivered at the University of California Centennial Program, "Studies in Violence," Los Angeles, June 1, 1968. For criticisms and ideas that have improved an earlier draft, I am indebted to Robert Wood,

Lincoln Bergman, and Gary Marx. As a good colonialist I have probably restated (read: stolen) more ideas from the writings of Kenneth Clark, Stokely Carmichael, Frantz Fanon, and especially such contributors to the Black Panther Party (Oakland) newspaper as Huey Newton, Bobby Seale, Eldridge Cleaver, and Kathleen Cleaver than I have appropriately credited or generated myself. In self-defense I should state that I began working somewhat independently on a colonial analysis of American race relations in the fall of 1965; see my "Whitewash Over Watts: The Failure of the McCone Report," *Trans-action*, 3 (March–April, 1966), pp. 3–9, 54.

2. Harold Cruse, *Rebellion or Revolution*, New York: 1968, p. 214.

3. Nationalism, including an orientation toward Africa, is no new development. It has been a constant tendency within Afro-American politics. See Cruse, *ibid*, esp. chaps. 5–7.

4. This was six years before the publication of *The Crisis of the Negro Intellectual*, New York: Morrow, 1968, which brought Cruse into prominence. Thus the 1962 article was not widely read until its reprinting in Cruse's essays, *Rebellion or Revolution*, *op. cit.*

5. Kenneth Clark, *Dark Ghetto*, New York: Harper and Row, 1965. Clark's analysis first appeared a year earlier in *Youth in the Ghetto*, New York: Haryou Associates, 1964.

6. Stokely Carmichael and Charles Hamilton, *Black Power*, New York: Random, 1967.

7. As Eldridge Cleaver reminds us, "Black people are a stolen people held in a colonial status on stolen land, and any analysis which does not acknowledge the colonial status of black people cannot hope to deal with the real problem." "The Land Question," *Ramparts*, 6 (May, 1968), p. 51.

8. *Youth in the Ghetto, op. cit.*, pp. 10–11; 79–80.

9. N. Glazer and D.P. Moynihan, *Beyond the Melting Pot*, Cambridge, Mass.: M.I.T., 1963, p. 37.

10. "When we speak of Negro social disabilities under capitalism, . . . we refer to the fact that he does not own anything—*even what is ownable in his own community*. Thus to fight for black liberation *is to fight for his right to own*. The Negro is politically compromised today because he owns nothing. He has little voice in the affairs of state because he owns nothing. The fundamental reason why the Negro bourgeois-democratic revolution has been aborted is because American capitalism has prevented the development of a black class of capitalist owners of institutions and economic tools. To take one crucial example, Negro radicals today are severely hampered in their tasks of educating the black masses on political issues because Negroes do not own any of the necessary means of propaganda and communication. The Negro owns no printing presses, he has no stake in the networks of the means of communication. Inside his own communities he does not own the house he lives in, the property he lives on, nor the wholesale and retail sources from which he buys his commodities. He does not own the edifices in which he enjoys culture and entertainment or in which he socializes. In capitalist society, an individual or group that does not own anything is powerless." H. Cruse, "Behind the Black Power Slogan," in Cruse, *Rebellion or Revolution, op. cit.*, pp. 238–39.

11. Harold M. Baron, "Black Powerlessness in Chicago," *Trans-action,* 6 (Nov., 1968), pp. 27–33.

12. R. Blauner, "Whitewash Over Watts," *op. cit.*

13. "The police function to support and enforce the interests of the dominant political, social, and economic interests of the town" is a statement made by a former police scholar and official, according to A. Neiderhoffer, *Behind the Shield,* New York: Doubleday, 1967 as cited by Gary T. Marx, "Civil Disorder and the Agents of Control," *Journal of Social Issues,* forthcoming.

14. Report of the National Advisory Commission on Civil Disorders, N.Y.: Bantam, March, 1968, p. 7.

15. This kind of attitude has a long history among American Negroes. During slavery, Blacks used the same rationalization to justify stealing from their masters. Appropriating things from the master was viewed as *"taking* part of his property for the benefit of another part; whereas *stealing* referred to appropriating something from another slave, an offense that was not condoned." Kenneth Stampp, *The Peculiar Institution,* Vintage, 1956, p. 127.

16. Report of the National Advisory Commission on Civil Disorders, *op. cit.,* p. 178.

17. Frantz Fanon, *Wretched of the Earth,* New York: Grove, 1963; Albert Memmi, *The Colonizer and the Colonized,* Boston: Beacon, 1967.

18. Robert Wood, "Colonialism in Africa and America: Some Conceptual Considerations," December, 1967, unpublished paper.

19. F. Fanon, *Black Skins, White Masks,* New York: Grove, 1967.

20. Harold Cruse has described how these two themes of integration with the larger society and identification with ethnic nationality have struggled within the political and cultural movements of Negro Americans. *The Crisis of the Negro Intellectual, op. cit.*

21. Memmi, *op. cit.,* p. 128.

22. *Ibid.,* p. 130.

23. *Ibid.,* p. 132.

24. *Ibid.,* p. 134.

25. In another essay, I argue against the standard sociological position that denies the existence of an ethnic Afro-American culture and I expand on the above themes. The concept of "Soul" is astonishingly parallel in content to the mystique of "Negritude" in Africa; the Pan-African culture movement has its parallel in the burgeoning Black culture mood in Afro-American communities. See "Black Culture: Myth or Reality" in Peter Rose, editor, *Americans From Africa,* Atherton, 1969.

26. Scholars and social commentators, Black and white alike, disagree in interpreting the contemporary Black Power movement. The issues concern whether this is a new development in Black protest or an old tendency revised; whether the movement is radical, revolutionary, reformist, or conservative; and whether this orientation is unique to Afro-Americans or essentially a Black parallel to other ethnic group strategies for collective mobility. For an interesting discussion of Black Power as a modernized version of Booker T. Washington's separatism and economism, see Harold Cruse, *Rebellion or Revolution, op. cit.,* pp. 193–258.

27. Memmi, op. cit., pp. 137–138.

28. For the New York school conflict see Jason Epstein, "The Politics of School Decentralization," New York Review of Books, June 6, 1968, pp. 26–32; and "The New York City School Revolt," ibid., 11, no. 6, pp. 37–41.

29. This dual split in the politics and psyche of the Black American was poetically described by Du Bois in his Souls of Black Folk, and more recently has been insightfully analyzed by Harold Cruse in The Crisis of the Negro Intellectual, op. cit. Cruse has also characterized the problem of the Black community as that of under-development.

30. A recent survey of police finds "that in the predominantly Negro areas of several large cities, many of the police perceive the residents as basically hostile, especially the youth and adolescents. A lack of public support—from citizens, from courts, and from laws—is the policeman's major complaint. But some of the public criticism can be traced to the activities in which he engages day by day, and perhaps to the tone in which he enforces the "law" in the Negro neighborhoods. Most frequently he is 'called upon' to intervene in domestic quarrels and break up loitering groups. He stops and frisks two or three times as many people as are carrying dangerous weapons or are actual criminals, and almost half of these don't wish to cooperate with the policeman's efforts." Peter Rossi et al., "Between Black and White—The Faces of American Institutions and the Ghetto," in Supplemental Studies for The National Advisory Commission on Civil Disorders, July 1968, p. 114.

31. "In the Gordon Riots of 1780 demonstrators destroyed property and freed prisoners, but did not seem to kill anyone, while authorities killed several hundred rioters and hung an additional 25. In the Rebellion Riots of the French Revolution, though several hundred rioters were killed, they killed no one. Up to the end of the Summer of 1967, this pattern had clearly been repeated, as police, not rioters, were responsible for most of the more than 100 deaths that have occurred. Similarly, in a related context, the more than 100 civil rights murders of recent years have been matched by almost no murders of racist whites." G. Marx, "Civil Disorders and the Agents of Social Control," op. cit.

32. Report of the National Advisory Commission on Civil Disorders, op. cit., p. 321. That Black officers nevertheless would make a difference is suggested by data from one of the supplemental studies to the Kerner Report. They found Negro policemen working in the ghettoes considerably more sympathetic to the community and its social problems than their white counterparts. Peter Rossi et al., "Between Black and White—The Faces of American Institutions in the Ghetto," op. cit., chap. 6.

33. Eldridge Cleaver has called this first stage of the anti-colonial movement community liberation in contrast to a more long-range goal of national liberation. E. Cleaver, "Community Imperialism," Black Panther Party newspaper, 2 (May 18, 1968).

34. For a discussion of this failure to deal with racism, see Gary T. Marx, "Report of the National Commission: The Analysis of Disorder or Disorderly Analysis," 1968, unpublished paper.

35. Such a statement is easier to assert than to document but I am attempting the latter in a forthcoming book tentatively titled *White Racism, Black Culture,* to be published by Little Brown, 1970.
36. Report of the National Advisory Commission on Civil Disorders, *op. cit.*, pp. 253–256.
37. Lee Rainwater, "The Revolt of the Dirty-Workers," *Trans-action,* 5 (Nov., 1967), pp. 2, 64.

SUGGESTED READINGS

Hannah Arendt, *On Violence* (New York: Harcourt, Brace & World, 1970).

David O. Arnold, "The American Way of Death: The Roots of Violence in American Society," Institute of Government and Public Affairs, University of California at Los Angeles, 1968.

Norman Birnbaum, *The Crisis of Industrial Society* (New York: Oxford University Press, 1969).

Dee Brown, *Bury My Heart at Wounded Knee* (New York: Holt, Rinehart, & Winston, 1971).

Claude Brown, *Manchild in the Promised Land* (New York: Macmillan, 1965).

Stokely Carmichael and Charles V. Hamilton, *Black Power: The Politics of Liberation in America* (New York: Random House, 1967).

Kenneth B. Clark, *Dark Ghetto* (New York: Harper & Row, 1965).

Eldridge Cleaver, *Soul on Ice* (New York: McGraw-Hill, 1968).

Robert Coles, *Children of Crisis* (Boston: Little, Brown, 1967).

Harold Cruse, *Rebellion or Revolution?* (New York: Morrow, 1968).

David Brion Davis, *The Problem of Slavery in Western Culture* (Ithaca, N.Y.: Cornell University Press, 1966).

John Dollard, *Caste and Class in a Southern Town,* 3rd ed. (Garden City, N.Y.: Doubleday Anchor, 1957).

William O. Douglas, *Points of Rebellion* (New York: Random House, 1970).

St. Clair Drake and Horace R. Cayton, *Black Metropolis* (New York: Harcourt, 1945).

Stanley M. Elkins, *Slavery* (Chicago: University of Chicago Press, 1959).

Frantz Fanon, *The Wretched of the Earth* (New York: Grove Press, 1968).

Frank Harvey, *Air War: Vietnam* (New York: Bantam Books, 1967).

George L. Jackson, *Soledad Brother* (New York: Coward-McCann, 1970).

Kenneth Keniston, *Young Radicals: Notes on Committed Youth* (New York: Harcourt, Brace & World, 1968).

Herbert R. Kohl, *36 Children* (New York: New American Library, 1967).

Jonathan Kozol, *Death at an Early Age* (Boston: Houghton Mifflin, 1967).

Eliot Liebow, *Talley's Corner* (Boston: Little, Brown, 1967).

Seymour Martin Lipset and Sheldon S. Wolin, eds., *The Berkeley Student Revolt* (Garden City, N.Y.: Doubleday Anchor, 1965).

Malcolm X, *The Autobiography of Malcolm X* (New York: Grove Press, 1965).

Malcolm X, "The Ballot or the Bullet," in *Malcolm X Speaks: Selected Speeches and Statements* (New York: Grove Press, 1965).

H. G. Nicholas, *Violence in American Society* (London: Oxford University Press, 1969).

Bobby G. Seale, *Seize the Time* (New York: Random House, 1970).

Kenneth M. Stampp, *The Era of Reconstruction: 1865–1877* (New York: Alfred A. Knopf, 1965).

Piri Thomas, *Down These Mean Streets* (New York: Alfred A. Knopf, 1967).

Eugene Victor Walter, *Terror and Resistance* (New York: Oxford University Press, 1969).

C. Vann Woodward, *The Strange Career of Jim Crow*, 2nd rev. ed.(New York: Oxford University Press, 1966).

V

PROBLEMS OF CRIME
AND JUSTICE ❧ ❧

CRIME, CORRUPTION, AND THE SEARCH FOR JUSTICE ✐

It can be said, in a variation of a statement that has been made innumerable times about an infinite variety of things, that if a society did not have crime, it would have to invent it. If to the resident of the modern world, particularly the American, this seems too far-fetched to be taken seriously, one can find such a concept, albeit in more sophisticated terms, in Emile Durkheim, for whom crime (or more exactly, the societal reaction induced by crime, including the act of labeling it as criminal and punishing the transgressor) was a method that societies used to reinforce the moral order and bring a sense of unity, cohesion, and self-righteousness to the punishers. Moreover, through the punishment of the offender, the members of the society had their confidence restored in the effectiveness of their moral order.

Whatever may be the antiquity and the ubiquity of crime (to borrow two words that were linked by Tumin in his discussion of social inequality), it takes on many forms, seems to be endless in its expansion into new sectors of the populace, and increasingly touches directly on the everyday life of everyday people. It has influence, real or alleged, in the highest echelons of business and government, vast influence on racial hostility, and strong roots embedded in the history and traditions, as well as the mythology and ideology of America. All these factors make crime at this time in the United States a social problem of the most challenging magnitude. If, as some have contended, a social problem comes into existence when it is identified and recognized as such by large sectors of the population (a statement we are not endorsing, but merely repeating), then by such a criterion crime is a major problem, and for many people the greatest.

Statistics themselves will relate this story although they are patently vulnerable. In criminology texts, it is commonplace to quote some social thinker or political campaigner to the effect that streets are unsafe, that young people of ever-decreasing age levels are molesting ordinary citizens,

419

that law and order are deteriorating to the point where they have almost disappeared, and so the statement continues until the reader is abruptly shocked by the date—usually the early nineteenth century. Although this is not made explicit, the intent is to imply that crime has always been with us and in a form as widespread and threatening to the people then as it is today. We are only more aware of it now, either because of mass media or because this is the period that we are living in. Such a view has an appeal because it is strangely reassuring; it tells us that things are not so bad because they have always been so bad. From this, one is expected to draw the conclusion that we will live through the present era without society deteriorating or disintegrating, for the increase in crime is illusory. This view has the further appeal of unconventionality: scholars and sociologists, in particular, like to assert and prove the very reverse of what everybody "knows" (when they are not busy proving precisely what everybody "knows").

The statistics tell another story, but they are challengeable. In the period from 1960 to 1970, the *crime rate* for a special category of what are often called "serious crimes" (that is, the number of such crimes reported and believed to have been committed, in proportion to the total population) increased appreciably, as did the chances of any person being the victim of a serious crime during any one-year period. It can be persuasively argued that reporting of crime has become more common (as a result of insurance, income tax deduction on losses, less fear of shame in cases of rape, better and more uniform statistical methods) and that information is generally more sophisticated than it was years before, thus causing an apparent increase that may be entirely illusory. Aside from homicide and automobile theft, studies recently conducted indicate that most serious crimes go unreported; in fact, the actual crime rate may be some three or four times as great as the official rate. While this may make the data even more alarming than without such a statement, some criminologists and commentators have interpreted this in a more reassuring manner: the official statistics could show a doubling or trebling of robbery, rape, and burglary, while, in fact, the number or rate of these crimes remained constant.

On the other hand, the very pervasiveness of crime as an everyday affair, the feeling of hopelessness among poor people, who believe that the police could not care less or are helpless, may have resulted in greater underreporting of certain crimes (rape excepted) than ever; and certainly organized crime, though so much in the news, never finds its way into statistics except in the form of an occasional corpse that increases by one digit the homicide figures. If organized crime has increased, as strongly appears to be the case, then it is an increase not reflected in crime statistics.

However one looks at it, however the statistics may be challenged, interpreted, or discounted subject to long overdue correction, some sociologists and many laymen contend that America today faces a problem far greater in scope and ramifications than ever known in its history. Crime may change its character, may vacillate in intensity from violations against property to those against persons, and then return to the former. It may become more visible or less, and it may reflect changes in life styles and technologies of the changing society. Yet the changing nature of criminality in America has manifested itself in the late sixties and the early seventies in two complementary forms: fear and suspicion. Of the first, who can deny that people are frightened on the streets of almost all major cities, in all parts of these cities, and not only at night but during the day? Not only restricted to the streets, this fear penetrates people in parks, in hallways, in elevators, and even in one's very home. Who ventures on the street alone for a walk after dark, even in the shadow of the White House? Who opens the door today for that once popular figure in American life, the door-to-door salesman, the Fuller brush man? How many people, when alone, walk up or down many flights, lest the elevator be stopped by a stranger on another floor, and one's property, even one's life, put in danger? Who would have dreamed, only a few years ago, that every self-service elevator in major cities of the United States would be required to be equipped with a rounded mirror, so that the dweller or visitor before entry could gain a glimpse of the corners and detect any crouching figure lying in wait for his prey?

Suspicion accompanies fear. Although the suspicion of one's neighbor, a stranger on the street, or the person walking idly by all exist, suspicion generally takes three more defined forms: (1) mutual hostility between police and civilians, particularly when the civilians are black, young, or poor; (2) hostility between large portions of members of different ethnic groups; and (3) a pervasive feeling or belief that everything has a price on it, that government, politics, and business are evil, and that the crime on the streets is only the poor man's reflection of the crime in the mansions. If you steal a loaf of bread, they send you to prison, but if you steal a railroad . . ., so the saying used to go. Today it might be concluded that they make your grandson a governor or a United States Senator.

As we approach the final quarter of this century, the widespread character of crime in America can hardly be gainsaid. It takes on many well-publicized yet far different forms: white collar and other "respectable" acts, organized crime, street crime, all different in forms and consequences, yet, interrelated in their cumulative effects on the deterioration of morality and respect for law. With the exclusion of certain crimes, an increase in a single type of illegal behavior cannot be quantified. The exceptions are automobile theft, murder, and violent rape, and kidnapping. There is no way of stating how many crimes of racketeering, extortion, smuggling, price-fixing, blackmail and numerous other illegal acts are committed by organized criminals and by men in high positions of government and business. Nor are the small, ordinary crimes easily countable, as they become taken-for-granted episodes in a way of life that is increasingly hazardous. Who calls the police to report that a mailbox has been pried open and the contents stolen, unless there is reason to believe that a check is missing? Who gets uptight over the crime (one is almost tempted to place the word in quotation marks) of officials who pocket a part of the money appropriated for feeding convicts, with dietary results that are not difficult to imagine? We have become inured to this as institutionalized immorality that is part of the deteriorating quality of life.

Crime has a long history in this country, with roots in its ideology and social institutions. It is a country founded on violence, not in the sense of the Revolutionary War of independence, but violence against natives who, the white settlers insisted, had to be subdued, and against black immigrants who were kidnapped and brought here by force, and then against new groups of immigrants as they came voluntarily, attracted by a world of hope, fleeing a world of oppression and often fleeing compulsory military service abroad, to come to a land that did not have such an outrageous institution. "Go West, young man," said Horace Greeley, several decades after the founding of the Republic, and the young man went, one gun in hand and the second in the holster. If Hollywood and television have parodied and caricatured the frontiersman that he became (a caricature not without its effect on the world view and the behavior of the beholder), certainly the law and order was hardly of a nonviolent kind. It was the law of the mighty and the order of the bullet, buttressed not even by such formalities as courts and jails, but by running one's opponents out of town, if merciful, and otherwise by using the whip, the rope, the tar and feather. The heritage of violence is strong and deeply ingrained as presidential commissions have recently been pointing out, but from which they tend to draw the unfortunate conclusion that the criminal violence of the 1960s and 1970s is no different, rather than the significant conclusion that it is a continuation and an escalation based upon a cherished heritage.

If the Nuremberg trials and principles are to be taken seriously, then in retrospect one must not only indict the founders of America, but note that this nation was built in a spirit of the institutionalization and legitimation of crime—the crime of abduction, genocide, and slavery. However, despite Nuremberg and despite the enormity of these acts as a part of our history, these crimes are better seen as grave social problems unlike those usually thought of as crimes. How clearly they have become interwoven and how inextricable the two strands are in relation to one another is seen as one glances back to the period of Reconstruction and the tragic years that followed. After the Civil War with the passage of the Thirteenth, Fourteenth, and Fifteenth Amendments to the Constitution, it appeared for a short time as if the American dream of liberty, freedom, and equality of opportunity for all would be transformed into a reality. Yet, a combination of *realpolitik,* two centuries of ingrained prejudice, the bitterness of the defeated in the war, and the fatigue of the victorious, who had likewise bled profusely, worked to reestablish the power of those who would continue, in only a slightly altered form, the oppression of the former slave.

Night riders and terror, the rule of rope and fagot, lynchings frequent enough to tranquilize an entire population, and all done in conspiracy with law officers, from local sheriffs to governors and senators, and with the silence (shall we say "benign neglect"?) of the authorities in Washington— these events marked the beginning of another century of oppression. The lesson of this period in American history is tragically self-evident and closely related to the present development and proliferation of crime. Postbellum America, particularly the South, was placed on its course, on its historic and manifest destiny, by criminal acts the enormity of which can hardly be exaggerated. This crime became institutionalized and became the heritage of which the present generation is reaping the bitter fruit.

America learned that it had to contend with more than merely a tradition of violence and politically accepted and institutionalized crime. The resulting racism, involuntary and illegal ghettoization, systematic deprivation, which created a land of people devoid of a sense of community and without any sense of belonging to one another, demanded attention and answering. The melting pot was not a dream, it was a chimera, from which the Indians and the Negroes were always to be excluded. In its place there grew what was euphemistically called "cultural pluralism," and what for moments there was a possibility of this land becoming. However, instead there developed an America in which people were deeply intertwined in each other's lives, in a single political, economic, and military structure, which separated people socially and culturally from one another by deep chasms that generated hatred and suspicion. The blacks believed, and with considerable justification, that they were ruled, judged, and imprisoned by whites, who were in power because of cheating, conniving, and outright criminality. It was difficult to teach people respect for a law that did not respect them— a law that they had not made and had never been used to protect them; a law, in fact, that was not respected by those who had themselves created it. The poor whites, many of them struggling to form unions and to protect themselves not only against employers but against competition from blacks as well, likewise cheated and tricked in company towns. Subjected to yellow dog contracts, they did not develop a respect for law, although they had a deep well of disrespect for others (blacks, immigrants, Mexicans, Orientals, just "them") whose pattern of law-breaking was dissimilar from their own. Then came Prohibition. Not only the heyday of institutionalized and often glamorized lawlessness, the men quick on the trigger were beyond the law if they did not own the law, or at least own some of the lawmakers. It was a period of wide, almost universal, contempt for the idea that a law was to be obeyed, especially when it did not seem useful or convenient to do so.

The contempt for law that arose particularly during Prohibition combined with the background of violence, the racial bitterness, lack of community belonging, and the resurgence of an old power structure by systematic criminal means in the post-Civil War South, formed some of the confluent heritages that have given America a crime problem even greater than that faced by other peoples. No doubt other forces have converged with these to create a proliferation of crime. Violence is an American heritage, but this theme, now so frequently repeated, can be overstated. Violence is a heritage in many other lands, as were peasant revolts, glorification of folk-hero villains, official corruption, racial tensions, and government-sponsored hostilities, but these did not lead to criminality as a social problem in the manner that it has in the United States. We may be in danger of creating a myth of violence to explain away crime and rioting, to blame it on a past that cannot be rewritten. We might be inventing a mechanism for our failing to examine *the contemporary institutions* from which contemporary crime and violence flow. Let us not forget that the American heritage was one of both violence and nonviolence, the land that gave us the Boston Tea Party also gave us Thoreau and his famed night in prison.

In fact, it may be out of some of the best strands in the American ethos that criminality is born. Look at the open-class society and the land of opportunity. Here is the American dream that every man can get ahead and make it in the world, and no one is fixed into a caste and forced to remain for life. It is the dream of Cinderella and Horatio Alger that one could make it to the top, if not by a Prince Charming then by hard work, starting at the bottom and climbing, ever climbing, always upward, and often upon the backs and over the trampled bodies of others. Yet, at least it was by work, by the penny earned being a penny saved, by early to bed and early to rise, not rising early to go out and burglarize the neighbor's house before he is awakened, but to go to field or shop and be industrious. Getting ahead by hard work led to the golden pot at the end of the rainbow, and the success stories were heartily publicized. In the theory of Merton (developed from Durkheim and in turn adapted by Cloward and Ohlin), many of those unable to reach the top of the ladder by legitimate means were motivated nonetheless to get there. In a country in which ethics, religiosity, and the means to reach the ends had not been stressed, some continued to strive by

using other (even condemned) means. If Cloward and Ohlin see this as the
key to an introduction into the life of delinquency among youths, from
which one graduates after a short apprenticeship into adult criminality, the
same thesis can be applied with equal or greater vigor to an understanding
of the robber barons, the founders of the major American fortunes, whose
descendants are now the ultra-elite of America's power elites.

The period after World War II saw increases in crime, and new causes
for such increases. A new form of Prohibition fell like a pall over the
country. It had its roots in the early years of the century but was only now
gaining wide publicity and resulting in ominous repercussions such as the
suppression of the use of narcotics, and even of several nonaddictive materials that might be considered mild intoxicants. The repercussions of this
movement were far more insidious than when the suppression was against
alcoholic beverages. A veritable subterranean social organization for the
importation, adulteration, and distribution of the materials came into being.
A government-like structure, it was at the top a prototype for organized
crime, and at the bottom it drove its victims either to recruit new adherents
in order to sell the illegal material, or to resort to ordinary crime to obtain
the funds they required for the costly drugs.

Here was a new criminal order, the rich and the lofty on top, who often
had strong connections with respected political authorities, and at the
bottom the outcasts of society, *lumpenproletariat,* men and women who
supported themselves at best as pimps and prostitutes, but more frequently
in a far less welcome manner. One can only estimate how much of what
became widespread as muggings on the streets, purse-snatchings, burglariz-
ing of slum homes, stealing of social security and welfare checks, using
fences for the disposition of stolen merchandise and storekeepers for the
cashing of stolen checks can be attributed to the criminalization of a sector
of the population by the anti-narcotic laws. In the large cities, where addicts
tend to gather, the estimate is 50 to 60 per cent.

Two other forms of crime came to the fore in America during the quarter
of a century following World War II. One was dubbed "white-collar crime,"
Sutherland's happy phrase for an unhappy condition. The history of law-
breaking by respectables was not itself startling, and as mentioned, many
of the great American fortunes were based on it. Not only had there been
embezzlement, bribery, and forgery by men in white collars, actions long
defined as criminal and sometimes prosecuted as such, but violations of laws
governing labor relations, advertising, adulteration, and numerous other
activities had taken place on a large scale. Sutherland painstakingly documented and insisted that these too should be conceptualized as crime and
prosecuted as such, even though such acts had been ignored and actually

approved in the past, and the perpetrators honored the more for having committed them. Had Sutherland chosen to document his work with studies of violations of laws governing race relations, his work on white-collar crime, offenses by respectable members of the community, might have been a hundred times as long, and, yet, would have contained nothing new. For who in America did not know of some such events?

Finally in the 1960s, there came the rising anger and protest against injustice, on the part of blacks, youth, welfare recipients, militant feminists, and many other groups and categories of people. It was a generation aroused to heights of moral indignation by Dr. Martin Luther King, Jr., and let down by Vietnam, Cambodia, and dreams unfulfilled. It was a generation that became increasingly angry, alienated, disillusioned, contemptuous of those in power, impatient for change, doubtful whether the much-vaunted democratic process could bring about such change before the whole world had become polluted, defoliated, regimented, and poisoned. In this type of world, people looked for and found other paths to express their anger or to insist upon meaningful steps toward the correction of social evils.

Another form of crime was introduced. It began with the deliberate lawbreaking of a nonviolent character which had been nobly advocated by King, and was to result in the moral confrontation with the immoral men in power. However, the crime continued and escalated into physical confrontation and brute force against brute force. Guerrilla warfare, a dramatic act to prevent an immoral or illegal one, a shaking of one's fist at humanity and a challenge to the system that it must come down or be brought down, if it does not make concessions. Buildings were seized and sometimes bombed and set afire. While here and there concessions were indeed made, little concessions involving what has been called student power, or a sop to the blacks by forcing a union to open its doors to the hitherto excluded, the oppression of whole races continued, the war in Vietnam dragged on, and students, white and black, and many black political protest organizers were shot and killed. In turn, they shot back, crime continued from both sides, and from the vantage point of each side only the other was criminal. The protesters saw themselves as carrying the banner of freedom, as being revolutionaries on the one hand, and as acting in self-defense on the other; the police saw themselves as protectors of law and order and regarded the bombers and snipers as ordinary criminals and murderers, not people caught in a political war.

Crime of at least the ordinary variety excluding from this political crime, which one believes in as a matter of principle, is usually thought of as being evil. Who needs it? To a certain extent, and within limits, we all do. Although there are functional alternatives that a society can use (such as education, rewards, and the like), crime is a mechanism by which a society is given the warning that social changes are urgently needed. In this sense, crime is like conflict, but a conflict in which the individual perpetrator, or criminal, usually is not motivated on a conscious level by political gains, but only by personal ones. Law violation calls to the attention of legislators and public that the penal code is outmoded (as violations of some sex laws) and that there are gross inequities that must be corrected.

However, there are two dangers in this view, correct as we believe it to be, and both dangers seem to be manifesting themselves in America at this stage of its history. First, the amount of crime and the type of crime may grow beyond that which a society "needs" or can tolerate. It can reach the point where it threatens the everyday existence and functioning of all citizens. Crime can, in this sense, jolt the ongoing society and interfere with its complacency, but it does not reach the point where that society ceases to be a continuing system. There is another danger, namely, that instead of responding to crime by examining its social roots and correcting what is correctable, the powers in society may respond with increasing oppression, harsher laws, longer but not more effective sentences, and the whittling away of civil liberties, not only for the accused, but for the general populace.

The victims of crime are all of us, but they are mainly the poor, the blacks, the victims of society itself. These people have been the victims of crime for generations, but it is only recently that they have risen in protest and that crime has extended its victimization to large sectors of middle- and even upper-class people. That is why America has become so crime-conscious. Were not the blacks always robbed, by each other and by whites? Were they not held in terror, illegally disenfranchised, systematically excluded, assaulted, and not even permitted the outlet of retaliation? Crime is not new to these people, nor has it increased considerably against them, but a society that has awakened to crime as a grave social problem now finds that its white citizens, and many not so poor, are among the victims. It is at this point that the government itself, particularly as there is pressure toward drifting in the direction of a welfare state, intervenes to study the problem of crime.

To understand the nature of crime as a social problem, one must delve into many concomitant and subsidiary phenomena: (1) the role of the police, the problem of police-community relations, and the question of police corruption; (2) the administration of justice, the rights of the accused, and the social class bias built into the court system; (3) the matter of deterrence, the protection of the citizen from victimization, and the com-

pensation of the victim; and (4) punishment (or as it is now euphemistically
called, "correction"), its rationale and justification, the forms it can take to
be effective, and the guarantees that society must make that it shall not be
dehumanizing.

Not all of the problems briefly summarized here are handled in the
selections that follow. One essay is an overall survey of crime in America,
the second a description of organized crime and its relationship to political
corruption in one American city, the third discusses the matter of criminal
justice for the impoverished, and the fourth deals with the problem of drugs,
their use and abuse. All but the last are government documents. Although
there are limitations on what a government is able or willing to state on
matters that embarrass it, it is nevertheless true that government has a
vested interest in the control of at least some types of illegal activities. The
documents reproduced here must be read with an understanding of these
limitations. If they downplay the place of the Protestant ethic and the
predatory economy in the creation of crime, if they omit institutionalized
racism as a source of crime, if they have nothing to say on police brutality,
they have other significant focal points of attention, and they come to us
from impeccable sources, and with the stamp of authority that should make
the reading all the more chilling because it is almost unchallengeable.

Completing our section on crime, and supplementing the material from
government reports, is an original article on drug use and abuse by Charles
Winick. Like many other aspects of the phenomenon of crime, the problem
of drug abuse can be solved in America on a personal basis, but not on a
mass basis, within the framework of contemporary society. For a mass
solution of the problem requires that we tackle many other and more
fundamental issues that are eroding the lives not only of many youths but
of large numbers of older people. Ghetto residents are angry and disaffected,
and many are turning to drugs out of a sense of hopelessness and helplessness. Youth is in rebellion against the morality of a society that represents
to them war, oppression, and hypocrisy. Some have embraced drugs as a
mechanism for demonstrating their contempt for the world of their elders,
while others find in drugs an escape from all that they see as evil in that
world.

To solve the problem of drug abuse, we must come together, bring about
a unity of races and generations. But more than that, there are today
powerful vested interests in drugs: organized crime, corrupt officials, and
others, a veritable political economy of junk. This situation has reached
such proportions that only a national commitment can change a deteriorating situation. The victims of drugs are the users, their families, and their
communities, and it is only when they make their voices heard and their
power felt that change will be forthcoming.

CRIME IN AMERICA
President's Commission on Law Enforcement and the Administration of Justice

The most natural and frequent question people ask about crime is "Why?" They ask it about individual crimes and about crime as a whole. In either case it is an almost impossible question to answer. Each single crime is a response to a specific situation by a person with an infinitely complicated psychological and emotional makeup who is subject to infinitely complicated external pressures. Crime as a whole is millions of such responses. To seek the "causes" of crime in human motivations alone is to risk losing one's way in the impenetrable thickets of the human psyche. Compulsive gambling was the cause of an embezzlement, one may say, or drug addiction the cause of a burglary or madness the cause of a homicide; but what caused the compulsion, the addiction, the madness? Why did they manifest themselves in those ways at those times?

There are some crimes so irrational, so unpredictable, so explosive, so resistant to analysis or explanation that they can no more be prevented or guarded against than earthquakes or tidal waves.

At the opposite end of the spectrum of crime are the carefully planned acts of professional criminals. The elaborately organized robbery of an armored car, the skillfully executed jewel theft, the murder of an informant by a Cosa Nostra "enforcer" are so deliberate, so calculated, so rational, that understanding the motivations of those who commit such crimes does

SOURCE: The President's Commission on Law Enforcement and Administration of Justice, *The Challenge of Crime in a Free Society* (Washington, D.C., 1967), pp. 17–53.

not show us how to prevent them. How to keep competent and intelligent men from taking up crime as a life work is as baffling a problem as how to predict and discourage sudden criminal outbursts.

To say this is not, of course, to belittle the efforts of psychiatrists and other behavioral scientists to identify and to treat the personality traits that are associated with crime. Such efforts are an indispensable part of understanding and controlling crime. Many criminals can be rehabilitated. The point is that looking at the personal characteristics of offenders is only one of many ways, and not always the most helpful way, of looking at crime.

It is possible to say, for example, that many crimes are "caused" by their victims. Often the victim of an assault is the person who started the fight, or the victim of an automobile theft is a person who left his keys in his car, or the victim of a loan shark is a person who lost his rent money at the race track, or the victim of a confidence man is a person who thought he could get rich quick. The relationship of victims to crimes is a subject that so far has received little attention. Many crimes, no matter what kind of people their perpetrators were, would not have been committed if their victims had understood the risks they were running.

From another viewpoint, crime is "caused" by public tolerance of it, or reluctance or inability to take action against it. Corporate and business— "white-collar"—crime is closely associated with a widespread notion that, when making money is involved, anything goes. Shoplifting and employee theft may be made more safe by their victims' reluctance to report to the police—often due to a recognition that the likelihood of detection and successful prosecution are negligible. Very often slum residents feel they live in territory that it is useless for them even to try to defend. Many slum residents feel overwhelmed and helpless in the face of the flourishing vice and crime around them; many have received indifferent treatment from the criminal justice system when they have attempted to do their duty as complainants and witnesses; many fear reprisals, especially victims of rackets. When citizens do not get involved, criminals can act with relative impunity.

In a sense, social and economic conditions "cause" crime. Crime flourishes, and always has flourished, in city slums, those neighborhoods where overcrowding, economic deprivation, social disruption and racial discrimination are endemic. Crime flourishes in conditions of affluence, when there is much desire for material goods and many opportunities to acquire them illegally. Crime flourishes when there are many restless, relatively footloose young people in the population. Crime flourishes when standards of morality are changing rapidly.

Finally, to the extent that the agencies of law enforcement and justice, and such community institutions as schools, churches and social service agencies, do not do their jobs effectively, they fail to prevent crime. If the police are inefficient or starved for manpower, otherwise preventable crimes will occur; if they are overzealous, people better left alone will be drawn into criminal careers. If the courts fail to separate the innocent from the guilty, the guilty may be turned loose to continue their depredations and the innocent may be criminalized. If the system fails to convict the guilty with reasonable certainty and promptness, deterrence of crime may be blunted. If correctional programs do not correct, a core of hardened and habitual criminals will continue to plague the community. If the community institutions that can shape the characters of young people do not take advantage of their opportunities, youth rebelliousness will turn into crime.

The causes of crime, then, are numerous and mysterious and intertwined. Even to begin to understand them, one must gather statistics about the amounts and trends of crime, estimate the costs of crime, study the conditions of life where crime thrives, identify criminals and the victims of crime, survey the public's attitudes toward crime. No one way of describing crime describes it well enough.

The Amount of Crime

There are more than 2800 Federal crimes and a much larger number of State and local ones. Some involve serious bodily harm, some stealing, some public morals or public order, some governmental revenues, some the creation of hazardous conditions, some the regulation of the economy. Some are perpetrated ruthlessly and systematically; others are spontaneous derelictions. Gambling and prostitution are willingly undertaken by both buyer and seller; murder and rape are violently imposed upon their victims. Vandalism is predominantly a crime of the young; driving while intoxicated, a crime of the adult. Many crime rates vary significantly from place to place.

The crimes that concern Americans the most are those that affect their personal safety—at home, at work, or in the streets. The most frequent and serious of these crimes of violence against the person are willful homicide, forcible rape, aggravated assault, and robbery. National statistics regarding the number of these offenses known to the police either from citizen complaints or through independent police discovery are collected from local police officials by the Federal Bureau of Investigation and published annually as a part of its report, "Crime in the United States, Uniform Crime Reports." The FBI also collects "offenses known" statistics for three property crimes: Burglary, larceny of $50 and over and motor vehicle theft. These seven crimes are grouped together in the UCR to form an Index of serious crimes.

THE RISK OF HARM

Including robbery, the crimes of violence make up approximately 13 percent of the Index. The Index reports the number of incidents known to the police, not the number of criminals who committed them or the number of injuries they caused.

The risk of sudden attack by a stranger is perhaps best measured by the frequency of robberies since, according to UCR and other studies, about 70 percent of all willful killings, nearly two-thirds of all aggravated assaults and a high percentage of forcible rapes are committed by family members, friends, or other persons previously known to their victims. Robbery usually does not involve this prior victim-offender relationship.

Robbery, for UCR purposes, is the taking of property from a person by use of threat of force with or without a weapon. Nationally, about one-half of all robberies are street robberies, and slightly more than one-half involve weapons. Attempted robberies are an unknown percentage of the robberies reported to the UCR. The likelihood of injury is also unknown, but a survey by the District of Columbia Crime Commission of 297 robberies in Washington showed that some injury was inflicted in 25 percent of them. The likelihood of injury was found higher for "yokings" or "muggings" (unarmed robberies from the rear) than for armed robberies. Injuries occurred in 10 of 91 armed robberies as compared with 30 of 67 yokings.

Aggravated assault is assault with intent to kill or for the purpose of inflicting severe bodily injury, whether or not a dangerous weapon is used. It includes all cases of attempted homicide, but cases in which bodily injury is inflicted in the course of a robbery or a rape are included with those crimes rather than with aggravated assault. There are no national figures showing the percentage of aggravated assaults that involve injury, but a survey of 131 cases by the District of Columbia Crime Commission found injury in 84 percent of the cases; 35 percent of the victims required hospitalization. A 1960 UCR study showed that juvenile gangs committed less than 4 percent of all aggravated assaults.

Forcible rape includes only those rapes or attempted rapes in which force or threat of force is used. About one-third of the UCR total is attempted rape. In a District of Columbia Crime Commission survey of 151 cases, about 25 percent of all rape victims were attacked with dangerous weapons; the survey did not show what percentage received bodily harm in addition to the rape.

About 15 percent of all criminal homicides, both nationally and in the District of Columbia Crime Commission surveys, occurred in the course of committing other offenses. These offenses appear in the homicide total rather than in the total for the other offense. In the District of Columbia Crime Commission surveys, less than one-half of 1 percent of the robberies and about 1 percent of the forcible rapes ended in homicide.

Some personal danger is also involved in the property crimes. Burglary is the unlawful entering of a building to commit a felony of a theft, whether force is used or not. About half of all burglaries involve residences, but the statistics do not distinguish inhabited parts of houses from garages and similar outlying parts. About half of all residential burglaries are committed in daylight and about half at night. A UCR survey indicates that 32 percent of the entries into residences are made through unlocked doors or windows. When an unlawful entry results in a violent confrontation with the occupant, the offense is counted as a robbery rather than a burglary. Of course, even when no confrontation takes place there is often a risk of confrontation. Nationally such confrontations occur in only one-fortieth of all residential burglaries. They account for nearly one-tenth of all robberies.

In summary, these figures suggest that, on the average, the likelihood of a serious personal attack on any American in a given year is about 1 in 550; together with the studies available they also suggest that the risk of serious attack from spouses, family members, friends, or acquaintances is almost twice as great as it is from strangers on the street. Commission and other studies, moreover, indicate that the risks of personal harm are spread very unevenly. The actual risk for slum dwellers is considerably more; for most Americans it is considerably less.

Except in the case of willful homicide, where the figures describe the extent of injury as well as the number of incidents, there is no national data on the likelihood of injury from attack. More limited studies indicate that while some injury may occur in two-thirds of all attacks, the risk in a given year of injury serious enough to require any degree of hospitalization of any individual is about 1 in 3,000 on the average, and much less for most Americans. These studies also suggest that the injury inflicted by family members or acquaintances is likely to be more severe than that from strangers. The risk of death from willful homicide is about 1 in 20,000.

Criminal behavior accounts for a high percentage of motor vehicle deaths and injuries. In 1965 there were an estimated 49,000 motor vehicle deaths. Negligent manslaughter, which is largely a motor vehicle offense, accounted for more than 7,000 of these. Studies in several States indicate that an even higher percentage involve criminal behavior. They show that driving while intoxicated is probably involved in more than one-half of all motor vehicle deaths. These same studies show that driving while intoxicated is involved in more than 13 percent of the 1,800,000 nonfatal motor vehicle injuries each year.

For various statistical and other reasons, a number of serious crimes against or involving risk to the person, such as arson, kidnapping, child molestation, and simple assault, are not included in the UCR Index. In a study of 1,300 cases of delinquency in Philadelphia, offenses other than the seven Index crimes constituted 62 percent of all cases in which there was physical injury. Simple assault accounted for the largest percentage of these injuries. But its victims required medical attention in only one-fifth of the cases as opposed to three-fourths of the aggravated assaults, and hospitalization in 7 percent as opposed to 23 percent. Injury was more prevalent in conflicts between persons of the same age than in those in which the victim was older or younger than the attacker.

PROPERTY CRIMES

The three property crimes of burglary, automobile theft, and larceny of $50 and over make up 87 percent of Index crimes. The Index is a reasonably reliable indicator of the total number of property crimes reported to the police, but not a particularly good indicator of the seriousness of monetary loss from all property crimes. Commission studies tend to indicate that such non-Index crimes as fraud and embezzlement are more significant in terms of dollar volume. Fraud can be a particularly pernicious offense. It is not only expensive in total but all too often preys on the weak.

Many larcenies included in the Index total are misdemeanors rather than felonies under the laws of their own States. Auto thefts that involve only unauthorized use also are misdemeanors in many States. Many stolen automobiles are abandoned after a few hours, and more than 85 percent are ultimately recovered according to UCR studies. Studies in California indicate that about 20 percent of recovered cars are significantly damaged.

OTHER CRIMINAL OFFENSES

The seven crimes for which all offenses known are reported were selected in 1927 and modified in 1958 by a special advisory committee of the International Association of Chiefs and Police on the basis of their serious nature, their frequency, and the reliability of reporting from citizens to police. In 1965 reporting for these offenses included information supplied voluntarily by some 8,000 police agencies covering nearly 92 percent of the total population. The FBI tries vigorously to increase the number of jurisdictions that report each year and to promote uniform reporting and classification of the reported offenses.

The UCR Index does not and is not intended to assist in assessing al serious national crime problems. For example, offense statistics are not sufficient to assess the incidence of crime connected with corporate activity, commonly known as white-collar crime, or the total criminal acts committed by organized crime groups. Likewise, offense and arrest figures alone do not aid very much in analyzing the scope of professional crime—that is, the number and types of offenses committed by those whose principal employment and source of income are based upon the commission of criminal acts.

Except for larceny under $50 and negligent manslaughter, for which there are some national offenses-known-to-the-police data, knowledge of the volume and trends of non-Index crimes depends upon arrest statistics. Since the police are not able to make arrests in many cases, these are necessarily less complete than the "offenses known" statistics. Moreover, the ratio between arrests and the number of offenses differs significantly from offense to offense—as is shown, for example, by the high percentage of reported cases in which arrests are made for murder (91 percent) and the relatively low percentage for larceny (20 percent). Reporting to the FBI for arrests covers less than 70 percent of the population. However, because arrest statistics are collected for a broader range of offenses—28 categories including the Index crimes—they show more of the diversity and magnitude of the many different crime problems. Property crimes do not loom so large in this picture.

Nearly 45 percent of all arrests are for such crimes without victims or against the public order as drunkenness, gambling, liquor law violations, vagrancy, and prostitution. Drunkenness alone accounts for almost one-third of all arrests. This is not necessarily a good indication of the number of persons arrested for drunkenness, however, as some individuals may be arrested many times during the year. Arrest statistics measure the number of arrests, not the number of criminals.

FEDERAL CRIMES

More than 50 percent of all Federal criminal offenses relate to general law enforcement in territorial or maritime jurisdictions directly subject to Federal control, or are also State offenses (bank robberies, for example). Police statistics for these offenses are normally reported in the UCR, particularly when local law enforcement is involved. Such other Federal crimes as antitrust violations, food and drug violations and tax evasion are not included in the UCR.

THE EXTENT OF UNREPORTED CRIME

Although the police statistics indicate a lot of crime today, they do not begin to indicate the full amount. Crimes reported directly to prosecutors usually do not show up in the police statistics. Citizens often do not report crimes to the police. Some crimes reported to the police never get into the statistical system. Since better crime prevention and control programs depend upon a full and accurate knowledge about the amount and kinds of crime, the Commission initiated the first national survey ever made of crime victimization. The National Opinion Research Center of the University of Chicago surveyed 10,000 households, asking whether the person questioned, or any member of his or her household, had been a victim of crime during the past year, whether the crime had been reported and, if not, the reasons for not reporting.

More detailed surveys were undertaken in a number of high and medium crime rate precincts of Washington, Chicago, and Boston by the Bureau of Social Science Research of Washington, D.C., and the Survey Research Center of the University of Michigan. All of the surveys dealt primarily with households or individuals, although some data were obtained for certain kinds of businesses and other organizations.

These surveys show that the actual amount of crime in the United States today is several times that reported in the UCR. The amount of personal injury crime reported to NORC is almost twice the UCR rate and the amount of property crime more than twice as much as the UCR rate for individuals. Forcible rapes were more than 3½ times the reported rate, burglaries three times, aggravated assaults and larcenies of $50 and over more than double, and robbery 50 percent greater than the reported rate. Only vehicle theft was lower and then by a small amount. (The single homicide reported is too small a number to be statistically useful.)

Even these rates probably understate the actual amounts of crime. The national survey was a survey of the victim experience of every member of a household based on interviews of one member. If the results are tabulated only for the family member who was interviewed, the amount of unreported victimization for some offenses is considerably higher. Apparently, the person interviewed remembered more of his own victimization than that of other members of his family.

The Washington, Boston, and Chicago surveys, based solely on victimization of the person interviewed, show even more clearly the disparity between reported and unreported amounts of crime. The clearest case is that of the survey in three Washington precincts, where, for the purpose of comparing survey results with crimes reported to the police, previous special studies made it possible to eliminate from police statistics crimes involving business and transient victims. For certain specific offenses against individuals the number of offenses reported to the survey per thousand residents 18 years or over ranged, depending on the offense, from 3 to 10 times more than the number contained in police statistics.

The survey in Boston and in one of the Chicago precincts indicated about three times as many Index crimes as the police statistics, in the other Chicago precinct about 1½ times as many. These survey rates are not fully comparable with the Washington results because adequate information did not exist for eliminating business and transient victims from the police statistics. If this computation could have been made, the Boston and Chicago figures would undoubtedly have shown a closer similarity to the Washington findings.

In the national survey of households those victims saying that they had not notified the police of their victimization were asked why. The reason most frequently given for all offenses was that the police could not do anything. As table 5 shows, this reason was given by 68 percent of those not reporting malicious mischief, and by 60 or more percent of those not reporting burglaries, larcenies of $50 and over, and auto thefts. It is not clear whether these responses are accurate assessments of the victims' inability to help the police or merely rationalizations of their failure to report. The next most frequent reason was that the offense was a private matter or that the victim did not want to harm the offender. It was given by 50 percent or more of those who did not notify the police for aggravated and simple assaults, family crimes, and consumer frauds. Fear of reprisal, though least often cited, was strongest in the case of assaults and family crimes. The extent of failure to report to the police was highest for consumer fraud (90 percent) and lowest for auto theft (11 percent). . . .

There has always been too much crime. Virtually every generation since the founding of the Nation and before has felt itself threatened by the spectre of rising crime and violence.

A hundred years ago contemporary accounts of San Francisco told of extensive areas where "no decent man was in safety to walk the street after dark; while at all hours, both night and day, his property was jeopardized by incendiarism and burglary." Teenage gangs gave rise to the word "hoodlum"; while in one central New York City area, near Broadway, the police entered "only in pairs, and never unarmed." A noted chronicler of the period delcared that "municipal law is a failure * * * we must soon fall back on the law of self preservation." "Alarming" increases in robbery and violent crimes were reported throughout the country prior to the Revolution. And in 1910 one author declared that "crime, especially its more violent forms, and among the young is increasing steadily and is threatening to bankrupt the Nation."

Crime and violence in the past took many forms. During the great railway strike of 1877 hundreds were killed across the country and almost 2 miles of railroad cars and buildings were burned in Pittsburgh in clashes between strikers and company police and the militia. It was nearly a half century later, after pitched battles in the steel industry in the late thirties, that the Nation's long history of labor violence subsided. The looting and takeover of New York for 3 days by mobs in the 1863 draft riots rivaled the violence of Watts, while racial disturbances in Atlanta in 1907, in Chicago, Washington, and East St. Louis in 1919, Detroit in 1943 and New York in 1900, 1935, and 1943 marred big city life in the first half of the 20th century. Lynchings took the lives of more than 4,500 persons throughout the country between 1882 and 1930. And the violence of Al Capone and Jesse James was so striking that they have left their marks permanently on our understanding of the eras in which they lived.

However, the fact that there has always been a lot of crime does not mean that the amount of crime never changes. It changes constantly, day and night, month to month, place to place. It is essential that society be able to tell when changes occur and what they are, that it be able to distinguish normal ups and downs from long-term trends. Whether the amount of crime is increasing or decreasing, and by how much, is an important question—for law enforcement, for the individual citizen who must run the risk of crime, and for the official who must plan and establish prevention and control programs. If it is true, as the Commission surveys tend to indicate, that society has not yet found fully reliable methods for measuring the volume of crime, it is even more true that it has failed to find such methods for measuring the trend of crime.

Unlike some European countries, which have maintained national statistics for more than a century and a quarter, the United States has maintained national crime statistics only since 1930. Because the rural areas were slow in coming into the system and reported poorly when they did, it was not until 1958, when other major changes were made in the UCR, that reporting of rural crimes was sufficient to allow a total national estimate without special adjustments. Changes in overall estimating procedures and two offense categories—rape and larceny—were also made in 1958. Because of these problems figures prior to 1958 and particularly those prior to 1940, must be viewed as neither fully comparable with nor nearly so reliable as later figures.

For crimes of violence the 1933–65 period, based on newly adjusted unpublished figures from the UCR, has been one of sharply divergent trends for the different offenses. Total numbers for all reported offenses have increased markedly; the Nation's population has increased also—by more than 47 percent since 1940. The number of offenses per 100,000 population has tripled for forcible rape and has doubled for aggravated assault during the period, both increasing at a fairly constant pace. The willful homicide rate has decreased somewhat to about 70 percent of its high in 1933, while robbery has fluctuated from a high in 1933 and a low during World War II to a point where it is now about 20 percent above the beginning of the postwar era. The overall rate for violent crimes, primarily due to the increased rate for aggravated assault, now stands at its highest point, well above what it has been throughout most of the period.

Property crime rates are up much more sharply than the crimes of violence. The rate for larceny of $50 and over has shown the greatest increase of all Index offenses. It is up more than 550 percent over 1933. The burglary rate has nearly doubled. The rate for auto theft has followed an uneven course to a point about the same as the rate of the early thirties.

The upward trend for 1960–65 has been faster than the long-term trend, up 25 percent for the violent crimes and 36 percent for the property crimes. The greatest increases in the period came in 1964, in forcible rape among crimes of violence and in vehicle theft among property crimes. . . .

The picture portrayed by the official statistics in recent years, both in the total number of crimes and in the number of crimes per 100,000 Americans, is one of increasing crime. Crime always seems to be increasing, never going down. Up 5 percent this year, 10 the next, and the Commission's surveys have shown there is a great deal more crime than the official statistics show. The public can fairly wonder whether there is ever to be an end.

This official picture is also alarming because it seems so pervasive. Crimes of violence are up in both the biggest and smallest cities, in the suburbs as well as in the rural areas. The same is true for property crimes. Young people are being arrested in ever increasing numbers. Offense rates for most crimes are rising every year and in every section of the country. That there are some bright spots does not change this dismal outlook. Rates for some offenses are still below those of the early thirties and perhaps of earlier periods. Willful homicide rates have been below the 1960 level through most of the last few years. Robbery rates continue to decline in the rural areas and small towns, and arrest rates for many non-Index offenses have remained relatively stable. . . .

The Economic Impact of Crime

One way in which crime affects the lives of all Americans is that it costs all Americans money. Economic costs alone cannot determine attitudes about crime or policies toward crime, of course. The costs of lost or damaged lives, of fear and of suffering, and of the failure to control critical events cannot be measured solely in dollars and cents. Nor can the requirements of justice and law enforcement be established solely by use of economic measures. A high percentage of a police department's manpower may have to be committed to catch a single murderer or bombthrower. The poor, unemployed defendant in a minor criminal case is entitled to all the protections our constitutional system provides—without regard to monetary costs.

However, economic factors relating to crime are important in the formation of attitudes and policies. Crime in the United States today imposes a very heavy economic burden upon both the community as a whole and individual members of it. Risks and responses cannot be judged with maximum effectiveness until the full extent of economic loss has been ascertained. Researchers, policymakers, and operating agencies should know which crimes cause the greatest economic loss, which the least; on whom the costs of crime fall, and what the costs are to prevent or protect against it; whether a particular or general crime situation warrants further expenditures for control or prevention and, if so, what expenditures are likely to have the greatest impact.

The number of policemen, the size of a plant security staff, or the amount of insurance any individual or business carries are controlled to some degree by economics—the balance of the value to be gained against the burden of additional expenditures. If the protection of property is the objective, the economic loss from crime must be weighed directly against the cost of better prevention or control. In view of the importance and the frequency of such decisions, it is surprising that the cost information on which they are based is as fragmentary as it is. The lack of knowledge about which the Wickersham Commission complained 30 years ago is almost as great today.

Some cost data are now reported through the UCR and additional data are available from individual police forces, insurance companies, industrial security firms, trade associations, and others. However, the total amount of information is not nearly enough in quantity, quality, or detail to give an accurate overall picture.

The information available about the economic cost of crime is most usefully presented not as an overall figure, but as a series of separate private and public costs. Knowing the economic impact of each separate crime aids in identifying important areas for public concern and guides officials in making judgments about priorities for expenditure. Breakdowns of money now being spent on different parts of the criminal justice system, and within each separate part, may afford insights into past errors. For example, even excluding value judgments about rehabilitative methods, the fact that an adult probationer costs 38 cents a day and an adult offender in prison costs $5.24 a day suggests the need for reexamining current budget allocations in correctional practice. . . .

ECONOMIC IMPACT OF INDIVIDUAL CRIMES

The picture of crime as seen through cost information is considerably different from that shown by statistics portraying the number of offenses known to the police or the number of arrests:

Organized crime takes about twice as much income from gambling and other illegal goods and services as criminals derive from all other kinds of criminal activity combined.

Unreported commercial theft losses, including shoplifting and employee theft, are more than double those of all reported private and commercial thefts.

Of the reported crimes, willful homicide, though comparatively low in volume, yields the most costly estimates among those listed on the UCR crime index.

A list of the seven crimes with the greatest economic impact includes only two, willful homicide and larceny of $50 and over (reported and unreported), of the offenses included in the crime Index.

Only a small proportion of the money expended for criminal justice agencies is allocated to rehabilitative programs for criminals or for research.

Employee theft, embezzlement, and other forms of crime involving business, which appear in relatively small numbers in the police statistics, loom very large in dollar volume. Direct stealing of cash and merchandise, manipulation of accounts and stock records, and other forms of these crimes, along with shoplifting, appear to constitute a tax of one to two percent on the total sales of retail enterprises, and significant amounts in other parts of business and industry. In the grocery trade, for example, the theft estimates for shoplifting and employee theft almost equal the total amount of profit. Yet Commission and other studies indicate that these crimes are largely dealt with by business itself. Merchants report to the police fewer than one-quarter of the known offenses. Estimates for these crimes are particularly incomplete for nonretail industries.

Fraud is another offense whose impact is not well conveyed by police statistics. Just one conspiracy involving the collapse of a fraudulent salad oil empire in 1964 created losses of $125–$175 million. Fraud is especially vicious when it attacks, as it so often does, the poor or those who live on the margin of poverty. Expensive nostrums for incurable diseases, home-improvement frauds, frauds involving the sale or repair of cars, and other criminal schemes create losses which are not only sizable in gross but are also significant and possibly devastating for individual victims. Although a very frequent offense, fraud is seldom reported to the police. In consumer and business fraud, as in tax evasion, the line between criminal conduct and civil fraud is often unclear. And just as the amount of civil tax evasion is much greater than the amount of criminal tax fraud, the amount of civil fraud probably far exceeds that of criminal fraud.

Cost analysis also places the crimes that appear so frequently in police statistics—robbery, burglary, larceny, and auto theft—in somewhat different perspective. The number of reported offenses for these crimes accounts for less than one-sixth the estimated total dollar loss for all property crimes and would constitute an even lower percentage if there were any accurate way of estimating the very large sums involved in extortion, blackmail, and other property crimes.

This is not to say, however, that the large amounts of police time and effort spent in dealing with these crimes are not important. Robbery and burglary, particularly residential burglary, have importance beyond the number of dollars involved. The effectiveness of the police in securing the return of better than 85 percent of the $500 million worth of cars stolen annually appears to be high, and without the efforts of the police the costs of these crimes would doubtless be higher. As with all categories of crime, the total cost of property crimes cannot be measured because of the large volume of unreported crimes; however, Commission surveys suggest that the crimes that are unreported involve less money per offense than those that are reported.

The economic impact of crimes causing death is surprisingly high. For 1965 there were an estimated 9,850 homicide victims. Of the estimated 49,000 people who lost their lives in highway accidents, more than half were killed in accidents involving either negligent manslaughter or driving under the influence of alcohol. An estimated 290 women died from complications resulting from illegal abortions (nearly one-fourth of all maternal deaths). Measured by the loss of future earnings at the time of death, these losses totaled more than $1½ billion.

The economic impact of other crimes is particularly difficult to assess. Antitrust violations reduce competition and unduly raise prices; building code violations, pure food and drug law violations, and other crimes affecting the consumer have important economic consequences, but they cannot be easily described without further information. Losses due to fear of crime, such as reduced sales in high crime locations, are real but beyond measure.

Economic impact must also be measured in terms of ultimate costs to society. Criminal acts causing property destruction or injury to persons not only result in serious losses to the victims or their families but also the withdrawal of wealth or productive capacity from the economy as a whole. Theft on the other hand does not destroy wealth but merely transfers it involuntarily from the victim, or perhaps his insurance company, to the thief. The bettor purchasing illegal betting services from organized crime may easily absorb the loss of a 10-cent, or even 10-dollar, bet. But from the point of view of society, gambling leaves much less wealth available for legitimate business. Perhaps more important, it is the proceeds of this crime tariff that organized crime collects from those who purchase its illegal wares that form the major source of income that organized crime requires to achieve and exercise economic and political power.

Crime and the Inner City

One of the most fully documented facts about crime is that the common serious crimes that worry people most—murder, forcible rape, robbery, aggravated assault, and burglary—happen most often in the slums of large cities. Study after study in city after city in all regions of the country have traced the variations in the rates for these crimes. The results, with monotonous regularity, show that the offenses, the victims, and the offenders are found most frequently in the poorest, and most deteriorated and socially disorganized areas of cities.

Studies of the distribution of crime rates in cities and of the conditions of life most commonly associated with high crime rates have been conducted for well over a century in Europe and for many years in the United States. The findings have been remarkably consistent. Burglary, robbery, and serious assaults occur in areas characterized by low income, physical deterioration, dependency, racial and ethnic concentrations, broken homes, working mothers, low levels of education and vocational skill, high unemployment, high proportions of single males, overcrowded and substandard housing, high rates of tuberculosis and infant mortality, low rates of home ownership or single family dwellings, mixed land use, and high population density. Studies that have mapped the relationship of these factors and crime have found them following the same pattern from one area of the city to another.

Crime rates in American cities tend to be highest in the city center and decrease in relationship to distance from the center. This typical distribution of crime rates is found even in medium sized cities. This pattern has been found to hold fairly well for both offenses and offenders, although it is sometimes broken by unusual features of geography, enclaves of socially well integrated ethnic groups, irregularities in the distribution of opportunities to commit crime, and unusual concentrations of commercial and industrial establishments in outlying areas. The major irregularity found is the clustering of offenses and offenders beyond city boundaries in satellite areas that are developing such characteristics of the central city as high population mobility, commercial and industrial concentrations, low economic status, broken families and other social problems. A detailed discussion of the relationship of crime to the conditions of inner-city life appears in chapter 3 of this report, in connection with programs aimed at reducing juvenile delinquency.

The big city slum has always exacted its toll on its inhabitants, except where those inhabitants are bound together by an intense social and cultural solidarity that provides a collective defense against the pressures of slum living. Several slum settlements inhabited by people of oriental ancestry have shown a unique capacity to do this. However, the common experience of the great successive waves of immigrants of different racial and ethnic backgrounds that have poured into the poorest areas of our large cities has been quite different.

An historic series of studies by Clifford R. Shaw and Henry D. McKay of the Institute of Juvenile Research in Chicago documented the disorganizing impact of slum life on different groups of immigrants as they moved through the slums and struggled to gain a foothold in the economic and social life of the city. Throughout the period of immigration, areas with high delinquency and crime rates kept these high rates, even though members of new nationality groups successively moved in to displace the older residents. Each nationality group showed high rates of delinquency among its members who were living near the center of the city and lower rates for those living in the better outlying residential areas. Also for each nationality group, those living in the poorer areas had more of all the other social problems commonly associated with life in the slums.

This same pattern of high rates in the slum neighborhoods and low rates in the better districts is true among the Negroes and members of other minority groups who have made up the most recent waves of migration to the big cities. As other groups before them, they have had to crowd into the areas where they can afford to live while they search for ways to live better. The disorganizing personal and social experiences with life in the slums are producing the same problems for the new minority group residents, including high rates of crime and delinquency. As they acquire a stake in urban society and move to better areas of the city, the crime rates and the incidence of other social problems drop to lower levels.

However, there are a number of reasons to expect more crime and related problems among the new migrants to the city than among the older immigrants. There have been major changes in the job market, greatly reducing the demand for unskilled labor, which is all most new migrants have to offer. At the same time the educational requirements for jobs have been rising. Discrimination in employment, education, and housing, based on such a visible criterion as color is harder to break than discrimination based on language or ethnic background.

What these changes add up to is that slums are becoming ghettos from which escape is increasingly difficult. It could be predicted that this frustration of the aspirations that originally led Negroes and other minority groups to seek out the city would ultimately lead to more crime. Such evidence as exists suggests this is true. . . .

The Victims of Crime

One of the most neglected subjects in the study of crime is its victims: the persons, households, and businesses that bear the brunt of crime in the United States. Both the part the victim can play in the criminal act and the part he could have played in preventing it are often overlooked. If it could be determined with sufficient specificity that people or businesses with certain characteristics are more likely than others to be crime victims, and that crime is more likely to occur in some places than in others, efforts to control and prevent crime would be more productive. Then the public could be told where and when the risks of crime are greatest. Measures such as preventive police patrol and installation of burglar alarms and special locks could then be pursued more efficiently and effectively. Individuals could then substitute objective estimation of risk for the general apprehensiveness that today restricts—perhaps unnecessarily and at best haphazardly—their enjoyment of parks and their freedom of movement on the streets after dark.

Although information about victims and their relationships to offenders is recorded in the case files of the police and other criminal justice agencies, it is rarely used for systematic study of those relationships or the risks of victimization. To discover variations in victimization rates among different age, sex, race, and income groupings in the population, the Commission analyzed information on these items obtained in the national survey by NORC.

Rather striking variations in the risk of victimization for different types of crime appear among different income levels in the population. The results shown in table 11 indicate that the highest rates of victimization occur in the lower income groups when all Index offenses except homicide are considered together. The risks of victimization from forcible rape, robbery, and burglary, are clearly concentrated in the lowest income group and decrease steadily at higher income levels. The picture is somewhat more erratic for the offenses of aggravated assault, larceny of $50 and over, and vehicle theft. Victimization for larceny increases sharply in the highest income group.

National figures on rates of victimization also show sharp differences between whites and nonwhites. Nonwhites are victimized disproportionately by all Index crimes except larceny $50 and over.

The rates of victimization shown for Index offenses against men are almost three times as great as those for women, but the higher rates of burglary, larceny and auto theft against men are in large measure an artifact of the survey procedure of assigning offenses against the household to the head of the household.

The victimization rate for women is highest in the 20 to 29 age group. In fact the victimization rates for women for all the Index offenses reported, with the exception of larceny, are greatest in this age group. The concentration of offenses against women in this age group is particularly noticeable for forcible rape and robbery and much less apparent in aggravated assault and the property crimes.

For men the highest Index total rate falls in the 30–39 age category, a result heavily influenced by the burglaries assigned to men as heads of households. Actually, all the Index property offenses against men show peak rates in the older age categories. This is probably due not only to their role as household heads but also to the fact that at older ages they are likely to possess more property to be stolen. Crimes against the person, such as aggravated assault and robbery, are committed relatively more often against men who are from 20 to 29 years of age.

Thus, the findings from the national survey show that the risk of victimization is highest among the lower income groups for all Index offenses except homicide, larceny, and vehicle theft; it weighs most heavily on the non-whites for all Index offenses except larceny; it is borne by men more often than women, except, of course, for forcible rape; and the risk is greatest for the age category 20 to 29, except for larceny against women, and burglary, larceny, and vehicle theft against men. . . .

Public Attitudes Towards Crime
and Law Enforcement

What America does about crime depends ultimately upon how Americans see crime. The government of a free society can act only in response to the desires of the governed. This is true in general and in detail. The Nation's overall effort against crime will be only as intense as the public demands that it be. The lines along which the Nation takes specific action against crime will be those that the public believes to be the necessary ones.

A chief reason that this Commission was organized was that there is widespread public anxiety about crime. In one sense, this entire report is an effort to focus that anxiety on the central problems of crime and criminal justice. A necessary part of that effort has been to study as carefully as possible the anxiety itself. The Commission has tried to find out precisely what aspects of crime Americans are anxious about, whether their anxiety is a realistic response to actual danger, how anxiety affects the daily lives of Americans, what actions against crime by the criminal justice system and the government as a whole might best allay public anxiety. It included questions about attitudes toward crime and law enforcement in the surveys of victimization it made, and it looked hard, as well, at those national opinion polls that asked questions about crime.

Before setting forth the results of these studies and discussing the conclusions that might be drawn from them, the Commission must make one general comment. There is reason to be alarmed about crime. In fact just because crime is alarming, those discussing it—and many people must discuss it often if it is ever to be controlled—have an obligation to be cool, factual, and precise. Thoughtless, emotional, or self-serving discussions of crime, especially by those who have the public's attention and can influence the public's thinking, are an immense disservice. They do not and cannot lead to significant action against crime. They can, and sometimes do, lead to panic.

PUBLIC CONCERN ABOUT CRIME

The public sees crime as one of the most serious of all domestic problems. The Commission's NORC survey asked citizens to pick from a list of six major domestic problems the one they were paying the most attention to. Crime was second to race relations as the most frequently mentioned problem, except in the case of nonwhites with annual incomes less than $6,000; they placed education second and crime third.

Crime is linked to other social problems by many people. In a 1964 Harris survey more people attributed increased crime in their neighborhood to "disturbed and restless teenagers" than to any other cause. A part of the crime problem that especially worries people is juvenile delinquency. A typical finding was reported by a Gallup poll in 1963. When persons were asked to name the top problems in their community from a list of 39 problems, "juvenile delinquency" was the second most frequent selection— exceeded only by complaints about local real estate taxes. Also related to the problems of youth was a third frequently chosen problem—the need for more recreation areas.

However, people are more inclined to think of crime in moral than in social terms. An August 1965 Gallup poll that asked people what they thought was responsible for the increase of crime found that most of the reasons people mentioned had to do directly with the moral character of the population rather than with changes in objective circumstances or with law enforcement. Over half of the answers fitted under the category "family, poor parental guidance." About 6 percent of the answers gave "breakdown of moral standards." A variety of other directly moral causes were given in addition, such as: "People expect too much," "people want something for nothing," and "communism." Relatively few (12 percent) of the responses cited objective conditions such as "unemployment," "poverty," "the automobile," or "the population explosion."

Public concern about crime is mounting. National polls by Harris and Gallup show that the majority of people think the situation in their own communities is getting worse, that a substantial minority think the situation is staying about the same, and that almost no one thinks the situation is improving. A Gallup survey in April 1965 showed that this pessimistic view of the crime trend was held by men and women of all ages, incomes, and degrees of education in all parts of the country. In July 1966, Harris surveys reported that in each recent year there has been an increase over the year before in the percent of persons worried about their personal safety on the streets.

PERSONAL FEAR OF CRIME

Perhaps the most intense concern about crime is the fear of being attacked by a stranger when out alone. One-third of Americans feel unsafe about walking alone at night in their own neighborhoods, according to the NORC survey. As one would expect, the percentage of people feeling unsafe at night on the street is, according to an April 1965 Gallup survey, higher in large cities than in smaller ones and higher in cities than in rural areas.

Recently studies have been undertaken to develop an index of delinquency based on the seriousness of different offenses. They have shown that there is widespread public consensus on the relative seriousness of different types of crimes and these rankings furnish useful indicators of the types of crime that the public is most concerned about. Offenses involving physical assaults against the person are the most feared crimes and the greatest concern is expressed about those in which a weapon is used.

A further index of the public concern about crime may be found in attitudes toward reporting crime when it occurs. Whether one reports a crime or not involves in many cases an assessment of the significance of the event to one's self or others. The results from the victim surveys indicate that the reporting of crime varies directly with a rough scale of seriousness of the offense in the public view. Other than vehicle theft, the crimes that are likely to be reported most frequently are crimes of violence, particularly those that cause great physical harm or psychological shock. Such acts as petty larceny, malicious mischief, and fraud, though the most frequent offenses as a group, are also considered the least serious and are the least likely to be reported to the police.

Fear of crime makes many people want to move their homes. In the four police precincts surveyed for the Commission in Boston and Chicago, 20 percent of the citizens wanted to move because of the crime in their neighborhoods, and as many as 30 percent wanted to move out of the highest crime rate district in Boston.

Fear of crime shows variations by race and income. In the survey in Washington, the Bureau of Social Science Research put together an index of anxiety about crime. It found that Negro women had the highest average score, followed by Negro men, white women, and white men. Anxiety scores were lower at the higher income levels for both Negroes and whites.

Fear of crime is not always highest in the areas where official crime rates are highest or where rates of victimization based on the survey findings are highest. For example, the BSSR Washington study found that the average level of concern with crime in a predominately Negro police precinct that has one of the highest crime rates in the city, according to police data, was lower than it was in another Negro precinct that had a very low rate relative to the first.

The surveys uniformly show that people feel safer in their own neighborhoods even if they actually have a higher crime rate than other areas. For example, the national survey revealed that crime is seen as a problem most characteristic of other places. Sixty percent of those questioned compared their own neighborhoods favorably to other parts of their communities with regard to the likelihood that their homes would be broken into. Only 14 percent thought their own neighborhoods were more dangerous. Similarly, two-thirds of the respondents said they felt safe walking alone after dark if they were in their own neighborhoods. On the other hand, when persons interviewed were asked whether there were places outside their neighborhoods where they would not feel personally safe, 53 percent said there were, and almost one-third of these respondents said they never go there.

A tendency to see the risk of victimization as greater in another neighborhood than one's own was also found among residents in high crime rate precincts by the BSSR survey in Washington. The surveys in Boston and Chicago showed that 73 percent of the respondents thought their own neighborhoods were very safe or average compared to other neighborhoods in relation to the chances of getting robbed, threatened, beaten up, or anything of that sort.

The NORC survey asked people whether there have been times recently when they wanted to go somewhere in town but stayed at home instead, because they thought it would be unsafe to go there. Sixteen percent of the respondents said that they had stayed home under these conditions. This type of reaction showed marked variation with race; one out of every three Negro respondents had stayed home as contrasted with one in eight whites.

People also take special measures at home because of the fear of unwanted intruders. The national survey showed that 82 percent of the respondents always kept their doors locked at night and 25 percent always kept their doors locked even in the daytime when the family members were at home. Twenty-eight percent kept watchdogs and 37 percent said they kept firearms in the house for protection, among other reasons.

The special city surveys disclosed that a substantial number of the people take other measures to protect themselves from crime. In Boston and Chicago 28 percent had put new locks on their doors primarily, as one might expect, because they had been victimized or were worried about the high crime rate in the area. Another 10 percent had put locks or bars on their windows; this occurred primarily in the highest crime rate areas. Nine percent said they carried weapons, usually knives, when they went out, and this figure rose to 19 percent in the highest crime rate district in Boston.

The close relationship between worry about crime and the taking of strong precautionary measures is further demonstrated by the results from the national survey. Respondents were asked how much they worried about being victimized by robbery or burglary and their responses were related to their tendency to take strong household security measures. Persons worried about both burglary and robbery are most likely to take such precautions, about 50 percent more likely than those who are worried about neither.

Perhaps the most revealing findings on the impact of fear of crime on people's lives were the changes people reported in their regular habits of life. In the high-crime districts surveyed in Boston and Chicago, for example, five out of every eight respondents reported changes in their habits because of fear of crime, some as many as four or five major changes. Forty-three percent reported they stayed off the streets at night altogether. Another 21 percent said they always used cars or taxis at night. Thirty-five percent said they would not talk to strangers any more.

One of the most curious findings of the surveys was that fear of crime is less closely associated with having been a victim of crime than might be supposed. The national survey showed that victims tended to have somewhat more worry about burglary or robbery. This was true for both males and females. However, females, whether they had been victimized or not, were more concerned about their safety than males. Furthermore, other data show that recent experience of being a victim of crime did not seem to increase behavior designed to protect the home. Almost identical proportions, 57 percent of victims and 58 percent of nonvictims, took strong household security measures.

In its Washington study BSSR found similar results. An index of exposure to crime was developed based on having personally witnessed offenses or on whether one's self or one's friends had been victimized. Scores on this index, in general, were not associated with responses to a variety of questions on attitudes toward crime and toward law enforcement that respondents were asked. Nor did exposure to crime appear to determine the anxiety about crime manifested in the interviews. The one exception appeared in the case of the Negro male. Negro men showed a tendency to be influenced in their attitudes and behavior by their actual exposure to crime.

CONCLUSIONS

The Commission cannot say that the public's fear of crime is exaggerated. It is not prepared to tell people how fearful they should be; that is something each person must decide for himself. People's fears must be respected; certainly they cannot be legislated. Some people are willing to run risks that terrify others. However, it is possible to draw some general conclusions from the findings of the surveys.

The first is that the public fears most the crimes that occur least often, crimes of violence. People are much more tolerant of crimes against property, which constitute most of the crimes that are committed against persons or households or businesses. Actually, the average citizen probably suffers the greatest economic loss from crimes against business establishments and public institutions, which pass their losses on to him in the form of increased prices and taxes. Nevertheless, most shoplifters never get to court; they are released by the store managers with warnings. Most employees caught stealing are either warned or discharged, according to the reports of businesses and organizations in the Commission's survey in three cities.

Second, the fear of crimes of violence is not a simple fear of injury or death or even of all crimes of violence, but, at bottom, a fear of strangers. The personal injury that Americans risk daily from sources other than crime are enormously greater. The annual rate of all Index offenses involving either violence or the threat of violence is 1.8 per 1,000 Americans. This is minute relative to the total accidental injuries calling for medical attention or restricted activity of 1 day or more, as reported by the Public Health Service. A recent study of emergency medical care found the quality, numbers, and distribution of ambulances and other emergency services severely deficient, and estimated that as many as 20,000 Americans die unnecessarily each year as a result of improper emergency care. The means necessary for correcting this situation are very clear and would probably yield greater immediate return in reducing death than would expenditures for reducing the incidence of crimes of violence. But a different personal significance is attached to deaths due to the willful acts of felons as compared to the incompetence or poor equipment of emergency medical personnel.

Furthermore, most murders and assaults are committed by persons known to the victim, by relatives, friends, or acquaintances. Indeed on a straight statistical basis, the closer the relationship the greater the hazard. In one sense the greatest threat to anyone is himself, since suicides are more than twice as common as homicides.

Third, this fear of strangers has greatly impoverished the lives of many Americans, especially those who live in high-crime neighborhoods in large cities. People stay behind the locked doors of their homes rather than risk walking in the streets at night. Poor people spend money on taxis because they are afraid to walk or use public transportation. Sociable people are afraid to talk to those they do not know. In short, society is to an increasing extent suffering from what economists call "opportunity costs" as the result of crime. For example, administrators and officials interviewed for the Commission by the University of Michigan survey team, report that library use is decreasing because borrowers are afraid to come out at night. School officials told of parents not daring to attend PTA meetings in the evening, and park administrators pointed to unused recreation facilities. When many persons stay home, they are not availing themselves of the opportunities for pleasure and cultural enrichment offered in their communities, and they are not visiting their friends as frequently as they might. The general level of social interaction in the society is reduced.

When fear of crime becomes fear of the stranger the social order is further damaged. As the level of sociability and mutual trust is reduced, streets and public places can indeed become more dangerous. Not only will there be fewer people abroad but those who are abroad will manifest a fear of and a lack of concern for each other. The reported incidents of bystanders indifferent to cries for help are the logical consequence of a reduced sociability, mutual distrust and withdrawal.

However, the most dangerous aspect of a fear of strangers is its implication that the moral and social order of society are of doubtful trustworthiness and stability. Everyone is dependent on this order to instill in all members of society a respect for the persons and possessions of others. When it appears that there are more and more people who do not have this respect, the security that comes from living in an orderly and trustworthy society is undermined. The tendency of many people to think of crime in terms of increasing moral deterioration is an indication that they are losing their faith in their society. And so the costs of the fear of crime to the social order may ultimately be even greater than its psychological costs to individuals.

Fourth, the fear of crime may not be as strongly influenced by the actual incidence of crime as by other experiences with the crime problem generally. For example, the mass media and overly zealous or opportunistic crime fighters may play a role in raising fears of crime by associating the idea of "crime" with a few sensational and terrifying criminal acts. Past research on the mass media's connection with crime has concentrated primarily on depictions and accounts of violence in the mass media as possible causes of delinquency and crime. Little attention has thus far been given to what may be a far more direct and costly effect—the creation of distorted perceptions of the risk of crime and exaggerated fears of victimization.

The greatest danger of an exaggerated fear of crime may well reside in the tendency to use the violent crime as a stereotype for crimes in general. For example, there may be a significant interplay between violence and the mass media and the reporting of general crime figures. Publicity about total crime figures without distinguishing between the trends for property crime and those for crimes against persons may create mistaken ideas about what is actually happening. If burglaries and larcenies increase sharply while violent crimes decrease or remain stable, the total figures will follow the property crime figures, since crimes against property are more than four-fifths of the total. Yet under these conditions people may interpret the increases in terms of the dominant stereotype of crimes of violence, thus needlessly increasing their fears. They may not only restrict their activities out of an exaggerated fear of violence but may fail to protect themselves against the more probable crimes. The fact is that most people experience crime vicariously through the daily press, periodicals, novels, radio and television, and often the reported experiences of other persons. Their fear of crime may be more directly related to the quality and the amount of this vicarious experience than it is to the actual risks of victimization.

The Commission believes that there is a clear public responsibility to keep citizens fully informed of the facts about crime so that they will have facts to go on when they decide what the risks are and what kinds and amounts of precautionary measures they should take. Furthermore, without an accurate understanding of the facts, they cannot judge whether the interference with individual liberties which strong crime control measures may involve is a price worth paying. The public obligation to citizens is to provide this information regularly and accurately. And if practices for disseminating information give wrong impressions, resources should be committed to developing more accurate methods.

Finally, public concern about crime need not have only the adverse effects that have been described so far. It can be a powerful force for action. However, making it one will not be easy. The Commission's Washington survey asked people whether they had ever "gotten together with other people around here, or has any group or organization you belong to met and discussed the problem of crime or taken some sort of action to combat crime." Only about 12 percent answered affirmatively, although the question was quite broad and included any kind of group meeting or discussion. Neither did most persons believe that they as individuals could do anything about crime in their own neighborhoods. Only slightly over 17 percent thought that they could do either a lot or just something.

Most people feel that the effort to reduce crime is a responsibility of the police, the courts and perhaps other public agencies. This was even true to some extent of administrators and officials of public agencies and utilities who were interviewed in the three city precinct surveys. However, when these officials were pressed they were able to think of many ways in which their organizatons might help reduce crime, such as cooperating to make law enforcement easier, donating and helping in neighborhood programs, providing more and better street lighting, creating more parks with recreational programs, furnishing more youth programs and adult education, and promoting integration of work crews and better community relations programs.

WINCANTON: THE POLITICS OF CORRUPTION
John A. Gardiner

Introduction

This study focuses upon the politics of vice and corruption in a town we have chosen to call Wincanton, U.S.A. Although the facts and events of this report are true, every attempt has been made to hide the identity of actual people by the use of fictitious names, descriptions and dates.

SOURCE: The President's Commission on Law Enforcement and Administration of Justice, *Task Force Report: Organized Crime* (Washington, D.C., 1967), pp. 61–79. This essay was written with the assistance of David J. Olson.

Following a brief description of the people of Wincanton and the structure of its government and law enforcement agencies, a section outlines the structure of the Wincanton gambling syndicate and the system of protection under which it operated. A second section looks at the corrupt activities of Wincanton officials apart from the protection of vice and gambling.

The latter part of this report considers gambling and corruption as social forces and as political issues. First, they are analyzed in terms of their functions in the communtiy—satisfying social and psychological needs declared by the State to be improper; supplementing the income of the participants, including underpaid city officials and policemen, and of related legitimate businesses; providing speed and certainty in the transaction of municipal business. Second, popular attitudes toward gambling and corruption are studied, as manifested in both local elections and a survey of a cross-section of the city's population. Finally, an attempt will be made to explain why Wincanton, more than other cities, has had this marked history of lawbreaking and official malfeasance, and several suggestions will be made regarding legal changes that might make its continuation more difficult.

Wincanton

In general, Wincanton represents a city that has toyed with the problem of corruption for many years. No mayor in the history of the city of Wincanton has ever succeeded himself in office. Some mayors have been corrupt and have allowed the city to become a wide-open center for gambling and prostitution; Wincanton voters have regularly rejected those corrupt mayors who dared to seek reelection. Some mayors have been scrupulously honest and have been generally disliked for being too straitlaced. Other mayors, fearing one form of resentment or the other, have chosen quietly to retire from public life. The questions of official corruption and policy toward vice and gambling, it seems, have been paramount issues in Wincanton elections since the days of Prohibition. Any mayor who is known to be controlled by the gambling syndicates will lose office, but so will any mayor who tries completely to clean up the city. The people of Wincanton apparently want both easily accessible gambling and freedom from racket domination.

Probably more than most cities in the United States, Wincanton has known a high degree of gambling, vice (sexual immorality, including prostitution), and corruption (official malfeasance, misfeasance and nonfeasance of duties). With the exception of two reform administrations, one in the early 1950's and the one elected in the early 1960's, Wincanton has been wide open since the 1920's. Bookies taking bets on horses took in several millions of dollars each year. With writers at most newsstands, cigar counters, and corner grocery stores, a numbers bank did an annual business in excess of $1,300,000 during some years. Over 200 pinball machines, equipped to pay off like slot machines, bore $250 Federal gambling stamps. A high stakes dice game attracted professional gamblers from more than 100 miles away; $25,000 was found on the table during one Federal raid. For a short period of time in the 1950's (until raided by U.S. Treasury Department agents), a still, capable of manufacturing $4 million in illegal alcohol each year, operated on the banks of the Wincanton River. Finally, prostitution flourished openly in the city, with at least 5 large houses (about 10 girls apiece) and countless smaller houses catering to men from a large portion of the State.

As in all cities in which gambling and vice had flourished openly, these illegal activities were protected by local officials. Mayors, police chiefs, and many lesser officials were on the payroll of the gambling syndicate, while others received periodic "gifts" or aid during political campaigns. A number of Wincanton officials added to their revenue from the syndicate by extorting kickbacks on the sale or purchase of city equipment or by selling licenses, permits, zoning variances, etc. As the city officials made possible the operations of the racketeers, so frequently the racketeers facilitated the corrupt endeavors of officials by providing liaison men to arrange the deals or "enforcers" to insure that the deals were carried out.

The visitor to Wincanton is struck by the beauty of the surrounding countryside and the drabness of a tired, old central city. Looking down on the city from Mount Prospect, the city seems packed in upon itself, with long streets of red brick row houses pushing up against old railroad yards and factories; 93 percent of the housing units were built before 1940.

Wincanton had its largest population in 1930 and has been losing residents slowly ever since.[2] The people who remained—those who didn't move to the suburbs or to the other parts of the United States—are the lower middle class, the less well educated; they seem old and often have an Old World feeling about them. The median age in Wincanton is 37 years (compared with a national median of 29 years). While unemployment is low (2.5 percent of the labor force in April 1965), there are few professional or white collar workers; only 11 percent of the families had incomes over $10,000, and the median family income was $5,453. As is common in many cities with an older, largely working class population, the level of education is low —only 27 percent of the adults have completed high school, and the median number of school years completed is 8.9.

While most migration into Wincanton took place before 1930, the various nationality groups in Wincanton seem to have retained their separate identities. The Germans, the Poles, the Italians, and the Negroes each have their own neighborhoods, stores, restaurants, clubs and politicians. Having immigrated earlier, the Germans are more assimilated into the middle and upper middle classes; the other groups still frequently live in the neighborhoods in which they first settled; and Italian and Polish politicans openly appeal to Old World loyalties. Club life adds to the ethnic groupings by giving a definite neighborhood quality to various parts of the city and their politics; every politician is expected to visit the ethnic associations, ward clubs, and voluntary firemen's associations during campaign time—buying a round of drinks for all present and leaving money with the club stewards to hire poll watchers to advertise the candidates and guard the voting booths.

In part, the flight from Wincanton of the young and the more educated can be explained by the character of the local economy. While there have been no serious depressions in Wincanton during the last 30 years, there has been little growth either, and most of the factories in the city were built 30 to 50 years ago and rely primarily upon semiskilled workers. A few textile mills have moved out of the region, to be balanced by the construction in the last 5 years of several electronics assembly plants. No one employer dominates the economy, although seven employed more than 1,000 persons. Major industries today include steel fabrication and heavy machinery, textiles and food products.

With the exception of 2 years (one in the early 1950's; the other 12 years later) in which investigations of corruption led to the election of Republican reformers, Wincanton politics have been heavily Democratic in recent years. Registered Democrats in the city outnumber Republicans by a margin of 2 to 1; in Alsace County as a whole, including the heavily Republican middle class suburbs, the Democratic margin is reduced to 3 to 2. Despite this margin of control, or possibly because of it, Democratic politics in Wincanton have always been somewhat chaotic—candidates appeal to the ethnic groups, clubs, and neighborhoods, and no machine or organization has been able to dominate the party for very long (although a few men have been able to build a personal following lasting for 10 years or so). Incumbent mayors have been defeated in the primaries by other Democrats, and voting in city council sessions has crossed party lines more often than it has respected them.

To a great extent, party voting in Wincanton follows a business-labor cleavage. Two newspapers (both owned by a group of local businessmen) and the Chamber of Commerce support Republican candidates; the unions usually endorse Democrats. It would be unwise, however, to overestimate either the solidarity or the interest in local politics of Wincanton business and labor groups. Frequently two or more union leaders may be opposing each other in a Democratic primary (the steelworkers frequently endorse liberal or reform candidates, while the retail clerks have been more tied to "organization" men); or ethnic allegiances and hostilities may cause union members to vote for Republicans, or simply sit on their hands. Furthermore, both business and labor leaders express greater interest in State and National issues—taxation, wage and hour laws, collective bargaining policies, etc.—than in local issues. (The attitude of both business and labor toward Wincanton gambling and corruption will be examined in detail later.)

Many people feel that, apart from the perennial issue of corruption, there really are not any issues in Wincanton politics and that personalities are the only things that matter in city elections. Officials assume that the voters are generally opposed to a high level of public services. Houses are tidy, but the city has no public trash collection, or fire protection either, for that matter. While the city buys firetrucks and pays their drivers, firefighting is done solely by volunteers—in a city with more than 75,000 residents. (Fortunately, most of the houses are built of brick or stone.) Urban renewal has been slow, master planning nonexistent, and a major railroad line still crosses the heart of the shopping district, bringing traffic to a halt as trains grind past. Some people complain, but no mayor has ever been able to do anything about it. For years, people have been talking about rebuilding City Hall (constructed as a high school 75 years ago), modernizing mass transportation, and ending pollution of the Wincanton River, but nothing much has been done about any of these issues, or even seriously considered. Some people explain this by saying that Wincantonites are interested in everything—up to and including, but not extending beyond, their front porch.

If the voters of Wincanton were to prefer an active rather than passive city government, they would find the municipal structure well equipped to frustrate their desires. Many governmental functions are handled by independent boards and commissions, each able to veto proposals of the mayor and councilmen. Until about 10 years ago, State law required all middle-sized cities to operate under a modification of the commission form of government. (In the early 1960's, Wincanton voters narrowly—by a margin of 16 votes out of 30,000—rejected a proposal to set up a council-manager plan.) The city council is composed of five men—a mayor and four councilmen. Every odd-numbered year, two councilmen are elected to 4-year terms. The mayor also has a 4-year term of office, but has a few powers not held by the councilmen; he presides at council sessions but has no veto power over council legislation. State law requires that city affairs be divided among five named departments, each to be headed by a member of the council, but the council members are free to decide among themselves what functions will be handled by which departments (with the proviso that the mayor must control the police department). Thus the city's work can be split equally among five men, or a three-man majority can control all important posts. In a not atypical recent occurrence, one councilman, disliked by his colleagues, found himself supervising only garbage collection and the Main Street comfort station! Each department head (mayor and councilmen) has almost complete control over his own department. Until 1960, when a $2,500 raise became effective, the mayor received an annual salary of $7,000, and each councilman received $6,000. The mayor and city councilmen have traditionally been permitted to hold other jobs while in office.

To understand law enforcement in Wincanton, it is necessary to look at the activities of local, county, State, and Federal agencies. State law requires that each mayor select his police chief and officers "from the force" and "exercise a constant supervision and control over their conduct." Applicants for the police force are chosen on the basis of a civil service examination and have tenure "during good behavior," but promotions and demotions are entirely at the discretion of the mayor and council. Each new administration in Wincanton has made wholesale changes in police ranks —patrolmen have been named chief, and former chiefs have been reduced to walking a beat. (When one period of reform came to an end in the mid-1950's, the incoming mayor summoned the old chief into his office. "You can stay on as an officer," the mayor said, "but you'll have to go along with my policies regarding gambling." "Mr. Mayor," the chief said, "I'm going to keep on arresting gamblers no matter where you put me." The mayor assigned the former chief to the position of "Keeper of the Lockup," permanently stationed in the basement of police headquarters.) Promotions must be made from within the department. This policy has continued even though the present reform mayor created the post of police commissioner and brought in an outsider to take command. For cities of its size, Wincanton police salaries have been quite low—the top pay for patrolmen was $4,856—in the lowest quartile of middle-sized cities in the Nation. Since 1964 the commissioner has received $10,200 and patrolmen $5,400 each year.

While the police department is the prime law enforcement agency within Wincanton, it receives help (and occasional embarrassment) from other groups. Three county detectives work under the district attorney, primarily in rural parts of Alsace County, but they are occasionally called upon to assist in city investigations. The State Police, working out of a barracks in suburban Wincanton Hills, have generally taken a "hands off" or "local option" attitude toward city crime, working only in rural areas unless invited into a city by the mayor, district attorney, or county judge. Reform mayors have welcomed the superior manpower and investigative powers of the State officers; corrupt mayors have usually been able to thumb their noses at State policemen trying to uncover Wincanton gambling. Agents of the State's Alcoholic Beverages Commission suffer from no such limitations and enter Wincanton at will in search of liquor violations. They have seldom been a serious threat to Wincanton corruption, however, since their numbers are quite limited (and thus the agents are dependent upon the local police for information and assistance in making arrests). Their mandate extends to gambling and prostitution only when encountered in the course of a liquor investigation.

Under most circumstances, the operative level of law enforcement in Wincanton has been set by local political decisions, and the local police (acting under instructions from the mayor) have been able to determine whether or not Wincanton should have open gambling and prostitution. The State Police, with their "hands off" policy, have simply reenforced the local decision. From time to time, however, Federal agencies have become interested in conditions in Wincanton and, as will be seen throughout this study, have played as important a role as the local police in cleaning up the city. Internal Revenue Service agents have succeeded in prosecuting Wincanton gamblers for failure to hold gambling occupation stamps, pay the special excise taxes on gambling receipts, or report income. Federal Bureau of Investigation agents have acted against violations of the Federal laws against extortion and interstate gambling. Finally, special attorneys from the Organized Crime and Racketeering Section of the Justice Department were able to convict leading members of the syndicate controlling Wincanton gambling. While Federal prosecutions in Wincanton have often been spectacular, it should also be noted that they have been somewhat sporadic and limited in scope. The Internal Revenue Service, for example, was quite successful in seizing gaming devices and gamblers lacking the Federal gambling occupation stamps, but it was helpless after Wincantonites began to purchase the stamps, since local officials refused to prosecute them for violations of the State antigambling laws.

The court system in Wincanton, as in all cities in the State, still has many of the 18th century features which have been rejected in other States. At the lowest level, elected magistrates (without legal training) hear petty civil and criminal cases in each ward of the city. The magistrates also issue warrants and decide whether persons arrested by the police shall be held for trial. Magistrates are paid only by fees, usually at the expense of convicted defendants. All serious criminal cases, and all contested petty cases, are tried in the county court. The three judges of the Alsace County court are elected (on a partisan ballot) for 10-year terms, and receive an annual salary of $25,000.

Gambling and Corruption: the Insiders

THE STERN EMPIRE

The history of Wincanton gambling and corruption since World War II centers around the career of Irving Stern. Stern is an immigrant who came to the United States and settled in Wincanton at the turn of the century. He started as a fruit peddler, but when Prohibition came along, Stern became a bootlegger for Heinz Glickman, then the beer baron of the State. When Glickman was murdered in the waning days of Prohibition, Stern took over Glickman's business and continued to sell untaxed liquor after repeal of Prohibition in 1933. Several times during the 1930's, Stern was convicted in Federal court on liquor charges and spent over a year in Federal prison.

Around 1940, Stern announced to the world that he had reformed and went into his family's wholesale produce business. While Stern was in fact leaving the bootlegging trade, he was also moving into the field of gambling, for even at that time Wincanton had a "wide-open" reputation, and the police were ignoring gamblers. With the technical assistance of his bootlegging friends, Stern started with a numbers bank and soon added horse betting, a dice game, and slot machines to his organization. During World War II, officers from a nearby Army training base insisted that all brothels be closed, but this did not affect Stern. He had already concluded that public hostility and violence, caused by the houses, were, as a side effect, threatening his more profitable gambling operations. Although Irv Stern controlled the lion's share of Wincanton gambling throughout the 1940's, he had to share the slot machine trade with Klaus Braun. Braun, unlike Stern, was a Wincanton native and a Gentile, and thus had easier access to the frequently anti-Semitic club stewards, restaurant owners, and bartenders who decided which machines would be placed in their buildings. Legislative investigations in the early 1950's estimated that Wincanton gambling was an industry with gross receipts of $5 million each year; at that time Stern was receiving $40,000 per week from bookmaking, and Braun took in $75,000 to $100,000 per year from slot machines alone.

Irv Stern's empire in Wincanton collapsed abruptly when legislative investigations brought about the election of a reform Republican administration. Mayor Hal Craig decided to seek what he termed "pearl gray purity"—to tolerate isolated prostitutes, bookies, and numbers writers—but to drive out all forms of organized crime, all activities lucrative enough to make it worth someone's while to try bribing Craig's police officials.

Within 6 weeks after taking office, Craig and District Attorney Henry Weiss had raided enough of Stern's gambling parlors and seized enough of Braun's slot machines to convince both men that business was over—for 4 years at least. The Internal Revenue Service was able to convict Braun and Stern's nephew, Dave Feinman, on tax evasion charges; both were sent to jail. From 1952 to 1955 it was still possible to place a bet or find a girl. But you had to know someone to do it, and no one was getting very rich in the process.

By 1955 it was apparent to everyone that reform sentiment was dead and that the Democrats would soon be back in office. In the summer of that year, Stern met with representatives of the east coast syndicates and arranged for the rebuilding of his empire. He decided to change his method of operations in several ways; one was by centralizing all Wincanton vice and gambling under his control. But he also decided to turn the actual operation of most enterprises over to others. From the mid-1950's until the next wave of reform hit Wincanton after elections in the early 1960's, Irv Stern generally succeeded in reaching these goals.

The financial keystone of Stern's gambling empire was numbers betting. Records seized by the Internal Revenue Service in the late 1950's and early 1960's indicated that gross receipts from numbers amounted to more than $100,000 each month, or $1.3 million annually. Since the numbers are a poor man's form of gambling (bets range from a penny to a dime or quarter), a large number of men and a high degree of organization are required. The organizational goals are three: have the maximum possible number of men on the streets seeking bettors, be sure that they are reporting honestly, and yet strive so to decentralize the organization that no one, if arrested, will be able to identify many of the others. During the "pearl gray purity" of Hal Craig, numbers writing was completely unorganized—many isolated writers took bets from their friends and frequently had to renege if an unusually popular number came up; no one writer was big enough to guard against such possibilities. When a new mayor took office in the mid-1950's, however, Stern's lieutenants notified each of the small writers that they were now working for Stern—or else. Those who objected were "persuaded" by Stern's men, or else arrested by the police, as were any of the others, who were suspected of holding out on their receipts. Few objected for very long. After Stern completed the reorganization of the numbers business, its structure was roughly something like this: 11 subbanks reported to Stern's central accounting office. Each subbank employed from 5 to 30 numbers writers. Thirty-five percent of the gross receipts went to the writers. After deducting for winnings and expenses (mostly protection payoffs), Stern divided the net profits equally with the operators of the subbanks. In return for his cut, Stern provided protection from the police and "laid off" the subbanks, covering winnings whenever a popular number "broke" one of the smaller operators.

Stern also shared with out-of-State syndicates in the profits and operation of two enterprises—a large dice game and the largest still found by the Treasury Department since Prohibition. The dice game employed over 50 men—drivers to "lug" players into town from as far as 100 miles away, doormen to check players' identities, loan sharks who "faded" the losers, croupiers, food servers, guards, etc. The 1960 payroll for these employees was over $350,000. While no estimate of the gross receipts from the game is available, some indication of its size can be obtained from the fact that $50,000 was found on the tables and in the safe when the FBI raided the game in 1962. Over 100 players were arrested during the raid; one business-man had lost over $75,000 at the tables. Stern received a share of the game's profits plus a $1,000 weekly fee to provide protection from the police.

Stern also provided protection (for a fee) and shared in the profits of a still, erected in an old warehouse on the banks of the Wincanton River and tied into the city's water and sewer systems. Stern arranged for clearance by the city council and provided protection from the local police after the $200,000 worth of equipment was set up. The still was capable of producing $4 million worth of alcohol each year, and served a five-State area, until Treasury agents raided it after it had been in operation for less than 1 year.

The dice game and the still raise questions regarding the relationship of Irv Stern to out-of-State syndicates. Republican politicians in Wincanton frequently claimed that Stern was simply the local agent of the Cosa Nostra. While Stern was regularly sending money to the syndicates, the evidence suggests that Stern was much more than an agent for outsiders. It would be more accurate to regard these payments as profit sharing with coinves-tors and as charges for services rendered. The east coasters provided techni-cal services in the operation of the dice game and still and "enforcement" service for the Wincanton gambling operation. When deviants had to be persuaded to accept Stern's domination, Stern called upon outsiders for "muscle"—strong-arm men who could not be traced by local police if the victim chose to protest. In the early 1940's, for example, Stern asked for help in destroying a competing dice game; six gunmen came in and held it up, robbing and terrifying the players. While a few murders took place in the struggle for supremacy in the 1930's and 1940's, only a few people were roughed up in the 1950's and no one was killed.

After the mid-1950's, Irv Stern controlled prostitution and several forms of gambling on a "franchise" basis. Stern took no part in the conduct of these businesses and received no share of the profits, but exacted a fee for protection from the police. Several horse books, for example, operated regularly; the largest of these paid Stern $600 per week. While slot machines had permanently disappeared from the Wincanton scene after the legislative investigations of the early 1950's, a number of men began to distribute pinball machines, which paid off players for games won. As was the case with numbers writers, these pinball distributors had been unorganized during the Craig administration. When Democratic Mayor Gene Donnelly succeeded Craig, he immediately announced that all pinball machines were illegal and would be confiscated by the police. A Stern agent then contacted the pinball distributors and notified them that if they employed Dave Feinman (Irv Stern's nephew) as a "public relations consultant," there would be no interference from the police. Several rebellious distributors formed an Alsace County Amusement Operators Association, only to see Feinman appear with two thugs from New York. After the association president was roughed up, all resistance collapsed, and Feinman collected $2,000 each week to promote the "public relations" of the distributors. (Stern, of course, was able to offer no protection against Federal action. After the Internal Revenue Service began seizing the pinball machines in 1956, the owners were forced to purchase the $250 Federal gambling stamps as well as paying Feinman. Over 200 Wincanton machines bore these stamps in the early 1960's, and thus were secure from Federal as well as local action.)

After the period of reform in the early 1950's, Irv Stern was able to establish a centralized empire in which he alone determined which rackets would operate and who would operate them (he never, it might be noted, permitted narcotics traffic in the city while he controlled it). What were the bases of his control within the criminal world? Basically, they were three: First, as a business matter, Stern controlled access to several very lucrative operations, and could quickly deprive an uncooperative gambler or numbers writer of his source of income. Second, since he controlled the police department he could arrest any gamblers or bookies who were not paying tribute. (Some of the local gambling and prostitution arrests which took place during the Stern era served another purpose—to placate newspaper demands for a crackdown. As one police chief from this era phrased it, "Hollywood should have given us an Oscar for some of our performances when we had to pull a phony raid to keep the papers happy.") Finally, if the mechanisms of fear of financial loss and fear of police arrest failed to command obedience, Stern was always able to keep alive a fear of physical violence. As we have seen, numbers writers, pinball distributors, and competing gamblers were brought into line after outside enforcers put in an appearance. Stern's regular collection agent, a local tough who had been convicted of murder in the 1940's, was a constant reminder of the virtues of cooperation. Several witnesses who told grand juries or Federal agents of extortion attempts by Stern, received visits from Stern enforcers and tended to "forget" when called to testify against the boss.

Protection. An essential ingredient in Irv Stern's Wincanton operations was protection against law enforcement agencies. While he was never able to arrange freedom from Federal intervention (although, as in the case of purchasing excise stamps for the pinball machines, he was occasionally able to satisfy Federal requirements without disrupting his activities), Stern was able in the 1940's and again from the mid-1950's through the early 1960's to secure freedom from State and local action. The precise extent of Stern's network of protection payments is unknown, but the method of operations can be reconstructed.

Two basic principles were involved in the Wincanton protection system —pay top personnel as much as necessary to keep them happy (and quiet), and pay something to as many others as possible to implicate them in the system and to keep them from talking. The range of payoffs thus went from a weekly salary for some public officials to a Christmas turkey for the patrolman on the beat. Records from the numbers bank listed payments totaling $2,400 each week to some local elected officials, State legislators, the police chief, a captain in charge of detectives, and persons mysteriously labeled "county" and "State." While the list of persons to be paid remained fairly constant, the amounts paid varied according to the gambling activities in operation at the time; payoff figures dropped sharply when the FBI put the dice game out of business. When the dice game was running, one official was receiving $750 per week, the chief $100, and a few captains, lieutenants, and detectives lesser amounts.

While number of officials receiving regular "salary" payoffs was quite restricted (only 15 names were on the payroll found at the numbers bank), many other officials were paid off in different ways. (Some men were also silenced without charge—low-ranking policemen, for example, kept quiet after they learned that men who reported gambling or prostitution were ignored or transferred to the midnight shift; they didn't have to be paid.) Stern was a major (if undisclosed) contributor during political campaigns —sometimes giving money to all candidates, not caring who won, sometimes supporting a "regular" to defeat a possible reformer, sometimes paying a candidate not to oppose a preferred man. Since there were few legitimate sources of large contributions for Democratic candidates, Stern's money was frequently regarded as essential for victory, for the costs of buying radio and television time and paying pollwatchers were high. When popular sentiment was running strongly in favor of reform, however, even Stern's contributions could not guarantee victory. Bob Walasek, later to be as corrupt as any Wincanton mayor, ran as a reform candidate in the

Democratic primary and defeated Stern-financed incumbent Gene Donnelly. Never a man to bear grudges, Stern financed Walasek in the general
election that year and put him on the "payroll" when he took office.
Even when local officials were not on the regular payroll, Stern was
careful to remind them of his friendship (and their debts). A legislative
investigating committee found that Stern had given mortgage loans to a
police lieutenant and the police chief's son. County Court Judge Ralph
Vaughan recalled that shortly after being elected (with Stern support), he
received a call from Dave Feinman, Stern's nephew. "Congratulations,
judge. When do you think you and your wife would like a vacation in
Florida?"

"Florida? Why on earth would I want to go there?"

"But all the other judges and the guys in City Hall—Irv takes them all
to Florida whenever they want to get away."

"Thanks anyway, but I'm not interested."

"Well, how about a mink coat instead. What size coat does your wife
wear? * * *"

In another instance an assistant district attorney told of Feinman's arriving at his front door with a large basket from Stern's supermarket just before
Christmas. "My minister suggested a needy family that could use the food",
the assistant district attorney recalled, "but I returned the liquor to Feinman. How could I ask a minister if he knew someone that could use three
bottles of scotch?"

Campaign contributions, regular payments to higher officials, holiday
and birthday gifts—these were the bases of the system by which Irv Stern
bought protection from the law. The campaign contributions usually en-
sured that complacent mayors, councilmen, district attorneys, and judges
were elected; payoffs in some instances usually kept their loyalty. In a
number of ways, Stern was also able to reward the corrupt officials at no
financial cost to himself. Just as the officials, being in control of the instruments of law enforcement, were able to facilitate Stern's gambling enterprises, so Stern, in control of a network of men operating outside the law,
was able to facilitate the officials' corrupt enterprises. As will be seen later,
many local officials were not satisfied with their legal salaries from the city
and their illegal salaries from Stern and decided to demand payments from
prostitutes, kickbacks from salesmen, etc. Stern, while seldom receiving any
money from these transactions, became a broker: bringing politicians into
contact with salesmen, merchants, and lawyers willing to offer bribes to get
city business; setting up middlemen who could handle the money without
jeopardizing the officials' reputations; and providing enforcers who could
bring delinquents into line.

From the corrupt activities of Wincanton officials, Irv Stern received little in contrast to his receipts from his gambling operations. Why then did he get involved in them? The major virtue, from Stern's point of view, of the system of extortion that flourished in Wincanton was that it kept down the officials' demands for payoffs directly from Stern. If a councilman was able to pick up $1,000 on the purchase of city equipment, he would demand a lower payment for the protection of gambling. Furthermore, since Stern knew the facts of extortion in each instance, the officials would be further implicated in the system and less able to back out on the arrangements regarding gambling. Finally, as Stern discovered to his chagrin, it became necessary to supervise official extortion to protect the officials against their own stupidity. Mayor Gene Donnelly was cooperative and remained satisfied with his regular "salary." Bob Walasek, however, was a greedy man, and seized every opportunity of profit from a city contract. Soon Stern found himself supervising many of Walasek's deals to keep the mayor from blowing the whole arrangement wide open. When Walasek tried to double the "take" on a purchase of parking meters, Stern had to step in and set the contract price, provide an untraceable middleman, and see the deal through to completion. "I told Irv," Police Chief Phillips later testified, "that Walasek wanted $12 on each meter instead of the $6 we got on the last meter deal. He became furious. He said, 'Walasek is going to fool around and wind up in jail. You come and see me. I'll tell Walasek what he's going to buy.' "

Protection, it was stated earlier, was an essential ingredient in Irv Stern's gambling empire. In the end, Stern's downfall came not from a flaw in the organization of the gambling enterprises but from public exposure of the corruption of Mayor Walasek and other officials. In the early 1960's Stern was sent to jail for 4 years on tax evasion charges, but the gambling empire continued to operate smoothly in his absence. A year later, however, Chief Phillips was caught perjuring himself in grand jury testimony concerning kickbacks on city towing contracts. Phillips "blew the whistle" on Stern, Walasek, and members of the city council, and a reform administration was swept into office. Irv Stern's gambling empire had been worth several million dollars each year; kickbacks on the towing contracts brought Bob Walasek a paltry $50 to $75 each week.

Official Corruption

Textbooks on municipal corporation law speak of at least three varieties of official corruption. The major categories are nonfeasance (failing to perform a required duty at all), malfeasance (the commission of some act which is positively unlawful), and misfeasance (the improper performance of some act which a man may properly do). During the years in which Irv Stern was running his gambling operations, Wincanton officials were guilty of all of these. Some residents say that Bob Walasek came to regard the mayor's office as a brokerage, levying a tariff on every item that came across his desk. Sometimes a request for simple municipal services turned into a game of cat and mouse, with Walasek sitting on the request, waiting to see how much would be offered, and the petitioner waiting to see if he could obtain his rights without having to pay for them. Corruption was not as lucrative an enterprise as gambling, but it offered a tempting supplement to low official salaries.

NONFEASANCE

As was detailed earlier, Irv Stern saw to it that Wincanton officials would ignore at least one of their statutory duties, enforcement of the State's gambling laws. Bob Walasek and his cohorts also agreed to overlook other illegal activities. Stern, we noted earlier, preferred not to get directly involved in prostitution; Walasek and Police Chief Dave Phillips tolerated all prostitutes who kept up their protection payments. One madam, controlling more than 20 girls, gave Phillips et al. $500 each week; one woman employing only one girl paid $75 each week that she was in business. Operators of a carnival in rural Alsace County paid a public official $5,000 for the privilege of operating gambling tents for 5 nights each summer. A burlesque theater manager, under attack by high school teachers, was ordered to pay $25 each week for the privilege of keeping his strip show open.

Many other city and county officials must be termed guilty of nonfeasance, although there is no evidence that they received payoffs, and although they could present reasonable excuses for their inaction. Most policemen, as we have noted earlier, began to ignore prostitution and gambling completely after their reports of offenses were ignored or superior officers told them to mind their own business. State policemen, well informed about city vice and gambling conditions, did nothing unless called upon to act by local officials. Finally, the judges of the Alsace County Court failed to exercise their power to call for State Police investigations. In 1957, following Federal raids on horse bookies, the judges did request an investigation by the State Attorney General, but refused to approve his suggestion that a grand jury be convened to continue the investigation. For each of these instances of inaction, a tenable excuse might be offered—the beat patrolman should not be expected to endure harassment from his superior officers, State police gambling raids in a hostile city might jeopardize State-local cooperation on more serious crimes, and a grand jury probe might easily be turned into a "whitewash" in the hands of a corrupt district attorney. In any event powers available to these law enforcement agencies for the prevention of gambling and corruption were not utilized.

MALFEASANCE

In fixing parking and speeding tickets, Wincanton politicians and policemen committed malfeasance, or committed an act they were forbidden to do, by illegally compromising valid civil and criminal actions. Similarly, while State law provides no particular standards by which the mayor is to make promotions within his police department, it was obviously improper for Mayor Walasek to demand a "political contribution" of $10,000 from Dave Phillips before he was appointed chief in 1960.

The term "political contribution" raises a serious legal and analytical problem in classifying the malfeasance of Wincanton officials, and indeed of politicians in many cities. Political campaigns cost money; citizens have a right to support the candidates of their choice; and officials have a right to appoint their backers to noncivil service positions. At some point, however, threats or oppression convert legitimate requests for political contributions into extortion. Shortly after taking office in the mid-1950's, Mayor Gene Donnelly notified city hall employees that they would be expected "voluntarily" to contribute 2 percent of their salary to the Democratic Party. (It might be noted that Donnelly never forwarded any of these "political contributions" to the party treasurer.) A number of salesmen doing business with the city were notified that companies which had supported the party would receive favored treatment; Donnelly notified one salesman that in light of a proposed $81,000 contract for the purchase of fire engines, a "political contribution" of $2,000 might not be inappropriate. While neither the city hall employees nor the salesmen had rights to their positions or their contracts, the "voluntary" quality of their contributions seems questionable.

One final, in the end almost ludicrous, example of malfeasance came with Mayor Donnelly's abortive "War on the Press." Following a series of gambling raids by the Internal Revenue Service, the newspapers began asking why the local police had not participated in the raids. The mayor lost his temper and threw a reporter in jail. Policemen were instructed to harass newspaper delivery trucks, and 73 tickets were written over a 48-hour period for supposed parking and traffic violations. Donnelly soon backed down after national news services picked up the story, since press coverage made him look ridiculous. Charges against the reporter were dropped, and the newspapers continued to expose gambling and corruption.

MISFEASANCE

Misfeasance in office, says the common law, is the improper performance of some act which a man may properly do. City officials must buy and sell equipment, contract for services, and allocate licenses, privileges, etc. These actions can be improperly performed if either the results are improper (e.g., if a building inspector were to approve a home with defective wiring or a zoning board to authorize a variance which had no justification in terms of land usage) or a result is achieved by improper procedures (e.g., if the city purchased an acceptable automobile in consideraton of a bribe paid to the purchasing agent). In the latter case, we can usually assume an improper result as well—while the automobile will be satisfactory, the bribe giver will probably have inflated the sale price to cover the costs of the bribe.

In Wincanton, it was rather easy for city officials to demand kickbacks, for State law frequently does not demand competitive bidding or permits the city to ignore the lowest bid. The city council is not required to advertise or take bids on purchases under $1,000, contracts for maintenance of streets and other public works, personal or professional services, or patented or copyrighted products. Even when bids must be sought, the council is only required to award the contract to the lowest responsible bidder. Given these permissive provisions, it was relatively easy for council members to justify or disguise contracts in fact based upon bribes. The exemption for patented products facilitated bribe taking on the purchase of two emergency trucks for the police department (with a $500 campaign contribution on a $7,500 deal), three fire engines ($2,000 was allegedly paid on an $81,000 contract), and 1,500 parking meters (involving payments of $10,500 plus an $880 clock for Mayor Walasek's home). Similar fees were allegedly exacted in connection with the purchase of a city fire alarm system and police uniforms and firearms. A former mayor and other officials also profited on the sale of city property, allegedly dividing $500 on the sale of a crane and $20,000 for approving the sale, for $22,000, of a piece of land immediately resold for $75,000.

When contracts involved services to the city, the provisions in the State law regarding the lowest responsible bidder and excluding "professional services" from competitive bidding provided convenient loopholes. One internationally known engineering firm refused to agree to kickback in order to secure a contract to design a $4.5 million sewage disposal plant for the city; a local firm was then appointed, which paid $10,700 of its $225,000 fee to an associate of Irv Stern and Mayor Donnelly as a "finder's fee." Since the State law also excludes public works maintenance contracts from the competitive bidding requirements, many city paving and street repair contracts during the Donnelly-Walasek era were given to a contributor to the Democratic Party. Finally, the franchise for towing illegally parked cars and cars involved in accidents was awarded to two garages which were then required to kickback $1 for each car towed.

The handling of graft on the towing contracts illustrates the way in which minor violence and the "lowest responsible bidder" clause could be used to keep bribe payers in line. After Federal investigators began to look into Wincanton corruption, the owner of one of the garages with a towing franchise testified before the grand jury. Mayor Walasek immediately withdrew his franchise, citing "health violations" at the garage. The garageman was also "encouraged" not to testify by a series of "accidents"—wheels would fall off towtrucks on the highway, steering cables were cut, and so forth. Newspaper satirization of the "health violations" forced the restoration of the towing franchise, and the "accidents" ceased.

Lest the reader infer that the "lowest responsible bidder" clause was used as an escape valve only for corrupt purposes, one incident might be noted which took place under the present reform administration. In 1964, the Wincanton School Board sought bids for the renovation of an athletic field. The lowest bid came from a construction company owned by Dave Phillips, the corrupt police chief who had served formerly under Mayor Walasek. While the company was presumably competent to carry out the assignment, the board rejected Phillips' bid "because of a question as to his moral responsibility." The board did not specify whether this referred to his prior corruption as chief or his present status as an informer in testifying against Walasek and Stern.

One final area of city power, which was abused by Walasek et al., covered discretionary acts, such as granting permits and allowing zoning variances. On taking office, Walasek took the unusual step of asking that the bureaus of building and plumbing inspection be put under the mayor's control. With this power to approve or deny building permits, Walasek "sat on" applications, waiting until the petitioner contributed $50 or $75, or threatened to sue to get his permit. Some building designs were not approved until a favored architect was retained as a "consultant." (It is not known whether this involved kickbacks to Walasek or simply patronage for a friend.) At least three instances are known in which developers were forced to pay for zoning variances before apartment buildings or supermarkets could be erected. Businessmen who wanted to encourage rapid turnover of the curb space in front of their stores were told to pay a police sergeant to erect "10-minute parking" signs. To repeat a caveat stated earlier, it is impossible to tell whether these kickbacks were demanded to expedite legitimate requests or to approve improper demands, such as a variance that would hurt a neighborhood or a certificate approving improper electrical work.

All of the activities detailed thus far involve fairly clear violations of the law. To complete the picture of the abuse of office by Wincanton officials, we might briefly mention "honest graft." This term was best defined by one of its earlier practitioners, State Senator George Washington Plunkitt who loyally served Tammany Hall at the turn of the century.

There's all the difference in the world between [honest and dishonest graft]. Yes, many of our men have grown rich in politics. I have myself.

I've made a big fortune out of the game, and I'm gettin' richer every day, but I've not gone in for dishonest graft—blackmailin' gamblers, saloonkeepers, disorderly people, etc.—and neither has any of the men who have made big fortunes in politics.

There's an honest graft, and I'm an example of how it works. I might sum up the whole thing by sayin': "I seen my opportunities and I took 'em."

Let me explain by examples. My party's in power in the city, and it's goin' to undertake a lot of public improvements. Well, I'm tipped off, say, that they're going to lay out a new park at a certain place.

I see my opportunity and I take it. I go to that place and I buy up all the land I can in the neighborhood. Then the board of this or that makes its plan public, and there is a rush to get my land, which nobody cared particular for before.

Ain't it perfectly honest to charge a good price and make a profit on my investment and foresight? Of course, it is. Well, that's honest graft.[3]

While there was little in the way of land purchasing—either honest or dishonest—going on in Wincanton during this period, several officials who carried on their own businesses while in office were able to pick up some "honest graft." One city councilman with an accounting office served as bookkeeper for Irv Stern and the major bookies and prostitutes in the city.

Police Chief Phillips' construction firm received a contract to remodel the exterior of the largest brothel in town. Finally one councilman serving in the present reform administration received a contract to construct all gasoline stations built in the city by a major petroleum company; skeptics say that the contract was the quid pro quo for the councilman's vote to give the company the contract to sell gasoline to the city.

How Far Did It Go? This cataloging of acts of nonfeasance, malfeasance, and misfeasance by Wincanton officials raises a danger of confusing variety with universality, of assuming that every employee of the city was either engaged in corrupt activities or was being paid to ignore the corruption of others. On the contrary, both official investigations and private research lead to the conclusion that there is no reason whatsoever to question the honesty of the vast majority of the employees of the city of Wincanton. Certainly no more than 10 of the 155 members of the Wincanton police force were on Irv Stern's payroll (although as many as half of them may have accepted petty Christmas presents—turkeys or liquor.) In each department, there were a few employees who objected actively to the misdeeds of their superiors, and the only charge that can justly be leveled against the mass of employees is that they were unwilling to jeopardize their employment by publicly exposing what was going on. When Federal investigators showed that an honest (and possibly successful) attempt was being made to expose Stern-Walasek corruption, a number of city employees cooperated with the grand jury in aggregating evidence which could be used to convict the corrupt officials.

Before these Federal investigations began, however, it could reasonably appear to an individual employee that the entire machinery of law enforcement in the city was controlled by Stern, Walasek, et al., and that an individual protest would be silenced quickly. This can be illustrated by the momentary crusade conducted by First Assistant District Attorney Phil Roper in the summer of 1962. When the district attorney left for a short vacation, Roper decided to act against the gamblers and madams in the city. With the help of the State Police, Roper raided several large brothels. Apprehending on the street the city's largest distributor of punchboards and lotteries, Roper effected a citizen's arrest and drove him to police headquarters for proper detention and questioning. "I'm sorry, Mr. Roper," said the desk sergeant, "we're under orders not to arrest persons brought in by you." Roper was forced to call upon the State Police for aid in confining the gambler. When the district attorney returned from his vacation, he quickly fired Roper "for introducing politics into the district attorney's office."

If it is incorrect to say that Wincanton corruption extended very far vertically—into the rank and file of the various departments of the city— how far did it extend horizontally? How many branches and levels of government were affected? With the exception of the local Congressman and the city treasurer, it seems that a few personnel at each level (city, county, and State) and in most offices in city hall can be identified either with Stern or with some form of free-lance corruption. A number of local judges received campaign financing from Stern, although there is no evidence that they were on his payroll after they were elected. Several State legislators were on Stern's payroll, and one Republican councilman charged that a high-ranking State Democratic official promised Stern first choice of all Alsace County patronage. The county chairman, he claimed, was only to receive the jobs that Stern did not want. While they were later to play an active role in disrupting Wincanton gambling, the district attorney in Hal Craig's reform administration feared that the State Police were on Stern's payroll, and thus refused to use them in city gambling raids.

Within the city administration, the evidence is fairly clear that some mayors and councilmen received regular payments from Stern and divided kickbacks on city purchases and sales. Some key subcouncil personnel frequently shared in payoffs affecting their particular departments— the police chief shared in the gambling and prostitution payoffs and received $300 of the $10,500 kickback on parking meter purchases. A councilman controlling one department, for example, might get a higher percentage of kickbacks than the other councilmen in contracts involving that department.

LEGAL PROTECTION AGAINST CORRUPTION

Later in this report, Wincanton's gambling and corruption will be tied into a context of social and political attitudes. At this point, however, concluding the study of official corruption, it might be appropriate to consider legal reforms which might make future corruption more difficult. Many of the corrupt activities of Wincanton officials are already covered sufficiently by State law—it is clearly spelled out, for example, that city officials must enforce State gambling and prostitution laws, and no further legislation is needed to clarify this duty. The legal mandate of the State Police to enforce State laws in all parts of the State is equally clear, but it has been nullified by their informal practice of entering cities only when invited; this policy only facilitates local corruption.

The first major reform that might minimize corruption would involve a drastic increase in the salaries of public officials and law enforcement personnel. During the 1950's Wincanton police salaries were in the lowest quartile for middle-sized cities in the Nation, and were well below the median family income ($5,453) in the city. City councilmen then were receiving only slightly more than the median. Since that time, police salaries have been raised to $5,400 (only slightly below the median) and council salaries to $8,500. Under these circumstances, many honest officials and employees were forced to "moonlight" with second jobs; potentially dishonest men were likely to view Stern payoffs or extortionate kickbacks as a simpler means of improving their financial status. Raising police salaries to $7,000 or $8,000 would attract men of higher quality, permit them to forego second jobs, and make corrupt payoffs seem less tempting. The same considerations apply to a recommendation that the salaries of elected officials be increased to levels similar to those received in private industry. A recent budget for the city of Wincanton called for expenditures of $6 million; no private corporation of that size would be headed by a chief executive whose salary was $9,500 per year.

A second type of recommendation would reduce the opportunities available to officials to extort illegal payoffs or conceal corruption. First, the civil service system should be expanded. At the time this report was written, Wincanton policemen could not be discharged from the force unless formal charges were brought, but they could be demoted from command positions or transferred to "punishment" details at the discretion of the chief or mayor. The latter option is probably a proper disciplinary tool, but the former invites policemen to seek alliances with political leaders and to avoid unpopular actions. Promotions within the force (with the possible exception of the chief's position) should be made by competitive examination, and demotions should be made only for proven cause. (While research for this report was being conducted, a full 18 months before the next local election, police officers reported that politicking had already begun. Men on the force had already begun making friends with possible candidates for the 1967 elections, and police discipline was beginning to slip. Command officers reported that the sergeants were becoming unwilling to criticize or discipline patrolmen. "How can I tell someone off?" one captain asked. "I'll probably be walking a beat when the Democrats come back into power, and he may be my boss.") A comprehensive civil service system would also give command officers control over informal rewards and punishments, so that they could encourage "hustlers" and harass slackers, but formal review of promotions and demotions is essential to guard against the politicking, which has been characteristic of the Wincanton police force.

Second, opportunities for corruption could be reduced by closing the loopholes in State laws on bidding for municipal contracts. While a city should be free to disregard a low bid received from a company judged financially or technically unable to perform a contract, the phrase "lowest responsible bidder" simply opens the door to misfeasance—either to accepting under-the-table kickbacks or to rewarding political friends. In this regard, the decision to ignore the bid of former Police Chief Phillips is just as reprehensible as the decision to give paving contracts to a major party contributor. Furthermore, there is no reason why service contracts should be excluded from the competitive bidding; while the professions regard it as undignified to compete for clients, there is no reason why road repair or building maintenance contracts could not be judged on the basis of bids (with a proviso regarding some level of competence). Finally, the exclusion of "patented or copyrighted products" is untenable—it is well known that distributors of say, automobiles, vary widely in their profit margins, or allowances for trade-ins, etc. City officials should be forced therefore to seek the best possible deal.

One mechanism, which is often suggested to guard against official misconduct, is an annual audit of city books by a higher governmental agency, such as those conducted of local agencies (e.g., urban renewal authorities) administering Federal programs. The evidence in Wincanton, however, seems to indicate that even while official corruption was taking place, the city's books were in perfect order. When a kickback was received on a city purchase, for example, the minutes of council meetings would indicate that

X was the "lowest responsible bidder," if bids were required, and X would slip the payoff money to a "bagman," or contactman, on a dark street corner. The books looked proper and auditors would have had no authority to force acceptance of other bids. It would seem that revision of the bidding laws would be more significant than an outside audit.

Finally, the problem of campaign contributions must be considered. As was stressed earlier, contributions to political candidates are regarded in this country as both a manifestation of free speech and the best alternative to government sponsorship of campaigns. The use of political contributions as a disguise for extortion and bribery could be curtailed, however, by active enforcement of the "full reporting of receipts" provision of State campaign laws (in Wincanton, candidates filed reports of receipts, but, of course, neglected to mention the money received from Irv Stern). Second, city hall employees should be protected against the type of voluntary assessment imposed by Mayor Donnelly. Third, State and local laws might more clearly prohibit contributions, from persons doing business with the city, which can be identified as payoffs for past or future preferment on city contracts. (Tightening of bidding requirements, of course, would make such activities less profitable to the contractors.)[4]

*   *   *

Public Attitudes Toward Gambling and Corruption

A clean city, a city free of gambling, vice, and corruption, requires at least two things—active law enforcement and elected officials who oppose organized crime. Over the last 20 years, Federal agents have been successful in prosecuting most of the leaders of Wincanton gambling operations. Slot machine king Klaus Braun was twice sent to jail for income tax evasion. Federal agents were also able to secure convictions against Irv Stern for income tax evasion (a 4-year sentence), gambling tax evasion (a 2-year sentence running concurrently with the income tax sentence), and extortion on a city contract to purchase parking meters (a 30-day concurrent sentence). Federal men also sent to jail lesser members of the Stern syndicate and closed down a still and an interstate dice game.

These Federal actions, however, had very little effect upon Wincanton gambling. Lieutenants carried on while Stern was in jail, and local police, at the direction of city officials, continued to ignore numbers writers, bookies, and prostitutes. As one Federal agent put it, "Even though we were able to apprehend and convict the chief racketeers, we were never able to solve the political problem—city officials were always against us." On the two occasions when Wincanton voters did solve the political problem by electing reform officials, however, organized crime was quickly put out of business. Mayor Hal Craig chose to tolerate isolated bookies, numbers writers, and prostitutes, but Stern and Braun were effectively silenced. Mayor Ed Whitton, in office since the early 1960's, has gone even further, and the only gamblers and prostitutes still operating in Wincanton are those whom the police have been unable to catch for reasons of limited manpower, lack of evidence, etc. The American Social Hygiene Association reported after a recent study that Wincanton has fewer prostitutes today than at any time since the 1930's. The police acknowledge that there are still a few gamblers and prostitutes in town, but they have been driven underground, and a potential patron must have a contact before he can do business.

If the level of law enforcement in a community is so directly tied to local voting patterns, we must look more closely at the attitudes and values of Wincanton residents. First, how much did residents know about what was going on? Were the events which have been discussed previously matters of common knowledge or were they perceived by only a few residents? Second, were they voting for open gambling and corruption; were they being duped by seemingly honest candidates who became corrupt after taking office; or were these issues irrelevant to the average voter, who was thinking about other issues entirely? Our conclusions about these questions will indicate whether long-range reform can be attained through legal changes (closing loopholes in the city's bidding practices, expanding civil service in the police department, ending the "home rule" policy of the State Police, etc.) or whether reform must await a change in popular mores.

PUBLIC AWARENESS OF GAMBLING AND CORRUPTION

In a survey of Wincanton residents conducted recently,[7] 90 percent of the respondents were able correctly to identify the present mayor, 63 percent recognized the name of their Congressman, and 36 percent knew the Alsace County district attorney. Seventy percent identified Irv Stern correctly, and 62 percent admitted that they did recognize the name of the largest madam in town. But how much did the people of Wincanton know about what had been going on—the extent and organization of Irv Stern's empire, the payoffs to city hall and the police, or the malfeasance and misfeasance of Bob Walasek and other city officials? Instead of thinking about simply "knowing" or "not knowing," we might subdivide public awareness into several categories—a general awareness that gambling and prostitution were present in the city, some perception that city officials were protecting these enterprises, and finally a specific knowledge that officials X and Y were being paid off. These categories vary, it will be noticed, in the specificity of knowledge and in the linkage between the result (e.g., presence of gambling or corruption) and an official's action.

While there is no way of knowing exactly how many Wincantonites had access to each type of knowledge about gambling and corruption during the period they were taking place, we can form some ideas on the basis of the newspaper coverage they received and the geographical distribution of each form of illegality. The dice game, for example, was in only one location (hidden and shifted periodically to escape Federal attention) and relied primarily on out-of-town gamblers. The newspapers said little about it, and it was probably safe to say that few residents knew of its existence until it was raided by the FBI in the early 1960's.

Prostitutes were generally found only in two four-block areas in the city —semi-slum areas that no outsider was likely to visit unless he was specifically looking for the girls. The newspapers, however, gave extensive coverage to every prostitution arrest and every report by the American Social Hygiene Association which detailed the extent of prostitution and venereal disease in the city. A series of newspaper articles, with photographs, forced the police to close (for a short period of time) several of the larger brothels. With regard to prostitution, therefore, it is likely that a majority of the adult population knew of the existence of commercialized vice; but, apart from innuendoes in the papers, there was little awareness of payoffs to the police. It was not until after the election of a reform administration, that Stern and Walasek were indicted for extorting payments from a madam.

In contrast to the dice games and prostitution, public awareness of the existence of pinball machines, horsebooks, and numbers writing must have been far more widespread. These mass-consumption forms of gambling depended upon accessibility to large numbers of persons. Bets could be placed in most corner grocery stores, candy shops, and cigar counters; payoff pinball machines were placed in most clubs and firehalls, as well as in bars and restaurants. Apart from knowing that these things were openly available, and thus not subject to police interference, there was no way for the average citizen to know specifically that Irv Stern was paying to protect these gambling interests until Police Chief Phillips began to testify—again after the election of reformer Whitton.

Public awareness of wrongdoing was probably least widespread in regard to corruption—kickbacks on contracts, extortion, etc. Direct involvement was generally limited to officials and businessmen, and probably few of them knew anything other than that they personally had been asked to pay. Either from shame or from fear of being prosecuted on bribery charges or out of unwillingness to jeopardize a profitable contract, those who did pay did not want to talk. Those who refused to pay usually were unable to substantiate charges made against bribes so that exposure of the attempt led only to libel suits or official harassment. As we have seen, the newspapers and one garage with a towing contract did talk about what was going on. The garageman lost his franchise and suffered a series of "accidents"; the newspapers found a reporter in jail and their trucks harassed by the police. Peter French, the district attorney under Walasek and Donnelly, won a libel suit (since reversed on appeal and dismissed) against the papers after they stated that he was protecting gamblers. Except for an unsuccessful citizen suit in the mid-1950's seeking to void the purchase of fire trucks (for the purchase of which Donnelly received a $2,000 "political contribution") and a newspaper article in the early 1960's implying that Donnelly and his council had received $500 on the sale of a city crane, no evidence—no specific facts—of corruption was available to the public until Phillips was indicted several years later for perjury in connection with the towing contracts.

Returning then to the three categories of public knowledge, we can say that even at the lowest level—general perception of some form of wrongdoing—awareness was quite limited (except among the businessmen, most of whom, as we noted in the "Introduction," live and vote in the suburbs). Specific knowledge—this official received this much to approve that contract—was only available after legislative hearings in the early 1950's and the indictment of Phillips in the early 1960's; on both occasions the voters turned to reform candidates.

If, therefore, it is unlikely that many residents of Wincanton had the second or third type of knowledge about local gambling or corruption (while many more had the first type) during the time it was taking place, how much do they know now—after several years of reform and a series of trials—all well-covered in the newspapers revealing the nature of Stern-Donnelly-Walasek operations? To test the extent of specific knowledge about local officials and events, respondents in a recent survey were asked to identify past and present officials and racketeers and to compare the Walasek and Whitton administrations on a number of points.

Earlier, we noted that 90 percent of the 183 respondents recognized the name of the present mayor, 63 percent knew their Congressman (who had been in office more than 10 years), and 36 percent knew the district attorney. How many members of the Stern organization were known to the public? Seventy percent recognized Stern's name, 63 percent knew the head of the numbers bank, 40 percent identified the "bagman" or collector for Stern, and 31 percent knew the operator of the largest horsebook in town. With regard to many of these questions, it must be kept in mind that since many respondents may subconsciously have felt that to admit recognition of a name would have implied personal contact with or sympathy for a criminal or a criminal act, these results probably understate the extent of public knowledge. When 100 of the respondents were asked "What things did Mr. Walasek do that were illegal?", 59 mentioned extortion regarding vice and gambling, 2 mentioned extortion on city contracts, 7 stated that he stole from the city, 8 that he fixed parking and speeding tickets, 4 that he was "controlled by rackets," and 20 simply stated that Walasek was corrupt, not listing specific acts.

Even if Wincantonites do not remember too many specific misdeeds, they clearly perceive that the present Whitton administration has run a cleaner town than did Walasek or Donnelly. When asked to comment on the statement, "Some people say that the present city administration under Mayor Whitton is about the same as when Mayor Walasek was in office," 10 percent said it was the same, 74 percent said it was different, and 14 percent didn't know. When asked why, 75 respondents cited "better law enforcement" and the end of corruption; only 7 of 183 felt that the city had been better run by Walasek. Fifty-eight percent felt the police force was better now, 22 percent thought that it was about the same as when Walasek controlled the force, and only 7 percent thought it was worse now. Those who felt that the police department was better run now stressed "honesty" and "better law enforcement," or thought that it was valuable to have an outsider as commissioner. Those who thought it was worse now cited "inefficiency," "loafing," or "unfriendliness." It was impossible to tell whether the comments of "unfriendliness" refer simply to the present refusal to tolerate gambling or whether they signify a more remote police-public contact resulting from the "professionalism" of the commissioner. (In this regard, we might note that a number of policemen and lawyers felt that it had been easier to secure information regarding major crimes when prostitution and gambling were tolerated. As one former captain put it, "If I found out that some gangster was in town that I didn't know about, I raised hell with the prostitutes for not telling me.")

Comparing perceptions of the present and former district attorneys, we also find a clear preference for the present man, Thomas Hendricks, over Peter French, but there is a surprising increase in "Don't knows." Thirty-five percent felt the district attorney's office is run "differently" now, 13 percent said it is run in the same way, but 50 percent did not know. Paralleling this lack of attitudes toward the office, we can recall that only 36 percent of the respondents were able to identify the present incumbent's name, while 55 percent knew his more flamboyant predecessor. Of those respondents who saw a difference between the two men, 51 percent cited "better law enforcement" and "no more rackets control over law enforcement."

In addition to recognizing these differences between past and present officials, the respondents in the recent survey felt that there were clear differences in the extent of corruption and gambling. Sixty-nine percent disagreed with the statement, "Underworld elements and racketeers had very little say in what the Wincanton city government did when Mr. Walasek was mayor;" only 13 percent disagreed with the same statement as applied to reform Mayor Whitton. When asked, "As compared with 5 years ago, do you think it's easier now, about the same, or harder to find a dice game in Wincanton?"; only one respondent felt it was easier, 8 percent felt it was about the same, 56 percent felt it was harder, and 34 percent didn't know. The respondents were almost as sure that Whitton had closed down horse betting; 51 percent felt it was harder to bet on horses now than it was 5 years ago, 11 percent felt it was about the same, and three respondents thought it was easier now than before. Again, 34 percent did not know.

PUBLIC ATTITUDES TOWARD CRIME AND LAW ENFORCEMENT

Earlier, we asked whether Wincanton's long history of gambling and corruption was based on a few bad officials and formal, structural defects such as the absence of civil service or low pay scales, or whether it was rooted in the values of the populace. The evidence on "public awareness" indicates that most Wincantonites probably knew of the existence of widespread gambling, but they probably had little idea of the payoffs involved. When we turn to public attitudes, we find a similar split—many citizens wanted to consume the services offered by Irv Stern, but they were against official corruption; few residents think that one produces the other. But in thinking about "public attitudes," several problems of definition arise. For one thing, "attitudes" depend on the way in which a question is phrased —a respondent would be likely to answer "no" if he were asked, "Are you in favor of gambling?", but he might also answer "yes" if he were asked whether it was all right to flip a coin to see who would buy the next round of drinks. As we will shortly see, it is very difficult to conclude that because a Wincantonite voted for candidate X, he was voting "for corruption"—in his mind, he might have been voting for a fellow Pole, or a workingman, or an athletic hero, etc., and the decision did not involve "corruption" or "reform."

Second, we have to ask whether "attitude," in the sense of a conscious preference for X over Y, is an appropriate concept. We must keep in mind that for Wincantonites, "reform" has been the exception rather than the rule. The vast majority of local citizens have lived with wide-open gambling all their lives, and the reform administrations of Craig and Whitton add up to only 7 of the last 40 years. As one lawyer said, "When I was a little kid, my dad would lift me up so I could put a dime in the slot machine at his club. We never saw anything wrong in it." In addition to knowing about gambling in Wincanton, the residents knew of other cities in the State in which gambling was equally wide open, and they believe that Wincanton is similar to most cities in the country. Fifty-four percent of the respondents in the survey agreed with the statement, "There is not much difference between politics in Wincanton and politics in other American cities." (Nineteen percent were undecided and only 25 percent disagreed.) Because of this specific history of gambling and this general perception that Wincanton is like other cities, it may be more accurate to speak of latent acceptance of gambling and petty corruption as "facts of life" rather than thinking of conscious choices, e.g., "I prefer gambling and corruption to a clean city and honest officials." Under most circumstances, the question has not come up.

In a series of questions included in the recent attitude survey, Wincantonites indicated a general approval or tolerance of gambling, but they frequently distinguished between organized and unorganized operations. Eighty percent felt that the State legislature should legalize bingo. Fifty-eight percent felt that a State-operated lottery would be a good idea. Fifty-four percent agreed with the general statement, "The State should legalize gambling." When asked *why* the State should legalize gambling, 42 percent of those favoring the idea felt that gambling was harmless or that people would gamble anyway; 44 percent thought that the State should control it and receive the profits; 8 percent felt that legalization would keep out racketeers. Forty-nine percent agreed that "gambling is all right so long as local people, not outsiders, run the game;" 35 percent disagreed; and 11 percent were uncertain. Forty-six percent felt that "the police should not break up a friendly poker game, even if there is betting." Here, 37 percent disagreed and 14 percent were uncertain.

If Wincanton residents are tolerant of gambling, they show little tolerance of official corruption: 72 percent of the respondents disagreed with a statement that, "A city official who receives $10 in cash from a company that does business with the city should not be prosecuted;" only 13 percent agreed. Sixty-one percent were unwilling to agree that, "It's all right for the mayor of a city to make a profit when the city buys some land so long as only a fair price is charged." Thirty-four percent agreed that, "It's all right for a city official to accept presents from companies so long as the taxpayers don't suffer," but 47 percent disagreed and 13 percent were undecided. Fifty-four percent did not believe that, "The mayor and police chief should be able to cancel parking and speeding tickets in some cases," but 36 percent thought it might be a good idea.

The intensity of feelings against corruption was brought out most strongly when the respondents were asked about the 30-day jail sentences imposed on Irv Stern and Bob Walasek for extorting $10,500 on city purchases of parking meters. Eighty-six percent felt that the sentences were too light; seven respondents felt that they were too severe, generally feeling that publicity arising from the trial had hurt Walasek's family. When asked why they felt as they did, 32 percent felt that Walasek had "betrayed a public trust;" 18 percent gave an answer such as, "If it had been a little guy like me instead of a guy with pull like Walasek, I'd still be in jail."

In light of the mixed feelings about gambling and corruption, we might wonder whether Wincantonites are hostile toward the police department's present antigambling policy. This does not appear to be the case: 55 percent of the respondents disagreed with the statement, "The Wincanton police today are concentrating on gambling too much"; only 17 percent agreed, and 21 percent were undecided. Further support for the local police was indicated by the respondents when asked to comment on the statement, "If there is any gambling going on in Wincanton, it should be handled by the local police rather than the FBI"; 57 percent agreed and 19 percent disagreed. The preference for local action was slightly stronger—58 percent— when the question stated "* * * the local police rather than State Police."

We have frequently mentioned that Walasek and Stern were convicted on the basis of testimony given by former Police Chief Dave Phillips. Phillips was given immunity from Federal prosecution, and perjury charges against him were dropped. What was the public response to Phillips having testified? Was he regarded as a "fink" or a hero? Fifty-nine percent of the respondents felt that it was right for Phillips to testify. Only 15 percent felt that he should have received immunity, 40 percent felt the grant of immunity was wrong, and 40 percent did not know whether it was right or wrong. The most common reaction was that Phillips was as guilty as the others, or "he only testified to save his own skin."

Finally, to ascertain how much citizens know about law enforcement agencies, the survey respondents were asked, first, "As you remember it, who was it who decided that bingo should not be played in Wincanton?" Five percent attributed the ban to the legislature. Forty-three percent correctly stated that a joint decision of Mayor Whitton and District Attorney Hendricks (declaring that the State gambling law included bingo) had led to the current crackdown. Thirty-four percent didn't know. Ironically, 13 respondents believed that Walasek, Donnelly, Police Chief Phillips, or District Attorney French had ended bingo (all had been out of office for at least 6 months and opposed the ban)!

Second, respondents[8] were asked, "Which of the Federal investigative agencies would you say was primarily responsible for most of the prosecutions of Wincanton people in the past 10 years?". Thirty-one percent correctly cited the Internal Revenue Service, 20 percent mentioned the Federal Bureau of Investigation (whose only major involvement had been in raiding the dice game), and 46 percent did not know.

The Politics of Reform. In every local election in Wincanton, it seems that some candidates are running on "reform" platforms, charging their opponents with corruption or at least tolerating gamblers and prostitutes. Usually, we see Republicans attacking Democratic corruption. But Democratic primary candidates also attack the records of Democratic incumbents, and in 1955, Democrats promised the voters that they would rid the town of the prostitutes and bookies that "pearl gray" Hal Craig had tolerated. Frequently, officials have become corrupt after they were elected, but Wincanton voters have never returned a known criminal to office. Following legislative investigations in the early 1950's, Mayor Watts lost the general election, receiving only 39 percent of the vote. After the Federal indictment of Police Chief Phillips in the early 1960's, Bob Walasek was defeated in the Democratic primary, running a poor third, with only 19 percent of the vote. Even with Walasek out of the running, the voters selected Republican Whitton over his Democratic opponent, a councilman in the Walasek administration. While the Republicans were able to elect councilmen in two elections, they were unable to make inroads in the off-year council elections despite wholesale Federal gambling raids in the months just prior to the elections in these years.

Looking at these voting figures, two questions arise—why corruption and why reform? As we have seen, Wincantonites have never voted for corruption, although they may have voted for men tolerant of the gambling citizens demanded. While the newspapers and the reformers have warned of the necessary connection between gambling and corruption, their impact has been deadened by repetition—Wincanton voters have acquired a "ho-hum" attitude, saying to themselves, "That's just the Gazette sounding off again." or "The Republicans are 'crying wolf' just like they did 4 years ago." As Lord Bryce said of Americans 80 years ago:

> The people see little and they believe less. True, the party newspapers accuse their opponents of such offenses, but the newspapers are always reviling somebody; and it is because the words are so strong that the tale has little meaning * * *.
>
> The habit of hearing charges promiscuously bandied to and fro, but seldom probed to the bottom, makes men heedless.[9]

If the Democrats have dominated Wincanton elections so consistently, why did they lose in two important elections? Those years were different because official corruption was being documented by Federal investigators; in other years investigations were only showing widespread gambling, and only newspaper inferences suggested that officials were being paid off. It is equally, perhaps more, significant to note that Federal investigations attracted national attention—instead of seeing allusions of corruption in the Wincanton Gazette, city voters were beginning to read about themselves and their city in *The New York Times* and the papers of the larger cities within the State. Just as national media coverage of the "War on the Press" may have forced Mayor Donnelly to back down, so the national interest during the two elections may have shamed local voters into deserting the Democratic Party. The years when the Republicans won were different because the voters were forced to recognize the conflict between their norms (honesty in government, no corruption, etc.) and the actions of local Democratic officials. Their "active sense of outrage"[10] produced a crisis leading to a readjustment of their normal patterns of behavior. Furthermore, even though the voters had been willing to tolerate petty corruption on the part of past officials , the national investigations indicated that officials were now going too far. As Irv Stern had predicted, Bob Walasek, unlike his predecessor, got "greedy," and pushed the voters too far, tolerating too much vice and gambling and demanding kickbacks on too many contracts and licenses. For the voters, the "price" of Democratic control had gotten too high.[11]

A city where the government has for its subjects acquaintances, whose interests and passions it knows and can at pleasure thwart or forward, can hardly expect a neutral government.

—Sir Ernest Barker,
"Greek Political Theory"[12]

THE FUTURE OF REFORM IN WINCANTON

When Wincantonites are asked what kind of law enforcement they want, they are likely to say that it is all right to tolerate petty gambling and prostitution, but that "you've got to keep out racketeers and corrupt politicians." Whenever they come to feel that the city is being controlled by these racketeers, they "throw the rascals out." This policy of "throwing the rascals out," however, illustrates the dilemma facing reformers in Wincanton. Irv Stern, recently released from Federal prison, has probably, in fact, retired from the rackets; he is ill and plans to move to Arizona. Bob Walasek, having been twice convicted on extortion charges, is finished politically. Therefore? Therefore, the people of Wincanton firmly believe that "the problem" has been solved—"the rascals" have been thrown out. When asked, recently, what issues would be important in the next local elections, only 9 of 183 respondents felt that clean government or keeping out vice and gambling might be an issue. (Fifty-five percent had no opinion, 15 percent felt that the ban on bingo might be an issue, and 12 percent cited urban renewal, a subject frequently mentioned in the papers preceding the survey.) Since, under Ed Whitton, the city is being honestly run and is free from gambling and prostitution, there is no problem to worry about.

On balance, it seems far more likely to conclude that gambling and corruption will soon return to Wincanton (although possibly in less blatant forms) for two reasons—first, a significant number of people want to be able to gamble or make improper deals with the city government. (This assumes, of course, that racketeers will be available to provide gambling if a complacent city administration permits it.) Second, and numerically far more important, most voters think that the problem has been permanently solved, and thus they will not be choosing candidates based on these issues, in future elections.

Throughout this report, a number of specific recommendations have been made to minimize opportunities for wide-open gambling and corruption— active State Police intervention in city affairs, modification of the city's contract bidding policies, extending civil service protection to police officers, etc. On balance, we could probably also state that the commission form of government has been a hindrance to progressive government; a "strong mayor" form of government would probably handle the city's affairs more efficiently. Fundamentally, however, all of these suggestions are irrelevant. When the voters have called for clean government, they have gotten it, in spite of loose bidding laws, limited civil service, etc. The critical factor has been voter preference. Until the voters of Wincanton come to believe that illegal gambling produces the corruption they have known, the type of government we have documented will continue. Four-year periods of reform do little to change the habits instilled over 40 years of gambling and corruption.

NOTES

·1. This study, part of a larger investigation of the politics of law enforcement and corruption, was financed by a grant from the Russell Sage Foundation. All responsibility for the contents of this report remains with the senior author. The authors wish gratefully to acknowledge the assistance of the people and officials of Wincanton who will, at their request, remain anonymous. The authors wish particularly to acknowledge the assistance of the newspapers of Wincanton; Prof. Harry Sharp and the staff of the Wisconsin Survey Research Laboratory; Henry S. Ruth; Jr., Lloyd E. Ohlin, and Charles H. Rogovin of the President's Commission on Law Enforcement and Administration of Justice; and many National, State, and local law enforcement personnel. The authors shared equally in the research upon which this report is based; because of the teaching duties of Mr. Olson, Mr. Gardiner assumed the primary role in writing this report. Joel Margolis and Keith Billingsley, graduate students in the Department of Political Science, University of Wisconsin, assisted in the preparation of the data used in this report.

2. To preserve the anonymity of the city, it will only be stated that Wincanton's 1960 population was between 75,000 and 200,000.

3. William L. Riordan, "Plunkitt of Tammany Hall" (New York: E. P. Dutton. 1963), p. 3.

4. See the excellent discussion of political campaign contributions in Alexander Heard, "The Costs of Democracy" (Chapel Hill: University of North Carolina Press, 1960), and Herbert Alexander, "Regulation of Political Finance" (Berkeley: Institute of Governmental Studies, and Princeton: Citizens' Research Foundation, 1966).

*   *   *

7. This survey was conducted by eight female interviewers from the Wisconsin Survey Research Laboratory, using a schedule of questions requiring 45 to 75 minutes to complete. Respondents were selected from among the adults residing in housing units selected at random from the Wincanton "City Directory." One hundred eighty-three completed interviews were obtained.

8. This question was inserted in the schedule after the survey was underway; only 87 respondents were asked this question.

9. James Bryce, "The American Commonwealth," vol. II (London: MacMillan, 1889), p. 204.

10. Arnold A. Rogow and Harold D. Lasswell, "Power, Corruption, and Rectitude" (Englewood Cliffs; Prentice-Hall, 1963), p. 72.

11. Cf. Eric L. McKitrick, "The Study of Corruption," 72 Political Science Quarterly 507 (December 1957).

12. Sir Ernest Barker, "Greek Political Theory" (London: Methuen, 1918), p. 13.

POVERTY AND CRIMINAL JUSTICE ✒ Patricia M. Wald

The great majority of those accused of crime in this country are poor. The system of criminal justice under which they are judged is rooted in certain

SOURCE: The President's Commission on Law Enforcement and Administration of Justice, *Task Force Report: The Courts* (Washington, D.C., 1967), pp. 139–151.

ideals: that arrest can only be for cause; that defendants, presumed innocent until shown guilty, are entitled to pretrial freedom to aid in their own defense; that a guilty plea should be voluntary; that the allegations of wrongdoing must be submitted to the truthfinding light of the adversary system; that the sentence should be based on the gravity of the crime, yet tempered by the rehabilitative potential of the defendant; that, after rehabilitation, the offender should be accepted back into the community.

To the extent, however, that the system works less fairly for the poor man than for the affluent, the ideal is flawed.

How *does* the system work for the poor?

On almost any night in any metropolitan jurisdiction in the United States a wide range of arrests is made: petty offenses, serious misdemeanors, felonies, juvenile misconduct. These are typical:

Defendant A is spotted by a foot patrol officer in the skid row district of town, weaving along the street.[1] When the officer approaches him, the man begins muttering incoherently and shrugs off the officer's inquiries. When the officer seizes his arm, A breaks the hold violently, curses the officer and the police. The patrolman puts in a call for a squad car, and the man is taken to the precinct station where he is booked on a double charge of drunk and disorderly.[2]

Defendant B, a woman, is apprehended for shoplifting a $10 dress in a downtown department store. A store detective who has been watching stops her near the door and finds the dress under her skirt. He calls a police officer who takes her to the precinct for booking on a charge of petty larceny.

Defendant C is charged with holding up a liquor store and seriously wounding the proprietor while making his getaway. His arrest follows an informer's tip and the victim's identification of his mug shot. The mug shot is a leftover from an "investigative arrest" two years before.[3]

Defendant D, a 17-year-old Negro male, unemployed and a school drop-out, is stopped by a Youth Division officer at 12:30 a.m. on a street corner while loitering with a noisy gang.[4] There is a 10:00 p.m. curfew in effect for juveniles. The officer tells the gang to disperse and go home; D retorts that he doesn't have to and "no . . . cop can make me." The officer takes him in custody, frisks him for weapons, marches him to the precinct station, and calls his home. A man answers the phone, but is either intoxicated or unable to understand what the officer says. D is taken to the juvenile detention center for the night.[5]

All of these defendants are poor. At every stage of the criminal process they will face the cumulative handicaps of poverty.

In the Stationhouse

Defendant A's belt is removed to balk any attempts at suicide, and he is put in the drunk tank to sober up.

"His cellmate lies slumped and snoring on the cell's single steel bunk, sleeping off an all-day drunk, oblivious to the shouts . . . There are at least two men in each 4 x 8 foot cell and three in some. . . . The stench of cheap alcohol, dried blood, urine and excrement covers the cell block. Except for the young man's shouts, it is quiet. Most of the prisoners are so drunk they gaze without seeing, unable to answer when spoken to. There are no lights in the cells, which form a square in the middle of the cell block. But the ring of naked light bulbs on the walls around the cell block throw light into the cells, each of which is equipped with a steel bunk. There are no mattresses. 'Mattresses wouldn't last the night,' a policeman explains. 'And with prisoners urinating all over them, they wouldn't be any good if they did last.' The only sound in the cell block is the constant flowing of water through the toilets in each cell. The toilets do not have tops, which could be torn off and broken."[6]

Every half hour or so a policeman checks to see if the inmates are "still warm."[7]

After sobering up, a drunk or disorderly can usually leave the lockup in four to five hours if he is able to post collateral, $10–$25. No matter how many times he has been arrested before, he will not have to appear in court if he chooses to forfeit the collateral. The drunk without money stays in jail until court the next morning. At 6 a.m., the police vans collect the residue of the precinct lockups and take them to the courthouse cell blocks to await a 10:00 arraignment.

Defendant B is booked at the precinct. Her offense is an "open and shut" case with witnesses; she is charged with petty larceny, and the files are checked to see if she has a record. Because of the frequent association among shoplifting, prostitution, and narcotics addiction, she is subjected to a compulsory physical examination. Clean, she is eligible for stationhouse bail of $500. This means cash in the full amount or a $50 premium for a bondsman. She may make one or several phone calls to a bondsman (a list hangs by the pay phone), a friend, relative, or an attorney if she knows one or can pick one out of the yellow pages. But the timing and the number of phone calls are usually a matter of police discretion, and it may be an empty right if no one answers, or if there is no telephone in the rented rooms or tenements of her friends and family. Unable to raise bail,[8] she must await arraignment—any time from an hour to several weeks after booking.[9]

Defendant C, suspected of robbery and aggravated assault, both felonies, is properly warned of his right to remain silent or to consult counsel before any questioning takes place. But he has no right to an appointed lawyer before his first court appearance, and since he cannot afford his own lawyer, his real choice is to keep quiet or sign a waiver of the right not to be questioned. For the present he prefers not to talk.

C's fingerprints and mug shot are taken, and a record check is made for any other arrests in the police files. The FBI is sent a copy of the fingerprints to check for out-of-jurisdiction offenses. He is taken to the hospital for identification by the owner-victim, then back to the liquor store so the police can replay the event and verify the victim's story as well as watch C's reaction. Street witnesses brought to the station point him out as the man they saw running from the store. C is placed in a lineup, made to strike a variety of poses and repeat the words of the holdup man.[10] A blood smear is taken to match against some stains on the sidewalk outside the store. His room is searched for weapons, and ballistics tests are made on a gun found there.

This investigative process, steady or interrupted, may go on for many hours, even days.[11] He is allowed to call or see his family, but their entreaties to tell all, their own woes—"what will happen to me and the kids now"— offer little solace.[12] He may not want to involve others who can help him because they, too, would come under police scrutiny and questioning.

The interrogation (if there is any) and the investigation often precede the actual booking, so he is unsure of what charges are lodged against him. The duration of his custody is open-ended; he is not told how long it will last. If he has not been able to reach a friend or relative, no one knows for sure where he is.

In the back of his mind may linger stories he has heard about police brutality: telephone books which leave no marks, psychological bullying.[13] Only the police are present to hear what he actually says or to observe in what condition he is when he says it.[14] Often, in the tension of the moment and the rush of later events, he forgets what he said.

The morning following juvenile defendant D's apprehension, the arresting officer finds he has a record of prior juvenile offenses, minor thefts, truancy, gang activity. Several years ago, he was put on juvenile probation, and completed the period without further incident. The officer goes to see his parents and finds the mother, unmarried with several younger children, working a 3:00–12:00 shift in a bar. The home consists of two rooms in a dilapidated, overcrowded tenement. The mother reacts to the news by bitterly complaining of the boy, the company he keeps, the troubles he has already caused her, and the miseries yet to come. Based on the interview and D's past record, the officer decides to petition the case to juvenile court.

Preliminary Hearing and Arraignment

Defendant A, charged with drunk and disorderly, is brought into court from the bullpen in a shuffling line of dirty, beat, unshaven counterparts, many still reeking of alcohol. Each spends an average of 90 seconds before the judge, time for the clerk to intone the charge and for the judge to ask if he desires counsel and how he pleads. Rarely does a request for counsel or a "not quilty" break the monotony of muttered "guilties."[15] Lawyers are not often assigned in police court, and anyone who can afford his own counsel will already have been released from jail on bond—to prepare for trial at a later date or to negotiate with the city prosecutor to drop the charges.

Occasionally, an unrepresented defendant will ask for trial. If the arresting officer is present, he will be tried on the spot. There are no jury trials in drunk court. The policeman will testify that the man was "staggering," "his breath smelled of some sort of alcoholic beverage," his speech was "slurred"—"his eyes were bloodshot and glassy." The man may protest that he had only a few drinks, but there are no witnesses to support his testimony, no scientific evidence to establish his alcoholic blood level at the time of arrest, no lawyers to cross-examine the officers.[16] If the defendant pleads not guilty and hopes he can get counsel (his own or court-assigned), he may have his trial postponed a week or two. Meanwhile, he must make bond or return to jail.[17]

Police Court sentencing is usually done immediately after a plea. A few courts with alcoholic rehabilitation court clinics may screen for likely candidates—those not too far along on the alcoholism trail—in the detention pens. Counsel, when available, can ask for a presentence report, but delay in sentencing means jail or bail in the meantime. On a short-term offense it is seldom worth it.

Other kinds of petty offenders—disorderlies, vagrants, street ordinance violators—follow a similar pattern in court. Guilty pleas are the rule. Without counsel or witnesses it is the defendant's word against the police. Even when counsel is present, defense efforts at impeachment founder on the scanty records kept by the police in such petty offenses. The only defense may be the defendant's word—impeachable if he has a record—and hard-to-find "character witnesses" without records from his slum neighborhood.

Defendant B, the shoplifter, is arraigned in a misdemeanor court the same morning:

"The audience section of the courtroom is usually jammed with relatives of the defendants involved, and with witnesses and complainants, as well as with defendants themselves who have been released on parole or bail. . . .
"The number of reserved seats is usually inadequate for all of the attorneys and police involved in the day's cases. As a result, the attorneys usually gather close to the bench; and the police invariably also congregate inside the rail close to the door leading to the detention pen. As each case is called, the policeman will fetch from the pen the defendant whom he has arrested and bring him before the judge."[18]

B is told of her rights, in a mass of a hundred other accused, crushed into the space between counsel table and spectators "like New Yorkers in a subway at rush hour." Marched slowly to the judge's bench "like assembly line workers in a factory, all parties operate under a climate which makes it appear that nothing may be permitted to interfere with the smooth operation of the line."[19]

When B is before the judge, the clerk reads her a summary statement of the charges against her and recites her rights to trial and counsel, phrased in the words of the pertinent statute or court ruling. "Spoken at high speed, in a dull monotone, phrased in legal jargon, the charges and the rights are frequently unintelligible."[20]

B can plead guilty at her first appearance or ask for a trial. She can also request an adjournment to consult or obtain counsel. The various jurisdictions differ on whether a misdemeanant who cannot afford counsel[21] is entitled to appointed counsel. Until recently in Washington, D.C., the court appointed counsel from a "mourners' bench" and left it to the lawyer and his new client to negotiate a fee. In New York City, a Legal Aid lawyer is appointed minutes before the arraignment of an indigent defendant. In Miami, there is no representation provided for indigent misdemeanants; in Los Angeles, less than 10% of all misdemeanants have counsel at arraignment. In all events, more misdemeanants than felons lack representation. It may be harder for the defendant to qualify as an indigent misdemeanant than as an indigent felon, either because he has scraped up a small, automatically disqualifying bail bond[22] or because the counsel fees involved are so small. Without counsel, defendant B is almost certain to plead quilty.

Even with counsel, however, pressures are strong in a high volume misdemeanor court to plead guilty and hope for, or bargain for, leniency. Assigned counsel often get no pay for representation at this level; retained counsel put into the case only the time equivalent of the $50 or $75 they can get out of it, and public defenders have only a few minutes' frantic conference with their clients outside the courtroom to decide on a plea or request for adjournment.[23]

Trial is not an attractive prospect for an indigent misdemeanant or his lawyer. It can mean a new round of bail bonds or weeks in jail awaiting trial.

Complexities of proof may be just as great as in felony trials; thorny legal issues can arise: problems of illegal search and seizure, unlawful arrests, or coerced confessions. But public funds are almost never available for investigators or expert witnesses in these courts.[24] Preliminary hearings are usually waived because lawyers cannot take the time. Witness fees—75 cents a day in misdemeanor cases in the General Sessions Court of the District of Columbia—are noncompensatory. Constant adjournments and calendar breakdowns wear down even a persevering defendant, his underpaid lawyer, and his reluctant witnesses. Few legal reputations are made in misdemeanor courts. The trials are more informal, the judges apt to be less learned in the law than in higher courts. There is generally no court reporter unless the defendant hires his own, which he seldom can afford. In general, upsetting the routine of misdemeanor court by demanding a trial is a risky proposition; it can operate as a lever to bargain with the prosecutor for a shorter sentence or dismissal, but it can also antagonize the prosecutor and judge, resulting in a stiffer sentence on conviction.[25]

Only defendants with money can afford to play the waiting game. Lawyers assured of reasonable fees can invest the time and energy to prepare for trial if bargaining for leniency ends in a stalemate. Their clients do not suffer from tactical maneuvers that delay the ultimate trial. The prosecutor, cannily recognizing their potential "follow through," may capitulate earlier in the game. In contrast the indigent's attempts at bargaining are confined to a few hours or days after arraignment and, declining in vigor, reflect the inescapable fact that he has the most to lose from each new delay.

After the police have completed their investigation, defendant C is brought before a judge for preliminary hearing. Charged with robbery and aggravated assault, a determination is made on whether he should be bound over to the grand jury.[26] If the police cannot justify the charges, they could be dismissed at this juncture, but if C has already confessed, his admissions can be introduced against him; so can other incriminating post-arrest developments, including lineup identifications, fingerprints, etc. At the preliminary hearing, the defendant has the option of asserting his right to have the government present its case. Appearance of counsel here may be crucial. The defendant may not fully understand that if he waives, he loses one of his best and most effective chances to discover the identity of the government's key witnesses and the nature of the government's evidence. Adroit cross-examination at the preliminary hearing can expose and freeze inconsistencies in testimony before government witnesses have time to reflect and to consult extensively with the prosecution: valuable ground work may be laid for later impeachment at trial.

But the indigent defendant may not always be offered assigned counsel at his first appearance before a judicial officer.[27] Without counsel, few felony suspects are adept enough to probe evidentiary weaknesses by cross-examining prosecution witnesses; few are experienced enough to weigh the pros and cons of taking the stand themselves.[26] Since he has been in police custody from the time of his arrest, the defendant has had no opportunity to line up defense witnesses. Even if, by some extraordinary effort, he succeeded in constructing a plausible defense or in challenging the government's case, no stenographic record of the preliminary examination would be available without costly advance arrangements.[29]

Bail in felony cases is ordinarily set for the first time at the preliminary hearing. For armed robbery and aggravated assault, it may be as high as $25,000, requiring a $2,500 premium that poor defendants cannot raise.[30] With no defense lawyer to argue for lower bail, the prosecutor's recommendation will ordinarily stand. Even in cities where projects are operating to release worthy defendants without bail, the indigent's roots in the community usually must be solid, his record comparatively clean of past felonies.[31] On the other hand, financial ability to make bail can be a mixed blessing. It may disqualify him from obtaining assigned counsel then, or later on arraignment.[32]

When he is bound over to the grand jury, the detained defendant enters a legal limbo. Even if counsel were appointed for the preliminary hearing, his duties have ceased, and appointment of new counsel awaits action of the grand jury. Without a lawyer, the defendant can do nothing to affect the grand jury's deliberations or to identify key witnesses.

In jail, the defendant is thrown among convicted criminals. He marks out his days in idleness.[33] Outside problems proliferate and contacts crumble.[34] He is the target of constant jailhouse advice on "copping a plea"[35] from fellow inmates. Weeks, months go by, often with no word from the courts or the lawyers on the progress of his case. If the grand jury finally declines to indict, his case may be "kicked downstairs" for reinstatement of misdemeanor charges. This process may take additional weeks while witnesses are recalled to swear to the new complaint and a new prosecutor assigned to the case. Only when the misdemeanor information is filed and a new arraignment date set is he notified that the felony charges have been dismissed.

When an indictment is handed down, the accused felon is brought from jail for arraignment, this time in the felony court where he will be tried. Counsel is now offered the indigent defendant.[36] Bail must be reset by the judge to cover the period until trial, sometimes months away. An adjournment may be necessary to decide on a plea. Many indigents, energies sapped by prolonged periods in jail, waive counsel and plead guilty immediately.[37] Yet a plea of not guilty is often necessary to buy time for negotiating with the prosecutor on reduction of the charges, dropping some charges in exchange for a plea to others, prosecuting multiple charges or indictments separately or concurrently.[38] Occasionally only a token bargaining effort is required because of the pressures of the calendar on the court and prosecutors,[39] but usually defense counsel's success is comprised of many factors: his reputation and the intensity of his commitment to the case; his capacity for engaging the prosecution with pretrial motion and writs; his resources for proceeding to a full-scale trial; his willingness to challenge illegal police or prosecutorial tactics. To bargain expertly, counsel must be able to probe the strengths and weaknesses of the prosecution's case, to realize and fulfill the potential of his own. He must acquire a sure knowledge of all the permutations and combinations of pleas and penalties that are possible under the indictment.[40] Intangibles enter the picture;[41] the defendant must impose full trust in his counsel's strategic judgment, be willing to accept his assessment of the prospects and alternatives.[42]

As soon as the petition involving defendant D is filed in juvenile court, the court's intake worker decides whether to proceed with the case. If she thinks the family can control the boy and he is likely to avoid trouble again, she can dismiss the case or place him on informal probation for a few months. To make the decision, she has to assess the child himself, his home situation, his school, and police record.

In D's case, the lack of home supervision, his mother's self-admitted defeat in holding him in line, and his record of one previous probation rule out dismissal. The decision is made to charge him with violation of the curfew and disorderly conduct and to bring him before the juvenile court that afternoon. (Had the offense been more serious, he might have been waived to an adult court for a full-scale criminal trial.)[43] In a few jurisdictions, the child and parents will be asked if they want a lawyer when a decision to petition the case is made; if they have no money, counsel will be assigned.[44] In most jurisdictions, however, there is no procedure for assignment of counsel before hearing.

The first hearing before the juvenile judge decides whether D has committed some act which, under the statute, gives the court jurisdiction. Juvenile court proceedings are informal, not open to the public, not usually recorded. The judge, in the presence of D's mother, will ask the boy if he wants counsel. Most juvenile court defendants lacking funds waive counsel.[45] The judge asks if D admits the allegation of the petition; nothing is said about his right to remain silent. Most juveniles concede "involvement" readily.[46] If the child denies the facts alleged, the case is set down for trial at a later date, and he is either sent back to the detention home or released to his own parents in the interim. D, who has been this route before, admits his offense, and the judge postpones disposition until a social study can be made by the court. In the meantime, out of school without a job or 24-hour supervision at home, he is remanded to detention.

At the detention home, D is one of the older inmates. In the group are other 16–18–year-olds awaiting waiver decisions, trials or dispositions for auto thefts, housebreakings, burglaries, and narcotics offenses. They are questioned by the police while detained. Because of the transient, short-term population, the school program is a haphazard, undisciplined one. D has been out of school over a year and has no interest in renewing his formal education. The home provides a different kind of education: He learns details of other inmates' exploits, tricks for dealing with the police, names of friends to contact or stay clear of in training schools; he gets a first exposure to the future jailhouse crowd, is initiated into homosexual rites.

"I could do everything I wanted to do—steal, fight, curse, play, and nobody could take me and put me anywhere. I was already in the only place they could put me. I had found a way to get away with everything I wanted to do . . . I was doing things to people that I never would have done out on the street, but I didn't care. It didn't make sense to be in the Youth House if you were only going to do the things you did out on the street."[47]

Preparation and Trial

C prepares for trial, although plea bargaining continues up to the time of entering the courthouse. As the momentum of pretrial preparation mounts, pressures to compromise increase. Pretrial motions involving full-scale hearings are time-consuming, require extensive research and investigation,[48] and can delay trial for months. Yet they are often the vitals of the defense strategy. The suspect should be taken to the scene of the arrest to replay his account of what happened. Other witnesses to the incident have to be located and their stories recorded. The legal precedents must be researched. New counsel must familiarize himself with any evidence adduced at an earlier preliminary hearing. All of this takes time and money while the defendant languishes in jail.

Challenging a confession before trial means obtaining a copy of the admission itself and since the *Miranda* decision a copy of any written waiver of the defendant's right to counsel. A moment-by-moment account of how and when it was obtained from the defendant must be developed by subpoenaing the police log in the case, and having the defendant examined —physically and psychologically—for signs of incapacity or compulsion, as soon as possible after he made the statements. A motion for severance means a painstaking analysis of the prejudice of a joint trial, as well as discovery motions to obtain a codefendant's admissions. Motions for a change of venue must assess the prejudice of pretrial publicity and obtain assurances that the new forum is in a jurisdiction willing to accept the burden of an indigent defendant. Efforts to exclude wiretaps or electronic bugs may demand acoustical engineers, debugging experts, blueprint specialists.[49] Search and seizure motions in narcotics cases require that the arresting officers be interviewed on the details of the seizure, and what probable cause they had for suspecting possession or making the arrest.

And there are larger problems. Motions for tactical delay have little appeal to a client in jail. Even a successful motion to dismiss the indictment —unless it concludes the case—merely signals the state of the process all over again and interminable months more in detention.

If he proposes to plead his client not guilty by reason of insanity, an indigent's counsel encounters formidable obstacles. He can have him committed to a public hospital for observation and diagnosed by government psychiatrists, who then report back to the court on the defendant's capacity to stand trial and his mental responsibility for the alleged criminal acts. If they report him sane and responsible, counsel has the option of abandoning the defense or relying on cross-examination to discredit the examiner. If, however, the defendant can afford to hire his own psychiatrist—or better still, several (at $25 an hour)—to examine the patient, he may produce a contradiagnosis to put before the jury. The defense psychiatrist can speak confidently of the quality of the state's psychiatric report, the talents of the staff, and the acceptability of the methodology employed. With an expert stalemate, the jury will be less inhibited in making up their own minds.[50]

Perhaps more important, the psychiatrist preparing the state's initial diagnosis does so in the sobering knowledge that it will undergo the close scrutiny of an outside professional who has had ample opportunity to observe and examine the patient. His participation in the psychiatric dialogue that precedes the formal report may make the difference between a contested and an uncontested plea.

Tracking down ordinary defense witnesses in the slums to support the defendant's alibi or to act as character witnesses often has a Runyanesque aspect to it. The defendant in jail tells his counsel he has known the witnesses for years, but only by the name of "Toothpick," "Malachi Joe," or "Jet." He does not know where they live or if they have a phone. If he could get out and look himself, he is sure he could find them at the old haunts, but his descriptive faculties leave something to be desired. Since a subpoena cannot be issued for "Toothpick," or no known address, counsel sets off on a painstaking, often frustrating, search of the defendant's neighborhood. He stops children at play; he attempts door-to-door conversations with hostile and suspicious slum-dwellers; he haunts the local bars; he even asks the police on the beat for help.[51] If he finally locates the witnesses, they must be "collared" and cajoled into coming to court; otherwise, they will probably ignore a subpoena.[52] They must be reassured—if possible—that there will be no retaliation from police or prosecutors,[53] that they will not themselves be held in jail as material witnesses. Fare for the trip to court must be dredged up from somewhere, lost days' pay replaced.[54] Rarely can they tolerate more than one trip, if their testimony is postponed, they slip back into oblivion.

A defendant in jail cannot help counsel locate witnesses, persuade them to testify, nor restage his story on the actual scene.[55] He is unavailable for spot calls to check details or last-minute conferences to plan strategy; jail may be on the edge of town and the visiting hours inconvenient for busy counsel.[56]

But often there is no alibi, no insanity plea, no defensive pyrotechnics. The indigent must meet the government's case head-on and seek to exploit evidentiary weaknesses. Ideally, he needs to size up his opposition in advance of trial, to know who the witnesses are and what they will say; to obtain the results of scientific tests on blood, narcotics, fingerprints, handwriting, ballistic tests on weapons, exhibits taken from the scene or from the defendant himself, and reports on medical examination of the victim.

In the absence of a cadre of independent investigators, the defendant has to rely for this information on pretrial criminal discovery. But neither the names of government witnesses nor their prior statements to the police or to the grand jury, even those of a codefendant, are generally available in advance through discovery;[57] their stories cannot be checked out for error —purposeful or inadvertent. They cannot even be contacted personally to see if they have any information helpful to the defense. Their FBI records cannot be secured.[58]

The indigent defendant, on the other hand, must often disclose what he expects his witnesses to testify in order to obtain a free subpoena.[59] The government has its corps of fingerprint, ballistics, and handwriting specialists; it has laboratories in which to test and analyze the evidence. The government also possesses the real evidence itself: the prints, the bullet, the blood, the signature. The results of these tests may be available through discovery[60] but to counter these tests effectively the defense needs its own experts to view the original evidence. This means double trips and double expert fees, once to analyze and again to testify. Funds from public sources for expert defense witnesses are always limited;[61] often they are nonexistent.

The defendant can have his case tried to a jury or a judge. Detained defendants and those with assigned counsel are more apt to choose a judge;[62] jury calendars are notoriously backlogged, and the penalty for demanding a jury trial may be a stiffer sentence.[63] Adjournments are frequent, and the attrition rate for defense witnesses high. There may be subtler reasons, too, for bypassing a jury. The make-up of many juries is middle-class oriented —small businessmen, accountants, housewives. Slum residents are not so likely to be on the voter registration lists from which the juries are drawn.[64] If they are, they are not attracted to jury duty; usually they cannot afford long absences from their jobs.

The outcome of C's trial depends on a number of factors: his counsel's ability to discredit government witnesses on cross-examination; his successful refutation of scientific evidence or tests; his ability to keep any confessions out of evidence; his success in convincing the judge that the defendant could not be the man involved or that he was somewhere else at the time.

Skillful cross-examination is most effective "when the questions are based on facts rather than on intuition . . . it often takes days or weeks to secure a witness or scientific proof which can destroy a fabricated story. If the fabricated story is not revealed until trial, it may be too late."[65]

But indigent defense counsel must rely too often on spotting surface inconsistencies in a witness' testimony or on comparing testimony on the stand with prior statements made available in the courtroom only after the witness has testified. The statements must then be perused under the impatient eyes of judge and jury while the trial is stalled.[66]

Defense witnesses pose strategic obstacles, even when they actually appear. They are likely to be shabbily dressed, inarticulate, unsophisticated, testy, nervous, and vulnerable to prosecution efforts at impeachment. The effect on a predominantly white collar jury can be prejudicial.

The defendant himself runs a similar risk. A detained defendant often comes to the courtroom pallid, unshaven, dishevelled, demoralized, a victim of the jailhouse blues.[67] He comes and goes through a special door that the jury soon learns leads to the detention pen beyond. He is always closely accompanied by a police escort or marshal.[68]

A defendant under courtroom guard raises tactical as well as psychological problems. During the trial his lawyer may need to consult with him privately in the courtroom, but his guard is always in range. There can be no productive lunch or recess conferences, no quick trips to locate last-minute rebuttal witnesses, no pretrial warm-ups or post-trial replays. Should surprise witnesses or evidence materialize, the indigent's defense counsel must face such crises alone.

In most cases, the trial will end in a guilty verdict.[69] But even an acquitted defendant often faces debts, no job, broken family ties.[70] Should there be a hung jury and retrial ordered, a transcript of the trial becomes an urgent necessity: to find contradictions in the prosecution's case, to prepare to impeach witnesses, to reevaluate trial strategy. But transcripts for retrial are not routinely provided indigents. Nor is the defendant now likely to be any freer to participate in the crucial work of preparing for his second trial than he was for the first.

After the verdict, the judge can admit the defendant to bail pending sentence, or he can refuse bail altogether. A new bail premium may be necessary to continue his freedom. If he has been detained to this point, it is unlikely that he will be released now.

Had defendant D chosen to deny the charges against him in juvenile court, he would have faced many of the same problems of locating witnesses and refuting prosecution evidence that confront his adult counterparts. In most juvenile courts, he would not, however, have had the benefit of assigned counsel, let alone investigative help. Even with counsel the chances of acquittal would be slim. The rules of evidence applicable in many juvenile courts do not bar hearsay or illegally obtained evidence to establish his involvement. He may even have been forced to testify himself. The child can be excluded from the courtroom at the judge's discretion. There may be no court record to appeal from; in only a few places can he demand a jury. The standard of proof is a preponderance of evidence, not guilt beyond a reasonable doubt.[71] If adjudicated a delinquent, there could be an immediate disposition at trial; more likely he will be sent back to the detention center while the court's staff conducts a social study into his background to recommend what should be done with him.[72]

NOTES

1. The majority of arrests for drunkenness, disorderly conduct, and vagrancy are made in the run-down sections of the city. A research project interviewing several hundred Philadelphia skid-row residents disclosed 71% had been arrested sometime during their lifetime. Blumberg, Shipley & Shandler, *The Homeless Man and the Law Enforcement Agencies*, 45 PRISON JOURNAL 29, 32 (1965). HARRINGTON, THE OTHER AMERICA, 95 (1963), reports impressions of the police pickups in the Bowery:

"I never understood how the exact number to be arrested was computed, but there must have been some method to this social madness. The paddy wagon would arrive on the Bowery; the police would arrest the first men they came to, at random; and that was that."

A variety of forces are at work to explain the disproportionate number of poor arrested. High crime and low income inhabit the same quarters. As a result, saturation patrols designed to deter major crime produce increased surveillance of slum residents, and a greater likelihood they will be picked up for minor offenses: noisy corner gatherings, neighborhood arguments, drunks staggering home. The slum resident lives a good part of his life "on the street" where the police can see him.

"The rooms of Harlem are, more often than not, small, dingy, and mean. Everyone wants to get out, to get away. . . . There are jukeboxes in the candy stores, so there is dancing in the streets . . . There are places to sit—fire escapes and car fenders and curbstones. In short, there is society in the street among neighbors from the block." STRINGFELLOW, MY PEOPLE IS THE ENEMY 8 (1964).

Yet failure to "move on" or "to give a good account" of one's presence to a policeman is an offense under many laws.

"Court: What did you do? How did you wind up in jail here?

"Def.: I don't know. I was just standing there.

"Court: I am going to give you 90 days in the Onondaga County Penitentiary but I am going to suspend that sentence on one condition, that in the future you don't give the cops a hard time. Am I getting through to you?

"Def.: Yes.

"Court: One more time, and if you are brought in for anything like this again you are going up to the Penintentiary for 90 days. Do I make myself clear?

"Def.: Yes.

"Court: The next time a cop tells you to move, you move, understand?

"Def.: Yes."

Transcript, *People v. Trotter,* City Ct., Syracuse, N.Y., June 29, 1965.

2. The more affluent drunk with money in his pocket is often put in a taxi and sent home instead of being arrested. PRESIDENT'S COMM'N ON CRIME IN THE DISTRICT OF COLUMBIA, REP. 475–76 (1966) [hereinafter cited as D.C. CRIME COMM'N REP.]

3. Dubious police practices like the investigative arrest fall heaviest in the slums. Slum residents bring few suits for false arrest, and the police are aware of this. The New York City newspapers reported the case of two young Puerto Ricans picked up by the police on their 119th Street stoop and held eight months in jail for murder before a ballistics test in another case implicated a different suspect. The boys were finally released, but:

" 'These people around here,' Ramon said, 'a lot of them still think we had something to do with it. Who's going to give me a job now? They don't want me.'

"Orlando is lucky. A relative gave him a job in a warehouse on Park Avenue a few days after he got out of jail.

" 'But I don't go nowhere,' he said the other day. 'I'm not going to give the police another chance to pick me up. When I go out, I don't go alone. I go with an adult, like my stepfather, someone who the police will believe.' "

N.Y. Herald Tribune, April 10, 1966.

The poor are also the most apt to suffer from illegal searches of their homes. In Baltimore, 300 Negro families were subjected to wholesale invasion of their homes by the police without warrants on unverified anonymous tips on the whereabouts of suspected police killers. *Lankford* v. *Gelston,* 364 F.2d 197 (4th Cir. 1966). "Four officers carrying shotguns or submachine guns and wearing bulletproof vests would go to the front door and knock . . . other men would surround the house, turning their weapons on windows and doors." *Id.* at 199. The Court of Appeals, in granting an injunction against such practices, said:

"The invasions so graphically depicted in this case 'could' happen in prosperous suburban neighborhoods, but the innocent victims know only that wholesale raids do not happen elsewhere and did happen to them. Understandably they feel that illegal treatment is reserved for those elements who the police believe cannot or will not challenge them." *Id.* at 204.

4. *Cf.* FRIEDENBERG, THE VANISHING ADOLESCENT 121 (1959):
"In our major cities merely to be young and cheaply dressed, in the company of friends like yourself and in such resorts as will let you hang around is to invite the grim attention of the Youth Squad."

Police have wide discretion not to refer minor cases to juvenile court. Some of the grounds on which a referral decision may be made are "uncooperative parents," "past failures with social agencies," "inadequate supervision." District of Columbia Metropolitan Police Dept., General Order No. 6.

In a questionnaire sent to over 6,000 police officers throughout the United States by the International Association of Police Chiefs, 50% of those replying considered the following statement correct:
"In most cases involving lower-class, under-privileged, slum-type juveniles, strong police and court action are necessary because the families of these offenders are incapable of exercising proper control." O CONNOR & WATSON, DELINQUENCY AND YOUTH CRIME—THE POLICE ROLE 134 (1964).

5. Typical detention criteria for juveniles include inability to locate a parent, presumption the parent cannot produce the child in court, lack of a "suitable home," failure of the parents adequately to control a child, "physical or moral danger" in the home. See, *e.g.,* District of Columbia Metropolitan Police Dept., General Order No. 6.

6. Hoagland, *Cell Blocks' Common Denominator: A Stench of Alcohol and Dried Blood,* Washington Post, March 29, 1966, p. A1, col 3.
A policeman complains: "We don't have the manpower for constant surveillance. We can't pull the men off the streets. . . . If a man really wants to commit suicide, he'll find a way. We've found them strangled by tying a handkerchief around the bars behind them and slumping forward, looking like they were asleep. It only takes a minute . . . as for the natural deaths . . . well, many of our 'clients' spend ¾ of their lives in jail. So they've got a 75% chance of being in a cell when they go." *Ibid.*

In 1964–65, 16 men arrested for intoxication died in Washington, D.C., lockups. D.C. CRIME COMMISSION REP. 476.

7. Hoagland, *supra* note 6.

8. In Silver Spring, Md., a man arrested for disorderly conduct and detained for want of $16 bond premium was "lost" two and one-half months in jail before coming to trial. Montgomery County (Md.) Sentinel, February 18, 1967, p. 1. A New York woman arrested for possession of narcotics subsequently found to be thyroid pills spent 20 days in jail for want of a $20 bond premium. Jackson, *Who Goes to Prison?* Atlantic Monthly, Jan. 1966, p. 54.

9. Between arrest and arraignment, a minor defendant out on bail with his own counsel can often negotiate successfully with the corporation counsel to drop the charges if he has no extensive record, can demonstrate the injury to his reputation

from such a conviction, and offer desirable alternatives to prosecution, such as medical or psychiatric treatment. The initiative in proposing such plans usually lies with the defense. See, *e.g.,* Washington Post, September 9, 1965, p. C24, col. 1 (charges of sexually assaulting a 17-year-old dropped against Virginia defendant on condition he undergo treatment with private doctor); The (Washington) Evening Star, January 28, 1966 (Maryland man who kept police at bay six hours by threatening to shoot infant placed on probation without verdict on condition he undergo psychiatric care). Similarly, if a potential defendant can offer immediate restitution to his victim, the complainant can often be persuaded not to pursue the case.

10. See Note, *Indigent Jailed for Lack of Bail is not Denied Equal Protection by Forced Participation in Lineup,* 79 HARV. L. REV. 844 (1966).

11. In Dallas, Texas, an accused may be held in jail for investigation up to seven days without being "filed on." During that period he cannot be released on bail without a writ of habeas corpus. The power of the court to appoint an attorney for an accused prior to his being "filed on" is in doubt. Vera Foundation News-letter, May 14, 1966, p. 1. Experienced defense counsel have ways of coping with such police practices. See *America's Foxiest Lawyer,* Life, April 1, 1966, p. 98.

"Three days after the murder was discovered Foreman's telephone rang. Melvin Lane Powers was being grilled by the Houston police. Just a couple of hours earlier, Powers had been hauled out of his office without being allowed to make a phone call. But on the way out he had said to his cousin, 'Get in touch with Percy Foreman.'

"Foreman responded instantly—but not by rushing down to the jail. First he called the Houston newspaper and announced that he was on his way to 'storm the Bastille.' He needed witnesses he could depend on and there were none more observant than reporters. Flanked by three reporters he descended on the Harris County jail demanding to see his client. But the police had Powers hidden away and wouldn't produce him until the next morning. Foreman's accusation of illegal police tactics blared in the newspapers."

12. See, *e.g.,* D.C. CRIME COMMISSION REP. 604 (suspects who consulted attorneys made admissions 23% of the time; those who consulted no one, 37%; those who consulted friends or relatives, 44%).

13. "There is no doubt . . . that a substantial segment of the community believes that Negroes in the custody of the police are physically mistreated. Twenty-five percent of the Negroes interviewed . . . expressed this opinion." *Id.* 207. See also Washington Post, March 28, 1966 (21-year-old Negro charged with assaulting a white police officer counter-charges officers "beat him to the ground, threw him into a patrol wagon, chained him to a radiator in the Tenth Precinct interrogation room, slapped him, kicked him and knocked a chair out from under him after telling him to sit down"); Washington Post, May 5, 1966, p. 22:

"When Robert arrives, he finds his brother sitting in a chair in an interrogation room, his face bloodied and bruised. Police refuse to send brother to hospital unless he signs a release. Robert refuses for him. After two hours they relent, drive brothers to D.C. General Hospital. At six a.m., the brother is treated. The official police report: 'Subject experienced a seizure and fell against the wall, scraping his face.' "

14. In the pre-*Miranda* period, "uneducated," "underprivileged," and "persons

of low social status" were considered peculiarly vulnerable to sophisticated interrogation techniques. See INBAU & REID, CRIMINAL INTERROGATION AND CONFESSION 72, 115 (1962). Less subtle pressures used with poor suspects in the past have included threatened cutoffs of welfare benefits to children. *Lynumn* v. *Illinois,* 372 U.S. 528 (1963).

15. Philadelphia interviews of "skid rowers," Blumberg, Shipley & Shandler, *supra* note 1, at 33–35, showed a "low verbal facility" among the men, characterized them as "extremely vulnerable" to dubious police and magistrate practices, unlikely to "express hostility verbally," and seeking to "survive by external conformity to the demands of authority such as the missions, the police, social welfare agencies."

16. See the following:

"At night, in the drama of dereliction and indifference called Night Court in New York, the alcoholics would be lined up. Sometimes they were still drunk. The magistrate would tell them of their legal rights; they would usually plead guilty, and they would be sentenced. Some of the older men would have been through this time and time again. It was a social ritual, having no apparent effect on anything. It furnished, I suppose, statistics to prove that the authorities were doing their duty, that they were coping with the problem."

HARRINGTON, *op. cit. supra* note 1, at 95.

In March 1965, 1,590 homeless men were arraigned in New York City's Criminal Court for disorderly conduct; 1,259 pleaded guilty, 325 were acquitted, and 6 were convicted after trial. In March 1966, after Legal Aid representation was introduced into the court, 1,326 were arraigned, 1,280 were acquitted, 45 pled guilty, and 1 was convicted after trial. Botein, N.Y. GOVERNOR'S CONFERENCE ON CRIME 149 (1966).

17. See the following:

Q. How do you plead to the charge?

A. I am not guilty of drinking. I don't think. I haven't drunk anything in several months. They might have thought I was drinking because I have epilepsy, but I don't drink.

Court: Then, I am not going to accept your plea of guilty. I will enter a plea of not guilty on your behalf and give you a week to get a lawyer. April 16th for counsel. Do you want any bail here, Mr. N. (the prosecutor).

Mr. N.: $250.00 bail.

Court: All right, bail is $250.00 property or cash. Have you got any relatives here in the city?

A. No.

Q. Do you have any friends here in the city?

A. No, not here. They are all in Rochester.

(Later, at the same session of Court.)

Court: Will you just listen to me for a moment? We have a procedure here that we have to follow. When you appeared before me earlier this morning, you pleaded not guilty to the charge. Do you now wish to change your plea?

A. I don't have no choice.

Q. No, you have a lot of choices. You can continue your plea of not guilty and get a lawyer and have a trial.

A. But they will take me back upstairs and I want to get out.

Q. If you plead not guilty to the charge, the only thing I can do is give you a trial
. . . I have no jurisdiction to do anything unless you are convicted after trial or unless you plead guilty.

A. I told you before I plead guilty.

Q. You understand that you are entitled to an attorney and that you can plead not guilty to the charge.

A. I know that, but I don't want to go back upstairs.

Transcript, *People* v. *Wimberly,* City Ct., Syracuse, N.Y., April 9, 1965.

18. JUDICIARY COMM. OF THE N.Y. ASSEMBLY, REPORT ON THE INVESTIGATION OF THE PRACTICES AND PROCEDURES IN THE CRIMINAL COURT OF THE CITY OF NEW YORK 67–68 (1963) [hereinafter cited as N.Y. ASSEMBLY REP.].
". . . there is great danger of undue influence by either Police Officer or defendant when the two are in frequent unsupervised personal contact, as they are on each court appearance day. . . . Many persons have told us that police officers have advised them, when they were being brought before the court, how they should plead, or what course of conduct they should follow." *Id.* at 68.

19. Nutter, *The Quality of Justice in Misdemeanor Arraignment Courts,* 53 J. CRIM. L., C. & P.S. 215 (1963).

20. N.Y. ASSEMBLY REP. 65. "We doubt that one in five of those persons to whom their rights are recited could assimilate . . . usefully the least part of what he has been told." *Ibid.*

21. A typical misdemeanant defense in New York City was estimated by lawyers interviewed for this paper to cost $250–$300 for a plea, up to $500 for a trial. The exact fee reflects the number of court appearances the lawyer has to make, which may be up to five in a misdemeanor case. Throughout the country 1,250,000 indigent misdemeanants go to court annually. In 175 out of 300 sample counties studied by the American Bar Foundation no counsel was assigned to misdemeanor cases. SILVERSTEIN, DEFENSE OF THE POOR 125, 132 (1965) [hereinafter cited as SILVERSTEIN].

22. Id. at 107–08.

23. See the following:
"The very frequency of assignment at times becomes so great that the Legal Aid lawyer can do no more than make a cursory examination of the case papers, without any hope of familiarizing himself sufficiently with the facts to determine whether a preliminary hearing, motion to suppress evidence, or some other preliminary relief, is indicated.

* * *

". . . the attorney . . . has no alternative but to exchange a few whispered words in the courtroom with his client. At very best, he may be able to spend a few moments outside the gates of the detention cell where he is compelled to speak to his client packed in along with dozens of other prisoners." N.Y. ASSEMBLY REP. 19–20.

24. An interview with a Legal Aid lawyer in New York City revealed that the eight investigators on the staff are used solely for felony cases; expert witnesses too are practically available to Legal Aid only in serious cases. Grand jury minutes (if an original felony charge has been ignored and the defendant recharged as a mis-

demeanant) often cannot be secured for use in misdemeanor trials because of a shortage of typists. In assigned counsel jurisdictions, there may be provision for investigative expenses for upper court but not lower court representation. See, *e.g.*, Montgomery County (Md.) Sentinel, Jan 13, 1966, p. B-10, col. 1.

25. Washington Post, February 5, 1966:

"In open court recently, [Judge X] told the lawyer for a man charged with negligent homicide (his speeding car had run down and killed a woman):

'I'll give your man probation if he pleads guilty right now.'

"Later, [Judge X] told the lawyer for another defendant appearing before him in court: 'So your client wants a jury trial. If he is found guilty by that jury and I ascertain that his defense was a lie, I'll throw the book at him.' "

26. The period from arrest to court appearance is as long as two to three weeks in Miami, Florida. Only warrant cases are immediately brought before a judge, despite a prompt arraignment statute. The public defender in Miami believes this period to be the greatest detriment to successful handling of an indigent's defense. Lineups, trips to the scene, and, before *Miranda*, questioning go on without any defense intervention. Interview with Robert Koeppel, Dade County Public Defender, April 15, 1966.

27. The majority of jurisdictions surveyed by the American Bar Foundation offered counsel in felony cases only after the indictment or information had been filed. SILVERSTEIN 75; *cf. White v. Maryland*, 373 U.S. 59 (1963).

28. On the other hand, some retained counsel advocate waiver of the preliminary hearing. They feel previewing the government's case on preliminary examination highlights and publicizes morbid details of the crime, commits the witness to the testimony he has given before any defense representative has a chance to discuss it with him, and identifies him in his own mind with the prosecution. They prefer to see the government witnesses privately, and to feel out the prosecutor on a plea bargain before there is a record in the case. Interview with Gary Bellow, former Deputy Director, Washington, D.C., Legal Aid Agency, April 9, 1966. The government itself can often forestall a preliminary hearing by asking for an adjournment and getting an indictment in the meantime.

29. See N.Y. ASSEMBLY REP. 23:

"One of the great values of requesting a preliminary hearing is that the defendant can thereby make a record of the evidence and testimony upon which the charge is based. But if the defendant cannot afford a certified transcript of the preliminary hearing, he is incapable of effectually refuting a change in the testimony of the complainant or a prosecution witness. For an indigent defendant, then, the preliminary hearing loses much of its value."

30. The higher the bail, the lower the percentage of defendants who can make it. In a New York City survey, 35% of defendants with bail of $500 or less could not make it, while 61% with bail above that amount could not. Rankin, *Effect of Pre-Trial Detention*, 39 N.Y.U.L. REV. 650 (1964); ATT'Y GEN. COMM. ON POVERTY AND THE ADMINISTRATION OF FEDERAL CRIMINAL JUSTICE, REP. 135 (1963) [hereinafter cited as ATT'Y GEN. REP.]. $500-$1000—60%; $5000-$10,000—80%. Ironically a richer defendant loses less in a bail transaction; he can put down cash or a property bond for the total amount and recover it all on his appearance. A

poorer man must use a commercial bail bondsman, and his 10% premium is nonrefundable.

31. See MOLLEUR, BAIL REFORM IN THE NATION'S CAPITAL—FINAL REPORT OF THE D.C. BAIL PROJECT 25 (1967) (two felony convictions or one conviction on the present charge render defendant ineligible for bail project recommendation).

32. This proved true in 21 out of 300 counties in the Silverstein study. Failure to make bail was a prime test for eligibility in 40 others, a serious factor to be considered in 181 counties. SILVERSTEIN 107.

"If a defendant owns a home occupied by his wife and two children, but owns nothing else, is he an indigent? If he has a couple of hundred dollars but can find no $200 lawyer, what does the judge do with him? If he is gainfully employed and can make all periodic payments, should counsel be appointed to serve without charge? Or if he is the son of rich parents or the husband of a rich wife, owning nothing of his own, does he qualify? The more common case and the one we see with increasing frequency is that the defendant who by some means has been able to raise $1000 or $1500 to pay a professional bondsman to assure him of freedom during a period of perhaps 60 days between his appearance before the Commissioner and the date of trial, but who stands in the court room and says that he cannot possibly raise another few hundred dollars to pay his lawyer." Conally, *Problems in the Determination of Indigency for the Assignment of Counsel,* 1 GA. S.B.H. 11, 12–13 (1964).

33. "Whether contaminated or not, however, we doubt whether any innocent person (as all before trial are presumed to be) can remain unscarred by detention under such a degree of security as New York's detention houses impose. The indignities of repeated physical search, regimented living, crowded cells, utter isolation from the outside world, unsympathetic surveillance, outrageous visitors' facilities, Fort Knox-like security measures, are surely so scaring that one unwarranted day in jail itself can be a major social injustice." N.Y. ASSEMBLY REP. 33.

34. See, *e.g.* memorandum to D.C. Crime Commission, October 25, 1965 from Workhouse Supt., M.C. Pfalzgraf, D.C. Dep't of Corrections, listing as a major "factor causing much unrest and anxiety among the inmates" "the difficulty of making contacts and getting welfare assistance for families of the incarcerated individual."

35. N.Y. Herald Tribune, April 10, 1966, quoting detainee:

"And those other guys in The Tombs (City Prison), they can drive you crazy. Asking questions: 'Why you kill a boy Tito? See you upstate Tito. If you got money, you'll get justice; if you ain't got no money you better cop-out.' They can get you crazy."

Cf. GLASER, EFFECTIVENESS OF A PRISON AND PAROLE SYSTEM 263 (1964) [hereinafter cited as GLASER]:

"The often long interval of idleness in jail, between arrest and delivery to prison, is frequently reported by prisoners as a period in which they and their jail mates assist each other in making out a rationalization of their failures, thus salvaging a favorable conception of themselves."

36. In 1964, 70% of indigent felony defendants were indicted in counties using an assigned counsel system (judges' panels, Bar Association lists, courtroom law-

yers). In 35 States the assigned lawyers were paid moderate fees ($25–500) for such representation, nothing elsewhere. SILVERSTEIN 15. New York City's Legal Aid Society handles over 60,000 cases on an annual $250,000 budget compared with the District Attorney's $4 million. See N.Y. ASSEMBLY REP. 18:

"The Legal Aid lawyer is so hampered by the case burden he must carry in the Criminal Court that he will seek shortcuts to the detriment of defendants. At times stalwart representation of a defendant requires counsel to do battle with the Assistant District Attorney or the judge. Where the penalty may be damage to the rapport between court and counsel, and defense counsel has 25 more defendants to represent the same day, he will be reluctant, perhaps, to seek a preliminary hearing or to challenge a bail failure, and eager to see the case disposed of somehow."

Public defender offices are often administratively forced to use different counsel at each stage of the proceedings to represent the same indigent.

"Persons who have been defended by Legal Aid have complained to us that they never knew who their lawyer was, and that they had to educate a new lawyer with respect to their case each time they appeared in court."

Id. at 17.

37. The great majority of unrepresented defendants apparently plead guilty to the principal offense. SILVERSTEIN 91–93. Fifteen counties in the Silverstein survey automatically assumed a waiver of counsel from a plea of guilty. Fifty counties merely asked if the defendant wanted counsel, *e.g.,* Baltimore: "Do you want counsel or to proceed without it?" The defendant may assume he must pay for it and say, "No," not wishing to impose on his family. In some cases it has been found he does not know what "counsel" is. Silverstein also relates the number of waivers to the stage at which counsel is offered; when it is offered at an early stage, more defendants appear to take advantage of it. SILVERSTEIN 89–90, 95.

38. SILVERSTEIN 72, indicates that clients of retained counsel get more dismissals than indigents.

39. See, *e.g.,* STRINGFELLOW, *op. cit. supra* note 1, at 52–53 (four boys picked up on heroin possession; one boy was designated to "take the rap"):

"I had decided, partly on the advice of another attorney, to go to court before it convened and discuss the case with the prosecutor and try to persuade him to reduce the charge, in exchange for a guilty plea. There were not any serious legal grounds for the district attorney to agree to this, but there were practical arguments in favor of it. For one thing, the defendant had been in prison three other times, and since this had not deterred his addiction, there was no reason to think that a long felony sentence would be of any help to him or advantage to society. For another thing, there is a shortage of prison space in New York, and that constitutes a pressure on the courts to hand down short sentences, at least in minor cases, which this was, even though it was a felony charge.

"When I arrived at the courtroom, several other lawyers were standing in line, waiting to speak to the D.A. I overheard their discussions of other cases on the day's calendar. They were terse to say the least, and seemed to me to be quite disinterested and even indifferent to the merits of the cases being negotiated. Finally my turn came. I identified myself to the district attorney, whom I had never met before, this being my first court case.

"I told him whom I represented, and then he said, 'Well, counselor, what do you want?' 'I want a misdemeanor,' I replied. And then to my astonishment he said, 'O.K. When the case is called, we'll talk to the judge.'

"We did. The judge agreed to the guilty plea to a misdemeanor and the defendant was sentenced to seven months in prison.

"It was all over in no more than two minutes. After the hearing, I went back to the 'pen'—where the prisoners are kept, pending their appearance in court and awaiting their return to jail—and talked with the defendant. He was very pleased with the way the case had gone. He assured me that this was the best solution, certainly better than for all four of them to be imprisoned. Besides, he said, he knew how to get along in jail, and some of the other guys did not, so it was better that he should go in their place."

40. A New York robbery indictment typically was 4 counts: robbery in 1st degree (10–30 years); assault in 1st degree (up to 10 years); grand larceny in 1st degree (up to 10 years); unlawful weapon (up to 7). There are 22 lesser pleas possible, many carrying the same penalty (*i.e.,* 5 years for attempted robbery in 3d degree, grand larceny in 2d degree, assault in 2d degree). A second or third conviction for robbery in 1st degree carries a mandatory sentence of 15–30 years and a 4th felony conviction, life.

41. Interviews with public defenders in New York City and Miami (April 1966) disclosed they did not feel at a disadvantage in plea bargaining to any but the most prominent criminal lawyers. They stressed that the rapport or lack of it between the prosecutor and defense is a personal matter. In this respect, the Legal Aid lawyer in New York City said that the big city defender offices had "devoted and rigorous lawyers—differing in abilities but all competent," superior to the "marginal" criminal lawyer who takes a case for a small fee ($100), is often "ignorant of the law, does not keep abreast of new developments, cannot command funds to hire investigators or experts or purchase transcripts," and is held in disdain by the district attorney's office.

42. Public defenders admit that their clients may view the relationship as too "impersonal"; this condition, they say, stems not from a lack of commitment on their part but "rather, from a vague feeling on the part of some defendants that because they have not paid for the services of a defense attorney, that attorney has no commitment to them and to their interests." Segal, *The Indigent Defendant and Defense Counsel,* 45 PRISON J. 22 (1965).

43. *Kent* v. *United States* 383 U.S. 541 (1966).

44. See N.Y. FAMILY CT. ACT § 242.

45. In the D.C. Juvenile Court, between 85% and 90% of the alleged delinquents waive counsel. D.C. CRIME COMM'N REP. 682; *cf.* New York City, where 92% of alleged delinquents used to be unrepresented. 17 RECORD OF N.Y.C.B.A. 10, 15 (1962). Under the new system, where counsel is offered before going to court and is physically available in the building, the vast majority of juvenile delinquency respondents (over 70%) take advantage of the right.

46. Seventy-four percent in the District of Columbia. D.C. CRIME COMMISSION REP. APPENDIX 484.

47. BROWN, MANCHILD IN THE PROMISED LAND 61 (1965).

48. The defendant in jail cannot aid in investigation, and investigative expenses are paid to assigned counsel in only a small minority of jurisdictions. Only 23 out of 72 public defender offices had paid investigators. SILVERSTEIN 16, 45. *Cf.* ATT'Y GEN. REP. 34: "In the judgment of the Committee, present practices sometimes induce a plea of guilty because appointed counsel recognizes the futility of electing a contest in the absence of resources to litigate effectively."

49. For a detailed account of the time-consuming requirements of defense preparation for a successful attack on evidence obtained by a spike microphone, see WILLIAMS, ONE MAN'S FREEDOM 80–81 (1962).

50. For a vivid step-by-step account of how this process works, see Arens, *The Defense of Walter X. Wilson—An Insanity Plea and a Skirmish in the War on Poverty,* 11 VILL. L. REV. 259 (1966). How skillful and detailed an examination the private psychiatrist conducts may depend, however, on whether his fee is $100 or $1,000. Travel time to the state mental hospital—usually far removed from his midtown offices—must be compensated as well as time spent examining the patient and studying his hospital files. Five such observations is considered a minimum for an adequate examination. A private doctor must also be paid for any wait in court as well as for time on the witness stand.

51. See HARRINGTON, *op. cit. supra* note 1, at 23:
"In almost any slums there is a vast conspiracy against the forces of law and order. If someone approaches asking for a person, no one there will have heard of him, even if he lives next door. The outsider is a 'cop,' bill collector, investigator (and, in the Negro ghetto, most dramatically, he is 'the Man')."
See also GEORGETOWN LAW CENTER, LAW AND TACTICS IN FEDERAL CRIMINAL CASES 9 (1963):
"It is extremely important for counsel attempting to locate a defense witness to properly identify himself as a lawyer for Mr. X and that he is not a police officer or a bill collector."
One poverty program neighborhood lawyer in Washington, D.C., commented it was equally hard to find his clients during this pretrial period. Typically, the client will not have a phone, and contacts will be limited to a few unscheduled "dropping in" visits to the lawyer's office. Interview with Brian Olmstead, attorney, D.C. Neighborhood Legal Services Program, April 5, 1966.

52. See the following:
"We are told that subpoenas issued by this Court are all too often disregarded. Among the very poor, any risk to one's job is to be avoided, and obedience to a subpoena means a day or more spent in court. As a result the best hope for a defendant (if he be detained in jail, as most Legal Aid's clients are) is to have an investigator personally seek out the witness and explain to him the importance of appearing." N.Y. ASSEMBLY REP. 18.

53. STRINGFELLOW, *op. cit. supra* note 1, at 60–62 gives an account of his futile attempts to persuade Harlem eyewitnesses to testify in a police assault case.
". . . a great effort was made to locate and interview eyewitnesses who could either confirm or refute the boy's testimony. Of the many who were contacted and questioned, six (as I recall) essentially repeated the boy's own version of what had happened—that he had been assaulted by the policeman rather than the other way

around. Each of them admitted this in private conversation; none was willing to be a witness for the defense. They all had many excuses for their reluctance. They wanted to stay out of trouble—any trouble, all trouble, especially trouble involving cops. It was none of their business, they kept saying. Clearly, they were afraid. These were the policemen from the beat; they would be around tonight and tomorrow and after that, and they might find something to arrest you for if you were going to be a witness against them in this case. Some had things to hide—illegal activities of their own—which argued against having anything to do with anybody else's problems with the law. Some—the most sympathetic—just had no confidence that, even if they did testify for the defense, their testimony (since they, too, were Negroes) would be given any credence by the court. They felt that since there was no chance for a fair and impartial hearing and verdict, why take the time from work or home to testify for this boy. . . . There were, in consequence, no witnesses for the defense respecting the policeman's alleged assault upon the defendant. Even the defendant refused, despite urgent entreaties, to testify in his own defense. He viewed the case as hopeless."

54. The public defender in Miami reports that an out-of-town defense witness must pay his own fare to court, refundable (up to $3) only after "a good deal of rigamarole." The state's attorney has a fund to advance transportation costs to prosecution witnesses. Interview with Robert Koeppel, Dade County Public Defender, April 15, 1966.

55. One defense lawyer interviewed emphasized the value of replaying the incident at the scene with the defendant. His man was charged with gouging his victim's eye out during a fight. On a visit to the scene the defendant pointed out the sharp pebbles in the gutter; defense counsel evolved a theory that the pebbles caused the eye injury when the victim fell. He was acquitted. Interview with Richard Arens, April 13, 1966.

56. District of Columbia appointed lawyers cited the inconvenient 8:00–3:00 weekday visiting hours at the D.C. Jail as a serious obstacle to defense participation. COMM. ON THE ADMINISTRATION OF BAIL OF THE JUNIOR BAR SECTION OF THE D.C. BAR ASS'N REPORT ON THE BAIL SYSTEM OF THE DISTRICT OF COLUMBIA 26 (1963) [hereinafter cited as D.C. BAIL STUDY].

57. See, *e.g.*, Edward Bennett Williams' account of an indigent defense:

"In 1947 I was assigned as court-appointed counsel to defend a forty-year-old musician named Paul Collins. He had been indicted by a grand jury and charged with the felony of embezzlement, a crime punishable by imprisonment. He had never before been arrested and, except for his alcohol problem, his record was unblemished.

"Collins was without funds or friends. Before I was assigned to the case he had languished in jail for twenty-three days because he couldn't afford a bail bond and no one had made any effort on his behalf. I was able to secure his release before trial by getting his bail sharply reduced.

"As I began preparation for trial of the case, my mind automatically turned toward the conventional weapons that I had so often employed for the firm's corporate clients when they were sued for money damages. But none of those weapons was now available to me. I could not get the names of the prosecution witnesses. I could not take their testimony before trial, even if I knew who they were.

"If the dairy had filed a civil suit against Collins for $700 alleging that he owed them this as a result of a shortage in his accounts, he would have had available to him all of the procedural safeguards that any civil litigant can employ. He could have ascertained the names of all the witnesses against him and taken their depositions before trial to find out what their testimony at trial would be. In other words, in the defense of $700 he could have availed himself of what we lawyers call pre-trial discovery procedures.

"But this was a criminal case. His liberty was at stake. He faced a possible sentence of five years in the penitentiary, the loss of his civil rights and the destruction of his reputation. Under the criminal rules, the procedural safeguards available to the parties in a civil case were not available to him.

"When we went to trial in the spring of 1947, for the first time in the two years I had been trying cases I had the feeling of going into court unprepared. It was not for lack of work. I had never before worked so hard on a case. It was just that under the criminal rules I couldn't prepare to defend Collins' liberty the way I had become accustomed to prepare for the defense of corporate bankrolls." WILLIAMS, *op. cit. supra* note 49, at 132–34.

58. Access to prior records of prosecution witnesses for impeachment is particularly vital in narcotics prosecutions.

"The pattern of testimony in these cases is frequently similar. An informant testifies that he received the narcotics from the defendant. An officer of the police department corroborates his testimony. The defendant testifies and claims either that he did not transfer the narcotics or that he was induced into making the sale under circumstances which constitute entrapment. The defendant usually has a criminal record which is used effectively to impeach his credibility. The informant frequently has a criminal record also. The FBI maintains a record of such convictions, but will not provide them to the defense. They cannot be reached by the present discovery procedure." Pye, *Discovery in Federal Criminal Cases,* 33. F.R.D. 47, 87–88 (1963).

59. Only recently has Rule 17(b) of the Federal Rules of Criminal Procedure eliminated this requirement.

60. The new amendment to Rule 16 of the Federal Rules of Criminal Procedure allows inspection and copying of recorded statements made by the defendant, scientific tests, the defendant's grand jury testimony, books, papers, tangible objects "material" to the defense. Witnesses' names are not available except in capital cases.

61. The public defender in Miami, Florida, commented that a judge who authorized a $1,000 fee to fly in a handwriting expert in an indigent forgery case would "never be elected next time around." Interview with Robert Koeppel, April 15, 1966. A New York City Legal Aid lawyer interviewed in April 1966 said his staff is forced to rely on charitable appearances by experts and to "improvise," *i.e.,* ask a psychiatrist to answer a hypothetical question about the defendant's sanity at the time of the offense.

62. See ATT'Y GEN REP. 138–44 (defendants with retained counsel or out on bail in four Federal districts pled guilty less often and chose jury trials more often than those with assigned counsel or those who were detailed in lieu of bail).

63. See D.C. CRIME COMM'N REP. 385, 396 (54% of those convicted in the felony court after a jury trial sentenced to over 5 years; only 21% of those who pled guilty received over 5 years in prison).

64. JACOB, JUSTICE IN AMERICA 111 (1965). Los Angeles, Milwaukee, and Baltimore studies have shown professionals, managers, and proprietors over-represented on juries, workingmen under-represented.

64. Pye, *supra* note 58. Professor Wigmore once said that the "difference between getting the same facts from other witnesses and from cross-examination is the difference between slow-burning gunpowder and quick flashing dynamite; each does its appointed work, but the one burns along its marked line only, the other rends in all directions." Quoted in WILLIAMS, *op. cit. supra* note 49, at 135.

66. See, *e.g.,* 18 U.S.C. § 3500.

67. See description of the average Women's Court defendant in New York City: "Against these highly skilled witnesses (Police Vice Squad officers) the usual testimony is that of the defendant herself, in most instances a person of limited intelligence, often suffering from addiction to narcotics, and frequently not articulate in the English language."

N.Y. ASSEMBLY REP. 72; *cf. People* v. *Moore* 274 N.Y.S.2d 518 (1966) (D.A. said, ". . . his wife tells us . . . that they are on welfare, and maybe he wanted to supplement that welfare allowance a little bit by a little extracurricular activity").

68. Defense lawyers in the District of Columbia agreed:
"There is an appearance of guilt that attaches to the accused's entry into the courtroom from the cell block with marshals and usually in attire not suitable to the occasion." D.C. BAIL STUDY 26.

69. See ATT'T GEN. REP. 138–44, for correlations in 4 federal district courts between pleas, trials, convictions and whether the defendants had assigned or retained counsel and were free on bail or detained pending trial: One example (N.D. Cal., S.F. Div.):

	BAIL	DETAINED	ASSIGNED COUNSEL	RETAINED
Initial plea:	(Percent)	(Percent)	(Percent)	(Percent)
Not guilty	51	25	20	42
Guilty	43	71	76	54
Mode or trial:				
Jury	18	7	6	31
Court	6	3	4	5
None	76	90	90	82
Outcome:				
Dismissal	20	13	9	17
Acquittal	2	1	1	2
Guilty plea	60	79	81	68
Guilty adjudged	18	7	8	13

But see the Committee's caveat, at 131, on drawing from such samples oversimplified causal conclusions between poverty and outcome.

70. See Pye, *The Administration of Criminal Justice,* 66 COLUMN. L. REV. 286, 298 (1966).
"A defendant who has been acquitted may need assistance as much as one who has been convicted and placed on probation. In the first place it is obvious that some defendants who have committed crimes are able to escape conviction. Furthermore, individuals who may not be guilty of an offense may be plunged back into an environment in which the probability of future crimes is great."
See also *Giaccio* v. *Pennsylvania,* 15 L. Ed. 2d 447 (1966) (Pennsylvania law authorizing jury to impose costs on defendant acquitted of misdemeanor and commit him to jail in lieu of payment held unconstitutional).
71. See Quick, *Constitutional Rights in Juvenile Court,* 12 HOW. L.J. 101 (1966).
72. In some jurisdictions the judge looks at the social study even before he adjudicates the child as a delinquent. *Ibid.*

DRUG ABUSE AS A SOCIAL PROBLEM 🎌 *Charles Winick*

This morning thousands of Americans awakened with one driving need—to obtain enough illegal drugs to see them through the day! They are victims of a habit so powerful and so expensive that many will commit crimes before the day is done in order to pay for their drugs.[1]

Today the drug addiction problem is news, but it is not new. It is centuries old. In this country it dates back at least to the Civil War period. Recognition by the American public of addicton as a public health problem, however, is relatively new. Such awareness has been developing only during the past few decades.

It is something of an anomaly that Thomas De Quincey's classic "Confessions of an English Opium-Eater," refuting many of the myths about addiction and presenting a grimly realistic portrait of the addict, was published in 1821; yet, the public continued to turn its back on the problem during most of the intervening years and today still accepts many of the myths of drug use.

De Quincey made it quite clear that opiates are depressants and that most addicts under the influence of drugs withdraw into their own private worlds, finding quiet satisfaction in a kind of make-believe existence. The term "dope fiend" persisted, however, calling up images of wild-eyed derelicts given to violence and crime. It is true that addiction is linked to crime but in a complex way. The addict's crimes are often the result of his urgent need for money to buy more drugs, although a substantial number of younger addicts today have a pre-addiction record of anti-social activity. It is difficult to replace the "image" of an addict with the facts about addiction.

Here is a complex human problem which has benefitted little from the remarkable advances in knowledge in related fields in recent years. Partial explanation lies, perhaps, in the very nature of the problem. Addiction is often a solitary habit—a quiet, unobtrusive habit. The addict associates chiefly with other addicts. It is when he is driven to criminal behavior to finance his habit that the addict attracts public attention.

Addiction is an illness, with frequently tragic consequences, but it is so linked in the minds of many with the underworld as the source of narcotics, that their attitude toward crime takes precedence over their attitude toward disease.[2] The public has felt justified over the years in considering addiction more of an immoral and criminal problem than a psychiatric, public health, or social condition.[3]

In numerical terms, the addiction problem seems small and insignificant when compared with alcoholism or venereal disease, for example. The truth is that no one can say, with complete certainty, how many people are addicted to drugs. Addicts are hardly eager to be counted in a census, knowing that their behavior is illegal. It is usually estimated that there are some 100,000 addicts in the United States.[4] However, there are those who believe that for every addict known to law enforcement agencies there may be one or even more unknown to such agencies.

The size and significance of the addiction problem must be measured, not only in terms of the number of addicts, but in terms of human suffering, disrupted lives, and financial cost to society. The family is frequently in the position of longing for help, not knowing where to turn for help and, at the same time, fearful lest its secret be discovered.

Cost of Addiction

The cost of the addiction problem to society is enormous. The typical addict requires from ten to thirty dollars or more daily for drugs. Male addicts usually turn to stealing in one form or another to obtain the necessary money for their habit. Since stolen merchandise brings the thief only a small proportion of its original cost, addicts must steal items worth far more than the cash they need for drugs. It can be safely said that the typical male addict may steal in a year's time merchandise valued from $30,000 to $90,000.[5]

On the other hand, the typical female addict usually resorts to prostitution to obtain the money she needs. She is, thereby, involved in two forms of illegal activity, one supporting the other. It is likely that more than half the women in the prisons of large cities are there because they were apprehended in this situation. Clearly society is paying an exorbitant price, through a variety of channels, for this continuing problem.

Drug Traffic: An International Problem

Many countries other than the United States report an addiction problem. The United Nations' Commission on Narcotic Drugs is responsible for administrative work in connection with those drugs that are kept under international control and also considers the problems of addiction to drugs, as does the World Health Organization study group on the treatment and care of drug addicts. After years of work on the part of many different countries, a single Convention on narcotic drugs was finally agreed upon in 1961 and is now in effect. The United States became a signatory in 1967.

Despite the controversy over some aspects of the addiction problem, there is total agreement that smuggling of illegal drugs is undesirable and that all possible effort must be made, through appropriate national and international action, to stop such illegal traffic. The United States has long been a world leader in international efforts to combat the illegal narcotics trade. Most recently, it has paid Turkish opium farmers not to grow opium and to divert their acreage to other products.

Although the need for money to buy illegal heroin is what leads so many persons to engage in criminal activity, many other forms of drug abuse— usually defined as the use of a chemical substance outside of medical supervision—have contributed to the "drug problem" in this country.

Non-opiate Forms of Drug Dependence

Many millions of Americans are dependent on non-addicting drugs, such as the following:

Depressants, which depress the nervous system: for example, alcohol, and tranquilizers, such as reserpine, thorazine, or equanil.

Stimulants, which stimulate the nervous system, for example, amphetamines, such as benzedrine.

Psychotomimetics, which simulate symptoms of mental illness and include LSD, mescaline, peyote, and psilocybin.

Marijuana, which combines a stimulus action (e.g., increased heart rate) and a depressant action (e.g., drowsiness and diminished anxiety).

In assessing the effect of a dependence drug it is necessary to consider the dose, the user's anticipations, and the social setting. Some drugs have an additive effect, so that the depressant action of alcohol may combine with the depressant action of barbiturates and prove lethal, as happened in the case of celebrities like Alan Ladd and Marilyn Monroe. Some drugs potentiate, or rapidly maximize, the effect of other drugs which have previously been ingested, so that $2+2$ equals 7 rather than 4. Thus, antihistamines potentiate the effect of alcohol.

One of the contributors to this country's drug problem is our over-reliance on chemical substances for a wide range of purposes, beyond those for which they were originally intended. Drugs are prescribed to help children be better students at school, assist adults in dealing with anxiety, and similar purposes related to the emotional challenges of daily living. Advertising for chemical substances is ubiquitous and helps to create a feeling of readiness for the benefits of "better living through chemistry." In such a climate of opinion, it is difficult to see how young people are going to be discouraged from "hard" drug use. Distinguishing "good" from "bad" drug use is likely to be very difficult.[6]

In addition, the years since the end of World War II have seen a variety of social forces which have facilitated the increase in drug use by middle-class youths.[7] A dozen reasons may be cited for this increase in drug abuse.

1. Young people are exploring life styles which involve questioning of such traditional American values as rationality and order.
2. There is a crisis in liberalism which has led many young people to regard the liberal as the enemy. As a result, the liberal traditional argument, in terms of its relevance to drug use, has little effect.
3. The post-World War II generation is the first one to grow up amid conspicuous affluence. As a result, many young people feel that they can have a second and third chance and are experimenting with drug use as one way of seeking authenticity.
4. Young people today do not believe what they are told about drug use by their seniors. Students feel free to explore the scientific literature, in which they may find material that disagrees with what they have learned in school.
5. A young man who may face the possibility of having his head blown off in Vietnam is hardly likely to be dissuaded from drug use by being told that he will go "out of his head" by taking hallucinogens. The Now Generation does not want

to delay its gratification, especially since it has little confidence in its ability to change the world in the future.

6. Many new heroes of rock music and other forms of mass communication publicly praise drug use and record music which celebrates the psychedelic drug experience.

7. Many young people, confused about their sex role, retreat from the challenges and uncertainties of masculinity and femininity into the degenderized and asexual world of chemical satisfaction.

8. Drug use, in many ways, is a "rite of passage" which has replaced many traditional benchmarks. Freshmen and seniors are the student groups most likely to use drugs.

9. Television commercials and magazine advertising have conditioned us to believe that there is a chemical remedy for everything from "nerves" to "housetosis." Illegal drugs are taken as a specific for many different conditions.

10. From a business point of view, drugs provide a continually expanding market, with all cash transactions, no income tax, and a geographic concentration of customers. With such favorable economic factors and the possibility of increasing a $10,000 investment to $1,000,000 in a very short time, many entrepreneurs will be happy to service this growing market.

11. The fact that over 50 per cent of the population is under the age of 27 has created conditions of enormous competition among youth, and drug abuse is one way of "tuning out" from competition.

12. Our society offers very few easily available forms of risk-taking behavior. Drug abuse represents one form of such behavior which is available to anyone.

Drugs Used by the Addict

True addiction occurs only with sedative drugs and is associated with the continued use of barbiturates and opiates.

Addiction is characterized by three separate but related phenomena: tolerance, habituation, and physical dependence. Tolerance is the diminishing effect of the same dose of a drug, or the need to increase the dose in order to get an effect similar to the initial one. Habituation is the emotional or psychological need which is met by the drug. Dependence is the body's need to get the drug.[8]

Opiates that have been used by addicts in this country are opium, morphine, heroin, and the synthetics (drugs that are manmade but have effective properties of an opium derivative). In the early 1930s, opium ceased to be the choice drug among American addicts, giving way to morphine, and a few years later heroin, a morphine derivative, became the preferred drug. Heroin is nearly twice as potent as morphine and is used by most of today's opiate addicts. Heroin is illegal in the United States, and anyone possessing it violates the law.

Although not an addicting drug, cocaine is habituating and is used by some opiate addicts. It gives an almost instantaneous "charge" which is very concentrated and intense, but of short duration. Addicts seldom use cocaine by itself consistently because it is extremely high-priced on the illegal markets and because its effects are so short-lived. Some experienced addicts like to mix heroin and cocaine into a "speed ball" which provides the immediacy and potency of cocaine with the extended afterglow of heroin. This mixture is also called a "love affair," as heroin is often referred to as "boy" and cocaine as "girl."

Other popular drugs which are under federal regulation, even though they are not opiates and not addicting, are marijuana and peyote. Approximately 300,000,000 people throughout the world are said to use marijuana as an intoxicant. Some prominent writers, including Aldous Huxley and Henri Michaux, have reported unusual sensory experiences with peyote, although medical opinion generally regards the comments of such amateur experimenters with great caution. A number of writers and artists have reported enthusiastically that peyote facilitates creative work, but their reports are impressionistic.

The barbiturates, or sleeping pills, are genuinely addicting drugs when used to excess. In the past few years, there has been evidence strongly suggesting that overuse of barbiturates may lead to an addiction as serious, if not more so, than the opiates. Some narcotic users take barbiturates if their regular drug is not available, and some take both opiates and barbiturates.

Recognition and Concealment

Many people still believe that an addict can be identified by his appearance. He cannot. As a matter of fact, members of an addict's immediate family may not be able to recognize changes in his appearance that are attributable to the drug. It is true, however, that heroin users may show scars or sores on their arms, resulting from repeated injections of the drug into the veins.

It is extremely difficult to recognize an opiate user who is receiving a regular supply of his drug. However, if the drug is withdrawn for one or two days, the addict is easily identified by a series of definite involuntary reactions called the withdrawal or abstinence syndrome. The severity of the addiction can be measured by the severity of this reaction pattern. A mild abstinence syndrome involves sneezing, yawning, perspiring, watering of the eyes and a running nose. A moderate response includes tremors of the body, goose flesh, loss of appetite, and dilation of the pupils.

A severe syndrome often involves fever, increased blood pressure, rapid breathing, insomnia, acute restlessness. In its most intense form, the response takes the form of vomiting, diarrhea, weight loss, and spasms of the limbs. The reaction pattern begins when the effect of the last "shot" starts to wear off. For the typical heroin addict, this period is nearly six hours; for the morphine addict, it is likely to be twelve hours; for the opium addict, twenty-four hours.[9]

Social Class and Addiction

Contrary to a widely held belief, drug addicts are not necessarily members of society's lowest class—economically, socially, or mentally. A considerable number of doctors, for example, are addicted to drugs and some of them, while they manage to keep their habit under control, may be among the most successful and highly respected physicians in their communities.[10] Rock musicians represent another occupational group found among drug users. The lives of brilliant performers, like Jimi Hendrix and Janis Joplin, have been destroyed by the habit.

Through history, there have been some highly intelligent, talented, well-known figures addicted to narcotics. This is true today, as well. Yet, the addict group attracting the greastest attention and eliciting the deepest public concern today is made up of teenagers. Some of them have been involved in delinquent and even criminal activities prior to their development of the drug habit. Their use of drugs represents one more aspect of the anti-social pattern of their lives. In this respect, today's young addict differs from the drug user of the 1930s who usually had a clean record until his need for narcotics drove him to criminal activity.[11]

Genesis and Causation

Most addicts begin using drugs as a result of association with those already using drugs. It must be pointed out, however, that many, if not most, persons who try drugs out of curiosity do not use them a second time and certainly do not become addicted. It is likely that only those persons who sense that drugs serve as a method of coping with serious personal problems continue to use narcotics and ultimately become addicts. It is not possible to make generalizations about the reasons for drug use because it appears that drugs meet different needs for different persons. For example, some addicts may begin using drugs to emulate the members of a group they admire, while others may develop the habit to accent their individuality and to set them apart from a group that does not take drugs.

A substantial number of addicts in large cities begin using narcotic drugs when they are about 16 years old, the age when adolescents are likely to be confronted by new challenges of maturity. Many of these teenagers are suffering from a personality disturbance so severe that they seek to "tune out" on reality and its commitments and decisions. Different kinds of inadequate persons may begin and sustain drug use. There is no general agreement about the type of personality makeup that is most likely to be found in addicts. There is urgent need for more research in this field to determine the common denominators of the addict personality, if there is one.

Treatment

The Narcotic Addict Rehabilitation Act of 1966 (NARA) established a new national policy: civil commitment of addicts—both those charged with, or convicted of, violating federal criminal laws and others seeking treatment.

To carry out this policy, Public Law 89–793 contained a sweeping mandate: total treatment rather than fragmented efforts. Institutional treatment was expanded to include the supervised return of the patient to the community. For the first time, provision was made for aftercare help and direction of addicts.

In the case of a narcotic addict charged with a federal offense who desires to be committed in lieu of trial on the criminal charge, Title I authorizes federal courts to commit him to the Surgeon General for examination, three years' treatment (initially in a hospital) and rehabilitation, including aftercare following release from institutional treatment. A patient who has made progress in treatment will be discharged to out-patient supervision.

California and New York also have programs for the civil commitment of persons dependent on opiates.[12] Typically, a court order sends the addict to a treatment center where he may stay for perhaps six months. He can then be discharged and transferred to the community under parole supervision. He may remain on parole for as long as two and one-half years. In both states, a wide range of modalities of treatment is available.

Another significant development in terms of treatment is the establishment of "total treatment" therapeutic communities like Synanon, Odyssey House, and Daytop Lodge. Synanon, originally in Santa Monica, was the pioneer in establishing a treatment center which has no professional staff and in which the residents themselves constitute the therapeutic personnel.[13] A variety of innovative small-group discussion procedures have been successfully employed by Synanon in order to effect personality changes in participants in its program. A number of communities are adapting the Synanon model, which has been presented on television and motion pictures. Its energetic program of public education has helped to make the general public more responsive to the plight of the addict and more willing to participate in programs of rehabilitation.

New York City has developed its own continuum of services for the narcotic addict. The program stresses the employment of former addicts as therapeutic personnel at all stages of the treatment process. The program begins with community orientation and intake procedures, followed by detoxification and psychotherapy. Reentry houses assist the former drug user in reestablishing himself in the community. Special units identify and treat young potential addicts and there is a network of community education activities that is built on the cooperation of employers and relatives of drug users.

Drugs Used in Treatment

Recent years have seen remarkable success in the use of drugs to treat narcotic addicts. Methadone and cyclazocine have been the two substances most effectively used. In the first phase of the methadone maintenance program, heroin addicts are given the synthetic opiate methadone in accelerated doses until they build up to a stabilizing dose. During the inpatient phase of approximately six weeks, the patient receives considerable support from the hospital staff.

In the second (out-patient) phase, the patients appear daily for their medication. Psychosocial and vocational support is always available, as needed. The patients are assisted in getting a job, returning to school, and increasing their vocational skills. Methadone has a blocking action which appears to eliminate the patients' previous craving for heroin. The New York methadone maintenance program, under Dr. Vincent Dole, has found that 88 per cent of its patients respond effectively to treatment.[14]

The Albert Einstein College of Medicine and New York Medical College have studied the effects of cyclazocine in the rehabilitation of narcotic addicts.[15] Cyclazocine is a long-acting narcotic antagonist in the benzomorphan series and, in proper doses, reduces the subjective and physiological effects of any opiate. The regular use of cyclazocine reduces or prevents the development of physical dependency on opiates. The studies have tentatively demonstrated that some compulsive narcotic users can be helped, with cyclazocine, to become abstinent, provided that individual and group helping services are available. Cyclazocine stabilized the patients, prevented occurrence of the usual effects of the drug they were using, and facilitated the process of rehabilitation.

The New York State Narcotic Addiction Control Commission (NACC) has developed the most substantial range of treatment facilities in the country. Some idea of the cost of adequate treatment can be obtained from the budget of the commission, which is around $150 million per year, although it only services a small proportion of the state's addict population.

The state of Illinois, under Dr. Jerome H. Jaffe, has pioneered in the establishment of a different approach, in which research seeks to identify which kinds of patients do best in which approach.

Problems of the Ex-addict

The former addict returns to his home from a hospital under extremely difficult circumstances.[16] He is back in the environment which helped to spawn his addiction, and people are likely to know he is a former addict. Usually, he returns with no money and when he goes looking for work, he finds that employers are very wary about hiring ex-addicts. Chances are that his family situation has been strained by his long absence and by the community's obvious disapproval of addiction. His non-addict friends may be suspicious of him, and his addict friends may be far too available. Social agencies often are reluctant to help the former addict because they feel the chances of his successful adjustment are too slight to warrant the necessary expenditure of time and counseling talent.

In view of the lack of supportive services for the former addict, it is not surprising that he often reverts to drug use as a way of expressing his disenchantment with the community, even though he may have been eager to break his habit and return to normal living, released from dependence on daily drugs.

The Process of "Maturing Out"

There is some evidence to support the belief that some—perhaps many— addicts go through a process of "maturing out" of their habit. They stop taking drugs, often without much treatment.[17]

The Federal Bureau of Narcotics maintains the only central file of addicts in the United States, and analysis of the Bureau's data suggests that a substantial number of addicts reported do not subsequently come to the attention of law enforcement authorities. Some authorities believe that the typical addict, who begins taking drugs in his teens to escape or to cope with certain problems of adjustment, continues taking drugs as long as those problems are important. Once the urgency of these problems has diminished, usually in his thirties, he may begin to adapt to reality without the crutch provided by drugs. The very passage of time is a major factor in this phenomenon of "maturing out."

Conflicting Theories

Prevention of addiction and rehabilitation of the addict are hampered by conflicting theories regarding the problem itself. The various branches of the social science and medical professions engaged in studying addiction have each emphasized one facet of this complex problem. There is need, in the field of narcotic addiction, to know the whole structure, to understand all facets of the problem. Only then can a truly effective program of rehabilitation and prevention be established. Ways must be found to pull together the interested professional workers so that each may have the benefit of the others' knowledge and achievements, and cooperatively work out an approach to addiction that embraces medical, sociological, psychiatric, physical, anthropological, legal, and statistical factors.

The sociologist sees addiction as a problem that develops in certain geographical areas, in specific environments. He points to the blacks and Puerto Ricans who form a large segment of the addict population and who are concentrated in a few big city neighborhoods which are economically depressed and culturally deprived and have a high rate of delinquent behavior. The psychologist, on the other hand, interprets addiction among minority groups as an expression of the frustration and hostility they feel and cannot express overtly. The psychoanalyst sees the addict developing in and responding to a specific kind of family situation which fosters an "oral passive" personality.

There are still many who hold fast to the concept of addiction as strictly a problem of law enforcement. They feel that if the smuggling rings are smashed and the "pushers" thrown in jail, drug addiction will disappear because there will be no illegal drugs available.

Still another group holds the opposite view, insisting that addiction is an illness and that law enforcement cannot cure an illness. Proponents of this view note that prohibition did not eliminate alcoholism. Drug use, they point out, is a symptom of other serious problems, and any treatment for addiction must take into consideration these causal factors. They also note that most addicts have "mixed drug dependencies" or "polydependencies," involving substances other than heroin. If the heroin miraculously became unavailable, the addict would use other substances.

In recent years, the extreme views have begun yielding to a more balanced approach, which seeks to create and sustain a climate of disapproval for drug abuse while providing sympathy and assistance for the drug abuser himself. Growing stress on techniques of resocialization and personality strengthening is improving the range of techniques available and improving our knowledge of what kinds of people respond best to what techniques.

NOTES

1. Charles Winick, "Drug Addiction and Crime," *Current History,* 52 (1967), 349–354.

2. Charles Winick, "The Drug Addict and His Treatment," *Legal and Criminal Psychology,* ed. Hans Toch (New York: Holt, Rinehart & Winston, 1961), pp. 357–380.

3. Joint Committee of the American Bar Association and American Medical Association, *Drug Addiction: Crime or Disease?* (Bloomington: Indiana University Press, 1961).

4. See annual reports of the Bureau of Narcotics and Dangerous Drugs, Department of Justice.

5. Harry J. Anslinger, and Will Oursler, *The Murderers: The Shocking Story of the Narcotic Gangs* (New York: Farrar, Straus and Cudahy, 1961); Edward Preble, and John J. Casey, "Taking Care of Business," *International Journal of Addictions,* 4 (1969), 1–24.

6. Henry L. Lennard, *et al., Mystification and Drug Misuse* (San Francisco: Jossey-Bass, 1971).

7. Edward A. Suchman, "The Hang-Loose Ethic and the Spirit of Drug Use," *Journal of Health and Social Behavior,* 9 (1968), 146–155; Richard H. Blum, *Students and Drugs* (San Francisco: Jossey-Bass, 1969).

8. Marie Nyswander, *The Drug Addict as a Patient* (New York: Grune & Stratton, 1956).

9. David W. Maurer, and Victor H. Vogel, *Narcotics and Narcotic Addiction* (Springfield: Charles C. Thomas, 1968).

10. Charles Winick, "Physician Narcotic Addicts," *Social Problems,* 9 (1961), 174–186.

11. Lee N. Robins, and George E. Murphy, "Drug Use in A Normal Population of Young Negro Men," *American Journal of Public Health,* 57 (1967), 1580–1596.

12. John C. Kramer, *et al,* "Civil Commitment for Addicts," *American Journal of Psychiatry,* 6 (1968), 816–824; Daniel Glaser, "Research for Rationality in Narcotics Policy," *The Analyst,* 1 (1969), 17–20.

13. D. Casriel, *So Fair A House* (Englewood Cliffs, N.J.: Prentice-Hall, 1967).

14. Vincent P. Dole, *et al.,* "Methadone Treatment of Randomly Selected Criminal Addicts," *New England Journal of Medicine,* 280 (1969), 1372–1375.

15. Alfred M. Freedman, "Blocked With Methadone, Cyclazocine, Naloxone," *International Journal of Addictions,* 5 (1970), 507–575.

16. Jerome H. Jaffe, "What Ever Turns You Off," *Psychology Today,* 3 (1970), 73–74.

17. Charles Winick, "The Life Cycle of the Narcotic Addict and of Addiction," *U.N. Bulletin on Narcotics,* 16 (1964), 22–32.

SUGGESTED READINGS

Abraham S. Blumberg, *Criminal Justice* (Chicago: Quadrangle Books, 1967).

Isidor Chein *et al., The Road to H: Narcotics, Delinquency & Social Problems* (New York: Basic Books, 1964).

Ramsey Clark, *Crime in America* (New York: Simon and Schuster, 1970).

Donald R. Cressey, *Theft of the Nation* (New York: Harper & Row, 1969).

John A. Gardiner, *The Politics of Corruption* (New York: Russell Sage Foundation, 1970).

Lester Grinspoon, *Marihuana Reconsidered* (Cambridge, Mass.: Harvard University Press, 1971).

Karl Menninger, *The Crime of Punishment* (New York: Viking Press, 1968).

Norval Morris and Gordon Hawkins, *The Honest Politician's Guide to Crime Control* (Chicago: University of Chicago Press, 1970).

Edwin M. Schur, *Crimes Without Victims* (Englewood Cliffs, N.J.: Prentice-Hall, 1969).

Edwin M. Schur, *Our Criminal Society* (Englewood Cliffs, N.J.: Prentice-Hall, 1969).

Stephen Schafer, *The Victim and His Criminal* (New York: Random House, 1968).

Jerome H. Skolnick, *Justice Without Trial* (New York: John Wiley, 1966).

VI

PROBLEMS OF THE FAMILY, AGE, AND SEX ROLES ❧ ❧

PRIVATE TROUBLES AS
PUBLIC PROBLEMS ✒

There are no strictly private troubles in society. All social problems affect us as individuals in the aloneness of our own lives or in the most intimate groups with which we are interlocked, a close friendship group, a couple, or a family. At the same time, the most personal and idiosyncratic features of our lives, whether they be our joys or our difficulties, are in part determined by the society in which they thrive. This is true in two senses. First, the nature of that society, its values and its institutions, must be at least partially responsible for the incidence and distribution of various types of life styles, for the quality of life, for the successes and failures that people have. Second, the nature of a social reaction to a private trouble determines, again in part, the continuation, aggravation, or alleviation of it and its consequences for all aspects of life.

Only recently has the public become aware of the extent to which ill health and disease are distributed according to social class. Whether one individual is stricken by a fatal or disabling illness is unpredictable, and in that sense more or less a matter of chance. Yet, the frequency of a disease within a part of the population, as well as the medical care available to the people so stricken, is a matter of how the society as a whole, and its most powerful groups in particular, sees the value of human lives. No longer are the mentally ill viewed as "by devil possessed," and while there are mentally ill of all social classes, the pressures of poverty, unemployment, and other social factors in creating mental illness are revealed in statistical studies. The differential treatment available to those who become mentally ill is quite apparent to those who have made even the most cursory study of the subject. It is also true that types of mental illness vary according to social and economic factors.

Considerable numbers of people in America and other societies suffer from private troubles and have a deep feeling of isolation, hopelessness, and

529

alienation, which prevents them from forming satisfactory family units or meaningful sexual relationships. This is an outgrowth of social institutions and a serious problem with which society must cope. If it were merely a matter of many people choosing and being satisfied with alternate forms of life styles in place of the traditional family or what has come to replace it, the nuclear family, one would not be greatly concerned. With regard to population, the society could well survive and perhaps even better survive if only a small minority of its members chose to form families. Many who do form families find only frustration and dissatisfaction with those they have chosen as a life mate. Others mature in families only to find themselves deeply alienated from the individuals most concerned (one might interject, perhaps overly concerned) with their welfare. Others have children sometimes unplanned and often unwanted, for whom they cannot provide the maternal and paternal care that appears to be essential for those children's successful socialization into reasonably happy and well-adjusted adults.

No longer are as many people in society uptight over deviations from person-to-person, monogamous, affectional sexuality confined to the marriage bed, or at least so it seems. Alternate forms of sexual expression are decreasingly seen as criminal or immoral. There is also evidence that many of these forms, including group sex or orgiastic relations, male and female prostitution, transvestism and transsexualism, and fixed or exclusive homosexuality, involve problems of gender disorientation, sexual exploitation, emotional or mental illness, all leading not to gratification but to frustration and a never-ending search.

All social problems are interwoven and interrelated but this is especially true of problems of family and sexuality. One cannot examine the questions of war and peace without looking at the nature of technology, the alienation of the young, and the new forms of social protest. Problems of poverty are also those of mental health, prejudice and racism, and attitudes toward the aged in the society and so it is with the family. That venerable, oft-changing but seemingly universal and indestructible institution becomes a microcosm in which is seen many, although not all, of the dilemmas and crises facing the American society. The family's forms and internal activities reflect the paradoxes of a society in flux, and its structure will have consequences for all sectors and aspects of that society.

The student who looks at the family in pursuit of an understanding of social problems must perforce examine social class differentiation, with its ramifications that extend from poverty to competitiveness. He must reflect on the place of divorce in a secular society, with consequences for children as well as for the once married who become mateless. He must examine the remnants of caste and the very viable continuity of prejudice and inequality of life chances based on race or other ethnic differentiation. He must look at the psychological, social, and economic consequences of illegitimacy. With Talcott Parsons and others, he must ask whether the nature of industrial economy has produced an absent father or a matrifocal family with severe consequences particularly for the male child.

Population problems of the society are family problems. Matters involving sexual mores involve of necessity the question of the desirability, not to speak of success of channeling sexual activity toward males and females committed to one another, if not as mates than at least as potential mates; and this means that the society is faced with a large number of its members who will not, or one might say cannot, make an adjustment satisfactory to themselves within such restrictive boundary lines. Prostitution, homosexuality, promiscuity, adultery by mutual consent, and adultery without consent or knowledge: should these phenomena be ignored, be deemed criminal and suppressed with the prosecution of the transgressor, be discouraged without criminalization or stigmatization, or be seen as outgrowths, the manifestations, and symptoms of the breakdown of a moral order?

The wide use of birth control methods does not seem to have contributed to the decline of illegitimacy, but it is still too early to know whether legal and easy-to-obtain abortions will affect illegitimacy rates. As Kingsley Davis has shown, though the stigmatization of the child is cruel, it is not entirely irrational, for societies seek to encourage such arrangements as will provide for socialization. The burden falls on the parents to care for the infant and young when he cannot fend for himself, to transmit the culture and values to the next generation, and particularly to provide the economic needs. This latter is usually the responsibility of the male, defined as the breadwinner in the nuclear family. Where that male is unknown or has not tied himself to the woman by legal and often religious bonds, how can the child be cared for without becoming a burden to the state? Today, this question is being broadened. We are asking whether, in an already matrifocal family system, the child brought up in a fatherless home can have satisfactory socialization even if the economic needs are taken care of, be this by the mother, the state, or some other source.

There are numerous social problems that revolve around the place of the family in society. Many have suggested that the relatively high divorce rate, the rather meager financial and other obligations of young adults to the aged, the generation gap, the challenge of youth to the world of their elders, the transformation of the home into a hotel, the allegedly widespread sexual promiscuity (particularly in something called suburbia), the decline of the family as an independent economic unit (at least as an economically *producing* unit, although it certainly exists as a *consuming* unit), the wider recreational activities that are outside rather than within the family: all these factors and many more suggest that the family is declining in our society and is on the verge of disappearance. Some mourn, and others celebrate. Still others challenge this whole picture of society. Dennis Wrong is among the latter. The family is not breaking up, he contends, but is changing as an adaptation and response to an altering technological situation. The nuclear family is as strong and necessary as ever, but because it is nuclear and not extended, the youth will marry people of their own choices and not those arranged for by others. This means that love, premarital and nonmarital sexuality, divorce, and diminished ties between the aged and their adult children will come into being.

In this section, we have sampled a few aspects of private troubles that are social problems, and particularly those that revolve around the family, sex roles, and sexuality. The scope of these issues carries us to the social protest movement of militant feminism, the searching demands of revolutionary and disaffected youth, and the loneliness and desolation of the aged. We start with that oft-used expression "the generation gap," that seems to have become an unbridgeable chasm. Even in our complex and pluralistic society with vastly different family lives among rich and poor, urban and rural dwellers, and different ethnic and racial groups, youth seems to have much in common. There is such a phenomenon as the youth culture with its rock, long hair, scorn for the old, and alienation from the world and the mores of the elders.

Generational conflict reveals some of the important sources of disorder and violence in modern society. Perhaps these strains are not based on mutual misunderstanding as much as on knowing each other's position too well. Social critic, educator, and sociologist Edgar Z. Friedenberg locates several structured discrepancies: (1) between what one is taught to be at home and the docility demanded by the schools, and (2) between the burdens that youth must bear in service to their country and their rights which have been specifically denied by law and lack of constitutional protection in the courts for what others claim to be their own good. Moreover, the law is often excessively enforced by the police and other custodial functionaries at the service of middle- and upper-class elites who feel threatened by young persons. Every hostile response to the autonomy of youth makes for an increasing acceptability of hostility, including violence, among the young, and the further delegitimation of American institutions.

Kenneth Keniston, who brings to his study a psychoanalytic and sociological orientation, examines the theme of youth's rebellion. He develops the thesis that the rebellion of contemporary youth results from a variety of structural changes in American society which have rendered invalid and obsolete the basic values encouraged by their elders. The extension of the period of youth into the late twenties, a product of an increasing need for graduate and postdoctoral work to handle the complex technology, has meant that the sharp separation between childhood and adulthood no longer exists. The luxury that this cohort of student-workers has in its presence in the academy and surrounding environs is itself a product of an abundant economy and highly developed division of labor. Now society has made it possible for some people to spend much time in reflection, and in so doing, the opportunity to develop new codes of morality, a sensibility at odds with the conventional world, and a freedom from responsibility. These members of post-industrial society, free from concern about necessity, can go beyond necessity to deal with problems of a strictly moral kind on the order of: (1) how resources are distributed in this country and (2) what kinds of reordering of social priorities and personal values are necessary to make sense out of life amidst abundance. Furthermore, Keniston points to the interrelationship between these two concerns. That is to say, it may well be that youth today can create new ways of living via the struggle to make the ideals of justice, equality, and economic security real, because they have been so long outside the mainstream of America that they bring a new consciousness to the scene. Through this endeavor, they diminish the extent of violence in America by creating new constituencies around new authoritative institutions.

A supposed index of the decline of the family is sexual promiscuity. In one sense, it is not a problem except to the people involved in it, and then only if they see it as such for it has no victims and does not turn the promiscuous into nonfunctioning persons or burdens to others. However, if promiscuity is an indicator of a malfunctioning socialization process, of discrepancy between the socially respectable and the real values, or of the failure to provide socially approved patterns of sexuality for the urban and secular world, then it becomes an issue which those concerned with social policy must face. If sexual promiscuity is a symptom of malaise and ill health, and if it leads to a nonrelenting sense of frustration, then it is indeed a social problem as are other private troubles, whether they be defined as such or not. While it is not the moral enforcers who create the problem in this instance, they might well aggravate it. Albert Ellis turns his attention to this question and finds that the extent and incidence of sexual promiscuity has probably been exaggerated. That there is a great deal of premarital (or what might better be called nonmarital) sexuality, probably more than before, does not suggest that there is widespread lack of discrimination in the choice of sex partners. Where promiscuity does take place, it seems to be more the domain of the male, and there is considerable doubt as to whether this is a new phenomenon.

In an age of protest, one of the most far-reaching assaults on the old order of things is that launched by the militant feminists. Their view of society was delineated some years back by Simone de Beauvoir who saw how wrongly women had been cast as the perennial other and denied any biological basis for masculine domination. Then came Helen Hacker who noted the striking similarity between the status of women and that of racial and ethnic minorities in society. Later Betty Friedan described what she saw as "the problem without a name"—millions of women without purpose in life because they had been relegated to home and motherhood and deprived of meaningful careers. There was an irreparable emptiness in the lives of women, coming upon them in their middle years and remaining as they grew old.

The new militant feminism, or women's liberation movement, embraces the outlook of these previous writers and goes beyond them. It not only demands equal economic and career opportunities for women, but launches an assault on the accepted sex role ascriptions that have prevailed in most human societies for centuries. Perhaps such sex role differentiations are grounded in biology, but whatever functions they may have performed for primitive and pre-industrial man, they are oppressive to the modern female and hence, to the male as well.

Out of this has come one of the most unexpected manifestations of this age of protest. Susan Brownmiller's essay "Sisterhood Is Powerful," is not so much a description of the problems that women face but of the way in which a group of them are reacting to such problems. It introduces us to their meetings, gives us windows on their minds and their outlooks; we meet some of the people as they reflect, examine, and forge tactics for their struggle. The women in these inner circles stand with Keniston's revolutionary youths, with black militants and antiwar demonstrators, who are seeking solutions for severe social problems, and who are, by various methods, urging upon the society the solutions that they are finding. Interestingly, many of these groups are supporting each others' movements. Possibly they find common cause in a common enemy, the established and establishment way, or they see that their problems cannot be solved while other major ones continue to erode the society.

This might have been an optimistic note on which to end this collection, but there is still another essay, the only one to come from the pen of one outside the United States, which describes the aged in England, their isolation and loneliness. Many of the people studied by Peter Townsend were spinsters or bachelors, while some of the married or formerly married likewise had no children. When it is considered that the desolation described by Townsend is taking place in a nation more welfare-oriented than our own, and in a land where the extended family has not declined to the point that it has in America, one can well understand the scope and depth of the problem transplanted to the United States.

THE GENERATION GAP
❧ Edgar Z. Friedenberg

The idea that what separates us from the young is something so passive that it may justly be called a "generation gap" is, I believe, itself a misleading article of middle-aged liberal ideology, serving to allay anxiety rather than to clarify the bases of intergenerational conflict. It is true, to be sure, that the phrase is strong enough to describe the barrier that separates many young people from their elders, for a majority still accept our society as providing a viable pattern of life and expectations for the future. Liberalism dies hard, and most young people, like some Negroes even today, are still willing to attribute their difficulties with their elders and society to mutual misunderstanding.

I believe, however, that this is a false position. Though most adults maintain a benevolent posture in expressing their public attitudes toward youth and—though, I think, steadily fewer—young people still accept this as what their elders intend in principle, both young and old seem trapped in a false view of what is actually a profound conflict of interest in our society. What appears to be a consequence of mere cultural lag in responding to a new social and political maturity in the young, with distressing but unintended repressive consequences, is rather the expression of what has become genuine class-conflict between a dominant and exploitive older generation and youth who are slowly becoming more aware of what is happening to them as demands on them are, in the language of the time, escalated.[1]

SOURCE: Edgar Z. Friedenberg, "The Generation Gap," *The Annals*, 382 (March 1969), 32–42. Reprinted by permission of the author and the publisher.

Discontinuity in an Open Society

In all societies, so far as I know, young people enter the social system in subordinate roles while older people run things. This is true even in technically primitive cultures where the crude physical strength of youth is still of real productive advantage. Is there always a generational conflict? And, if so, does it always reflect as profound a division, and as severe a conflict in America today?

There is, I believe, indeed an inherent basis for such a conflict in the fact that the old dominate the young and the young wish to replace them, but it is not as severe in most societies as in ours. Here, it has become different in kind, as the brightest and most articulate of the young declare that they will not even accept, when their turn comes, the kinds of roles—in the kind of society—which their parents have held. As Bruno Bettelheim[2] pointed out in a classic paper some years ago, factors that have traditionally mitigated generational conflict have become feeble or inoperative even in this country. The family, for example, which is the context within which the strongest—albeit ambivalent—affectual ties between the generations are formed, plays a decreasing role in the lives of its members and, certainly, in the socialization of the young. It has less effect on their life-chances than it once had. If the Victorian father or the head of a traditional rural household was often a tyrant, and more or less accepted as such by his neighbors and his children, he was also a man who felt that he could transmit his wealth, his trade, and his position in the community, by inheritance. His relationship to his sons was not purely competitive but complementary as well: it was they who would have to carry on his work as his own powers failed, and on whom he was therefore ultimately dependent if his accomplishment in life was to lead to anything permanent. The proper attitude of father to son—both the authority and the underlying tenderness —took account of this mutual though unequal dependency. And while excessive and inconsiderate longevity in a father might make his son's position grotesque, as that of mad old George III did to the Prince Regent's position, the problems of succession were usually made less abrasive by the recognition of mutual need.

Moreover, so long as society changed slowly, elders really knew more that was useful than the young did; they were wiser; their authority was based on real superiority in the subtle techniques of living. This was never a very strong bond between the generations in America, where the sons of immigrants have always been as likely to find their greenhorn parents a source of embarrassment as of enlightenment; and generational conflict has probably always been more severe here than in more stable cultures—or would have been had there not also been a continent to escape into and develop.

But, today, the older generation has become not merely an embarrassment, but often an obstructive irrelevance to the young. We cannot even defend our former functions with respect to youth; for the ethos of modern liberalism condemns as inequitable, and a violation of equal opportunity, the arrangements on which continuity between the generations has been based. Bourgeois emphasis on private property and the rights of inheritance gave to the family the function of providing this continuity, which, under feudal conditions, would have been shared among several institutions—apprenticeship, for example. But the development of an open, bureaucratic society has weakened the influence of the family, and has transferred the task of distributing status among claimants primarily to the schools, which profess to judge them, so far as possible, without regard to their antecedents.

Today, college admissions officers agree that the sons of alumni should not be favored over more gifted applicants who seek admission solely on the basis of their academic record and recommendations. But this amounts to redefining merit to mean the kind of performance and personality that high school teachers and, increasingly, counselors like. Counselors now virtually control many a high school student's future chances, by their decision whether to assign him to a college-preparatory course, and by monitoring his applications for admission. Whether this whole process makes the contest more open or merely changes the criteria for preferment, is hard to say.[3]

The effect of the high school, and especially of the counselor, on continuity of status between the generations, and hence on the bond between the generations, is the subject of a fascinating study—still little known after five years—by Aaron V. Cicourel and John I. Kitsuse.[4] While the entire work bears on this issue, one particular interview-excerpt is worth quoting here because of the clarity with which it shows a high school student from an upper-status suburban home being punished for his lack of humility in school by restriction of his future chances. This young man had already been classed by his counselor as an "underachiever." Here are some of the counselor's comments to Cicourel and Kitsuse's interviewer:

COUNSELOR: His mother says he's a pleasant outgoing boy. His teachers will say he's either a pleasant boy or that he's a pest. I think he's arrogant. He thinks he's handsome. He's nice-looking, but not handsome. He thinks he owns Lakeshore. He talks to his teachers as if they were stupid. He's a good student. He's in biology and algebra honors.
INTERVIEWER: Is he going to college?
COUNSELOR: He plans college. I think he said he plans to go East like MIT, Harvard, etc. He won't make it. He's a candidate for a midwestern school.[5]

This excerpt, of course, illustrates certain very positive reasons for conflict between youth and older people: the constraint imposed by the school and its basic disrespect for its young captive. But I have introduced it here specifically to call attention to the fact that the school is here destroying the basis for continuity in the home by making it a condition—for higher- as well as for lower-status students—that the student *unlearn* what the home has taught him about himself if he wishes to retain access to his family's present socioeconomic status. In this way, older middle- and upper-class life-patterns are made positively dysfunctional for the young, just as lower-class life-patterns are, in the equalizing process of the school. Unless the tendency of the home is toward docile acceptance of the common-man pattern of life and expectation, the school will run counter to its influence.

The influence of the school itself is, in a matter of this complexity, difficult to isolate and appraise. But it is clear—and, I think, significant—that disaffection in the young is heavily concentrated among both the bright middle-class and upper-middle-class youth, on the one hand, and the lower-class, especially Negro, youth, on the other. The working class, young and old, is, in contrast, much more likely to be hostile to dissent, and especially to demonstrations, and to regard the school as the pathway to opportunity; its children are more willing to put on a clean shirt and tie and await the pleasure of the draft board or the interviewer from industry. For them, the school and family have worked together, and adult role-models retain their quite possibly fatal appeal.

Youth as a Discriminated-Against Class

I have already asserted that conflict between the generations is less a consequence of the ways in which old and young perceive, or misperceive, each other than of structurally created, genuine conflicts of interest. In this, as in other relationships, ideology follows self-interest: we impute to other people and social groups characteristics that justify the use we plan to make of them and the control over them that use requires. The subordinate group, in turn, often develops these very characteristics in response to the conditions that were imposed on them. Slaves, slum-dwellers, "teen-agers," and enlisted men do, indeed, often display a defensive stupidity and irresponsibility, which quickly abates in situations which they feel to be free of officious interference, with which they can deal, by means of their own institutions, in their own way.

For American youth, these occasions are few, and have grown relatively fewer with the escalation of the war in Vietnam. The Dominican intervention, the scale and permanence of our military investment in Southeast Asia, and the hunch that our economic system requires the engagement of its youth at low pay, or none, in a vast military-academic complex, in order to avoid disastrously widespread unemployment—even under present circumstances far greater among youth than among older persons—suggest to thoughtful young people that their bondage may be fundamental to the American political system and incapable of solution within its terms.

That bondage is remarkably complete—and so gross, in comparison to the way in which other members of the society are treated, that I find it difficult to accept the good faith of most adults who declare their sympathy with "the problems of youth" while remaining content to operate within the limits of the coercive system that deals with them, in any official capacity. To search for explanations of the problems of youth in America in primarily psychological terms while suggesting ways of easing the tension between them and the rest of society is rather like approaching the problem of "the American turkey in late autumn" with the same benign attitude. Turkeys would have no problem, except for the use we make of them, though I can imagine clearly enough the arguments that a cadre of specialists in poultry-relations might advance in defense of Thanksgiving, all of them true enough as far as they went: that wild turkeys could not support themselves under the demanding conditions of modern life; that there are now more turkeys than ever before and their general health and nutritional status, if not their life-expectancy, is much more favorable than in the past; that a turkey ought to have a chance to fulfill its obligations and realize the meaning of its life as a responsible member of society; that, despite the sentimental outcries of reformers, most turkeys seem contented with their lot—those that are not content being best treated by individual clinical means and, if necessary, an accelerated program; and that the discontented are not the fattest, anyway, only the brightest.

Young men in America, like most Negroes, are excluded from any opportunity to hold the kind of job or to earn the kind of money without which members of this society committed to affluence are treated with gross contempt. In a sense, the plight of youth is more oppressive, for the means by which they are constrained are held to be lawful, while discrimination against Negroes is now proscribed by law and what remains, though very serious indeed, is the massive toxic residue of past practice rather than current public policy.

Students are not paid for attending school; they are held to be investing in their future—though if, in fact, they invested as capital the difference between the normal wage of an employed adult high school graduate for four to seven years and what little they may have received as stipends during their academic careers for the same length of time, the return accrued to them might easily exceed the increment a degree will bring. But, of course, they have not got it to invest, and are not permitted to get it to live on. The draft siphons off working-class youth, while middle-class youth are constrained to remain in college to avoid it. If there were no draft, their impact on the economy would probably be ruinous. Trade-union restrictions and child-labor laws, in any case, prevent their gaining the kind of experience, prior to the age of eighteen—even as part of a high school program—that would qualify them for employment as adults by the time they reach their legal majority, though young workers could be protected by laws relating to working conditions, hours, and wage-rates, if this protection were indeed the intent of restrictive legislation, without eliminating his opportunity for employment.

Even the concept of a legal majority is itself a social artifact, defining the time at which the social structure is ready to concede a measure of equality to those of its members whom youthfulness has kept powerless, without reference to their real qualifications which, where relevant, could be directly tested. Nature knows no such sharp break in competence associated with maturation, except in the sexual sphere; and comparatively little of our economic and political behavior is overtly sexual. Perhaps if more were, we would be more forthright and less spiteful. Nor is there any general maturational factor, gradual but portentous in its cumulative effect, which is relevant to society's demands.

Neither wisdom nor emotional stability is particularly characteristic of American adults, as compared to the young; and where, in this country, would the electoral process become less rational if children were permitted to vote: southern California? Washington, D.C.? If there should be any age limitation on voting, it ought to apply, surely, to those so old that they may reasonably expect to escape the consequences of their political decisions, rather than to those who will be burdened and perhaps destroyed by them. Certainly, the disfranchisement of youth is impossible to square, morally, with the Selective Service Act—though politically, there is no inconsistency: the second implies the first. But the draft is pure exploitation, in a classical Marxian sense. The question of the need for an army is not the issue. A volunteer army could be raised, according to the conservative economist Milton Friedman,[6] for from four to twenty billion dollars per year; and to argue that even the larger sum is more than the nation can afford is merely to insist that draftees support the nation by paying, in kind, a tax-rate several times greater than the average paid by civilian taxpayers in money, instead of being compensated for their loss in liberty and added risk. To argue that military service is a duty owed to one's country seems quite beside the point: it is not owed more by a young man than by the old or the middle-aged. And, at a time when a large proportion of enlisted military assignments are in clerical and technical specialties identical with those for which civilians are highly paid, the draft seems merely a form of involuntary servitude.

Without a doubt, the Selective Service Act has done more than any other factor not only to exacerbate the conflict between generations, but to make it clear that it is a real conflict of interest. The draft makes those subject to it formally second-class citizens in a way to which no race is subjected any longer. The arrogance and inaccessibility of Selective Service officials, who are neither elected nor appointed for fixed terms subject to review; the fact that it has been necessary to take court action even to make public the names of draft-board members in some communities; the fact that registrants are specifically denied representation by counsel during their dealings with the Selective Service System and can only appeal to the courts after risking prosecution for the felony of refusing induction—all this is without parallel in the American legal process.

But the laws of the land are, after all, what define youth as a discriminated-against class. In fact, it is their discrimination that gives the term "youth" the only operational meaning it has: that of a person who, by reason of age, becomes subject to special constraint and penalties visited upon no other member of the commonwealth—for whom, by reason of age, certain conduct, otherwise lawful, is defined as criminal and to whom special administrative procedures, applicable to no other member of the commonwealth, are applied. The special characteristics of "youth culture" are derived from these disabilities rather than from any inherent age-graded characteristics. "Youth culture" is composed of individuals whose time is pre-empted by compulsory school attendance or the threat of induction into the Armed Service, who, regardless of their skills, cannot get and hold jobs that will pay enough to permit them to marry and build homes, and who are subject to surveillance at home or in school dormitories if they are detected in any form of sexual activity whatever. Youth and prisoners are the only people in America for whom *all* forms of sexual behavior are defined as illicit. It is absurd to scrutinize people who are forced to live under such extraordinary disabilities for psychological explanations of their resistance or bizarre conduct, except insofar as their state of mind can be related to their real situation.[7]

Law Enforcement and Legal
Process Applied to Youth

In their relationship to the legal structure, youth operate under peculiar disabilities. The educational codes of the several states provide for considerably more restraint even than the compulsory attendance provisions provide

—and that provision would be regarded as confiscatory, and hence doubtless unconstitutional, if applied to any member of the commonwealth old enough to be respected as having the right to dispose of his own time. Soldiers are at least paid *something.* But the code does more than pre-empt the students' time. It is usually interpreted by school authorities as giving them power to set standards of dress and grooming—some of which, like those pertaining to hair length, of a kind that cannot be set aside while the student is not in school. It becomes the basis for indoctrination with the values of a petty, clerical social subclass. Regulations on dress, speech, and conduct in school are justified by this subclass as being necessary because school is supposed to be businesslike; it is where you learn to behave like a businessman. This leaves the young with the alternative of becoming little-league businessmen or juvenile delinquents, for refusal to obey school regulations leads to charges of delinquency—which seems a rather narrow choice among the possibilities of youthful life.

But I have written so much more elsewhere[8] about education as a social sanction that it seems inappropriate to devote more space to the functioning of the school as such. I have introduced the topic here simply to point out that the educational code, from the viewpoint of those subject to it, constitutes the most pervasive *legal* constraint on the movements and behavior of youth. It is not, however, from the viewpoint of legal theory, the most fundamental. The juvenile code and the juvenile court system provide even more direct contradictions to the standard of due process afforded adults in American courts.

For the juvenile court is, ostensibly, not a criminal court. It is technically a court of chancery before which a respondent is brought as a presumptive ward—not as an adversary, but as a dependent. It is assumed—the language is preserved in the legal documentation used in preparing juvenile court cases—that the authorities intervene *on behalf of the minor,* and with the purpose of setting up, where necessary, a regime designed to correct his wayward tendencies. The court may restrict; it may, as a condition of probation, insist that a respondent submit to a public spanking; it may detain and incarcerate in a reformatory indistinguishable from a prison for a period of years—but it may not punish. It is authorized only to correct.

Because action in juvenile court is not, therefore, regarded as an adversary proceeding, the juvenile courts provide few of the legal safeguards of a criminal court. There is considerable public misunderstanding about this, because the effect of recent Supreme Court decisions on the juvenile court process has been widely exaggerated, both by people who endorse and by people who deplore what the Court has done. What it *has* done, in effect, is to require the juvenile court to provide the usual safeguards if its actions are ever to become part of an adversary proceeding in a regular criminal court. Since the state may at its discretion, try as adults rather than as juveniles youngsters over a certain minimum age who are accused of actions that violate the criminal code, and since the more serious offenses are usually committed by older adolescents, it may choose to provide these accused with the safeguards granted adults from the time of arrest rather than impair its chances for subsequent successful prosecution. It is, therefore, becoming usual, for example, to provide counsel for juveniles in serious cases; to exclude, in the event of a subsequent criminal prosecution, statements taken by probation officers or youth-squad members in a legally improper manner; and to permit juvenile respondents to summon and cross-examine witnesses—procedures which have not been part of juvenile court practice in the past.

These are improvements, but they leave untouched the much vaster potential for intergenerational conflict afforded by the summary treatment of casual offenders, and, particularly, of those youngsters of whose behavior the law could take no cognizance if they were older; for example, truants, loiterers, runaways, curfew-violators, and twenty-year-olds who buy beer in a tavern. For such as these, there is no question of compromising future prosecution in a formal court, and their treatment has been affected very little, if at all, by high-court decisions. The law still presumes that its intervention in their lives is beneficial *per se,* and they have few enforceable civil rights with respect to it. If young people are "troublemakers," they are punished for it—that is all. Step out of line, and the police "take you away," as the Buffalo Springfield described it—on the occasion of a Los Angeles police roundup of the youngsters strolling on the Sunset Strip in the autumn of 1968—in the song, "For What It's Worth," that gained them a national reputation among teen-agers.

It is quite clear that one's moral judgment of the legal position of youth in American society depends very largely on the degree to which one shares the fundamental assumption on which juvenile proceedings are based: that they are designed to help; that the adults who carry them out will, by and large, have the wisdom and the resources, and the intent to help rather than to punish. Legal authorities have caviled at this assumption for some time. Thus, Paul W. Alexander writes in a paper on "Constitutional Rights in Juvenile Court":

> In the area of the child's constitutional rights the last decade has seen a minor but interesting revolt on the part of some highly distinguished judges. So repellent were some of the juvenile court practices that the judges were moved to repudiate the widely held majority rule that a delinquency hearing in a juvenile court is a civil, not a criminal action. . . . This doctrine appeared so distasteful to a California appellate court that the following language appeared in the opinion: "While the juvenile court law provides that adjudication of a minor to be a ward of the court

should not be deemed to be a conviction of crime, nevertheless, for all practical purposes, this is a legal fiction, presenting a challenge to credulity and doing violence to reason."[9]

Youth Today Have No Respect for the Law

The kind of legal structure which youth face would appear to be, of itself, sufficient to explain why young people are often inclined to be skeptical rather than enthusiastic about law and order—and about those of their number who are enthusiasts for law, as student leaders and prominent athletes tend to be. Yet, the hostile relations that develop between youth and law-enforcement agencies are, even so, probably more attributable to the way in which police generally respond to young people than to the oppressive character of the legal system itself—though the two factors are, of course, causally related, because the fact that youth have few rights and many liabilities before the law also makes it possible for law-enforcement agencies to behave more oppressively.

With respect to youth, law-enforcement agencies assume the role of enforcers of morals and proper social attitudes, as well as of the law, and —having few rights—there is not much the young can do about it. Police forces, moreover, provide a manpower-pool by "moonlighting," while off duty, as members of private enforcement squads hired to keep young people from getting out of hand, a task which they often try to perform by making themselves as conspicuous as possible in order to keep the young people from starting anything—exactly what police would *not* do in monitoring a group of orderly adults in a public place.

My own observations at folk-rock concerts and dances, for example, which are among the best places for learning how young people express themselves and communicate with one another, confirm that surveillance on these occasions is characteristically officious and oppressive. It often expresses a real contempt for the customs of the youngsters, even when these are appropriate to the occasion. Police, clubs in hand, will rush onstage or into the pit at any sign that the performers are about to mingle with the dancers or audience—if a soloist jumps down from the stage, say, or if members of the audience attempt to mount it; or they will have the lights turned up to interrupt a jam session or freakout that has gone on too long, or with too great intensity, for their taste; or insist on ruining a carefully designed and well-equipped light-show by requiring that the house-lights be kept bright. All this is done smirkingly, as if the youngsters at the concert knew that they were "getting out of line" in behaving differently from a philharmonic audience. It should be borne in mind, considering the fiscal basis for rights in our culture, that tickets for the Beach Boys or Jefferson Airplane are now likely to cost more than tickets for a symphony concert, and the youngsters are poorer than symphony subscribers, but they rarely enjoy the same right to listen to their music in their own way, unmolested.

The music itself provides some of the best evidence of the response of the "further-out" youngsters to police action, which, indeed, sometimes inflicts on them more serious damage than the annoyance of having a concert ruined. In Watts, San Francisco, and Memphis, the civil disorders associated with each city in recent years were triggered by the slaying of a Negro youth by a police officer. "Pot busts" are directed primarily against young people, among whom the use of marijuana has become something of a moral principle evoked by the destructive hostility of the legal means used to suppress it: thirty students at the State University of New York at Stony Brook, for example, were handcuffed and herded from their dormitories before dawn last winter, before the lenses of television cameras manned by news agencies which the Suffolk County police had thoughtfully notified of the impending raid.[10] Rock artists, speaking to, and to some degree for, youth, respond to the social climate which such incidents, often repeated, have established. I have already cited the Buffalo Springfield's song "For What It's Worth." The Mothers of Invention are even more direct in their new album, *We're Only In It for the Money,* where they represent the typical parent as believing that police brutality is justified toward teen-agers who look "too weird" and make "some noise."[11]

Bringing It All Back Home

Finally, exacerbating the confrontations between youth and adults is the fact that the control of youth has largely been entrusted to lower-status elements of the society. Custodial and control functions usually are so entrusted, for those in subjection have even lower status themselves, and do not command the services of the higher grades of personnel that their society affords. Having low status, moreover, prevents their being taken seriously as moral human beings. Society tends to assume that the moral demands made on the criminal, the mad, and the young by their respective wardens are for their own good and to reinforce those demands while limiting the subjects' opportunities for redress to those situations in which the grossest violations of the most fundamental human rights have occurred. The reader's moral evaluation of the conflict that I have described will, therefore, depend very largely, I believe, on the degree to which he shares society's assumption.

As has surely been obvious, I do not share it. The process by which youth is brought into line in American society is almost wholly destructive of the dignity and creative potential of the young, and the condition of the middle-aged and the old in America seems to me, on the whole, to make this proposition quite plausible. Nevertheless, the violation of the young in the process of socialization fulfills an essential function in making our society cohesive. And curiously—and rather perversely—this function depends on the fact that custody and indoctrination—education is not, after all, a very precise term for it—are lower-status functions.

American democracy depends, I believe, on the systematic humiliation of potential elites to keep it going. There is, perhaps, no other way in which an increasingly educated middle class, whose technical services cannot be spared, can be induced to acquiesce in the political demands of a deracinated and invidious populace, reluctant to accept any measure of social improvement, however generally advantageous, which might bring any segment of the society slightly more benefits than would accrue to it. Teachers, police, and parents in America are jointly in the business of rearing the young to be frightened of the vast majority who have been too scarred and embittered by the losses and compromises which they have endured in the process of becoming respectable to be treated in a way that would enrage them. Anything generous—or perhaps merely civil, like welcoming a Negro family into a previously white community, or letting your neighbor "blow a little grass" in peace—does enrage them, and so severely as to threaten the fabric of society. A conference of recent American leaders associated with a greater measure of generosity toward the deprived—John and Robert Kennedy, Martin Luther King, Jr., and Malcolm X, for a start —might, perhaps, agree, if it could be convened.

Many of today's middle-class youth, however—having been spared, by the prevailing affluence, the deprivations that make intimidation more effective in later life—are talking back; and some are even finding support, rather than betrayal, in their elders—the spectacle of older folks helping their radical sons to adjust their identifying armbands during the spring protests at Columbia University is said to have been both moving and fairly common. The protest, in any case, continues and mounts. So does the rage against the young. If the confrontation between the generations does pose, as many portentous civic leaders and upper-case "Educators" fear, a lethal threat to the integrity of the American social system, that threat may perhaps be accepted with graceful irony. Is there, after all, so much to lose? The American social system has never been noted for its integrity. In fact, it would be rather like depriving the Swiss of their surfing.

NOTES

1. I am indebted to John and Margaret Rowntree, of York University and the University of Toronto, respectively, for demonstrating, in their paper "The Political Economy of Youth in the United States," the class-dynamics of generational conflict. This document, prepared for presentation at the First Annual Meeting of the Committee on Socialist Studies in Calgary, Alberta, in June 1968, was published in the Montreal quarterly journal *Our Generation,* Vol. 6, No. 1, 1968. Their radical analysis simplifies many apparent paradoxes in the relationship between the generations.

2. Bruno Bettelheim, "The Problem of Generations," *Daedalus,* Vol. 91, No. 1 (Winter 1962), pp. 68–96.

3. Christopher Jencks and David Riesman, in *The Academic Revolution* (Garden City, N.Y.: Doubleday, 1968), pp. 146–154, provide a thoughtful, if rather gingerly, discussion of this issue.

4. Aaron V. Cicourel and John I. Kitsuse, *The Educational Decision-Makers* (Indianapolis: Bobbs-Merrill, 1963).

5. *Ibid.,* p. 72.

6. Quoted in *Newsweek,* December 19, 1966, p. 100.

7. To be sure, as we become more sophisticated in our conception of mental illness, this becomes more and more clearly true of all forms of mental illness. All states of mind have their psychodynamics; but, regardless of the school of psychodynamic thought to which one adheres, the most basic possible definition of mental illness seems to be "a chronic or recurring mental or emotional state which disturbs other people more powerful than the victim." Sometimes, of course, as in the case of certain kinds of paranoid schizophrenics, with good reason.

As a corollary to this, it seems to follow that the head of a modern, centralized, national state—unlike his poor, royal predecessors—can never go officially mad until his government is overthrown.

8. See *The Vanishing Adolescent* (1959), *Coming of Age in America* (1965), *The Dignity of Youth and Other Atavisms* (1965), and *Society's Children* (1967, in collaboration with Carol Nordstrom and Hilary Gold).

9. Included in Margaret K. Rosenheim (ed.), *Justice for the Child* (New York: Free Press of Glencoe, 1962), p. 83.

10. *The New York Times,* January 18, 1968.

11. Copyright by Frank Zappa Music Company, Inc., a subsidiary of Third Story Music, Inc. (BMI)

YOU HAVE TO GROW UP IN SCARSDALE TO KNOW HOW BAD THINGS REALLY ARE

✥ Kenneth Keniston

The recent events at Harvard are the culmination of a long year of unprecedented student unrest in the advanced nations of the world. We have learned to expect students in underdeveloped countries to lead unruly demonstrations against the status quo, but what is new, unexpected and upsetting to many is that an apparently similar mood is sweeping across America, France, Germany, Italy and even Eastern European nations like Czechoslovakia and Poland. Furthermore, the revolts occur, not at the most backward universities, but at the most distinguished, liberal and enlightened —Berkeley, the Sorbonne, Tokyo, Columbia, the Free University of Berlin, Rome and now Harvard.

This development has taken almost everyone by surprise. The American public is clearly puzzled, frightened and often outraged by the behavior of its most privileged youth. The scholarly world, including many who have devoted their lives to the study of student protest, has been caught off guard as well. For many years, American analysts of student movements have been busy demonstrating that "it can't happen here." Student political activity abroad has been seen as a reaction to modernization, industrialization and the demise of traditional or tribal societies. In an already modern, industrialized, detribalized and "stable" nation like America, it was argued, student protests are naturally absent.

SOURCE: Kenneth Keniston, "You Have to Grow Up in Scarsdale to Know How Bad Things Really Are," *The New York Times Magazine* (April 27, 1969), 27–29, 122, 124, 126, 128–30. Copyright © 1969 by The New York Times Company. Reprinted by permission of *The New York Times.*

548

Another explanation has tied student protests abroad to bad living conditions in some universities and to the unemployability of their graduates. Student revolts, it was argued, spring partly from the misery of student life in countries like India and Indonesia. Students who must live in penury and squalor naturally turn against their universities and societies. And if, as in many developing nations, hundreds of thousands of university graduates can find no work commensurate with their skills, the chances for student militance are further increased.

These arguments helped explain the "silent generation" of the nineteen-fifties and the absence of protest, during that period, in American universities, where students are often "indulged" with good living conditions, close student-faculty contact and considerable freedom of speech. And they helped explain why "superemployable" American college graduates, especially the much-sought-after ones from colleges like Columbia and Harvard, seemed so contented with their lot.

But such arguments do not help us understand today's noisy, angry and militant students in the advanced countries. Nor do they explain why students who enjoy the greatest advantages—those at the leading universities—are often found in the revolts. As a result, several new interpretations of student protest are currently being put forward, interpretations that ultimately form part of what Richard Poirier has termed "the war against the young."

Many reactions to student unrest, of course, spring primarily from fear, anger, confusion or envy, rather than from theoretical analysis. Governor Wallace's attacks on student "anarchists" and other "pin-headed intellectuals," for example, were hardly coherent explanations of protest. Many of the bills aimed at punishing student protesters being proposed in Congress and state legislatures reflect similar feelings of anger and outrage. Similarly, the presumption that student unrest *must* be part of an international conspiracy is based on emotion rather than fact. Even George F. Kennan's recent discussion of the American student left is essentially a moral condemnation of "revolting students," rather than an effort to explain their behavior.

If we turn to more thoughtful analyses of the current student mood we find two general theories gaining widespread acceptance. The first, articulately expressed by Lewis S. Feuer in his recent book on student movements, "The Conflict of Generations," might be termed the "Oedipal Rebellion" interpretation. The second, cogently stated by Zbigniew Brzezinski and Daniel Bell, can be called the theory of "Historical Irrelevance."

The explanation of Oedipal Rebellion sees the underlying force in all student revolts as blind, unconscious Oedipal hatred of fathers and the older generation. Feuer, for example, finds in all student movements an inevitable tendency toward violence and a combination of "regicide, parricide and suicide." A decline in respect for the authority of the older generation is needed to trigger a student movement, but the force behind it comes from "obscure" and "unconscious" forces in the child's early life, including both intense death wishes against his father and the enormous guilt and self-hatred that such wishes inspire in the child.

The idealism of student movements is thus, in many respects, only a "front" for the latent unconscious destructiveness and self-destructiveness of underlying motivations. Even the expressed desire of these movements to help the poor and exploited is explained psychoanalytically by Feuer: Empathy for the disadvantaged is traced to "traumatic" encounters with parental bigotry in the students' childhoods, when their parents forbade them to play with children of other races or lower social classes. The identification of today's new left with blacks is thus interpreted as an unconscious effort to "abreact and undo this original trauma."

There are two basic problems with the Oedipal Rebellion theory, however. First, although it uses psychoanalytic terms, it is bad psychoanalysis. The real psychoanalytic account insists that the Oedipus complex is universal in all normally developing children. To point to this complex in explaining student rebellion is, therefore, like pointing to the fact that all children learn to walk. Since both characteristics are said to be universal, neither helps us understand why, at some historical moments, students are restive and rebellious, while at others they are not. Second, the theory does not help us explain why some students (especially those from middle-class, affluent and idealistic families) are most inclined to rebel, while others (especially those from working-class and deprived families) are less so.

In order really to explain anything, the Oedipal Rebellion hypothesis would have to be modified to point to an unusually *severe* Oedipus complex, involving especially *intense* and unresolved unconscious feelings of father-hatred in student rebels. But much is now known about the lives and backgrounds of these rebels—at least those in the United States—and this evidence does not support even the modified theory. On the contrary, it indicates that most student protesters are relatively *close* to their parents, that the values they profess are usually the ones they learned at the family dinner table, and that their parents tend to be highly educated, liberal or left-wing and politically active.

Furthermore, psychological studies of student radicals indicate that they are no more neurotic, suicidal, enraged or disturbed than are nonradicals. Indeed, most studies find them to be rather more integrated, self-accepting and "advanced," in a psychological sense, than their politically inactive contemporaries. In general, research on American student rebels supports a "Generational Solidarity" (or chip-off-the-old-block) theory, rather than one of Oedipal Rebellion.

The second theory of student revolts now being advanced asserts that they are a reaction against "historical irrelevance." Rebellion springs from the unconscious awareness of some students that society has left them and their values behind. According to this view, the ultimate causes of student dissent are sociological rather than psychological. They lie in fundamental changes in the nature of the advanced societies—especially, in the change from industrial to post-industrial society. The student revolution is seen not as a true revolution, but as a counterrevolution—what Daniel Bell has called "the guttering last gasp of a romanticism soured by rancor and impotence."

This theory assumes that we are moving rapidly into a new age in which technology will dominate, an age whose real rulers will be men like computer experts, systems analysts and technobureaucrats. Students who are attached to outmoded and obsolescent values like humanism and romanticism unconsciously feel they have no place in this post-industrial world. When they rebel they are like the Luddites of the past—workers who smashed machines to protest the inevitable industrial revolution. Today's student revolt reflects what Brzezinski terms "an unconscious realization that they [the rebels] are themselves becoming historically obsolete"; it is nothing but the "death rattle of the historical irrelevants."

This theory is also inadequate. It assumes that the shape of the future is already technologically determined, and that protesting students unconsciously "know" that it will offer them no real reward, honor or power. But the idea that the future can be accurately predicted is open to fundamental objection. Every past attempt at prophecy has turned out to be grievously incorrect. Extrapolations from the past, while sometimes useful in the short run, are usually fundamentally wrong in the long run, especially when they attempt to predict the quality of human life, the nature of political and social organization, international relations or the shape of future culture.

The future is, of course, made by men. Technology is not an inevitable master of man and history, but merely provides the possibility of applying scientific knowledge to specific problems. Men may identify with it or refuse to, use it or be used by it for good or evil, apply it humanely or destructively. Thus, there is no real evidence that student protest will emerge as the "death rattle of the historical irrelevants." It could equally well be the "first spark of a new historical era." No one today can be sure of the outcome, and people who feel certain that the future will bring the obsolescence and death of those whom they dislike are often merely expressing their fond hope.

The fact that today's students invoke "old" humanistic and romantic ideas in no way proves that student protests are a "last gasp" of a dying order. Quite the contrary: *All* revolutions draw upon older values and visions. Many of the ideals of the French Revolution, for example, originated in Periclean Athens. Revolutions do not occur because new ideas suddenly develop, but because a new generation begins to take *old* ideas seriously—not merely as interesting theoretical views, but as the basis for political action and social change. Until recently, the humanistic vision of human fulfillment and the romantic vision of an expressive, imaginative and passionate life were taken seriously only by small aristocratic or Bohemian groups. The fact that they are today taken as real goals by millions of students in many nations does not mean that these students are "counter-revolutionaries," but merely that their ideas follow the pattern of every major revolution.

Indeed, today's student rebels are rarely opposed to technology *per se*. On the contrary, they take the high technology of their societies completely for granted, and concern themselves with it very little. What they *are* opposed to is, in essence, the worship of Technology, the tendency to treat people as "inputs" or "outputs" of a technological system, the subordination of human needs to technological programs. The essential conflict between the minority of students who make up the student revolt and the existing order is a conflict over the future direction of technological society, not a counter-revolutionary protest against technology.

In short, both the Oedipal Rebellion and the Historical Irrelevance theories are what students would call "put-downs." If we accept either, we are encouraged not to listen to protests, or to explain them away or reject them as either the "acting out" of destructive Oedipal feelings or the blind reaction of an obsolescent group to the awareness of its obsolescence. But if, as I have argued, neither of these theories is adequate to explain the current "wave" of student protest here and abroad, how can we understand it?

One factor often cited to explain student unrest is the large number of people in the world under 30—today the critical dividing line between generations. But this explanation alone, like the theories just discussed, is not adequate, for in all historical eras the vast portion of the population has always been under 30. Indeed, in primitive societies most people die before they reach that age. If chronological youth alone was enough to insure rebellion, the advanced societies—where a greater proportion of the population reaches old age than ever before in history—should be the *least* revolutionary, and primitive societies the *most*. This is not the case.

More relevant factors are the relationship of those under 30 to the established institutions of society (that is, whether they are engaged in them or not); and the opportunities that society provides for their continuing intellectual, ethical and emotional development. In both cases the present situation in the advanced nations is without precedent.

Philippe Aries, in his remarkable book, "Centuries of Childhood," points out that, until the end of the Middle Ages, no separate stage of childhood was recognized in Western societies. Infancy ended at approximately 6 to

7, whereupon most children were integrated into adult life, treated as small men and women and expected to work as junior partners of the adult world. Only later was childhood recognized as a separate stage of life, and our own century is the first to "guarantee" it by requiring universal primary education.

The recognition of adolescence as a stage of life is of even more recent origin, the product of the 19th and 20th centuries. Only as industrial societies became prosperous enough to defer adult work until after puberty could they create institutions—like widespread secondary-school education —that would extend adolescence to virtually all young people. Recognition of adolescence also arose from the vocational and psychological requirements of these societies, which needed much higher levels of training and psychological development than could be guaranteed through primary education alone. There is, in general, an intimate relationship between the way a society defines the stages of life and its economic, political and social characteristics.

Today, in more developed nations, we are beginning to witness the recognition of still another stage of life. Like childhood and adolescence, it was initially granted only to a small minority, but is now being rapidly extended to an ever-larger group. I will call this the stage of "youth," and by that I mean both a further phase of disengagement from society and the period of psychological development that intervenes between adolescence and adulthood. This stage, which continues into the 20's and sometimes into the 30's, provides opportunities for intellectual, emotional and moral development that were never afforded to any other large group in history. In the student revolts we are seeing one result of this advance.

I call the extension of youth an advance advisedly. Attendance at a college or university is a major part of this extension, and there is growing evidence that this is, other things being equal, a good thing for the student.

Put in an oversimplified phrase, it tends to free him—to free him from swallowing unexamined the assumptions of the past, to free him from the superstitions of his childhood, to free him to express his feelings more openly and to free him from irrational bondage to authority.

I do not mean to suggest, of course, that all college graduates are free and liberated spirits, unencumbered by irrationality, superstition, authoritarianism or blind adherence to tradition. But these findings do indicate that our colleges, far from cranking out only machinelike robots who will provide skilled manpower for the economy, are also producing an increasing number of highly critical citizens—young men and women who have the opportunity, the leisure, the affluence and the educational resources to continue their development beyond the point where most people in the past were required to stop it.

So, one part of what we are seeing on campuses throughout the world is not a reflection of how bad higher education is, but rather of its extraordinary accomplishments. Even the moral righteousness of the student rebels, a quality both endearing and infuriating to their elders, must be judged at least partially a consequence of the privilege of an extended youth; for a prolonged development, we know, encourages the individual to elaborate a more personal, less purely conventional sense of ethics.

What the advanced nations have done is to create their own critics on a mass basis—that is, to create an ever-larger group of young people who take the highest values of their societies as their own, who internalize these values and identify them with their own best selves, and who are willing to struggle to implement them. At the same time, the extension of youth has lessened the personal risks of dissent: These young people have been freed from the requirements of work, gainful employment and even marriage, which permits them to criticize their society from a protected position of disengagement.

But the mere prolongation of development need not automatically lead to unrest. To be sure, we have granted to millions the opportunity to examine their societies, to compare them with their values and to come to a reasoned judgment of the existing order. But why should their judgment today be so unenthusiastic?

What protesting students throughout the world share is a mood more than an ideology or a program, a mood that says the existing system—the power structure—is hypocritical, unworthy of respect, outmoded and in urgent need of reform. In addition, students everywhere speak of repression, manipulation and authoritarianism. (This is paradoxical, considering the apparently great freedoms given them in many nations. In America, for example, those who complain most loudly about being suffocated by the subtle tyranny of the Establishment usually attend the institutions where student freedom is greatest.) Around this general mood, specific complaints arrange themselves as symptoms of what students often call the "exhaustion of the existing society."

To understand this phenomenon we must recognize that, since the Second World War, some societies have indeed begun to move past the industrial era into a new world that is post-industrial, technological, post-modern, post-historic or, in Brzezinski's term, "technectronic." In Western Europe, the United States, Canada and Japan, the first contours of this new society are already apparent. And, in many other less-developed countries, middle-class professionals (whose children become activists) often live in post-industrial enclaves within pre-industrial societies. Whatever we call the post-industrial world, it has demonstrated that, for the first time, man can produce more than enough to meet his material needs.

This accomplishment is admittedly blemished by enormous problems of economic distribution in the advanced nations, and it is in terrifying contrast to the overwhelming poverty of the Third World. Nevertheless, it is clear that what might be called "the problem of production" *can*, in principle, be solved. If all members of American society, for example, do not have enough material goods, it is because the system of distribution is flawed. The same is true, or will soon be true, in many other nations that are approaching advanced states of industrialization. Characteristically, these nations, along with the most technological, are those where student unrest has recently been most prominent.

The transition from industrial to post-industrial society brings with it a major shift in social emphases and values. Industrializing and industrial societies tend to be oriented toward solving the problem of production. An industrial ethic—sometimes Protestant, sometimes Socialist, sometimes Communist—tends to emphasize psychological qualities like self-discipline, delay of gratification, achievement-orientation and a strong emphasis on economic success and productivity. The social, political and economic institutions of these societies tend to be organized in a way that is consistent with the goal of increasing production. And industrial societies tend to apply relatively uniform standards, to reward achievement rather than status acquired by birth, to emphasize emotional neutrality ("coolness') and rationality in work and public life.

The emergence of post-industrial societies, however, means that growing numbers of the young are brought up in family environments where abundance, relative economic security, political freedom and affluence are simply facts of life, not goals to be striven for. To such people the psychological imperatives, social institutions and cultural values of the industrial ethic seem largely outdated and irrelevant to their own lives.

Once it has been demonstrated that a society *can* produce enough for all of its members, at least some of the young turn to other goals: for example, trying to make sure that society *does* produce enough and distributes it fairly, or searching for ways to live meaningfully with the goods and the leisure they *already* have. The problem is that our society has, in some realms, exceeded its earlier targets. Lacking new ones, it has become exhausted by its success.

When the values of industrial society become devitalized, the élite sectors of youth—the most affluent, intelligent, privileged and so on—come to feel that they live in institutions whose demands lack moral authority or, in the current jargon, "credibility." Today, the moral imperative and urgency behind production, acquisition, materialism and abundance has been lost.

Furthermore, with the lack of moral legitimacy felt in "the System," the least request for loyalty, restraint or conformity by its representatives—for example, by college presidents and deans—can easily be seen as a moral outrage, an authoritarian repression, a manipulative effort to "co-opt" students into joining the Establishment and an exercise in "illegitimate authority" that must be resisted. From this conception springs at least part of the students' vague sense of oppression. And, indeed, perhaps their peculiar feeling of suffocation arises ultimately from living in societies without vital ethical claims.

Given such a situation, it does not take a clear-cut issue to trigger a major protest. I doubt, for example, that college and university administrators are in fact *more* hypocritical and dishonest than they were in the past. American intervention in Vietnam, while many of us find it unjust and cruel, is not inherently *more* outrageous than other similar imperialistic interventions by America and other nations within the last century. And the position of blacks in this country, although disastrously and unjustifiably disadvantaged, is, in some economic and legal respects, better than ever before. Similarly, the conditions for students in America have never been as good, especially, as I have noted, at those élite colleges where student protests are most common.

But this is *precisely* the point: It is *because* so many of the *other* problems of American society seem to have been resolved, or to be resolvable in principle, that students now react with new indignation to old problems, turn to new goals and propose radical reforms.

So far I have emphasized the moral exhaustion of the old order and the fact that, for the children of post-industrial affluence, the once-revolutionary claims of the industrial society have lost much of their validity. I now want to argue that we are witnessing on the campuses of the world a fusion of *two revolutions* with distinct historical origins. One is a continuation of the old and familiar revolution of the industrial society, the liberal-democratic-egalitarian revolution that started in America and France at the turn of the 18th century and spread to virtually every nation in the world. (Not completed in any of them, its contemporary American form is, above all, to be found in the increased militancy of blacks). The other is the new revolution, the post-industrial one, which seeks to define new goals relevant to the 20th and 21st centuries.

In its social and political aspects, the first revolution has been one of universalization, to use the sociologist's awkward term. It has involved the progressive extension to more and more people of economic, political and social rights, privileges and opportunities originally available only to the aristocracy, then to the middle class, and now in America to the relatively affluent white working class. It is, in many respects, a *quantitative* revolution. That is, it concerns itself less with the quality of life than with the amount of political freedom, the quantity and distribution of goods or the amount and level of injustice.

As the United States approaches the targets of the first revolution, on which this society was built, to be poor shifts from being an unfortunate fact of life to being an outrage. And, for the many who have never experienced poverty, discrimination, exploitation or oppression, even to *witness* the existence of these evils in the lives of others suddenly becomes intolerable. In our own time the impatience to complete the first revolution has grown apace, and we find less willingness to compromise, wait and forgive among the young, especially among those who now take the values of the old revolution for granted—seeing them not as goals, but as *rights*.

A subtle change has thus occurred. What used to be utopian ideals—like equality, abundance and freedom from discrimination—have now become demands, inalienable rights upon which one can insist without brooking any compromise. It is noteworthy that, in today's student confrontations, no one requests anything. Students present their "demands."

So, on the one hand, we see a growing impatience to complete the first revolution. But, on the other, there is a newer revolution concerned with newer issues, a revolution that is less social, economic or political than psychological, historical and cultural. It is less concerned with the quantities of things than with their qualities, and it judges the virtually complete liberal revolution and finds it still wanting.

"You have to have grown up in Scarsdale to know how bad things really are," said one radical student. This comment would probably sound arrogant, heartless and insensitive to a poor black, much less to a citizen of the Third World. But he meant something important by it. He meant that *even* in the Scarsdales of America, with their affluence, their upper-middle-class security and abundance, their well-fed, well-heeled children and their excellent schools, something is wrong. Economic affluence does not guarantee a feeling of personal fulfillment; political freedom does not always yield an inner sense of liberation and cultural freedom; social justice and equality may leave one with a feeling that something else is missing in life. "No to the consumer society!" shouted the bourgeois students of the Sorbonne during May and June of 1968—a cry that understandably alienated French workers, for whom affluence and the consumer society are still central goals.

What, then, are the targets of the new revolution? As is often noted, students themselves don't know. They speak vaguely of "a society that has never existed," of "new values," of a "more humane world," of "liberation" in some psychological, cultural and historical sense. Their rhetoric is largely negative; they are stronger in opposition than in proposals for reform; their diagnoses often seem accurate, but their prescriptions are vague; and they are far more articulate in urging the immediate completion of the first revolution than in defining the goals of the second. Thus, we can only indirectly discern trends that point to the still-undefined targets of the new revolution.

What are these trends and targets?

First, there is a revulsion against the notion of quantity, particularly economic quantity and materialism, and a turn toward concepts of quality. One of the most delightful slogans of the French student revolt was, "Long live the passionate revolution of creative intelligence!" In a sense, the achievement of abundance may allow millions of contemporary men and women to examine, as only a few artists and madmen have examined in the past, the quality, joyfulness and zestfulness of experience. The "expansion of consciousness"; the stress on the expressive, the aesthetic and the creative; the emphasis on imagination, direct perception and fantasy—all are part of the effort to enhance the quality of this experience.

Another goal of the new revolution involves a revolt against uniformity, equalization, standardization and homogenization—not against technology itself, but against the "technologization of man." At times, this revolt approaches anarchic quaintness, but it has a positive core as well—the demand that individuals be appreciated, not because of their similarities or despite their differences, but because they *are* different, diverse, unique and noninterchangeable. This attitude is evident in many areas: for example, the insistence upon a cultivation of personal idiosyncrasy, mannerism and unique aptitude. Intellectually, it is expressed in the rejection of the melting-pot and consensus-politics view of American life in favor of a post-homogeneous America in which cultural diversity and conflict are underlined rather than denied.

The new revolution also involves a continuing struggle against psychological or institutional closure or rigidity in any form, even the rigidity of a definite adult role. Positively, it extols the virtues of openness, motion and continuing human development. What Robert J. Lifton has termed the protean style is clearly in evidence. There is emerging a concept of a lifetime of personal change, of an adulthood of continuing self-transformation, of an adaptability and an openness to the revolutionary modern world that will enable the individual to remain "with it"—psychologically youthful and on top of the present.

Another characteristic is the revolt against centralized power and the complementary demand for participation. What is demanded is not merely the consent of the governed, but the involvement of the governed. "Participatory democracy" summarizes this aspiration, but it extends far beyond the phrase and the rudimentary social forms that have sprung up around it. It extends to the demand for relevance in education—that is, for a chance for the student to participate in his own educational experience in a way that involves all of his faculties, emotional and moral as well as intellectual. The demand for "student power" (or, in Europe, "co-determination") is an aspect of the same theme: At Nanterre, Columbia, Frankfurt and Harvard, students increasingly seek to participate in making the policies of their universities.

This demand for participation is also embodied in the new ethic of "meaningful human relationships," in which individuals confront each other without masks, pretenses and games. They "relate" to each other as unique and irreplaceable human beings, and develop new forms of relationships from which all participants will grow.

In distinguishing between the old and the new revolutions, and in attempting to define the targets of the new, I am, of course, making distinctions that students themselves rarely make. In any one situation the two revolutions are joined and fused, if not confused. For example, the Harvard students' demand for "restructuring the university" is essentially the second revolution's demand for participation; but their demand for an end to university "exploitation" of the surrounding community is tied to the more traditional goals of the first revolution. In most radical groups there is a range of opinion that starts with the issues of the first (racism, imperialism, exploitation, war) and runs to the concerns of the second (experimental education, new life styles, meaningful participation, consciousness-expansion, relatedness, encounter and community). The first revolution is personified by Maoist-oriented Progressive Labor party factions within the student left, while the second is represented by hippies, the "acid left," and the Yippies. In any individual, and in all student movements, these revolutions co-exist in uneasy and often abrasive tension.

Furthermore, one of the central problems for student movements today is the absence of any theory of society that does justice to the new world in which we of the most industrialized nations live. In their search for rational critiques of present societies, students turn to theories like Marxism that are intricately bound up with the old revolution.

Such theories make the ending of economic exploitation, the achievement of social justice, the abolition of racial discrimination and the development of political participation and freedom central, but they rarely deal adequately with the issues of the second revolution. Students inevitably try to adapt the rhetoric of the first to the problems of the second, using concepts that are often blatantly inadequate to today's world.

Even the concept of "revolution" itself is so heavily laden with images of political, economic and social upheaval that it hardly seems to characterize the equally radical but more social-psychological and cultural transformations involved in the new revolution. One student, recognizing this, called the changes occurring in his California student group, "too radical to be called a revolution." Students are thus often misled by their borrowed vocabulary, but most adults are even more confused, and many are quickly led to the mistaken conclusion that today's student revolt is nothing more than a repetition of Communism's in the past.

Failure to distinguish between the old and new revolutions also makes it impossible to consider the critical question of how compatible they are with each other. Does it make sense—or is it morally right—for today's affluent American students to seek imagination, self-actualization, individuality, openness and relevance when most of the world and many in America live in deprivation, oppression and misery?

The fact that the first revolution is "completed" in Scarsdale does not mean that it is (or soon will be) in Harlem or Appalachia—to say nothing of Bogotá or Calcutta. For many children of the second revolution, the meaning of life may be found in completing the first—that is, in extending to others the "rights" they have always taken for granted.

For others the second revolution will not wait; the question. "What lies beyond affluence?" demands an answer now. Thus, although we may deem it self-indulgent to pursue the goals of the new revolution in a world where so much misery exists, the fact is that in the advanced nations it is upon us, and we must at least learn to recognize it.

Finally, beneath my analysis lies an assumption I had best make explicit. Many student critics argue that their societies have failed miserably. My argument, a more historical one perhaps, suggests that our problem is not only that industrial societies have failed to keep all their promises, but that they have succeeded in some ways beyond all expectations. Abundance was once a distant dream, to be postponed to a hereafter of milk and honey; today, most Americans are affluent. Universal mass education was once a Utopian goal; today in America almost the entire population completes high school, and almost half enters colleges and universities.

The notion that individuals might be free, en masse, to continue their psychological, intellectual, moral and cognitive development through their teens and into their 20's would have been laughed out of court in any century other than our own; today, that opportunity is open to millions of young Americans. Student unrest is a reflection not only of the failures, but of the extraordinary successes of the liberal-industrial revolution. It therefore occurs in the nations and in the colleges where, according to traditional standards, conditions are best.

But for many of today's students who have never experienced anything but affluence, political freedom and social equality, the old vision is dead or dying. It may inspire bitterness and outrage when it is not achieved, but it no longer animates or guides. In place of it, students (and many who are not students) are searching for a new vision, a new set of values, a new set of targets appropriate to the post-industrial era—a myth, an ideology or a set of goals that will concern itself with the quality of life and answer the question, "Beyond freedom and affluence, what?"

What characterizes student unrest in the developed nations is this peculiar mixture of the old and the new, the urgent need to fulfill the promises of the past and, at the same time, to define the possibilities of the future.

SEXUAL PROMISCUITY
IN AMERICA ✦ *Albert Ellis*

Strictly speaking, there has never been any sexual promiscuity in America—nor, for that matter, anywhere else in the world—except in restricted areas, under certain special conditions, for distinctly limited periods of time. For the main dictionary definitions of the term *promiscuous* are:

1. consisting of different elements mixed together or mingled without sorting or discrimination; 2. characterized by a lack of discrimination; specifically, engaging in sexual intercourse indiscriminately or with many persons.

Even the male of the human species is rarely indiscriminate in his choice of female objects: since he usually rejects as sex partners members of the other sex who are ugly, old, very young, physically handicapped, sexually listless, very stupid, or closely related to him by blood. And, barring prostitutes, only the exceptional female is unselective in her choice of a sex mate. So, when true promiscuity exists, we can be virtually certain that it is the product of a special time and place, and that it almost never applies to more

SOURCE: Albert Ellis, "Sexual Promiscuity in America," *The Annals*, 378 (July 1968), 58–67. Reprinted by permission of the author and publisher.

than a small percentage of the populace who are sexually undiscriminating all their lives.

In the more usual sense of the term, especially as it is used in the United States, promiscuity refers to an individual's having a good many (say, two dozen or more) sex partners during his entire lifetime or to his having a few bed mates simultaneously or in fairly rapid succession. Such an individual, of course, especially if "he" is a "she," may actually be quite discriminating, for he or she may have chosen from a very large potential number of partners and may have slept with a small percentage of those who were easily available. Thus, an attractive female in our society may be propositioned by a hundred or more males each year for three decades of her life; and even if she ends by copulating with a hundred of them before she dies, she has quite discriminatingly granted her sexual favors to only about 3 percent of her most importuning suitors!

Assuming, however, that a promiscuous individual is one who has sex affairs on a rather casual basis, who does not require that his amours be truly amative, and who beds with a respectable (or should we say unrespectable?) number of members of the other sex during his lifetime, then it can safely be said that promiscuity has always to some extent been a part of the American scene. Thus, we find that in the very first century of colonization, our forefathers were hardly noted for their chastity. Baber[1] tells us that "in 1642 governor Bradford complained of the incontinence of both married and unmarried persons in Plymouth. Early church records in many communities reveal frequent cases of discipline for fornication and adultery." Bridenbaugh[2] notes:

Early New Amsterdam was not conspicuous for its virtue. . . . As contrasted with Boston, sexual laxity ran vertically through all classes. . . . At Philadelphia, the number of sailors of every nationality and of foreign merchants . . . led to the introduction of many of the sorts of debauchery which naturally attach to active seaport towns. . . . All observers reported an increase in sexual immorality at Boston. . . . Cases of adultery and bastardy multiplied.

In the eighteenth-century America, as Calhoun[3] has shown, sexual morality was "a very scarce commodity among people of the ruling class." And during the nineteenth century, various kinds of promiscuity were rampant among white Southerners, mining-camp followers, church-led polygamists and communal-society residents, freed Negroes, and many other groups.[4]

In recent decades, evidence of both premarital and extramarital promiscuity has continued to be shown. Although most Americans still lead lives of quiet sexual desperation and have actual coitus with but few partners during their lifetime, a sizable number of males and, seemingly, an increasing number of females deviate considerably from this norm and, for a few or many years, have multiple affairs. Virtually every objective study of contemporary sex behavior that has been done during the last thirty years conclusively indicates that we are far from being a truly monogamous (one mate for a lifetime) or even a very monogymous (one mate at a time) people.[5]

Is sexual promiscuity increasing at the present time? Most probably, yes. Petting to orgasm is becoming the rule rather than the exception among large segments of our young people; and it is the general tendency of many of these youngsters to "make out" with almost any members of the other sex whom they date. Premarital intercourse is considered to be a requisite to marrying by a large percentage of college-level individuals and is also widely engaged in by less-educated members of the population who are theoretically opposed to it. Certain groups, such as the beatniks and the hippies, think nothing of going to bed with each other the very first day they meet, and are also highly enthusiastic about group sex experiences. Not only are literally hundreds of thousands of Americans promiscuously homosexual, but many basically heterosexual individuals now actively seek and find occasional homosexual encounters as well. Mate-swapping is openly practiced by an increasing number of people and is encouraged by several widely sold, as well as by many privately circulated publications. While common prostitution has considerably decreased, the call-girl business openly flourishes, and is largely supported by highly respectable business concerns. Nude living is increasing both in organized groups (such as nudist camps, which tend to be far more sexually liberal today than they were a decade ago) and among unorganized individuals (who frequently mix it with sexual participations). Even group marriage, which is a difficult practice to sustain for any length of time because of the problems inherent in finding suitable partners who can maintain domestic compatibility with all the other members of a group, has been increasingly espoused and carried out during the last several years by several enthusiastic bands of Americans.

Attitudes Toward Promiscuity

Although there are many signs, as just noted, that sexual promiscuity in America is increasing at the present time, there is no reason to believe that it is doing so in enormous leaps and bounds. As the Kinsey studies showed, and as other sex surveys seem to substantiate, human sexual behavior does not tend to vary enormously over the years. Certainly, there is a difference between the young male of the nineteenth century consorting with prostitutes and his counterpart of the twentieth century fornicating with the girls he meets at high school or college; but in terms of the overt number of sex acts with females that he performs each year, the difference may be slight. The male's frequency of sex outlets, from decade to decade, does not seem to vary that much.

In the case of overt female sexuality, the case may be significantly different. In the old days, relatively few prostitutes or "loose women" could service most of the males in their communities who desired nonmarital affairs. Today, much larger percentages of females than ever before seem to be engaging in pre-marital and extramarital unions. Even here, however, the published figures are often somewhat deceptive. If, for example, the Kinsey figures show (as they do) that more than 50 per cent of American females have premarital intercourse and about 25 per cent engage in adultery, it looks as if our feminine populace is highly promiscuous. The fact remains, however, that a very large proportion of these females fornicated only (a) with their future husbands, (b) with males to whom they were emotionally attached, (c) with one or a few males in their entire premarital life, and (d) relatively infrequently with the males with whom they did participate. Similarly, probably the vast majority of the females committing adultery did so on a few occasions with a total of one or two sex partners. Although, therefore, the number of these *women* is surprisingly high (especially considering the fact that the bulk of the Kinsey data was accumulated almost three decades ago), the number of nonmarital *acts* is not. And there is good reason to believe that the number of *times* that American females in the 1960's have premarital and extramarital unions is higher than the number of times they participated in such unions half a century ago.

What has changed in the last decade or two is the liberalization of attitude toward sexual promiscuity—not that this has always been absent. As I showed in two research presentations in the early 1950's—*The Folklore of Sex* and *The American Sexual Tragedy*[6]—we have always tended to have contradictory attitudes in this country toward unconventional sex behavior. On the one hand, we legally proscribe and socially condemn it; but on the other hand, our mass media clearly indicate that it is highly delightful, exciting, love-inducing, and worthy of seeking. We are, indeed, highly hypocritical, in our movies, television, shows, novels, magazines, billboards, songs, and other popular means of communication, in flaunting sex as an unusually shameful, but exceptionally delectable act.

Only recently has this hypocrisy shown real signs of coming to a halt. Our newsstands are now full of magazines and paperback books—including *Playboy*, which is phenomenally successful—which portray most forms of human sexuality as an unalloyed joy and which vigorously campaign against puritanical views. Our movies are becoming incredibly revealing, including presentations of nudity and sex activity which would have been clearly banned only a few years ago; and even our home television screens are now showing films like *Never on Sunday* and *La Dolce Vita*, which they never allowed before. We now have sex education in many public schools; radio and television discussions on sex that were previously entirely taboo; assigned readings in college courses of books that were once considered downright pornography; published reports, including photographs, of many young people who are openly living together in "sin"; and many other manifestations of openly espoused sexual liberalism. I can add a personal note to this by stating that less than five years ago when I spoke to groups of college students on sexual topics, there was frequently an outcry of protest from members of the administration and the citizens of the community in which I lectured. Today, there is much less hue and cry in this respect, and I am increasingly asked to speak on sexual subjects by Young Men's Christian Associations, by religious departments of various universities, and by Catholic colleges.

A definite change in sex attitudes has therefore recently occurred, in many respects, indeed, a kind of American sex revolution. I have stated for the last several years that, as a result of this revolution, our people are not necessarily engaging in considerably more overt nonmarital acts than they did in previous years, but they are leading unconventional sex lives with much less shame, guilt, and self-deprecation than they ever did at any other time in American history. How do I come to this conclusion? From talking to hundreds of psychotherapy and marriage-counseling clients; from discussing sexual attitudes with scores of individuals in many parts of the country; from reading many psychological and sociological surveys; from talking with numerous educators, counselors, clergymen, writers, and other professionals; from corresponding with large numbers of readers of my articles and books. Although this kind of information is hardly definitive, I am happy to note that it has just been corroborated by the latest finding of the Institute for Sex Research, Inc., founded by Dr. Alfred C. Kinsey at Indiana University. Giving a preliminary statement on the updated study of sex behavior that the Institute has been conducting during the past year, Dr. Paul H. Gebhard has just announced to the press that young Americans are now engaging in premarital affairs with much less feeling of self-condemnation and guilt than they did when the first Kinsey survey was made several decade ago.

Promiscuity and Love

The main barrier to promiscuity today no longer seems to be the time-honored religious and social codes of the Judeao-Christian culture, but the seeming incompatibility of casual sex and love. Almost all important educated groups in the United States—including even liberal Catholics like Mary Perkins Ryan and her husband, John Julian Ryan[7]—agree that premarital sex relations are hardly heinous as long as they are engaged in within the context of an affectional relationship between the partners. But this very standard has its obvious neopuritanical overtones: for it strongly implies that there *is* something terribly wrong about fornication without love. Consequently, innumerable Americans who tolerate or even espouse antenuptial sexuality are practically horrified at the mere thought of anyone's engaging in this kind of activity *promiscuously*.

The fact that one can truly love several members of the other sex in rapid succession or even simultaneously is blithely ignored by most of those who violently oppose promiscuity. So is the fact that just as love leads to sex, sex frequently leads to love.[8] Sparked, however, by the experiences and the values of the hippies of the last few years, who have emphasized group love as well as group sex participations, a new concept of what might be called promiscuous love is beginning to arise. The *Modern Utopian* has recently carried several articles espousing group marriage; and the latest issue includes an article by T. Pascal[9] on group dating. Pascal writes:

At the uni-level way of life, we are led to believe that educationally, emotionally and otherwise, each of us can possibly fit into only ONE social and professional slot. . . . Millions of men and women, brainwashed by this only portal to development and happiness, cannot even conceive that there are many other human beings who can bring some joy and interest into their private life. . . . We believe that an attempt to devise a new level of human relationships is mandatory for those fully aware of the implications of our times. We use the term "multi-level" for need of a better word but it is precisely what Group-Dating is aiming for: offering to each person within a Group a larger context to enhance their emotional, personal and spiritual growth. . . . The act of interdating is fully conscious and willing, and bears no innuendoes, no "games." It is done in the open and, we must add, with definite personal interest toward all the other members of a particular group. In such an approach, the ultimate aim is to allow a greater consciousness of others' existence, not merely in the forms of abstractions, but as living beings. Through such an expanding awareness, we can generate deeper and greater love than those stuck in their uni-level transactory relationship.

Whether the latest proposals for amative promiscuity will bear any better or longer-lasting fruit than those which were started in several utopian American communities in the 1840's and thereabouts remains to be seen. But modern promiscuity, in both theory and some practice, has gone far beyond mere sex play, and it will be interesting to watch future developments in promiscuous love.

Reasons for Modern Promiscuity

Assuming that both talk about and action favoring promiscuity have significantly increased in recent years, what are some of the reasons for this trend?
Major causes of this "revival" may include the following:

TECHNOLOGICAL ADVANCES

No society in human history has had as effective contraceptive methods
as we now possess. Birth control pills and intrauterine coils have not only
offered women a much more aesthetic and practical method than was
previously available to them, but have also provided *continuous* protection
that is highly conducive to spontaneous, last-minute adventures. Unlike the
highly restricted would-be sex partners of a century ago, who might well
find difficulty finding a suitable place in which comfortably to have their
affairs, today's fornicators and adulterers have a very wide choice of hotels,
motels, station wagons, motor boats, weekend resorts, Caribbean cruises,
and the like, with which, in a highly respectable manner, they can abet the
satisfaction of their sexual appetites.

MARITAL DISILLUSIONMENT

Innumerable individuals, today, are disillusioned and jaded with conventional ways of courtship and marriage. From firsthand experiences or from
observation of the sex-love joylessness of others, they have decided that
going steadily with one member of the other sex and eventually marrying
one such person for a lifetime is just not their cup of tea. Consequently, they
are more than eager to experiment with all kinds of untraditional modes of
sexuality, including promiscuity.

SOCIOPOLITICAL ALIENATION

Faced by what they consider to be onerous school and career demands,
confronted by an army draft and a possible active involvement in a war
situation about which they are most unenthusiastic, and worried about the
ultimate eventuality of a full-scale atomic holocaust, literally millions of our
young people (and not a few of our older citizens) feel that the only sensible
"solution" to their problem is a form of short-range hedonism: an *eat, drink,
and be merry today for tomorrow you may die* philosophy. Such individuals,

quite logically deducing from their major attitudinal premises, often see promiscuity as a glorious diversion.

INCREASING LIBERTARIANISM

Almost all our major institutions—including state, church, and school—have become much more liberally oriented during the last decade than they ever were before. American individualism has—in spite of our still prevalent swamping conformity—made at least enormous theoretical strides since World War II. Although few Americans are really, as yet, their "true selves," a vast number at least have the concept of so being and in some ways are valiantly striving to be. Such strivers after selfhood are frequently more than willing to experiment with new forms of economic, political, and sex-love ideas; and some of their experimentation includes promiscuous sex.

PSYCHOTHERAPY

One form of social-educational encounter which you could be fairly certain your friend, neighbor, business associate, or family member did *not* experience twenty-five years ago was intensive psychotherapy. But no longer! In every highly literate area of our country today—and especially in the northeastern cities and the urban areas of the West Coast—some form of participation in psychotherapy seems to be becoming the rule rather than the exception for the sensitive, educated person. Almost innumerable forms of individual therapy—ranging from classical psychoanalysis to behavior therapy and rational-emotive psychotherapy—are now extant; and group therapy includes analytic groups, sensitivity training, sensory awareness, Yoga classes, marathon groups, rational training, and a host of other methods which are no longer restricted to the therapist's office, but are also conducted in schools, weekend seminars, management training programs, boat cruises, and every other place imaginable.[10] Almost all kinds of psychotherapy tend to help the individual become less rigid, more interested in finding himself, and more prone to various kinds of experimentation, including sexual experimenting. Although psychotherapists and counselors rarely push their clients into promiscuous sex behavior, I think that there is little doubt that the loosening-up process that they abet does often encourage this mode of activity.

Is Sexual Promiscuity Compatible with Mental Health?

Recent psychological literature has been highly equivocal about diagnosing promiscuous individuals as being emotionally aberrated. On the one hand, some studies have strongly stated or implied that promiscuous people, especially women, are distinctly disturbed.[11] On the other hand, as noted above, psychotherapists have published innumerable clinical reports indicating that their clients, when they were behaving in a sexually loose manner, were considered by them to be healthier than when they were sexually conventional, and various kinds of promiscuity are encouraged in the course of many individual and group therapy sessions.

Actually, there seem to be both healthy and disturbed reasons why men and women are promiscuous—just as there are sane and neurotic reasons for adultery and various other kinds of unconventional sex behavior.[12] Some of the healthy reasons for promiscuity are as follows.

EXPERIENCE EXPANSION

The human individual largely learns about himself and others by engaging in wide-ranging relationships. Promiscuous sex participations enable many males and females to discover exactly what they want, sexually and nonsexually, and to know many other people quite intimately. Several primitive cultures have found that monogamous mating is best fostered by a period of sexual unselectivity before marriage; and many modern Americans are discovering the same thing. Only experimentation and practice is likely to lead to maximum change and growth in the individual, as I have noted in several of my psychotherapeutic writings;[13] and considerable sex-love experimenting tends notably to expand one's experiential outlook.

FREEDOM-SEEKING

Monogamic marital and family patterns of living foster several important values, including those of responsibility, patience, and high frustration tolerance. The freeing of the human spirit, however, is also a most important value; and in regard to sex-love and even family attachments, many people find that they are freer, more labile, and more truly themselves (as distinct from well-behaved conformists) when having promiscuous than when having conventional mating relationships.

SEXUAL VARIETISM

Although some sexual varietists, as I shall indicate below, believe that they *need* plural sex-love affairs for neurotic reasons, almost all healthy individuals, at some times during their lives, strongly *want* such affairs for normal biological and social reasons. When such individuals manage to have their varietist inclinations fulfilled without seriously defeating their other goals and desires and without coming into great conflict with other members of their community, they may well be enhancing their own existence (as well as those of their chosen partners) in a quite harmless manner.

LOVE ENHANCEMENT

It is often wrongly believed that sexual promiscuity interferes with deep, abiding love relationships. On the contrary, individuals who have only one sex partner during their entire lives more frequently than not end up in relationships where they take each other for granted, are romantically loveless, and even loathe one another; while those who have many sex partners often eventually find one or more with whom they maintain prolonged and intense involvements. As many novelists and playwrights have indicated, sexual experimentation is almost the only path that ultimately will lead many of us to "real" love, and some people deliberately take this path for that very reason.

SEX ENLIGHTENMENT

Practice makes perfect in virtually all physical pastimes, including petting and intercourse—which is why so many counselors and psychotherapists actually encourage their sexually inept clients to get a wider range of experience. Quite on their own, literally millions of Americans discover, every decade, that if they really want to know the facts of life, and to bring to their marriage beds the best technical know-how they can command, they had better try some degree of promiscuity prior or subsequent to legal mating.

ADVENTURE-SEEKING

Although excitement-seeking, as I shall show below, has its neurotic aspects, some forms of adventure are harmless and productive—especially in a society, such as our own, where frontiers are gone and where fun and games of a game-hunting or mountain-climbing nature are relatively rare. One of the few remaining areas in which modern Americans can fairly easily find real novelty and adventure is through having somewhat promiscuous sex-love affairs; and many of our most respectable citizens engage in such affairs for precisely this reason.

So much for some of the main healthy reasons for contemporary promiscuity. Unhealthy reasons include the following:

LOW FRUSTRATION TOLERANCE

The emotionally disturbed individual characteristically convinces himself that he *needs* what he *wants,* and that he will be utterly miserable if some of his sexual or nonsexual desires are not fulfilled. A person with this kind of low frustration tolerance—and his name is legion today—frequently finds that even a good nonmarital or marital relationship is highly intolerable, since it rarely gives him *everything* he wants. So he sometimes becomes compulsively promiscuous and ruins his existing involvement by running after another and another and another one.

EGO-BOLSTERING

A considerable amount of promiscuity, on the part of both sexes, is for ego-bolstering reasons. The male who feels inadequate wrongly concludes that he can become a "real man" by adding sexual notches to his belt; so he seeks one conquest after another. The woman who feels that she *must* be loved, in order to compensate for her own feelings of worthlessness, discovers that hopping into bed with males is the easiest and quickest way to gain at least a small measure of masculine approval. Few highly promiscuous women, in fact, have intercourse for sex reasons; most of them seem to do so in order falsely to enhance their egos—instead of truly raising their self-confidence by convincing themselves that they can fully accept themselves *whether or not* other people, including males, approve of them.[14]

ESCAPISM

When life tends to be drab, either sexually or nonsexually, large numbers of people refuse to face what *they* are doing or not doing to make it so and look for easily available, highly exciting diversions. This is particularly true of anxious and self-hating individuals, who are afraid to be by themselves for any length of time and to confront their own basic disturbances. Many of these individuals find an easy out in promiscuous sex-love affairs, which temporarily distract them but which do nothing to help them solve their basic problems.

HOSTILITY AND REBELLIOUSNESS

Hostile individuals have great difficulty in loving and therefore often resort to casual, sometimes sadistic affairs. Some people in our society also resort to promiscuity because it is a socially disapproved form of behavior and because by engaging in it they can thereby ostentatiously rebel against their families, their religious upbringing, or their entire community. Such individuals may neurotically derive much more pleasure from *not* doing what they are "supposed" to do than the real joy and personal growth they might experience from being healthfully promiscuous.

The Future of Sexual Promiscuity

No one can accurately predict, from past and present trends, what the future of promiscuity is going to be in our country or abroad. At the moment, it seems to be distinctly increasing; and, as noted above, it is being engaged in with much less anxiety, guilt, and depression than were its main concomitants previously. The best guess at the moment is that this trend will continue and that sex-love promiscuity in America will become somewhat more widespread, especially among the higher socioeconomic and educated segments of our populace, during the next several decades, and that it will increasingly be experienced for healthy rather than for unhealthy reasons. A return to Victorianism, with its one-sided allowances for promiscuity (largely on a prostitutional basis) for males, is difficult to imagine. But a sudden overthrow of the basic ideals and practices of American monogyny is also improbable. A slow advance to new levels of sane and enlightened sexual freedom seems much more likely to occur.

NOTES

1. Ray E. Baber, *Marriage and the Family* (New York: McGraw-Hill, 1939).
2. Carl Bridenbaugh, *Cities in the Wilderness* (New York: Ronald Press, 1938).
3. Arthur W. Calhoun, *A Social History of the American Family* (Cleveland: Clark, 1917).
4. James G. Leyburn, *Frontier Folkways* (New Haven: Yale University Press, 1935); A. P. Richard, *Marriage and Divorce* (Chicago: Rand, McNally, 1899); Nevil L. Sims, *A Hoosier Village* (New York: Columbia University, 1912); Calhoun, *op. cit.*
5. G. V. Hamilton, *A Research in Marriage* (New York: Boni, 1929); Alfred C. Kinsey, et. al., *Sexual Behavior in the Human Female* (Philadelphia: Saunders, 1953); Winston W. Ehrmann, *Premarital Dating Behavior* (New York: Holt, Rinehart and Winston, 1960); Ira L. Reiss, *Premarital Sexual Standards in America* (Glencoe, Ill.: Free Press, 1960); Paul H. Gebhard, *et al., Sex Offenders* (New York: Harper and Row, 1965); Harry Benjamin and R. E. L. Masters, *Prostitution and Morality* (New York: Julian Press, 1964); Albert Ellis, *The Case for Sexual Freedom* (Tucson: Seymour Press, 1965).

6. Albert Ellis, *The Folklore of Sex* (New York: Boni, 1951; rev. ed., New York: Grove Press, 1961); Albert Ellis, *The American Sexual Tragedy* (New York: Twayne, 1954; rev. ed., New York: Lyle Stuart and Grove Press, 1962).

7. Mary Perkins Ryan and John Julian Ryan, *Love and Sexuality; A Christian Approach* (New York: Holt, 1967).

8. Albert Ellis, *Sex Without Guilt* (New York: Grove Press and Lyle Stuart; rev. ed., 1965); Albert Ellis, *If This Be Sexual Heresy* (New York: Lyle Stuart and Tower Publications, 1966).

9. T. Pascal, "Group Dating," *Modern Utopian,* Vol. 2, No.2 (October–November 1967), pp. 3, 12.

10. Robert A. Harper, *Psychoanalysis and Psychotherapy; 36 Systems* (Englewood Cliffs, N.J.: Prentice-Hall, 1959); Alvin R. Mahrer, *The Goals of Psychotherapy* (New York: Appleton-Century-Crofts, 1967).

11. E. G. Lion, *et al., An Experiment in the Psychiatric Treatment of Promiscuous Girls* (San Francisco: Department of Health, 1945); B. Safier, *A Psychiatric Approach to the Treatment of Promiscuity* (New York: American Social Hygiene Association, 1949); Celia Deschin, *Teenagers and Venereal Disease* (Washington, D.C.: United States Department of Health, Education, and Welfare, 1961); Stanley E. Willis, "Sexual Promiscuity as a Symptom of Personal and Cultural Anxiety," *Medical Aspects of Human Sexuality,* Vol. 1 (October 1967), pp. 16–23.

12. Albert Ellis, "Healthy and Disturbed Reasons for Having Extramarital Relations," Paper presented at the American Psychological Association Convention, September 5, 1967. To be included in Gerhard Neubeck (ed.), *Extramarital Relations* (Englewood Cliffs, N.J.: Prentice-Hall, 1968).

13. Albert Ellis, *Reason and Emotion in Psychotherapy* (New York: Lyle Stuart, 1962); Albert Ellis and Robert A. Harper, *A Guide to Rational Living* (Englewood Cliffs N.J.: Prentice-Hall, 1961; and Hollywood: Willshire Books, 1967).

14. Albert Ellis and Edward Sagarin, *Nymphomania: A Study of the Oversexed Woman* (New York: Julian Messner-Gilbert Books and Macfadden-Bartel, 1965).

SISTERHOOD IS POWERFUL
✥ *Susan Brownmiller*

"Women are an oppressed class. Our oppression is total, affecting every facet of our lives. We are exploited as sex objects, breeders, domestic servants and cheap labor. We are considered inferior beings whose only purpose is to enhance men's lives. . . ."

—REDSTOCKINGS MANIFESTO.

"While we realize that the liberation of women will ultimately mean the liberation of men from the destructive role as oppressor, we have no illusion that men will welcome this liberation without a struggle. . . ."

—MANIFESTO OF THE NEW YORK

RADICAL FEMINISTS

There is a small group of women that gathers at my house or at the home of one or another of our 15 members each Sunday evening. Our ages range from the early twenties to the late forties. As it happens, all of us work for a living, some at jobs we truly like. Some of us are married, with families, and some are not. Some of us knew each other before we joined the group and some did not. Once we are settled on the sofa and the hard-backed chairs brought in from the kitchen, and the late-comers have poured their own coffee and arranged themselves as best they can on the floor, we begin our meeting. Each week we explore another aspect of what we consider to be our fundamental oppression in a male-controlled society. Our conversation is always animated, often emotional. We rarely adjourn before midnight.

Although we are pleased with ourselves and our insights, we like to remind each other now and then that our small group is not unique. It is merely one of many such groups that have sprung up around the city in the last two years under the umbrella of that collective term, the women's liberation movement. In fact, we had been meeting as a group for exactly four Sundays when one of us got a call from a representative of C.B.S. asking if we would care to be filmed in our natural habitat for a segment on the evening news with Walter Cronkite. We discussed the invitation thoroughly, and then said no.

Women's liberation is hot stuff this season, in media terms, and no wonder. In the short space of two years, the new feminism has taken hold and rooted in territory that at first glance appears an unlikely breeding ground for revolutionary ideas: among urban, white, college-educated, middle-class women generally considered to be a rather "privileged" lot by those who thought they knew their politics, or knew their women. From the radical left to the Establishment middle, the women's movement has become a fact of life. The National Organization for Women (NOW), founded by Betty Friedan in 1966, has 35 chapters across the country.

SOURCE: Susan Brownmiller, "Sisterhood is Powerful," *The New York Times Magazine* (March 15, 1970), 27, 128–30, 132, 134, 136, 140. Copyright © 1970 The New York Times Company. Reprinted by permission of *The New York Times.*

Radical feminist groups—creators of the concept of women's liberation, as opposed to women's *rights*—exist in all major cities side by side with their more conservative counterparts.

Without doubt, certain fringe aspects of the movement make "good copy," to use the kindest term available for how my brethren in the business approach the subject matter. ("Get the bra burning and the karate up front," an editor I know told a writer I know when preparing one news magazine's women's liberation story.)

But the irony of all this media attention is that while the minions of C.B.S. News can locate a genuine women's liberation group with relative ease (they ferreted out our little group before we had memorized each other's last names), hundreds of women in New York City have failed in their attempts to make contact with the movement. I have spoken to women who have spent as much as three months looking for a group that was open to new members. Unclaimed letters have piled up at certain post office box numbers hastily set up and thoughtlessly abandoned by here-today-and-gone-tomorrow "organizations" that disappeared as abruptly as they materialized. The elusive qualities of "women's lib" once prompted the writer Sally Kempton to remark, "It's not a movement, it's a state of mind." The surest way to affiliate with the movement these days is to form your own small group. That's the way it's happening.

Two years ago the 50 or so women in New York City who had taken to calling themselves the women's liberation movement met on Thursday evenings at a borrowed office on East 11th Street. The official title of the group was the New York Radical Women. There was some justification at the time for thinking grandly in national terms, for similar groups of women were beginning to form in Chicago, Boston, San Francisco and Washington. New York Radical Women came by its name quite simply: the women were young radicals, mostly under the age of 25, and they come out of the civil rights and/or peace movements, for which many of them had been full-time workers. A few years earlier, many of them might have been found on the campuses of Vassar, Radcliffe, Wellesley and the larger coed universities, a past they worked hard to deny. What brought them together to a women-only discussion and action group was a sense of abuse suffered at the hands of the very protest movements that had spawned them. As "movement women," they were tired of doing the typing and fixing the food while "movement men" did the writing and leading. Most were living with or married to movement men who, they believed, were treating them as convenient sex objects or as somewhat lesser beings.

Widely repeated quotations, such as Stokeley Carmichael's wisecrack dictum to S.N.C.C., "The position of women in our movement should be prone," and, three years later, a similar observation by Black Panther

Eldridge Cleaver had reinforced their uncomfortable suspicion that the social vision of radical men did not include equality for women. Black power, as practiced by black male leaders, appeared to mean that black women would step back while black men stepped forward. The white male radical's eager embrace of *machismo* appeared to include those backward aspects of male supremacy in the Latin culture from which the word *machismo* is derived. Within their one-to-one relationships with their men, the women felt, the highly touted "alternate life style" of the radical movement was working out no better than the "bourgeois" life style they had rejected. If man and wife in a suburban split-level was a symbol of all that was wrong with plastic, bourgeois America "man and chick" in a Lower East Side tenement flat was hardly the new order they had dreamed of.

In short, "the movement" was reinforcing, not eliminating, their deepest insecurities and feelings of worthlessness as women—feelings which quite possibly had brought them into radical protest politics to begin with. So, in a small way, they had begun to rebel. They had decided to meet regularly —without their men—to talk about their common experience. "Our feminism was very underdeveloped in those days," says Anne Koedt, an early member of the group. "We didn't have any idea of what kind of action we could take. We couldn't stop talking about the blacks and Vietnam."

In Marxist canons, "the woman question" is one of many manifestations of a sick, capitalist society which "the revolution" is supposed to finish off smartly. Some of the women who devoted their Thursday evening meeting time to New York Radical Women believed they were merely dusting off and streamlining an orthodox, ideological issue. Feminism was bad politics and a dirty word since it excluded the larger picture.

But others in the group, like Anne Koedt and Shuli Firestone, an intense and talkative young activist, had begun to see things from a different, heretical perspective. Woman's oppressor was Man, they argued, and not a specific economic system. After all, they pointed out, male supremacy was still flourishing in the Soviet Union, Cuba and China, where power was still lodged in a male bureaucracy. Even the beloved Che wrote a guidebook for revolutionaries in which he waxed ecstatic over the advantages to a guerrilla movement of having women along in the mountains—to prepare and cook the food. The heretics tentatively put forward the idea that feminism must be a separate movement of its own.

New York Radical Women's split in perspective—was the ultimate oppressor Man or Capitalism?—occupied endless hours of debate at the Thursday evening meetings. Two warring factions emerged, dubbing each other "the feminists" and "the politicos." But other things were happening as well. For one thing, new women were coming in droves to the Thursday evening talk fest, and a growing feeling of sisterhood was permeating the room. Meetings began awkwardly and shyly, with no recognized chairman and no discernible agenda. Often the suggestion, "Let's sit closer together, sisters," helped break the ice. But once the evening's initial awkwardness had passed, volubility was never a problem. "We had so much to say," an early member relates, "and most of us had never said it to another woman before."

Soon *how* to say it became an important question. Young women like Carol Hanisch, a titian-haired recruit to the civil rights movement from a farm in Iowa, and her friend Kathie Amatniek, a Radcliffe graduate and a working film editor, had spent over a year in Mississippi working with S.N.C.C. There they had been impressed with the Southern-revival-style mass meeting at which blacks got up and "testified" about their own experience with "the Man." Might the technique also work for women? And wasn't it the same sort of thing that Mao Tse-tung had advocated to raise political consciousness in Chinese villages? As Carol Hanisch reminded the group, Mao's slogan had been "Speak pain to recall pain"—precisely what New York Radical Women was doing!

The personal-testimony method encouraged *all* women who came to the meeting to speak their thoughts. The technique of "going around the room" in turn brought responses from many who had never opened their mouths at male-dominated meetings and were experiencing the same difficulty in a room full of articulate members of their own sex. Specific questions such as, "If you've thought of having a baby, do you want a girl or a boy?" touched off accounts of what it meant to be a girl-child—the second choice in a society that prizes boys. An examination of "What happens to your relationship when your man earns more money than you, and what happens when *you* earn more money than him?" brought a flood of anecdotes about the male ego and money. "We all told similar stories." relates a member of the group. "We discovered that, to a man, they all felt challenged if we were the breadwinners. It meant that we were no longer dependent. We had somehow robbed them of their 'rightful' role."

"We began to see our 'feminization' as a two-level process," says Anne Koedt. "On one level, a woman is brought up to believe that she is a girl and that is her biological destiny. She isn't supposed to want to achieve anything. If, by some chance, she manages to escape the psychological damage, she finds that the structure is prohibitive. Even though she wants to achieve, she finds she is discouraged at every turn and she still can't become President.

Few topics, the women found, were unfruitful. Humiliations that each of them had suffered privately—from being turned down for a job with the comment, "We were looking for a man," to catcalls and wolf whistles on the street—turned out to be universal agonies. "I had always felt degraded, actually turned into an object," said one woman. "I was no longer a human being when a guy on the street would start to make those incredible animal noises at me. I never was flattered by it, I always understood that behind that whistle was a masked hostility. When we started to talk about it in the group, I discovered that every woman in the room had similar feelings. None of us knew how to cope with this street hostility. We had always had to grin and bear it. We had always been told to dress as women, to be very sexy and alluring to men, and what did it get us? Comments like 'Look at the legs on that babe' and "would I like to—her.""[1]

"Consciousness-raising," in which a woman's personal experience at the hands of men was analyzed as a *political* phenomenon, soon became a keystone of the women's liberation movement.

In 1963, *before* there was a women's movement, Betty Friedan published what eventually became an American classic, "The Feminine Mystique." The book was a brilliant, factual examination of the post-World War II "back to the home" movement that tore apart the myth of the fulfilled and happy American housewife. Though "The Feminine Mystique" held an unquestioned place as *the* intellectual mind-opener for most of the young feminists—de Beauvoir's "The Second Sex," a broad, philosophical analysis of the cultural restraints on women, was runner-up in popularity—few members of New York Radical Woman had ever felt motivated to attend a meeting of Friedan's National Organization for Women, the parliamentary-style organization of professional women and housewives that she founded in 1966. Friedan, the mother of the movement, and the organization that recruited in her image were considered hopelessly bourgeois. NOW's emphasis on legislative change left the radicals cold. The generation gap created real barriers to communication.

"Actually, we had a lot in common with the NOW women," reflects Anne Koedt. "The women who started NOW were achievement-oriented in their professions. They began with the employment issue because that's what they were up against. The ones who started New York Radical Women were achievement-oriented in the radical movement. From both ends we were fighting a male structure that prevented us from achieving."

Friedan's book had not envisioned a movement of young feminists emerging from the college campus and radical politics. "If I had it to do all over again," she says, "I would rewrite my last chapter." She came to an early meeting of New York Radical Women to listen, ask questions and take notes, and went away convinced that her approach—and NOW's—was more valid. "As far as I'm concerned, we're *still* the radicals," she says emphatically. "We raised our consciousness a long time ago. I get along with the women's lib people because they're the way the troops we need come up. But the name of the game is confrontation and action, and equal employment is the gut issue. The legal fight is enormously important. Desegregating The New York Times help-wanted ads was an important step, don't you think? And NOW did it. The women's movement *needs* its Browns versus Boards of Education."

Other older women, writers and lifetime feminists, also came around to observe, and stayed to develop a kinship with girls young enough to be their daughters. "I almost wept after my first meeting. I went home and filled my diary," says Ruth Herschberger, poet and author of "Adam's Rib," a witty and unheeded expostulation of women's rights published in 1948. "When I wrote 'Adams's Rib,' I was writing for readers who wouldn't accept the first premise. Now there was a whole roomful of people and a whole new vocabulary. I could go a whole month on the ammunition I'd get at one meeting."

In June of 1968, New York Radical Women produced a mimeographed booklet of some 20 pages entitled "Notes from the First Year." It sold for 50 cents to women and $1.00 to men. "Notes" was a compendium of speeches, essays and transcriptions of tape-recorded "rap sessions" of the Thursday evening group on such subjects as sex, abortion and orgasm. Several mimeographed editions later, it remains the most widely circulated source material on the New York women's liberation movement.

The contribution to "Notes" that attracted the most attention from both male and female readers was a one-page essay by Anne Koedt entitled, "The Myth of Vaginal Orgasm." In it she wrote:

"Frigidity has generally been defined by men as the failure of women to have vaginal orgasms. Actually, the vagina is not a highly sensitive area and is not physiologically constructed to achieve orgasm. The clitoris is the sensitive area and is the female equivalent of the penis. All orgasms [in women] are extensions of sensations from this area. This leads to some interesting questions about conventional sex and our role in it. Men have orgasms essentially by friction with the vagina, not with the clitoris. Women have thus been defined sexually in terms of what pleases men; our own biology has not been properly analyzed. Instead we have been fed a myth of the liberated woman and her vaginal orgasm, an orgasm which in fact does not exist. What we must do is redefine our sexuality. We must discard the 'normal' concepts of sex and create new guidelines which take into account mutual sexual enjoyment. We must begin to demand that if a certain sexual position or technique now defined as 'standard' is not mutually conducive to orgasm, then it should no longer be defined as standard."

Anne Koedt's essay went further than many other women in the movement would have preferred to go, but she was dealing with a subject that every woman understood. "For years I suffered under a male-imposed definition of my sexual responses," one woman says. "From Freud on down, it was *men* who set the standard of my sexual enjoyment. *Their* way was the way I should achieve nirvana, because their way was the way it worked for them. Me? Oh, I was simply an 'inadequate woman.' "

By September, 1968, New York Radical Women felt strong enough to attempt a major action. Sixty women went to Atlantic City in chartered buses to picket the Miss America pageant. The beauty contest was chosen as a target because of the ideal of American womanhood it extolled— vacuous, coiffed, cosmeticized and with a smidgen of talent.

But New York Radical Women did not survive its second year. For one thing, the number of new women who flocked to the Thursday evening meetings made consciousness-raising and "going around the room" an impossibility. The politico-feminist split and other internal conflicts— charges of "domination" by one or another of the stronger women were thrown back and forth—put a damper on the sisterly euphoria. An attempt to break up the one large group into three smaller ones—by lot—proved disastrous.

Several women felt the need for a new group. They had become intrigued with the role of the witch in world history as representing society's persecution of women who dared to be different. From Joan of Arc, who dared to wear men's clothes and lead a men's army, to the women of Salem who dared to defy accepted political, religious mores, the "witch" was punished for deviations. Out of this thinking grew WITCH, a handy acronym that the organizers announced, half tongue-in-cheek, stood for Women's International Terrorist Conspiracy from Hell.

Much of WITCH was always tongue-in-cheek, and from its inception its members were at great pains to deny that they were feminists. The Yippie movement had made outrageous disruption a respectable political tactic of the left, and the women of WITCH decided it was more compatible with their thinking to be labeled "kooks" by outsiders than to be labeled man-haters by movement men.

In the WITCH philosophy, the patriarchy of the nuclear family was synonymous with the patriarchy of the American business corporation. Thus, four women took jobs at a branch of the Travelers Insurance Company, where a fifth member was working, and attempted to establish a secret coven of clerical workers on the premises. (For the Travelers' project, WITCH became "Women Incensed at Travelers' Corporate Hell.") In short order, the infiltrators were fired for such infractions of office rules as wearing slacks to work. Undaunted, a new quintet of operatives gained employment in the vast typing pools at A.T. & T. "Women Into Telephone Company Harassment" gained three sympathizers to the cause before Ma Bell got wise and exorcised the coven from her midst. Two WITCHes were fired for insubordination; the rest were smoked out and dismissed for being "overqualified" for the typing pool.

WITCH's spell over the women's movement did not hold. "At this point," says Judith Duffet, an original member, "you could say that WITCH is just another small group in women's liberation. We're concerned with consciousness-raising and developing an ideology through collective thinking. We don't do the freaky, hippie stuff any more."

While WITCH was brewing its unusual recipe for liberation, another offshoot of New York Radical Women emerged. The new group was called Redstockings, a play on *bluestockings,* with the blue replaced by the color of revolution. Organized by Shuli Firestone and Ellen Willis, an articulate rock-music columnist for the New Yorker and a serious student of Engels's "Origins of the Family," Redstockings made no bones about where it stood. It was firmly committed to feminism and action.

Redstockings made its first public appearance at a New York legislative hearing on abortion law reform in February, 1969, when several women sought to gain the microphone to testify about their own abortions. The hearing, set up to take testimony from 15 medical and psychiatric "experts" —14 were men—was hastily adjourned. The following month, Redstockings held its *own* abortion hearing at the Washington Square Methodist Church. Using the consciousness-raising technique, 12 women "testified" about abortion, from their own personal experience, before an audience of 300 men and women. The political message of the emotion-charged evening was that *women* were the only true experts on unwanted pregnancy and abortion, and that every woman has an inalienable right to decide whether or not she wished to bear a child.

Redstockings' membership counts are a closely held secret, but I would estimate that the number does not exceed 100. Within the movement, Redstockings push what they call "the prowoman line." "What it means," says a member, "is that we take the woman's side in *everything.* A woman is never to blame for her own submission. None of us need to change ourselves, we need to change men." Redstockings are also devout about consciousness-raising. "Whatever else we may do, consciousness-raising is the ongoing political work," says Kathie Amatniek. For the last few months, the various Redstocking groups have been raising their consciousness on what they call "the divisions between women that keep us apart" —married women *vs.* single, black women *vs.* white, middle class *vs.* working class, etc.

While Redstockings organized its abortion speak-out, the New York chapter of NOW formed a committee to lobby for repeal of restrictive abortion legislation. These dissimilar approaches to the same problem illustrate the difference in style between the two wings of the women's movement.

But within New York NOW itself, a newer, wilder brand of feminism made an appearance. Ti-Grace Atkinson, a Friedan protégée and the president of New York NOW, found herself in increasing conflict with her own local chapter and Friedan over NOW's hierarchical structure, a typical organization plan with an executive board on top. Ti-Grace, a tall blonde who has been described in print as "aristocratic looking," had come to view the power relationship between NOW's executive board and the general membership as a copycat extension of the standard forms of male domination over women in the society at large. She proposed to NOW that all executive offices be abolished in favor of rotating chairmen chosen by lot from the general membership. When Atkinson's proposal came up for a vote by the general membership of the New York chapter in October, 1968, and was defeated, Ti-Grace resigned her presidency on the spot and went out and formed her own organization. Named the October 17th Movement —the date of Ti-Grace's walkout from NOW—it made a second debut this summer as The Feminists, and took its place as the most radical of the women's liberation groups. (New York NOW suffered no apparant effects from its first organizational split. Over the last year it has *gained* in membership as feminism has gained acceptability among wider circles of women.)

The Feminists made antiélitism and rigorous discipline cardinal principles of their organization. As the only radical feminist group to take a stand against the institution of marriage they held a sit-in at the city marriage license bureau last year, raising the slogan that "Marriage Is Slavery." Married women or women living with men may not exceed one-third of the total membership.

Differences over such matters as internal democracy, and the usual personality conflicts that plague all political movements, caused yet another feminist group and another manifesto to make their appearance this fall. In November, Shuli Firestone and Anne Koedt set up a plan for organizing small groups—or "brigades," as they prefer to call them—on a neighborhood basis, and named their over-all structure the New York Radical Feminists. Eleven decentralized neighborhood units (three are in the West Village) meet jointly once a month.

The Radical Feminists coexist with the Feminists and the Redstockings without much rivalry, although when pressed, partisans of the various groups will tell you, for instance, that Redstockings do too much consciousness-raising and not enough action, or that the Feminists are "fascistic," or that the Radical Feminists are publicity hungry. But in general, since interest in the women's liberation movement has always exceeded organizational capacity, the various groups take the attitude of "the more the merrier."

Despite the existence of three formal "pure radical feminist" organizations, hundreds of women who consider themselves women's liberationists have not yet felt the need to affiliate with any body larger than their own small group. The small group, averaging 8 to 15 members and organized spontaneously by friends calling friends has become *the* organizational form of the amorphous movement. Its intimacy seems to suit women. Fear of expressing new or half-formed thoughts vanishes in a friendly living-room atmosphere. "After years of psychoanalysis in which my doctor kept telling me my problem was that I wouldn't accept—quote—*my female role,*" says a married woman with two children who holds a master's degree in philosophy, "the small group was a revelation to me. Suddenly, for the first time in my life, it was *O.K.* to express feelings of hostility to men." Says another woman: "In the small group I have the courage to think things and feel feelings, that I would never have dared to think and feel as an individual."

The meetings have often been compared to group therapy, a description that most of the women find irritating. "Group therapy isn't political and what we're doing is highly political," is the general response. In an early paper on the nature and function of the small group, Carol Hanisch once wrote, "Group therapy implies that we are sick and messed up, but the first function of the small group is to get rid of self-blame. We start with the assumption that women are really 'neat' people. Therapy means adjusting. We desire to change the objective conditions."

The groups are usually leaderless and structureless, and the subjects discussed at the weekly meetings run the gamut of female experience. The Radical Feminists offer to new groups they organize a list of consciousness-raising topics that includes:

Discuss your relationships with men. Have you noticed any recurring patterns?
Have you ever felt that men have pressured you into sexual relationships? Have you ever lied about orgasm?
Discuss your relationships with other women. Do you compete with women for men?
Growing up as a girl, were you treated differently from your brother?
What would you most like to do in life? What has stopped you?
"Three months of this sort of thing," says Shuli Firestone, "is enough to make a feminist out of any woman."

The kind of collective thinking that has come out of the women's liberation movement is qualitatively different from the kinds of theorems and analyses that other political movements have generated. "Women are different from all other oppressed classes," says Anne Koedt. "We live in isolation, not in ghettos, and we are in the totally unique position of having a master in our own houses." It is not surprising, therefore, that marriage and child care are two subjects that receive intensive scrutiny in the small group.

If few in the women's movement are willing to go as far as the Feminists and say that marriage is slavery, it is hard to find a women's liberationist who is not in some way disaffected by the sound of wedding bells. Loss of personal identity and the division of labor within the standard marriage (the husband's role as provider, the wife's role as home maintenance and child care) are the basic points at issue. "I have come to view marriage as a built-in self-destruct for women," says one divorcée after 12 years of marriage. "I married early, right after college, because it was expected of me. I never had a chance to discover who I was. I was programed into the housewife pattern." Many married women's liberationists will no longer use their husbands' last names; some have gone back to their maiden names, and some even to their mothers' maiden names.

One paper that has been widely circulated within the movement is entitled "The Politics of Housework," by Pat Mainardi, a Redstocking who is a teacher and painter. "Men recognize the essential fact of housework right from the beginning," she wrote. "Which is that it stinks. You both work, you both have careers, but *you* are expected to do the housework. Your husband tells you, 'Don't talk to me about housework. It's too trivial to discuss.' MEANING: *His* purpose is to deal with matters of significance. *Your* purpose is to deal with matters of insignificance. So *you* do the housework. Housework trivial? Just try getting him to share the burden. The measure of his resistance is the measure of your oppression."

Not only the oppression of housework, but the oppression of child care has become a focus of the women's movement. Much of the energy of young mothers in the movement has gone into setting up day-care collectives that are staffed on an equal basis by mothers and fathers. (Thus far they have proved difficult to sustain.) "Some of the men have actually come to understand that sharing equally in child care is a political responsibility," says Rosalyn Baxandall, a social worker and an early women's liberationist. Rosalyn and her husband, Lee, a playwright, put in a morning a week at an informal cooperative day nursery on the Lower East Side where their 2-year-old, Finn, is a charter member.

In November, at the Congress to Unite Women, a conference that drew over 500 women's liberationists of various persuasions from the New York area, a resolution demanding 24-hour-a-day child care centers was overwhelmingly endorsed. Women in the movement have also suggested plans for a new kind of life style in which a husband and wife would each work half-day and devote the other half of the day to caring for their children. Another possibility would be for the man to work for six months of the year while the woman takes care of the child-raising responsibilities—with the roles reversed for the next six months.

The "movement women" who did not endorse the separatism of an independent radical feminist movement last year and chose to remain in what the feminists now call "the male left" have this year made women's liberation a major issue in their own political groups. Even the weatherwomen of Weatherman meet separately to discuss how to combat male chauvinism among their fellow revolutionaries. The women of Rat, the farthest out of the underground radical newspapers, formed a collective and took over editorial management of their paper last month, charging that their men had put out a product filled with sexist, women-as-degraded-object pornography. Twenty-two-year-old Jane Alpert, free on bail and facing conspiracy charges for a series of terrorist bombings, was spokesman for the Rat women's *putsch*. A black women's liberation committee functions within S.N.C.C., and its leader, Frances M. Beal, has said publicly, "To be black and female is double jeopardy, the slave of a slave."

The new feminism has moved into some surprisingly Establishment quarters. A spirited women's caucus at New York University Law School forced the university to open its select national scholarship program to women students. Women's caucuses exist among the editorial employes at McGraw Hill and Newsweek. Last month, 59 women in city government, sent a petition to Mayor Lindsay demanding that he actively seek qualified women for policy-making posts.

The movement is a story without an end, because it has just begun. The goals of liberation go beyond a simple concept of equality. Looking through my notebook, I see them expressed simply and directly. *Betty Friedan: "We're going to redefine the sex roles." Anne Koedt: "We're going to be redefining politics."* Brave words for a new movement, and braver still for a movement that has been met with laughter and hostility. Each time a man sloughs off the women's movement with the comment, "They're nothing but a bunch of lesbians and frustrated bitches," we quiver with collective rage. How can such a charge be answered in rational terms? It cannot be. (The supersensitivity of the movement to the lesbian issue, and the existence of a few militant lesbians within the movement once prompted Friedan herself to grouse about "the lavender menace" that was threatening to warp the image of women's rights. A lavender *herring,* perhaps, but surely no clear and present danger.)

The small skirmishes and tugs of war that used to be called "the battle of the sexes" have now assumed ideological proportions. It is the aim of the movement to *turn men around,* and the implications in that aim are staggering. "Men have used us all their lives as ego fodder," says Anne Koedt. "They not only control economics and the government, they control us. There are the women's pages and the rest of the world." It is that rest of the world, of course, that we are concerned with. There is a women's rights button that I sometimes wear and the slogan on it reads, "Sisterhood is Powerful." If sisterhood were powerful, what a different world it would be.

Women as a class have never subjugated another group; we have never marched off to wars of conquest in the name of the fatherland. We have never been involved in a decision to annex the territory of a neighboring country, or to fight for foreign markets on distant shores. Those are the games men play, not us. *We* see it differently. We want to be neither oppressor nor oppressed. The women's revolution is the final revolution of them all.

How does a sympathetic man relate to a feminist woman? Thus far, it has not been easy for those who are trying. The existence of a couple of *men's* consciousness-raising groups—the participants are mostly husbands of activist women—is too new to be labeled a trend. "When our movement gets strong, when men are forced to see us as a conscious issue, *what are they going to do?*" asks Anne Koedt. And then she answers: "I don't know, but I think there's a part of men that really wants a human relationship, and that's going to be the saving grace for all of us."

NOTES

1. My small group has discussed holding a street action of our own on the first warm day of spring. We intend to take up stations on the corner of Broadway and 45th Street and whistle at the male passersby. The confrontation, we feel, will be educational for all concerned.

ISOLATION, LONELINESS AND THE HOLD ON LIFE

✵ Peter Townsend

The poorest people, socially as well as financially, were those most isolated from family life. The questions of social isolation and loneliness in old age have not so far been examined in this book and will be discussed here. A

SOURCE: Peter Townsend, "Isolation, Loneliness and the Hold on Life," *The Family Life of Old People: An Inquiry in East London* (London: Routledge & Kegan Paul, 1957), pp. 166–182.

distinction is made between the two: to be socially isolated is to have few contacts with family and community; to be lonely is to have an unwelcome *feeling* of lack or loss of companionship. The one is objective, the other subjective and, as we shall see, the two do not coincide.

Social isolation needs to be measured by reference to objective criteria. The problem is rather like that of measuring poverty. "Poverty" is essentially a relative rather than an absolute term, and discovering its extent in a population is usually divided into two stages. Most people agree on the first stage, which is to place individuals on a scale according to their income; they often disagree about the second, which involves deciding how far up the scale the poverty "line" should be drawn. The task of measuring isolation can also be divided in this way by placing individuals on a scale according to their degree of isolation and by drawing a line at some point on the scale so that those below the line would, by common consent, be called "the isolated. . . ."

The Isolated

There were 20 people . . .[who were] very isolated. Their ages ranged from 64 to 83. They comprised two married women, two widowers, eight widows, five spinsters and three bachelors. Thirteen of them lived alone; 12 had no children and half of the rest had sons only. It is worth examining their circumstances, taking first those with children. Four of the eight with surviving children had daughters. One was a widow living with her only daughter, unmarried; she had few other relatives and all lived outside London. The second was a widow who had come with her only daughter from Scotland after the war, leaving friends and relatives behind. They were together until the housing authorities gave them two separate homes, several miles apart; now one of her daughter's children lived with her but she saw the rest of the family once a week or less. The third was a very infirm widow whose only daughter was married to a naval officer, obliged to live near Portsmouth; she lived in the same house as a widowed and childless sister and saw her every day but infirmity prevented other social contacts. The fourth was a widower of 80 who said his daughter and son living in Bethnal Green visited him twice a week to see he was all right but did not spend much time with him, now his wife was dead; he had a drink with a friend twice a week but infirmity precluded other activities.

The other four very isolated people with children had sons only. One was a married woman whose only son had moved into his wife's home district outside London; she and her husband had only one relative in Bethnal Green, the wife's unmarried sister, who was seen each week, and they had no friends or outside social activities, largely because the husband could not walk. Another was a widower, living with an unmarried son, who saw two married sons about once a week; he had no other surviving relatives. The two remaining people were both widows living alone. One had three sons living outside London, two of them visited her once a week; she saw a sister and two aged aunts in Bethnal Green every week but she spent much of her time on her own. The other had two illegitimate sons but no other relatives; she saw these sons occasionally.

There remain the childless and the unmarried. Most were in a worse position. The 10 most isolated people of the 203 interviewed were all unmarried or childless. The circumstances of two are summarized below.

Miss Paley, aged 67, lived in a one-room tenement flat. It was a large airless room with dismal orange-brown wallpaper peeling off in huge strips. Two or three mats, ingrained with dirt, covered the floor. There was an old iron bedstead propped up in the middle by two bits of wood and on this was a heap of gray and brown blankets. An ancient iron mangle stood in a corner and there was a gas stove, a gas mantel for lighting, three or four wooden chairs and a table with a flat-iron propping up one of its legs. Miss Paley wore a pair of stockings, extensively patched and tied around her knees, and a ramshackle navy-blue skirt and slip. Her skin had the whiteness of someone who rarely went out and she was very shy of her appearance, particularly the open sores on her face. She said she suffered from blood poisoning, but had not seen her doctor since the war. (This was confirmed by the doctor.) She was the only child of parents who had been street traders and who had died when she was young, in the 1880s. "I was with my aunt until I was nearly 40. She was 85 when she died. I had cousins in the street but they were my aunt's children. In the war they got scattered. They all had families to bring up and I haven't met them since the war. I don't know where they are. They had to leave me behind. I don't want them people. I do my work in my own way. They wouldn't have the patience with me." Persistent questioning failed to reveal a single relative with whom she had any contact. She did not go to the cinema, to a club or to church, and had no radio. She had spent Christmas on her own and had never had a holiday away from home. She sometimes made conversation with her neighbors in the street but because of her appearance did not go into their homes or they into hers. She had only one friend, a young woman who "used to live in the street where I lived," and they visited one another about once a week. Her answer to a question about membership of a club was typical of much she said. "No, I can't be shut in. I don't go to those clubs. They'd be too much excitement for me." At one point she said she went to bed about 8 pm and got up between 10 and 11 the next day. I also found she had an hour or two in bed in the afternoons.

Mr. Fortune, aged 76, lived alone in a two-room council flat. There were two wooden chairs, an orange-box converted into a cupboard, a gas stove, a table covered with newspaper, a battered old pram with tins and boxes inside, a pair of wooden steps and little else in the sitting-room. There was no fire, although the interview took place on a cold February morning. Mr. Fortune had been a cripple from birth and he was partly deaf. He was unmarried and his five siblings were dead. An older widowed sister-in-law lived about a mile away with an unmarried son and daughter. These three and two married nieces living in another East London borough were seen from once a month to a few times a year. Asked how often he saw his sister-in-law Mr. Fortune said, "Only when I go there. It's a hard job to walk down there in winter time and I haven't seen her for three or four months." Asked about an old people's club he said, "No. I'm simply as I am now. I shouldn't like to join. Walking is such a painful job for me. I can't get any amusement out of it." He spoke to one or two of the neighbors outside his flat but he had no regular contact with any of them. He had one regular friend, living a few blocks away, who came over to see him on a Sunday about once a month, "more when there's fine weather." He was not a churchgoer, never went to a cinema, rarely went to a pub because he could not afford a drink, had never had a holiday in his life and spent Christmas on his own. "My nephew came down for an hour. He gave me a little present, 2s. 6d. No, I didn't get any cards." He received a non-contributory pension and supplementary assistance through the National Assistance Board, which recently arranged for him to have a woman home-help for two hours a week. Her regular call was the main event of the week. "I sit here messing about. Last week I was making an indoor aerial. I made those steps over there. I like listening to the wireless and making all manner of things. My time's taken up, I can tell you, with that and cooking and tidying-up."

The most striking fact about the most isolated people was that they had few surviving relatives, particularly near-relatives of their own or of succeeding generations. This lent special significance to familiar references to fathers having weaker ties with children than mothers, to sons being drawn into their wives' families, and to distant relatives being lost sight of after the death of "connecting" relatives. The isolated included a comparatively high number of unmarried and childless people, of those possessing sons but not daughters and of those without siblings. Rarely did they have friends, become members of clubs or otherwise participate in outside social activities in compensation. Nearly all of them were retired and most were infirm; some were shy of revealing to others how ill or poverty-stricken they were or how they had "let themselves go." They had little or no means of regular contact with the younger generation, and for one reason or another could not be brought into club activities.

Loneliness in Old Age

. . . One of the most striking results of the whole inquiry was that those living in relative isolation from family and community did not always say they were lonely.

Particular importance was attached during the interviews to "loneliness."

The question was not asked until most of an individual's activities had been discussed and care was taken to ensure as serious and as considered a response as possible. One difficulty had to be overcome. A few people liked to let their children think they were lonely so the latter would visit them as much as possible. This meant they were not inclined to give an honest answer if children were present. In an early interview one married woman, asked whether she ever got lonely, said, "Sometimes I do when they are all at work." But she hesitated before answering and looked at two married daughters, who were in the room. On a subsequent call, when this woman was alone, she told me she was "never lonely really, but I like my children to call." A widow, who was alone when interviewed, said she was never lonely. In fascinating contrast to this was a statement of one of her married daughters, who was interviewed independently. "She's not too badly off. The most she complains of is loneliness. She's always wanting us to go up there." Care was therefore taken to ask about loneliness so far as possible when the old person was alone and to check any answer which seemed doubtful.

Some people living at the center of a large family complained of loneliness and some who were living in extreme isolation repeated several times with vigor that they were never lonely—such as Miss Paley and Mr. Fortune, described above. . . . Despite there being a significant association between isolation and loneliness about a half of the isolated and rather isolated said they were not lonely; over a fifth of the first group said they were.

What is the explanation? Previous investigations have pointed to the multiplicity of causes of loneliness. In his Wolverhampton study Sheldon showed that those experiencing loneliness tended to be widowed and single people, to be living alone, to be in their eighties rather than in their sixties, to be men rather than women and to be the relatively infirm. He concluded, "Loneliness cannot be regarded as the simple direct result of social circumstances, but is rather an individual response to an external situation to which other old people may react quite differently."[1] There seemed to be no single cause of severe loneliness in old people.

In several respects the present inquiry reached similar results. Forty-six per cent of widowed people said they were very or sometimes lonely, 42 per cent of those living alone, 53 per cent of those in their late seventies and eighties and 43 per cent of those who were infirm, compared with 27 per cent in the sample as a whole. But it is possible that less emphasis should be given to personal differences and to a multiplicity of causes. The results also suggested that a single social factor may be fundamental to loneliness. This is the recent deprivation of the company of a close relative, usually a husband or wife or a child, through death, illness or migration.

Recent Bereavement

Examination of individual interview-reports showed that of the 56 people saying they were very or sometimes lonely, 28 had been recently bereaved and 17 separated from children. This seemed to be the chief cause of their loneliness. A further 11 had experienced other drastic changes in family circumstances. It is necessary to consider these lonely people.

All but four of the 28 who had been recently bereaved had lost a husband or wife within the previous 10 years. "No one knows what loneliness is till your partner happens to go." "You don't realize it until you know it. But loneliness is the worst thing you can suffer in life." The men in particular talked about their bereavement with very deep feeling. "I miss her. Every time I look over there—that's her seat. People kept telling me to have someone to look after me but I said to myself, there'll never be another woman who will take her place." Three of them did not talk, they wept.

Mr. Heart had lost his wife seven years earlier. He lived with an unmarried son but he had no daughter. "Sometimes I get lonely. I think of her. There's not a day passes but she's in my mind. When she died I don't know how I stood on my feet. You don't know what it is when you don't have a wife. . . . I wish I had a daughter. If you had a daughter it would put you in mind of your wife. Sometimes I think I hear her calling in the next room. She was what you call exceptional, exceptional good. You never had to run round any public house for her. My son still goes and puts flowers on her grave. . . . You can't tell how you miss someone until they go. Death's a terrible thing, to lose someone you love."

One of the major consequences of a wife's death was that the man saw less of his children. He acknowledged it was the mother who held the family together. "When my missus was alive I had to come and have tea in the bedroom because there wasn't room in here. The place was crowded out with them (married children and their families on Saturdays and Sundays)." "My daughters used to come round often when my wife was alive, but I don't see so much of them now. But they like to know I'm comfortable and being looked after." Widowers in fact saw less of their children, particularly of their sons, than married men and married or widowed women, as judged by average frequency of contact. But this falling-off did not apply to all a widower's children. A close relationship with one child was usually maintained. Several lived with a single or married daughter, or visited a married daughter daily, and then described the pleasure grandchildren gave them. "My young granddaughter likes swinging and I pick her up and she swings

between my legs. And then she climbs up on me. Playing with my grandchildren is my greatest pleasure." They found some consolation here. "I'm
a grandfather," said one man, "and that's the only goodness I get out of
life."

The loss of the marriage partner was not quite such a disaster for women.
They had always depended less on husbands than husbands on them, and
they found it easier to console themselves with their families. Nevertheless,
many of them were lonely, particularly if their husbands had died recently
and particularly if infirmity or shortage of relatives prevented them from
finding comfort readily in the companionship of others. One woman's husband had died eight years previously. She had no children. "I get so lonely
I could fill up the teapot with tears."

> Mrs. Pridy was very infirm and her husband had died only a year previously,
> when she was 80. She lived with a daughter and grandchildren. "I sit here for hours
> and hours sometimes thinking about it. I get depressed and I start crying. We was
> always together. I can remember even his laughing. 'Come on, girl,' he'd say, 'don't
> get sitting about. Let's liven 'em up.' They say what is to be will be. I never thought
> he'd. . . . But we've all got to go. A good many of them don't even know he's gone
> (neighbors). I sit here for hours thinking about him. I can't get over it."

Almost every man and woman whose husband or wife had died within
the previous five years, compared with a half between five and ten years and
a quarter over that limit, felt lonely. The shorter the period since the death
the more likely were people to complain of loneliness. . . . Although practically everyone felt lonely at first after about five or six years the presence
or not of an affectionate family seemed to determine how long such feelings
persisted.

Four people had lost a child and not a husband recently. Three were
women widowed in the 1914 war who said a son had died in the previous
few years. One had lost two sons in the 1939 war and another three years
previously. "I could cry my heart out sometimes when I sit here." There
was also a married woman whose only son had been killed at Arnhem in
1944. "He's never out of my mind. I always see him in my mind and they're
still talking about wars." In speaking of the loss of children and other
relatives it was notable how long people felt grief and how indelible was the
memory of these people. The "In Memoriam" column of a local East
London newspaper provides many examples of the feelings of relatives
for those who have died, some of them severalyears previously. In the
following three illustrations, printed in 1955, only the names have been
changed.

HOWARD—To the beautiful memory of my beloved daughter, Alice, who fell asleep June 17th, 1949.
> Time takes away the edge of grief,
> But memories turn back every leaf.
> Ever in our thoughts—Mum and all.

TALEWILL—In treasured memory of our dear Mum, who fell asleep June 7th, 1945.
> Not a day do we forget you, Mum,
> In our hearts you are ever near,
> Loved, remembered, longed for always,
> Bringing many a silent tear.
> Sadly missed—Loving sons and daughters.

HUGGINS—In loving memory of a dear nephew who passed away June 6th, 1953.
> Sad and sudden was the call,
> To one so dearly loved by all,
> This month of June comes with regret,
> It brings back a tragedy we shall never forget.
> —From Aunt Caroline, Uncle Bill, Uncle Herbert, Uncle
> Steve and cousins Mary, Alice and children.

Recent Separation

After bereavement, recent separation from children and grandchildren was the most important reason for loneliness, affecting 17 of the 56 people. Eleven of the 17 had no contact with a child living in the district although recently at least one child had been there. What happened was that, if the last child to get married moved out of the district or was unable to find a home in it and there were no other children living nearby, the old person greatly missed their daily companionship, particularly if widowed. A further three old persons had a son living nearby but the daughters had recently moved away. And three widows who had been living with married children now lived alone, although some of their children still lived in the same district.

Mrs. Marvel was 80 and she lived alone in a new council flat. Her husband had been dead for 30 years. None of her six surviving children lived in Bethnal Green although five of the six visited her regularly once or twice a week. A married daughter lived with her until she obtained a council house outside London five years previously. Mrs. Marvel wanted to stay in the district where she had lived nearly all her life. Speaking of her former home, which was recently demolished, she said, "We went in ten and came out one." Later she said, "I'm sometimes lonely, especially as my children are away. Still, I count my blessings. They're all good children."

Mrs. Foreman had been a widow for over 30 years. She had no daughters and until twelve months previously had been living with her married son. He had now moved to a new housing estate. Although she stayed with him every weekend she was lonely at home. "I don't like coming back here. I get the hump."

There remained 11 whose loneliness seemed to be due to other causes. All had recently experienced a marked change in their social circumstances. The husband of one and the daughter of another were in hospital, and had been there for some months. A third complained bitterly about the new council flat to which she had been moved a year previously; she was among neighbors she did not know or like and she was further from two of her relatives. Two married men were infirm and could not leave the house; both had retired within the past three years. A married woman had experienced several drastic changes in the past few years and was one of the most lonely of all those interviewed. As an extreme example, she is worth noting.

Mrs. Austin, in her late sixties, lived in a council flat with her husband. She said she missed not having her seven children around her and that she was "very lonely. I can't account for it at all. I get so depressed." Five of the seven had married within a space of three years around 1950 and had left home one after another. All but two had moved to housing estates outside London or in other East London boroughs. These two lived about a mile away. One son, to whom she was particularly attached, had been killed in an accident several years previously. Soon after the children had married Mr. and Mrs. Austin had to leave their home, because it was to be demolished. "I can't settle here. I'd been over 40 years in one house. Since it's been pulled down and we've come here I've hardly spoken to my next-door neighbors. All the old neighbors have gone. You can't go in and out like you used to." She saw much less of her children than formerly, although her two youngest visited her twice a week and three of the others once a fortnight. Her only sister had died three years ago. Because of headaches she could no longer read and because of a fall which damaged her hand she could no longer knit. Her husband had been in ill-health for several years and was on bad terms with some of the children. Mrs. Austin had made two attempts at suicide and had recently spent six months in a mental hospital.

In this example nearly all the disturbing social changes that can occur in the life of an old person had occurred. Close relatives had died, the children had migrated, the old home and neighborhood had to be given up and many activities had to be abandoned because of increasing infirmity. This was desolation with a vengeance. Now to be *desolate,* as defined earlier, is to have been deprived recently of the companionship of someone who is loved. And the main conclusion of this analysis is that people saying they were lonely were nearly all people who had been deprived recently of the companionship of someone they loved. They were *desolates* and not necessarily *isolates.* They were isolated only in the sense that they had *become* isolated, relative to their previous situation. Many were not short of company. Several widowed people, in particular, lived with children and grandchildren and had many social activities.

The Hold on Life

We have seen that desolation, or the loss of someone who is loved, is more important than social isolation in explaining the loneliness of old people. Such a change may explain much more than loneliness, for it affects a person's health and whole state of mind. The problems of the physical and mental health of old people need to be studied against their known social condition and the sudden changes in that condition. In Bethnal Green many people talked of the drastic effects of retirement on men and of bereavement on both men and women. Remarks about people who had just retired or who had been recently widowed suggested they had less will to live and deteriorated quickly. "He didn't want to live any more." "Men break up when they give up work. They soon go." "He just went to pieces when she died." "She was left all alone in the world and didn't want to go on living." "I've got nothing left to live for." "He won't be long in following her." These remarks deserve careful attention. They imply the possibility of sudden physical degeneration, after retirement, for men, and after bereavement, for men and women.

While this is a very complex matter which cannot be discussed in detail here, three separate points seem to be worth making. The first concerns widows and widowers. The difficulties of old people in adapting themselves to new situations are well known.[2] It may be particularly difficult for them to adjust their lives to the fact of bereavement. This is strongly supported by what they say about loneliness. The suggestion is that the mortality rates for people widowed in old age are likely to be higher than the rates for single and married people, and even than people, of the same age, widowed when young.

Precise statistical data are not available to test this supposition. What evidence there is does not distinguish between those widowed late in life and other widowed people. But it is certainly not in conflict with the supposition. Mortality rates, by age and marital status, are available. These show higher death rates among older widowed people than others. . . . There may be a number of reasons why the death rates for older widowed people tend to be higher than those for single and married people. Some may catch the illnesses from which their husbands or wives died. On the face of it, however, the influence of recent bereavement upon the rates may be worth careful study.

The second point concerns the higher death rates for older men than for older women. The differences between men and women may not be explained entirely by biological and physiological differences. Social factors may play a significant part here too. It was shown earlier, for example, that the man in Bethnal Green, on retirement, had to change virtually his whole style of living; he was deserted by workmates and friends and while he was thrown back on his family, he could rarely do other than play second fiddle to his wife. On the other hand his wife, to whom the affairs of household and family had always been dominant, could usually go on to a ripe old age doing most of the things she had always done. Sheldon observed that fewer women than men were in extreme good- or ill-health and while more of them had subnormal health their hold on life was tenacious. The present limited findings, so far as they go, confirm his observation. It is possible that the effect of retirement on men and that the security of women in job and family may contribute to the woman's greater expectation of life.[3] This complicated question cannot be entered into here: a plea is made only for further study of these social influences.

The third point in this matter of the effect of social factors upon health concerns social isolation. The trials and tribulations of old age may be harder for isolated people to bear, because they are not sustained by family and friends. A crude hypothesis may be put forward. Those who are socially isolated in old age, particularly those with the fewest contacts with relatives, tend to make greater claims on hospital and other health and social services and to die earlier than others.

. . . In old age the death rates for bachelors are higher than those for married men but lower than those for widowers. The differences between single and married women seem to be very slight, except at the oldest ages.[4] The subject is, however, very complex because of the influence of physical selection for marriage and of diseases associated with childbearing, to say nothing of the changes in patterns of marriage. There has been a rise in marriage rates since 1939. As those who marry are likely, on average, to be in better health than the unmarried it seems that as the number of spinsters becomes progressively smaller, a higher proportion will have inferior vitality. Recent evidence has shown that death rates of single women, relatively to married women, have increased in the last 20 years.[5] Safer child-bearing has also contributed to the relative improvement in the death rates of married women. Even so, in a long analysis comparing the mortality of single and married women before the war the Registrar General stated, "It is difficult to escape the conclusion that in the present state of society the married condition *per se* for women is more favorable to vitality than the single condition at ages up to 60."[6]

Other data concern the once-married but childless. Since 1938 information has been obtained, at the registration of deaths of women who were or had at any time been married, as to whether they had had children. The number of such children, and whether they were live or still-born, is not recorded. Infertility rates, derived from such information, are published from time to time. The infertility rates for older deceased widows are lower than those for older deceased married women. This "unexpected" relationship, as it is described in the Statistical Review,[7] may be due to a number of factors. One is that women with children may live longer, or may more often outlive their husbands, than childless women because the company of children helps them to keep a hold on life. All the available information about death-rates is, however, rather scanty. None of it—so far as the writer is aware—allows any exact test of an association between death and social isolation or, more generally, any systematic study of the relation between longevity and social circumstances.[8]

Some of these speculations may deserve further inquiry. Comfort has stated that senescence is a change in the behavior of an organism with age, which leads to a decreased power of survival and adjustment.[9] Here it is suggested that the social and especially the family circumstances of individuals are a major determinant of the rate of decline in the power of self-adjustment and self-defense in later life. Broadly speaking there may be a marked association between each of three social factors, these being social isolation, social desolation, and retirement, and the expectation of life of old people. Biological, physiological and health factors aside, one would expect, on the rather limited evidence from the present study, that old women and, to a lesser extent, old men who are at the center of a secure family live longer than those who are socially isolated or desolated, particularly the latter.

The chief purpose of this chapter has been to distinguish between *isolates* and *desolates* in old age and show the importance of the distinction. Those who are secluded from family and society, as objectively assessed on the basis of defined criteria, are the isolates. Those who have been recently deprived by death, illness or migration of the company of someone they love —such as a husband or wife or child—are the desolates. A major conclusion of the present analysis is that, though the two are connected, the underlying reason for loneliness in old age is desolation rather than isolation. The method of defining the isolates described above was to place those interviewed on a scale according to the number of social contacts they had. About a tenth had an average of only three social contacts a day or less; these were the most isolated, and they included a relatively high number of unmarried and childless people. The problems of such people seem to be acute and it has been suggested they are likely to make by far the greatest claim on the social services. This suggestion will now be examined; if true the implications for social policy are many.

NOTES

1. Sheldon, J. H., *The Social Medicine of Old Age*, 1948, p. 130. He added, in parenthesis, that the main exception to this statement was when the death of a spouse was recent.

2. Welford, A. T., *et al., Skill and Age*, 1950.

3. One interesting fact is that suicide rates increase much more quickly with age for men than for women. Sainsbury suggests this is partly due to the greater susceptibility of men to change and economic stress. He also pointed out that "during the War, for example, when elderly men were able to obtain useful employment, the suicide rate among them fell more than that of younger men" (Sainsbury, P., *Suicide in London*, 1955, p. 81).

4. For comment, see *Registrar General's Decennial Supplement for England and Wales*, 1931, Part I, 1936, p. 12.

5. *Registrar General's Decennial Supplement for England and Wales*, 1951.

6. *Registrar General's Statistical Review of England and Wales for the Year 1933* (Text), pp. 42–43.

7. *Registrar General's Statistical Review of England and Wales for the Five Years, 1946–1950* (Text, Civil), 1954, p. 147.

8. Death rates by social class provide some informantion, but perhaps not in enough detail. See the *Registrar General's Decennial Supplement, England and Wales, 1951* (Occupational Mortality, Part I). This suggests, among other things, that the differences between the death rates of the five social classes tend to narrow with advancing age and for men aged 65 and over death rates in Social Class V are lower than those for all other classes. There is some doubt, however, about the reliability of the information on social class. [Editors' note: Social Class V comprises manual workers, as distinct from professional and clerical.]

9. Comfort, A., *The Biology of Senescence*, 1956, p. 190.

SUGGESTED READINGS

Simone de Beauvoir, *The Second Sex* (New York: Alfred A. Knopf, 1953).
Albert Ellis, *The American Sexual Tragedy* (New York: Grove Press, 1963).
Erik Erikson, *Childhood and Society* (New York: W. W. Norton, 1950).
Erik Erikson, *Youth: Change and Challenge* (New York: Basic Books, 1963).
Betty Friedan, *The Feminine Mystique* (New York: W. W. Norton, 1963).

Edgar Z. Friedenberg: *The Vanishing Adolescent* (New York: Delta, 1968).

Paul Goodman, *Growing up Absurd* (New York: Random House, 1960).

Germaine Greer, *The Female Eunuch* (New York: McGraw-Hill, 1971).

James Herndon, *How to Survive in Your Native Land* (New York: Simon and Schuster, 1971).

Kenneth Keniston, *The Uncommitted: Alienated Youth in American Society* (New York: Harcourt, Brace & World, 1965; reprint, New York: Delta).

Lester A. Kirkendall and Robert N. Whitehurst, eds., *The New Sexual Revolution* (New York: Donald W. Brown, 1971).

Kate Millett, *Sexual Politics* (Garden City, N.Y.: Doubleday, 1970).

Charles E. Silberman, *Crisis in the Classroom* (New York: Random House, 1970).

Philip Slater, *The Pursuit of Loneliness* (Boston: Beacon Press, 1970).

Charles Winick, *The New People: Desexualization in American Life* (New York: Pegasus, 1968).

Charles Winick and Paul M. Kinsie, *The Lively Commerce: Prostitution in the United States* (Chicago: Quadrangle Books, 1971).

EPILOGUE ❧ ❧

LOOKING FORWARD ❧

The recitation of major problems facing a society can be a rather dreary and depressing affair. One describes poverty, militarism, alienation, racism, and the decline of the environment, and it may appear from such descriptions and analyses that a society is falling apart, or has reached a point of no return. Here and there, in our material on confrontation and again in the essays on youth and on women, there was a view of how some people were responding to these felt needs: with organization, sometimes a threat of disorder or actual disorder, and by the exertion of tremendous pressure for social change.

Somehow, there is a tendency in an analysis of social problems to focus on the negative aspects of a society. By definition, a public or private issue is a social problem if it has negative connotations for the society or for large numbers of its people. When one has gone through some thirty or so descriptions of various difficulties in the society, knowing that there are many other problems that have remained untouched (mental health, suicide, poor medical care, tax inequities, and one could go on almost indefinitely), one searches for perspectives and for responses. In what direction is the American society going in each of these areas of trouble, and what can be done to ameliorate a situation that is obviously in need of massive aid?

First with regard to perspectives it is difficult to be enthusiastic about the outlook on militarism as one notes not only the length and casualties of the war in Indochina, but also the character of that war: defoliation, the spoiling of entire villages, the brutalization of American youths, and the realization that My Lai was not unique and may even have been common. As we write, the war in Indochina seems to be grinding toward an American disinvolvement leaving a wartorn subcontinent indescribably devastated and an American-supported government incredibly corrupt. Little likelihood exists that power groups in the United States will examine the roots of the war, will challenge the legality of its entry, or will look to place responsibility. Perhaps this will be the task of the academicians on the one hand and the youth on the other.

600

Although disengagement presents a glimmer of brightness in this very bleak picture, there are other factors over which our society can take heart. We refer to the challenge to nationalism, patriotism, and chauvinism; the widespread refusal of Americans to accept the war and to engage in it; the organizations, marches, and prestigious men of the cloth speaking out from their pulpits. Even the veterans of that war have on foot, on crutches, and in wheelchairs, expressed their scorn by discarding medals.

The United States is a country of paradoxes: one in which a brutal war in a far-off place can be fought and one in which people can openly express their condemnation of that war and of the leaders responsible for it. In no other country could there be a serious call to try national leaders as war criminals, but in no other country is there a Viet Nam as a blot on its contemporary history. If the democratic process is to be of any service to a society, and we are convinced that it is both of service and indispensable to America, then it must express itself by just such manifestations of public pressure, bent toward a constant challenge to the way things are and a constant demand for modification.

Yet, if we stop there, we can be caught in still a greater paradox. For the democratic process with its dissent and continuous opposition can serve to delude a populace into believing that it has been effective in modifying policy. While the manifestos are distributed and the demonstrators go home, the old policy remains the same. "Let them march, we shall listen and do just as we please," may be the modern equivalent of "let them eat cake." If the demonstration is only an ego trip and is being used by the power groups in the society as a safety valve for dissatisfaction and as a showpiece to display a democratic face to the world while undemocratic policies continue unabated, it will have defeated its purpose.

Should this be the case, and the danger is real, and even if some protestors employ tactics that are counterproductive because they create hostility among those who might have been at least neutral, the protest's significance nonetheless is never completely lost. The pressures on a government come from many and varied sources, and those that derive from oppositionists cannot be completely ignored or discounted.

What shall we say about the direction of race relations in this country, particularly the question of black and white? The greatest single advance, in our view, has been the decline and almost complete eradication of any respectability in the *idea* of racism. This does not mean that racism has disappeared or even that it has seriously diminished in its intensity. It is rooted in the traditions and institutions of American society. Yet, as an *idea,* as a concept that one can espouse, teach, and propagate, openly embrace for political and other advantages, the scene has changed.

America has travelled a long way in the past half century. What is interesting to note about a motion picture like "The Birth of a Nation" is not whether its revival today should be suppressed because of the hate that it might engender, but rather that it was possible for such a picture, as vicious as the worst anti-Semitism that came out of Hitler Germany, to have been produced by the leading intellectuals in American cinema art less than six decades ago. It was hailed by our critics and elevated to a heroic pedestal by the men in the White House and the Cabinet.

It has also been a long way since the lynchings that were commonplace in American life, although much of the underlying prejudice that motivated lynch crowds may be unchanged. Today's political leaders appeal to a racist populace by speaking in what has come to be called "code words." The phrase is interesting for what it implies is that the open appeal to race hatred is unacceptable in the United States, but it also implies that such race hatred remains rampant throughout the land. One may seriously debate whether code words and concealed hostility are not more difficult to combat than the overt and ugly manifestations of racism that marked American history until only a few years ago.

Camouflaged racism may be more difficult to combat, but the ideas of the racist society are probably going to diminish in force and effect as their propaganda and dissemination recede. Simply as an index of where America stands and of the progress or lack of progress on racial confrontation, we can say some things about this decline in the respectability of the idea of racism. First, it is itself the sign of welcome and long overdue change; second, it may very well be the result of international competition for the favor of new and underdeveloped countries; and third, it can be a dynamic force for bringing about newer and greater change.

It is a society in flux in an era of rapid technological and social change and with manifestations of upheaval all around it. Is it possible that a land of unprecedented wealth cannot solve (or will not solve) its problems of poverty? Is it possible that remarkable scientific manpower (of which the moon landing was only a dramatic incident) cannot dispose of waste, keep its rivers and lakes from becoming sewers, keep its air fresh and breathable? Is it possible . . . one can continue. And the answer is always in the affirmative. Yes, these things are possible, but not necessary, certainly not inevitable. They are possible because there are people in powerful positions (the wealthy, the corporate enterprises, and others) who have vested interests, albeit short-term to their own advantage, for the continuation of things as they are. However, counterforces can be put into effect, and America, in particular, offers an outlook for a future in which they may be triumphant.

All of this requires knowledge and analysis, uncontaminated by ideology, continuous enlightened dissent by an informed and vigilant public, and a deepgoing commitment by significant sectors of the society. Furthermore, it requires that we implement, and not simply repeat as rhetoric, the demand for the reordering of priorities; and finally that all of us understand that social change, to be effective, must be daring, imaginative, and carefully planned.

LIBRARY OF DAVIDSON COLLEGE

Books on regular loan may be checked out for **two weeks.** Books must be presented at the Circulation Desk in order to be renewed.

A fine of **five cents** a day is charged after date due.

Special books are subject to special regulations at the discretion of library staff.